V Grammar

22 Questions About Subject-Verb Agreement? 406
23 Questions About Verb Tense, Voice, and Mood? 419
24 Questions About Verbals? 435
25 Questions About Plurals, Possessives, and Articles? 441
26 Questions About Pronoun Reference? 451
27 Questions About Pronoun Agreement? 457
28 Questions About Pronoun Case? 466
29 Questions About Pronoun Choices? 478
30 Questions About Modifiers? 488
31 Are You an ESL Writer? 505
32 ESL Questions About Verbs? 512
33 ESL Questions About Gerunds, Infinitives, Articles, or Number? 529

VI Punctuation and Mechanics

34 How Do You Punctuate Sentence Endings? 542
35 Questions About Sentence Boundaries: Fragments, Comma Splices, and Run-ons? 547
36 Questions About Commas? 559
37 Questions About Semicolons and Colons? 576
38 Questions About Quotation Marks and Ellipses? 585
39 Questions About Parentheses and Brackets? 593
40 Questions About Dashes, Hyphens, and Slashes? 597
41 Questions About Italics and Capitalization? 604
42 Questions About Abbreviations and Numbers? 615

VII

43 .... .oject? 626
44 H............................ ..ation? 640
    a. ....rary and Library Catalogs 6..
    b. Finding Research Materials 644
    c. Choosing Electronic Resources 653
    d. Searching with Keywords 659
    e. Conducting Field Research 664
45 How Do You Evaluate and Use Sources? 670
    a. Evaluating Research Sources 670
    b. Using Research Materials 677
46 How Do You Acknowledge Sources? 693
    a. Documenting a Research Project 693
    b. Understanding Academic Responsibility 696
    c. Handling Quotations 701
47 How Do You Complete a Project? 709

VIII Documentation

48 How Do You Use MLA Documentation? 722
49 How Do You Use APA Documentation? 773
50 How Do You Use CMS Documentation? 803
51 How Do You Use CBE Documentation? 820
52 How Do You Use COS Documentation? 826

Glossary of Terms and Usage 856
Index 907

Be sure you understand your responsibility as an academic writer. Take the "Avoiding Plagiarism" tutorial on the CD-ROM that accompanies your handbook to learn to identify and correct the seven common causes of plagiarism.

The Scott, Foresman Media Program

Writers today work in a variety of print and online media, and *Scott, Foresman* keeps pace. In print, on the Web, and on CD-ROM, *The Scott, Foresman Handbook for Writers* offers you the information and tools you need to succeed.

In the handbook . . .

 E-tips throughout the book guide you to Web resources and give helpful strategies for using the Web to write and conduct research.

On the Web . . .

The companion Web site for *The Scott, Foresman Handbook for Writers* includes a wide array of resources, tutorials, and tools to help you. Log on at http://www.ablongman.com/sfhandbooks.

The Scott, Foresman Handbook for Writers E-book gives you a completely online, searchable version of *The Scott, Foresman Handbook for Writers*. You'll need a PIN number to access the e-book at http://www.ablongman.com/sfhandbooks.

On CD-ROM . . .

The Longman ExerciseZone and *Avoiding Plagiarism CD-ROM* offers thousands of practice exercises on key handbook topics, as well as an interactive tutorial designed to help you identify the major causes of plagiarism. You'll receive immediate feedback as you work throughout these exercises and the tutorial.

In addition, the entire text of *The Scott, Foresman Handbook for Writers* is available as an Interactive Edition CD-ROM, supplemented with video and audio clips, web links, and exercises.

The Scott, Foresman Handbook for Writers

SIXTH EDITION

Maxine Hairston
University of Texas at Austin

John Ruszkiewicz
University of Texas at Austin

Christy Friend
University of South Carolina

Longman

New York   San Francisco   Boston
London   Toronto   Sydney   Tokyo   Singapore   Madrid
Mexico City   Munich   Paris   Cape Town   Hong Kong   Montreal

Editor-in-Chief: Joseph P. Terry
Acquisitions Editor: Lynn M. Huddon
Development Manager: Janet Lanphier
Development Editor: Leslie Taggart
Supplements Editor: Donna Campion
Marketing Manager: Christopher Bennem
Senior Production Manager: Bob Ginsberg
Design Manager and Text Designer: Wendy Ann Fredericks
Cover Designer: Kay Petronio
Cover Photo: © PhotoDisc
Art Studio: ElectraGraphics, Inc.
Photo Researcher: Photosearch, Inc.
Electronic Production Manager: Heather A. Peres
Senior Manufacturing Buyer: Dennis J. Para
Electronic Page Makeup: York Production Services
Printer and Binder: Quebecor World
Cover Printer: Phoenix Color

For permission to use copyrighted material, grateful acknowledgment is made to the copyright holders on pages 901–05, which are hereby made part of this copyright page.

Hairston, Maxine.
  The Scott, Foresman handbook for writers/Maxine Hairston, John Ruszkiewicz, Christy Friend.—6th ed.
    p. cm.
  Includes index.
  ISBN 0-321-12561-4
  1. English language—Rhetoric—Handbooks, manuals, etc. 2. English language—Grammar—Handbooks, manuals, etc. 3. Report writing—Handbooks, manuals, etc. I. Ruszkiewicz, John J., 1950- II. Friend, Christy.

PE1408 .H2968 2001
808'.042—dc21   2001022350

Please visit our website at http://www.ablongman.com/sfhandbooks

ISBN 0-321-12561-4

12345678910—QWT—040302

Contents

Preface   *xxvi*

PART 1

Writing Processes   1

1. What Does Writing Involve?   2
   a. Why write?   2
   b. What does it take to write well?   3
       Resist myths that can discourage writers   *3*
   c. How does writing work?   4
   d. How do you define a writing situation?   6
   e. How do you define your purpose(s) in writing?   7
       1. Decide on your goals   *7*
       2. Consider your writing situation   *7*
   f. How do you write for an audience?   9
   g. How do you present yourself to readers?   11
       1. Show readers that you are credible   *11*
       2. Present material fairly and honestly   *12*
       3. Use a civil tone   *13*

2. How Do You Find and Explore a Topic?   15
   a. How do you find a topic?   15
       1. Think beyond traditional topics   *15*
       2. Consider your interests and strengths   *16*
       3. Choose a topic in your world   *16*
       4. Browse in the library   *17*
       5. Look for ideas online   *17*
   b. How do you refine your topic?   18
       1. Don't try to cover everything   *19*
       2. Make a tree diagram   *19*
       3. Make an idea map   *20*
       4. Investigate a question or hypothesis   *21*

     5. *State a tentative goal*   22
  c. How do you explore and develop a topic?   23
     1. *Freewrite*   23
     2. *Use the journalist's questions*   24
     3. *Try different perspectives*   24
     4. *Write a zero draft*   25
     5. *Read up on your topic*   25
     6. *Talk to others*   26
  d. How do you write a topic proposal?   27
     GOING PUBLIC: *A Topic Proposal*   27

3. How Do You Focus and Organize a Writing Project?   29

  a. How do you craft a thesis?   29
     1. *Make a strong point*   29
     2. *Sharpen your focus*   31
     3. *Preview the direction of your paper*   32
     4. *Place your thesis effectively*   32
     5. *Revise your thesis as your project evolves*   33
     GOING PUBLIC: *An Opening Paragraph with Thesis*   34
  b. How do you organize a writing project?   35
     1. *Introduction/body/conclusion*   36
     2. *Narrative or process design*   37
     3. *Comparison/contrast*   38
     4. *Division or classification*   40
     5. *Cause and effect*   41
     6. *Problem and solution*   42
  c. How do you outline a paper?   43
     1. *Use a working list*   44
     2. *Use an informal (scratch) outline*   45
     3. *Use a formal (sentence) outline*   46
     4. *Use an outlining program*   47
  d. How do you choose a title?   48
     1. *Experiment with a working title*   48
     2. *Revise the working title*   48
     3. *Keep your readers in mind*   48

4. How Do You Write a Draft?   50

  a. How do you start a piece of writing?   50
     1. *Find a place to write*   50
     2. *Keep the ideas coming*   50

3. *Avoid premature criticism*   *51*
4. *Set your own pace*   *51*
5. *Get feedback*   *51*
6. *Draft on a computer*   *52*
b. How do you keep a draft on track?   52
   1. *Highlight key ideas*   *52*
   2. *Maintain proportion*   *53*
   3. *Leave time for conclusions*   *54*
c. When should you take a break?   54
   GOING PUBLIC: *One Writer's Drafting Process*   *55*
d. How do you know when you have a solid draft?   56
e. How do you work on a draft collaboratively?   57
   1. *Decide on shared goals*   *58*
   2. *Assign sections of the project*   *58*
   3. *Try collaborative writing*   *59*
   4. *Address disagreements promptly*   *59*

5. How Do You Revise, Edit, and Proofread?   60

a. What does revising involve?   61
   1. *Read your draft thoughtfully*   *61*
   2. *Refine the focus*   *62*
   3. *Consider your purpose*   *62*
   4. *Examine the proportions of your paper*   *63*
   5. *Check that you have kept your promises*   *63*
   6. *Check for adaptation to audience*   *63*
   7. *Check the organization*   *64*
   8. *Check the content*   *64*
   9. *Revise from hard copy*   *65*
   GOING PUBLIC: *A Revised Opening Paragraph*   *65*
b. What does editing involve?   67
   GOING PUBLIC: *Edited Sentences from Student Papers*   *70*
c. What does proofreading involve?   71
d. How do you help another writer revise, edit, and proofread?   73
   GOING PUBLIC: *Draft with Peer Comments*   *76*

6. How Is Writing Evaluated?   83

a. How do you deal with letter grades?   83
   1. *Understand grading criteria*   *84*
   2. *Clarify any criteria that are confusing*   *86*
   3. *Find out which parts of your work will be evaluated*   *86*

4. *Read your instructor's responses carefully*   87
b. How do you prepare a portfolio?   89
   1. *Understand writing portfolios*   90
   2. *Design your portfolio*   90
   3. *Comment on your work*   91
   GOING PUBLIC: *One Student's Self-Assessment*   91
   4. *Work steadily on your portfolio*   94
c. What are your rights and responsibilities in the evaluation
   process?   95
   1. *Have reasonable expectations*   95
   2. *Question a grade responsibly*   96

PART II

Writing for Academic and Public Forums   99

7. How Do You Write in College?   100

a. How do you write a successful academic paper?   100
   1. *Review the assignment*   100
   2. *Don't take on too much*   101
   3. *Support your claims with reasons and evidence*   101
   4. *Understand what counts as evidence*   101
   GOING PUBLIC: *Writing an Annotated Bibliography*   103
   5. *Document your sources and give credit to others*   104
   6. *Follow the conventions of your subject area*   104
   7. *Turn in professional-looking work*   106
b. How do you write on essay examinations?   108
   1. *Know the material*   108
   2. *Find out as much as you can about the exam*   109
   3. *Use your study time intelligently*   109
   4. *Devise strategies for coping with pressure*   110
   5. *Figure out what the question asks you to do*   110
   6. *Budget your time*   111
   7. *Make a plan*   113
   8. *Know what a good response looks like*   113
   GOING PUBLIC: *Framing a Successful*
   Examination Essay   114

8. How Do You Write for the Public?   116

a. How do you write outside the classroom?   116
  1. *Understand the range of writing you may do*   *116*
  2. *Learn to spot opportunities for public writing*   *118*
  3. *Find out what your readers expect*   *119*
  4. *Seek out models and advice*   *119*
  5. *Recognize the benefits and risks of public writing*   *120*
  6. *Be professional*   *121*
  GOING PUBLIC: *Shaping an Argument for a Public Audience*   *121*
b. How do you write in service-learning courses?   125
  1. *Understand the dual purpose of service learning*   *126*
  2. *Be aware of the different audiences for your writing*   *126*
  3. *Find out how your work will be evaluated*   *127*
  4. *Be willing to learn and to collaborate*   *128*
  GOING PUBLIC: *Collaboration and Service Learning*   *129*

9. How Do You Read and Think Critically?   130

a. How do you read to understand complex material?   130
  1. *Preview the text*   *131*
  2. *Look up unfamiliar terms and concepts*   *131*
  3. *Slow down*   *132*
  4. *Annotate the text*   *132*
  5. *Adapt your reading process to online settings*   *134*
b. How do you think critically about your reading?   136
  1. *Read as a believer and a doubter*   *136*
  2. *Assess the writer's qualifications*   *137*
  3. *Look carefully at the evidence*   *137*
  4. *Assess the writer's claims and evidence*   *138*
  5. *Look for what's not there*   *138*
  6. *Note contradictions*   *139*
  7. *Examine word choices for bias*   *139*
  8. *Resist black-and-white thinking*   *140*

10. How Do You Interpret and Use Visual Texts?   142

a. How do you understand visual representations of information?   142
  1. *Using pie charts*   *143*
  2. *Using bar graphs*   *144*

      3. *Using line graphs*   145
      4. *Using tables*   145
      5. *Judging the accuracy of visuals*   148
  b. How do you interpret layout, graphics, and other visual
     elements?   149
      1. *Assess layout and design*   149
      2. *Evaluate images critically*   150
      3. *Assess visual media critically*   150

11. How Can You Write Powerful Arguments?   153

  a. What does argument involve?   153
      1. *Distinguish between arguments and disagreements*   153
      2. *Look for claims supported by reasons and evidence*   154
      3. *Consider unstated beliefs, or warrants*   155
      4. *Recognize qualifiers*   157
  b. How do you construct a solid written argument?   158
      1. *Clarify your claim*   158
      2. *Gather reasons and evidence*   158
      3. *Evaluate your evidence*   159
      4. *Identify your warrants, or unstated beliefs*   159
  c. How do you write an argument that appeals to readers?   160
      1. *Draw on shared beliefs and values*   161
      2. *Present opposing arguments fairly*   162
      3. *Refute an opposing argument*   163
     GOING PUBLIC: *An Argument That Addresses*
       Opposing Views   164
      4. *Make concessions to another position*   169
  d. How can you recognize and avoid fallacies?   170

12. How Do You Write a Literary Analysis?   176

  a. What approaches can you take to literary analysis?   176
     GOING PUBLIC: *Two Approaches to Literary Analysis*   179
  b. What sources can you use in producing literary analyses?   180
      1. *Understand primary texts*   180
      2. *Consult secondary sources*   181
  c. How do you develop a literary project?   182
      1. *Begin by reading carefully*   183
      2. *Develop a thesis*   184
      3. *Read the works again*   185
      4. *Use scratch outlines*   186

5. *Follow the conventions of literary analysis*   *187*
GOING PUBLIC: *A Literary Analysis Paper*   *188*

PART III

Style   193

13. What Makes Paragraphs Work?   194

a. How do you construct unified paragraphs?   194
  1. *Find a focus and stick with it*   *194*
  2. *Anchor your paragraph with a topic sentence*   *195*
  3. *Use internal transitions*   *197*
b. How can you organize paragraphs?   199
  1. *Illustration*   *199*
  2. *Question and answer*   *200*
  3. *Narration or process*   *200*
  4. *Definition*   *201*
  5. *Classification*   *201*
  6. *Comparison and contrast*   *202*
  7. *Cause and effect*   *202*
  8. *Analogy*   *203*
c. How can you create polished paragraphs?   204
  1. *Revise for variety*   *204*
  2. *Revise for economy*   *206*
d. How can you improve paragraph appearance?   207
  1. *Break up long paragraph blocks*   *208*
  2. *Use short paragraphs for effect*   *208*
  3. *Adapt paragraph length to your writing situation*   *209*

14. How Do You Manage Opening and Closing Paragraphs?   211

a. What makes an opening paragraph effective?   211
  1. *Begin with a narrative*   *211*
  2. *Begin with a description that establishes tone and forecasts content*   *212*
  3. *Begin with a question or a series of questions that relates to your topic*   *212*
  4. *Begin by quoting a key source*   *213*
  5. *Start with your thesis*   *213*
  GOING PUBLIC: *Using a Narrative to Revise an Opening Paragraph*   *214*

   b. What makes a closing paragraph effective?   215
      1. *Summarize the main points you have made*   216
      2. *Make a recommendation when one is appropriate*   216
      3. *Link the end to the beginning*   216
      4. *Place your argument in a larger context*   217
      5. *Stop when you're finished*   218

15. How Do You Manage Transitions?   220

   a. How do you spot problems with transitions?   220
      1. *Check for a series of short, disconnected sentences*   220
      2. *Check for vague sentence openings like* it is, there are,
        and there is   221
      3. *Check for gaps between paragraphs*   222
   b. How can you strengthen transitions?   223
      1. *Use transition words*   223
      2. *Repeat key terms*   224
      3. *Use demonstrative pronouns*   225
      4. *Use relative pronouns*   225
      5. *Use parallelism*   225
      6. *Use semicolons*   226
      7. *Use headings or other visual markers*   226
      GOING PUBLIC: *Using Transitions to Strengthen*
        an Argument   227

16. What Kinds of Language Can You Use? 229

   a. How formal should your writing be?   229
      1. *Choose the appropriate level of formality*   229
      2. *Formal language*   230
      3. *Informal language*   231
      4. *Casual language*   233
   b. How emotionally charged should your language be?   235
      1. *Understand denotation and connotation*   236
      2. *Choose neutral language in informative research papers,*
        case studies, and reports   237
      3. *Avoid strong connotation in newsletters, press releases,*
        and informative brochures   237
      4. *Use connotation in arguments, reviews, editorials,*
        and opinion pieces   238
      5. *Be alert to connotative language*   239
   c. How do you choose reader-friendly language?   240
      1. *Choose familiar language*   240

    2. Balance abstract and concrete language   *241*
    3. Limit your use of jargon   *242*
    4. Use a civil tone   *242*
    5. Build common ground   *244*
  d. How do you avoid stereotyped language?   245
    1. Avoid sexist language   *246*
    2. Avoid ethnic, racial, and religious stereotypes   *248*
    3. Avoid stereotypes about age, physical condition,
      and sexual orientation   *250*
    4. Avoid bias against professions and social class   *251*
    5. Use good judgment and keep your sense of humor   *252*
  e. How do you handle language varieties?   253
    1. Appreciate dialects   *254*
    2. Understand limitations of dialect   *254*
    3. Use dialect when appropriate   *255*
    4. Use languages other than English when appropriate   *256*

17. How Do You Construct Effective Sentences?   **257**
  a. How are sentences structured?   257
    1. Sentence patterns   *257*
    2. Compound subjects, verbs, and objects   *262*
  b. What do modifiers do?   263
    1. Adjectives modify nouns and pronouns   *264*
    2. Adverbs modify verbs, adjectives, and other adverbs   *266*
    3. Nouns can operate as modifiers   *267*
    4. Verbals can operate as modifiers   *268*
  c. What are phrases?   268
    1. Prepositional phrases   *268*
    2. Verbals and verbal phrases   *270*
    3. Absolute phrases   *273*
    4. Appositive phrases   *274*
  d. What do clauses do in sentences?   275
    1. Independent clauses   *276*
    2. Dependent clauses   *276*
  e. What types of sentences can you write?   280
    1. Simple sentences   *280*
    2. Compound and complex sentences   *281*
  f. How does coordination build sentences?   282
    1. Coordinating conjunctions   *282*
    2. Correlative constructions   *284*

    3. Semicolons, colons, and dashes   284
    4. Conjunctive adverbs with semicolons   285
  g. How does subordination build sentences?   287
    1. Use subordination to clarify relationships between clauses   288
    2. Use subordination to shift emphasis   289
    3. Use subordination to expand sentences   289
    4. Use subordinate clauses sensibly   290
  h. How does parallelism work?   292
    1. Recognize sentence patterns that require parallel
       construction   293
    2. Use parallelism in comparisons and contrasts   293
    3. Recognize expressions that require parallel structure   294
    4. Use parallelism to show a progression of ideas   294
    5. Use parallelism for emphasis   295
    6. Correct faulty parallelism   295
  i. How do you craft balanced sentences?   298
  j. How do you craft cumulative sentences?   299

18. How Do You Write Stylish Sentences?   303
  a. What are agent/action sentences?   303
    1. Make persons or things the subjects of sentences
       and clauses   303
    2. Don't overload the subjects of sentences   304
    3. Make sure verbs convey real actions   305
    4. Make sure subjects can do what their verbs demand   306
    5. Replace to be verbs whenever possible   307
    6. Reduce the number of passive verbs   308
  b. How can you achieve clarity?   310
    1. Use specific details   310
    2. State ideas positively   311
    3. "Chunk" your writing   311
    4. Use charts and graphs   313
  c. How can you write more economically?   313
    1. Condense sprawling phrases   313
    2. Cut nominalizations   315
    3. Condense long verb phrases   316
    4. Eliminate doublings and redundancies   317
    5. Eliminate surplus intensifiers   318
    6. Cut down on expletive constructions   318
    7. Cut down on prepositional phrases   319
    8. Cut that, which, who, whom   321

　　　9. *Condense sentences into clauses, clauses into phrases*
　　　　or words　　321
　　d. How can you achieve sentence variety?　　322
　　　　1. *Vary sentence types*　　322
　　　　2. *Vary sentence patterns*　　323
　　　　3. *Vary sentence length*　　324
　　e. How do you use figurative language?　　326
　　　　1. *Look for fresh images*　　326
　　　　2. *Use similes and metaphors*　　327

PART IV

Design and Shape of Documents　　329

19. What Is Document Design?　　330

　　a. How do documents work?　　330
　　　　1. *Understand document format*　　331
　　　　2. *Consider the different requirements of print and*
　　　　　electronic formats　　332
　　　　3. *Know when to combine formats*　　334
　　　　4. *Understand document style*　　334
　　b. How do you prepare and plan your design?　　336
　　　　1. *Identify suitable formats for your documents*　　336
　　　　2. *Explore possible document styles*　　337
　　　　3. *Assess the design resources available to you*　　338
　　c. How do you draft and revise your design?　　338
　　　　1. *Start with standard formats*　　339
　　　　2. *Work with accessible formats*　　339
　　　　3. *Experiment with document style*　　339
　　　　4. *Revise for readability, impact, and flow*　　340
　　d. How do you edit and proof your design?　　341
　　　　1. *Fine-tune fonts, colors, and type styles*　　342
　　　　2. *Add functional graphics and images*　　342
　　　　3. *Adjust alignment, spacing, and positioning*　　343
　　　　4. *Make document style consistent*　　343
　　　　5. *Test a final draft in your audience's viewing environment*　　344
　　e. How do you copyright your work?　　344
　　　　1. *Copyright your final product*　　345

2. *Document or credit borrowed images*   345
3. *Respect software copyrights*   345

20. How Do You Create Documents and Web Sites?   347

a. How do you design documents with a computer?   347
   1. *Explore the design features of your word processor*   347
   2. *Consider using other kinds of software*   349
b. How do you organize long documents?   349
   1. *Divide long documents into sections*   349
   2. *Insert a table of contents*   350
   3. *Attach appendices, indexes, and glossaries*   350
c. How do you lay out pages?   351
   1. *Choose a manageable size and orientation*   351
   2. *Break material into units*   351
   3. *Arrange material according to relevance*   353
   4. *Align material to direct readers' eyes down and across*   353
   5. *Format paragraphs for readability*   354
   6. *Use white space to avoid clutter*   354
d. How do you choose type?   355
   1. *Select a suitable typeface*   355
   2. *Use type styles strategically*   356
   3. *Adjust type size for readability*   356
e. How do you use graphics and images?   357
   1. *Present numerical data with graphs*   357
   2. *Clarify details through charts and diagrams*   358
   3. *Enliven writing with photos and illustrations*   358
   4. *Separate material with borders and rules*   359
f. How do you work with color?   359
   1. *Select a readable color scheme*   360
   2. *Create a mood for your document*   360
   3. *Use color to highlight or soften elements of your layout*   360
g. How do you design Web pages?   361
   1. *Plan your Web project carefully*   361
   2. *Choose a method for creating HTML pages*   363
   3. *Choose a single-page or a multi-page format*   364
   4. *Storyboard pages*   366
   5. *Gather materials*   367
   6. *Draft HTML documents*   369
   7. *Consider drafting with an HTML text editor*   369
   8. *Consider drafting with a visual HTML editor*   376

9. *Consider drafting by exporting from your word processor*   *380*
10. *Edit and proof your Web page*   *381*
11. *Upload your page to a Web server*   *382*

21. Model Documents   383

a. Email   384
b. Business letters   386
c. Letters of application   388
d. Résumés   390
e. Professional memos   394
f. Messages to online forums   396
g. Newsletters   398
h. Brochures   400
i. Web pages   402
j. Academic papers   404

PART V

Grammar   405

22. Questions About Subject–Verb Agreement?   405

a. Agreement: Is the subject singular or plural?   405
b. Agreement: Is the subject an indefinite pronoun?   411
c. Agreement: Is the subject a collective noun?   413
d. Agreement: Is the subject separated from its verb?   415
e. Agreement: Is the subject hard to identify?   416

23. Questions About Verb Tense, Voice, and Mood?   419

a. How do you choose verb tenses?   419
   1. *Verb tenses and what they do*   *419*
   2. *Perfect tenses*   *422*
b. Questions about tense in parallel constructions?   423
c. Questions about tense consistency in longer passages?   425
d. Questions about irregular verbs?   426
e. Do you understand active and passive voice?   429
f. What is the subjunctive mood and how do you use it?   431

24. Questions About Verbals?   435

   a. What are verbals?   435
   b. How do verbals cause sentence fragments?   438
   c. What is a split infinitive?   438

25. Questions About Plurals, Possessives,
   and Articles?   441

   a. Questions about plurals of nouns?   441
   b. Questions about possessives?   445
   c. Are possessives needed before gerunds?   448
   d. Is it *a* or *an?*   449

26. Questions About Pronoun Reference?   451

   a. Do pronouns lack antecedents?   451
   b. Are pronoun references ambiguous?   453
   c. Questions about *this, that, which,* and *it?*   454

27. Questions About Pronoun Agreement?   457

   a. Are pronoun antecedents lost?   457
   b. Questions about agreement with indefinite pronouns?   460
   c. Questions about agreement with collective nouns?   462
   d. Questions about agreement with *or, nor, either . . .
      or, neither . . . nor?*   464

28. Questions About Pronoun Case?   466

   a. Do you understand case: subjective/objective/possessive?   466
   b. Questions about pronoun case in prepositional phrases?   468
   c. Questions about pronoun case in comparisons?   469
   d. Questions about pronoun case after linking verbs?   471
   e. Is it *who* or *whom?*   472
   f. Questions about possessive pronouns?   474
   g. Special problems: *Its/It's* and *Whose/Who's*   475

29. Questions About Pronoun Choices?   478

   a. Questions about reflexive and intensive pronouns?   478
   b. Questions about *that, which,* and *who?*   480
   c. When to use *I, we, you,* or *one?*   482
   d. Do your pronouns treat both sexes fairly?   485

30. Questions About Modifiers?   488

a. Questions about misplaced or dangling modifiers?   488
b. How do you place adjectives effectively?   491
c. How do you handle predicate adjectives?   492
d. Questions about absolute adjectives?   494
e. Questions about adverb form?   495
f. Where do you place adverbs?   496
g. Questions about double negatives?   498
h. Questions about comparatives and superlatives?   500
i. Questions about nonessential and essential modifiers?   502

31. Are You an ESL Writer?   505

a. Common Problem Areas for ESL Writers   506
   1. Making sure each clause has a subject   *506*
   2. Making sure sentences have main verbs   *506*
   3. Checking the -s on third person singular verbs   *506*
   4. Checking for -ed endings on past participles   *507*
   5. Checking adjective pairs   *507*
   6. Avoiding repetition of sentence elements   *508*
   7. Checking for correct placement of adverbs   *509*
b. Finding Other ESL Resources   510

32. ESL Questions About Verbs?   512

a. Which verb tense should you use?   512
   1. Simple present and present progressive   *515*
   2. Nonaction verbs and the present tense   *515*
   3. Simple past and present perfect   *516*
   4. Present perfect and present perfect progressive   *516*
b. How do you use transitive and intransitive verbs?   518
c. How do you use two-word and three-word verbs?   520
   1. Separable verbs   *521*
   2. Inseparable verbs   *521*
d. Which modal should you use?   523
   1. Choosing the modal that best expresses your idea   *523*
   2. Selecting the correct form of the modal and the main
   verb that follows it   *523*
   3. Using the perfect form to express past time   *526*

33. ESL Questions About Gerunds, Infinitives, Articles, or Number?   529

a. How do you use gerunds and infinitives?   529

1. *Learning which form—gerund or infinitive—to use*   530
2. *Knowing when a verb must be followed by a noun or a pronoun*   530
3. *Using the base form of the verb after* have, make, *and* let   532
4. *Using a gerund after a preposition*   533
b. Questions about articles and number agreement?   534
1. *Count and noncount nouns*   534
2. *Definite and indefinite articles*   535
3. *Articles before general nouns*   536
4. *Noncount nouns*   537
5. *Quantifiers*   537

PART VI

Punctuation and Mechanics   541

34. How Do You Punctuate Sentence Endings?   542

a. When do you use periods?   542
b. When do you use question marks?   543
c. When do you use exclamation marks?   545

35. Questions About Sentence Boundaries: Fragments, Comma Splices, and Run-ons?   547

a. How do you repair sentence fragments?   547
1. *Complete subjects and verbs*   547
2. *Dependent clauses*   548
3. *Relative clauses and appositives*   548
4. *Verbals*   549
5. *Disconnected phrases*   550
6. *Lists*   550
b. Do you understand intentional fragments?   551
c. How do you avoid comma splices?   552
1. *Avoiding commas to join complete sentences*   553
2. *Substituting a semicolon for the comma*   554
3. *Substituting a period for the comma*   554

4. *Inserting a coordinating conjunction*   *554*
5. *Making one of the clauses subordinate*   *554*
d. Questions about run-on sentences?   556
    1. *Inserting a period*   *557*
    2. *Inserting a semicolon*   *557*
    3. *Using a comma and a coordinating conjunction*   *557*
    4. *Making one of the clauses subordinate*   *557*

36. Questions About Commas?   559

a. Do you understand commas that separate?   559
    1. *To set off long introductory phrases*   *559*
    2. *To set off introductory subordinate clauses*   *558*
    3. *To set off an additional or contrasting thought*   *558*
    4. *To follow conjunctive adverbs*   *561*
    5. *To set off absolute phrases*   *561*
    6. *To mark contrasts*   *562*
    7. *To replace omitted verbs or predicates*   *562*
    8. *To keep ideas clear and distinct*   *562*
    9. *To set off conversational expressions*   *562*
b. Do you understand commas that enclose?   563
    1. *To mark nonessential (nonrestrictive) modifiers*   *563*
    2. *To enclose nonessential (nonrestrictive) appositives*   *563*
    3. *To enclose interrupting elements*   *564*
c. Do you understand commas that link?   565
    1. *Compound sentences*   *566*
    2. *Comma splices*   *566*
    3. *Items in a series*   *567*
    4. *Coordinate adjectives in a series*   *567*
    5. *Noncoordinate adjectives in a series*   *568*
d. Do you put commas where they aren't needed?   569
    1. *No commas that interrupt the flow of a sentence*   *569*
    2. *No commas that separate a subject and its verb*   *570*
    3. *No commas in compound elements*   *571*
    4. *No commas to introduce a series*   *571*
    5. *No commas around essential modifiers*   *572*
e. Do you understand the conventional uses of commas?   573
    1. *For introducing quotations*   *573*
    2. *Within numbers*   *573*
    3. *In dates*   *574*
    4. *In addresses*   *574*
    5. *After names with titles and degrees*   *574*
    6. *After the salutation in personal letters*   *574*

37. Questions About Semicolons and Colons? 576

a. Do you have questions about semicolons? 576
  1. *Separating items of equal grammatical weight* 576
  2. *Joining independent clauses* 577
  3. *Separating independent clauses joined by conjunctive adverbs* 578
  4. *Connecting independent clauses with phrases* 578
  5. *Using in clauses, phrases, or series to avoid confusion* 579
  6. *Not using to introduce quotations* 579
  7. *Not using to introduce lists* 579
  8. *Using semicolons with quotation marks* 580
b. Do you have questions about colons? 581
  1. *Using with examples and explanations* 581
  2. *Using with lists* 581
  3. *Using with quotations or dialogue* 583
  4. *Using to join two complete sentences* 583
  5. *Using between titles and subtitles* 583
  6. *Using in conventional situations* 583

38. Questions About Quotation Marks and Ellipses? 585

a. When do you use quotation marks? 585
  1. *Using with material borrowed word for word from sources* 585
  2. *Using with dialogue* 585
  3. *Using with titles of short works* 586
  4. *Using to draw attention to specific words* 586
  5. *Using quotation marks with commas or periods* 587
  6. *Placing quotation marks and other punctuation* 587
b. When do you use ellipses? 589
  1. *Using to indicate omission from a direct quotation* 589
  2. *Using to indicate pauses or continuing action* 590
  3. *Using correct spacing and punctuation with ellipsis marks* 590
  4. *Keeping ellipses to a minimum* 591
  5. *Using to indicate omission of more than a line of verse* 591

39. Questions About Parentheses and Brackets? 593

a. When do you use parentheses? 593

b. When do you use brackets?   595

40. Questions About Dashes, Hyphens, and Slashes?   597

a. When do you use dashes?   597
b. When do you use hyphens?   599
c. When do you use slashes?   602

41. Questions About Italics and Capitalization?   604

a. When do you use italics?   604
b. How do you capitalize sentences, titles, and poems?   606
c. When do you capitalize persons, places, and things?   609

42. Questions About Abbreviations and Numbers?   615

a. How do you handle abbreviations?   615
b. How do you handle numbers?   621

PART VII

Research and Writing   625

43. How Do You Design a Research Project?   626

a. How do you claim a topic?   628
  1. Size up the assignment   628
  2. Browse your topic area   629
b. How do you plan a project?   631
  1. Write a research proposal   631
  2. Classify your materials   632
  3. Prepare a working bibliography   633
  4. Make photocopies and note cards for printed sources   634
  5. Print or download electronic sources   635
  6. Consider collaborative research   636

c. How do you schedule a project? 637
1. *Determine the hard points of your project* 637
2. *Create a calendar* 638

44. How Do You Find Information? 640

a. How do you use a library? 640
1. *Explore your library* 640
2. *Use traditional and online catalogs* 642
b. How do you find research materials? 644
1. *Bibliographies* 644
2. *Periodical indexes and databases* 646
3. *Biographical resources* 648
4. *Statistics* 649
5. *News sources* 650
6. *Book and film reviews* 652
7. *Professional organizations* 652
8. *Image collections* 653
c. How do you choose electronic resources? 653
1. *The World Wide Web* 654
2. *Electronic conversations* 657
d. How do you search by keywords? 659
1. *Simple keyword searches* 660
2. *The principles of Boolean searching* 661
3. *Searching by exact phrase* 663
4. *Focusing your search* 663
e. How do you do field research? 664
1. *Conduct interviews* 664
2. *Conduct surveys* 665
3. *Make systematic observations* 669

45. How Do You Evaluate and Use Sources? 670

a. How do you evaluate research sources? 670
1. *Consider the purpose of a source* 670
2. *Consider the authority and reputation of a source* 671
3. *Consider the credentials of authors and sponsoring agencies* 671
4. *Consider the timeliness and stability of a source* 674
5. *Consider the biases of a source* 675
6. *Consider how well a source presents key information* 676
7. *Consider commercial intrusions into a source* 676

b. How do you use research materials?   677
    1. Position your sources   *677*
    2. Annotate your research materials   *682*
    3. Summarize or paraphrase a source   *684*
    4. Relate and connect your research materials   *691*
    GOING PUBLIC: *Using Sources*   *692*

46. How Do You Acknowledge Sources?   693

a. How do you document a research project?   693
    1. Provide a source for every direct quotation   *693*
    2. Document everything not considered common knowledge   *694*
    3. Document materials readers might question   *694*
    4. Furnish dates and credentials to assist readers   *695*
    5. Use links to document electronic sources   *695*
    6. Use computer programs to document your project   *695*
b. Do you understand academic responsibility?   696
    1. Acknowledge all direct uses of anyone else's work   *696*
    2. Summarize and paraphrase carefully   *698*
    3. Appreciate the unique features of electronic discourse *698*
    GOING PUBLIC: *Copying and Pasting*   *699*
    4. Understand the special nature of collaborative projects *701*
c. How do you handle quotations?   701
    1. Select direct quotations strategically   *702*
    2. Introduce all direct and indirect borrowings in some way *702*
    3. Fit direct quotations into the grammar of your sentences *704*
    4. Use ellipses (three spaced periods) for omitted material *704*
    5. Use square brackets to add necessary information   *706*
    6. Use [sic] for an error copied faithfully from a source *707*
    7. Use quotation marks around short quotations
        (MLA, APA)   *707*
    8. Indent more than three lines of poetry (MLA)   *707*
    9. Indent long prose quotations (MLA, APA)   *708*
    10. Refer to events in works of fiction in the present tense *708*

47. How Do You Complete a Project?   709

a. Is the organization solid?   709
    1. Narrow or qualify your claim   *709*
    2. Test your organization   *711*
b. Is the format correct?   712
    1. Pay attention to the format of your work   *712*
    2. Insert tables and figures as needed   *713*

3. Be consistent with headings *715*
c. Are the details correct? 717
   1. Include all necessary components *717*
   2. Follow documentation rules exactly *718*
   3. Submit your project professionally *718*

PART VIII

Documentation   721

48. How Do You Use MLA Documentation? 722
a. How to use MLA documentation 722
b. MLA models 728
c. How to use footnotes or endnotes 757
d. Sample MLA paper: "Can Quality Survive the
    Standardized Test?" 759

49. How Do You Use APA Documentation? 773
a. How to use APA documentation 773
b. APA models 777
c. Sample APA paper: "The Genome Project:
    Opportunities and Ethics" 788

50. How Do You Use CMS Documentation? 803
a. CMS notes 803
b. CMS bibliographies 806
c. CMS models 806
d. Sample CMS paper: "Diomedes as Hero of *The Iliad*" 812

51. How Do You Use CBE Documentation? 820
   1. Include in-text citations *820*
   2. List sources used at the end of your paper *821*

52. How Do You Use COS Documentation? 826
a. How to use COS documentation 826
b. COS models—Humanities (MLA) 831

c. Sample COS Works Cited page—Humanities (MLA)   841
d. COS models—Sciences (APA)   843
e. Sample COS References page—Sciences (APA)   853

Glossary of Terms and Usage   *856*
Credits   *901*
Index   *907*

Preface

Readers may not stand in line for the new edition of a reference work as they do for the latest Tom Clancy thriller or Harry Potter adventure. Yet volumes like *The Scott, Foresman Handbook for Writers,* aren't quite the staid items they once were. The world is changing too fast, especially for writers and readers producing documents with technologies that would have seemed like science fiction a generation ago. *The Scott, Foresman Handbook* remains the friendly, thorough guide to English composition, grammar, mechanics, punctuation, research, and documentation that has made it a best seller since its debut in 1987. But this sixth edition, like its predecessors, once again breaks new ground.

After all, innovation has been a hallmark of *The Scott, Foresman Handbook.* In matters large and small, it has accurately mapped the terrain that writers (and writing instructors) have been exploring for the past decade and more. It featured the first serious treatment of document design in a college handbook, the first appearance in a handbook of Alliance for Computers and Writing (ACW) and Columbia Online Style conventions for citing electronic sources, the first extended discussion of civic and public writing, and a groundbreaking discussion of Web and online research. It was also the first reference work of its kind to address readers in an informal style, the first to take a problem-solving approach to issues of writing, and even the first to index and color-code its documentation pages for quick reference. *The Scott, Foresman Handbook* is, we believe, the most imitated book in its field.

We expect the sixth edition to be similarly flattered. Our mantra for this revision has been "writer friendly," and we have interpreted that theme in dozens of ways to keep a popular volume surprising and fresh. We have introduced new material that we believe writers need today, and we have renovated familiar sections to make them clearer, more inviting, and more efficient. Here are the highlights.

- **Concerned about grades?** *The Scott, Foresman Handbook* is the first book of its kind to offer a full chapter exploring how writing is evaluated: Chapter 6, "How Is Writing Evaluated?" Designed to demystify an activity that scares or demoralizes many writers, this important new chapter provides answers to writers' questions about grading processes and criteria. Chapter 6 examines both traditional grading systems and writing portfolios. The chapter also outlines a writer's rights and responsibilities in the evaluation process.

● **Hope to make a difference?** The fifth edition of *The Scott, Foresman Handbook* provided support for writers reaching beyond academic assignments to do work in their local communities. This concern for civic and public writing is augmented in the sixth edition with new "Going Public" materials and enhanced attention to both service learning and distance learning programs. In addition to a newly expanded Chapter 8, "How Do You Write for the Public?" the handbook emphasizes civic and public issues throughout. For instance, in the new model MLA paper, a student teacher explores the consequences of using competency examinations in high school courses. It's an issue that matters to him because he faces it every day.

● **Need to craft a Web page?** Long a leader in explaining how contemporary technology is changing the way people write, *The Scott, Foresman Handbook* now includes a full chapter on creating Web pages:

Chapter 20, "How Do You Create Documents and Web Sites?" This fully illustrated chapter is designed to serve both Web novices and more experienced writers. For instance, it offers a flow chart to provide writers with a step-by-step sequence to Web site creation, whether they choose to work with a basic HTML editor or more helpful Web authoring software. Web design never looked quite so easy.

● **Want to look good?** The handbook that introduced document design to college writing classes takes the next step to examine the process of document design for both paper and electronic texts. The sophisticated tutorial in Chapter 19, "What Is Document Design?" asks writers to consider design the same way they treat writing, as a process shaped by rhetorical strategies and choices. Chapter 20, "How Do You Create Documents and Web Sites?" and Chapter 21, "Model Documents," follow up with specific advice on everything from choosing fonts to selecting a color palette and are richly illustrated with models that embody principles of successful design.

• **Want a book that practices what it preaches?** The sixth edition of *The Scott, Foresman Handbook for Writers* features a new four-color look that embodies the best features of contemporary design. Every effort has been made to create a more open and writer-friendly handbook, one less cluttered and *textbookish* than previous editions. Headings and fonts are crisper, graphic elements are more stylish, and colors used throughout the four-color volume are both more vivid and better coordinated. Even the reference system used to locate information in the book has been simplified, eliminating or reducing complicated cross-references.

• **Believe that less is more?** To make the new writer-friendly design work, we rethought the sequence and length of many chapters, hoping to give each section a distinct focus. For instance, we've broken the slightly mysterious and bulging "Problems with Other Punctuation Marks?" into three concise chapters with far more helpful titles: "Questions About Quotation Marks and Ellipses?" "Questions About Parentheses and Brackets?" and "Questions About Dashes, Hyphens, and Slashes?" (Note, too, that "Questions" replaces "Problems"—a more upbeat way of looking at these issues, we think.) A more serious restructuring occurs in the section on research, where we've broken three long chapters into a more manageable and inviting five. And throughout the book we've looked for similar opportunities to reframe material for clarity and efficiency.

- **Want to see real writers at work?** We wanted to fill this edition of *The Scott, Foresman Handbook* with images of writers. So, whenever possible, we've collected photographs of the students and professionals whose work appears in this volume. (Some writers chose not to appear.) We are happy to put a more human expression on a reference volume. We've also introduced illustrations to make memorable points about issues of writing, style, and mechanics. A few of the photographs are mainly for fun, but we suspect most readers won't mind.

Organizing Paragraphs **199**

EXERCISE 13.2 Examine critically one or two paragraphs of a draft you're currently working on: Do the paragraphs seem adequately unified? What unifying strategies have you used? Can you think of others that might be useful?

13b How can you organize paragraphs?

We don't know how many skilled writers consciously choose specific organizational patterns when they draft their essays or articles. Perhaps during the writing process certain patterns just emerge because they so closely resemble typical ways of thinking. Or perhaps some writers say to themselves, "I think I'll try a comparison-and-contrast pattern here" or "This would be a good place to use cause and effect." Whatever their origins, the paragraph patterns discussed in this section are common, and writers looking for a way to get started on a draft can profit by trying them.

13b ¶

SUMMARY *Common Paragraph Patterns*

illustration	classification
question and answer	comparison and contrast
narration or process	cause and effect
definition	analogy

1 Illustration. A paragraph of illustration begins with a general statement or claim and develops it with supporting details, evidence, or examples. This paragraph opens an essay by the professional writer Anna Quindlen; she follows a general statement about interaction between boys and girls with vivid descriptive details.

Perhaps we all have the same memory of the first boy-girl party we attended. The floors were waxed, the music loud, the air thick with the smell of cologne. The boys stood on one side of the room and the girls on the other, each affecting a nonchalance belied by the shuffling male loafers and the occasional high bird-like sound of a female giggle.
—Anna Quindlen, "Between the Sexes, a Great Divide"

In an argument paper, writers often follow a general claim with one or more pieces of supporting evidence.

---

200 What Makes Paragraphs Work?

The popularity of McDonald's holds true across the world except, ironically, in the United States, where sales have slumped. McDonald's now makes 59 percent of its profit outside the United States, [company spokesperson Brad] Trask said. In Moscow, where the world's busiest McDonald's opened in 1990, lines still spill out the door.
—Lini Kadaba, "No Beef"

2 Question and answer. Asking and answering a question is another way to organize a paragraph. Here's an example from the well-known science writer Carl Sagan.

What do we actually see when we look up at the Moon with the naked eye? We make out a configuration of irregular bright and dark markings—not a close representation of any familiar object. But almost irresistibly, our eyes connect the markings, emphasizing some, ignoring others. We seek a pattern, and we find one. In world myth and folklore, many images are seen: a woman weaving, stands of laurel trees, an elephant jumping off a cliff, a girl with a basket on her back, a rabbit, . . . a woman pounding tapa cloth, a four-eyed jaguar. People of one culture have trouble understanding how such bizarre things could be seen by the people of another.
—Carl Sagan, *The Demon-Haunted World*

When you're having real trouble finding an opening sentence, beginning with a question will often get your paragraph started.

13b ¶

3 Narration or process. One popular and simple way to develop a paragraph is to relate events or the steps of a process in chronological order. This pattern is obviously appropriate for writing personal or historical accounts, but you can also use it effectively to describe a scientific or technical process. Here is a narrative written by a naturalist studying wolves.

Quite by accident I had pitched my tent within ten yards of one of the major paths used by the wolves when they were going to, or coming from, their hunting grounds to the westward; and only a few hours after I had taken up residence one of the wolves came back from a trip and discovered me and my tent. He was at the end of a hard night's work and was clearly tired and anxious to go home to bed. He came over a small rise fifty yards from me with his head down, his eyes half-closed, and a preoccupied air about him. Far from being the preternaturally alert and suspicious beast

---

- **Need to look it up?** No part of *The Scott, Foresman Handbook* has been more admired (or imitated) than its chapters on research and documentation. This leadership is enhanced in the sixth edition with a thorough reworking of material that long ago anticipated professional calls to take undergraduate research more seriously. (*The Scott, Foresman Handbook* has always done that.) The restructured chapters now give more focused attention to the design and planning phase of a research project. There is enhanced coverage of field research too, as well as updated and expanded material on electronic tools and resources. Even more attention is given to techniques for evaluating and using sources than in the previous edition, which set a new standard for this coverage. All the documentation chapters have been refined and simplified to make it easier to figure out how to document an item. Once again, we cover a full range of documentation styles: MLA, APA, Chicago, CBE, and COS.

- **Want to search online?** For the first time, *The Scott, Foresman Handbook* supplements its discussions of writing processes, research, and mechanics with Web links called "E-Tips" that guide writers to valuable information online. We've resisted the temptation to provide URLs at every possible opportunity; instead, we've selected links that genuinely extend the discussion in *The Scott, Foresman Handbook* and offer writers more than we can fit into the handbook. We've also looked for links that should age gracefully, though we can't guarantee their longevity. Web addresses change about as often as the weather.

- **Need to know how English does it?** We wanted to offer more help to writers whose native language is not English. So we revised our material significantly, dividing one lengthy chapter into three more focused ones. The material is more engaging too, with the rhetorical issues faced by ESL writers addressed more directly.

- **How has *The Scott, Foresman Handbook* been revised in this sixth edition?** When we began this revision, we compiled a list of changes as we made them—and soon found ourselves slowed down by the effort to record all refinements. Suffice to say that every chapter has been reviewed and hundreds of items have been improved. Some changes are major ones—for example, the addition of lively new models of undergraduate writing in Chapter 11,

"How Can You Write Powerful Arguments?" and Chapter 12, "How Do You Write a Literary Analysis?" Other changes are more limited but no less important. Exercises have been improved, cultural references have been updated, and the style has been smoothed in section after section. Again and again, our list of changes records modifications made "for clarity and economy." Many changes reflect the fact that the authors of *The Scott, Foresman Handbook* teach writing to undergraduates (especially first-year students) every semester, year after year. We want this book to work for them.

- **What's not new?** *The Scott, Foresman Handbook for Writers* retains its authoritative discussion of the writing process; its full coverage of critical thinking, argumentation, and academic writing; its engaging coverage of grammar, mechanics, and usage; its lively discussion of research; and its exhaustive treatment of documentation. Perhaps most important, it retains its commitment to writers, addressing them throughout in language that is both personal and encouraging. We realize that writing is hard work and that even a volume as thick as this one just begins to address the complexities writers face in sharing their ideas. We want them to succeed.

···

Supplements

An extensive package of supplements accompanies *The Scott, Foresman Handbook for Writers,* Sixth Edition, for both instructors and students.

For Instructors

- *The Instructor's Resource Manual: Creating a Community of Writers,* by John Clark and Ann Recker Westrick of Bowling Green University and Christy Friend, offers guidance to new and experienced teachers in using the handbook and the ancillary package to its best advantage.
- A separate *Answer Key for The Scott, Foresman Handbook for Writers,* Sixth Edition, provides answers to all the exercises in the book.
- *An Introduction to Teaching Composition in an Electronic Environment,* by Eric Hoffman and Carol Scheidenhelm of Northern Illinois University, offers a wealth of computer-related classroom activities. It also provides detailed guidance for both experienced and inexperienced instructors who wish to make creative use of technology in a composition environment.
- An extensive assessment package includes Competency Profile tests, and sample CLAST and TASP exams. In addition, *Diagnostic and Editing Tests,* Third Edition, includes diagnostic tests for analyzing common errors. The additional exercise sets on grammar, punctuation, and mechanics topics supplement those found in the handbook. (It is also available in computerized Windows and Macintosh formats.)
- *Model Research Papers Across the Disciplines,* Fifth Edition, by Diane Gould of Shoreline Community College, is a collection of student papers in the humanities, social sciences, and natural sciences, and contains photo-reproducible material that can be distributed to students.
- *The Allyn & Bacon Sourcebook for College Writing Teachers,* Second Edition, edited by James McDonald of the University of Louisiana at Lafayette, provides instructors with a varied selection of readings written by composition and rhetoric scholars on both theoretical and practical subjects.
- Longman Resources for Instructors also includes these helpful texts: *Teaching in Progress: Theories, Practices, and Scenarios,* Third Edition; *Using Portfolios,* by Kathleen McClelland; *Comp Tales,* a collection of writing teachers' accounts of their teaching

experiences, edited by Richard Haswell and Min-Zhan Lu; and the videos *Writing, Teaching, and Learning,* by David Jolliffe and *Writing Across the Curriculum: Making It Work,* produced by Robert Morris College and the Public Broadcasting System.

For Students

- A handy *Documentation Guide* offers up-to-date documentation guidelines for MLA, APA, CMS, CBE, and COS styles, as they are presented in *The Scott, Foresman Handbook for Writers,* Sixth Edition. It also includes complete sample MLA and APA student papers.
- *Researching Online,* Fifth Edition, by David Munger and Shireen Campbell of Davidson College, gives students detailed, step-by-step instructions for performing electronic searches; for using e-mail, listservs, Usenet newsgroups, IRC, and MUDs and MOOs to do research; and for assessing the validity of electronic sources.
- *ESL Worksheets,* Third Edition, by Jocelyn Steer and Dawn Schmid of California State University, San Marcos, provides non-native speakers with extra practice in areas that tend to be more troublesome for them.
- The Literacy Library Series (*Public Literacy,* by Elizabeth Ervin; *Workplace Literacy,* by Rachel Spilka; and *Academic Literacy,* by Stacia Neeley) offers additional models and instruction for writing for each of these three different contexts.
- *The Longman Writer's Journal* by Mimi Markus, provides students with their own personal space for writing. It contains journal writing strategies, sample journal entries by other students, and many writing prompts and topics to help get students writing.
- Additional Longman Resources for Students include: *The Longman Researcher's Journal,* by Mimi Markus; *Visual Communication,* Second Edition, by Susan Hilligoss and Tharon Howard; *A Guide for Peer Response,* by Tori Haring-Smith, Brown University and Helon Raines; *Analyzing Literature: A Guide for Students,* by Sharon James McGee; and *Reading Critically: Text, Charts, Graphs,* Second Edition, by Judith Olson-Fallon.
- This handbook may also be packaged with other books at a discount. Two dictionaries are available: *Merriam-Webster's Collegiate Dictionary,* Tenth Edition, a hardcover desk dictionary; and *The New American Webster Handy College Dictionary,* Third Edition, a briefer paperback. Also, in conjunction with Penguin Putnam, Longman is proud to offer a variety of Penguin titles, such as Arthur Miller's *Death of a Salesman,* Julia Alvarez's *How the Garcia Girls Lost Their Accents,* and Mike Rose's *Lives on the Boundary.*

For Instructors and Students

- A companion website, *The Scott, Foresman Handbook for Writers Online* (at <www.ablongman.com/sfhandbooks>), offers chapter overviews, self-testing exercises, and Web links for each chapter of the handbook. Students will also find several additional model research projects, and tutorials on topics like drafting and revising, oral presentations, analyzing visuals, academic responsibility, and more. Sample syllabi, sample quizzes and assignments, teaching suggestions, and other resources are also provided for instructors.

- A complete **e-book edition** of *The Scott, Foresman Handbook for Writers,* Sixth Edition, is also available via this companion website.

- *The Scott, Foresman Handbook for Writers Interactive Edition CD-ROM* contains the complete, searchable text of the Sixth Edition, with additional live Web links, some audio and video explanations of key concepts, and interactive exercises.

- *The Longman English Tutor Center* is a new service being offered by Longman. Students who register with our Tutor Center can receive feedback to their draft writing assignments from experienced college instructors of English composition.

- *The Longman ExerciseZone and Plagiarism Tutorial CD-ROM* is a cross-platform CD-ROM that offers two interactive resources in one. "Exercise Zone" has over 2,500 exercises in ten topic areas of grammar, style, and punctuation with a diagnostic test to help students identify the areas where they need the most practice. The "Plagiarism Tutorial" includes a series of modules which allow students to explore issues of plagiarism, with advice, self-scoring tests, and sample papers to help them learn to avoid and recognize plagiarism.

- *Take Note!* is a complete research information-management tool for students working on projects that require the use of outside sources. This cross-platform CD-ROM integrates note taking, outlining, and bibliography management into one easy-to-use package.

- *The Writer's ToolKit Plus* is a cross-platform CD-ROM offering a wealth of tutorials, exercises, and reference material for writers and is flexible enough to be used either occasionally for practice or regularly in class lab sessions.

- *CourseCompass* is a nationally-hosted, dynamic, interactive online course management system powered by BlackBoard. This easy-to-use and customizable program enables professors to tailor content and functionality to meet individual course needs. Every CourseCompass course includes a range of pre-loaded content such as testing and assessment questions, chapter-level objectives, chapter summaries, illustrations, web activities and the complete text in electronic form—all designed to help students master core course objectives. For more information, or to see a demo, visit <www.coursecompass.com>.

- *Daedalus Online* (<http://daedalus.pearsoned.com>) is the next generation of the highly regarded Daedalus Integrated Writing Environment (DIWE), uniting writing pedagogy with the inherently cooperative tools of the Web. Students can explore online resources, participate in real-time conferences, and use "Invent" and "Respond" prompts to develop their ideas and collaborate with their peers. *Daedalus Online's* online course management tools also enable instructors to create and post assignments effortlessly, link them to online educational resources, tie lessons to a specific textbook, and customize materials for their classroom.

Acknowledgements

Since a project of this size and scope is necessarily (and fortunately) a collaborative effort, we have many people to thank for their work on *The Scott, Foresman Handbook*. Our acquisitions editor Lynn Huddon supported the new ideas we presented at the proposal stage and provided sound guidance as the book developed and grew. Leslie Taggart, our developmental editor, brought her wealth of experience to this complex effort, coordinating the hundreds of changes we were making with precision and good cheer. Text designer Wendy Ann Fredericks gave our pages a handsome new look and helped us to incorporate dozens of new images into the project. Kay Petronio designed the striking new cover and Donna Campion coordinated the massive package of text supplements. And then there is Bob Ginsberg, our senior production manager who, edition after edition, leaves us in awe of his patience, skill, and book-making sensibility. He is the consummate professional.

We owe a special debt, too, to Carol Rhoades for her fine update of our ESL chapters and to Dan Seward who is largely responsible for the three chapters in *The Scott, Foresman Handbook* on document design. Dan crafted not only the chapters themselves, but the detailed illustrations that accompany them and make them come alive. We would like to thank Lee Bauknight for his fine work on the answer key and Chris Fosen, Eileen Hart, and Ray McManus for useful editing suggestions. Our sincere thanks goes to all the students whose papers, projects, and smiling faces appear in these pages. It is an honor to publish their work. Finally, we thank all of the instructors who have used *The Scott. Foresman Handbook* over its many editions, most especially those reviewers whose comments contributed directly to this latest revision:

Other reviewers who have given us the benefit of their expertise are J. Robert Baker, Fairmont State College; Sue Beebe, Southwest Texas State University; Bill Bolin, Texas A&M University, Commerce; Andrew Burke, University of Georgia; Peggy Cheng, Southern Oregon University; John M. Clark, Bowling Green State University; John Coakley, New Jersey Institute of Technology; Deborah Core, Eastern Kentucky University; Lauren S. Coulter, University of Tennessee at Chattanooga; Aleta J. Crockett, Bluefield State College; Laurie Delaney, Kent State University; Dawn L. Elmore-McCrary, San Antonio College; April Fallon, Kentucky State University; Jim Frazer, University of Arkansas at Little Rock; Cassy Gilson, Broward Community College; Tami Haaland, Montana State University, Billings; Ashan Hampton, Morehouse College; Candy A. Henry, Penn State University, New Kensington; Mary Lynch Kennedy, State University of New York at Cortland; Judith Kerman, Saginaw Valley State University; Scott Orme, Spokane Community College; Jennifer Palmgren, University of Kansas; Pennie Pflueger, Louisiana State University; Susan Pratt, Concordia University, St. Paul; William Provost, University of Georgia; Dave Rieder, University of Texas at Arlington; David Sandell, University of Texas; Karah Stokes, Kentucky State University; Jennifer Turley, DeVry Institute of Technology; Pauline Uchmanowicz, State University of New York at New Paltz; Ted Walkup, Clayton College and State University; Lori Watts, McLennan Community College; June West, Bates Technical College.

Maxine Hairston

John J. Ruszkiewicz

Christy Friend

Writing Processes

1 What Does Writing Involve?

2 How Do You Find and Explore a Topic?

3 How Do You Focus and Organize a Writing Project?

4 How Do You Write a Draft?

5 How Do You Revise, Edit, and Proofread?

6 How Is Writing Evaluated?

CHAPTER 1

What Does Writing Involve?

1a Why write?

- Students at the University of Arizona designed and created Web sites for local nonprofit agencies, including the Tucson Ronald McDonald House, as part of a business writing class.
- A first-year English student at the University of South Carolina regularly attends a community writers' group to get feedback on papers she's drafting for classes and poetry she writes for fun.
- An education major at Trinity University wrote a letter that alerted her employer to potentially dangerous staffing shortages at the summer day camp where she worked.
- A psychology major at the University of Oklahoma earned the opportunity to present her research to professionals in her field when she submitted a course paper she had written to a statewide academic conference.

As these examples suggest, writing is not a mysterious activity at which only a talented few can succeed. Nor is it a purely academic skill that you will leave behind at graduation. On the contrary. In our information-based society, almost everyone writes. Through writing, people share what they know, debate issues, promote their beliefs, and advocate change. Whether you are drafting a letter to your senator about student loan funding or posting an online notice to recruit players for your intramural volleyball team, writing gives you a public voice.

Writing is also a rich medium for intellectual inquiry. As the novelist E. M. Forster put it, "How do I know what I think until I see what I say?" Many people use writing to work through their ideas on an issue or to help organize complex material they learn in school or on the job.

The ability to write has become even more important with the explosion of electronic media during the past decade. People once could get along in school by writing papers that would be seen only by their teachers, or at work by writing an occasional memo to the boss. But today writers must address wider audiences as part of a typical day's work. In school, you may communicate with classmates and instructors online—in fact, if you are taking distance education courses, email may be your primary mode of communication. At work, computerized conferencing software makes it easy to network with colleagues worldwide. Citizens now also have computerized access to a multitude of government agencies and archives.

Years ago, futurists predicted that computers would make writing obsolete. Now we know that these technologies have only expanded its possibilities. As you begin this handbook, then, don't approach it as a dusty collection of rules that you can forget at the end of the term. Instead, read it knowing that writing is a powerful medium for communication and for learning. Writing matters.

E-Tips   To see more examples of student writing projects from a variety of majors, see the "Model Research Projects" feature in the "Student Resources" section of our Web site, at <http://www.ablongman.com/hairston>.

1b What does it take to write well?

To take full advantage of the opportunities writing offers, you first need to *see* yourself as a writer. Many people underestimate their potential as writers because they don't realize that writing is a skill that almost anyone can master.

Resist myths that can discourage writers. The following myths about writing have been around for a long time; don't let them fool you.

- **Myth:** *Good writers are born, not made.*
  Fact: People become good writers by working at writing. If you want to write well, you can if you invest the time.
- **Myth:** *Good writers know what they want to say before they start writing.*
  Fact: Many good writers begin with only a general notion of what they want to say. They know that the process of writing can help them generate new ideas and rethink what they already know.
- **Myth:** *Good writers get it right the first time.*
  Fact: Although experienced writers sometimes produce polished work on the first try, they usually must work through several drafts.

- **Myth:** *Good writers work alone.*
  Fact: Writers often rely on colleagues for ideas and help, even if they will do much of the actual composing alone. They may also co-author articles, reports, or essays.
- **Myth:** *Writing won't be important once you leave school.*
  Fact: Most people write every day, whether or not they are in school. Even professionals in technical fields like engineering, medicine, and computer science spend a significant portion of their time communicating their expertise through written reports and proposals.
- **Myth:** *Only professional authors publish their work.*
  Fact: Now that technology makes it so easy to preserve and distribute documents, even the writing you do in school may reach large audiences online via the World Wide Web or campus publications.

EXERCISE 1.1 Make a list of every piece of writing you've produced during the past three days. Then discuss these questions with a group of classmates: What activities in your everyday life require writing? What kinds of tasks do you accomplish through writing? With whom do you communicate when you write? Do you do most of your writing in or outside school?

EXERCISE 1.2 When you think of the term *writer,* what kind of person comes to mind? Many people reserve the terms *author* and *journalist* for those who make their living solely by writing. But can you think of other people who write frequently? What kinds of writing do they do? Discuss your answers with your classmates.

1c How does writing work?

It's tempting to believe that there's a secret formula for writing well and that if you could just discover it, your life would be much easier. We assure you that no such formula exists—there's no quick or foolproof way to turn an initial idea into a polished final paper. Nonetheless, researchers agree that most people, when they write, follow general thinking patterns similar to those that occur in other creative activities. Chart 1.1 on page 5 outlines these general stages and describes some of the activities writers engage in during each.

Remember, though, that any formal diagram of these stages can only hint at what writers really do. Writing is a complex activity that

Chart 1.1

Stages of Writing

- **Preparing**
  Read, brainstorm, browse online, and talk to people in order to decide what you want to write about and to generate ideas about it.

- **Researching**
  Gather facts or examples from reading, conversations with others, field research, or your own experiences, to support your ideas.

- **Planning**
  Develop and organize your ideas further, perhaps preparing working lists, outlines, summaries, or note cards.

- **Drafting**
  Begin to put words down on a page or screen. Compose one or more drafts, rethinking and reshaping your materials as necessary.

- **Incubating**
  Take time off to let your ideas simmer. New ideas may come to you after you've taken a break.

- **Revising**
  Critically review what you have written and make any large-scale changes you need in topic, organization, content, or audience adaptation.

- **Editing**
  Critically review your draft to make smaller-scale changes in style, clarity, and readability.

- **Proofreading**
  Read carefully to rid your project of mechanical problems such as spelling and punctuation errors and to be sure that you have met any formatting requirements.

Figure 1.1 *Like any creative activity, writing is dynamic and flexible. It can't be approached as a predictable sequence of steps, because the process may be different for different writing projects—just as a painter can take different approaches to presenting a visual image.*

involves rich and mutually reinforcing skills. A chart can't show nuances in the process, overlap among the various stages, or differentiate among individual writers and varied writing situations. Some successful writers—like Justin Cone, whose paper draft appears at the end of Chapter 5—shift freely among the preparing, researching, planning, and revising stages as they work. Others, like Barbara Westbrook, whose work appears in Chapter 9, delay major revisions until they have a first draft. Still others—like Christy Friend, co-author of this book—revise as they go along. For complex projects, writers may need to repeat steps in the process several times.

Writers also adjust their approach to their purpose, their audience, and the specific demands of the project. Writing a 15-page term paper for a professor requires extensive planning and research; sending an email to ask your lab partner about an upcoming homework assignment may require very little. So don't think of the writing process as a lockstep march from outlining to proofreading. It's a dynamic, flexible network of choices. Writers adapt the process to their needs.

EXERCISE 1.3 Think back to a piece of your writing you were proud of—perhaps a letter to the editor that was published, a personal statement that won you a scholarship, or an *A* paper in a difficult class—and write a paragraph describing the preparation you put into it, how many times you revised it, and why you think it was successful.

EXERCISE 1.4 Write a paragraph or two candidly describing your most hectic writing experience, when you were most pressed to get an assignment done. What did you have to do to finish the paper? Was it successful? Why or why not? What, if anything, would you do differently if you had the chance to do it again?

1d   How do you define a writing situation?

Writing is a *social activity,* a way of interacting with others. Every time you write, you enter into a *writing situation* in which

- *You*
- Say *something*
- To *somebody*
- For *some purpose*

Experts on *rhetoric,* the art of persuasive communication, believe that people communicate more effectively when they think in these terms: *what* do I want to say, to *whom,* and *why?* Thus, every time you write, you should think carefully about your purpose, your audience, and how you want to come across to your readers. Probably no other single habit will do more to help you become a skilled writer.

1e How do you define your purpose(s) in writing?

When you begin a writing project, consider why you are writing in the first place. Do you need to show an instructor that you've mastered a difficult concept or reading assignment? Do you have an idea you care about and want others to care about too? Is there an ongoing debate you wish to enter? We don't mean that every time you write you have to come up with an earth-shattering idea or that everything you write must aim at a serious and lofty goal. Nonetheless, having a general purpose in mind will help you to focus and to think about the kinds of supporting materials you will need. This section will help you understand some common purposes for writing.

1 Decide what you hope to accomplish. You will usually write more effectively if you think about your purpose ahead of time and use it to shape your first draft. Centuries ago, theorists of rhetoric identified three basic purposes for writing: writing *to inform,* or writing that teaches readers new information; writing *to persuade,* or writing that convinces readers to believe or act in new ways; and writing *to entertain,* writing that diverts and engages readers.

Sometimes you may want to achieve more than one of these goals within a single paper. To review a restaurant for a campus magazine, for example, your primary aim might be to *evaluate* the food and service, but you would also want to *persuade* readers to visit or avoid the restaurant and perhaps to *entertain* them as well. See Section 3b for specific methods for organizing papers to suit particular purposes.

Thinking about these purposes isn't just an exercise; it's a practical matter. When you don't know why you're writing, you can't produce a coherent paper. If you find that you are starting a draft without any idea of your goals, you may need a clearer explanation of the task.

Sometimes you may not be completely sure of your purpose until you've explored the topic by writing a first draft. You may look into several angles on an idea before you figure out what you want to say. Eventually, though, even the most exploratory essay must articulate a purpose that satisfies both writer and readers. The purpose checklist below will help you think about your goals in writing.

Checklist 1.1

Purpose

1. If you are writing a paper for a course, list any description of purpose in the assignment. Target words like *narrate, explain, argue, evaluate.*

2. What do you want readers to get from your piece? Do you want to inform, explain, persuade, or entertain? If you have more than one goal, which is the most important, and which are secondary?

3. What supporting materials will you draw on to achieve your goal(s)? What research, examples, or personal experience will you use?

4. How will you present these supporting materials in your paper? Will you narrate, define, describe, compare and contrast, explain, or argue?

5. What form will this project take? Will you write a letter, editorial, report, Web page, or review, for example? Where might you publish this piece?

2 Consider how other elements in the writing situation shape your purpose(s). Although we discuss each aspect of the writing situation separately in this chapter, in practice it's difficult to consider any of these elements in isolation. For any project, your purpose(s) will help you define your audience, the form in which you present your ideas, and the impression you want to make. Suppose, for example, that you are angry about a proposal to stop offering evening courses at your college. If you want to convince people that these courses should continue, you have a choice of audiences. Here is where your purpose becomes important.

If you want direct action, you need to write to the person in charge of scheduling courses—the college scheduling office or the provost's office, for example. For this audience, your purpose might be to construct a calm, well-supported argument demonstrating the harmful effects of cancellation—potential graduation delays for working students who can attend class only in the evening, shrinking college enrollment if angry evening students transfer to other local colleges, and so on. If, however, you want to get fellow students to join you in a protest, you might draft and circulate a petition or publish a newspaper editorial condemning the proposed cancellation in more passionate terms.

1f How do you write for an audience?

Suppose that you are concerned about the lack of after-school programs for children in your city.

- You decide to write a research paper for a government course, documenting that such programs help prevent juvenile crime.
- The next week, your city council debates whether to enter into a partnership with the local YMCA to pilot an after-school activities program at a local elementary school. You compose a short statement supporting the project and read it during the town-hall portion of the meeting.
- Months later, as part of a volunteer team, you prepare a flyer to distribute to elementary school students, encouraging them to sign up for the YMCA program.

Although the topic and your viewpoint remain the same, your three pieces of writing will differ dramatically. The academic paper will use technical terminology, academic source materials, and a sophisticated organizational structure. The statement to the city council might draw on the same sources, but it will be shorter and it will argue a position more strongly. The children's flyer will rely on simple language and visual elements. All these differences represent *audience adaptations,* the ways in which a writer tailors a piece to appeal to readers' interests and needs.

Each time you write, you will have to think carefully about who your audience might be and how they will respond to the material you are writing about. Perhaps the examples above—the differences among writing for a college professor, a panel of city officials, and a group of fourth-graders—make audience adaptation seem simple. It's not. Even seasoned writers sometimes misjudge their readers, offering material that baffles or bores them.

Sometimes writers have to contend with multiple and possibly conflicting audiences: men and women; young, middle-aged, and older people; liberals and conservatives; teacher and classmates. In other cases, identifying an audience at all seems nearly impossible. When you create a Web page, for example, literally anyone in the world who has access to the Internet might read it.

Don't let these complexities discourage you. Even though you cannot always pinpoint your readers or predict their responses, knowing even a few parameters will help you focus. To help you reach your audience, try the following two-step process.

1. **Analyze your audience.** Brainstorm a list of all the groups who are likely to read your work. Then, for each group, consider what knowledge, attitudes, and needs they are likely to bring to your topic.

2. **Tailor your work to respond to these characteristics.** With your audience in mind, decide how much background information you need to provide, whether you can use specialized terminology, and whether readers will need to be persuaded to accept your ideas. Think about which kinds of examples and arguments might entice and which might alienate them.

For example, an audience of local business owners would be unlikely to respond to a request for computer funds for a high school on the grounds that computers enhance students' artistic skills. They might, however, get excited at the prospect of preparing students for the workforce. See Sections 16c and 16d for more on appealing to particular audiences.

Learning how to appeal to an audience takes time and practice, but it is a skill that any writer can master. As you begin to think about your readers, consult the audience checklist below. If within a single project you will reach several potential audiences, run through the checklist for each group. Then you'll need to reconcile the differences among those groups as you write—admittedly not an easy task. But at least you'll have a clearer idea of the challenge.

Checklist 1.2

Audience

1. Does the assignment specify a particular audience? If so, describe that audience. If not, whom do you visualize as the audience(s) for this project?

2. What reasons might they have for reading your work?

3. What do they already know about your subject? What kinds of information will they need you to provide?

4. What general values and beliefs are important to them? To what kinds of examples and arguments are they likely to respond?

5. What is their attitude about your subject? How will you convince them of the value of your ideas?

EXERCISE 1.5 Briefly analyze what you think readers would want to know if you were writing

1. a personal statement for a scholarship application.

2. a letter disputing a charge on your credit card account.

3. a description of an experiment you carried out for a chemistry class.

4. a message to several listservs encouraging students to attend a performance by your best friend's blues band.

EXERCISE 1.6 Working with a classmate, select a magazine—some possibilities are *Sports Illustrated, Spin, Harper's, Maxim, Money, Wired, Good Housekeeping, Jet*—and study the advertisements and the kinds of articles it carries. Then draft a description of the kind of people you think the editor and publisher of the magazine assume its readers to be. Use the audience checklist on page 10 to guide your work.

1g How do you present yourself to readers?

Just as important as audience and purpose is knowing what kind of impression you want to make on readers. Readers respond most favorably when they trust and respect the person sending the message. This is why we see Olympic athletes pitching tennis shoes on television and successful entrepreneurs selling books about investment strategies. But presenting an effective image isn't just about "selling" something. It's also about showing readers that you are a person whose ideas are worth listening to. This section will help you do just that.

1 Show readers that you are credible. Would you take driving lessons from someone whose license has been revoked? Or let someone with no computer training replace your hard drive? Of course not. It's a question of credibility, of having enough knowledge about or experience with the topic to be believable. Readers expect you to show that you know what you are talking about before they will give your ideas serious consideration.

One way to achieve credibility is to learn everything you can about a topic before you begin writing. Do your homework. Find out who the authorities are on your subject and become familiar with their work. Read background sources to get a sense of key terminology, concepts, and the debates within the field and to find out about recent developments. Once you have this knowledge, you will be able to write about the subject with confidence. And you will project this confidence to readers. See Sections 44a and 44b for more on researching a topic.

Your personal experiences can also build credibility. In writing about U.S. immigration policy, for example, don't hesitate to share your childhood experience of coming with your family to this country from Taiwan. Even though your experience doesn't make you an authority on every aspect of the subject, it gives you knowledge that is richer and in some ways more powerful than what you can learn from books. Of course, there are forums—such as scientific writing—in which personal expression is generally inappropriate. But when the assignment allows it, readers will respect your close involvement with a topic.

Finally, to win readers' respect, you must come across as a professional. Format your work appropriately, edit carefully, and proofread thoroughly to show your audience that you are serious about your work.

The self-presentation checklist below will help you to credibly present yourself to readers.

Checklist 1.3

Presenting Yourself to Readers

1. How can you show readers that you are knowledgeable about your subject? What research, reading, or personal experience will you draw upon?

2. How will you show readers that you are trustworthy? What will you do to present information accurately and fully?

3. How will you show readers that you are reasonable and fair? What tone will you adopt, and how will you talk about opposing views?

2 Present material fairly and honestly. Some television commercials annoy viewers because they make grand claims about a product or denigrate competitors without sufficient supporting evidence. If you're like most people, this kind of dishonesty turns you off.

Readers believe writers whom they perceive as trustworthy, so you'll need to present material accurately and fairly in a paper. Base your arguments on reputable sources, and be open about any gaps or limitations in what you know. Suppose you're writing a paper about the negative effects of day care on young children. You will need to acknowledge that some studies indicate that day care is not especially harmful. Otherwise, readers who have heard of such studies will think that you are trying to hide something.

1g
image

You will also need to cite the sources of your information, to show that the materials you've consulted are reliable and authoritative. When readers see that you treat your subject honestly, they'll be more open to your ideas. See Chapters 45 and 46 for more about evaluating and documenting sources.

■ **3 Use a civil tone.** Being polite to those who disagree with you may seem a bit naive given the hostile tone of much public discussion in our society. It sometimes seems that the more outrageous the statement, the more attention it gets, and you may be tempted to follow this trend in your writing. Don't be fooled—the loudest voices aren't always the ones that people end up listening to.

When animal rights activists deride meat eaters as "murderers" or yell obscenities at medical researchers whose experiments involve animals, they offend far more of their audience than they convince. When a radio talk-show host jokes about shooting a politician whose views annoy him, more listeners are disgusted than impressed. Readers don't want to identify with a bully. They will resist your ideas if you come across as mean-spirited.

You will project a more credible image when you treat different viewpoints fairly and generously. It's fine to disagree strongly with another's ideas; without vigorous disagreement, neither democracy nor intellectual exchange can thrive. But confine your criticism to the issues rather than attack your opponent's worth as a human being. Avoid name-calling ("idiot," "Religious Right fanatic," "tax-and-spend liberal"), inflammatory language (calling a viewpoint "evil," "stupid," "un-American"), and ethnic or gender stereotypes. Not only will you sound more professional, but your fairness will lay the groundwork for ongoing conversation with readers who hold different views.

For more about avoiding bias in your language, see Section 16d. For detailed advice about addressing opposing views, see Section 11c.

EXERCISE 1.7 Writers of political advertisements are especially sensitive to the importance of creating a positive image for their candidates. Obtain copies of campaign advertisements and literature from a recent election, or look up an elected official's home page on the World Wide Web. Then, working with a group of classmates, discuss how successfully the politician presents himself or herself as credible, honest, and likable. Circle words, phrases, and details that suggest these qualities. Are you persuaded by this image?

1g
image

EXERCISE 1.8 Select a subject that you know a lot about, and imagine that you have been asked to write about it for several different venues: a college research paper, a televised public-service announcement, and a letter for the editorial page of a local newspaper. How would each element of the writing situation—your purpose, your audience, and the image you want to project as a writer—affect the written product? Which task appeals to you the most? Discuss your responses with your classmates.

CHAPTER 2

How Do You Find and Explore a Topic?

2a How do you find a topic?

Sometimes you will start a writing project knowing exactly what you want to write about. When you don't have to find your topic, you can begin immediately to generate ideas, plan, and start a draft.

Often, however, college instructors encourage students to choose their own topics, believing that students write better when they can investigate subjects that interest them. "Having a choice is great," you may say, "but how do I find a topic that both my readers and I will enjoy?"

1 Think beyond broad, traditional topics. Too often students think that they should always write about issues of earthshaking importance. Does this list look familiar?

Abortion	Gun Control	Euthanasia
Child Abuse	Capital Punishment	Pollution

These issues *are* important. And if you feel passionately enough about one of them to be willing to do the research that will add something current, fresh, or informative to the debate on that issue, don't shy away from it. However, be aware that so much has already been written about these issues that you risk bogging down in generalities and clichés. Tired old material won't impress readers, no matter how serious its subject.

If you do choose one of these broad topics, make your paper unique by focusing on a recent controversy or a local case. Rather than write a general paper on gun control, you might concentrate on recent proposals that aim to prevent school shootings by requiring every public school to install metal detectors. Similarly, while a generic paper on capital punishment would probably rehash arguments that are decades old, one that investigates a local death penalty case might yield new insights. Checklist 2.1 on page 16 can help you find original angles on a traditional issue.

2a
topic

Checklist 2.1

To Find a Topic, Ask Yourself . . .

* **What three subjects do you enjoy reading about most?** What magazines do you pick up? What kinds of books do you browse through? Which newspaper headlines catch your eye?

* **What three subjects do you know the most about?** What topics could you discuss for half an hour without notes? What problems lead people to seek your advice or expertise? What could you teach someone else to do?

* **What three subjects are you most curious about?** What issues or subjects have you always wanted to learn more about, but never had the time? On what topics would you like to become an expert?

* **What three subjects do you enjoy arguing about most?** On what subjects can you hold your own with just about anyone? What opinions do you advocate most strongly? For what causes do you volunteer your time?

* **What three issues in your community do you care about the most?** What issues affect you or people you know? What opinions and ideas would you like to communicate to government officials or to the community at large?

2 Consider your interests and strengths. When you have to invest as much energy in a task as you do in a writing project, be good to yourself. Choose a topic that interests you, preferably one that you already have some knowledge and ideas about. Begin by brainstorming a list of possibilities: current issues on campus or in your neighborhood, activities you're involved in, experiences you've had, or subjects that you've always been curious about. Some writers carry an "idea book" or journal so that they can jot down interesting thoughts whenever they occur. Look over your list and select one or two ideas that seem best suited for the assignment and the amount of time you have to complete the project. Checklist 2.1 above will help you discover such topics.

3 Choose a topic in your world. You may be used to heading straight for the library when you receive a paper assignment. But some of the best issues for writing are unfolding right in front of you. Perhaps your local school board is debating whether to require uniforms in city high schools, or a branch of your city's library system that serves a low-income neighborhood is slated for closure. Or maybe you're concerned about increased gang activity in your grandparents' neighborhood.

Even if your instructor has assigned a topic, try to connect that topic to your own experience or to issues in your community. For example, an assignment to research the civil rights movement for your history class could lead you to inquire about local concerns: Was your school or community ever segregated? How did your city or town react to civil rights initiatives or legislation? Do contemporary concerns for women's or gay rights have roots in this earlier political movement?

Any one of these issues could make a promising paper topic. Because such topics connect to your everyday life, you're bound to have a strong interest in finding out more about them. Additionally, when you concentrate on local events, you are more likely to do original research; expert sources of information—newspapers, community organizations, government offices, and interested citizens—are close at hand. And should you decide to publish your writing outside the classroom, perhaps as a guest newspaper editorial or as a letter to an elected official, you may even influence public opinion on your topic.

4 Browse in the library. If you have a general subject area in mind, try looking it up in the library catalog or in the directory of the Library of Congress (better known as the *Subject List*). Just the way a broad subject is broken down into headings and subheadings should suggest many topic possibilities. Consult such reference sources as specialized encyclopedias, too. If you want to learn about endangered animal species in your state, for example, a glance at the *Encyclopedia of the Environment* might provide several topic ideas.

Even when you don't have a general subject area to direct your library search, try browsing in the periodicals room or the new book section for topics that spark your curiosity. For more on finding library sources, see Sections 44a and 44b.

E-Tips
> Now that most college libraries have put part or all of their card catalogs and reference databases online, you can browse the library without leaving your desk. Visit your college or university's Web site to find out how to access your library's resources.

5 Look for ideas online. In addition to the library materials your school offers online, the Internet offers a multitude of resources for writing. If you have a general subject in mind, look for newsgroups to see what others are saying about it. Usenet newsgroups exist for almost every conceivable topic, as examples like *rec.sport.golf, talk.politics.guns,* *alt.ufo.reports,* and *soc.culture.african.american* suggest. Newsgroups are convenient places to browse because they are open to everyone.

Listservs are more difficult to browse because you have to subscribe to a list in order to participate in its discussions. However, some listservs maintain archives of past exchanges that are open to anyone; these can be excellent resources.

E-Tips You can usually access newsgroups from your Web browser and explore them with a search engine. See <http://www.liszt.com> for a directory of electronic mailing lists, newsgroups, and IRC chat groups. To search Usenet groups, try <http://groups.google.com>.

To explore a wider variety of materials, try conducting a Web search. A keyword search on a subject that interests you will elicit a wealth of diverse and interesting materials. But be forewarned: it may also call up materials you find irrelevant or distracting. And because it's so easy to link from one site to another, you may spend hours following an unproductive trail of associations. To ensure that you don't lose valuable information, save bibliographic information for any useful sources you encounter on the Web. For more advice on using online resources, see Chapter 44.

E-Tips A powerful way to search for topic ideas is to use a Web search engine such as Yahoo (www.yahoo.com), Google (www.google .com), or Lycos (www.lycos.com) that is arranged by categories. The groupings themselves offer a range of general topic areas (Arts & Humanities; Health; Science), but the topics get more intriguing when you push deeper into them, especially *Yahoo*'s "Society and Culture." Check out "Issues and Causes" at <http://dir.yahoo.com/Society_and_Culture/Issues_and_Causes/>.

2b How do you refine your topic?

Once you have found a promising topic, you'll probably need to narrow it down. If you don't focus your efforts, you may end up writing a superficial paper of little interest to anyone, no matter how promising your initial subject seemed to be. You may have read professional articles that seem out of focus. Their titles promise exciting information ("How to Win a Scholarship," "The Best Career Fields for the New Millennium"), but the pieces themselves deliver few new facts or ideas.

Problems of focus can also happen in college papers, when writers try to cover more material than they can within the parameters of their project. The result is papers that are long on generalities but short on lively details and thoroughly developed ideas.

◼ 1 Don't try to cover everything. You may be excited about your subject and eager to learn more about it. But remember that your time to develop a project is usually quite limited. You can't discover all there is to know about a topic such as single parenthood in a few weeks. Even if you could, you wouldn't be able to fit all that material into one paper. It's better to narrow your research to something more manageable, perhaps the difficulties involved in being an unmarried teenage father. Better yet, focus on whether providing counseling and parent-education classes can help these fathers stay more involved in their children's lives.

Does that kind of topic reduction seem too drastic? It's probably not, especially when you consider that any paper you write should contain only a portion of what you know about its subject. To write an authoritative and interesting piece, you need to select material carefully to suit your purpose and audience—not just reproduce every single thing you've read.

Think about refining your topic in the same way that you'd think about focusing a flashlight. If you adjust the beam to its broadest range, you will throw diffused light over a larger territory but you won't be able to see details. If you want to see the details, you'll have to narrow the focus of your light and concentrate its beam on a small area. In other words, learn to write *more* about *less*.

◼ 2 Make a tree diagram. One way to narrow a topic to manageable size is to draw a tree diagram. To do this, make a chart on which you divide and subdivide the topic into smaller and smaller parts, each of which branches out like an inverted tree. The upside-down tree helps you see many potential areas within each division as well as the relationships among them. You can choose to develop the branch that seems to offer the most promising material.

Suppose you've become interested in writing about college student debt after watching your roommate run up several thousand dollars in credit card bills during a single semester. Your tree diagram exploring this topic might look something like this:

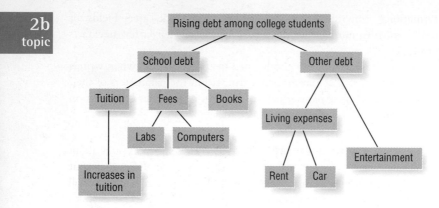

Now select the most promising branch from your first diagram and make a new diagram to refine that idea further.

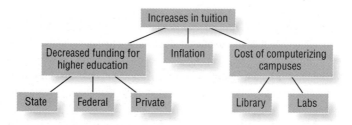

■ **3 Make an idea map.** Another way to narrow a topic is to look within the subject for patterns of related ideas worth exploring. Making an idea map is an easy way to do this. In the middle of a blank sheet of paper, write down a phrase that describes your general subject. Circle that term—say, *college expenses*—and then, for about ten minutes, attach every word you can think of either to that original term or to others that you have linked to it. Circle all those additional words as you write them, and draw lines connecting them to the words that triggered them.

It's important here not to concentrate too much on every single word you write. An idea map is an exercise in free association; you want to see what your mind comes up with. Your finished map might look something like the one on page 21. When you're done, examine the map to see whether any clusters of words suggest topics you might develop. For example, one group of ideas (tuition—increases—state funding cuts—fees—student loans) suggests a paper about government funding for higher education. Another (credit cards—"student card" promotions—spring break trip—football weekends—club-hopping) might lead you to explore the kinds of luxuries that easy credit allows students to purchase. As with tree diagrams, you can use any promising concept from your first idea map as the focal point of a second exercise, starting again with the narrowed subject to develop more ideas.

4 Investigate an interesting question or hypothesis. Another way to narrow a topic is to pursue an interesting problem involving your topic for which you do not yet have a satisfactory answer—much as investigative reporters look for "leads" that will turn into breaking news stories.

Sometimes a promising issue will take the form of a question. Reading a headline about decreased national crime rates, for example, might spur you to ask this question.

> QUESTION   Why is violent crime increasing among juveniles at a time when the overall crime rate is decreasing?

Rather than ask an open-ended question, some writers prefer to start a project with a hypothesis, a statement that makes a tentative claim to be tested in a paper. Scientists often begin research projects with these kinds of educated guesses. Here is an initial hypothesis on the topic of juvenile violence.

> HYPOTHESIS   Despite a drop in the overall crime rate, violence among juveniles is increasing because of the harmful influence of television.

A guiding question or hypothesis will usually help you focus your topic. But at this stage it is probably too early to commit to a definite position. Until the evidence comes in and you have more information, remain flexible in your thinking and willing to revise your focus and approach.

How can you find a promising question or hypothesis to focus on? In your preliminary reading and discussion about the topic, look for clues:

- Titles, headings, and focal points of published pieces on the topic
- Names of important people, experts, events, or institutions related to the topic
- Issues or questions that come up repeatedly
- Issues about which people disagree

5 State a tentative goal. If you are working on a topic that you understand well, or are engaged in an informational or service-learning project for which you already know the purpose or goal, you might compose a brief mission statement. Here is an example:

> **Goal:** This Web site will create an environment in which users can interact with proposals for the new city veterans' monument, thus helping to shape its design, its function, and associated community outreach programs.

Remember, though, that even when you begin a paper with a well-established goal, you should be prepared to shift your focus as your knowledge about the topic and the writing situation grows.

EXERCISE 2.1 Suppose you want to write a short paper for a composition course on one of the following subjects. Write down several promising subtopics that you might focus on; then use a tree diagram or an idea map to generate ideas about the subtopic that you find most interesting.

Affirmative action
Hazing at colleges and universities
Illegal drug use
"Extreme" sports

EXERCISE 2.2 Obtain a copy of today's editorial page from your local or campus newspaper. Working with a group of your classmates, identify the topic of each piece. Then answer these questions: How broad is the writer's topic? How do you think the writer decided on that focus? How adequately does he or she cover the topic?

2c How do you explore and develop a topic?

Now you have a topic. What's the next step? It's to push your idea further by exploring its implications, finding supporting evidence, and filling in specific details. Since classical times rhetoricians have looked for ways to stimulate this kind of thinking. They came up with the term *invention* to describe the techniques writers use to generate subject matter for a paper.

This section explains invention techniques that can help you explore and develop a thesis. You can use any of these techniques at any point in your writing process. Although it's logical to review them before starting a draft, you may want to return to them while writing or even when revising—in short, anytime you need to expand and develop your ideas.

1 Freewrite about the topic. Freewriting is writing nonstop for ten or fifteen minutes on a topic in order to explore what you already know and to discover areas you'd like to learn more about. Don't worry about grammar, spelling, or other niceties while you're freewriting—concentrate on generating words and ideas.

The point of freewriting is to spark ideas, so continue to write as long as ideas come, and don't cross out or reject anything prematurely. But be alert for phrases and concepts that extend your thesis in promising directions.

Here is a sample from a freewrite that Justin Cone did before writing the paper that appears in Section 5d. Note that he has not always capitalized, that he doesn't always write complete sentences, and that his style is very informal. But note also how many ideas even this short excerpt articulates.

> I want to write about the Internet. that is, is it a threat to our society? . . . I mean, why books when you can have full-color, action packed, digital sound, excitement at the click of the button? why take part in the painstakingly slow process of reading when there are so many other quicker ways to gather information, the nightly

news for instance? there are answers to these whys, but what? I'll get back to that later. the point is, new media technology is far more appealing to society than books. and as technology grows, books as we know them today would logically die out. actually I don't believe that books will ever die out, they will merely switch, people will read books for different reasons than they read them now. . . .

2 Use the journalist's questions. Beginning journalists are taught to keep six questions in mind when writing a news story.

Who?   What?   Where?
When?   Why?   How?

Simple as they may seem, these questions can help you be sure you have covered all the bases, especially when you are writing an informative paper (though not every question will apply to every topic).

3 Look at your topic from different perspectives. One way to do this is to consider some frameworks people have traditionally used to organize and generate ideas. Among the oldest are the four categories of questions that classical rhetoricians used to explore topics: questions of *fact, definition, value,* and *policy.* Originally designed to develop speeches for the law courts of ancient Greece and Rome, these questions move from simple to more complex ways of examining an issue.

- Questions of **fact** involve things already known about your topic: What has already happened? What factual information is already available? What policies are already in place?
- Questions of **definition** interpret these facts and place them in a larger context: What category does your topic fit into? What laws or approaches apply?
- Questions of **value** ask you to make a judgment: Is the idea you're talking about a good thing or a bad thing? Is it ethical or unethical? Workable or unworkable?
- Questions of **policy** allow you to consider specific courses of action: What exactly should be done in response to the issue? Are old solutions working, or is a new approach needed?

You won't be able to answer all these questions in a single paper, but they are useful for comprehensively examining a topic. Here, for example, are ways a writer might use these questions to find material for a paper on whether the fashion industry's use of thin models in advertising indirectly encourages eating disorders among young women.

HIGHLIGHT *Looking at a Topic from Different Perspectives*

* **Questions about the facts:** What kinds of clothing and models do most fashion advertisements feature? To what extent do young women draw their beauty ideals from fashion ads? How many fashion ads feature unusually thin models? How many young women have eating disorders?

* **Questions about key definitions:** How does our culture define "beauty"? How preoccupied with thinness must one be to be defined as having an "eating disorder"?

* **Questions about values:** Is it ethical for fashion designers to display their clothes on models who are much thinner than most women can hope to be? Is it sensible for the industry to produce clothing that doesn't look good on most of the population? Does the artistic value of fashion trends outweigh any harmful social effects they may cause?

* **Questions about policy:** What could the fashion industry do to promote a healthier ideal of beauty? How might young women be discouraged from trying to look like models?

Once you've run through all the questions, decide which one(s) you want to treat most fully in your paper. For example, an editorial on this topic might focus on the definitional question "How does our culture define 'beauty'?" A report, however, might gather information that answers the factual question "How many fashion ads feature unusually thin models?" For more on how these questions can help you construct a thesis statement, see Section 43a.

4 Write a zero draft. You may find that your best device for generating material is just to start a draft. The very act of writing will often get the creative juices flowing and help you to organize your thoughts. Think of this first try as a "zero draft," a trial run that doesn't really count. Zero drafts are easy to write, and after they're complete, you can select the best material to use in your next draft. Some experts suggest writing several zero drafts to try out several possible approaches to a project.

5 Read up on your topic. No one ever said you have to come up with all your ideas on your own. Get to the library or get on the Internet, look up your subject, and read. You'll find detailed instructions on doing library research in Section 44a.

But don't read just to find facts; read to discover how other writers have treated topics like yours. Perhaps you want to write about a bicycle trip you took across the American Northwest. Then look up some travel literature. Your eyes may be opened by the sheer variety of approaches available to record your adventures, everything from serious day-by-day field accounts written by anthropologists to the rollicking narratives in travel magazines. The same might be true if you're writing a review of a book or a movie. Seeing how others have reviewed works for different kinds of publications will suggest possibilities for your own review.

6 Talk to others about your topic. From the start, invite others to join in exploring your topic. Look for campus events, clubs, or forums that might be connected to the subject. Check the local papers for information about lectures, film groups, or community meetings where you might meet people interested in your work. And when you find such people, network with them to find more people and organizations tied to your subject.

Online newsgroups and listservs offer instant access to an even wider network of contacts. Once you have a good sense of the issues you want to write about, consider posting to one of these forums a short description of your project and a request for input. You're likely to get valuable suggestions from experts in the field that will guide your reading and research. However, at this stage in your work, you must be cautious about online exchanges: most are unmonitored, so the accuracy and quality of information will vary. You should also be careful to observe the etiquette appropriate to online forums. See Section 44c for more on entering online discussions.

Classmates are another useful resource. In many writing classes, the instructor arranges for groups of students to meet before they start work on a project so they can help each other to generate ideas. Even if there's no standing arrangement, try to meet with classmates informally. You can also explore subjects via a class listserv (if your instructor sets one up) or through conventional email exchanges with instructors and colleagues.

Even if you haven't decided exactly what your paper will cover, you'll find that as you start to explain your ideas to others, more ideas will come to you. You may see arguments you hadn't considered and learn about new examples or potential sources.

EXERCISE 2.3 Use any two of the techniques described in this section to generate ideas about one of your writing projects in progress. Then discuss your experience with your classmates: Which strategy yielded the best ideas? Which would you be likely to use again as a regular part of your writing process?

EXERCISE 2.4 Choose a controversy currently under debate in your neighborhood, campus, or city. (If no ideas come to mind, consult a local or campus newspaper.) Use the four categories outlined on pages 24–25 to identify major questions about facts, definitions, values, and policies regarding that issue. Which questions generate the most disagreement? Which questions have already been settled? Which ones could provide the focus for an interesting paper? Discuss your responses with a group of classmates.

2d How do you write a topic proposal?

Occasionally an instructor may ask you to write a preliminary proposal defining your topic and analyzing the writing situation for a course paper. Even when it's not assigned, such a proposal can help you to refine your ideas about your topic, audience, purpose, and tone early so that your conclusions can guide your research and shape your first draft.

When your instructor asks you to write a topic proposal for a writing project, you should include the following elements. Also be sure to check with your instructor to find out if he or she has additional requirements.

Checklist 2.2
Writing a Topic Proposal

1. Identify your topic.

2. Articulate a working thesis statement, research question, hypothesis, or key issue that you plan to focus on in the paper (see Section 3a).

3. Indicate what kinds of research you plan to do and what supporting materials you will draw on in the paper (see Section 7a).

4. Offer a brief analysis of your writing situation (see Section 1d).

Going Public   *A Topic Proposal*

In the following sample proposal, first-year composition student Justin Cone describes his goals for the paper shown in draft form on pages 76–81. The assignment asked him to write a research paper explaining and exploring a current controversy for the instructor and the class. Justin starts his proposal by explaining his topic and purpose, and then he identifies his audience. He ends by considering the kind of impression he wants to make on readers.

Note that while he has done a lot of thinking about his topic, at this point in the process Justin is still refining and developing his ideas.

He hasn't yet formulated a definite thesis statement or identified specific research materials—and his language is less formal than his instructor will expect to see in the finished paper.

Justin Cone

Topic Proposal

Where Exactly Are We Surfing To?

The Information Superhighway. The Net. The World Wide Web. Cyberspace. These are the buzzwords of the fastest growing technological craze since floppy disks. Yet although an estimated 30 million users of the Internet can wield these words skillfully, a question remains unanswered: What value does this new technology possess? How can society benefit from the cyber-revolution? How can individuals benefit? Is there something good for everyone on the Internet? Or is it a quick, cheap substitute for real knowledge? Is it bad that my peers would rather surf the Net than read classic novels?

In an attempt to speak above the growing chatter of keyboards across the planet, I hope to find some answers to these questions. Although I will do library and online research, I can also draw on my own personal experience here. I was born into this age of information. My mother admits to plopping me down in front of a computer game while she did laundry; I grew up teaching myself to program in BASIC and trading lingo with the computer store clerks like I was Bill Gates.

My audience will be my classmates, who, like me and the rest of our generation, have been shaped by media technology. By drawing on our common experience, I hope to write a paper that will engage their interest and make them look closely at our lifestyle--without coming across as moralistic.

CHAPTER 3

How Do You Focus and Organize a Writing Project?

Now you have an interesting, workable topic for your writing project. You've thought about it carefully, talked with others about it, and gathered a satisfyingly deep pool of information about it. What's next? It's time to sort through these raw materials and make some decisions about the direction your paper will take.

This chapter offers strategies to guide you from the invention stage through the planning and organizing stages of a paper, so that when you sit down to write that first draft, you can do so with purpose and confidence.

3a How do you craft a thesis?

As you explore your topic, you will likely discover one or two issues that you know you want your paper to focus on. These issues will shape your *thesis statement*. A *thesis* is a sentence (sometimes two or three sentences) that explicitly identifies the point of a paper. Depending on the project, it may be a conclusion you draw as a result of doing research, your answer to a puzzling question about your topic, or a claim you will spend the rest of the paper explaining or supporting.

Many writers like to construct a tentative thesis statement early in their writing process and use it as a framework for organizing the rest of the paper. By keeping your tentative thesis in mind, you can be sure of covering all the important points. This section will help you develop a solid thesis and incorporate it effectively into your paper.

■ 1 **Make a strong point.** A thesis statement is more than just an observation; it is a statement that might be questioned or challenged. This means that your thesis should not be so obvious that most readers already agree with it ("Domestic violence harms families"), so wishy-washy that readers can't tell where you stand ("There are many strengths and weaknesses in our town's current zoning law"), or so subjective that you can't cite credible evidence to support it ("My child is the most beautiful child at his preschool"). Rather, it should offer a clearly stated analysis, critique, or position on your topic that readers will find new and significant.

When you construct a thesis, ask yourself whether an intelligent member of your audience might respond to it with a hostile "So what's your point?" or a disappointed "Big deal!" If you suspect he or she might, look for a more significant idea or sharpen the point you intend to make. The following examples illustrate the difference.

> BORING   Brought to Boston as a slave in 1761, Phillis Wheatley would become the first African-American woman recognized for her poetry. *So what's your point? What makes this fact interesting?*

> BETTER   Because Phillis Wheatley was the first African-American woman to achieve fame as a poet, it is surprising that her work contains so few references to slavery and racial injustice.

> BORING   Boxing is one of the most dangerous sports. *Everyone knows that. What's new?*

> BETTER   Because professional boxers often sustain severe injuries or brain damage in the ring, the sport should be outlawed or at least be subject to strict safety regulations.

In argument papers, the thesis statement often makes a *claim* that the rest of the paper is devoted to supporting. For more on claims, see Section 11b. The checklist below contains guidelines for constructing a strong thesis.

Checklist 3.1

What Makes a Strong Thesis?

• Does it focus on a substantive issue, one that deserves readers' attention?

• Is the thesis debatable—could reasonable people disagree with it?

• Does it address an issue that affects the public? Is the issue current? Will readers care about this thesis?

• Can you support your thesis adequately, using research or your own experiences? Do you need to narrow or qualify your claim?

• Is your thesis clearly stated? Can readers tell where you stand?

■ **2 Sharpen your focus.** For many writers, developing a manageable thesis is a major challenge. Especially when you are exploring a broad or complicated topic, it may be tempting to settle for a thesis statement that breaks a sprawling subject into several parts rather than present a focused idea. Take these examples.

SPRAWLING   Child abuse is a serious problem with three major aspects: causes, detection, and prevention.

SPRAWLING   Among the most commonly prescribed medications in the United States are antidepressant, weight-loss, and behavior-altering drugs.

Broad categories like these can, in fact, work well if you *need* to divide an issue into basic components—as you might when designing a home page on the Web. The home page introducing a Web site on child abuse might quite logically link to additional pages that separately explore causes, detection, and prevention. The simplicity of the design would help to make the site user-friendly and coherent.

But for projects that require more extensive development and discussion of ideas, like academic research papers or argument pieces, such a thesis might seem more like a shopping list than a compelling claim. Broad statements like these deaden the argument by preventing readers (and writers too) from examining underlying concepts fully, whereas a more sharply focused thesis allows for extended examination of an issue.

FOCUSED   Since most citizens know little about how to respond appropriately when they suspect someone of abusing a child, better public education in this area could significantly reduce child abuse.

FOCUSED   Doctors are increasingly willing to prescribe antidepressant drugs to populations other than the clinically depressed, including people who undergo minor mood swings and children with normal adjustment anxieties. This trend raises troubling questions about whether normal levels of unhappiness have become unacceptable in our culture.

One way to avoid an unmanageably broad thesis is to limit it to one or two of the most urgent questions connected to your topic. In your reading and conversations, look for issues that demand strong evidence from you but that also encourage readers to rethink their ideas about the topic. For general advice on narrowing your topic, see

Section 2b. For help finding compelling research questions related to your topic, see Section 43a.

Checklist 3.1 on page 30 offers guidelines for constructing a strong thesis statement.

3 Preview the direction your paper will take.

Write a complete sentence or two that forecasts in some detail the ideas you expect to write about, in roughly the same order in which you plan to address them. Your thesis sentence(s) should be *succinct* yet *comprehensive*—that is, it should be short yet indicate the major points you want to make. Suppose you are writing an article for the pre-law student newsletter on your campus. This thesis tells readers what to expect:

> When you start looking for that summer job or
> internship, you need to think beyond hourly pay and
> congenial working companions and look for jobs where
> you can learn something about the law--as a runner in
> a law firm, a junior staff member for a state
> legislator, or a research assistant for a lobbying
> organization.

4 Place your thesis effectively.

Don't assume that your thesis must be the first sentence of your paper, although it can be. Your decision about where to put your thesis depends on the writing situation: your audience, your purpose, and the position you want to take on the topic.

When you are presenting information or arguments in a straightforward, no-nonsense fashion—as you should in an essay examination or a business letter—you'll want to state your thesis very early. It may even be your first sentence. At other times you'll need to provide a context for your thesis, by defining key terms or giving background information. That's why, in academic papers, thesis statements often appear at the end of the introductory paragraph.

In other situations, you may want to delay your thesis even more. You may be writing to explore a question rather than to present a settled opinion on it. Or, if your thesis is controversial, you may want to present all your evidence first, then lead readers gradually to your point. In the social sciences, writers often begin research reports by describing their methods and data and end with their larger conclusions. In such cases, your thesis may not be stated until the last paragraph.

Remember, though, that a delayed thesis doesn't give you license to write an unfocused paper. Even if you don't clarify your specific claim until late in the essay, readers should understand what central ideas your paper will address from its very beginning, or they won't be able to follow your discussion.

Suppose you interviewed a group of children about their television viewing habits for a communications course. Your introductory paragraph might contain a framing statement like this.

> My interviews with 22 second-graders explored this question: Do children really like the kinds of programs that the networks and the general public assume are their favorites?

This question sets the stage for a more developed thesis statement later in the paper, one which might look something like this.

> These data indicate that these children gravitate toward educational and family-oriented programming rather than the violent cartoons that many people assume children like—a finding that has important implications for parents and the television networks.

■ **5 Revise your thesis as your project evolves.** Don't be surprised if your thesis shifts as you continue to explore, research, and plan your project. Most writers will revise their working thesis statement to make it more precise or to reflect changes in the paper's direction. Don't worry about such changes. This is the time when you should be testing your preliminary assumptions and ideas so that your final paper will be stronger. Learn from every part of the process, and don't be discouraged easily. Your final thesis may be nothing like what you imagined at the outset—and that's okay.

EXERCISE 3.1 Review the guidelines for an effective thesis, then rate the following thesis statements as "good," "not too bad," or "needs a lot of work." Revise the statements that don't merit a "good" rating to make them stronger.

1. In trying to promote meaningful campaign finance reform, organizations like Common Cause run into opposition from lobbyists, major companies, the news media, and, most of all, the candidates themselves.

2. Scientists will soon possess enough information about genes to cure virtually all diseases.

3. Recent films like *The Matrix* and *Men in Black II* show that today's action movies rely more than ever on high-tech special effects.

4. Some drivers in our city are too dangerous to be allowed on public roads.

Going Public   *An Opening Paragraph with Thesis*

Sometimes a thesis statement pulled out of context, like the previous examples in this chapter, can seem pretty bland. Fortunately, in a real paper, a thesis isn't solely responsible for shaping a reader's first impression. The sentences that surround it also play an important part. In this opening paragraph for a course paper, Justin Cone uses personal experiences to set his thesis into context and to spark his instructor's and classmates' interest in his topic. Justin's thesis is highlighted. See pages 76–81 for a finished draft of this paper.

> Technology's Children: Has Media Technology
>
> Intellectually Stunted Our Generation?
>
> I was the 5-year-old learning ABCs from Kermit
> the Frog. I was the 7-year-old programming in BASIC
> at 5:30 in the morning, just before Bugs Bunny aired.
> I was the 10-year-old successfully installing a
> modem, sans instructions. But I was also the 16-year-
> old who couldn't finish reading Thomas Hardy's Tess
> of the D'Urbervilles for junior English because I
> didn't have the concentration or mental stamina to
> read anything longer than a computer screen. I was
> raised during the computer craze. Now my peers and I
> stand on a shore as technology's children, looking
> across the growing technological divide to a chunk of
> land sliding into the sea, where our parents swim,
> where our teachers worry, and where traditional kinds
> of literacy sink--dragging much of our culture and
> history with it. My experience is part of a larger
> phenomenon in our culture. Media technology has
> shaped young adults' ways of processing knowledge in

ways that make books seem slow and out of date. In
leaving books behind, our generation may lose
priceless cultural archives, but we may also pioneer
exciting new ways of learning.

3b
org

3b How do you organize a writing project?

No matter how good your ideas are, if you don't make the effort to organize them, readers will get lost and blame you for their confusion. Coherent organization is the foundation of any writing project.

It is true that many writers never consciously select a design before they start a paper. They may know intuitively what events they want a story to contain or what order the information in a report should follow. Still, understanding the options available when you organize a paper can help you. When you begin a writing project, look for models that show how other writers have approached similar tasks. Whether you are writing a biology lab report or a research paper for your world literature course, examples give you valuable clues about how to organize your argument. (If you're not sure where to find such models for a course assignment, ask your instructor. For documents you write at work or in the community, ask an experienced colleague.) See Chapters 7 and 8 for more on writing within particular genres.

Figure 3.1 *Frank O. Gehry's Guggenheim Museum Bilbao (Spain) has been hailed as a triumph of contemporary architecture. Its unusual structure both challenges and delights visitors.*

Some basic patterns for organizing papers are discussed below, arranged from the simplest to the most complex.

■ 1 Consider an introduction/body/conclusion structure.

This basic pattern works for many kinds of projects. Lawyers, scientists, and writers in many academic fields favor this design because it suggests a logical movement from statement to proof.

- In the **introduction** you begin by telling your readers clearly and simply what topics your paper will cover.
- In the **body** of the paper you follow with examples and explanations for each of your main points.
- In your **conclusion** you tie your points together and leave readers with a sense of closure.

Another way of describing this basic structure is to call it a commitment and response pattern. That's because in the first section of the paper a writer promises to cover certain issues or address particular questions. The opening commitment can be direct or indirect. In a *direct commitment,* the writer addresses an issue squarely, almost as if making an announcement. Such an opening obliges the writer to cover every point mentioned.

> While there is some evidence that modern-day reptiles and dinosaurs are genetically related, recent fossil finds in China and Mongolia suggest that birds may be the closest links to our dinosaur predecessors.

A commitment can also be made *indirectly* by narrating an anecdote or an incident.

> Did you leave fall registration today with a rearranged schedule because two of the courses you planned to take had been canceled? Did you find that all the courses you want had prerequisites that you can't meet because all the prerequisite courses are filled? If so, welcome to the biggest club on campus.

Through this indirect commitment, the writer has clearly indicated without actually saying so that the subject of the paper will be registration problems.

Papers that result from the basic introduction/body/conclusion pattern will usually take a simple shape.

Basic Introduction/Body/Conclusion Pattern

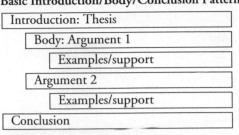

Such papers can also incorporate significant variations. When you make a point or support an argument, for example, you must usually deal with opposing views; if you don't address them, the paper will seem to evade key questions. Counterarguments—discussions of opposing views—inevitably make the structure of the paper more complex. They can be addressed immediately, near the beginning of the paper, or they can be dealt with as they arise in the body of the piece (but don't end with a counterargument, or you'll weaken your own case).

Here's how the basic model might look when counterarguments are added to the mix. (See Section 11c for more on handling different views in a paper.)

Introduction/Body/Conclusion Pattern with Counterarguments

```
  Introduction: Thesis
      Body: Argument 1
          Examples/support
          Counterargument 1 addressed
      Argument 2
          Examples/support
          Counterargument 2 addressed . . .
  Conclusion
```

This pattern—or any of its numerous variations—works especially well for essay exams or other impromptu writing when you have to organize your ideas quickly. It's easy to outline and readily expandable.

2 Consider a narrative or a process design. When you narrate a story, you usually describe events in the order they occurred. The structure can be quite straightforward.

Narrative Pattern

Introduction: Thesis

Body: Event 1

Event 2

Event 3 . . .

Conclusion

If for an astronomy course you wanted to narrate the discovery of pulsar stars, you might begin with the scientists at Bell Laboratories who thought that they were receiving messages from extraterrestrial beings when they first intercepted radio signals from pulsars. A narrative can also be more complicated—for instance, by moving back in time as a movie does with flashbacks.

A process pattern is essentially the same as a narrative pattern, but instead of telling a story you are explaining how something works. You list and describe each step in the process.

Process Pattern

Introduction: Thesis

Body: Step 1

Step 2

Step 3 . . .

Conclusion

Be careful to include all the necessary steps in the proper order. You can find good examples of process patterns in instructional and technical manuals.

3 Consider a comparison and contrast structure. In many kinds of papers you will have to examine different objects or ideas in relation to each other, especially when you are evaluating or arguing. In organizing such papers you can use one or two basic plans, either describing the things you are comparing one at a time (*subject by subject*) or describing them in an alternating sequence (*feature by feature*). The models here are followed by sample outlines.

Comparison/Contrast Pattern 1: Subject by Subject

Introduction: Thesis

Body: Subject 1 features examined

Feature A

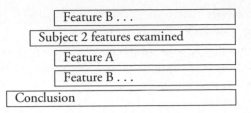

| Feature B . . . |
| Subject 2 features examined |
| Feature A |
| Feature B . . . |
| Conclusion |

Subject by Subject:
Sport-Utility Vehicles vs. Family Sedans

I. **Thesis:** Sport-utility vehicles, while currently more popular than family sedans, have environmental and safety drawbacks that should make potential buyers beware.

II. **Subject 1:** Features of sport-utility vehicles
   A. *Feature A: Popularity of sport-utility vehicles*
   B. *Feature B: Environmental impact of sport-utility vehicles*
   C. *Feature C: Safety of sport-utility vehicles*

III. **Subject 2:** Features of family sedans
   A. *Feature A: Popularity of family sedans*
   B. *Feature B: Environmental impact of family sedans*
   C. *Feature C: Safety of family sedans*

IV. **Conclusion:** Buyers who value safety and the environment over style should bypass sport-utility vehicles in favor of a traditional family sedan.

Comparison/Contrast Pattern 2:
Feature by Feature

| Introduction: Thesis |
| Body: Feature A examined |
| In subject 1 |
| In subject 2 |
| Feature B examined |
| In subject 1 |
| In subject 2 |
| Feature C examined |
| In subject 1 |
| In subject 2 |
| Conclusion |

**Feature by Feature:
Sport-Utility Vehicles vs. Family Sedans**

 I. **Thesis:** Sport-utility vehicles, while currently more popular than family sedans, have environmental and safety drawbacks that should make potential buyers beware.
 II. **Feature A:** *Popularity*
   A. Popularity of sport-utility vehicles
   B. Popularity of family sedans
 III. **Feature B:** *Environmental impact*
   A. Environmental impact of sport-utility vehicles
   B. Environmental impact of family sedans
 IV. **Feature C:** *Safety*
   A. Safety of sport-utility vehicles
   B. Safety of family sedans
 V. **Conclusion:** Buyers who value safety and the environment over style should bypass sport-utility vehicles in favor of a traditional family sedan.

The subject-by-subject plan works best in short papers involving only a few comparisons; in such pieces readers don't have to recall a large quantity of information to make the necessary comparisons. When you're doing a longer paper, however, use the feature-by-feature pattern; otherwise readers may lose track of the features you're comparing.

■ **4 Consider a division or classification structure.** These two ways of organizing a paper are quite different, though both involve creating categories to make material more manageable. A paper organized according to the principle of *division* breaks a topic into its components—its separate parts. A paper on the solar system might devote a section to each planet; a paper on a political candidate might describe her positions on several major issues in an order that seems appropriate:

Division Pattern

| Introduction: Thesis: Candidate X's platform for City Council |

| Body: Issue 1: X's views on crime prevention |

| Issue 2: X's stand on local tax rates |

| Issue 3: X's views on traffic control |

| Issue 4: X's views on the environment |

| Conclusion |

Classification involves breaking a large subject into categories according to some consistent and useful principle of division. Classification must follow rules that don't apply to division. First, classifications must be *exhaustive:* every member of the class must fit into a category. A classification of the planets might divide those that have significant moons from those that do not; obviously all of the nine planets fall into one of these classes.

> With no moon
> With one moon
> With more than one moon

Any principle of division you use must also be *consistent.* You can't classify by more than one principle at a time—for example, if you group planets according to the number of moons they have *and* whether or not they have rings, you are not really classifying. Finally, classes *must not overlap.* That means you should be able to place an object in only one category.

Classification Pattern

> Introduction with thesis: This year's most popular college bands represent a variety of musical genres.
>> Body: Class 1: Rock
>>> Class 2: Country
>>> Class 3: Hip hop
>>> Class 4: Folk
> Conclusion

Yet most systems of classification break down at one point or another, like the one in the model above. What do you do with acts—such as the Dixie Chicks or Bob Dylan—who play more than one kind of music? Well, you can create yet another class (country-rock or folk-rock), or you can classify by the band's major body of work. But you won't always be able to eliminate every exception.

■ **5 Consider a cause-and-effect design.** This design is appropriate when you write a paper explaining why something has happened. The typical cause-and-effect paper moves from an explanation of some existing condition to an examination of its particular causes. In other words, you see what has happened and you want to know why. For example, you might wonder why so many people did their Christmas shopping online last year. Possible causes might include the increased number of shopping outlets on the Web, the fact that more people have access to the Internet, and unusually cold winter weather that kept shoppers indoors.

Typically you'll see more than one explanation for a given event, so a cause-and-effect paper may examine various causes, from the least important to the most important.

Cause-and-Effect Pattern

Introduction: Thesis
Body: Effect(s) explained
Cause 1 (least important) explained
Cause 2 explained
Cause 3 explained
Cause 4 (most important) explained
Conclusion

You can begin your essay by identifying an effect and then go on to hypothesize about the causes, or you can start by listing a number of causes and then show how they contribute to a particular effect.

6 Consider a problem-and-solution pattern. You can use this pattern effectively for papers in which you argue for change or propose an idea to settle a problem.

Problem-and-Solution Pattern

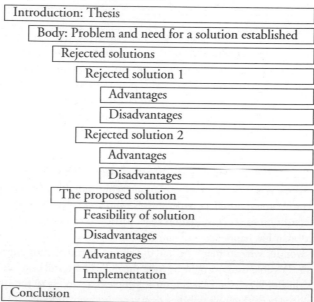

Introduction: Thesis
Body: Problem and need for a solution established
Rejected solutions
Rejected solution 1
Advantages
Disadvantages
Rejected solution 2
Advantages
Disadvantages
The proposed solution
Feasibility of solution
Disadvantages
Advantages
Implementation
Conclusion

The first part of this pattern says, "We've got a problem and we've got to solve it—now." Here's how one student began a problem-and-solution essay.

> In a 1997 issue of The American Prospect, a team
> of public health professors argues that Americans who
> live in areas where there is little "social
> cohesion"--where individuals feel isolated and
> neighbors don't trust each other--have a higher risk
> of disease and a shorter average life span.

The nature of the problem is evident from just this single sentence.

The second part of the problem-and-solution pattern steers the reader through proposals for solving the problem. Since most of these ideas will be rejected (or furnish only a part of the recommended solution), the advantages and limitations of each are examined carefully. This section of the essay assures readers that no plausible approach has been ignored.

In the third part of this pattern you propose a solution to the problem. You may then want to discuss the disadvantages and advantages of this proposal, highlighting the advantages. Readers need to feel that nothing is under wraps and that no hidden agendas guide your proposal. You can then conclude by explaining how the change can be put into place.

EXERCISE 3.2 Working with a group of classmates, consider what patterns you might use for writing about two of the topics listed below. Give reasons why you think those patterns would work well in each case.

Where to eat out near your campus
The popularity of *The X-Files*
Your experience volunteering at a local agency
Rising health care costs
The results of a recent election

3c How do you outline a paper?

No question about it, an outline can help you keep a writing project on track, whether you are following one of the patterns described in Section 3b or following one of your own. But a blueprint for essay doesn't have to be a full-sentence outline. You can choose number of organizational devices, including the working list and the scratch outline. Just be sure that if you're writing a paper for a class, you follow any instructions on outlining given by your instructor.

Outlining works well for some writers. John McPhee, who writes for the *New Yorker,* claims that he can compose a piece more easily and quickly when he invests time in making a preliminary outline. But Jacques Barzun, also a famous author and a philosopher, finds outlines "useless and fettering." He favors lists. Neither approach is necessarily right. You'll want to experiment with several techniques until you find out what works best for you.

1 Try a working list. The working list is the most flexible of all organizational devices. You start by jotting down the key points you want to make, leaving plenty of room under each major idea. This strategy works best as a preliminary planning device because it allows you to add examples and points under the main ideas they support as they occur to you.

Here are headings you might use for a cause-and-effect paper titled "The Case for Reviving the Family Dinner."

- How family eating patterns have changed
- Benefits of family dinners for children
- Benefits of family dinners for parents

Working from a brainstorming list or perhaps from freewriting on the subject, you select subpoints to fit under these major headings. You might also want to jot "cue notes" in the margin of the working list to remind yourself of anecdotes that illustrate specific points, as in the following example.

Working List
The Case for Reviving the Family Dinner

- **How family eating patterns have changed** vs. families in
  Families today eat fewer meals together 1960s-1970s
  More single-parent families and two-career families
  Increase in fast-food intake microwave dinners, delis
  More prepackaged single-portion foods in stores
  Family members often eat separately or in front of TV
- **Benefits of family dinners for children**
  Spend more time with family use story about dad's
  Better nutrition spaghetti dinners?
  Learn table manners
  Participate in cooking and cleanup

- **Benefits of family dinners for parents**
  Quality time with children
  More economical
  Can be sure that children are eating well
  Research study: children who eat with families fare better in
  school and are better-adjusted   *Check article in last Sun. newspaper*

When you think you have enough material, look over your list
and decide which points you want to treat first and how you can
arrange the others. Then start writing and, as you work, refer to your
list to check that you are staying on track. Add and delete items from
the list as you need to—nothing in a working list is untouchable.

▋2 Make an informal (scratch) outline. Many writers like
working from careful plans but dislike the formality and restrictions of
formal outlines. For them the informal or scratch outline—which
arranges points into categories and subcategories—provides a happy
medium.

A scratch outline should begin with a thesis that states your claim
or main idea. Then decide what major points you'll use to support
that thesis. For each major point you'll need subpoints that support,
explain, or illustrate the main point. However, your statement of
points and subpoints can be quite loose since the conventions of the
full-sentence outline need not be followed. Here's a sample scratch
outline on reviving family dinners, following a cause-and-effect pattern of the sort described in Section 3b-5. Note that the scratch outline is considerably fuller than the working list; thus it provides more
organizational guidance.

Scratch Outline
The Case for Reviving the Family Dinner

Thesis: Because eating meals together offers so many social and emotional benefits, parents need to restore family dinner as a top priority in
their homes.

1. Contemporary American families eat meals together much less
   frequently than previous generations did.

   - Most families used to eat breakfast and dinner together—now
     both children and parents may be away from home for long
     hours and hardly see each other.
   - Statistics show that fast-food intake and restaurant sales have
     risen steadily since 1980.

- Even grocery stores offer a variety of single-portion convenience foods, microwave dinners, and other items designed for people eating alone.

2. While eating alone may be convenient, family meals offer important benefits for children.

   - Family dinners ensure that children spend time with their parents and siblings each day. (childhood examples)
   - A recent study showed that children whose families eat dinner together at least once a week do better in school and have fewer behavioral problems. (cite article)
   - Children who eat with their families have a chance to learn table manners and basic cooking and cleanup skills.

3. Parents also benefit from family meals.

   - Parents can ensure that children are eating a healthy diet.
   - Family dinners allow parents to spend quality time with children.
   - Cooking and eating at home is cheaper than eating out.

3 Make a formal (sentence) outline. A formal outline is a fairly complex structure that compels you to think rigorously about how the ideas in a piece of writing will fit together. (That's why instructors often require them.) If your major points really aren't compatible or parallel, a formal outline will expose the problems. When your supporting evidence is thin or inconsistent, those flaws may show up too.

In a formal sentence outline you state every point in a complete sentence, and you make sentences within each grouping parallel, according to the following scheme.

Chart 3.1

Framework of a Formal Outline

I. _____

  A. _____

    1. _____

    2. _____

  B. _____

    1. _____

    2. _____

    3. _____

  C. _____

II. _____

Here's how a formal outline of the article on family dinner might begin. We haven't detailed the entire argument, but you can see from this excerpt how the material would be organized.

Formal Outline
The Case for Reviving the Family Dinner

Thesis: Because eating meals together offers so many social and emotional benefits, parents need to restore family dinner as a top priority in their homes.

I. Contemporary American families eat meals together much less frequently than previous generations did.
   A. Most families in the 1960s and 1970s ate dinner and breakfast together.
      1. Dad's Sunday-night spaghetti dinners were a tradition in my family.
      2. Popular TV shows from the era, such as *The Brady Bunch,* frequently feature family meals.
   B. However, today families' schedules are so complicated that family members often eat separately.
      1. According to the federal government, nearly one-third of families are headed by a single working parent, and more than 60 percent of mothers now work outside the home.
      2. Children also participate in more extracurricular activities, including sports leagues and after-school programs, so they spend less time at home.
      3. When family members' schedules conflict, it is difficult to plan shared mealtimes. . . .

4 Use an outlining program on a computer. What makes outlining on a computer preferable to doing the job on paper is the ease with which an on-screen outline can be expanded, contracted, rearranged, and otherwise altered. Rather than constraining ideas, a computer outline encourages a writer to be flexible because adding and rearranging ideas is as easy as moving the cursor and pressing a few keys.

E-Tips "The Arrow," at <http://www.nwlink.com/~cawilcox/index.html>, offers an online outlining program with accompanying tutorials and advice on transforming an initial outline into a finished paper.

EXERCISE 3.3 Make a working list for a writing project you're currently working on. When you are done, make a formal outline of the same project. What additions and changes did you make to construct the formal outline? Which outline will you find most helpful when you sit down to begin a draft of the project? Why?

3d How do you choose a title?

It may seem odd to choose a title while you are still planning and organizing a project. But titles are surprisingly important. Readers want and expect them; in fact, they may be annoyed if they don't find one that helps them anticipate what they will be reading. So don't make your title an afterthought; make it an important element in your planning process.

■ **1 Experiment with a working title.** Choose a working title (one you can change as the work progresses) that will keep you on track as you move through the planning and drafting stages of your project. For example, when Justin Cone wrote the topic proposal that appears on pages 27–28, he knew that he wanted his paper to explore the positive and negative effects of the Internet, so he crafted this initial title: "Where Exactly Are We Surfing To?"

This title contains cues that helped Justin to shape his first draft: *surfing* focuses the paper on the Internet; *where* suggests that the paper will explore the effects and implications of Internet use. These focuses led him to choose a cause-and-effect pattern of organization.

■ **2 Revise the working title to reflect your finished product.** As you plan and draft, check your working title periodically to be sure it still fits the paper. Justin made exactly these kinds of revisions as his research progressed, when he decided to shift his focus from the Internet to the intellectual effects of all electronic gadgets, including television, computers and video games, on his generation. His final title—"Technology's Children: Has Media Technology Intellectually Stunted Our Generation?"—reflects this new focus. Justin's full paper appears on pages 76–81.

■ **3 Keep your readers in mind.** Be sure your title accurately reflects the content of your paper. No cute titles, please. People doing computer searches look for keywords that help to identify the content of a book or an article and direct the researcher to the place where he or she can find it. An essay on Napoleon called "Short Guy, Big Ego" would be hard to find. So it's essential that your title let readers know what your paper is really about.

If you have your heart set on a clever phrase that's not particularly descriptive, try a two-part title. Start with the unconventional phrase and follow it with a colon. The second part of the title, after the colon, should clarify exactly what the paper is about, as in "Short Guy, Big Ego: A Psychological Analysis of Napoleon's Military Strategy."

EXERCISE 3.4 Which of these titles seem as if they'd be good predictors of content in a paper? Why?

1. Cruising the Universe with Physicist Stephen Hawking
2. The Growing Crime Problem
3. Evaluating the New Diet Plans
4. What's in a Name?
5. Cowboys and Commies: Politics in the Hollywood Western, 1942–1973

CHAPTER 4

How Do You Write a Draft?

4a How do you start a piece of writing?

For many people, getting started is the hardest part of writing. Even professional authors describe the paralyzing anxiety they sometimes feel as they sit and stare at a blank page or computer screen. Beginnings *are* hard, but remember that a first draft doesn't have to be perfect. It's simply a place to start. In this section we offer suggestions to help you through the drafting process—so that you can stop worrying, take the plunge, and *start writing*.

1 Find a place to write and gather the things you'll need. If you can, find a spot away from friends, family, and noise, where you won't be distracted. Collect your materials—computer disks, notes, source materials, dictionary, and a copy of the assignment—and lay them out where you can see them. Turn your computer on and let it hum. In making preparations like these, you're not procrastinating; you're creating a working environment.

2 Keep the ideas coming. Some people agonize over their first few sentences, tinkering endlessly in a quest to get them just right. Don't let an awkward beginning stall the entire draft. Remember that what appears in a draft won't necessarily become part of the finished essay. So treat your first paragraph as a device to get rolling. Write three or four sentences nonstop to build momentum, no matter how imperfect they may be. You may be surprised at how quickly words begin to flow once you've warmed up to your topic.

Remember too that you don't have to write the opening paragraph first. You can always begin with whatever section of the paper seems easiest to write and come back to the introduction later, after you have a better sense of where your argument is headed. See Section 14a for more on writing opening paragraphs.

3 Don't criticize yourself or edit your writing prematurely. As you work on a first draft, cut yourself some slack. Don't moan, "This is awful!" or "I hate my writing!" Recognize that writing can be a slow and difficult business; you should congratulate yourself when you're making any progress at all. Most pieces of good writing develop over time. You can't expect something to be perfectly polished when you first start working on it.

4a
draft

Nor should you fiddle with problems of mechanics and style in your early drafts. You can go back and fix difficulties with spelling, punctuation, parallelism, word choice, and the like *after* you've gotten your ideas down on paper. If you bog down in details of form too early, you may lose your momentum for writing, letting your brightest ideas fade while you hunt for the spelling of *nitpicker*. Worse, you may find yourself always playing it safe, writing only the kinds of sentences you can compose easily, never pushing yourself to grapple with difficult ideas or to try out a more interesting style.

4 Set your own pace. When you're not sure what pace best suits you, try writing quickly at first. If you hit a snag or can't produce the specific phrase or example you need, skip the troublesome spot and move on. Above all, keep writing. A draft in hand, even a sketchy one, will give you a sense of accomplishment. You'll have material to develop and refine.

But if you're the kind of writer who isn't comfortable composing quickly, don't feel that you must change your routine. Especially when they are working on a project that incorporates a lot of research materials, many skilled writers do work slowly. They may take several hours to turn out a few paragraphs, but their first drafts are often quite polished. In the long run, slow writers may not spend much more time completing a project than writers who produce material faster but rework that material through more drafts.

5 Get feedback from other writers. One of the best ways to get writing done is to share ideas with other people. In college courses, in the workforce, and in community forums, groups of writers routinely brainstorm for ideas, compare findings, evaluate organizational strategies, and test out arguments. Such groups serve as important first audiences for drafts and keep writers motivated—after all, no one wants to let colleagues down.

In Section 4e you'll find tips for approaching collaborative writing projects; Section 43b-6 offers suggestions for doing collaborative research. See Section 5d for guidelines on helping another writer revise a draft.

▉ 6 Draft on a computer. Working on a computer makes it easy to accumulate material even before you begin a draft. You can start a file that records your initial impressions about a project days or weeks before the deadline. You can bookmark online sources that you want to refer to in your paper or download and store copies of relevant articles. Over time you'll accumulate a surprising amount of material to use in your draft. If you are comfortable working this way, you'll be gratified at how easy the process of assembling a paper can become. (Be sure, however, to keep track of and to cite material in your draft that comes from other sources. See Section 46a for more details.)

With a computer it's also easy to take risks. You can experiment with major changes without losing the work you've already done, by saving alternate versions of your draft until you decide which one you want to use. (Revising a text doesn't automatically improve it.)

Finally, computers make it easy to experiment with different formats and to incorporate graphic or multimedia elements. See Chapters 19 and 20 for more on document design.

4b   How do you keep a draft on track?

When you begin a draft, you will probably have a thesis and a general organizational plan in mind. You may have gathered the resources you plan to use in the paper (articles, interview data, Web sites, statistics) and even developed an outline. But the real work of constructing your paper doesn't start until you begin putting words on a page. Only then can you see precisely how your plan may have to be altered to fit the particular material and your particular writing situation. As a writer you have to be both focused and flexible: focused enough to guide readers through your material and flexible enough to shift strategies when necessary. This section will help you keep your draft on track.

▉ 1 Highlight key ideas. Know what main points you want to cover and keep them in mind as you compose the draft. One way to do this is to summarize your thesis up front, in the first paragraph. Beginning with key points gives readers a notion of what to expect; then you can follow with supporting material. For example, here is an opening paragraph that forecasts what the rest of the paper will be about. The thesis sentence is underlined.

```
     At the beginning of this decade, one-third of the

doctors graduating from medical schools were women.

Now the figure is around 40 percent. Women doctors

will soon be in the majority in specialties such as

obstetrics-gynecology, pediatrics, and psychiatry,

and they are rapidly making inroads into

traditionally male territories such as surgery and

orthopedics. This shifting balance in what up to now

has been a male-dominated profession is changing

American medicine in a number of ways. One can

already see changes in medical education as the

number of women professors in medical school

increases.
```

Even if you choose to ease your readers into your thesis by opening the paper with background information or an attention-getting anecdote (see Section 14a), you still need to keep your main point in mind so that the opening doesn't wander too far astray.

Continue to highlight main ideas throughout the draft. Use phrases like these to snap readers to attention.

> The points we must consider are . . .
> The chief issue, however, is . . .
> Now we have come to the crucial question.

You can also keep readers focused on key points with constructions that express your own thoughts about the topic or that draw their attention to contrasting viewpoints.

> I believe that . . .
> Other researchers say . . .
> Opponents have argued . . .
> Still, we should recognize that . . .

Even cues as simple as *first, second,* and *third* can help readers follow the structure of your paper. For more guidance on using transitional words and phrases, see Section 15b.

■ 2 Keep the amount you write about each point roughly proportionate to its importance in the paper. Be careful not to write a lopsided draft that misleads readers. If what you intend as an introduction takes up half the paper, it's no longer an introduction. If

your thesis promises to develop a new solution to a problem yet mentions this solution only in the last paragraph, you haven't fulfilled that promise. Should you find yourself writing at length on a minor point, or quoting at length from one source while neglecting others, step back and return to your central argument.

However, while you should respect the principle of proportion, don't be too stingy with words and ideas in a first draft. You'll discover in editing that it is easier to prune material you don't like than it is to fill in where your ideas are thin. Obviously you don't want to stray too far from your thesis. But you do want to capture any fresh thoughts that emerge as you write. The same is true of examples, illustrations, facts, figures, and details: If they don't work, you can always cut them later or find a better place in the draft to use them.

■ **3 Allow yourself enough time to draw conclusions.** Conclusions are important. Don't put so much energy into the introduction and body of a paper that you skimp on the final paragraphs. You can weaken your paper badly if you do, since the ending often determines what impression readers will take from your piece.

When you approach the end of a draft, take time to reread what you have written. Then consider what remains to be done: What are the larger implications of the ideas you've discussed? What do you want readers to know, believe, or do as a result of your piece? What loose ends need to be tied up? Let these concerns help shape your concluding paragraph(s). If you have time, try out several endings and choose the one that you think best fits your audience and purpose. See Section 14b for more on closing paragraphs.

4c When should you take a break?

In the midst of a writing project you may suddenly find yourself stumped. You gaze at your computer screen or look at a blank page, but nothing happens. No ideas come. Such a lull can be scary, especially when a deadline looms. But don't panic; you may simply need to kick back and let your thoughts *incubate*.

Incubation is an interval during which a writer stops composing for a time to let ideas germinate or develop. You can't force or rush incubation; you can only be ready to grab a new idea when it surfaces.

■ **1 Allow time for both long and short incubation periods.** When possible, start a writing project well before its deadline, since you may need several incubation periods. For authors who work consistently, such rest periods are absolutely necessary. When they've written themselves out for the day, they know it's fruitless to sit at the computer or writing desk any longer.

The periods that lapse between writing the first, second, and even third drafts of a paper can be similarly productive. But shorter incubation periods help too. When you are stuck for a word or can't think of the example you need to illustrate a point, get away from the desk long enough to do an errand or chat with someone. Even such a brief pause can trigger an insight. So you don't have to keep yourself glued to the chair all the time in order to write—minor interruptions can actually be productive.

4c
draft

2 Don't use incubation as an excuse for procrastination.

You should take occasional breaks while writing, but you can't afford to wait forever for inspiration. If you're still having problems with a project after a few hours (or a weekend) of rest, get back to work anyway. Review your notes or outlines; consult your research; reread what you've already written; try focusing on a new section of the paper. Most important, just write!

Going Public *One Writer's Drafting Process*

Even professional writers typically compose documents in several stages. When communication specialist Brad Stratton was asked to write a brochure publicizing a workshop sponsored by his employer, he spent parts of three days working toward his first draft, as the diary below illustrates. Note how often Brad moved back and forth among writing, researching, incubating, and revising during the drafting process.

Monday–Day 1

3:00–3:25	Reviewed content information and handwrote introduction
3:25–3:30	Shared draft of introduction with colleague
3:30–4:45	Put draft away; focused on other work
4:45–5:00	Typed introduction draft into computer, making some changes

Tuesday–Day 2

9:30–10:00	Reviewed other brochures for ideas

10:00–10:45	Made scratch outline of entire brochure in a new document
10:45–11:00	Break
11:00–11:25	Reviewed outline; did additional research on Internet to fill gaps in previous research
11:25–12:05	Wrote main text
12:05–12:45	Imported introduction from other document; experimented with layout
12:45–1:00	Reviewed text and corrected typos
1:00	Printed text of brochure and gave copies to colleagues for review

Wednesday—Day 3

9:00–9:30	Made additions and changes to text based on readers' suggestions
9:30–11:00	Worked on design: added logo, borders, and background graphics
11:00–12:00	Break
12:00–12:30	Proofread draft; printed out and submitted copy to boss

4d How do you know when you have a solid draft?

Many writing instructors ask students to submit a draft of an assignment for feedback before turning in the final version. You might also be asked to share a preliminary version of a report or memo with co-workers or to show a first version of an editorial to a news editor. As the deadline to turn in your draft approaches, relax. Although the paper you are laboring over may not be as good as you'd like, remember that you'll have a chance to revise and polish later. Don't relax too much, though: you'll waste your readers' time if you settle for a draft that's incomplete or rushed.

How do you know when you've made a solid effort? When you've met the three standards listed in Checklist 4.1, you can probably rest assured that readers will find your draft worth reading and responding to.

Checklist 4.1
Knowing When You Have a Solid Draft

Before you give a draft to your instructor, colleague, or peer reviewer for comments, be sure you've met these standards.

1. **Have you made a good-faith effort?**
   Be sure you've invested substantial time and thought in your paper. If you haven't, you're passing up an opportunity you may not get again: the chance to get useful criticism of your paper while it's still in progress.

2. **Is the draft reasonably complete?**
   Have you stated a thesis, developed it with supporting arguments and examples, and finished with a defensible conclusion? A few paragraphs don't qualify as a working draft. Nor does a carefully written opening followed by an outline of what the rest of the paper will cover.

3. **Is the draft readable?**
   You can't expect instructors, classmates, or colleagues to respond carefully to a paper that's hard to read.

   • Be sure to double-space your draft, leaving ample margins all the way around the page for comments.

   • Be sure that your printer or photocopier has made dark, legible copies.

   • If you must hand-write a draft, *print* in ink on every other line.

   • Write or print on one side of the paper only and number your pages.

EXERCISE 4.1 Evaluate a draft you have recently written against the three criteria in the checklist. Does your paper meet the standards? If not, what changes would you have to make to remedy the problems?

4e How do you work on a draft collaboratively?

It's challenging enough to stay focused when you're writing a draft by yourself. But the challenges multiply when you co-author a paper with classmates or colleagues. Being able to write collaboratively is an important skill. In business, project teams prepare presentations; in college, instructors sometimes ask groups of students to undertake service-learning or other joint writing projects; and in community settings, groups must create statements of their policies or goals.

It's always a relief to share the workload. But pundits don't joke about the ineffectiveness of committees for no reason. Without a shared focus and careful planning, group efforts can become frustrating exercises.

The kind of collaborative drafting we discuss in this section is different from the work of peer revision groups that meet to help individual writers improve an already-written draft. For more on peer revision, see Section 5d.

■ **1 Decide on shared goals.** Suppose your instructor has asked you and several classmates to develop a promotional Web site for a local historical museum as part of a service-learning project. Before you even turn on the computer, you should come to a consensus on what your group hopes to accomplish.

- Do you want to construct a primarily informational site where readers can find the museum's address, hours of operation, major exhibits, and admission fees?
- Will your site also try to persuade readers to serve as volunteer tour leaders or to donate funds to build a new children's wing?
- Will your Web site be technically sophisticated or very basic?

Once you've agreed on general goals, you can plan the actual research and writing. See Section 43b-6 for specific advice on doing collaborative research.

Of course, you may not be able to sharply define your project in a first meeting. You may need to brainstorm or do background research. If group members have different ideas about the project, you'll need to negotiate these differences over several meetings. You'll also need to consider the goals of your instructor and of the museum staff. It may take time to hammer out a shared purpose, but it's time well spent. If you rush to begin a project when each person has different ideas, you'll wind up with a mishmash of material that no one can agree how to put together.

■ **2 Consider assigning separate sections of the project to each writer.** You may find it efficient to divide a group assignment into sections. Ask each writer to research and compose a section individually, then schedule a group meeting to combine and edit the sections into a coherent document. Students working on the museum Web site might ask one writer to take responsibility for constructing an informational home page, another to compose pages on current exhibits, and another to create and monitor an email forum.

When you compose a group project in this way, set aside plenty of time to pull the pieces together. You'll need to eliminate overlap, address gaps in your coverage, and revise for consistency. The finished product shouldn't read like several short pieces awkwardly cobbled to-gether.

Splitting a document into individually authored parts is the quickest way to complete a group writing assignment. However, this approach doesn't work well for texts that aren't easily separated into components or for a document that you want to represent the perspective of the entire group.

▓ 3 Consider writing the document collaboratively.

Collaborative drafting—when an entire group participates in composing a text—can yield impressive results. Many powerful public documents, including the Declaration of Independence, were written in this way. The advantage of this method is that several ideas and viewpoints are often better than one: you'll have diverse input and ideas at every point in the composing process.

The primary disadvantage of this method, of course, is the amount of time required. You'll need to schedule plenty of group meetings or frequent email exchanges to write and discuss the text in progress. Consider assigning one person to be the group's "recorder," in charge of maintaining the draft in progress and recording new text and ideas.

▓ 4 Address disagreements promptly.

Like most group activities, collaborative writing isn't always smooth sailing. Many students resist group work because they've had bad experiences with classmates who monopolized a project or neglected their responsibilities.

The best way to deal with such problems is to do your best to avoid them in the first place. After you've decided on your group's goals, work out a schedule of meetings and deadlines that everyone can agree on. Distribute a copy of the schedule to each group member and to your instructor, if possible. If one writer fails to abide by the agreement, raise the issue in your next meeting. Remind him or her of the schedule and offer encouragement. You may need to ask your instructor to help if the problem persists.

Other difficulties arise when group members disagree about the direction a project is taking. Suppose that in a persuasive paper for an English composition course, some members of a group want to create a multimedia presentation on the health risks of body piercing, while the rest want to write a traditional report. Or one group member strongly opposes using school taxes for private school vouchers while the others favor it. If you can't settle on an approach that satisfies everyone, consult your instructor. He or she may allow you to compose two smaller subprojects or to incorporate a statement of minority views into your document.

CHAPTER 5

How Do You Revise, Edit, and Proofread?

Why make a fuss distinguishing among terms as similar as *revising, editing,* and *proofreading?* It's because revising, editing, and proofreading are different phases of the writing process, each of which involves thinking about a different aspect of the paper.

Chart 5.1

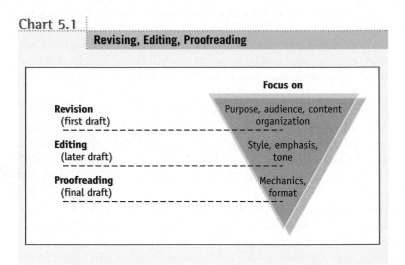

Revising, Editing, Proofreading	
	Focus on
Revision (first draft)	Purpose, audience, content organization
Editing (later draft)	Style, emphasis, tone
Proofreading (final draft)	Mechanics, format

When you start *revising* your draft, don't think in terms of *fixing* or *correcting* your writing—that's not really what you are doing. Rather you are *shaping a work in progress*, reviewing what you have written and looking for ways to improve it. You may get new ideas and shift the focus of the paper entirely; you may cut, expand, and reorganize. At this point you are making large-scale changes.

When you *edit* a paper, you are less concerned with the big issues. Instead you turn your attention to matters of style that affect clarity, emphasis, and tone. You may rewrite sentences you find awkward or correct problems with parallelism and repetition. Your goal is to create sentences and paragraphs that present your ideas effectively. These are small-scale changes.

When you *proofread* a paper, you go back over it line by line, reading carefully to correct typographical errors, to check for words that may have been omitted, to verify details, to eliminate inconsistencies, and to remove embarrassing gaffes. This is the fix-it stage, when you're finally preparing the paper to appear in public. However, it's a good idea to postpone proofreading until the end of a project. If you begin correcting errors while you are composing or revising, you're liable to waste time repairing sentences that later might be deleted.

5a   What does revising involve?

When you revise a draft, don't try to work through it paragraph by paragraph, making changes as you go. The problems of a first draft are likely to involve large-scale issues of content and rhetorical strategy that affect every paragraph in the paper, concerns that must be addressed before you can polish individual sentences. That's the point of serious revision—to reconsider everything you have written. At this point THINK BIG, don't tinker.

Large-scale changes include revising for focus, purpose, proportion, commitment, adaptation to audience, organization, and content. Begin by reading your first draft from start to finish, thinking about these major elements. If you are working with a computer, you need to print out a copy and revise from that (see Section 5a-9).

1 Read your draft thoughtfully. Review the original assignment and any feedback you have received from your instructor, classmates, or colleagues. Ask yourself frankly how you feel about the paper. What's good that you definitely want to keep? Where does it seem weak?

Ideally you should appraise your draft several days (or at a minimum several hours) after you have completed it so that you can read it more objectively. Obviously you can enjoy the advantages of setting a draft aside only if you start on an assignment early.

One bold option to consider at this point is writing a second, entirely new draft. Take this radical path when you really dislike what you've written, when editors have found little to praise in your first effort, or when you just need a fresh start. Creating a new draft may seem discouraging, but in the long run, starting from scratch may be easier than repairing a draft that just won't work. Even then, your first draft need not be a waste of effort. Often an unsuccessful version points a writer toward what he or she really wanted to write about. So don't mourn a discarded first draft; it can lead to a stronger new version.

2 Refine the focus of the paper. Once you've determined that your draft is workable, be sure that it makes and develops a central point. You have a problem with focus if the draft makes a lot of general statements without supporting and developing them. Check your examples and supporting material. Have you relied mostly on common knowledge? If so, your draft may lack the credibility that comes from specific information. To check for focus, ask yourself these questions.

Checklist 5.1

Revising for Focus

• Have you taken on a larger topic or more material than you can handle?

• Are you generalizing about your topic instead of stating specific positions?

• Have you supported your ideas with sufficient evidence and examples?

See Section 2b for more on focusing a topic.

3 Consider your purpose. Ask yourself whether someone reading your draft would immediately understand what you're trying to achieve. If you lacked a sense of purpose when you began drafting the paper, you now need to decide exactly what you want to accomplish. Be sure that your intentions are evident to yourself and to your readers. You can't seriously revise the paper further unless you know what its goals are. Here are three questions to ask yourself.

Checklist 5.2

Revising for Purpose

• Do you clearly state in the first paragraph or two what you intend to do?

• Does the draft develop all the main points you intended to make?

• After reading the draft, will most readers be able to summarize your main idea?

See Section 1e for more on refining your purpose.

■ **4 Examine the proportions of your paper.** *Proportion* means the distribution and balance of ideas in a piece. You should develop your ideas in relation to their importance. Ask yourself these questions.

Checklist 5.3

Revising for Proportion

- Are the parts of the paper out of balance? For example, have you gone into too much detail at the beginning and then skimped on the rest of the paper?
- Can your readers tell what points are most important by the amount of attention you've given to them?
- Does the conclusion do justice to the ideas it summarizes?

■ **5 Check that you have kept your promises to readers.** The introduction and thesis of your paper will create certain expectations in your readers. When you revise, check your response to any commitments you've made. Now is the time to tie up loose ends, so ask these questions.

Checklist 5.4

Revising for Commitment

- What exactly do you promise your readers at the beginning of the paper? Do you fulfill those promises?
- Do you support all the points you made in your thesis?
- Do you finish what you started? Have you inadvertently raised questions you can't or don't intend to answer?
- Does your conclusion agree with your opening?

■ **6 Check for adaptation to audience.** Sometimes a first draft is what we call *writer-centered;* that is, the writer has concentrated on expressing his or her ideas without thinking much about the audience. Such an approach can be productive in a first draft, but a major goal of revising should be to change *writer-centered* writing to *reader-centered* writing. You do that by trying to put yourself in the place of your readers. Consider these questions.

Checklist 5.5

Revising for Audience

- Do you spend too much time discussing material that most of your readers already know?

- Do you answer important questions that readers might have about your topic?

- Do you define all the concepts and terms that your readers need to know?

- Do you use language your readers will understand?

See the audience checklist on page 10 for more advice.

■ 7 Check the organization. A well-organized paper has a plan and a clear direction. Readers can move from the beginning to the end of a paper without getting lost. To revise the structure of a draft, you'll need a printed copy because organizational problems can be hard to detect on a computer screen. You need a sense of the whole to see how the parts are meshing. To check your organization, ask these questions.

Checklist 5.6

Revising for Organization

- Does your paper state a clear thesis or claim? Does it then develop key points related to that thesis?

- Does the development of your points follow a pattern readers will recognize?

- Do the transitions move readers sensibly from point to point?

- Would the paper work better if you moved some paragraphs around?

See Section 3b for more detailed tips on organization and Section 15b for more on making smooth transitions between ideas.

■ 8 Check the content of the paper. When you revise, you may need to add information to give a paper more substance. A college paper needs the weight of evidence to advance its argument. Ask yourself these questions.

Checklist 5.7

Revising for Content

* Do you fully develop and support each main idea?

* Do you need to add specific information and concrete examples that will make your case stronger? Do you need to do more research?

* Do you cite reliable, credible sources to back up your ideas?

* Does the title of your paper reflect its content?

If the content of your draft seems thin, return to the library or to other sources. See Chapter 44 for more on doing research.

9 Revise from hard copy if you are working on a computer. Whether you are revising, editing, or proofreading, you'll probably work better from a hard copy of your paper than from an on-screen text. Problems that seem all but invisible on the screen (weak organization, sprawling paragraphs, poor transitions, repeated words) show up more clearly on a printed page.

After you've marked up your draft, transfer all corrections made on the printed version to the computer file.

EXERCISE 5.1 Apply the criteria for large-scale revision described above to a draft you have written.

Going Public *A Revised Opening Paragraph* _____

Carl Jackson wanted to write a paper for his first-year composition course exploring the corrupt practices used by some colleges to recruit high school basketball players. Here's the opening paragraph of his first draft exactly as he wrote it.

        Basketball is one of the most exciting games to
    watch because of the nonstop action at every minite
    of the game. Unlike football where time is taken to
    huddle and the average play last only about five
    seconds, or even worse, baseball which is America's
    sport, seems to drag on forever until something

exciting happens. My opinion of basketball being the
most exciting sport to watch is arguable but what is
not arguable is the amount of unethical practices
found in the sport. It seems that every year another
team has been placed on probation or a school has had
to suspend its program. Among these are recruiting
violations and payments to recruits and active
players by alumni. These are the areas on which
I would like to focus and possibly give a
few suggestions on how to clean up college
basketball.

If Carl were to begin editing and proofreading this paragraph before undertaking larger-scale revisions, he'd probably make these corrections: (1) change *minite* to *minute;* (2) change *average play last* to *average play lasts;* (3) simplify the sentence that begins *Unlike football;* (4) change *amount* to *number.*

But Carl's classmates who reviewed the paper thought that the paragraph had bigger problems. For one thing, they were confused about Carl's focus. If he was interested in basketball, why does he comment on football and baseball? The first few sentences seem unrelated to the conclusion of the paragraph, and that conclusion isn't very intriguing. They doubted that this opener would keep readers interested. Clearly Carl needed to overhaul the paragraph.

Here's the heavily revised paragraph that opened his second draft. The new version gets to the point more quickly and catches readers' attention with the possibility of a solution to the recruitment problem. Though open to additional changes, this new paragraph demonstrates what we mean by large-scale revision.

Basketball is one of the most exciting games to
watch, with its fast-paced, nonstop action, but even
avid fans might be hard pressed these days to keep up
with NCAA investigations of the sport. It seems that
every year another college basketball program has
been placed on probation by the NCAA for recruiting
violations. This widespread problem has generated

```
much debate on what should be done to clean up the

sport of basketball. The suggestions range from

cutting athletic scholarships to paying the athletes

to play. Although a case can be made for both of

these extreme measures, I believe that there is a

better way to bring back the integrity of basketball.
```

Notice that the mechanical and grammatical errors of the first version are not present in the second draft. To have spent time fixing them before making the needed revisions would have been a waste of time.

5b What does editing involve?

Revision should have given you a better-focused, better-organized, more interesting draft. If you're reasonably satisfied with your revised paper, you're ready to *edit,* that is, to make the small-scale changes that you put on hold while you were adding, cutting, and rearranging material. Now you will consider concrete and specific language, word choice, wordiness, transitions, and a better introduction and conclusion.

Now is the time to use the handbook to check on details of style (Part III), grammar and usage (Part V), and mechanics (Part VI).

1 Make your language concrete and specific. Language is *concrete* when it describes things as they are perceived by the senses: colors, textures, sizes, sounds, actions. Language is *specific* when it names particular people, places, and things.

Although generalizations and abstract terms are appropriate in some writing situations, readers usually need vivid descriptions that bring concepts to life. As you edit, look for ways to add people to your discussions, to illustrate generalizations with examples, and to supply your readers with facts and images. Give your writing texture.

2 Strive for a readable style. Look at your word choices to see where they can be improved. Do you achieve the right level of formality for the writing situation? Do you balance technical terms with everyday language? Are your subjects specific and do your verbs express powerful actions? Are your modifiers vivid and accurate?

Different writing styles are appropriate in different settings. When in doubt about what kinds of language you should use in a piece, take a look at similar pieces others have written. For example, if you are writing a textbook review for an education course, look at similar reviews in education journals to see whether their authors use contractions and first-person pronouns, or whether more formal constructions are the rule.

Finally, look carefully at any questions your instructors or colleagues have raised about word choice. Check words you're not sure of in a dictionary to be certain the meaning you intend is appropriate and contemporary. Careful use of a thesaurus is appropriate at this stage. See Chapters 16 through 18 for more detailed suggestions on style.

3 Be sure that your tone is appropriate.
For most writing projects, you'll want to avoid polarizing or hostile language that might alienate readers. Replace any name-calling ("bleeding-heart liberal," "conservative fat cat," "so-called expert"), stereotypes, or unduly extreme descriptions ("man-hating ideology" to describe feminism or "religious fanatics" to describe an evangelical movement) with more moderate references.

If you want to make a reasoned argument, beware of relying too much on intensely emotional language ("I am unspeakably disgusted by the tobacco industry because . . ."). Although a well-timed expression of feeling can move readers, your personal anger shouldn't become the focus of an argument. Of course, such language might be perfectly suitable in other kinds of writing, such as an autobiographical narrative.

For more information about tone, consult Sections 11c and 16e. Section 1g discusses the importance of presenting a fair and responsible image in a paper.

4 Cut wordiness.
Many writers produce wordy first drafts, especially when they are generating ideas. In subsequent drafts, however, it's time to cut. In particular, go after sprawling verb phrases ("make the evaluation" → "evaluate"), redundancies ("initial start-up" → "start-up"), and boring strings of prepositional phrases ("in the bottle on the shelf in the refrigerator" → "in the bottle on the refrigerator shelf"). Be ruthless. You can usually cut as much as 25 percent of your prose without losing anything but verbiage (see Sections 13d and 18c).

5 Test your transitions.
Transitions are words and phrases that connect sentences, paragraphs, and whole passages of writing. When transitions are faulty, a paper will seem choppy and disconnected. To decide whether that's the case, read your draft aloud. If you pause, stumble, and detect gaps, you should improve the connections between ideas. Often you'll just need to add words or phrases to the beginnings of sentences and paragraphs—expressions such as "on the other hand," "however," and "nonetheless." In some cases you'll have to edit more deeply, rearranging whole sections of the piece to put ideas in a more coherent order. See Chapters 13 and 15 for additional suggestions.

6 Polish the introduction and the conclusion. Most of us know intuitively that the introduction of a draft is important enough to merit special attention. It makes sense, however, not to edit the first paragraph until you know precisely how your paper is going to come out. Then you can make sure that the introduction is both accurate and interesting.

Conclusions also warrant special care, but they may be even harder to write than introductions. So don't fuss too much with the conclusion until you have the main part of the paper under control. Then try to work out a strong ending that pulls the paper together and leaves your readers satisfied.

For more specific suggestions on how to improve introductory and concluding paragraphs, see Chapter 14.

7 Use a computer style checker—carefully. Style and editing programs have various functions: they may calculate the readability level of sentences in a paper, locate expletive constructions (*it is, there is*), spot clichés, detect repetitions, and so on. But for all their cleverness, such programs deal with stylistic problems chiefly by counting items. They can't assess context. And it is usually context that determines, for example, whether expletives or repetitions are appropriate. If you have access to a style checker, use it, but don't assume that it can create a polished paper for you.

When you don't have access to a commercial style checker, you can create a simple version on your own. Use the search command in your word-processing program to look for specific weaknesses in your writing. If you use *to be* verbs too frequently, direct the computer to find all uses of *be, is, are, was,* and *were* so that you can replace them, when possible, with action verbs. If punctuation around the word *however* baffles you, double-check each occurrence of the word. The longer your paper, the more helpful the search command can be.

Checklist 5.8

When Editing . . .

- Sharpen your language—make it concrete and specific.
- Check your word choice—make it readable and clear.
- Lop out wordiness.
- Be sure your tone is appropriate.
- Test your transitions.
- Polish your opening and closing.
- Use a style checker if you find it helpful.

5b

edit

Going Public   *Edited Sentences from Student Papers*

Here are sentences from student papers that have been improved by judicious editing. Notice that the changes do not greatly alter the meaning of the selections.

ORIGINAL

wordy, passive opening

It has been maintained throughout history by some of

hyphen needed   wrong connotation

the most well‸trained and (notorious) nutritionists

redundant?

and (specialists) that a vegetarian diet is superior to

a nonvegetarian diet.

EDITED

Over the years, many well-trained and respected

nutritionists have maintained that a vegetarian diet

is superior to a nonvegetarian diet.

ORIGINAL

Be specific. Which border?

The immigrants cross the border believing that they

where?

will not be here forever. They come to make more

"to" repeated too often

money to take home to Mexico to build a better life.

EDITED

These immigrants cross the Texas-Mexico border

believing that they will not be in the United States

forever. They hope to make enough money in the United

States to return to Mexico and build better lives.

EXERCISE 5.2 Apply the criteria for editing to a draft you are working on. Give your paper all the attention to detail it deserves. And don't back away from making more complicated changes when they are necessary.

5c What does proofreading involve?

When you are reasonably satisfied with the content, organization, and style of your paper, you're ready to put it in final form. Like checking your appearance in the mirror before an important meeting, *proofreading* provides a final measure of quality control. The more you care about the impression a paper makes, the more important it is *not* to neglect this last step.

At this stage use the handbook—Parts III, V, and VI—to check punctuation, correct usage, and the conventions of edited American English.

1 Check your weakest areas. If you are a poor speller, pick out words that might be misspelled and look them up in a dictionary. If you are inclined to put commas where they're not needed, check to be sure commas don't interrupt the flow of ideas. And see that you have used the correct forms of the troublesome words *its/it's, your/you're, there/their/they're.*

2 Check for inconsistencies. Have you switched your point of view in ways that might be confusing—for example, addressing readers initially as *you* and later referring to them as *we* or *they?* Do you use contractions in some parts of the paper but avoid them in others? Make certain the tone of the paper is consistent throughout, not inappropriately light in some places and formal in others.

3 Check punctuation. Look for comma splices—that is, places where a pair of independent clauses are mistakenly joined with a comma instead of a semicolon. Take a moment to review all semicolons. See that proper nouns and adjectives (*England, African*) and *I* are capitalized. And check that you have used quotation marks and parentheses in pairs. (See Chapters 34–42.)

4 Use a computer spelling checker. If you are using a word-processing program that includes a spelling checker, run your text through it. However, a spelling checker won't catch many serious misspellings, such as *where* for *were* or *no* for *know,* because it can't determine whether the word works within the context of a sentence. Thus you'll need to follow up with a final check of your own.

5 Check for typographical errors. Look especially for transposed letters, dropped endings, faulty word division, and omitted apostrophes.

6 Check the format of your paper. Be sure to number your pages, to keep accurate and consistent margins, to italicize or underline titles of sources as needed, to put other titles between quotation marks (see Chapters 38 and 39), and to clip your pages together. Be sure that you've cited outside sources appropriately and listed them in your bibliography (see Chapters 46 and 48–52).

Also be sure you've instructed the computer to paginate the paper in the right place and to add a running head (often your name) when required.

Rodriguez 2

Set the margins correctly and review the page breaks. You don't want the computer to leave a heading at the bottom of a page or to separate an illustration from its caption.

Checklist 5.9

When Proofreading . . .

* Check spelling, grammar, and usage.

* Eliminate inconsistencies.

* Get the punctuation right.

* Double-check spelling.

* Eliminate typographical errors.

* Check the format of your paper.

EXERCISE 5.3 Proofread a writing project you've recently completed, looking at all the areas listed in the checklist above. Which problems do you spot most often? How do you think you might avoid them in future projects?

5d How do you help another writer revise, edit, and proofread?

It's common these days for students in writing classes to work together on their papers. Meeting in small groups, writers read photocopies of each other's drafts and respond to them. The instructor may also comment on the drafts and make suggestions. In this way each writer in the class can receive feedback from several readers.

This method of responding to drafts (sometimes called *peer revision*) gives writers the benefit of real audiences. Colleagues, acting as friendly editors, can tell you whether you've included all the information you need and whether your argument is clear; they may also be able to suggest alternative approaches or to point out where you could rein in ideas that have gone too far. Even if you don't have the chance to participate in a formal peer editing session, try to get several readers' reactions to your work in progress. You can only profit from their responses—just as a professional author profits from an editor's comments before a book goes into print.

But it takes skill to be an honest and critical reader of another person's writing. When you do so, remember that you aren't taking the place of that person's writing teacher: you're an editor, not a grader. You can help a fellow writer most by showing an interest in what he or she has written, asking questions, giving encouragement, and making constructive suggestions for future drafts.

Similarly, you should use peers' criticism of your own drafts constructively, listening closely and selecting the comments that best suit your goals for the project. This section provides tips to help you get the most out of a draft revision session, whether you're giving or receiving feedback.

1 When you are reviewing a writer's draft, read it straight through once. Read it as a real piece of writing intended to inform, persuade, or entertain. Get a feel for the big issues before worrying about details of mechanics and usage. Do you understand what the writer is trying to achieve? Could you summarize the point of the paper? Do you find it informative, persuasive, or pleasurable reading? First impressions are important; if you don't think the draft works, try to explain why.

2 Read the paper a second time. Use the guidelines in Checklist 5.10 on page 75 to help you formulate responses to particular features of the paper. It's important that you say more than "I really like your paper" or "Maybe you could add some examples." Explain *what* you like about it, such as well-researched facts, colorful turns of phrase, or memorable examples. Show *where* you believe the paper needs more development. At this stage keep your critical focus on large-scale issues, not on misspellings or editing problems to be dealt with later.

3 Make marginal comments. If you are working with a photocopy of the draft, jot comments in the margins as you read it the second time. Editorial comments should be genuine queries or pointed observations, not stinging criticisms. Even when you're pointing out a weakness in a paper, use a courteous and supportive tone, not a sarcastic or unkind one. A question can sometimes be the most helpful remark.

> Can you say more about this?
> Have you left something out here?
> Would your opening be stronger if you cut this sentence?

Be as specific as you can about your reaction to the paper. Show precisely where you got lost when the organization is faulty. And let the writer know where something is working well.

4 Write out your responses to the paper. After you have read the paper carefully and annotated it in the margins, you still want to give the writer a general comment—something to ponder. That comment should come in a paragraph at the end of the paper, and it should be a thoughtful note summarizing your reaction to the draft.

It often helps a writer if you begin by saying what you think the paper has accomplished. That way the writer knows whether the paper has achieved at least part of what he or she hoped. Then you can say something about how well the paper works. Conclude your comment with suggestions for revision, stressing what you believe the writer's priorities might be.

The response memo to Justin Cone's essay (see page 76) is a good example of this kind of written response. A nice touch is to open this paragraph of commentary with your colleague's name and to conclude it with your signature.

5 Use a limited number of proofreading symbols. When reading a first draft, you don't want to waste time editing minor points of mechanics and usage that the writer can deal with in later versions. On the other hand, you may occasionally be asked to read a late draft of a paper, or you may know that the writer wants special help with a weakness such as spelling or punctuation. In such cases give the draft one last careful reading and look for mechanical problems only. At this time circle misspelled words (but don't correct them). Place words you think might be omitted in parentheses (but don't cross them out). Put a wavy line under words or phrases you think don't represent the writer's best choice.

> Books have <u>detailed</u> our culture since it began. When
> we wonder what life was like in eighteenth-century
> ⟨American⟩we turn to volumes written then. Historical
> events are preserved in print documents, and where
> history leaves blanks, literature⟨and poetry⟩step in.
> Can the new media take over this function?

To mark other items, consult the back of this book for proofreading symbols.

Checklist 5.10

Responding to a Draft

- What do you like most about the paper?

- How well does the paper achieve its purpose? Where does the purpose come through clearly?

- How well does the writer tailor the piece to his or her audience? What suggestions might you make for better adapting the paper for its intended readers?

- What suggestions can you make about focusing the topic? Should the focus be narrower? Does the paper need a sharper thesis?

- Does the writer come across as credible? What suggestions can you make that might add greater authority to the paper?

- What questions does the paper raise? What additional information, discussion, or examples would you like to have?

- How effectively does the writer use language? Are sentences clear and readable? How appropriate is the tone? What recurring problems with grammar, usage, and mechanics do you notice?

- What general comments do you have for the writer?

Going Public   *Draft with Peer Comments* _____

Here is a draft of a paper by a first-year composition student, Justin Cone. The assignment asked him to write a research paper exploring an ethical or social issue relevant to his classmates. It's a fine draft in many respects, interesting and thoughtful. It uses personal experiences and clever turns of phrase to catch readers' attention, drawing them into the argument. The paper also incorporates source materials effectively.

The draft also has some weaknesses. To get at them we've written comments in the margins and a concluding memo of the sort you might prepare in responding to a colleague's draft. These comments are a composite of real responses Justin received from several classmates; we've combined them in a single response from "Maria." Notice that most of the comments target large issues for revision rather than editing and mechanical problems.

Note too that Justin's paper cites and documents sources in MLA format. Some writers prefer to use the newer Columbia Online Style format for citing electronic sources. Check with your instructor to find out which style he or she prefers. You'll find information about MLA Style in Chapter 48 and on Columbia Online Style in Chapter 52.

Justin Cone

Topics in Writing

    Technology's Children: Has Media Technology

        Intellectually Stunted Our Generation?

        I was the 5-year-old learning ABCs from

Kermit the Frog. I was the 7-year-old programming

in BASIC at 5:30 in the morning, just before Bugs

Bunny aired. I was the 10-year-old successfully

installing a modem, sans instructions. But I was

also the 16-year-old who couldn't finish reading

Thomas Hardy's Tess of the D'Urbervilles for   *Interesting*
                                                      opening!
junior English because I didn't have the

concentration or mental stamina to read anything

longer than a computer screen.

        I was raised during the computer craze. Now

my peers and I stand on a shore as technology's

children, looking across the growing technological divide to a chunk of land sliding into the sea, where our parents swim, where our teachers worry, and where traditional kinds of literacy sink-- dragging much of our culture and history with it. In this paper, I will explore how media technology has shaped young adults' ways of processing knowledge so that books seem slow and out of date. In leaving books behind, our generation may lose priceless cultural archives amassed over thousands of years. But we may also pioneer exciting new ways of learning.

Nice image, but I get a little confused because the sentence is so long & complicated

Clear, interesting thesis

5d
collab

   When exploring a cause-and-effect relationship, the first thing I try to do is identify the cause. But in this case the cause is hard to tag. If there were some way to round up all the music videos, TV programs, fax transmissions, Internet sites, email, and online conversations (to name a few), we could heap the entire blinking, vibrating mass into a corner and point our fingers as if to say, "That's what did it." I am not foolish enough to blame media technology for all America's problems, but I can see the amazing impact it has had on my generation. As Boston area school superintendent Robert Calabrese notes, "You have to remember that the children of today have grown up with the visual media. . . . They know no other way" (qtd. in Birkerts 125). Fifty years ago, children did not grow up with computers in their homes or remote control access to instant news, sports, music videos, cartoons, and video games.

   This difference is the foundation for both advantages and disadvantages for my generation. We are privileged in that we are familiar with new

why is this an advantage?

forms of communication. Kids and computers "click"--
we "revel in having mastered a medium that often
befuddles [our] parents" (Silver and Perry). As new
media promise to move us faster and farther into
the future, "to surmount impedances and hasten
transitions," we embrace them (Birkerts 121).

Yet we are disadvantaged because much of the
world still plods along the old, slow route of
print. Thus our schools still demand that we be
able to read and comprehend lengthy writings from
heavy books. In an online article titled "Obsolete
Skill Set: The 3 R's," professor Seymour Papert
observes:

> A child who has grown up with the freedom to
> explore provided by . . . machines will not
> sit quietly through the standard curriculum
> dished out in most schools today. Already,
> children are made increasingly restive by
> the contrast between the slowness of school
> and the more exciting pace they experience
> in video games and television. (2)

This quiet war between print and new media
will, like all wars, claim casualties. Leaving
behind books means walking away from a storehouse
of cultural treasures. Books have detailed our
culture since it began. When we wonder what life
was like in eighteenth-century American, we turn
to volumes written then. Historical events are
preserved in print documents, and where history
leaves blanks, literature (and poetry) step in. Can
the new media take over this function? James *Will you answer*
Morris notes that while books are physical *this question?*
artifacts that can survive for many years,
"Hardware and software mutate at a giddy pace and

leave their forebears in the dust. The new machines cannot read the old software" (11). Books provide us with a continuity that electronic media cannot.

Sven Birkerts explains another quality associated with books, which he argues is found only in reading books. He explains, "As we read we are gradually engulfed by a half-familiar set of sensations. Because the characters walk, we walk; because they linger by roadsides or market squares, we do too. And by subtle stages we are overwhelmed" (25). I can remember reading One Flew Over the Cuckoo's Nest for a couple of hours and then taking a break. Leaning back in my chair for a stretch, I was surprised to see that I wasn't in a mental hospital, observing all the patients through Chief's eyes. The book had helped me build an imaginary world, but I believed in the world because I had experienced it.

Yet regardless of their merits, books are dying. Their death is not a choice, but the inevitable result of an unstoppable technological momentum carrying us into the future. Writer Neil Postman fears such a future, prophesying, "When a culture becomes overloaded with pictures; *Why? Explain. I'm confused.* when logic and rhetoric lose their binding authority . . . then a culture is in serious jeopardy." Such pessimistic predictions weigh heavily on our social conscience. Yet while scholars like Birkerts and Postman define the problems with technology beautifully, they offer no alternatives or suggestions, not even a "good luck" pat on the back *Good point* for my generation. Are we to allow ourselves to plummet into cultural despair? Or can we use our unique knowledge to go upward instead of down? I'll go out on a limb and say it: Yes, we can.

On a recent Sunday I decided to surf the Internet and found myself looking at a page on Shakespeare. After browsing some online pictures of Stratford-upon-Avon, I clicked a tiny icon and read a short biography of him. A list of play titles blinked at the bottom of the screen, and I clicked on Hamlet. An hour later I was reading Act II, Scene 1 with my roommate. When we happened upon a strange word, we clicked over to the online glossary. Once, we surfed all the way to ancient Rome before realizing that we had abandoned the play. With a simple click, we leaped back into the dialogue (http://the-tech.mit.edu/Shakespeare/works.html).

This is fun, but does it really have learning value? I'm not convinced.

No matter how large or well indexed, a book simply cannot offer such a rich experience. As Papert describes it, "the knowledge I gained was not the collection of propositions I read in books, but the web of connections that formed as my mind bounced here and there in a non-linear fashion" (2). The point of all this is simply that we can, through the hypertextual visual media, learn effectively: differently, maybe, but effectively just the same.

I'm confused by this quote. Is this a good thing or a bad thing?

What is "hypertextual"?

Granted, the transition from books to "bookless" may be a difficult one. But it is one that will not be completely good or completely bad until our generation makes it so.

I think you need a fuller conclusion.

Works Cited

Birkerts, Sven. <u>The Gutenberg Elegies: The Fate of Reading</u>

<u>in an Electronic Age</u>. New York: Ballantine, 1995.

Morris, James M. "The Human Touch." <u>Wilson Quarterly</u> 22.4

(Autumn 1998): 11-12.

Papert, Seymour. "Obsolete Skill Set: The 3 R's."

<u>HotWired</u>. 8 Dec. 1996

<http://www.feedmay.com/95.05dialog4.html>.

Postman, Neil. <u>Conscientious Objections: Stirring Up</u>

<u>Trouble About Language, Technology, and Education</u>.

New York: Knopf, 1988.

Silver, Marc, and Joellen Perry. <u>U.S. News and World</u>

<u>Report</u> 22 Mar. 1999: 57.

Here is Maria's memo with additional comments on Justin's paper.

Subject: your paper
From: Maria
To: Justin

1 Item   0 Bytes

Message Text 1

Justin,

I found your paper both interesting and informative. I think that almost anyone could identify with your opening examples. They illustrate just how dependent on electronic media we all are. Your thesis caught my attention, too. I've heard a lot of people complain about how television and computers make kids lazy, but I've never seen anyone look at both sides. I'm intrigued by the idea that all those video games and television cartoons might actually make us smarter.

The examples you use throughout are very good. You use a mix of research sources and your own experiences to illustrate your points. It's much more entertaining than a straight research paper. Sometimes though, I would have liked to see a broader perspective than just your own. For example, it's great that you were so enthralled by reading _One Flew Over the Cuckoo's Nest_, but isn't your focus on our whole generation? Do they have the same experiences? How do you know? Some more research on exactly what young people read or don't read would have been more convincing. In other words, you may need more data rather than relying so much on your own experiences. I have only one more complaint: You spend the whole paper leading up to your big point (that electronic media may have advantages that reading doesn't) and then don't really take time to develop that point. The only example you give is your experience with the Shakespeare Web site. I can see that the Web site is more fun than reading the play in a book, but does it really make us smarter? Does it help us learn something that we couldn't also get from a book? You aren't very specific in explaining this. I think you need to discuss this point much more--maybe in two or three more paragraphs--because, after all, it is the whole point of your essay.

Some of your sentences are also a little wordy and confusing, and you may want to develop a longer conclusion. Other than these suggestions, I think your paper is excellent. Please email me if you have any questions.

Maria

5d
collab

EXERCISE 5.4 Review Maria's comments on Justin's draft. If you had written this paper, would you find the advice helpful? Does it give enough guidance for improving the next draft? Working with a classmate, make a list of additional suggestions you might have made if Justin had asked you for feedback on his draft.

EXERCISE 5.5 Arrange with a classmate to exchange drafts of a writing assignment or project that you're both working on. Use the guidelines in Section 5d to write a memo responding to each other's drafts. Refer to your classmate's memo as you revise and edit the paper.

CHAPTER 6

How Is Writing Evaluated?

No matter how interesting or satisfying a project may be, most writers, sooner or later, ask the inevitable question: How will this be evaluated? Most of the academic, public, and professional writing you do will be judged by someone. In a college course, evaluation may certify that you have reached a specific level of proficiency, describe the progress you have made, or signal your readiness for new assignments and challenges. In public and professional settings, evaluation may simply assess how well your project was received by its intended audience. In fact, evaluations can be as varied and complex as any other part of the writing process.

But evaluations need not be mysterious or anxiety-producing. This chapter explains some of the most common methods college instructors use to evaluate writing, and suggests strategies for successfully dealing with them. We recognize, of course, that different instructors bring different ideas, strategies, and expectations to the courses they teach—and that's as it should be. You should adapt our general suggestions to fit the particular requirements of your courses and instructors. We realize too that you'll face evaluation outside the classroom, when you write in workplace and community settings; however, the assessment methods used in these settings vary widely and are generally less explicitly defined than those you'll encounter in college courses—so we don't address them here. Fortunately, the strategies you learn for dealing with grades in college may help you anticipate the standards your writing must reach outside of school.

6a How do you deal with letter grades?

Letter grades are so familiar to us all that they seem like a natural part of the academic landscape. Yet you shouldn't assume that you have nothing to learn about the marks assigned to your work. You may be surprised to discover that you have more control over the process of evaluation than you suspect.

■ **1 Understand your school's and your instructor's grading criteria.** At the beginning of any graded writing course, gather as much information as you can about the standards your work will be expected to meet. For instance, how does your instructor or school define an *A* or a *C* or an *F*? Does the system regard *D* as a passing mark? Can a course be taken pass/fail for credit?

Typically, a college or university will have fairly general criteria for coursework. Many—but not all—schools offer some version of the following scale.

A	excellent
B	above average
C	average
D	below average
F	unsatisfactory

Some institutions add plus and minus grades (*A–*, *C+*) or assign numerical equivalents to the letter grades. There are no nationwide standards for writing evaluation; in fact, even on a single campus, standards may vary from department to department and from one instructor to another. That's why it's so important to find out which standards will apply to you.

Some writing instructors distribute their own detailed grading criteria for the courses they teach. One instructor provides this description of a *C* paper to his first-year composition students:

AN EXCERPT FROM ONE INSTRUCTOR'S GRADING CRITERIA

C Paper (Average)

A *C* paper responds adequately to the assignment. Its treatment of an appropriate topic is thoughtful and reasonably well developed. A clear claim or thesis is supported by logical warrants and adequate, reliable evidence. The writer anticipates counterarguments and offers appropriate rebuttals. The structure of the paper is solid and logical. Paragraphs are organized around clear topic sentences. Transitions connect sentences to sentences and paragraphs to paragraphs. Sentences are correctly structured and reasonably varied. The handling of documentation (if any) is adequate. A *C* paper is generally correct though it may have a few comma splices, common subject-verb agreement errors, or difficulties with pronoun agreement/reference. The paper is double-spaced, paginated, titled, printed on clean white paper, and either clipped or stapled.

Such a description is more helpful than the term "average" in explaining what an instructor expects in a *C* paper. But it may still be too broad to explain exactly what features an instructor looks for in a particular assignment. For instance, not all papers will have paragraphs introduced by topic sentences or make claims that require evidence or documentation. For this reason, some instructors provide grading standards tailored to each assignment. Here's an example of a list of criteria one instructor developed for a researched argument assignment in a first-year composition course:

RHE 309S Critical Reading and Persuasive Writing
Professor Ruszkiewicz
Paper #1—Identity

Name: _____   Date: _____

Title of Paper: _____

1. Quality of your discussion of *identity*   Excellent___:___:___:___:___Poor

2. Clarity of your claim & argument   Excellent___:___:___:___:___Poor

3. Persuasiveness of your evidence   Excellent___:___:___:___:___Poor

4. Use of appropriate sources   Excellent___:___:___:___:___Poor

5. Handling of rebuttal/qualifiers   Excellent___:___:___:___:___Poor

6. Organization
   (including paragraph structures)   Excellent___:___:___:___:___Poor

7. Interest/adaptation to audience   Excellent___:___:___:___:___Poor

8. Sentence structures and style   Excellent___:___:___:___:___Poor

9. Handling of quotations/documentation   Excellent___:___:___:___:___Poor

10. Grammar/mechanics/word choice   Excellent___:___:___:___:___Poor

11. Presentation/format   Excellent___:___:___:___:___Poor

GRADE   _____

In schools that use "contract grading" in writing courses, the expectations will be markedly different. In this system, students and instructor agree beforehand that a particular grade will be earned by doing specified kinds of work or by completing a specific set of assignments. In such a course, a student might contract to earn an *A* by satisfactorily completing six papers or a *B* by satisfactorily completing five. The terms of the contract may be quite detailed and may involve activities such as participation in online forums in distance learning courses. If a project submitted is deemed "acceptable" and meets the contracted types and amounts of work, the grade follows automatically. Under a contract system, you have considerable power to determine your final grade.

2 Work to clarify any criteria that seem confusing. Whatever the system of evaluation you are working with, you should examine it critically and ask questions *before* and *while* you prepare your projects, not after. If you are told that an average paper will earn a *C,* you might ask your instructor these questions:

- What does a *C* (or *B,* or *A*) paper or project do?
- What does a *C* paper look like? May I see models?
- What does "average" in this case mean—an average performance in the section, in the first-year class as a whole, in the entire school?

When your instructor hands out detailed grading criteria, go over them with each new assignment, perhaps with a highlighting pen so you don't overlook important requirements.

Even when instructors don't spell out clear-cut standards, you can still learn much about their evaluation strategies by observing what they do in class. Did your instructor spend days teaching forms of argument or transitional phrases? She will likely pay attention to these features in your papers. Does the assignment sheet for a project mention "audience awareness," "cumulative sentences," or "MLA documentation"? Be sure you understand these concepts and handle them well in your project. Again, when you don't understand your instructor's expectations, don't be shy—ask for help.

3 Understand which portions of your work will be evaluated. The grade you receive on any assignment may depend on more than the quality of the final project. You should read any assignment sheet like a contract, to be sure you know what will count in the evaluation. Many instructors evaluate an entire writing process, assigning credit, for example, to your topic proposal, working bibliography, peer editing, first draft, and so on. Don't dismiss early stages of the writing process as busywork; your instructor may see them, with good reason, as points at which much learning takes place.

6a
eval

Similarly, examine carefully the formulas used to compute your final course mark. Sometimes an instructor designs a grading formula to place heavier emphasis on work produced later in the term. That way, he or she can reward students who make substantial progress. Here is one example:

Paper #1	10%
Paper #2	20%
Paper #3	30%
Paper #4	30%
Quizzes/participation	10%

In other cases the grading formula may include elements that carry the same weight throughout a term—items such as quizzes, exams, class participation, and credit for peer editing. Even faithful attendance may play a role in determining your final grade.

You should also be sure you know exactly who will be evaluating your work. You'll find it easier to satisfy your evaluators when you know precisely who they are. If your writing course includes a service-learning or internship component, will your supervisor in that setting help to decide on your grade? At some institutions, grades in writing courses may be decided by a panel of instructors so that standards stay consistent across course sections. In courses that include collaborative writing projects, your team members may have a voice in determining your grade.

4 Read your instructor's responses carefully. Your instructor and your colleagues may comment in a variety of ways on your drafts and final essays. It's important to read and respond to those comments appropriately.

Most papers come back from instructors (or peer editors) with comments in the margin. Whether written on paper or added electronically, these brief comments are usually directed at specific issues in your writing.

Some comments may just be proofreading symbols of the kind you'll find in this handbook at the beginning of the chapters on grammar and mechanics: "sp"; "cs"; "no ¶." These symbols tell you that the text contains a specific mechanical problem, one you should be able to fix by consulting a corresponding chapter in a handbook. Many instructors simply place an *X* next to a line that contains a slip in grammar, mechanics, or usage, leaving it to you to discover the particular problem. When you encounter an *X* or its equivalent and don't immediately detect a problem, you might review a list of proofreading symbols (see inside the back cover of this book). Consider, too, those problems instructors have noted before in your work: do you typically have difficulty with subject-verb agreement? with pronoun references? with wordiness? Look for patterns in the errors marked by teachers or peer editors, and then work to eliminate your most persistent problems.

Some marginal comments may be aimed at larger issues. Look especially at any questions posed by an instructor or peer editor: *Where's your thesis? Can you provide a better example? Have you considered possible rebuttals to your case?* Such questions tell you that a serious reader expects more from your writing and that serious revision should follow. Even if you won't have an opportunity to revise that assignment, you can use such comments to improve your next project.

Finally, look carefully at any summary comments you receive at the end of a draft or graded project. Some instructors write lengthy responses to a paper; others offer briefer feedback. Typically, instructors use their final comments to describe the overall strengths and weaknesses of a draft and to suggest strategies for revision or future work. Don't be defensive when you read these remarks—you can learn a lot from them.

Chart 6.1

Interpreting Marginal Comments

Marginal comments tend to be brief, even when they are attached to a paper electronically. Standard proofreading symbols and comments are reprinted on the inside back cover of this handbook. But you may encounter other, more cryptic remarks on your drafts. Following are suggestions for dealing with a few of them. (Remember, however, that different instructors may use correction symbols in different ways. Be sure to ask your instructor if you have questions about his or her comments.)

AWK means AWKWARD

Your sentence or phrase doesn't read quite right. The language may be grammatical, but the item needs to be reworked for clarity. See Chapter 17.

WDY means WORDY

State the idea more directly. Cut *be* verbs, eliminate passive verbs, excise redundancies. See Section 18c.

LOG? means LOGIC?

Your editor is challenging your thinking in this passage. Maybe you've made an unsupported (or unsupportable) claim, committed a logical fallacy, or offered unreliable evidence. See Chapter 11.

? means HUH?

Your reader is puzzled by something you've said, not by a problem in mechanics or usage. Review how you've phrased your ideas, or reconsider the evidence you have offered.

X means PROBLEM

Your reader has found a problem in mechanics or usage somewhere in the line next to the *X.* You'll have to find it on your own.

✓ means GOOD

Your reader likes the point you've made or the way you have phrased an idea. Be happy.

EXERCISE 6.1

1. Check your school's official handbook or catalog for its statement about evaluation and grading. How does it define and measure success in a course? How detailed are the criteria of evaluation? How well do those criteria fit written work?

2. On a Web search engine such as *Google* (at <http://www.google.com>) use a search term such as "grading standards" or "evaluating writing" to locate statements about grading policy from several writing courses. Compare the policies: How do they differ? How are they alike? What do they emphasize? Which do you find most helpful as a writer?

6b How do you prepare a portfolio?

In the last decade, many writing instructors have moved to *portfolio* evaluation of their students' progress as writers. Portfolio systems can vary as much as conventional grading, but they do share consistent elements. Writers are typically asked to assemble printed or online collections of their work produced over a term to show how they have developed. The writers may even control some aspects of the evaluation, such as choosing which projects to include in their final portfolios.

As you might guess, the emphasis in portfolio systems, in theory at least, is on the process of writing rather than solely on final products and grades. Portfolios are designed to make evaluation a fuller and richer experience, one that focuses on a body of work rather than on individual assignments. Portfolios also emphasize the relationship between writers, their colleagues, and their instructors. Yet grades still play a role in portfolio systems because most institutions still demand them.

▮1 Understand what writing portfolios do.

Portfolios can be shaped in many ways, so it's important to know the purpose of a portfolio you are asked to prepare. Will it be used for course placement or to certify that you have met a specific writing requirement? Will it serve as a record of your work over an extended period of time, perhaps an entire college career? Or will it be a component of your grade for a specific writing course?

Because portfolios serve different purposes, their contents vary enormously. Portfolios designed to provide a look at a writer's development over an extended period of time might include the following:

- Materials generated at the invention stage of writing, including freewriting, scratch outlines, topic proposals, and in-class or homework exercises
- Multiple drafts of papers
- Peer editing and instructors' comments on projects
- Transcripts from online forums or MOO sessions
- Creative work in multiple genres and forms
- Final versions of projects
- Self-assessments of written work

Other types of portfolios may be more restrictive; your instructor may specify exactly what the final portfolio should include. It's not unusual for an evaluation project to include two portfolios: a *working portfolio,* which includes all the relevant material generated during a specific time, and a briefer *final portfolio,* in which writers select their best or most representative materials to demonstrate what they've learned both about themselves and the process of writing. These choices are often the most revealing aspect of presenting a portfolio.

▮2 Design your portfolio to create a record of learning.

A good portfolio not only demonstrates that you have progressed as a writer, it actually contributes to that development by making you think more about your learning. That's why portfolios often incorporate so many kinds of items. You may not take the invention stage of writing or peer editing seriously until you see it fitted into the overall process of writing. Portfolios encourage this kind of reflection.

Portfolios should also encourage you to think of yourself as a writer, not as a student graded for each item you produce. As a result, portfolios sometimes include items you don't create yourself, such as the remarks of peers and instructors on your work. And some of that work may be tentative or open-ended. While a final portfolio typically includes several polished final products, your instructor may encourage you to select fragmentary pieces or exercises that ended up as interesting dead ends. The overall package should represent a full range of your talents.

3 Comment thoughtfully and purposefully on your work.

In many portfolio projects, writers are asked to prepare statements in which they reflect on their writing and learning process. These statements, often required at specific stages, demand a self-scrutiny that may not be instinctive, especially since such reflection is not a typical part of most college courses. Your statements should be thoughtful and scrupulously honest. If you try to write what you think your instructor wants to hear, or if you exaggerate in order to make your progress sound more impressive, you won't learn much about yourself as a writer and you probably won't fool your instructor either. If you aren't sure what to write, focus on specific aspects of your experience as a writer in the course: how you found a topic for a paper; why you made specific revisions to a piece; what you discovered in the library. Begin with the details of composing and consider, too, the connections you have made with other writers. Such statements will often be informal, even colloquial in tone, but they should be serious too.

Going Public *One Student's Self-Assessment* _____

Here is a self-assessment written at the end of a semester by student writer Sarah Davis, who had just completed a nonfiction writing course. Christy Friend, her instructor, had asked her to write a two- to three-page letter explaining the items in her portfolio, evaluating her progress during the term, and estimating her course grade.

May 3, 2000

Final Portfolio

English 460

Dear Dr. Friend,

The reason I enrolled in English 460 was simply to become a better writer. I considered writing to be a weak area for me, since my background is in biology and health sciences. As a biology major, I have written numerous lab reports and scientific research papers, and I consider that my strength. These papers are easy for me because I already have the information; I just have to arrange it. The challenge occurs when I have to write about a book I read, a character, or what an idea means to me. However, the strategies I have learned in this class (freewriting, thought questions, journal, constant feedback) have helped me tremendously. As I explain below, during the semester I have greatly improved my ability to collaborate, write in a variety of genres, and revise and polish my work.

Collaboration has helped me improve the most. I enjoy consulting with different people on each draft in progress. My revision group can tell me if my essay makes sense to them, does it flow, is there anything they don't understand. Although I participated in all the workshops, peer feedback helped me especially in writing my final draft of "The Track" because they gave me a sense of which words and details worked to further my theme. I have also worked hard to incorporate your feedback in all of my finished papers and to provide detailed advice to my group members.

Practicing with a range of nonfiction genres has also been a challenging and helpful experience. In my portfolio, you will see humor writing, place writing, a memoir essay, an argumentative piece, and a draft of a profile. I had the most success with the argument genre, as you will see in my editorial, "Response to Edward Lewis," where I collect all the facts about the topic of athletes' scholastic record on campus, take a stance, and defend it against the opposition.

I have also improved my revision and editing skills this semester. The continual revisions to my memoir piece, "The Track," were overwhelming at times. I had so many memories and it was tough to condense the material into one essay. As the final structure developed (using vignettes organized within the framework of a single workout) it was a lot easier to streamline. I am proud of the way I was able to incorporate flashbacks to deepen the focus while still keeping the events clear. The most important thing in this revision was explaining the importance of running, my overriding focus, to my readers. I had to keep asking myself, "Does my passion interest the reader?" and "How can I make them understand why this is important to me?"

While the other pieces I've included here are finished, I slashed the idea of finishing the profile piece I started about my Dad, because it is too personal a topic to deal with for this audience. Instead, I opted to include a humor piece about college life and time management. I first suggested this piece to Allen and Katie in a revision workshop, and they helped me to brainstorm ideas that eventually led up to this piece. The final piece in

the portfolio, "Hospital," has incorporated your
suggestion to bring my own voice in and acquire a
clearer focus. In my final draft, I have clarified why
I was at the hospital and focused on the irony of the
ICU. For awhile, the conclusion of this piece gave me
trouble, but by taking your advice to focus on the
ironies of the hospital, I was able to maintain my
focus and successfully conclude the piece.

Finally, this class has helped me as a writer
to express myself more clearly and fully on paper. I
am more confident not just about my own writing, but
also about helping others improve their work. I have
worked hard in this class to improve and polish the
papers selected here, participate in all the in-class
writing activities and journal, experiment with new
forms of writing, and participate in the revision
workshops. Taking all these things into
consideration, I believe I deserve an "A" for my work
in this class.

Sincerely,
Sarah Davis

4 Work steadily on your portfolio. A portfolio system of evaluation doesn't demand less from you than more traditional systems. To prepare a substantial portfolio, you'll have to work steadily and consistently over a full school term (or longer). You can't expect to make up work you've deferred in a burst of energy at the last minute—portfolios don't work that way. You need to determine at the start what items your portfolio will have to contain and when they must be in place. Often, portfolios are submitted several times during a term, not just at the end. Remember, too, that you'll likely be asked to work with other writers in the construction of their portfolios. Be just as conscientious in responding to their work as you want them to be with your own.

Finally, take the time to present a handsome portfolio, whether the work you produce is on paper or online. "Handsome" doesn't mean overproduced or slick; rather, your portfolio ought to show that you have given every element the time it merits—documents should be organized, clearly labeled, and displayed in a folder, notebook, or other format recommended by your instructor.

E-Tips Some instructors use a *Learning Record*, a systematic way of evaluating progress in literacy over extended periods of time. Created originally to serve students in elementary and secondary schools, Learning Records have begun to appear in college courses as well, especially in an online form. For detailed information on the *Online Learning Record*, see <http://www.cwrl.utexas.edu/~syverson/olr/>. For more general information about the *Learning Record*, see <http://www.learningrecord.org>.

EXERCISE 6.2 Write a self-assessment of a recent writing project or series of projects written in a single course. What are the strengths and satisfactions of the piece(s)? What do you think you might have managed better?

6c What are your rights and responsibilities in the evaluation process?

Evaluating writing may not be a hard science, but neither is it a completely mysterious, subjective process—even though it might sometimes seem so when you are puzzling over why the world literature paper you thought was great received a *C,* or why your first history essay got an *A* but the second rated only a *B–.*

Because writing is a human activity, it provokes human responses that are subtle and variable. Yet evaluations under such conditions can also be rigorous and consistent. If you take responsibility for your part in the process and assume good faith on the part of those who are assessing your work, your experiences with evaluation will be more productive.

1 Bring reasonable expectations to the evaluation process. When your writing is evaluated in a college course, you can reasonably expect your instructor to give you some basic information.

You should know what work you're expected to complete, which assignments will be graded, and how your final mark will be computed. Many instructors provide this information in a course syllabus or policy statement handed out during the first few days of class.

You should also receive periodic feedback on your work, in the form of grades or evaluative comments on your writing, and sometimes both. When an instructor returns a graded project, you should receive some indication of why your work received the mark it did. Not all instructors provide such justifications in written comments, but most are willing to meet with you to talk about a grade. It's part of your instructor's job to give this kind of information and feedback—and you have a right to expect it.

But just as your instructor should set reasonable policies, you should be sure that your own expectations are reasonable. First, recognize that standards are typically much higher in college courses than they are elsewhere—especially in high school English courses. Complaining that you don't deserve a *C* on a paper because you always got *A*'s before is a fallacy of argument that you probably don't want an instructor to point out. Similarly, don't blame a lower-than-expected grade on details in the assignment you should have paid more attention to (such as due dates or the form of documentation required).

Understand, too, that teachers will usually give you feedback at some stages of your project, from the topic proposal to the first draft. But they can't and shouldn't do everything. They can't comment on every underdeveloped thought, sharpen every unfocused paragraph, catch every error, reword every less-than-sterling sentence. To do so would intrude upon your rights as an author. At some point you must take charge of the writing project and move it beyond what others might have imagined. You won't always succeed on your own, but you will learn more about writing when you take responsibility for your work—both the failures and the successes.

2 Question a grade responsibly. There will be times when you wish to inquire about a grade. When this is the case, don't run up to your instructor and demand satisfaction immediately after an assignment is returned. Instead, take time to weigh the mark and any comments on your paper against the specific grading criteria, the performance you may have seen from other students, and your own frank assessment of what you have achieved.

It may be hard to do, but you should approach a grade inquiry as an opportunity to learn more about your writing. Ask yourself what might account for the difference between your perception of the work and your instructor's. If you think you did everything an instructor required, would merely doing what was required earn the kind of evaluation you hoped to receive? You also have to be honest about *effort*. Some instructors will reward writers for the time put into a project, but effort alone cannot be the entire story. All writers have the experience at times of laboring mightily to produce average or unsatisfying work.

If you decide to pursue a grading inquiry, build a reasonable argument (see Chapter 11): be sure you have a substantive claim to make, good reasons to support it, and specific evidence to draw upon. Many instructors expect inquiries about grades to be put into writing. (It's a good exercise even when such a statement is not required.) If you can draw attention to genuine strengths or strategies in a project that your teacher might have overlooked or undervalued, you may have a case. Be as specific as possible and focus on large-scale rhetorical issues such as your response to the assignment, your sensitivity to an audience, or the quality of your thinking and research. Make your case on substantive claims, not on quibbles or technicalities.

 E-Tips

What issues do instructors face when they evaluate writing? You can gain insight into the question at "Evaluating Student Writing: Methods and Measurement," compiled by Nancy Hyslop, at <http://www.indiana.edu/~eric_rec/ieo/digests/d50.html>.

SUMMARY | *When Your Writing Is Evaluated in a Course . . .*

You have the *right* to

- Know what work you need to complete and what assignments will be graded.

- Know how your course mark will be computed.

- Receive periodic feedback to tell you how well your writing matches your instructor's standards.

You have the *responsibility* to

- Assume that your instructor is acting in good faith.

- Recognize that you can learn from evaluations of your writing.

(Continued)

6c
eval

> ### *When Your Writing Is Evaluated in a Course* (*Continued*)
>
> • Bring reasonable expectations to the grading process.
>
> • Pay attention to instructions and grading criteria.
>
> • Pay attention to instructor's comments on your work.
>
> • Pursue grading inquiries responsibly.

PART

11

Writing for Academic and Public Forums

7 How Do You Write in College?

8 How Do You Write for the Public?

9 How Do You Read and Think Critically?

10 How Do You Interpret and Use Visual Texts?

11 How Can You Write Powerful Arguments?

12 How Do You Write a Literary Analysis?

CHAPTER 7

How Do You Write in College?

7a How do you write a successful academic paper?

As a college student, you can count on having to write. That's a fact of life, regardless of your major. But if you wrote only a few papers in high school, or if you have been out of school for several years and have written little during that time, you may feel uncertain when you think about starting to write again, not only in English classes but in history, philosophy, and science courses. Understandably, you wonder what instructors expect.

The answer is that academic writing is not necessarily tricky, but it differs from high school writing because college instructors have unique requirements in mind. While expectations vary somewhat from instructor to instructor and from subject to subject, most projects will ask you to approach topics with a critical eye, to justify your ideas with logical reasons and evidence, and to cite the sources of your information. These expectations are not optional; they are the *responsibilities* of any college writer. Once you understand these responsibilities, you can address academic audiences with confidence.

1 Review the assignment. When instructors assign a writing project, they usually have specific expectations in mind: a certain approach to a topic, certain kinds of research, a set number of pages, and a particular due date. Take all these instructions into account as you plan your paper. Think about what you can realistically accomplish, and focus your work accordingly.

Before you get too far into a topic, ask yourself these practical questions: Does the assignment call for an impersonal, factual account or for a creative approach? How much research will you have to do? What special materials will you need? How much time do you have? Some books may not be immediately available, or the library may not carry the periodical you want. If you need to do interviews, you'll have to allot time to contact people and keep appointments. And if the paper is due in the same week as two papers for other courses, you'll need to start extra early.

In other words, assess the requirements and think ahead, just as you would for any other big project—planning a family reunion or mailing your income tax forms by the deadline—so you can avoid last-minute snags.

2 Don't take on too much in a writing project. When you make a claim in a paper, think of yourself as having staked out a piece of territory: you've asserted what you believe and drawn lines around it, and now you have to defend it. You don't want to find out when you're halfway through that your claims are overextended and you can't back up the commitments you've made. You'll do better to stake out a smaller topic that you can manage. Then you'll have a chance to think and write about it in detail. See Section 2b for advice on how to narrow a topic.

3 Support your claims with reasons and evidence. If one word could describe college instructors and professors, it would be *skeptical,* especially when they read an explanation or an argument. Unless you're doing an informal assignment like a journal entry or writing a personal piece for a creative writing course, it's usually not enough for a writer to claim on the basis of personal opinion or feelings that something is true or that something should be done. In most courses, instructors want students to support their claims with reasons and evidence. Thus the best topics for academic assignments are generally those that are amenable to factual evidence and research. A passionate account of your belief in the afterlife, your relationship with your spouse, or your love for the great outdoors is better suited to personal writing than to most academic assignments.

4 Understand what constitutes good reasons and acceptable evidence in academic writing. We've all read popular magazine articles that generalize about a trend or a phenomenon on the basis of a single perspective or a few dramatic examples: "How I Helped My Children Say No to Drugs" and "IRS Scare Tactics: A Taxpayer Speaks Out." These kinds of pieces dramatize issues vividly; however, their approach wouldn't satisfy an instructor seeking a thorough academic treatment of a topic. Academic writing has its own standards of argument and proof that are more rigorous than what's expected in many other kinds of writing.

In academic writing, readers expect you to support your arguments with logical reasons and sufficient evidence. These supporting materials should come from reliable, recent sources, and you should be able to produce enough of them to show that you're knowledgeable about the topic. This often means doing research. Depending on the paper you're writing, you might look for the following kinds of data:

- Historical documents
- Research findings
- Case studies
- Eyewitness accounts
- Statements from experts on the subject
- Statistics

You'll find such evidence in reference volumes, scholarly books and articles, government archives, and publications produced by professional organizations.

When undergraduate student Matt Valentine decided to write a research paper about the Holocaust, he already had general opinions about the subject. But he didn't stop there; he did research to compile reputable data. In the library he consulted historical books and articles; he asked a history professor to direct him to relevant government documents from World War II; he consulted Web sites maintained by non-profit organizations concerned with the Holocaust; and he interviewed a local Holocaust survivor. When he sat down to write his paper, Matt had on hand an impressive amount of supporting evidence that he knew would satisfy his readers.

However, academic evidence isn't "one size fits all." Some arguments and evidence are more appropriate to some writing tasks than to others. If Matt Valentine were writing his paper for a history class, his historical sources would be the most relevant. If he were writing a survivor's profile for a journalism course, he might draw primarily on material he collected in personal interviews. For his writing course he decided to examine the language that people use to talk and write about the Holocaust, so he concentrated on literary and popular works about the topic. The Going Public section on page 103 summarizes some sources Matt incorporated into his final paper. (See Sections 44b and 44c for more on finding and selecting academic sources.)

Going Public *Writing an Annotated Bibliography* ———————

An instructor may ask you to turn in an *annotated bibliography* that briefly describes and evaluates the sources you plan to use in a paper. This excerpt from Matt Valentine's annotated bibliography details some of the materials he eventually included in his term paper about the Holocaust. Note the breadth and variety of his sources. Do you think he's chosen materials that his instructor will find valid and reliable? Are they the right kinds of evidence for an academic paper?

7a
college

Working Bibliography for

"The Rhetoric of Atrocity:

How People Write and Talk About the Holocaust"

American Jewish Committee. The Jews in Nazi Germany: A

Handbook of Facts Regarding Their Present Situation.

1935. New York: Fertig, 1982. This republished book

gives perspectives held by American Jews in the

years preceding the Holocaust.

Keegan, John. "Code of Silence." New York Times 25 Nov.

1996: A13. This news article reports on the release

of government records suggesting that officials of

the Allied forces were aware of the Holocaust death

camps but chose to keep the information away from

the public and not to act upon it.

Meyer, Walter. Personal interview. 24 Nov. 1996. First a

member of the Hitler Youth and later a concentration

camp prisoner, Dr. Meyer talks about propaganda,

attitudes in urban Germany and in the camps, and the

reactions of the Allied occupation forces after the

war.

Pehle, Walter H. From "Reichskristallnacht" to Genocide.

Nov. 1938. Trans. William Templer. New York: Berg,

1991. This book, which contains scholarly essays by

historians, deals with the development of anti-

Semitic sentiments in Germany leading to the

Holocaust. Also, some essays explore the civilian

```
        population: to what extent were the German citizens
        aware of what was going on?
Spiegelman, Art. Maus II: A Survivor's Tale. New York:
        Pantheon, 1991. This best-selling, Pulitzer Prize-
        winning comic book tells the story of one survivor's
        experience of the Holocaust.
```

5 Document your sources and give credit to others where appropriate. College instructors expect writers to cite their sources and to give credit for any quotations or ideas that have come from someone else. If you write, "It is generally believed that . . ." or "Experts agree on . . . ," your instructor is likely to ask, "By whom? Where?" When you cite statistics or research, your teacher will want to know where you got your data. And if you use *any* material that someone else thought of or wrote first, you're obligated to give that source credit. If you don't, you're committing plagiarism, a serious offense. (See Section 46b for more about plagiarism.)

Documenting sources takes time, but it's an essential part of college writing. It's not difficult to do once you know where to look for guidelines. Sections 46a and 46c offer comprehensive information on documenting sources.

6 Follow research and writing conventions appropriate to your subject area. While the guidelines we discuss in this chapter apply generally to the writing you'll do in any course, be aware that some expectations differ from subject area to subject area. Suppose that you wanted to write a paper on alcoholism. Imagine the various forms it might take in different courses: In a creative writing course you might craft a poem about a character's struggle with recovery. In a sociology course you might write a formal case study based on interviews with a member of Alcoholics Anonymous. In a biology course you might collect and report on data about the physical effects of alcohol on laboratory rats. All three projects would require critical thought, research, and the ability to construct a clear argument. Their differences grow out of the different *goals* and *approaches* valued in each discipline—the humanities, the social sciences, and the natural sciences:

- **Goals:** What kinds of questions interest scholars in this discipline? What do they want to find out? Do they want to know how physical objects and processes work? Are they interested in discovering how people throughout history have interpreted the world?

- **Methods:** How do scholars in a particular discipline go about finding out what they want to know? Do they test hypotheses systematically and empirically? Do they critically interpret texts and other artifacts?
- **Evidence:** What kinds of materials do scholars in a subject area typically use to support their arguments—numerical data, historical artifacts, quotations from literary or philosophical texts?
- **Genres:** What kinds of documents do scholars in a field typically produce—lab reports, critical analyses, case studies, personal commentaries? What organizational and stylistic conventions are typical? Is it appropriate to use first-person pronouns or passive verb constructions, for example?
- **Documentation:** What system do scholars in the field use for citing and documenting sources?

7a
college

The chart below lists some basic characteristics of research and writing in the humanities, social sciences, and natural sciences. Keep these in mind as you approach your writing in other courses, and ask your instructor when you're unsure about what rules apply.

HIGHLIGHT **Writing in Academic Disciplines**

HUMANITIES

Subject areas. Literature, philosophy, history, classics, and related areas

Purposes. To study how people use language or other symbols to interpret experience

Methods. Close reading and analysis of texts

Sources. Literary, philosophical, and historical works and critical commentaries on them

Formats. Critical and interpretive essays, book reviews, personal and reflective pieces, creative writing

Documentation. Usually MLA

SOCIAL SCIENCES

Subject areas. Sociology, psychology, anthropology, social work, education, and related areas

Purposes. To study how people create and live within social systems

Methods. Field work and other observational research; statistical analysis of data

Sources. Data collected from interviews, surveys, field observations; previous research by other scholars

Formats. Field notes, case studies, research reports, reviews of research

Documentation. Usually APA

NATURAL SCIENCES

Purposes. To study the structure and workings of the physical world
Methods. The scientific method, experimental testing of hypotheses
Sources. Data collected through systematic observation in controlled settings
Formats. Lab reports; research reports; summaries of research; process analyses
Documentation. Often CBE

7a college

■ **7 Remember that college instructors expect professional-looking work.** When you turn in a paper, you send your instructor a message about the kind of student you are. Just as you wouldn't come to class barefoot or smoke cigars during a lecture, you shouldn't tarnish your image with a poorly presented essay. Even if your instructors have been lenient about usage or punctuation errors when they read your drafts or haven't issued special warnings about grammatical correctness, they care about such details in the final product. If your paper looks good, it will make a good impression.

Before you submit an essay for a grade, proofread for faulty punctuation, agreement errors, and spelling. If you have trouble with any of these areas, get a second opinion from a friend or consult the grammar and usage portions of this book. Run your computer's spelling checker. Then check to see that your paper complies with any formatting instructions included in the assignment: Has the instructor specified MLA or APA style? A particular font size? Single or double spacing? See Section 5c for advice on proofreading and Chapters 48–52 for help with particular formats.

Instructors hate to get papers they can barely read. Word-process all writing projects, double spaced, with numbered pages. Be sure your printer produces letter-quality output. Fasten the whole package with a staple or a paper clip.

If the assignment allows it, you may want to experiment with layout, typefaces, and other graphic elements to create an even more attractive finished product. Chapter 20 provides comprehensive advice on document design.

Checklist 7.1

Writing for College Assignments

When you write in college, remember to

• Assess the assignment and plan to meet its requirements.

• Limit your thesis to one that you can adequately cover and support.

* Support your claims with reasons and evidence.

* Keep in mind what constitutes acceptable evidence in academic writing.

* Follow conventions appropriate for the subject area

* Document your sources.

* Hand in only carefully edited, proofread, professional-looking papers.

7a
college

EXERCISE 7.1 Here are several claims from undergraduate writing assignments. For each claim, suggest specific kinds of supporting evidence you think the writer's instructor would find appropriate and convincing.

1. *From a research project for a social work course:* For children who come from severely abusive families, high-quality institutional care is a better option than programs that try to reform the parents in an effort to keep the family together.

2. *From a research paper for a first-year writing course:* Professional athletes are poor role models because so many of them engage in unsportsmanlike or illegal behavior, on and off the playing field.

3. *From an essay exam for an ethics course:* Circuses are unethical because they exploit animals purely for entertainment.

4. *From a research review for a human biology course:* A growing body of data suggests that asthma has a strong genetic component.

EXERCISE 7.2 From a popular magazine, select an article on a current topic. Then go to the library and find a scholarly journal article on the same topic. Compare and contrast the kinds of evidence used in the two pieces: How much evidence does each writer cite? What kinds of sources does each draw on? Which piece do you find more interesting? more convincing?

EXERCISE 7.3 Evaluate a paper you've recently written for a college course against Checklist 7.1 on pages 106–07. Then ask yourself these questions: Does your paper meet the standards? Where does it fall short? If you could write the paper over again, to which item on the list would you pay the most attention? Why?

7b How do you write on essay examinations?

If you're like many writers, you'll do most of your writing outside the classroom—in your room, the library, or another familiar and relatively comfortable setting. However, when you write in a test situation, your approach will be drastically different. Whether you're taking a midterm exam in a history course or a competency examination required by your job, you can count on less flexibility and more pressure. You may have to write in response to questions that you have not chosen and have never seen before. You'll compose in a classroom setting, and you'll usually have only an hour or two to shape your ideas into a single draft that convinces readers you know the material.

Every writer should know how to compose under pressure. Researchers estimate that up to half the writing you do during college will occur on exams. After you leave school, you'll find that many jobs require the ability to write quickly and efficiently. Journalists must create news stories on tight deadlines. Engineers and other technical workers frequently write on-the-spot progress reports. And many government agencies base promotions for police officers, social workers, and other employees partly on competency test scores. Unfortunately, many writers resign themselves to failure at this kind of writing, believing, "I freeze under pressure."

Don't give up before you start. You *can* write well in an exam setting if you understand the unique skills involved and work to master them.

1 Know the material. Preparation is half the battle in an essay exam. Lay the foundation for success well in advance by attending class regularly, keeping up with required readings, and participating actively in class discussions.

But simply absorbing the material is not enough. You also need to organize and think critically about what you know. Look for clues in course lectures and readings about what ideas and examples are important—"*Three basic arguments for . . .*"; "*A central figure in . . .*"—and organize your notes accordingly. As you read, summarize important theories and concepts in your own words to be sure that you understand them. Review your notes periodically and ask yourself how new material fits with the old. And when you have questions, speak up.

If your teacher often asks students to express their views on course material or apply it to new situations, you can bet that he or she will include these kinds of questions on the exam. Prepare yourself by rehearsing your views about key points in the lecture and readings: Do you agree? Do you disagree? What approaches or theories make the most sense to you?

To practice applying your knowledge, look occasionally at the newspaper and imagine how the material you're studying might relate to a current event or controversy. For example, that article you read in your U.S. history course about the debates between the Federalists and the Anti-Federalists in the Revolutionary period might help you understand what's at issue in a contemporary Supreme Court decision about states' rights. See Chapter 9 for detailed advice on getting the most out of your reading.

7b
exams

2 Find out as much as you can about the exam. Because many exams cover hundreds or even thousands of pages of material, focus your preparation on those portions most likely to appear on the exam. As the exam date approaches, ask your instructor for details: How many questions will the test include? What kinds of questions? What topics will be emphasized? Will you get to choose from several questions? Knowing some parameters will help guide your study: for instance, if the test consists of four short essays, you won't have time to list many examples or details, so you should concentrate on learning main ideas.

If your instructor provides copies of exams from previous semesters, seize the opportunity. An old exam can help you anticipate what kinds of items will appear, and you can use it for a practice run. If your instructor does not offer sample exams, many schools maintain test files that archive exams from a variety of courses. The more you know about what to expect, the more comfortable you'll feel.

3 Use your study time intelligently. This advice may seem obvious, but it's true. An exam requires you to quickly pull together what you know—so you'll need to be in top academic form. Forgo extreme studying techniques, such as cramming or pulling all-nighters that leave you exhausted at the time of the test. And don't try to learn every piece of information covered in class; you'll only feel overwhelmed.

Instead, spend your time practicing the thinking and writing skills that exam essays require. Make scratch outlines of important theories or arguments you think are likely to be covered, along with one or two key examples or details, and use these as the basis for your review. Once you have a solid command of the material, devise questions similar to those you think might appear on the exam and practice answering them. Use a timer to accustom yourself to thinking under pressure.

Classmates can be another valuable resource. If you enjoy working collaboratively, try forming a study group with colleagues. Meet once or twice before the exam to compare notes, puzzle out gaps in your knowledge, and practice explaining key points to each other. But don't substitute group meetings for individual study. Allow yourself plenty of time to go over group insights and integrate them with your own knowledge.

4 Devise strategies for coping with pressure. Many writers have trouble adapting their writing process to a stressful, inflexible test environment. But don't panic. You can anticipate certain difficulties and decide beforehand how you will deal with them.

First, eliminate unnecessary stress. Get a good night's sleep, eat a healthful meal, and keep anxiety-producing cramming to a minimum before the exam. Gather all your materials—examination booklets, pens, calculator, and notes or books when the instructor allows them—well in advance. Arrive a few minutes early, but not too early; sitting in an empty classroom for too long may make you nervous.

Plan also to head off specific problems that can happen during the exam: If you haven't had much experience writing under pressure, time yourself on practice questions beforehand so that you won't stall during the exam. If you tend to panic when you see an unfamiliar question, plan to work on the easiest items first, then come back to the more challenging ones. If you fall apart when time runs short, give yourself a safety net by outlining each response before you start writing, so you can attach the outline to any unfinished response. And if you will write the exam on a computer, remind yourself to save frequently so that you don't inadvertently lose something important. This kind of troubleshooting will free you to focus on the actual writing.

5 Figure out what the question is asking you to do. Exam questions generally give writers much more specific instructions than out-of-class paper assignments do. So it's vital that you analyze each exam question carefully before you begin writing.

Start by locating all the key terms—usually nouns or noun phrases—that *identify* or *limit* the subject: "Discuss the *major components* of *Plato's educational ideal* as elaborated in *The Republic*"; "Explain *four kinds of confounding* that can occur in *observational research*"; "What are the *clinical indications* of *bipolar disorder*, and how do they differ from *cyclothymia*?" Next, underline key verbs that tell you what to do with the topic: *analyze, compare, discuss, explain, trace.* Each of these instructions means something a bit different, as the chart on pages 112–13 shows.

Finally, cross out any material that does not seem relevant to the question. Instructors sometimes begin an exam with a quotation, example, or introductory discussion that serves primarily to clarify the main question. Such material may make the question look intimidatingly long, but you need to pay attention to it only if it helps you focus. In this rather daunting example from a British literature course, for instance, the core question is stated only in the last sentence.

7b
exams

> The scholar Cornel West said, "At the heart of modernism is the fact of the decentering of European civilization." Since the beginning of the semester, we have seen thinkers such as Freud, Marx, and Nietzche describe the philosophical contradictions that inhabit the twentieth century. *Choose one major text we have read this semester and trace the ways that work describes contradictions in private, public, or intellectual activities.*

Here the quotation and the references to Freud, Marx, and Nietzche only introduce the idea of "contradiction," the focus of the main question. To answer this question, you don't need to comment on any of these thinkers; you just have to explain how contradiction shows up in one of the literary texts you studied for the class.

EXERCISE 7.4 Identify key terms in an examination question from another course or from a standardized test for college admission, job certification, or other purpose. What specific topics does the question stake out? Which verbs tell you what to do with those topics? If you have a copy of your response, analyze how well you fulfilled these instructions.

■ 6 Budget your time. Keep the amount of time you spend on each question roughly proportionate to its importance. If you squander all your time on a single question, you're likely to jeopardize your chance for a good grade. Here is a simple way to figure out how to allocate your time: Divide the number of points each question is worth by the number of points on the whole exam. The result equals the percentage of time you should devote to that question. For example, suppose you have a 50-point question on a one-hour test that is worth 200 total points. You should probably spend about 15 minutes, or 25 percent of the hour, on that response.

If you run out of time in the middle of a response, resist the temptation to steal time set aside for other questions. Instead, jot a note to your instructor explaining that you ran out of time, and attach your outline. Many instructors will give partial credit for outlined responses.

Chart 7.1

7b
exams

Common Exam Terms

Analyze: Break an argument or a concept into parts and explain the relationships among them; evaluate or explain your interpretation or judgment.

Analyze the effects of ketosis on the digestive system.

Apply: Take a concept, formula, or theory and adapt it to another situation.

Apply Bernard's elements of sound executive management to President Ronald Reagan's management practices during his first term.

Argue, prove: Take a position on an issue and provide reasons and evidence to support that position.

Argue whether or not you believe it is possible to run government agencies like private sector businesses.

Compare: Point out similarities between two or more concepts, theories, or situations.

Compare the educational philosophies of Dewey and Rousseau. How did each conceptualize the learner? the function of education? the role of the teacher?

Contrast: Point out differences between two or more concepts, theories, or situations.

Contrast the uses of imagery in Yeats's "The Second Coming" and Hardy's "The Darkling Thrush."

Critique, evaluate: Make and support a judgment about the worth of an idea, theory, or proposal, accounting for both strengths and weaknesses.

Evaluate spanking as a method of discipline for each of these age groups: infants, preschoolers, school-age children, and adolescents.

Define: State a clear, precise meaning for a concept or object, and perhaps give an illustrative example.

Define the three measures of central tendency (mean, median, mode); then explain which would provide the most accurate gauge of annual income in a given community.

Discuss, explain: Offer a comprehensive presentation and analysis of important ideas relating to a topic, supported with examples and evidence. These questions usually require detailed responses.

Discuss the Ebonics controversy, drawing on the research we have studied this semester to clarify key points of difference.

Enumerate, list: Name a series of ideas, elements, or related objects one by one, perhaps giving a brief explanation of each.

List Jean Piaget's developmental stages, and give an example of how moral choices are negotiated at each stage.

Review, summarize: Briefly lay out the main points of a larger theory or argument.

Summarize the definitions of legal discrimination presented in the decisions *Sweatt v. Painter* and *Hopwood v. The University of Texas*.

Trace: Explain chronologically a series of events or the development of a trend or idea.

Trace the pathway of a nerve impulse from stimulus to response.

7 Make a plan. A test setting doesn't allow false starts. In order to pack as much writing as possible into the allocated time, you'll need a good sense of where you're going before you begin. Once you've determined what kind of response an essay question requires, take five minutes or so to map out your answer. If the question asks for independent argument or analysis, consider brainstorming or freewriting to generate ideas. If the question asks you to synthesize course material, try an idea map that organizes information under key categories. (See Section 2b for more on prewriting techniques.)

Use these initial ideas as the foundation for a list or scratch outline of the full response. Whatever format you choose, it should include your thesis, main supporting ideas, and important examples. Once your outline is in place, you are ready to begin the actual writing. See Sections 3b and 3c for more on organizing and outlining an essay.

8 Understand what a good response looks like. Because grading standards vary from course to course and from instructor to instructor, no single formula can guarantee you perfect marks on every test you take. Nonetheless, a study by the researcher Randall Popken found that instructors across disciplines share some similar expectations. Most want a tightly organized response that contains the following elements.

- **A clear thesis statement** in the first paragraph or, better yet, in the first sentence. Don't worry about crafting a dramatic introduction—there isn't time.
- **Logical organization** with a single key idea developed in each paragraph and with clear transitions between points.

- **Adequate support and evidence** for each point, drawn from course readings and lectures.
- **Your own views or analysis** when the question asks for them. Remember, though, to justify your ideas with evidence and support.
- **A conclusion** that ties together main points and summarizes their importance, even if you have time for only a sentence or two.
- **Clear prose** free of major grammatical and mechanical errors.

If you have covered these basics, don't worry about adding creative flourishes. A powerful introduction, a scintillating style, or an encyclopedic coverage of a topic beyond what the question requires may dazzle, but your instructor doesn't expect them. A realistic goal in a test setting is to produce a solid first draft that demonstrates your command of the material.

Finally, before you set aside a lot of time for editing and proofreading, ask your instructor how he or she deals with grammatical and mechanical problems. Many teachers don't penalize minor mistakes unless they hinder the clarity of your argument, but others are sticklers for correctness.

Going Public   *Framing a Successful Examination Essay* _____

Undergraduate writer Jena Gentry encountered this question on the midterm for a U.S. history course: "Discuss some important causes of the Great Crash of 1929. How did Presidents Hoover and Roosevelt try to deal with the resulting Great Depression? How successful were they?" Note how the opening paragraph of her response, excerpted here, summarizes basic concepts and forecasts the direction of her argument.

The economic boom of the 1920s had a dramatic impact on the U.S. economy. While corporate profits were large, they weren't being recycled into the consumer market, but rather invested into an inflated stock market whose prices were continually increasing. The terrible result--the Great Crash of 1929--came as a result of four main causes: the saturation of the consumer market, a rigid price structure and speculative market, an unequal distribution of wealth, and Republican public policies that favored the rich. Two presidents, Hoover and Roosevelt, tried to deliver Americans out of the subsequent Great Depression. However, Hoover believed that the government should stay out of the economy, and his modest program of legislation didn't do much. Roosevelt's ambitious New Deal was more successful, bringing many Americans a measure of relief, recovery, and reform.

The rest of Jena Gentry's essay contains twelve paragraphs: one devoted to each cause of the Great Crash, three discussing Hoover's efforts to deal with the Depression, four explaining and evaluating Roosevelt's New Deal, and a brief conclusion.

Here is a less successful beginning, written in response to the same question. This writer knows the material but has not framed her observations within the terms laid out in the question. There is no explicit reference to causes of the Great Crash, and there is no mention of Hoover or Roosevelt. As a result, the instructor has no framework for understanding the facts and details the writer includes.

7b
exams

Throughout the 1920s, everything was produced at much speed and production increased 40 percent. Wages increased a slight 12 percent while corporate profits went up an incredible 70 percent. So much money was kept out of the market that the economy began to fail. Wage increases weren't enough to allow workers to be economically stable when prices were so high, and the wealthy were only putting their money into the stock market. When all this occurred, terrible results followed. The economy crashed and America went into the biggest depression in its history.

CHAPTER 8

How Do You Write for the Public?

8a How do you write outside the classroom?

Knowing how to write a solidly argued academic paper is crucial to your success in college. However, college writers often need to adapt their writing to settings outside the classroom. You may write letters to friends or elected officials, applications for jobs or scholarships, publicity materials for campus groups, or editorials for local publications. What do all these tasks have in common? They are all *public* statements of one kind or another. Anytime you write, you are presenting yourself and your ideas in a way that you hope will favorably impress your audience.

Yet what impresses readers in one setting may offend them in another, just as the same joke might get a big laugh at a family dinner but raise eyebrows at a church banquet. When you adapt your writing to different situations, think about what those readers expect and what seems appropriate under the circumstances. This chapter will help you understand important conventions of nonacademic writing so that you will come across as a skilled, responsible writer—no matter whom you find yourself addressing.

It would take several handbooks of this size to tell you exactly how to complete every writing task you may face. But even if we could provide such comprehensive advice, we wouldn't need to. You already know a lot about how to adjust your writing to different situations. You know that every time you begin a writing project, you must define your purpose, analyze your audience, and decide what kind of impression you want to make on readers. You should also realize that writing outside the classroom can differ from college writing in important ways. This section will help you identify these differences and make the transition from school to more public settings.

1 Understand the range of writing you may do outside the classroom. Most college students write for many audiences and purposes beyond the classroom. Writing instructors at many universities now require students to compose documents for nonprofit groups, to publish pieces in local media, or to post their writing on the World Wide Web, in addition to writing traditional papers. You may also have to produce documents as part of your job or for campus or community groups. At other times, you may become so excited about a topic you've studied in class that you want to express your views more publicly.

8a
public

You'll be better prepared to use your skills as a writer when you understand the range of situations you'll address and the kinds of documents you may be asked to produce. To give you a sense of this range, we asked several of the student writers featured in this book to list projects they'd recently completed that weren't part of a course assignment. Their list appears in the following box.

HIGHLIGHT : *Examples of Public Writing Projects*

WRITING AT WORK
- Articles for employee newsletter
- Information updates to office Web site
- Responses to complaint letters from customers
- Research report for boss on a legal issue
- Memo requesting vacation time

WRITING FOR CAMPUS GROUPS
- Letter inviting governor to speak at banquet
- Dramatic sketch for campus acting troupe
- Scholarship application essay for alumni association
- Funding proposal for speaker series

WRITING ON CIVIC AND COMMUNITY ISSUES
- Letter to the editor on proposed library closure
- Guest editorial on proposed capital punishment legislation
- Message to student listserv about proposed cuts in financial aid
- Letter to senator on whether the Confederate flag should fly over the state capitol
- Lesson plans for nonprofit after-school program

PERSONAL WRITING PROJECTS
- Personal Web page
- Poems to share with local writers' group
- Article on dance submitted to magazine
- Messages to newsgroup on go-cart racing

■ **2 Learn to spot opportunities for public writing.** Writing can be a powerful way to make your views heard and to get things done. But not all situations lend themselves equally well to it. Before you undertake a writing project, ask yourself these questions to decide whether the circumstances are right:

- **Is writing the most effective response to this situation?** Some problems call for direct or immediate action. Suppose that your neighbor's dog has just bitten the mail carrier. Would it be more effective to write a letter to your neighbor warning her to keep her dog inside or to simply pry the dog off the mail carrier's ankle? The answer is obvious (at least, we know which answer the mail carrier would prefer). However, if you believe that your neighbor's dog is part of a larger problem caused by lax leash laws in your city, that problem might be addressed by writing letters to the city council or circulating a citizen petition.
- **Is there an audience who cares (or can be persuaded to care) about your message?** Each year thousands of preteens write love letters to pop idols like the Backstreet Boys and Britney Spears. Are these letters examples of effective public writing? No, because no matter how passionately the writers feel about their arguments, neither the stars the letters are directed to nor any other audience has strong feelings about the issue. The question of who wins Backstreet Boy Howie D's heart is unlikely to have significant effects either on the larger community or on the letter writers. On the other hand, a group of students might successfully write to request that Howie D make an appearance at a school fund-raiser since he and his agent would presumably be interested in the opportunity to help a good cause.
- **Is the timing right?** Public writing is most effective if it appears when an issue seems most relevant to readers. April 14, the night before income taxes are due and the busiest day of the year at the accounting firm where you work, is not the best time to confront your boss with a memo calling for more stylish upholstery on the office chairs. (Best hold your proposal until budget deliberations later in the year.) Nor does a newspaper editor want to print a letter responding to a column that appeared nine months ago, though she might print responses submitted within a week or two.

Writing is challenging and time-consuming—too much so to be wasted where it's unlikely to have an impact. When you choose to write, choose the setting and the timing carefully to make sure that every word counts.

3 Find out as much as you can about your readers' expectations. When you write in a public setting—especially a setting new to you—don't automatically fall back on familiar academic conventions. The kind of writing your instructors reward in college will not always be received with enthusiasm in other forums.

Say that you've just received an *A* on an English paper you wrote on a recent police brutality case in your city and you've decided to write an editorial for the campus newspaper on the same topic. You'll quickly find that the news editors expect a piece that is much shorter, more attuned to the events in that week's news, more partisan, and simpler in organizational structure than your course paper. You'll also discover that the conventions for citing sources are simpler in journalism than in academic writing. If you take the time to learn these conventions, you'll be able to produce a publishable editorial.

8a
public

Before you begin any project for an unfamiliar audience or situation, find out what is expected.

- What kinds of genres and topics are typical for this forum?
- What are the typical length, style, and tone of documents published in this setting?
- What kinds of arguments and evidence do writers typically draw on?
- What are the expectations for formatting and for citing sources?

Many publications make submission guidelines available to prospective writers. In other cases, you'll have to ask someone in charge what the accepted practices are. See Section 1f for more tips on adapting your writing to particular audiences.

4 Seek out models and advice. One of the best ways to discover your readers' expectations in a new setting is to look at examples of similar documents. If you're entering an essay to win a scholarship, request a copy of the previous year's winning essay. If you hope to publish an article in a local music magazine, skim previous issues to get a feel for the kinds of topics and stories it prints. Find a couple of pieces that appeal to you and use them as models for organizing your own. You shouldn't imitate every sentence, but a familiarity with your models will help you get started. You can and should add individual touches once you've laid out your basic argument. Chapter 21 contains models of several kinds of academic and nonacademic writing projects.

Also feel free to ask experienced writers for advice. Call on colleagues, instructors, friends, and the staff of your university writing center to read your draft and offer general feedback. When you're unsure, it's better to head off a potential mistake than to recover from one that appears in print.

E-Tips

Garbl's Active Writing Links, at <http://www.garbl.com>, offers advice, templates, and links for writing a variety of public documents, including letters to the editor, letters to legislators, and editorials.

8a
public

5 Recognize that public writing offers benefits and risks that academic writing does not.

Although you may feel anxious when you turn in a course paper, your instructor and classmates are a relatively private audience. Slips in logic or punctuation won't usually damage anything other than your grade, and you can generally experiment with new ideas without fear of offending your instructor. But when you write for larger public audiences, responses may be more direct and less predictable. If you write an email message to your office listserv criticizing the company scheduling policy, your boss, unlike your writing instructor, may take your complaints personally—and may be less sympathetic the next time you ask for a night off.

For this reason, it's especially important to consider the impression you hope to make on readers when you undertake a public writing project. When Jesse Faleris wrote the letter advocating gun control that appears on pages 121–24—a letter he submitted to National Rifle Association (NRA) leadership at their annual convention—he faced a tricky rhetorical situation. As a longtime member of the organization, he understood their entrenched resistance to gun control measures of any kind and knew that such arguments would have to be carefully presented in order to be heard. Moreover, he valued his membership and wanted to avoid antagonizing fellow members in ways that would be unproductive. He solved this problem by prefacing his arguments with a statement of his commitment to gun ownership rights and to the organization's general goals, a statement that he hoped would build consensus with his audience. He recognized that his letter might nonetheless evoke negative responses, but he felt that the argument was important enough to justify the risk. (See Section 1g for more on creating a positive impression on readers.)

Knowing that your ideas have reached and affected others is precisely what makes public writing so rewarding. While Jesse's Faleris's English instructor probably wouldn't penalize him for his views on gun control, neither does she have the power to change NRA policy. So don't allow the directness of writing to a public audience scare you into confining your ideas to the classroom. But be prepared: *Before* you publish or mail your piece, think through the possible responses your writing might elicit. When you've anticipated these consequences, you can decide how you want to address them.

6 Be professional. You'll be taken seriously as a writer if you submit attractive, polished, and carefully edited and proofread documents. That rule applies to virtually every writing situation. See Section 5a-6 for more on this topic.

8a
public

Going Public   *Shaping an Argument for a Public Audience* ____

As you read this letter that student writer Jesse Faleris addressed to NRA leaders at the group's annual national convention, note how he shapes his argument to defuse potential negative responses from his readers. Consider, too, the ways in which his letter differs from an academic research paper on gun control.

To Fellow Members of the National Rifle Association:

   I am greatly concerned about the current escalation of gun legislation and how our organization's position may affect the rights of American citizens to own firearms. Unfortunately, I believe that our organization's current philosophy of "Guns do not kill--people do" is no longer an effective stance, and that if the Second Amendment is to survive future abolition legislation, our organization must transform its image.

   Before I continue with my suggestions, let me offer a summary of my background. I am a military careerist with ten years' United States armed forces active duty service. I am the son of an accomplished gunsmith who is actively involved in Canadian firearms legislation. I have four years' experience in military public relations, and I am currently a public relations and law philosophy student at the University of South Carolina. I am the coach of the

USC ROTC pistol team. Most importantly, I am a gun
owner and an advocate of all Americans' right to bear
arms.

8a
public

It is this last concern that prompts me to
write to you today. While I have not found a succinct
mission statement of the NRA, the literature produced
by our organization defines us as the protectors of
Americans' rights to own and use firearms for sport as
well as self-defense. But the majority of our
literature centers around the media's exploitation of
the gun debate, and the government's misdirected
attempts at firearms legislation. For example, the
August issue of the NRA's *American Guardian* magazine
criticizes a bill introduced into the U.S. Senate,
which would ban "Saturday Night Specials." Senator
Barbara Boxer introduced this bill in hopes of
ridding cities of the small inexpensive handguns that
are often used in crimes. The NRA rebuts by saying
that the government wants to stop America's
impoverished peoples from protecting themselves.

I understand why the NRA maintains the Second
Amendment posture that ". . . the right of the people
to keep and bear arms, shall not be infringed," but
at what cost do we deny any infringement? I
understand that need for a firm conviction from a
philosophical standpoint, but philosophy does not
solve social problems any more than misdirected
legislation does. This is because the general
populace will no longer accept "guns don't kill"
logic. In the midst of heightened awareness to hate
crimes and random violence, the handgun is quickly
becoming the social icon of America's violence
problem. Polls from the Gallup Organization, the
Associated Press, and others reveal that upwards of

85 percent of Americans favor further gun legislation.

For these reasons, the NRA must drop our current anti-legislation attitude in favor of a "responsible gun owner" persona. We must demand that not only our members, but also the gun owners outside our membership, as well as the manufacturers, actively advance responsible gun ownership. As gun owners, we must take responsibility to safeguard our firearms against use by irresponsible persons with the following steps:

- We must protect unsupervised minors from access to firearms. Yes, trigger locks! If used, trigger locks are a responsible means of regulating who uses a firearm. Again, I understand the NRA's slippery slope argument that any infringement will lead to abolition, but if we look at Canada as an example we may find voluntary compliance unrealistic.

- The manufacturers must contribute to the effort of safeguarding the public from firearm products. Including trigger locks with the purchase of new firearms is a necessity. Providing additional trigger locks for existing guns at manufacturers' cost is reasonable and would be recognized as a positive and responsible response to consumer America's concerns.

- Finally, we must work with legislators, particularly those supportive of gun owners, to draft and introduce effective and responsible gun legislation. This legislation should focus on criminal use of guns. We must find a way to keep criminals from using guns, without limiting the law-abiding citizens' right to keep and bear arms.

As a linchpin between gun owners, Congress, and gun manufacturers, the NRA possesses the influence to arbitrate these responsible proposals. These are our guns, our streets, our children and our legislatures-- let us take responsible action to safeguard all we hold precious.

I hope that my honest intentions are clear. I do not want to lose my rights, nor my children's, nor my grandchildren's rights to keep and bear arms. I am convinced that the NRA and Gun Owners of America organizations want to protect our rights in a changing social atmosphere. What I hope is that we can use our influence to effect positive changes in the average American's beliefs about gun ownership.

Respectfully,

Jesse M. Faleris

8a
public

SUMMARY *When You Write for the Public . . .*

* Choose an appropriate audience and forum.
* Be sure the timing is right.
* Learn your readers' expectations.
* Use models to help you get started.
* Recognize that your writing may elicit responses.
* Be professional.

EXERCISE 8.1 Here is a list of four public writing projects completed by undergraduate students. For each project answer these questions: How do you think the piece differs from an academic treatment of the same topic? What kinds of adjustments do you think the writer made for audience, purpose, and setting? Discuss your responses with classmates.

1. An article on aging and nutrition for a nursing home newsletter.

2. A proposal directed at the city arts commission requesting funding for Diversity Week activities sponsored by a local cultural organization.

3. An informational Web site that rates local landlords and apartment complexes according to the number of renters' complaints filed against them.

4. A review of the latest Eddie Murphy film for the local paper.

8b How do you write in service-learning courses?

While much of the writing you do in college will never leave the classroom, an increasing number of composition courses nationwide now incorporate one or more *service-learning projects*—projects that ask students to apply what they've learned by writing "real" documents for community agencies or groups. Service learning can take many shapes. Composition students at Carnegie Mellon University, for example, work with inner-city teenagers to produce newsletters and videos that explore the young people's views on drug use, violence, and gender issues. Students at Michigan State University are placed in community agencies for which they write newsletters, publicity materials, reports, and other documents. Business writing students at the University of Arizona collaborate with local nonprofit groups to write grant proposals. And students in other programs across the country serve in tutoring programs, homeless shelters, local arts agencies, and many other public settings as part of their academic work in a writing course.

If you're taking a writing class that includes a service-learning component, you can look forward to valuable opportunities: You'll learn more about organizations in your community and the work they do. You'll have a chance to do work that affects your community. You'll gain experience working collaboratively with others, and you'll make contacts that may help you find future volunteer work or a job after graduation. And perhaps most important, you'll have a chance to test your research and writing skills on real audiences.

But because they combine several audiences, purposes, and sets of expectations for writing, service-learning projects pose special challenges. This section offers general guidance for dealing with these challenges and introduces you to Ray McManus, a student writer who completed a service-learning project at the University of South Carolina.

> **E-Tips**
>
> Consult your university's Web page to learn more about service-learning programs on your campus. Campus Compact, a national alliance of colleges and universities committed to community service, has compiled information on service-learning opportunities nationwide, at <www.compact.org>.

■ 1 Understand the dual purpose of service learning.

Service-learning projects differ from strictly academic writing projects because they involve real writing for community audiences. They also differ from the volunteer work that you do outside school, even when that work involves writing. Service learning always involves an academic dimension—your instructor asks you to write for the community not just because it's a civic-minded thing to do but so that you can also explore concepts and strategies that you're learning in the course. In service-learning projects, both the service and the academic dimensions of the course are equally important: one reinforces the other.

When you begin a service-learning course, ask yourself:

* How does my work in the community reflect, reinforce, or problematize the material I'm learning in class?
* How does the material I'm learning in class help me to effectively approach the work I'm doing in the community?

Ray McManus, the student writer whose work is featured in this section, engaged in a service-learning project as part of a course on teaching writing. The project, in which he and other students designed and led several poetry workshops for teenagers at the local library, had both practical and academic components. On the one hand, his experiences with the workshops allowed him and his classmates to test strategies and approaches to teaching poetry that they'd read about in class. On the other, the workshops gave Ray, who hopes to become a teacher of creative writing, valuable experience in his chosen field and useful contacts with interested local librarians, teachers, and schools.

■ 2 Be aware of the different audiences your writing will address.

The dual purpose of service learning means that you'll be

writing for at least two audiences—your instructor and the community readers of any document you produce. Sometimes you'll write for both audiences simultaneously. Be aware of their differences and tailor your work accordingly, since the expectations in one setting are likely to differ from those in another. If you have questions about what's expected, don't hesitate to ask.

The chart below gives you an idea of the kinds of audiences and documents Ray McManus produced over the course of his project.

8b
service

HIGHLIGHT | *Writing Projects for One Service-Learning Course*

During the course of Ray McManus's service-learning project, he created a variety of documents for a variety of audiences. Some work was turned in to his professor, some was seen only by library staff and patrons, and some was directed to both audiences.

WORK PRODUCED FOR PROFESSOR
Annotated bibliography of resources on children's poetry writing
Reflective journal entries on workshop sessions
Lesson plans for workshop sessions
Final research paper reporting on and analyzing experience

WORK PRODUCED FOR LIBRARY STAFF OR PATRONS
Collaboratively written publicity flyers
Interview with newspaper
Thank-you letter to library director

WORK PRODUCED FOR PROFESSOR AND LIBRARY STAFF OR PATRONS
Lesson plans for workshop sessions
Exercises and materials for workshops

■ **3 Find out how your work will be evaluated.** The fact that you must write for several audiences sometimes makes it hard to figure out whether you're doing a good job with a service-learning project. For example, what if your instructor expects you to write very detailed lesson plans for tutoring sessions in an adult literacy program, when most tutors in the program take a more relaxed approach to planning by jotting down just a sentence or two?

When you encounter different sets of expectations, you'll feel more confident if you know how your work will be evaluated: Which pieces of your writing will your instructor grade? Will he evaluate them according to academic criteria? Will the community members you work with judge some or all of your writing? If so, what criteria will they use, and will they determine part of your course grade? Once you know these parameters, you can make decisions to adjust your work accordingly. In the above situation, knowing that your instructor will be grading your lesson plans, you might jot down a rough draft for the program's records, then use that draft to develop a more polished plan to turn in to your professor. See Chapter 6 for more on how writing is evaluated.

8b

service

4 Be willing to learn and to collaborate. When you engage in community service, it may be tempting to adopt a "savior" mentality—that is, to feel that your job is to bestow your knowledge and skills on needy individuals. Certainly a key goal of service-learning programs is to make university students' energy and talents available to others in the community. But remember that anytime you enter a new writing situation, *you're* the novice. Be ready to learn from the people you work with and to collaborate productively with them.

When Ray McManus and his classmates began designing poetry workshops for local teenagers, he had had plenty of experience with writing poetry and had researched ways to engage teenagers in learning about it. But when it was time to craft publicity materials for the sessions, they knew little about how to reach young people likely to attend. They knew that they wanted to make the sessions sound "cool," rather than something that was too much like school. Ray came up with the title "Split P Soup," which he thought reflected that goal. But Ray and his partners needed the expertise of library staff who had advertised previous youth programs, who had contacts with local teachers and youth and educational organizations, to determine how best to attract potential attendees. They also needed the library's publication office to translate their ideas into an eye-catching format. The flyer that resulted from this collaboration is featured on page 129.

Once the workshops began, Ray and his classmates worked collaboratively with the participants. While he and his co-leaders set a basic agenda for each session, participants took charge in selecting topics for writing and discussion and in recruiting new participants. By asking the young people to take part in shaping the sessions, Ray could be sure that the workshops met their interests and needs.

Community work involves exactly that—working in a community. As Ray McManus found, if you cultivate an open mind and are willing to learn from others, you'll likely be successful in your service-learning project.

Going Public   *Collaboration and Service Learning* _____

Here's the publicity flyer that resulted from the collaborative efforts of Ray McManus and numerous library staff. Do you think the flyer is effective? Why or why not? Do you think Ray could have created it alone?

8b
service

Checklist 8.1

When You Write in a Service-Learning Course . . .

• Understand that your writing has both academic and practical goals.

• Be aware of the different audiences you will address.

• Find out how your writing will be evaluated.

• Learn from and collaborate with others.

CHAPTER 9

How Do You Read and Think Critically?

As a student and as a citizen, you are bombarded each day with messages that try to influence you—that urge you to buy a particular brand of toothpaste, to give money to a certain charitable organization, to vote for one candidate rather than another, and to see the latest blockbuster film. Dealing with these competing texts requires that you examine ideas, ask questions, challenge arguments, and decide which viewpoints are worth accepting—in other words, that you think *critically*. Much of the information you absorb in college will be obsolete ten years from now, but the critical and analytical skills you develop in school will serve you the rest of your life.

In college, a crucial element of critical thinking involves learning to read critically, because much of what you write and think about is in response to textbooks, articles, research reports, and other readings. This chapter will guide you through the basic steps of the reading process and suggest ways that you can bring your critical abilities to bear on the texts you read, inside and outside the classroom.

9a How do you read to understand complex material?

College reading assignments pose special challenges. In high school, teachers may cover a textbook chapter in a week; in college, in-structors often assign several chapters in the same amount of time, along with supplementary readings from scholarly journals, literary texts, and other sources. College assignments may also address more abstract ideas and use more complicated language than you're accustomed to. Whereas you may be accomplished at reading sources that summarize and analyze issues *for* you—like high school textbooks or popular magazines do—in college you'll often have to weigh conflicting approaches to an issue or interpret research findings and data on your own.

But the classroom isn't the only place you'll encounter difficult texts. You'll also sift through competing viewpoints and complex terminology when you research current issues as a voter, when you use the Internet to become expert on a topic, when you draft a report at work or critique the news coverage of an important local event. These challenges present complex material that you can't read in the same way you'd read a paperback mystery novel or a grocery list. You'll need to develop specialized skills that help you become an active, engaged reader.

9a
crit

■ **1 Preview the text.** Just as you can navigate an unfamiliar city more easily when you have a map, you'll find it easier to read an unfamiliar text if you first preview its important features.

- **Genre:** What kind of document is it? An introductory textbook? An opinion piece? A literary work? A commercial Web site? Different genres have different purposes and audiences, which you should keep in mind as you read.
- **Title:** What does it tell you about the piece's content and purpose?
- **Organization:** If you're reading a printed text, are there headings or subheadings? If you're reading a Web site online, are major sections listed in the left frame or on a home page? What do these divisions suggest about what the text will cover?
- **Sources:** Inspect the bibliography and index. What do the sources listed there tell you about the kinds of information the writer will draw on?

Before reading a piece, determine your goals: Are you skimming the piece to see if it's relevant to a paper you're writing? Are you mainly interested in major concepts and arguments, or do you need to know details? Do you want to develop your own opinions on the subject? These goals should influence how much time you spend reading and which of the strategies discussed in the following sections you decide to use.

■ **2 Look up unfamiliar terms and concepts.** It's always easier to understand difficult material if you have the relevant background knowledge. When you preview a text, circle major terms, concepts, or topics that sound unfamiliar. For instance, you'll feel completely at sea reading an article about the African diaspora if you don't know what *diaspora* means and your knowledge of the continent is limited to vague memories from eighth-grade social studies. A look at a dictionary and an encyclopedia entry on Africa will put you on more solid ground.

Even if you have some general knowledge about a topic, it's not a bad idea to keep a dictionary at hand while you read so that you can clarify confusing references as they crop up.

■ **3 Slow down.** The best readers usually aren't the fastest ones. When you're reading about ideas new to you, expect to read slowly and to reread two or three times before you fully grasp an argument or explanation. Some experts advise making it a habit to read everything twice: the first time just to understand what the writer is saying, the second to focus on your own reactions and opinions. But whatever your strategy, don't rush. Speed-reading may sound good on "infomercials," but it doesn't produce a thorough understanding of a text.

■ **4 Annotate the text to clarify and respond to its content.** You can often spot a skilled reader by looking at the condition of his or her books: dog-eared pages, heavily underlined or highlighted passages, and margins overflowing with notes are sure signs. Critical readers understand that reading involves more than passively absorbing words on a page. It's an active process of creating a new understanding.

If you're not accustomed to taking notes on your reading, here are some useful strategies.

- **Content notes.** Most college students highlight key passages in their texts. But if you want to get the most from your reading, don't stop there. When you arrive at an important point or get tangled in a difficult passage, translate it into your own words. Expressing a concept or argument in your own language helps you to clarify its meaning.
- **Context notes.** Notes can also help you follow a text's structure. At crucial transitions, jot down a key word or two that explains where the argument is going or how a new point fits in: "Opposing argument," "Previous theories," "Example 3," for instance.
- **Response notes.** When you're reading something difficult, don't just accept what it says; talk back. Does a proposal excite or anger you? Write "Yes!" or "Bad logic." If the text raises questions, write them down: "But what about the innocent victims?" or "Does this argument follow?" Carrying on this kind of dialogue with your reading develops your own perspective on the issues being raised.

Here's how one reader used these three strategies to annotate the opening passage of an opinion piece she read while researching a paper on moral education. She made response notes in the left margin and content and context notes in the right margin; notice how these notes help her follow a fairly complicated argument.

9a
crit

"Second Thoughts on Civil Society"

by Gertrude Himmelfarb

? look up

I would like to think that it is not just contrariness on my part that makes me wince, these days, on hearing talk of civil society. Liberals and conservatives, communitarians and libertarians, Democrats and Republicans, academics and politicians appeal to civil society as the remedy for our dire condition. They agree upon little else but this, that mediating structures, voluntary associations, families, communities, churches, and workplaces are the correctives to an inordinate individualism and an overweening state.

these = "civil society"

The ubiquity of the phrase is enough to make it suspect. What can it mean if people of such diverse views can invoke it so enthusiastically? I am as critical as anyone (perhaps more so than most) of an individualism that is self-absorbed and self-indulgent, obsessively concerned with the rights, liberties, and choices of the "autonomous" person. And I am no less critical of a state that has usurped the authority of those institutions in civil society which once mitigated that excessive individualism. But I am also wary of civil society used as a rhetorical panacea, as if the mere invocation of the term is a solution to all problems—an easy, painless solution, a happy compromise between two extremes.

?

Civil society is indeed in a sorry condition. But one reason is that some of its institutions have been complicitous in fostering the very evils that civil society is supposed to mitigate. The welfare state is a classic case of the appropriation by government of the functions traditionally performed by families and localities. Neighbors feel no obligation to help one another when they can all upon the government for assistance. Private and religious charities are often little more than conduits of the state for the distribution of public funds (and are obliged to distribute those funds in accord with the requirements fixed by government bureaucrats.)

?

But what about people whose communities can't help?

But it is not only weakness of civil society that is at fault. Some of the institutions of civil society—private schools and universities, union and nonprofit foundations, civic and cultural organizations—are stronger and more influential than ever. The individualistic ideology of rights and the statist ideology of big government are reflected in the causes that these institutions have promoted: feminism, multiculturalism, affirmative action, political correctness.

Is she saying all these beliefs are wrong? Not sure I agree.

Everyone is saying that civil society can solve the probs. caused by big gov't.

But she is suspicious.

2 reasons

①Churches charities now rely on gov't $

②Other institutions are promoting big gov't.'s ideas

When you're working on a project that involves substantial research, it's especially important to take careful notes. Your annotations can identify ideas and information worth returning to, highlight passages you want to quote in your paper, and, more important, help you synthesize and engage in dialogue with the authors and texts you are encountering. See Chapter 45 for more on incorporating material you've read into a research paper.

5 Adapt your reading process to online settings. While most of the reading strategies described in the preceding sections apply to both print and online environments, electronic texts pose special challenges. Experts on reading have even coined a new term—*screen literacy*—to describe the skills readers need to navigate online texts.

Online texts are often less stable and more loosely structured than printed texts. Reading a Web site or an electronic book, for example, you may scroll through long passages without page markers, follow complicated series of hyperlinks, or encounter sophisticated audio and visual components. The text may look different on your home computer than it does in the campus computer lab, and its content or format may change periodically. These features can make it hard to find your place within a text, to return to important material, and to figure out how the pieces of a text fit together.

The boundaries that separate one online text from another are also blurred. When you follow hyperlinks, you may find it hard to distinguish where one text begins and another ends. In researching a paper for your American literature class, for example, you may wonder whether a link to biographical information on the poet Walt Whitman that's embedded in an online text of *Leaves of Grass* is a part of that text or a separate text.

These differences mean that when you go online, you have to adjust your reading process accordingly. James Sosnoski, a composition theorist, has identified several strategies you may find especially useful.

- **Filtering.** Skillful online readers are especially selective about what they choose to read, **skimming** and **pecking** to find the most relevant items.
- **Imposing.** Online readers approach reading with their own agendas rather than always following the author's preferred path through a text.

- **Filming.** Online readers pay as much attention to visual elements as they do to the words in a text. (See Section 10b for more on this topic.)

Cultivating these skills will help you navigate the vast array of materials on the Internet without feeling overwhelmed.

Once you've browsed through material online, you'll need to develop strategies for keeping track of it. The safest strategy is this: when you want to read an online text carefully or return to it later, download and print it. Having the document in hand will help you follow the arguments and see how components of the text work together. Also consider using your browser's "bookmark" feature to mark sites that you refer to frequently, so that you don't lose them. You can "bookmark" all sites or pages relevant to a project, arranging the items in folders that reflect its overall structure, one folder for each major section or theme. If a site is likely to change frequently, download and save material that you want to return to.

Finally, online texts support different methods of responding to your reading. You can use the annotation features of many word-processing programs to record your reactions to files you download onto your computer. (But be careful to clearly separate your comments from the original text.) Pages from the World Wide Web can be marked with comments and, in some cases, annotated as part of an ongoing online discussion. It's even possible to annotate bookmarks you've created to remind yourself why a particular site or page is important. (See Section 45b for more advice on organizing research materials and Sections 46b and 47c for advice on incorporating research into a writing project.)

9a
crit

EXERCISE 9.1 Use the three note-taking strategies described in Section 9a-4 to annotate a reading assignment in one of your other courses. How do these strategies compare to your typical approach to reading? Which strategy helped you learn the most, and why?

EXERCISE 9.2 Find and read a text that is published in both print and online versions. Possibilities include magazines (like *Newsweek* and Newsweek .MSNBC.com), informational materials about a nonprofit organization or political candidate, and university documents. Which version do you find more difficult to read? Why? How did your reading process differ in the two settings? Discuss your answers with a group of classmates.

> SUMMARY **Reading and Understanding Complex Material**
>
> When you're reading new or difficult material . . .
>
> • Preview the text.
>
> • Look up unfamiliar terms and concepts.
>
> • Take your time.
>
> • Take notes to clarify content and target points of confusion.
>
> • Adapt appropriately to online settings.

9b How do you think critically about your reading?

Critical thinking is only an extended and focused version of the kind of thinking we all do every day when we set out to solve problems: we gather evidence, we examine options, we look at advantages and disadvantages, and we weigh others' opinions for possible bias.

A voter thinks and reads critically when he or she researches candidates' backgrounds and positions on major issues before approaching the ballot box. So does the person who reads *Consumer Reports* and does some comparative shopping before buying a cellular phone. So do you when you wade through all the information you need to consider in deciding whether to find a second part-time job or to take out a student loan to pay next year's tuition. All these situations demand that you cultivate an attitude of inquiry—that you *inquire* and *reflect* on complex material in order to arrive at the best possible judgment.

1 Read as a believer and as a doubter. You'll get the most from your reading if you approach it with an open mind—if you appreciate that it's possible to learn something even from perspectives contrary to your own. An excellent way to engage with readings that present difficult or unfamiliar arguments is to play what the writing expert Peter Elbow calls the "believing and doubting game." This approach asks you to read and respond to a piece twice, each time adopting a dramatically different attitude.

To play the "believing" half of the game, read the piece with as much generosity as you can muster. Try to see what makes the argument so compelling to the writer, and look for claims, examples, or beliefs that seem reasonable or persuasive. Even if you don't agree with the writer's overall position, you may find enough common ground to understand it better than you would have if you had rejected it out of hand. Write a paragraph exploring whatever seems most worth believing in the piece. Then read the piece a second time as a "doubter." Scrutinize every statement for gaps, exaggerations, errors, and faulty reasoning. Ferret out any problems you can see in the writer's perspective, even if you agree with it. Again, summarize your conclusions in a paragraph. Keying in on weaknesses will guard against your accepting the argument too readily.

Here's how one writer played the "believing and doubting game" with the excerpt from the article on civil society in Section 9a-4.

9b
crit

> believing   I agree with Himmelfarb that neighbors, families, churches, etc., are less likely to get involved and help others if they think that the government will step in. They think it's not their job or even that "experts" know more about how to help. This does weaken community ties and make people more isolated from each other.
>
> doubting   What about the people whose families, neighbors, and churches can't or won't help them? Isn't that why government took over welfare programs to begin with, because too many people were slipping through the cracks? That's how tragedies happen; think of children who are abused for years because their relatives and neighbors don't want to intervene.

■ **2 Assess the writer's qualifications.** Get into the habit of checking the author's qualifications for everything you read. Does the writer have special expertise on a subject from either personal experience or academic training? Does he or she demonstrate adequate knowledge? You might find, in reading a debate about violent lyrics in "shock rock," that some of the loudest calls for censorship come from writers who admit they have never listened to the music. Or you may find that the author of a Web site on managing your investments has neither a business degree nor a substantial stock portfolio. A lack of expert qualifications doesn't necessarily invalidate a writer's arguments, but it should make you examine them with extra care. See Section 45a-3 for more on evaluating a writer's credentials. Section 45a-2 tells how to evaluate the credibility of different kinds of publications.

■ **3 Look carefully at the evidence presented.** A strong academic argument must adequately back up its claims. When you read an argument, size up the quantity and quality of its supporting evidence.

- **How much evidence does the writer present?** Does the amount of support seem substantial enough for the claims being made, or does the writer rely on just one or two examples?
- **Where does the evidence come from?** Is it recent, or is it so old that it may no longer be accurate? Does it seem trustworthy, or does the writer rely on sources of dubious credibility?
- **Is the evidence fairly and fully presented?** Do you suspect that the writer has manipulated information in order to make his or her case look better?

Critical thinkers guard themselves against the tendency we all have to gravitate toward arguments that confirm our own beliefs and to avoid those that don't. Thus, when you're researching an issue, seek out readings that reflect different perspectives—for example, *Slate* as well as *The Wall Street Journal, Ms.* as well as *Esquire.* Try to find arguments written by women and men, liberals and conservatives, and supporters as well as opponents of a proposal. See Section 11b-3 for more on evaluating the evidence presented in an argument.

4 Assess whether the writer's claims go beyond what the evidence actually supports. Closely allied to the quality of the evidence in an argument is how the writer applies that evidence. Does the writer draw conclusions that go beyond what his or her support warrants? For instance, some safety experts once made claims about the safety of air bags based on crash-test data calculated for crash dummies the size of adult men. These claims didn't hold true for children and small women. Faced with dozens of fatalities attributed to injuries caused by air bags, those experts admitted that their original claims went beyond what the data had established.

Although overstating one's claims doesn't usually result in such tragic consequences, you can and should question any argument that stretches its conclusions too far.

5 Look for what's *not* there: the unstated assumptions, beliefs, and values that underlie the argument. Does the writer take it for granted that he or she and the audience share certain knowledge or beliefs when in fact they don't? If what someone takes for granted in an argument can reasonably be disputed, then you should challenge the author's claims.

Consider the assumptions made in this sentence, taken from an article advocating the legalization of drugs.

> The violence brought about by the black market in drugs is attributable in large part to the fact that we have chosen to make criminals out of people who have a disease.

The statement makes two assumptions: (1) People who buy and sell drugs do so primarily because they suffer from a sickness—addiction—beyond their control. (2) It's wrong to criminalize behavior that results from illness. Both assumptions may well be true, but without further explanation and support, a reader might question them on the following grounds: (1) Drug offenders may engage in illegal behavior not because they're sick but for profit, for sheer kicks, as a response to peer pressure, or because they can't find legal work. (2) Even if drug abuse results from illness, so do many other crimes punishable by law; we don't legalize serial murder just because most perpetrators are mentally ill or legalize drunk driving because many drunk drivers are alcoholics.

9b
crit

See Sections 11a-3 and 11b-4 on how to spot and evaluate hidden assumptions in an argument.

6 Note any contradictions. One mark of critical thinkers is that they look for places where pieces of an argument don't fit together. Suppose a political candidate advocates mandatory prison sentences for first-time drug offenders yet dismisses as "immature behavior" her own abuse of alcohol and other drugs as a young woman. One should question why the candidate excuses for herself behavior that she condemns in others. One might even conclude that the contradiction weakens the candidate's arguments on drug policy.

7 Examine the writer's word choices to identify underlying biases. Everyone has biases—it's unavoidable. We wouldn't be human if we weren't influenced by our experiences, values, and opinions. So it's only natural that writers who want to convince others use language that favors their own point of view. But critical reading requires that you be sensitive to such biases so that you aren't unwittingly swayed by them.

Here's a passage from an article arguing that governments and businesses should work as partners in urban planning. It describes one such project.

> Addison Circle is not just a group of buildings; it is a dream, a vision that has brought together a city, a major landowner, and a developer renowned for producing unique, unusual, and highly successful projects. The result is a new "city center" for Addison, where there will be housing, retail, offices, theaters, and even a park.

This kind of sentence should make your bias detector buzz—it's all good words and positive connotations. Sure enough, checking the byline reveals that the writer who made the statement works for the real-estate developer who helped to create Addison Circle. Her claims may be true, but given her built-in bias, you should withhold judgment until you get more information.

Being a critical reader doesn't mean you have to distrust everything you read. But we should be alert when writers overload their prose with what rhetoricians call "god terms" (words like *democratic, responsible, natural*) or "devil terms" (words like *destructive, immoral, selfish*). See Section 16d for a more detailed discussion of biased language.

8 Be skeptical of simple solutions to complex problems, and resist black-and-white thinking. Be wary of arguments or explanations that offer quick, easy answers to difficult problems. Critical thinkers realize that most serious problems in our society are so complex that anyone who hopes to write about them intelligently must resist casting those involved as "good guys" and "bad guys" or suggesting that the problem could be solved quickly if someone would just do the right thing. There is seldom one "right thing."

Consider the complex issue of affirmative action in college admissions and the calls from many sectors that schools judge prospective students on merit rather than taking racial, ethnic, and economic background into account. Here are a few of the questions that complicate this issue.

1. What, exactly, constitutes "merit"? Test scores and grades? Special talent in a single area, like music or sports? The ability to overcome hardship? If all these factors count, how should each be weighed?
2. Should students who come from educationally disadvantaged groups be judged by the same standards as more privileged students?
3. Do some measures of merit favor certain groups of students over others? For example, some studies indicate that standardized college admission tests often underestimate how well women, members of ethnic and racial minorities, and students with learning disabilities will fare in college.
4. Do schools have a responsibility to make up for past discrimination against particular groups? If so, how long should this responsibility last and what should it entail?

Any solution to a problem, however perfect it may seem, has consequences. As you read an argument, look for evidence that the writer has neglected to consider the long-term implications of his or her position. Don't settle for easy answers.

SUMMARY   *Critical Reading Strategies*

To respond critically to a text . . .

• Read both as a believer and as a doubter.

• Assess the writer's credibility.

• Scrutinize the evidence presented.

• Decide whether the writer's claims are overstated.

• Look for what's left out.

• Check for contradictions.

• Be alert to biased language.

• Be suspicious of easy answers to complex problems.

EXERCISE 9.3 Read the lead editorial in today's newspaper twice, playing the "believing and doubting game" described in Section 9b-1. Which did you find more challenging, reading as a believer or reading as a doubter? Why? Did you notice anything using this method that you might not have noticed if you had read the piece just once?

CHAPTER 10

How Do You Interpret and Use Visual Texts?

Decades ago, your grandparents learned about events primarily through words—they read books, magazines, and newspapers, and they talked with others in their community. Today you may catch the evening news on television, watch political debates on C-SPAN, and choose your new school clothes from pictures on an Internet site. Literacy researchers say that over the past century or so, our society has shifted from being a "print culture," where people got information primarily through words, to an "image culture," where people learn just as much through visual media like film, television, and photography. Even traditional print media like newspapers and books increasingly make use of eye-catching charts, pictures, and other graphic devices.

Since images are so ingrained in our everyday lives, it's important to know how to approach them critically, how to "read" them just as carefully as we do words. This skill is called *visual literacy*. Like any critical thinking, visual literacy means cultivating an attitude of inquiry. It means learning to ask the right questions about what you see, so that you can make informed decisions about it rather than letting what you see control *you*.

10a How do you understand visual representations of information?

When writers present information through charts, graphs, and tables, they draw pictures for readers. These pictures help readers grasp a complex body of data that could be hard to absorb through words alone. Imagine, for example, that you want to rent an apartment and can afford to pay no more than $600 a month. If you could find a fact sheet that used a bar graph to show the price ranges for two-bedroom, two-bath apartments in four areas close to your college, you could quickly determine where you should look for an apartment.

Charts, graphs, and tables present information in different ways. This section explains how each works.

1 A pie chart shows how the parts of a whole are distributed. A pie chart is a simple graphic that shows percentages (the slices) of a total (the whole pie). The following two examples present basic information about property taxes in Indiana: who pays them and how they are spent. Using these charts, you could answer various questions: Do individual homeowners pay most of the taxes? How much of the state's revenue goes to local and county governments? Do schools receive a substantial share? And so on.

10a
visuals

But pie charts can't tell readers everything. They don't reveal fine distinctions. Since pie charts generally can't include more than six or seven slices without becoming visually confusing, writers often collapse

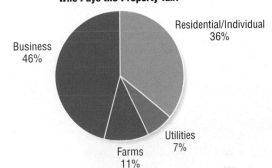

Who Pays the Property Tax?

Residential/Individual
36%

Business
46%

Utilities
7%

Farms
11%

Source: Indiana Handbook of Taxes, Revenues and Appropriations, by Indiana Legislative Services Agency, Fiscal Year 1994

Figure 10.1

Who Receives the Property Tax?

Cities/Towns
16%

Townships
3%

Schools
52%

Counties
19%

Libraries
3%

Other
7%

Source: State Board of Tax Commissions Database, Information supplied by IU Center for Urban Policy and the Environment

Figure 10.2

several smaller categories into a single "slice." Figure 10.1 doesn't tell you what proportion of taxes from farms comes from large commercial farms (which are really businesses) rather than family farms, and you can't tell from Figure 10.2 exactly which county and city services (police, water, roads) are funded by the property tax.

Sometimes writers may vary the design of a basic pie chart. For example, the information depicted in Figure 10.1 could be formatted in the shape of a piggy bank, as shown in Figure 10.3, with the different revenue sources represented as proportional areas within the piggy bank. Don't let the difference in shape confuse you; the basic information remains the same.

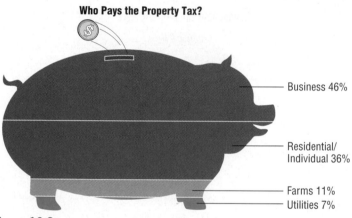

Figure 10.3

2 A bar graph shows the relationship between two variables. It does this by charting the data for one variable along a horizontal scale and the data for the other variable along a vertical scale, using vertical bars to depict data in several categories. In the bar graph in Figure 10.4, major racial and ethnic groups (White, Black, Hispanic, and Other) are shown on the horizontal axis; numerical data (percentage of households with home email access) are measured on the vertical scale. By depicting this information visually, the graph dramatizes both the general increase in email access over the four-year period and the differences among the four groups.

Bar graphs are easy to read, and they can give more information than pie charts. Not only can they show general trends, but they can show subtle distinctions within categories of data. For example, each bar in Figure 10.4 could be divided into two or three subcategories, perhaps using different colors for different age groups within each demographic category or for different parts of the country.

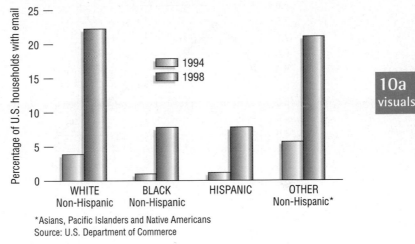

Figure 10.4

3 Line graphs also show relationships but depict trends more emphatically. Like bar graphs, line graphs chart the relationship between two variables, one depicted along the horizontal axis and one along the vertical axis. The sharply declining line in Figure 10.5 makes a strong impact on readers, who will immediately grasp the sense of what they're seeing.

Writers can also use the impact of a line chart to mislead readers. Figures 10.5 and 10.6 present exactly the same data on unemployment rates in the United States, but Figure 10.5 appears to show a sharp drop in the national unemployment rate during the 1990s, while Figure 10.6 makes the decrease in unemployment look insignificant by plotting it on a grid that shows the full range of rates, from 0 to 100% of the population. The writer who prepared Figure 10.6 has unfairly manipulated data to deceive readers by including numbers on his scale that aren't typically part of the range of this phenomenon. Even though it's theoretically possible to have 100% unemployment, the rate in this country has rarely been below 4% or above 10%. In this context, a drop of one percentage point is extremely significant.

4 Tables organize categories of information into vertical columns and horizontal rows that show relationships. Tables can provide more detailed information than graphs or charts, but they're visually less appealing because readers must read more carefully, analyze data for themselves, and draw their own conclusions.

To get the most out of a table, don't just plow through it from top to bottom. First look at the heading to identify the data being

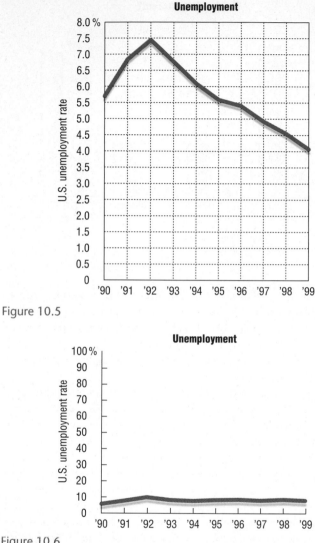

Figure 10.5

Figure 10.6

given, then look at the categories to see how the data are broken down. Like Figure 10.5, Table 10.1 provides information about unemployment in the United States, but the table shows data for a single year, and it breaks down that data by state and ranks each state according to its unemployment rate and the size of its labor force. Here you could find which regions of the United States have the greatest unemployment and use that data in an essay.

TABLE 10.1 Unemployment in the United States, 1999

	Unemployed Persons	Unemployment Rate	Unemployment Rate Rank	Total Labor Force	Labor Force as % of Population	% of Population Rank
Alabama	87,600	4.0%	24	2,170,300	49.9%	41
Alaska	19,100	6.0	2	316,700	51.6	34
Arizona	106,900	4.4	19	2,406,100	51.5	35
Arkansas	58,500	4.7	14	1,258,000	49.6	45
California	881,700	5.3	6	16,605,300	50.8	38
Colorado	69,000	3.0	39	2,286,900	57.6	2
Connecticut	44,800	2.6	46	1,706,500	52.1	30
Delaware	13,300	3.3	36	398,200	53.6	18
Florida	286,100	3.8	26	7,468,500	50.1	39
Georgia	148,900	3.7	28	4,059,600	53.1	22
Hawaii	32,000	5.4	5	596,700	50.0	40
Idaho	33,300	5.0	8	659,900	53.7	17
Illinois	293,500	4.6	15	6,388,700	53.0	23
Indiana	73,100	2.4	50	3,081,100	52.2	27
Iowa	42,800	2.7	45	1,597,300	55.8	7
Kansas	48,600	3.4	35	1,449,700	55.1	8
Kentucky	80,200	4.1	22	1,955,000	49.7	43
Louisiana	97,100	4.7	12	2,054,500	47.0	48
Maine	27,800	4.1	21	670,000	53.8	15
Maryland	108,900	3.9	25	2,815,300	54.8	10
Massachusetts	105,500	3.2	37	3,286,700	53.5	20
Michigan	175,300	3.4	31	5,092,000	51.9	31
Minnesota	81,000	3.0	42	2,740,600	58.0	1
Mississippi	60,300	4.7	13	1,281,700	46.6	49
Missouri	103,100	3.5	29	2,911,800	53.5	19
Montana	22,600	4.8	11	475,300	54.0	14
Nebraska	22,400	2.4	49	933,400	56.1	6
Nevada	36,600	3.8	27	955,500	54.7	11
New Hampshire	16,600	2.5	48	671,300	56.6	5
New Jersey	206,000	4.8	9	4,250,900	52.4	26
New Mexico	50,000	6.0	3	832,100	47.9	47
New York	461,800	5.2	7	8,910,200	49.0	46
North Carolina	113,900	3.0	41	3,845,900	51.0	37
North Dakota	9,800	2.9	43	341,100	53.4	21
Ohio	266,400	4.6	16	5,848,600	52.2	28
Oklahoma	57,500	3.5	30	1,661,600	49.6	44
Oregon	97,200	5.5	4	1,763,000	53.7	16
Pennsylvania	255,200	4.3	20	5,979,200	49.8	42
Rhode Island	20,800	4.1	23	509,400	51.5	36
South Carolina	66,600	3.4	34	1,980,200	51.6	33
South Dakota	10,300	2.6	47	400,400	54.2	13
Tennessee	96,000	3.4	33	2,813,700	51.8	32
Texas	464,500	4.5	18	10,308,800	52.2	29
Utah	37,900	3.4	32	1,105,400	52.6	25
Vermont	10,700	3.1	38	340,000	57.5	3
Virginia	96,300	2.7	44	3,593,900	52.9	24
Washington	148,600	4.8	10	3,120,600	54.9	9
West Virginia	49,800	6.1	1	813,900	44.9	50
Wisconsin	88,200	3.0	40	2,964,100	56.7	4
Wyoming	11,800	4.5	17	261,600	54.4	12
DC	16,300	6.0	—	271,500	51.9	—
US	5,947,200	4.3	—	139,254,000	51.5	—

Source: U.S. Bureau of Labor Statistics

10a
visuals

■ **5 Learn to judge the accuracy of charts, graphs, and ta-bles.** You should approach visual representations of data with a critical eye. Numbers *themselves* don't lie, but they can be presented in misleading ways.

Here are examples of misleading tactics. Say that a writer superimposes a drawing of a broken teddy bear onto a bar graph tracing cuts in Head Start funding. Recognize that he or she is trying to shape your views on the issue, and don't allow yourself to be distracted from the factual information itself. If the dates on the same graph end with 1992, ask why. Would more recent data alter the apparent downward trend? (See Section 10a-3 on the use of scales to overemphasize or downplay a drop or a rise in a line graph.)

The following checklist will help you detect problems that commonly appear in visual representations of information.

Checklist 10.1

Evaluating Charts, Graphs, and Tables

When you read a chart, a graph, or a table, ask yourself . . .

• Are the data up to date?

• What is the source of the data? Is that source credible?

• Does the writer try to argue for more than the data can actually prove?

• Does the writer use color or emotionally loaded graphics to influence my opinion?

• Does the writer manipulate the scale or select information in a way that distorts the data?

Writers will use charts, graphs, and tables just as they do other sorts of evidence: to persuade readers. It's your responsibility to read critically and carefully so that you aren't fooled into accepting weak or inaccurate claims. It's also your responsibility to be fair and accurate when you use charts, graphs, and tables to present information.

E-Tips

For more information on how numbers are used in charts, graphs, and tables, and for useful definitions of common statistical terms, consult Robert Niles's "Statistics Every Writer Should Know" at <www.robertniles.com/stats/>.

EXERCISE 10.1 Imagine that you want to give a talk that uses data on umemployment according to region. Read Table 10.1 with this focus in mind. Working with another student, decide what information from the table would be most useful for your talk. Share your findings with the class.

EXERCISE 10.2 Pick up a copy of *USA Today, Time, Newsweek*, or another popular publication that uses charts, graphs, and tables to present information. See if you can find an example that you think presents data in an inaccurate, oversimplified, or misleading way. Bring your example to class for discussion.

10b
visuals

10b How do you interpret layout, graphics, and other visual elements?

Have you ever bought a novel just because the cover design caught your eye? Or opened by mistake a piece of junk mail formatted to look like a legitimate business letter? Graphic representations, photos, other images, and the way a document is laid out on a page often work together to shape a writer's message. Such strategies can be powerful and useful, but you need to be aware of how they're used so that you can approach them critically.

1 Recognize that writers use layout and design to influence readers. The "body language" of a document—the way a page is laid out and the choice of such graphic features as font, color, and headings—can influence readers' responses to a text. (See Chapter 20 for an extended discussion of graphics and layout.) When you look at a page that obviously has been carefully planned, ask yourself these questions.

- **What ideas or information does the writer emphasize?** Are particular items boxed or set in boldface or in a larger font size than the rest of the text?
- **What ideas or information does the writer downplay?** What information is buried in the middle of the text or in small print?
- **What formatting devices does the writer use?** Does the writer use decorative borders, unusual fonts, or the formatting conventions of a particular genre—headlines and columns like a news article, or a business letter format, for example?

▪ **2 Evaluate images critically.** Pictures trigger impressions that are stronger and more immediate than those most writers can convey with words. And because images can be so powerful, it pays to view them with caution. When you look at pictures or graphic images in a magazine or brochure, on a Web site, or in a fund-raising letter, ask yourself these questions.

- **How does the picture or graphic reinforce or add to the written information?** Is this addition helpful, or is it only decoration? For example, you've probably seen personal Web pages that make distracting use of flashy graphics—multicolored backgrounds, blinking lights, animated characters—that don't relate clearly to the content.
- **What emotions, values, or beliefs does the illustration appeal to?** Is this appeal relevant and fair? Suppose that an organization that opposes animal research includes a photograph of injured rabbits in its annual fund-raising letter without providing a clear explanation of what's depicted in the photo and how it relates to the organization's work. Such emotional appeals are unfair.
- **What does the graphic or picture reveal about the writer's opinions or biases?** If a newspaper story on successful local entrepreneurs includes only pictures of men, you might wonder whether the story slights women business owners.
- **Does the picture or image exaggerate or distort the content of the document?** This might happen if a report on a city-sponsored summer camp featured only photos showing well-attended activities, when the text of the report indicates that the camp was sparsely attended.

▪ **3 Assess visual media critically.** Visual literacy means more than simply attending to the graphical features of printed or written texts. Many of the messages you encounter every day come through mass media (television and film) that consist almost entirely of images. When we watch a music video, drive by a billboard, or tune in the evening news, we take in information so quickly that we have little time to critically reflect on it. But it's important to remember that, like printed texts, the visual media are carefully constructed to appeal to readers, and we must read them as critically as we would any other text.

The mass media are so complex that trying to explain all their components would take us well beyond the scope of this book. However, the basic critical skills discussed in this chapter can generally be extended to apply to these media.

The nonprofit Center for Media Literacy suggests these useful starting points for critically approaching visual media.

- **Remember that visual media texts are purposefully constructed for a particular audience and purpose.** In a single news story, for example, a team of people filmed footage, interviewed sources, wrote an announcer's script, and combined all that raw material into a selective, carefully produced package. We never see what the film crew *didn't* shoot, what the story would have looked like with a different headline or "lead," or what portions of film the producer edited out. Because visual media texts are the products of human choices, they generally reflect their creators' values, viewpoints, and biases.

- **Be aware that visual texts come in many genres, each of which operates according to its own conventions.** Think how different your expectations are when you watch a daytime talk show, a late-night talk show, and a documentary film. These different formats govern how information can be presented.

- **Recognize that visual media may be interpreted differently by different viewers.** Parents often say that they can't make any sense of the music videos their teenaged children watch; it's all just noise and disconnected images, they complain. On the other hand, adults who watch the Disney cartoons they loved as kids often catch cultural references or jokes that eluded them when they were younger. Creators of visual media rely on these differences when they try to reach several audiences at once.

Being aware of these basic ways in which visual media persuade viewers will help you sharpen your visual literacy skills as you apply them to various situations.

E-Tips Interested in learning more about visual literacy? Here are two excellent resources. "The On-line Visual Literacy Project" offers useful and detailed explanations of basic visual literacy terminology at <www.pomona.edu/Academics/courserelated/classprojects/Visual-lit/intro/intro.html>. The Center for Media Literacy provides materials and links for writers who are interested in becoming more media-savvy. Visit <http://www.medialit.org>.

EXERCISE 10.3 Examine the Web site of an organization, public figure, or government agency that interests you. How has its author used layout, graphics, and images to emphasize and de-emphasize certain information or to influence readers? Discuss your findings with a group of classmates.

10b
visuals

EXERCISE 10.4 Keeping in mind the principles discussed in Section 10b-3, watch a television show, movie, music video, or commercial with a critical eye. What features do you notice that you hadn't noticed before? Do you enjoy the text more or less than you would have had you watched it less critically? Why or why not? Bring your answers to class for discussion.

CHAPTER 11

How Can You Write Powerful Arguments?

11a What does argument involve?

Many of the writing projects you undertake will involve constructing an argument. If you write a letter to convince your instructor that your last paper merited a *B* rather than a *C*, that's an argument. So is a flyer urging fellow students to get their free flu shots at the campus clinic or an editorial that takes a position on federal income tax reform. Each of these documents tries to persuade a particular audience to accept a general claim, using *logical reasoning* supported by facts, examples, statistics, or other kinds of *evidence*. The ability to construct powerful arguments is an advantage in almost any writing situation. This chapter introduces you to the basic structures and strategies of argument.

1 Know the difference between genuine arguments and other kinds of disagreements. In everyday life, people use the term *argument* to refer to any disagreement. But rhetoricians use the term in a more specialized way. When we talk about *argument* in this chapter, we mean a discussion of an issue with two qualities:

1. People might reasonably disagree about it.
2. There are *reasonable* grounds for supporting one viewpoint over another.

This narrow definition disqualifies some kinds of exchanges. An assertion that no one would dispute is not an argument. Statements like "Pain is bad" and "If you drop that chair, it will hit the ground" can be immediately proved, so there's no need to engage in debate about whether they're true.

Disputes about subjective personal tastes aren't true arguments either. It's possible to disagree about whether vanilla ice cream is tastier than chocolate and whether Brad Pitt is more handsome than Harrison Ford, but it's impossible to come up with solid support—that is, support that most people would regard as reliable—to prove one opinion more valid than the other.

One *could* logically argue that vanilla ice cream is more popular than chocolate and that Brad Pitt has a narrower range as an actor than Harrison Ford—because there exists evidence about these assertions that most readers would consider logical and convincing. Statistics on ice cream sales and flavor preference polls could support the former argument, and examples from particular films and quotations from reviews and experts on acting could build a case for the latter.

11a
arg

Finally, a statement is not an argument when it seeks to persuade others with threats, emotional manipulation, or trickery rather than with reasoning. An employer who persuades workers to sign up for weekend shifts by hinting that their annual raises depend on it is using threat, not argument. When a campaign advertisement depicts a candidate alongside cooing babies and proud veterans, it's appealing to viewers' emotions, not their intelligence. Although writers who use these techniques may present them as though they were arguments, don't be fooled. Arguments draw on different strategies entirely.

EXERCISE 11.1 Read a brochure, a flyer, or some other promotional literature from a political organization or an advocacy group (for example, College Republicans, Planned Parenthood, Campus Crusade for Christ, People for the Ethical Treatment of Animals, the American Federation of Teachers). Does the document meet the criteria for argument outlined above? Why or why not? Share the document and discuss your conclusions with a group of classmates.

2 Understand an argument as a claim supported by reasons and evidence. British logician and philosopher Stephen Toulmin has developed a useful model for understanding how arguments are structured. (Note: We follow the Toulmin model throughout this chapter because it is a comprehensive, useful, and commonly used way of understanding argument, but your instructor or classmates may use different terminology to refer to the basic parts of an argument. Ask your instructor to clarify any confusion you may have about these terms.)

The Toulmin model says that in every argument, a writer begins by making a general assertion—a *claim*—and then produces one or more grounds for supporting that claim. Support for a claim may include *reasons* (smaller assertions that often begin with the word *because*) and *evidence* (relevant examples, facts, statistics, or experts' statements).

Here's a simple way of outlining how an argument is put together:

Argument = Claim + Reason(s) and Evidence.

Suppose that you're writing an article for your campus magazine on the benefits of working during college. Using Toulmin's model, you might develop your argument as follows.

CLAIM   First-year students at large universities benefit academically from having a job.

REASON   (Because) The social contacts they make at work help them feel less isolated on campus.

EVIDENCE   1. A recent poll conducted by the admissions office found that working students have more friends than students who do not work.
2. My ex-roommate developed a network of friends and study partners while working part time in a campus copy shop.

11a
arg

▐ 3 Recognize that arguments rest on unstated beliefs, or warrants.
Simply laying out a claim and some kind of support isn't enough to make a solid argument. For example, the argument "Mina should do well in college because she's wealthy" would convince no one. A thinking person would respond, "That's an unwarranted conclusion. Being rich has nothing to do with excelling in school." Obviously some ways of connecting claims with reasons and evidence are more persuasive than others.

Toulmin's model uses the term *warrant* to describe the justification—a general belief, rule, or principle—that links together the claim and its support in an argument. A persuasive argument must rest on warrants that readers find satisfactory, or readers will reject it.

Sometimes a warrant is so self-evidently true that it's left unstated. The writer assumes that once the claim and its support are presented, readers will supply and accept the warrant on their own. For example, one might assert, "Mina should do well in college because she made straight *A*'s in high school." The writer doesn't really need to state and support the warrant—that making straight *A*'s is a good indicator of success in college—because just about everybody believes this connection is true. To predict college success based on previous good grades is a "warranted," or justified, conclusion.

But sometimes an argument rests on a warrant that not all readers will agree with. Consider this statement: "Mina should do well in college because she has worked at her parents' restaurant for six years." While the connection may seem reasonable to some readers, others might need convincing. The writer needs to state the warrant and provide some explanation and support for it. Reasons and evidence used to support the warrant in an argument are called *backing*. Here's how the argument would look with warrant and backing.

Parts of an Argument

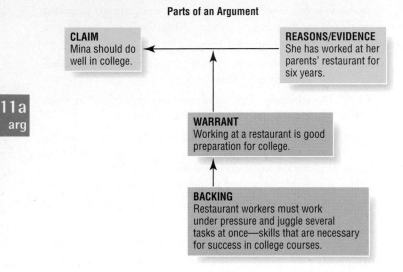

Figure 11.1

EXERCISE 11.2 Each argument below contains a claim and supporting reasons or evidence. Supply the unstated warrant(s) that link each claim to its data, then evaluate the warrant. Do you find the warrant convincing? Why or why not? We've done the first one for you.

ARGUMENT   *Claim:* The federal government should spend more money on cutting-edge cancer research.
Reason/evidence: Studies show that the treatments developed in this kind of research save lives.

RESPONSE   *Warrant:* The government should fund programs that save lives.
Analysis: This warrant is fairly convincing. However, it's possible that the government doesn't have enough money to fund *every* program that might save lives. What if a program is very expensive but will save only a few lives? This argument needs some support to show that cancer research saves more lives than other kinds of programs.

1. *Claim:* The push to legislate tougher safety standards for the trucking industry is misguided.
Reason/evidence: Federal data show that trucks are responsible for only a small percentage of highway accidents.

2. *Claim:* State governments should not approve lotteries as a way to avoid raising taxes.
   Reason/evidence: Lotteries make the state a partner in the legalized gambling business, whose tactics include airing misleading advertisements that entice citizens to play.

■ **4 Recognize that many claims include a qualifier that clarifies the limited circumstances in which that claim holds true.** Because most claims aren't true in every single case, many arguments include a limiting phrase or statement called a *qualifier—probably, in most cases, primarily in urban areas,* for example. The argument about student jobs laid out in Section 11a-2 would overstate its case if it claimed that *all* students benefit academically from holding *any* kind of job. Students who need extra time for studying and students whose work hours cut into class time are obvious exceptions. A more solid statement of this argument would add what Toulmin calls a *qualifier: "Except in cases where work hours interfere with school,* first-year students at large universities benefit academically from having a job."

11a
arg

EXERCISE 11.3 Working with a group of classmates, analyze the following argument taken from a magazine article reviewing recent perspectives on women, welfare, and work. Identify the statements that come after each number as claim, reason, evidence, warrant, backing, or qualifier. You may use some terms more than once and others not at all.

There are two [...] big reasons why [1] the responsible choice for a low-income single mother might be welfare rather than work. [2] Welfare provides health insurance for her children, and most low-wage jobs don't. [3] And welfare, however miserly, provides security that most jobs don't—at least before [welfare reform laws passed in] 1997. [4] In the jobs available to many low-skilled or unskilled women, such as fast food or home health care, workers can never be sure of getting enough hours to make enough money while they have a job, and they are always subject to firing or layoffs. [5] When insecurity doesn't just mean a little less of something but the possibility of starvation or homelessness, the rational risk-benefit calculation counsels taking the secure but less rewarding option.

—Deborah Stone, "Work and the Moral Woman"

11b How do you construct a solid written argument?

Dissecting the logical elements of an argument is one thing; constructing an argument that interests and persuades readers is another. But you'll find that Toulmin's model offers a helpful framework for generating material to include in an argumentative paper.

Start by asking yourself, "What's my claim going to be?" You may not need to spell it out completely to begin with, but you do need to know the general position you plan to take. When you determine your claim, ask yourself

- What reasons and evidence can I gather to support my claim? Can I get them? Are they solid? (Whether or not you can develop a strong case may depend on your answers.)
- What is the warrant that will tie the evidence to the claim? Will readers accept it without question, or should I state and support it with backing?
- Do I need to qualify the claim in some way?

Once you've roughed out your answers to these preliminary questions, you'll have a good start.

■ **1 Clarify your claim.** Figure out what you want readers to take from your piece: Do you want readers to look at some phenomenon in a new way? Do you want them to be aware of a problem they hadn't noticed before? To hold a particular position on a current issue? To take action? Your answer is your claim.

Suppose that, after reading in a child development course some studies about the influence of movies on children, you decide to write an article for the parents' newsletter of the preschool where you work. You want to argue that parents should avoid buying many of the films sold as children's classics because they are not in fact suitable for children. That assertion is your claim, the one set forth in the diagram on page 160. (For more detailed advice about discovering and narrowing a topic and developing a thesis, see Sections 2a and 2b. For more on building a research project around a particular claim, see Chapter 43.)

■ **2 Gather reasons and evidence to support your claim.** What material can you find to develop and strengthen your claim? Check the library for books, periodical articles, research reports, and government documents on the topic. Conduct a search on the World

Wide Web. For expert testimony, consider setting up an interview with a professor or teacher who specializes in children's development, or subscribe to a listserv devoted to children's entertainment.

Depending on the audience for your newsletter article, you might also explore more personal and anecdotal kinds of support. Say your interest in writing about films for children stems from your memories of being terrified at seeing certain so-called children's classics. To use that experience, you'll need firsthand evidence from the films themselves. You might rent several films that frightened you as a child—*The Wizard of Oz, 101 Dalmatians, The Little Mermaid*—and take notes on the scariest scenes. You could also ask friends whether their children had similar responses.

11b
arg

As you gather evidence, cast a wide net. You may not include everything you find in the finished article, but new evidence may help you adjust claims that might have been overstated or misguided. Evidence can also suggest supporting reasons that hadn't initially occurred to you. For example, even if your planned focus is the violence in children's classics, reviewing the films may remind you that many of the stories also promote sexist stereotypes—a point you can then add to your argument.

For more information about finding sources, see Chapter 44.

3 Evaluate your evidence. A skilled arguer knows how to select the supporting materials most appropriate to his or her writing situation. If you're writing a paper for a course, you'll probably concentrate on scholarly research and theories. If you're writing for a preschool newsletter, you might balance academic sources with real-life anecdotes that will catch busy parents' interest.

No matter where your evidence comes from, be sure that it meets certain basic requirements.

- **Timeliness.** Are the statistics, information, and examples you use recent, or are they so old that they may no longer be accurate?
- **Comprehensiveness.** Do you have enough support for your claim, or are you making generalizations based on one or two examples?
- **Credibility.** Do you draw your evidence from sources that both you and your readers trust?

For detailed discussions of how to evaluate evidence, see Sections 9b and 45a.

4 Identify the warrants, or beliefs, that underlie your argument and consider whether readers will accept them. The fact that your arguments seem reasonable to you is no guarantee that readers will immediately embrace them. If you suspect that readers may doubt or disagree with any of your assumptions, be prepared to explain and support them.

This step is especially important when you're writing for a hostile or unfamiliar audience. In the newsletter article on children's movies, you'd need to consider whether some parents might question your warrant that watching frightening, violent scenes is harmful to children. Some parents might believe that such scenes do no real damage. Here's where the research studies from your child development course might fit in: since they establish a causal link between violent films and emotional harm, you can cite them as *backing* for your warrant.

Here's how the fully developed argument might look.

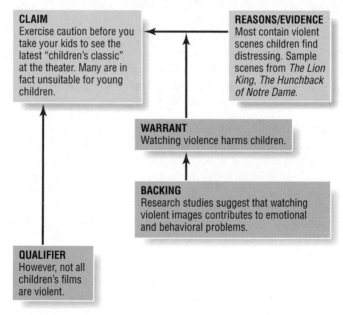

A Developed Argument

CLAIM
Exercise caution before you take your kids to see the latest "children's classic" at the theater. Many are in fact unsuitable for young children.

REASONS/EVIDENCE
Most contain violent scenes children find distressing. Sample scenes from *The Lion King*, *The Hunchback of Notre Dame*.

WARRANT
Watching violence harms children.

BACKING
Research studies suggest that watching violent images contributes to emotional and behavioral problems.

QUALIFIER
However, not all children's films are violent.

Figure 11.2

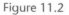 **11c How do you write an argument that appeals to readers?**

Some people see an argument as a sort of verbal war, in which enemies line up on opposing sides of an issue, each with the goal of demolishing the other side. To find samples of this "take no prisoners" attitude, you need only turn on a television talk show, visit a courtroom, or attend a political debate. Certainly competitive, winner-take-all arguments have their place in settings where compromise is impossible or undesirable, but they're not appropriate for much of the writing you'll do.

When you want your readers to accept your arguments and perhaps act on them, remember that you won't persuade people by making them angry. You'll only make them stick to their positions more stubbornly. For this reason, we suggest that you think of argument not as a battle but as a dialogue. In a dialogue, both sides exchange ideas as they search for a solution. The following section explores strategies for working productively with readers who disagree with you. (See also Section 16d on inclusive language.)

11c
arg

1 Draw on shared beliefs and values. Even if you're addressing readers whose position is completely opposed to your own, search for common ground. Any shared belief or value, no matter how general, may serve as a warrant on which you can build an argument those readers will find reasonable. For instance, both proponents and opponents of gun-control legislation value public safety, though they have different ideas about how to achieve it, and both supporters and opponents of school vouchers are concerned about the quality of public education. An argument that begins from these common beliefs may not change anyone's mind immediately. But it probably will get a fair hearing, and it may initiate a civil exchange of ideas.

Here's how one professional writer drew on shared values to make an unpopular argument. The following passage comes from an anti-abortion editorial that Mary Meehan wrote for *The Progressive*, a liberal magazine. To appeal to a strongly pro-choice readership, she invokes the political left's traditional concern with protecting society's downtrodden.

It is out of character for the Left to neglect the weak and helpless. The traditional mark of the Left has been its protection of the underdog, the weak, and the poor. The unborn child is the most helpless form of humanity, even more in need of protection than the poor tenant farmer or the mental patient or the boat people on the high seas. The basic instinct of the Left is to aid those who cannot aid themselves—and that instinct is absolutely sound. It is what keeps the human proposition going.

Did Meehan's argument change many readers' minds? Perhaps not, but her respect for their values won readers' respect and gave them something to think about. And that's what public argument is all about. (See Section 16c for more strategies for building consensus with readers.)

2 Present opposing arguments fairly. If you're going to write about controversial issues, you can't simply pretend that your position is the only one. You'll need to acknowledge that other arguments exist, or readers will think that you haven't done your homework. It is equally important that you learn to describe other positions accurately and respectfully. In doing so you enhance your own credibility.

11c
arg

Here are two rules to follow.

- **Don't oversimplify** another position to make it look weaker than yours.

This tactic is not only uncivil, it's bad argument. Logicians use the term *straw man fallacy* to describe this kind of misleading practice, in which a writer reconstructs another position in an oversimplified way that makes it easy to knock down. The following statement, made on a talk-radio program addressing the trial of a nanny whose infant charge died in her care, slips into this tactic. The speaker derides the infant's working mother.

> It's obvious that she didn't really care about the child, or she wouldn't have allowed a stranger to raise him just so she could earn a few dollars. By putting her paycheck ahead of her children, she got what she deserved.

Parents go to work for numerous reasons, including economic necessity; to pretend that selfishness is their sole reason is inaccurate, unjustified, and ungenerous.

- **Don't use hostile language** to describe another viewpoint.

It's natural to have strong feelings about positions you disagree with, but name calling, stereotyping, and overly emotional terminology hurt your credibility and may offend readers. This kind of language, unfortunately, is all too common—you can find many examples in the "flame wars" that frequently erupt in online discussion forums and in partisan political debates. Here are two examples, one from a Republican and one from a Democrat.

> Midnight basketball [a government-funded recreational program for inner-city youths] is based on the theory that the person who stole your car, robbed your house, and assaulted your family is no more than a would-be NBA star.
> —Lamar Smith, U.S. Representative (R–Texas),
> "Midnight Basketball Is Winner on Street"

Does it scare you to think that many prominent Republicans now sound like the members of an Idaho militia? It scares the hell out of me. The party has swung so far to the anarchistic right that a reasonable Republican like Dwight Eisenhower simply wouldn't be able to recognize today's GOP.

—James Carville, Democratic campaign adviser, *We're Right, They're Wrong: A Handbook for Spirited Progressives*

11c
arg

Both statements rely on negative stereotypes (that inner-city youths are all criminals, that all conservatives sympathize with the militia movement) and emotionally loaded examples and terms ("assaulted your family," "anarchistic"). Exaggerating the negative qualities of an opponent in this way commits what logicians call the *fallacy of special pleading*. This kind of language won't appeal to anyone but the most die-hard believers in your position. You'll find guidelines for using more civil kinds of language in Section 16d-5.

3 Consider refuting an opposing argument. Once you've acknowledged other viewpoints, what do you do with them? Don't just let them sit there; readers want to know how they affect the strength of your argument.

One option is to *refute* an opposing position—that is, to disprove the argument by pointing out its weaknesses or fallacies. It's possible to critique an argument on several grounds.

- **Question the claim.** Is it overstated? Is it insufficiently supported? (See Section 9b-5 for more on how to spot a flawed claim.)
- **Question the evidence.** Does the evidence come from reliable sources? Is there enough of it? Is it recent enough to be accurate? (Sections 9b-4 and 45a contain guidelines for evaluating evidence.)
- **Question the warrants and backing.** Does the argument rest on beliefs, values, or assumptions that you think are invalid? Does the writer need to justify and support those assumptions? (See Section 9b-6 for more on critiquing warrants and backing.)

When you've identified problems in one or more of these areas, point them out and call on readers to reject the argument. But again, even if you feel strongly about your rebuttal, be fair and avoid uncivil language.

Going Public *An Argument That Addresses Opposing Views* ___

Barbara Westbrook wrote the paper excerpted below in response to a class assignment that asked her to refute opposing arguments to a position she felt strongly about. As you read, notice how she describes and discusses these arguments. Is she fair? How does she attempt to create common ground between her position and that of others? Does she support her own position adequately?

Barbara Westbrook

Professors Matalene and Friend

October 14, 1999

A $20,000 Signing Bonus Won't Fill Empty Classrooms

The day that Evelyn Lasky decided to quit teaching high school wasn't her first day of teaching when she arrived to find 36 students, 22 desks, and no textbooks. And it wasn't the day when she calculated the time it would take for her to pay off her college loans. Evelyn Lasky decided to quit teaching on the day that her assistant principal required her to pass a student who had clearly failed but whose father, an influential member of the PTA, had threatened to sue her. "It's not worth it," the assistant principal told Lasky. "Just change the grade and save us all a lot of headaches."

Lasky felt like she had been dropped in a combat zone only to find that those she thought were her allies--administrators, parents, and other teachers--were fighting against her. She ultimately agreed that it <u>wasn't</u> worth the battle. That June, she was among the one-third of the faculty at that school who chose not to renew their contracts.

Unfortunately, Lasky is not unusual. She reflects a larger phenomenon in American education-- the mass exodus of bright new teachers from the profession. Several studies estimate that up to 50 percent of new teachers leave the profession within five years (Colbert and Wolff 193; Odell and Ferraro 200), with urban schools showing the highest attrition rate (Adams and Dial 90). As if this outlook weren't dismal enough, Richard Murnane and Randall J. Olsen's study found even more disturbing news: the higher teachers score on aptitude tests, the more likely they are to leave the profession (118). In other words, we are losing the brightest teachers at the very time when we need them most.

11c
arg

To address the national teacher shortage, schools across the nation have instituted aggressive recruiting strategies. Boston has begun to offer new teachers a signing bonus of $20,000. Baltimore has not only boosted teachers' starting salary by $3,000 but has also offered to pay teachers' relocation expenses and to assist them with down payments on homes (Streisand and Tote).

A low salary is certainly one of teachers' perennial complaints. But higher pay is only one way-- and a relatively ineffective one--to keep good teachers. According to a poll by the National Center for Education Information, 55 percent of teachers feel that they are underpaid. Yet over 90 percent say that they wouldn't quit teaching because of salary alone (Flanagan). Unfortunately, keeping good teachers won't be as simple as padding their wallets because good teachers don't go into teaching for money. They won't stay unless other things change.

As Kathleen Brady documents, many men and women who give up higher earning potential for teaching do so because they find working with students rewarding and fulfilling (36). David James, who plans

11c
arg

to return to his middle school classroom after earning a master's in English, exemplifies this kind of teacher. He told me, "The personal interaction with students was probably the most satisfying" aspect of teaching. Researcher Mary Shann has found that David is typical; teachers consistently rank teacher-pupil relationships as the factor most important to their job satisfaction (70). (Salary ranked thirteen out of fourteen.)

If salary is, as Dominic J. Brewer writes, "a factor [in retaining teachers] but a small one" (320), then we will have to find more effective ways to attract new teachers. I believe there is a better, cheaper way: administrators and parents need to go out of their way to support beginning teachers! It <u>is</u> that simple.

One of the best ways to keep idealistic young teachers in the classroom is to offer them plenty of administrative support. I learned just how powerfully a school administrator can affect her teachers when for an education class I wrote an ethnography of a diverse and unusually high performing urban elementary school. The principal, Thea Jacomides, had her work cut out for her when she came to the school that was experiencing "white flight" (of students <u>and</u> teachers) as a result of recent demographic changes in the neighborhood. Nevertheless, five years after arriving at the school, Ms. Jacomides had a fiercely loyal following of students, parents, and teachers.

How did Thea Jacomides win the respect of her teachers? As she told me herself, she subscribed to an administrative philosophy based on trust and support; she hired teachers whom she would want to teach <u>her</u> children, and then she did everything she could to help them do a good job. And teachers <u>did</u> a good job; they raised student achievement scores to the highest in the city.

In addition to having support from administrators in their schools, new teachers also need support from community members outside the school, especially parents. In fact, researcher Mary H. Shann (70) found that teachers value parent-teacher relationships even above collegial relationships. Teachers value parents because they know that when parents support them, kids behave, try harder, and succeed more often in school. Yet Shann found that although most teachers recognize the importance of parent-teacher relationships, they are dissatisfied with their contact with parents (69-70).

Probably because of the negative press that public schools receive, many Americans are skeptical and critical of teachers--especially new ones. Parents often question grades, attendance, discipline, and make-up work policies. And too often questions of policy become personal attacks on a teacher. During the time that Evelyn Lasky taught, for example, two parents threatened to sue her over the grades their children received in her courses. Parents should make sure that competent teachers are teaching their children, but they need to recognize that supporting a teacher who holds every student to high academic standards is in the best interest of their children.

If the high turnover rate of new teachers is any indication, K-12 teaching poses challenges that most new teachers aren't willing to endure alone. As we are considering ways to recruit and retain new teachers, we need to expand our strategies beyond increasing salaries to consider a few simple, inexpensive, and ultimately more effective methods. If we care deeply about our children's education, the

11c
arg

best chance we may have of keeping classrooms filled
with bright, idealistic, committed teachers is to
support them.

[New Page]

Works Cited

Adams, Gerald J., and Micah Dial. "Teacher Survival:
A Cox Regression Model." Education and Urban
Society 26.1 (Nov. 1993): 90-99.

Brady, Kathleen. "In Search of Meaning . . . Not
Money." Techniques 72.4 (Apr. 1997): 34-36.

Brewer, Dominic J. "Career Paths and Quit Decisions:
Evidence from Teaching." Journal of Labor
Economics 14.2 (Apr. 1996): 313-27.

Colbert, Joel A., and Diana E. Wolff. "Surviving in
Urban Schools: A Collaborative Model for a
Beginning Teacher Support System." Journal of
Teacher Education 43.3 (May-June 1992): 193-97.

Flanagan, Anna. "Administrative Support Is Key
Element in Job Satisfaction." English Journal
86.4 (Apr. 1997): 54.

Jacomides, Thea. Personal interview. 4 April 1997.

James, David. Personal interview. 13 Oct. 1999.

Lasky, Evelyn. Personal interview. 12 Oct. 1999.

Murnane, Richard J., and Randall J. Olsen. "The
Effects of Salaries and Opportunity Costs on the
Length of Stay in Teaching." Journal of Human
Resources (Winter 1990): 106-36.

Odell S., and D. Ferraro. "Teacher Mentoring and
Teacher Retention." Journal of Teacher Education
43 (May-June 1992): 200-04.

Shann, Mary H. "Professional Commitment and
Satisfaction Among Teachers in Urban Middle
Schools." Journal of Educational Research 92.2
(Nov. 1998): 67-73.

Streisand, Betsy, and Thomas Tote. "Many Millions of
Kids, and Too Few Teachers: Across America,
Teaching Jobs Go Wanting." US News and World
Report 14 Sept. 1998: 24.

4 Consider making concessions to another position. Often you won't be able to reject an opposing argument completely; most reasoned arguments do have some merit. In such cases you'll do well to concede that some of your opponent's points are valid and then argue that under the circumstances you believe yours are stronger. When you do this, you not only seem fair-minded but you avoid backing yourself into an untenable position.

11c
arg

One community organizer successfully used this strategy when she convinced the city council to grant her a permit to locate a homeless shelter across the street from a popular playground.

> I agree with you that safety concerns often make it inappropriate to locate shelters in areas frequented by children. The people served by homeless shelters are often troubled and difficult for shelter staff to monitor. However, the shelter I am proposing is different, because it will serve only mothers with small children who have been recommended by churches and social service agencies as good candidates for job training. These mothers will pose little danger to the neighborhood and their children will make good use of the playground.

By admitting that the city council's concerns are valid in many situations, she established valuable common ground with her audience. In addition, she freed herself from having to argue about the safety of homeless shelters in general, allowing her to focus on the special features of her particular shelter.

SUMMARY *Writing Arguments That Appeal to Readers*

- Draw on shared beliefs and values.
- Present opposing arguments fairly.
- Use civil language.
- Refute opposing views when appropriate.
- Make concessions to other views when appropriate.

11d How can you recognize and avoid fallacies?

Critical thinkers learn to recognize *fallacies*, those shoddy imitations of well-reasoned arguments. Most fallacies are flashy shortcuts that look good at first but turn out to be based on dubious assumptions and careless generalizations. Here are ten kinds of fallacy you're likely to encounter frequently.

■ **1 Avoid argument to the person (in Latin, *ad hominem*).** This fallacy makes a personal attack on an opponent rather than focusing on the issue under discussion. *Ad hominem* arguments become smear tactics when a speaker or a writer attacks an opponent's personality or personal life. Here are two examples.

A legislator arguing for a bill that would raise taxes on alcohol to provide low-cost housing claims that those who oppose the bill are heartless people more concerned with keeping down the price of their evening cocktails than with helping others.

A candidate for city council suggests that anyone who opposes his proposal to establish an agency he claims will help minority women is automatically a racist and a sexist.

The speaker who resorts to such abusive rhetoric may well be avoiding the real issues, such as whether a proposal is practical.

But don't confuse the *ad hominem* fallacy with relevant questions about credibility. It's perfectly legitimate to question a writer whose qualifications or motives are dubious, as long as those considerations are relevant to the issues being discussed. In the examples above, it might be appropriate to note that an opponent of the alcohol tax owns a brewing company whose sales might suffer if prices rise, and that an opponent of an agency to help minority women has a history of voting to limit women's rights.

■ **2 Avoid circular reasoning.** This fallacy—also called *begging the question*—happens when instead of supporting a claim, the writer simply restates the claim in different words. Take this faulty argument: "We should not raise taxes to build the new airport because doing so would cost taxpayers more money." Because raising taxes is the same thing as costing taxpayers more money, this statement basically says, "We should not raise taxes because doing so would raise taxes." It asks us to accept the claim at face value rather than providing substantive reasons and evidence.

Here's another example: "The death penalty is wrong because the state should not have the power to end a criminal's life." But that's exactly what the death penalty is—state-sanctioned execution. Unless the writer goes on to explain *why* it's wrong to end a criminal's life and provides supporting data, this claim begs the question.

If you hope to make effective arguments, you have to guard against this fallacy. An unsubstantiated claim is just that—it's not a reasoned argument.

11d
arg

3 Avoid hasty generalization. This fallacy involves drawing conclusions from too little evidence.

It's not safe to travel now because terrorists set off a bomb in the Tel Aviv airport last month, and two weeks later another bomb blew up at Heathrow Airport in London.

Terrorist incidents at two airports do not provide sufficient evidence on which to base a broad claim about travel safety all over the world.

Be careful about making claims that use absolute terms such as *always, never, everyone, no one, all,* and *none.* When you're talking about human events, absolutes are seldom accurate, so cover yourself by using qualifiers like *some, in most cases,* and *many.* And as a reader and a listener, you should always be skeptical about arguments that overstate their claims in this way. (See Section 11a-4 for more about using qualifiers in an argument.)

4 Avoid false cause arguments (in Latin, *post hoc, ergo propter hoc,* or "after this, therefore because of this"). These arguments incorporate the faulty assumption that because one event follows another, the first event caused the second. Setting up false cause arguments is a form of oversimplification that grows out of the desire we all have to believe in easy answers rather than wrestle with complex questions about who caused what and why.

Consider how silly the following argument sounds.

Starting in June of this year, per capita ice cream consumption increased significantly. Just one month later, the number of drownings increased. It's clear that eating ice cream causes people to drown.

Obviously, both ice cream consumption and drownings increase during the summer months. But one doesn't cause the other—more likely, hot weather causes people both to crave ice cream and to want to go swimming. Swimming accidents cause drowning.

It's easy to see the flaws in this example, but false cause arguments about social and political issues can be harder to spot. Consider this statement.

> In the years since the highway speed limit was raised to 70 miles per hour, the annual number of traffic fatalities in our state has doubled. Clearly, the new speed limit is causing unnecessary deaths.

11d
arg

Too many factors enter into changes in traffic fatality numbers for such a conclusion to be legitimate. Increased numbers of drivers on the road, altered traffic patterns due to new construction, an increase in the number of large trucks or other dangerous vehicles on the road, changes in how law enforcement monitors and enforces speeding or reckless driving—any of these factors might have influenced the number of fatal accidents. Without evidence *directly* linking the speed limit to traffic fatalities, one cannot reasonably infer a causal relationship.

5 Avoid either/or arguments (also called *false dilemma* or the *fallacy of insufficient options*).

This type of faulty reasoning states an argument in terms that imply that one must choose between only two options—right/wrong, good/bad, moral/immoral, and so forth. This is another form of simplistic reasoning that glosses over complex issues and instead attacks the opposition.

> If we allow that factory to come into our town, we are dooming ourselves and our children to a lifetime of breathing filthy air.

Many other options are available between the extremes of no factory and filthy air; one might be to require the factory to install scrubbers to clean its emissions.

The loaded rhetorical question that allows for only one acceptable answer is another form of the either/or argument.

> Are we going to increase the number of police officers in this city, or are we going to abandon it to thugs, gangs, and drug dealers?

When an arguer tries to force a false dilemma on you, your best response is to challenge your opponent's polarized thinking immediately and point out other alternatives to his or her oversimplified view. And be careful to avoid either/or statements in your own writing: at best, they make you look naive; at worst, they make you seem like a fanatic.

6 Avoid red herrings. This tactic involves diverting the audience's attention from the main issue by bringing up an irrelevant point. (The phrase refers to the practice of dragging a strong-smelling smoked herring across a trail to confuse hunting dogs and send them in the wrong direction.) Arguers who fear they have a weak case may employ a red herring by bringing in some emotionally charged but irrelevant point in the hope they can distract their audience and keep them from focusing on the real issue. For example, a mayor might complain:

11d
arg

> While it may be true that my press secretary submitted false expense account vouchers, my administration is just being targeted by a hostile media.

The charges of press bias might be true, but the attitude of the media has no bearing on the official's misbehavior.

7 Avoid slippery slopes. This fallacy occurs when a writer assumes that taking an initial action will automatically set in motion an unstoppable chain of events. Parents of teenagers slip into this fallacy when they make dire predictions based on a single incident.

> "If I allow you to stay out until 2 a.m. this weekend, you'll want to stay out until 3 a.m. next time, and pretty soon you'll be staying out all night every weekend."

This statement offers no real proof that one late night will set off a never-ending sequence of later and later curfews.

You'll encounter slippery slopes most often when writers are promoting or opposing a particular course of action. For instance, a politician who supports funding a new complex to house agencies dealing with homelessness might argue that when homeless people have easy access to services under one roof, they will be able to get the help they need, find jobs, and become productive citizens. Perhaps so, but without explanation and argument to support each link in that chain, these predictions have no real foundation, and you shouldn't readily accept them.

8 Avoid false analogies. These are comparisons that do not hold true or prove misleading. Analogies can be invaluable in helping readers to understand abstract or elusive ideas and concepts—for instance, a writer might clarify how the turbocharger in an automobile works by comparing it to a windmill or a waterwheel. Sometimes, however, in trying to make an argument more attractive to readers, writers create a false analogy in which the comparison drawn simply won't hold up. For example:

> A corporation couldn't operate without the leadership of a CEO to set priorities and make the big decisions. A family operates the same way: one spouse must be the head of the household, or chaos will result.

Certainly a business and a household share superficial similarities, but the two entities have completely different functions, involve different kinds of interpersonal relationships, and operate according to different value systems (profit and efficiency vs. nurturance and loyalty). To assume that what holds true in one environment should hold true in the other is a logical leap that readers won't be willing to take.

As a critical thinker, you'll want to pay attention to the analogies you use and those you encounter. Ask yourself this: Are the similarities between the things being compared strong enough to warrant the conclusions being drawn? If they're not, reject the analogy.

9 Avoid *non sequitur*. Latin for "it does not follow," this fallacy occurs when writers draw on irrelevant evidence or reasons to support a claim. *Non sequitur* is similar to the red herring fallacy, but whereas red herrings are designed to distract a reader from the central argument, *non sequitur* asks readers to accept the irrelevant material as proof. Here are two examples.

> That candidate would be an excellent mayor—after all, he was a successful businessman for years.

> I'm sure that it can't be a top-notch university. It's in a rundown area of the city, surrounded by housing projects and abandoned warehouses.

What does past business success have to do with being mayor? About as much as being in a bad neighborhood has to do with the quality of faculty and curriculum at a university: that is to say, little.

10 Avoid bandwagon appeal. This tactic argues that an activity or a product must be worthwhile because it is popular. Youngsters who try to persuade their parents that they must have a particular brand of sneakers or a new kind of in-line skates because "everybody has them" are using bandwagon tactics. As millions of parents have pointed out, popularity doesn't necessarily guarantee merit.

SUMMARY *Ten Common Fallacies*

1. **Argument to the person** (*ad hominem*): attacking the person instead of focusing on the issues involved.

2. **Circular reasoning:** restating instead of proving a claim.

3. **Hasty generalization:** drawing conclusions from scanty evidence.

4. **False cause:** presuming that if *B* follows *A*, *A* caused *B*.

5. **Either/or:** suggesting that only two choices are possible when in fact there may be several.

6. **Red herring:** bringing in an irrelevant issue to deflect attention from the main point.

7. **Slippery slope:** assuming that one event will set off an unstoppable chain reaction.

8. **False analogy:** making a comparison between things that are too dissimilar for the comparison to be useful.

9. *Non sequitur:* drawing a conclusion from irrelevant data.

10. **Bandwagon:** claiming that widespread popularity makes an object or idea valuable.

EXERCISE 11.4 Work with other students in a group to spot the fallacies in these arguments. In some instances you may find more than one.

1. Two kinds of young women come into corporations at the entry level: those who just want to work for a few years before they start a family and those who take their careers seriously. A company has to be careful not to hire the first kind.

2. Everyone knows that the next decade will be a poor time to go into medicine because government regulation is ruining the profession.

3. The great peasant rebellions in the Middle Ages happened because the rulers taxed the peasants to the limit to pay for foreign wars and neglected conditions in their own country; the United States can expect similar uprisings if it doesn't drastically cut its defense budget and invest in domestic social programs.

4. As a legislator, I can't get too upset about the proposed tuition raise when every time I drive by our state university I get caught in a traffic jam of students in their new four-wheel-drive vehicles and pricey convertibles.

CHAPTER 12

How Do You Write a Literary Analysis?

To write a literary analysis is a common assignment in most English courses, even in composition classes. But requirements and approaches vary from teacher to teacher and course to course. Instructors *do* think about literature in different ways, depending on their background, training, inclinations, and familiarity with literary theory. Critical approaches to literature today can range from close readings of individual texts to wide-ranging confrontations with issues of politics, gender, and culture. So how you write about works of literature or popular culture (movies, plays, music, television) may depend as much on how you are taught as on what you read or view.

What, then, is the point of a literary analysis or project? It can be to heighten your appreciation for literature, to demonstrate your ability to support a thesis about a literary work, to explore what it means to read, to understand how readers respond to texts, to enhance your skill at interpretation, to expand your knowledge of a particular era or literary movement, or to heighten your sensitivity to other cultures, races, and peoples. It can also be a creative activity—a way to go public with your writing.

In these few pages we can't give you advice for dealing with all these possibilities. What we can offer is a little practical advice for finding a subject and working with literary or cultural materials. Whatever your teachers' predilections, we hope that reading literature makes you wiser and gives you pleasure. Those two aims of literature have stood the test of time.

12a What approaches can you take to literary analysis?

There are dozens of ways to read, think about, and respond to literary works. When you write an analytical paper or create a literary project (a Web site, a literary magazine), you will usually make your point by using one or two of these approaches.

- **Read and analyze a text closely.** When doing a "close reading" of a poem, a play, a novel, or a longer work, you carefully explain the meaning and possible interpretations of a selected passage, sometimes line by line. In a close reading, you ordinarily consider how the language of a work (including its sounds, rhythms, and patterns) makes readers entertain specific ideas and images. If a work includes visual images, you may examine how they interact with elements of a written text. (See Section 9b on how to read critically.)

12a
lit

- **Analyze the theme(s) in a work.** Reading a work carefully, you might discover certain key themes (some common themes are *anger, jealousy, ambition, hypocrisy*). In examining a theme, you might show how the various parts of a work convey their meanings to readers.

- **Analyze plot or structure.** You may study the way a work of literature is put together and consider why a writer/creator chooses a particular arrangement of ideas or plot elements. With visual works (including films), structure is just as important and can be discussed in great detail.

- **Analyze character and setting.** You may study the behavior of characters in a novel, poem, play, or short story to understand their motivations and the ways different characters relate to each other. Or you can explore how a writer creates characters through description, action, reaction, and dialogue and embodies them with specific themes and ideas. See the student paper excerpted on page 179 for an example of a character analysis.

  Similarly, you might study an artist's creation of a setting to figure out how the environment of a work (where things happen in a novel, short story, or play) affects what happens in the plot or to the characters. Settings can also be analyzed as the exterior representations of characters' inner being or as manifestations of cultural values.

- **Analyze literary archetypes.** Certain recurring themes, plots, characters, and settings—such as (in Western society) the quest, the sacrificial lamb, the harrowing of hell—can be said to represent the myths or *archetypes* of a culture. You can explore literary texts to reveal the cultural patterns they embody and the archetypes they incorporate, modify, or even parody.

- **Analyze literary types or genres.** You can study a particular work by evaluating its form—tragedy, comic novel, sonnet, detective story, epic, situation comedy, film noir, and so on. You compare the work to other literary pieces of that genre, looking for similarities and differences and perhaps comparing the relative quality of the achievement.

- **Perform a historical or cultural analysis.** You can study a literary work as it reflects the society that produced it or as it was accepted or rejected by that society when it was published. Or you can study the way historical information makes a literary work from an earlier time clearer to a reader today.

You can similarly explore how a work of art embodies the culture that produced it, that is, the assumptions about the beliefs and values of a society that can be found in the literary work. Such analysis may reveal how certain groups gained or maintained power through the manipulation of literary myths or symbols.

- **Analyze a work from the perspective of gender.** You might examine how a literary work portrays women or men and defines their roles in society. Feminist analyses in particular have greatly influenced the reading of literary works in the last generation, though such interpretations vary as much as any other form of criticism. Many feminist critics explore the way literary works embody relationships of power between men and women. Sally Shelton's paper, which appears at the end of this chapter, is an example of this kind of analysis.

- **Study the biography of an author or the creative process.** You might examine how a writer's life is expressed in or through a literary work. Such analyses may be related to cultural and political studies, but they may also focus on the individual psychology of a writer. Similarly, you might learn all you can about the way a particular work was created. You might examine the sources, notes, influences, manuscripts, and revised texts behind a finished book, poem, or film: Or you might compare different versions of the same work.

- **Edit a text or produce a literary Web site.** One type of literary work surprisingly common in college settings is the production of literary journals or, more recently, Web sites that focus on cultural ideas and themes. Introducing new works is an important creative responsibility that requires the careful selection and editing of texts—an important way of going public with writing. Whether in print or on the Web, you can present and comment on new works or edit older, neglected texts in the public domain. (For an example of poems edited by undergraduate students, see *Women of the Romantic Period* at <http://www.cwrl.utexas.edu/~worp/index.html>.)

Going Public   *Two Approaches to Literary Analysis* _____

The following selections demonstrate two approaches to literary analysis. Both paragraphs are from papers by students at the University of South Carolina.

The first is from an essay by Joshua Michael French, "Bartleby: The Lost Follower," that offers a close reading of the central character in Herman Melville's short story "Bartleby the Scrivener." In the essay, French has already argued that Bartleby's problems stem from the psychological process of denial. Now he uses evidence (highlighted) from the short story to explore another psychological weakness in Bartleby's character.

12a
lit

> By denying his responsibilities and avoiding
> conflict with the narrator of the story, Bartleby
> displays a second psychological flaw: isolation. . . .
> The narrator calls the scrivener into his office to ask
> him a few simple questions and even offers Bartleby
> his friendship, but there is no emotional response.
> Instead, Bartleby stares blankly and refuses the
> narrator's advances as usual. The narrator notes that
> Bartleby "[keeps] his glance fixed upon [his] bust of
> Cicero" (122) instead of looking directly at him.
> Even when the narrator comments, "I feel friendly
> towards you" (122) there is no response from
> Bartleby. Strangely enough, however, Bartleby does
> show a need for the narrator's presence, meaning that
> he desires companionship even if he does not react to
> it. For instance, Bartleby "refuses to do any
> copying" (130) for anyone in the office but the
> narrator.

Kathryn R. Samra takes a more historical approach to a poem by Langston Hughes, a major artist of the Harlem Renaissance, in her paper "Theme for Langston Hughes." Samra draws on information about Hughes's life to interpret "Theme for English B," a poem about the only black person in a literature class. Throughout the paper she places Hughes within his cultural setting and uses the remarks of critics to position him as a major literary figure. This is Samra's opening paragraph.

> Known for his ability to mix popular culture and
> radical politics with poetry and a few jazzy beats,
> Langston Hughes became a prominent figure of the
> Harlem Renaissance (Sundquist 56). Born in 1902,
> Hughes lived during a time when African Americans
> were finally able to express the types of music and
> literature that were a part of their cultural
> history. And when he died at the age of 65, it was at
> the pinnacle of the Civil Rights Movement, when
> African Americans were beginning to be treated as
> equals. Most of Hughes's poetry reflected this point
> in his life. His poem "Theme for English B," for
> instance, mirrors the way he felt about his place in
> society. Although not written as a protest poem, it
> demonstrates how he felt as a black person growing up
> in Harlem.

12b What sources can you use in producing literary analyses?

The resources available to you as you begin a literary analysis can seem overwhelming. But many of them will in fact make your work easier, more authoritative, and more interesting.

■ **1 Understand the primary texts you are reading.** In working with literary and cultural texts, you may first need to establish certain basic facts about them. Are you reading (or viewing) a first edition of a work or a revised version, an edited version, a translation, or, in the case of a film, a later "director's cut" that differs from the version shown in theaters? Each of these considerations may have a bearing on your subsequent analysis. Evaluate any publication information you find in the prefaces or front matter of works of literature to discover when they were written, by whom they were published, how they might have been transmitted to readers, and how they may have changed over the years. In general, the older a work, the more complicated (and fascinating) its publication history might be. But even more recent texts deserve your attention. The techniques of "positioning" that you apply to research materials (see Section 45b-1) can be modified to work with literary and cultural texts before you analyze them.

■ **2 Consult secondary sources on literary subjects.** To locate secondary sources on literary topics, begin with the following indexes and bibliographies available in a library reference room.

> *Essay and General Literature Index*
> *MLA International Bibliography*
> *New Cambridge Bibliography of English Literature*
> *Year's Work in English Studies*

Many other useful reference works and Web sites are available; see the following checklist.

12b
lit

Checklist 12.1

Reference Works for Literary Analyses

PRINTED TEXTS

Altick, Richard D., and John J. Fenstermaker. *The Art of Literary Research.* 4th ed. New York: Norton, 1993.

Beacham, Walton, ed. *Research Guide to Biography and Criticism.* Washington, DC: Research, 1990.

Bloom, Harold. *American Women Fiction Writers, 1900–1960.* 3 vols. Philadelphia: Chelsea, 1997–.

Crystal, David. *The Cambridge Encyclopedia of Language.* 2nd ed. New York: Cambridge UP, 1997.

Drabble, Margaret, ed. *The Oxford Companion to English Literature.* Rev. ed. 2nd rev. Oxford: Oxford UP, 1998.

Encyclopedia of World Literature in the 20th Century. 3rd ed. Farmington Hills, MI: St. James, 1999.

Evans, Gareth L., and Barbara Evans. *The Shakespeare Companion.* New York: Scribner's, 1978.

Gates, Henry Louis, Jr., et al. *The Norton Anthology of African American Literature.* New York: Norton, 1997.

Gibaldi, Joseph. *MLA Handbook for Writers of Research Papers.* 5th ed. New York: MLA, 1999.

Gilbert, Sandra M., and Susan Gubar, *The Norton Anthology of Literature by Women: The Traditions in English.* 2nd ed. New York: Norton, 1996.

(Continued)

12c
lit

Reference Works for Literary Analyses *(Continued)*

Harner, James L. *Literary Research Guide: A Guide to Reference Sources for the Study of Literature in English and Related Topics.* 3rd ed. New York: MLA, 1998.

Hart, James D., ed. *The Oxford Companion to American Literature.* 6th ed. New York: Oxford UP, 1995.

Harmon, William, and C. Hugh Holman. *A Handbook to Literature.* 8th ed. New York: Prentice, 1999.

Howatson, M. C. *The Oxford Companion to Classical Literature.* 2nd ed. New York: Oxford UP, 1989.

Inge, M. Thomas, et al. *Black American Writers: Bibliographical Essays.* New York: St. Martin's, 1978.

Marcuse, Michael J. *A Reference Guide for English Studies.* Berkeley: U of California P, 1990.

Ousby, Ian. *The Cambridge Guide to Literature in English.* 2nd ed. New York: Cambridge UP, 1993.

Sage, Lorna. *The Cambridge Guide to Women's Writing in English.* Cambridge: Cambridge UP, 1999.

Sampson, George. *The Concise Cambridge History of English Literature.* 3rd ed. Cambridge: Cambridge UP, 1972.

WEB RESOURCES

The Complete Works of William Shakespeare. <http://the-tech.mit.edu/Shakespeare/>.

The English Server. <http://eserver.org/>.

Literary Resources on the Net. <http://andromeda.rutgers.edu/~jlynch/Lit/>.

MLA Online. <http://www.mla.org/>.

The On-Line Books Page. <http://digital.library.upenn.edu/books/>.

University of Virginia Library Electronic Text Center. <http://etext.lib.virginia.edu/>.

Voice of the Shuttle. <http://vos.ucsb.edu/index.asp/>.

Web Resources of Interest to Literary Scholars. The University of Texas at Austin. <http://www.lib.utexas.edu/subject/english/sites.html>.

Yahoo! Arts: Humanities: Literature. <http://www.yahoo.com/Arts/Humanities/Literature/>.

12c How do you develop a literary project?

How you develop a literary paper or project will depend on your course assignment and your own purpose. In some courses you'll be asked to do a close reading of an individual poem, novel, or short story;

in others you may be expected to contribute to a Web site that places artists or works in their historical or political contexts. Here we assume that you are most likely to write a paper with a thesis—but the principles we discuss will apply to other projects as well. For example, if you are participating in a Web forum or editing a literary journal, you still need to read carefully, formulate clear ideas about your subjects, report information accurately, and design a project that will be interesting and enlightening to others.

12c
lit

■ **1 Begin by reading carefully.** The evidence you'll need to write a thoughtful, well-organized analysis may come from within the literary work itself and from outside readings and secondary sources. Your initial goal is to find a point worth making, an assertion you can prove with convincing evidence.

To find your point, begin by *positioning* the work (or works) and then reading and *annotating* them carefully (see Sections 9a and 45b-2).

If you were assigned to read Shakespeare's *Macbeth,* you might position the work by doing a little background reading (see Section 12b). You'd quickly learn that *Macbeth* is a tragedy written by the most famous of English playwrights around 1605–06, though not published until 1623. An unusually brief tragedy, *Macbeth* may have been designed expressly to please the English monarch James I, who was fascinated by witches and whose legendary ancestor appears in the work.

You can position works in many ways to enhance your initial understanding. Yet you should also read with an open mind, being certain to savor the literary experience. Do, however, annotate texts in some way to record your immediate responses. You might simply ask yourself a series of questions.

- What issues engage me immediately as I read the work?
- What questions does the work raise that I'd like to explore?
- What puzzles or surprises me?
- What characters or literary devices seem most striking or original?
- What upsets me or seems most contrary to my own values and traditions?

Make a list of such queries as you read, and reexamine them when you have finished. While experiencing Shakespeare's *Macbeth,* you might produce annotations such as these.

- Is ambition the cause of Macbeth's defeat?
- What is the nature of the relationship between Lady Macbeth and her husband? How is Lady Macbeth inhibited by her gender?
- How old are the Macbeths? Does their age affect their actions?

- Is the story of Macbeth historically true?
- Why do some lines in this tragedy seem awkward or even funny?
- Can Macbeth blame the witches for his tragedy?
- What exactly makes this play a tragedy? What *is* a tragedy?

To stimulate more questions, you may want to compare and contrast the work(s) you have read with other similar works.

- Is Macbeth as ambitious as King Claudius in *Hamlet?*
- Is Lady Macbeth a more influential character in *Macbeth* than Queen Gertrude is in *Hamlet?*
- Why does Shakespeare use so much comedy in his tragedies, including *Hamlet, Romeo and Juliet,* and *Macbeth?*

At this point you might stimulate your thinking both by considering specific ways of approaching a literary text (see Section 12a) and by using one of the techniques we describe for finding and focusing ideas, particularly brainstorming and idea mapping (see Sections 2a and 2b).

2 Develop a thesis about the literary work(s) you are studying. You might begin with questions you are eager to explore in depth, a research query or hypothesis generated perhaps by your reading of secondary sources or by your discussions with classmates and other readers. A paper on *Macbeth* might lead to research questions such as the following.

- Are some scenes missing from *Macbeth?*
- What limits on the power of women in Elizabethan England might explain the behavior of Lady Macbeth?
- Did the term *equivocation* have particular political significance to the original audience of *Macbeth?*
- Did Shakespeare tailor *Macbeth* to please England's Scottish monarch, King James?

When you've put your question into words, test its energy. Is the answer to your inquiry so obvious that it isn't likely to interest or surprise anyone?

- Is Shakespeare's *Macbeth* a great play?

If so, discard the issue. Try another. Look for a surprising, even startling question—one whose answer you don't necessarily know. Test that question on classmates or your instructor. Would they want to read a paper or examine a Web page that explores the issue you are considering?

- Could Shakespeare's *Macbeth* actually be a comedy?
- What role do the lower classes play in a dynastic struggle like the one depicted in *Macbeth?*
- Are the witches really the physical embodiment of Macbeth's own mind?

When you have found your question, turn it into an assertion—your preliminary thesis statement.

12c
lit

- Shakespeare's *Macbeth* is really a comedy.
- The welfare of the lower classes seems to have been ignored in dynastic struggles like those depicted in *Macbeth.*
- The witches in Macbeth are a physical representation of the state of Macbeth's mind.

Is this an assertion you are interested in proving? Is it a statement other readers might challenge? If so, write it down and continue. If not, modify it or explore another issue.

3 Read the work(s) again with your thesis firmly in mind. Read even more slowly and critically this time. Look for characters, incidents, descriptions, speeches, dialogue, or images that support or refute your thesis. Take careful notes. If you are using your own text, highlight significant passages in the work.

When you are done, evaluate the evidence you have gathered from a close reading. Then modify or qualify your thesis to reflect what you have learned or discovered. In most cases, your thesis will be more specific and more limited after you have gathered and assessed your evidence.

- The many unexpected comic moments in *Macbeth* emphasize how disordered the world becomes for murderers like Macbeth and his wife.

If necessary, return to secondary sources or other literary works to supplement and extend your analysis. (For many papers, much of your reading will be in secondary sources and journals of literary criticism.) Play with ideas, relationships, implications, and possibilities. Don't hesitate to question conventional views of a work or to bring your own experiences to bear on the act of reading and interpreting literature.

Begin drafting your paper, drawing together your specific observations into full paragraphs. The following are two draft paragraphs analyzing lines from *Macbeth* that some readers find comic. Notice in particular how lines from the play are woven neatly into the analysis as specific evidence.

The first such comic lines come early in <u>Macbeth</u>
and might even pass unnoticed if actors play them
with straight faces. Yet one has to laugh when Lady
Macbeth boasts after drugging the grooms who guard
Duncan's bedchamber: "That which hath made them
drunk hath made me bold" (<u>Mac.</u> 2.2.1). Then, just
the way a drunken person would, she apologizes
gruesomely for not killing Duncan herself, almost
surprised by her reluctance to murder: "Had he [King
Duncan] not resembled / My father as he slept, I had
done't" (12-13).

Macbeth has the next comic line, this one his
reaction to Lennox's description of a horrible storm
that shakes Scotland while Macbeth is murdering
Duncan. Deadpans Macbeth: "'Twas a rough night"
(2.3.61). The audience laughs uneasily, knowing much
better than Lennox how rough the night really has
been for the new Thane of Cawdor. Then, when a
horrified Macduff discovers that Duncan has been
murdered, Lady Macbeth screams, "Woe, alas! / What,
in our house?" (2.3.87-88). Any audience that hears
those lines wants to laugh at Lady Macbeth's self-
centeredness. Even Banquo seems to notice her
callousness when he replies, "Too cruel any
where" (88).

If you consult secondary sources while writing the paper, take
careful notes from the books and articles you read. Be sure also to prepare accurate bibliography cards for your Works Cited page. (See
Chapter 43 on planning a research project.)

■ **4 Use scratch outlines to guide the first draft.** Try out
several organization plans for the paper (see Section 3b), then choose
the one you find most solid or most challenging. Working on a Web
project, you might similarly sketch out the overall site as well as individual pages (see Section 20g). Here's how a scratch outline for a paper
on comic elements in *Macbeth* might look.

```
Thesis: Comic moments in Macbeth emphasize how
disordered the world becomes for the Macbeths after
they murder the king.

I. Comic moments after the murder of King Duncan

II. Comedy at the feast for Banquo

III. Comedy in the sleepwalking scene

IV. Conclusion
```

12c
lit

When you have a structure, write a complete first draft. Stay open to new ideas and refinements of your original thesis, but try not to wander off into a biography of the author or a discussion of the historical period unless such material relates directly to your thesis. If you do wander, consider whether the digression in your draft might be the topic you *really* want to write about.

Avoid the draft that simply paraphrases the plot of a literary work. Equally ineffective is a paper that merely praises its author for a job well done. Avoid extremely impressionistic judgments: "I feel that Hemingway must have been a good American." And don't expect to find a moral in every literary work, or turn your analysis into a search for "hidden meanings." Respond honestly to what you are reading—not the way you think your teacher expects you to. (For a full example of a literary paper, see the paper demonstrating Chicago documentation style in Section 50d.)

5 Follow the conventions of literary analysis. One of those conventions is to introduce most direct quotations. Don't just insert a quotation from a literary work or a critic into your paper without identifying it and explaining its significance. And be sure quotations fit into the grammar of your sentences.

> **When an audience hears Macbeth call his cowering servant a** "cream-fac'd loon," it begins to understand why Macbeth's men hate and distrust him.

> **The doctor in *Macbeth* warns the gentlewoman,** "You have known what you should not" (5.1.46-47).

> **Commenting on the play, Frank Kermode observes that** "*Macbeth* has extraordinary energy; it represents a fierce engagement between the mind and its guilt" (1311).

In shaping the paper, you may want to follow the conventions of the MLA research paper or the *Chicago Manual of Style* paper (see Chapters 48 and 50).

Checklist 12.2

Conventions in a Literary Paper

• Use the present tense to refer to events occurring in a literary work: Hester Prynne *wears* a scarlet letter, Hamlet *kills* Polonius. Think of a literary work as an ongoing performance.

• Identify passages of short poems by line numbers: ("Journey of the Magi," lines 21–31). Avoid the abbreviations *l.* or *ll.* for *line* or *lines* because they are sometimes confused with Roman numerals; spell out *line* or *lines*. See Section 40c for advice on punctuating lines of poetry that appear within a paper.

• Provide act and scene divisions (and line numbers as necessary) for passages from plays. Act and scene numbers are now usually given in Arabic numbers, although Roman numbers are still common and acceptable: *Ham.* 4.5.179–85 or *Ham.* IV.v.179–86. The titles of Shakespeare's works are commonly abbreviated in citations: *Mac.* 1.2; *Oth.* 2.2. Check to see which form your instructor prefers.

• Provide a date of publication in parentheses after your first mention of a literary work: Before publishing *Beloved* (1987), Toni Morrison had written. . . .

• Use technical terms accurately. Spell the names of characters correctly. Take special care with matters of grammar and mechanics.

Going Public *A Literary Analysis Paper* _____

In the following literary analysis, "Queen Jane Approximately" (a clever allusion to a song by Bob Dylan), Sally Shelton from the University of South Carolina does a close reading of a poem by Sharon Olds, "The One Girl at the Boy's Party." She approaches the work from a feminist perspective, examining the interplay of gender roles between one young girl and a group of boys. Shelton supports her analysis by carefully citing passages from the poem, which we have reprinted in its entirety. The paper was written for a course taught by Anna Moore. We have edited the paper for concision.

The One Girl at the Boy's Party

By Sharon Olds

When I take my girl to the swimming party	1
I set her down among the boys. They tower and	2
bristle, she stands there smooth and sleek,	3

her math scores unfolding in the air around her.   4
They will strip to their suits, her body hard and   5
indivisible as a prime number,   6
they'll plunge in the deep end, she'll subtract   7
her height from ten feet, divide it into   8
hundreds of gallons of water, the numbers   9
bouncing in her mind like molecules of chlorine   10
in the bright blue pool. When they climb out,   11
her ponytail will hang its pencil lead   12
down her back, her narrow silk suit   13
with hamburgers and french fries printed on it   14
will glisten in the brilliant air, and they will   15
see her sweet face, solemn and   16
sealed, a factor of one, and she will   17
see their eyes, two each,   18
their legs, two each, and the curves of their sexes,   19
one each, and in her head she'll be doing her   20
wild multiplying, as the drops   21
sparkle and fall to the power of a thousand from her body.   22

12c
lit

Sally Shelton

Ms. Anna Moore

April 21, 2000

Queen Jane Approximately

Sharon Olds' "The One Girl at the Boys' Party"
examines the tense competition between the sexes. The
poem illustrates the innate vulnerability of men
while portraying females as winning the attention and
respect they rightfully deserve. Olds achieves these
insights by examining the isolation of a young girl
at a party of boys. She infuses the situation with
ironies, symbols, and repeated images that probe
themes of gender, sexuality, and domination.

The poem deceives the reader initially by
putting the youths in typical gender roles. The
speaker takes her daughter (1) to a party where she
"set[s] her down among the boys" (2) like a toy or
doll for their amusement. She is placed within a

situation where she must prove herself. The boys, in
turn, "tower and / bristle" (2-3) at the intrusion of
this showcase item. While she is being "set down,"
these boys move like a gang, intimidating and,
perhaps, angry. Yet suddenly, the attention of the
poem shifts from the girl to the boys as the young
woman quickly and nonchalantly asserts her dominance
over the unwitting youths.

    The schism between the girl and the group of
boys begins early in the poem. While the boys "tower
and bristle," the lone girl "stands there smooth and
sleek" (3), firmly placed, establishing her ground,
unabated in her delicate sensuality, and controlling
the air about her. It is in this "brilliant air" (15)
that her "math scores" (4) begin to unfold.
References to mathematics throughout the poem
illustrate how this ingenue, and perhaps the speaker
of the poem, have conquered society already. They
have figured the boys out through methodical and
meticulous calculations.

    To complete the reversal of gender roles, the
boys, who were the first to dominate in the poem,
assume a subordinate and effeminate role. As if to
expose themselves as sensual and enticing beings,
"[t]hey will strip to their suits" (5), leaving
themselves vulnerable (she can count the "curves of
their sexes" (19)) and hoping that the girl will
"strip" to her vulnerability as well. The girl,
however, remains in control, "her body hard and /
indivisible as a prime number" (5-6). The pool of
males will forever attempt to figure her, but she has
solved them. She stands before the boys in the pool,
with "the numbers / bouncing in her mind" (9-10), her
calculations racing. She, who was initially perceived

as an outcast, a toy to be discarded, has now silently attracted the desire and curiosity of the boys.

Now that the girl's presence has consumed the scene, the boys become enchanted by her sensuality. The infinite "molecules of chlorine" (10) that comprise the girl's ricocheting intelligence intoxicate the lads, who have by now succumbed to the innocent appeal of "the bright blue pool" (11). Sexual desires come into play: her tomboyish ponytail catches their gaze. Although it "hang[s] its pencil lead" (12), a phallic symbol with piercing connotations, the boys still allow their gaze to follow the ponytail "down her back" (13). Then they notice the girl's figure, more "smooth and sleek" (3) than before, in "her narrow silk suit" (13) with the mouth-watering "hamburgers and french fries" (14) that "glisten in the brilliant air" (15). Lastly, they notice her face, "sweet," "solemn," and "sealed" (16-17). No longer an object to discard, the girl becomes for the boys an embodiment of a desire that will never be satiated.

Again, the speaker widens the schism between the girl and the youths. It began with the girl doing all the observing and calculating, but soon the boys catch on. Threatened by her magnitude and ability to strip them, they "plunge the deep end" (7), hoping to hide their vulnerability while attempting to entice the girl. The act of plunging is risky and the boys nearly drown in their attempts to impress her. Defeated and weakened, they have to "climb out" (11), still fragile and susceptible, and, moreover, they discover how badly they are getting beaten. Then they enter the game, the observed becoming the observers.

12c
lit

While the boys "see her sweet face . . . a factor of
one" (16-17), the girl outnumbers them when she
"see[s] their eyes, two each, / their legs, two each,
and the curves of their sexes, / one each" (18-20).
She sheds some power when she lets her "drops /
sparkle and fall" (21-22), but they will never gain a
hold on her because she will forever be "doing her
wild multiplying" (20-21). The boys cannot enumerate
her "to the power of a thousand" (22) so her "power"
controls them and overwhelms them. She has reduced
these once towering and bristling boys to vulnerable,
starstruck, and curvy subordinates by daring them to
plunge into the deep end of womanhood.

Through the girl, the speaker offers insight
into how women encompass an infinite magnitude, power,
and elegance that men miscalculate and misunderstand.
The girl triumphs while the boys sink into her deep
intelligence, stamina, and sensuality. In the game of
relationships, here staged as a pool party, there are
those who tower, those who plunge, and those who
calculate.

PART

III

Style

13 What Makes Paragraphs Work?

14 How Do You Manage Opening and Closing Paragraphs?

15 How Do You Manage Transitions?

16 What Kinds of Language Can You Use?

17 How Do You Construct Effective Sentences?

18 How Do You Write Stylish Sentences?

CHAPTER 13

What Makes Paragraphs Work?

Paragraphs aren't natural units of writing in the way that sentences are. People don't think in paragraphs, even though researchers believe that we do think in sentences. But paragraphs exist for an important reason: they help readers. If you want readers to stick with your writing, you need to master the art of paragraphing.

Imagine how you'd feel if you opened a newspaper and saw pages filled with a single, unbroken stretch of print. You'd probably think, "I'll never be able to keep this straight in my head"—and you'd be right. Readers need to process information in chunks. When writers organize material into paragraph form, treating a single idea in each paragraph and connecting the paragraphs to each other, readers can follow the material more easily. Paragraphing also makes a text look visually inviting, drawing readers in and encouraging them to read on.

An effective paragraph has four characteristics:

- It is **unified**, focused on one point.
- It is **clearly organized**, following a coherent pattern.
- It is **polished**, conveying ideas in concise and readable language.
- It is of an **appropriate length** for the writing situation.

This chapter suggests ways to achieve all four goals.

13a How do you construct unified paragraphs?

When we say that a paragraph is *unified*, we mean that it is tightly focused: it makes a single point and develops it, without detours into irrelevant or tangential information.

■ **1 Find a focus and stick with it.** In a unified paragraph, you can follow the author's thinking because he or she concentrates on a single idea. Here's a professional example:

Prairie dogs have long been viewed, particularly by urban dwellers, as the epitome of cute. The scene here a few days ago was typical. When the animals emerged from their dens, some touched teeth in "kisses" of recognition. They romped, rolled, wrestled, and chased each other around. They assiduously tended their burrows, dirt flying from their busy paws, bundles of grass for lining underground nests drooping from their mouths.

> —William K. Stevens, "Prairie Dog Colonies
> Bolster Life in the Plains"

Suppose, however, that this writer had written his first sentence and then gone off in another direction, jotting down sentences as they occurred to him. The paragraph might have turned out like this:

13a
¶

Prairie dogs have long been viewed, particularly by urban dwellers, as the epitome of cute. Tourists often think of other wild animals as cute too. It seems to be an American habit to attribute human characteristics to animals. People make themselves look silly when they do this, and they sometimes put themselves in danger. One has to wonder if animals look at us humans and think we're like animals.

Now the paragraph rambles and sprawls. It lacks unity because the writer opens with a statement and then, instead of expanding on it or following through with connected examples, jumps into a completely new subject.

When you begin a paragraph, first ask yourself, "What point am I trying to make?" and then check your draft periodically to be sure you haven't strayed from your purpose.

2 Anchor your paragraph with a topic sentence. One way to keep a paragraph focused is to use a **topic sentence** that states your main idea clearly and directly. The topic sentence doesn't have to be the first one in the paragraph, although it often is, particularly in academic writing. Wherever it is located, a topic sentence acts like a magnet around which related sentences cluster. Here is a paragraph from a professional writer; the topic sentence is boldfaced.

Sleep has become another casualty of modern life. According to sleep researchers, studies point to a "sleep deficit" among Americans, a majority of whom are currently getting between 60 and 90 minutes less a night than they should for optimum health and performance. The number of people showing up at sleep disorder clinics with serious problems has skyrocketed in the last decade. Shift work, long working hours, the growth of a global economy (with its attendant continent-hopping and twenty-four-hour business culture), and the accelerating pace of life have all contributed to sleep deprivation. If you need an alarm clock, the experts warn, you're probably sleeping too little.

—Juliet Schor, *The Overworked American*

Schor leads into her topic with the opening sentence, going on to develop it with supporting research and evidence.

A writer can also lead up to a topic sentence, first giving readers details that build their interest and then summarizing the content in one sentence. Here is another example from a professional writer; the topic sentence is boldfaced.

13a

¶

Felix is in his 20s and gangly. Heinrich is in his 40s, a solid block of a man who has survived three avalanches. He is one of a team of scientists at the University of Bern. With the big drills that he designed and built in the university machine shop, the Bern team brings up cylindrical cores of ice from hundreds of feet below the surface of Swiss glaciers, and from many thousands of feet down in the Antarctic and Greenland ice sheets. The ice holds an abundance of bubbles the size of seltzer fizz. **The bubbles hold a wealth of stories on themes that encompass the planet: the death of the fabled island of Atlantis; the history of the greenhouse effect; the cause of ice ages; scenarios of the Earth's climate in the next hundred years.**

—Jonathan Weiner, "Glacier Bubbles"

Not all paragraphs have topic sentences, nor do they need them, since writers can unify paragraphs in a number of ways. But you may find them useful when you're searching for a way to start a paragraph. Think about a main point you want to make in a paper and construct a statement that expresses it. For example:

If one were looking for an example of a powerful and autonomous woman from an earlier age, no one could fill the role better than Eleanor of Aquitaine, the twelfth-century queen of both France and England.

Part of the phenomenal growth of the Internet undoubtedly comes from its appeal to a streak in the American personality that loves to circumvent authority.

Both of these topic sentences make assertions that must be elaborated and supported. As writers, we all know that once we've written such a sentence, we can't just go off and leave it. We've committed ourselves to following through.

Topic sentences work especially well to anchor and control the flow of ideas in academic writing—analyses, reports, arguments, and so forth. They help keep your writing organized and on track. By reading from one topic sentence to the next in the paragraphs that make up your paper, you can usually tell if you're developing your thesis as you have planned. For more on organizing a draft around a thesis, see Section 3b.

■ 3 Use internal transitions to unify your paragraphs.

Even when you have a clear focus, the connections among sentences or ideas in a paragraph may not always be immediately apparent to readers. In such cases, you'll need to incorporate *internal transitions*—words and phrases that act like traffic signals to move readers from one point in an argument or explanation to another.

Consider this paragraph from a student draft. It is focused on a single issue—the rise of cheating on campus—but the first version seems choppy and disconnected because it lacks internal transitions. Notice how much clearer and more readable the revised version is.

WEAK TRANSITIONS

Cheating has become frighteningly common. My roommate brought her mother to campus to complain when she failed her Spanish course for copying her term paper from a Web site. My English professor reported two students in my English literature course to the dean for allowing a high school teacher to write a paper for them. The Academic Affairs office reported last week that academic misconduct is up by 30 percent over last year. What is happening on our campus? Parents and teachers once instilled in students the value of doing one's own work instead of cheating.

INTERNAL TRANSITIONS ADDED

Cheating is becoming frighteningly common **on our campus.** **Last week** my roommate brought her mother to campus to complain when she failed Spanish for copying her term paper from a Web site. **Earlier this semester,** my English literature professor reported two students to the dean for allowing a high school teacher to write a paper for them. **Unfortunately, these cases are not unusual, campus officials say.** The Academic Affairs office reported last week that academic dishonesty cases are up by 30 percent over last year. What is happening on our campus? Parents and teachers **used to** instill in students the value of doing their own work; **now** many are encouraging them to **cheat.**

13a
¶

To incorporate internal transitions into a paragraph you've written, try these strategies:

- **Use transition words** such as *first, next, however,* and *in addition* to show the relationships among sentences and ideas. Section 15b-1 lists many of these words and explains when you can use each.
- **Repeat key words or phrases** to tie related sentences together. The paragraph above that gives several examples of a rise in cheating on campus, for example, repeats terms like *dishonesty* and *cheating,* to connect the examples. See Section 15b-2 for more on using repetition.
- **Use parallel phrases**—phrases that begin with the same word or that share the same grammatical structure—to emphasize connections among similar examples or related pieces of information. If you were writing a paragraph that summarized three arguments against capital punishment, you could connect them by beginning each with the phrase "Opponents believe that . . ." For more on using parallel structure to unify a paragraph, see Section 15b-5.

13a
¶

See Chapter 15 for a detailed discussion of transitions and for advice on using them within and between paragraphs.

EXERCISE 13.1 Working with a group of classmates, identify the strategies the writer has used to unify the following paragraph: Is there a topic sentence? Do you see transition words? repetition? parallel structure? Then discuss whether and how these devices helped you follow the writer's ideas.

> These things are known about Houdini. The same tireless ingenuity, when applied to locks and jails, packing cases and riveted boilers; the same athletic prowess, when applied at the bottom of the East River or while dangling from a rope attached to the cornice of the *Sun* building in Baltimore—these talents account for the vast majority of Houdini's exploits. As we have mentioned, theater historians, notably Raymund Fitzsimons in his *Death and the Magician,* have carefully exposed Houdini's ingenuity, knowing that nothing can tarnish the miracle of the man's existence. Their accounts are technical and we need not dwell on them, except to say they mostly support Houdini's oath that his effects were achieved by natural, or mechanical, means. The Houdini problem arises from certain outrageous effects no one has ever been able to explain, though capable technicians have been trying for more than sixty years.
> —Daniel Mark Epstein, "The Case of Harry Houdini"

EXERCISE 13.2 Examine critically one or two paragraphs of a draft you're currently working on: Do the paragraphs seem adequately unified? What unifying strategies have you used? Can you think of others that might be useful?

13b How can you organize paragraphs?

We don't know how many skilled writers consciously choose specific organizational patterns when they draft their essays or articles. Perhaps during the writing process certain patterns just emerge because they so closely resemble typical ways of thinking. Or perhaps some writers say to themselves, "I think I'll try a comparison-and-contrast pattern here" or "This would be a good place to use cause and effect." Whatever their origins, the paragraph patterns discussed in this section are common, and writers looking for a way to get started on a draft can profit by trying them.

13b
¶

SUMMARY | *Common Paragraph Patterns*

illustration	classification
question and answer	comparison and contrast
narration or process	cause and effect
definition	analogy

1 Illustration. A paragraph of illustration begins with a general statement or claim and develops it with supporting details, evidence, or examples. This paragraph opens an essay by the professional writer Anna Quindlen; she follows a general statement about interaction between boys and girls with vivid descriptive details.

Perhaps we all have the same memory of the first boy-girl party we attended. The floors were waxed, the music loud, the air thick with the smell of cologne. The boys stood on one side of the room and the girls on the other, each affecting a nonchalance belied by the shuffling male loafers and the occasional high bird-like sound of a female giggle.
—Anna Quindlen, "Between the Sexes, a Great Divide"

In an argument paper, writers often follow a general claim with one or more pieces of supporting evidence.

The popularity of McDonald's holds true across the world except, ironically, in the United States, where sales have slumped. McDonald's now makes 59 percent of its profit outside the United States, [company spokesperson Brad] Trask said. In Moscow, where the world's busiest McDonald's opened in 1990, lines still spill out the door.

—Lini Kadaba, "No Beef"

2 Question and answer. Asking and answering a question is another way to organize a paragraph. Here's an example from the well-known science writer Carl Sagan.

13b
¶

What do we actually see when we look up at the Moon with the naked eye? We make out a configuration of irregular bright and dark markings—not a close representation of any familiar object. But almost irresistibly, our eyes connect the markings, emphasizing some, ignoring others. We seek a pattern, and we find one. In world myth and folklore, many images are seen: a woman weaving, stands of laurel trees, an elephant jumping off a cliff, a girl with a basket on her back, a rabbit, . . . a woman pounding tapa cloth, a four-eyed jaguar. People of one culture have trouble understanding how such bizarre things could be seen by the people of another.

—Carl Sagan, *The Demon-Haunted World*

When you're having real trouble finding an opening sentence, beginning with a question will often get your paragraph started.

3 Narration or process. One popular and simple way to develop a paragraph is to relate events or the steps of a process in chronological order. This pattern is obviously appropriate for writing personal or historical accounts, but you can also use it effectively to describe a scientific or technical process. Here is a narrative written by a naturalist studying wolves.

Quite by accident I had pitched my tent within ten yards of one of the major paths used by the wolves when they were going to, or coming from, their hunting grounds to the westward; and only a few hours after I had taken up residence one of the wolves came back from a trip and discovered me and my tent. He was at the end of a hard night's work and was clearly tired and anxious to go home to bed. He came over a small rise fifty yards from me with his head down, his eyes half-closed, and a preoccupied air about him. Far from being the preternaturally alert and suspicious beast of fiction, this wolf was so self-engrossed that he came straight on to within fifteen yards of me, and might have gone right past the tent without seeing it at all, had I not banged my elbow against the teakettle, making a resounding clank. The wolf's head came up and his eyes opened wide, but he did not stop or falter in his pace. One brief, sidelong glance was all he vouchsafed to me as he continued on his way.

—Farley Mowat, *Never Cry Wolf*

4 Definition. Paragraphs of definition often work well in the first part of a report or article that explains or argues. They help to establish the meaning of important terms the author is going to use. In this example from an essay on linguistic diversity, Gloria Anzaldúa defines one of several dialects she spoke as a child.

13b
¶

From kids and people my own age I picked up *Pachuco.* *Pachuco* (the language of the zoot suiters) is a language of rebellion, both against Standard Spanish and Standard English. It is a secret language. Adults of the culture and outsiders cannot understand it. It is made up of slang words from both English and Spanish. *Ruca* means girl or woman, *vato* means guy or dude, *chale* means no, *simon* means yes, *churro* is sure, talk is *periquar*, *pignionear* means petting, *que gacho* means how nerdy, *ponte aguila* means watch out, death is called *la pelona*. Through lack of practice and not having others who can speak it, I've lost most of the *Pachuco* tongue.

—Gloria Anzaldúa, "How to Tame a Wild Tongue"

5 Classification. A classification paragraph that divides a subject into the categories to be discussed can work well as the opening paragraph of an essay or a section of the essay. Used this way, it helps to unify the essay by forecasting its organization. Here's the opening paragraph of an essay by a well-known conservationist.

There are, as far as I can tell, three kinds of conservation currently operating. The first is the preservation of places that are grandly wild or "scenic" or in some way spectacular. The second is what is called "the conservation of natural resources"—that is, of the things of nature that we intend to use: soil, water, timber, and minerals. The third is what you might call industrial troubleshooting: the attempt to limit or stop or remedy the most flagrant abuses of the industrial system. All three kinds of conservation are inadequate, both separately and together.

—Wendell Berry, *Sex, Economy, Freedom & Community*

■ 6 Comparison and contrast. A paragraph can be built quite naturally on a comparison-and-contrast pattern. Here's an easy-to-follow paragraph that sets up a comparison in the first sentence, discusses each item in alternating sentences, and concludes with a sentence that again compares both objects.

13b
¶

> Counselors and psychologists often point out that much of the conflict between men and women stems from the very different ways in which they use language. Linguistics expert Deborah Tannen supports this theory in her book *You Just Don't Understand.* She says men use language for "report talk" while women use it for "rapport talk." She believes that for women, conversation is a way of establishing connections and negotiating relationships; the emphasis is on finding similarities and matching experience. For men, talk is used to show independence and maintain status; this is done by exhibiting knowledge and skill and holding center stage by verbal performance. Thus men are usually more comfortable doing public speaking and can be taciturn at home while many women talk little in public situations but are articulate in small groups.

■ 7 Cause and effect. Cause-and-effect paragraphs can proceed in two ways: they can mention the effect first and then describe the causes, or they can start by giving causes and close with the effect. We illustrate both patterns here. The first paragraph illustrates cause to effect; the second illustrates effect followed by causes.

CAUSE TO EFFECT

> Problem gambling leads to other socially destructive and costly behavior. According to [Johns Hopkins University researcher Valerie C.] Lorenz, problem gamblers not only tend to have a high number of auto accidents, but they often don't have insurance to cover the costs of damages. This not only results in economic losses and physical problems to themselves, but to others involved in the accidents. "These accidents occur most often on the way home after a long day of gambling at the casino or race track," she says. "Often these accidents are not accidents; instead, they are deliberate suicide attempts." In one study, gamblers were shown to have a suicide rate ten times higher than the rest of the population.

—Robert Goodman, *The Luck Business*

EFFECT FOLLOWED BY CAUSES

One reason for the good teaching in Japan is that the profession attracts excellent people. The respect for teachers in Japan emerges in opinion polls, where teachers are awarded higher prestige than engineers or officials in city hall. Teachers are also paid very well, earning salaries that are generally higher than those of pharmacists or engineers, and so in a typical year there are five applicants for every teaching job.

—Nicholas Kristoff, "Where Children Rule"

8 Analogy. Writers who are explaining a concept they want to elaborate on or make vivid often turn to analogy to communicate better with their readers. An **analogy** is an extended comparison. One especially good use of analogy is to help readers understand a concept by showing a resemblance between the known and the unknown, as the physicist John Wheeler does in this paragraph on black holes. In the preceding paragraph, he asks his readers to imagine that they are flying over a city and see a domed stadium. Then he writes:

13b
¶

The domed-over stadium gives no evidence to the traveler of the crowd within. However, he sees the lines of traffic converging from all directions, becoming more and more tightly packed in traffic jams as they approach the center of attraction. A black hole whirling about, and being whirled about in orbit by, a normal star will also be the recipient of clouds of gas from this companion, with all the puffs and swirls that one can imagine from watching a factory chimney belch its clouds of smoke. This gas will not fall straight in. It will orbit the black hole in ever tighter spirals as it works its way inward, making weather on its way. It, like the traffic approaching the stadium, will be squeezed more and more.

—John Wheeler, "Black Holes and New Physics"

EXERCISE 13.3 Use the paragraph patterns discussed and illustrated in Section 13-b to write paragraphs in two of the following situations.

1. Summarize the arguments on one side of a local controversy you feel strongly about—for example, a new city ordinance, an upcoming school bond election, a controversial public event or program.

2. Explain how to operate a machine you use regularly—for instance, a food processor, a jet ski, a cash register, a computer scanner.

3. Set up a classification of your relatives at a family get-together, the students in your major, or the passengers you encounter every day on a bus or subway.

13c How can you create polished paragraphs?

A paragraph that's merely focused and well organized is like a family station wagon: it gets your readers where they need to go, but the ride may lack pizazz. If you want readers to enjoy and respond strongly to your writing, you'll need to craft paragraphs that are stylish and engaging as well as clear. This section shows you how.

1 Revise for variety. Good paragraphs move readers up and down what the linguist S. I. Hayakawa calls "the abstraction ladder." That is, they offer readers a mix of general statements and vivid, specific details. This sort of variety adds texture to your paragraphs and keeps readers interested. Just as important, it helps communicate your ideas: details help to illustrate abstract concepts that readers might otherwise find difficult, and general statements tie together details that might initially seem unrelated.

One way to be sure your paragraphs are engagingly varied is habitually to use examples to illustrate general statements or ideas. Readers like to see ideas in solid form, as the following example illustrates.

> We live in a society that is convinced of the benefits of taller stature. Conventional wisdom has it that taller, larger people are more powerful, effective, and intelligent. **Men, especially, are often obsessed with height, hoping to reach the magical six-foot mark.**
> —Thomas T. Samaras, "Let's Get Small"

You can also illustrate a general idea by showing something happening, using a colorful scene or anecdote. Here is a writer clarifying a hard-to-grasp, abstract concept by helping us to picture it very specifically:

> The distinction between Newton and Einstein's ideas about gravitation has sometimes been illustrated by picturing **a little boy playing marbles in a city lot. The ground is very uneven, ridged with bumps and hollows. An observer in an office ten stories above the street would not be able to see these irregularities in the ground. Noticing that the marbles appear to avoid some sections of the ground and move toward other sections,** he might assume a "force" is operating which repels the marbles from certain spots and attracts them toward others. But **another observer on the ground would instantly perceive that the path of the marbles is simply governed by the curvature of the field.**
> —Lincoln Barnett, *The Universe and Dr. Einstein*

You may notice that the writing in textbooks, professional journals, and periodicals such as *Scientific American* can be abstract and unspecific—not incomprehensible, but difficult nonetheless. To some degree, that's inevitable since writers for these publications are often addressing complex and technical issues; they may want to use an efficient professional vocabulary familiar to many of their readers. But writers especially concerned to reach a broader audience—including educated nonspecialists outside their fields—find ways to include specific details, helpful analogies, anecdotes, and narration. Here is an example of a lively passage from a Pulitzer Prize–winning historian that begins with a generalization (a comparison between two Presidents) that is illustrated through increasingly specific details.

In background, interests, personality, in everything from the sound of their voices to the kind of company they enjoyed to the patterns of their careers, [Franklin Roosevelt and Harry Truman] could not have been much more dissimilar. Roosevelt was now in his **twelfth year of office**. He had been president for so long and through such trying times that it seemed to many Americans, including the junior senator **from Missouri**, that he was virtually the presidency itself. His wealth, education, the social position he had known since boyhood were everything Harry Truman had never had. **Life and customs at the Roosevelt family estate on the upper Hudson River** were as far removed from **Jackson County, Missouri**, as some foreign land. Roosevelt fancied himself a **farmer**. To Truman, **Roosevelt was the kind of farmer who had never pulled a weed, never known debt, or crop failure, or a father's call to roll out of bed at 5:30 on a bitter cold morning.**
— David McCullough, *Truman*

13c
¶

EXERCISE 13.4 Imagine that you are writing a magazine article that includes one of the following paragraphs. Revise the paragraph, incorporating specific details, examples, or other material to add variety.

1. "Reality-based television" is becoming increasingly popular in the United States. There are more shows of this type each year, and their ratings are increasing. These shows often depict real people in physically dangerous or emotionally charged situations. This intensity level keeps viewers coming back for more.

2. College and university officials see binge drinking as a serious problem on campuses nationwide. Recent studies have documented its widespread occurrence across different demographic groups and different types of schools. The problem affects retention and graduation rates, student health, academic life, and campus safety.

■ 2 Revise for economy. Well-crafted paragraphs don't waste words. They move readers smoothly from point to point without bogging down in unnecessary verbiage or repetition. When you revise a paragraph, you'll often have to gut whole phrases or sentences when they contribute little to your meaning. (See Section 18c for advice on streamlining sentences.)

In the following paragraph on bicycling in China, the writer has realized he could eliminate most of his first two sentences, which are tedious generalizations. A sentence about the number of bicycles is also expendable because it contains no information—it might have been worth keeping if it had estimated the number of cycles. A complex sentence describing people riding bikes in Beijing colorfully illustrates a key point about cycling in China, so it is worth revising. The last two sentences need to be pared back for readability and focus, but they're valuable because they introduce ideas that play a role in the next paragraph (not shown). Here's the original draft of the paragraph, with major cuts indicated, followed by a revised version.

13c
¶

INFLATED FIRST DRAFT

~~Bicycles are a major form of transportation in many Third World countries because they are inexpensive and easy to maintain. Asians in particular seem to depend on them heavily.~~ Nowhere are they more important than they are in China, where one can see masses of them on the streets in every city. ~~Probably no one knows how many bicycles there are in China, nor does there seem to be a way of finding out.~~ Virtually everyone seems to ride—well-dressed businessmen with their briefcases strapped to the frame; a husband with his wife riding behind him and their child on the handlebars; women of all ages, some even in long, narrow dresses; and college students carrying their books on their backs. The newly arrived American cyclist in ~~Beijing or Shanghai,~~ however, would be astonished ~~not only~~ to see ~~the great numbers of bicycles, but to see what kinds of bicycles the Chinese ride and~~ how many other uses, besides simply riding, the Chinese have been able to figure out for bicycles. ~~They're an amazingly ingenious people when it comes to adapting the common bicycle.~~

REVISED FOR ECONOMY

Although bicycles are a major form of transportation in all Asian countries, nowhere are they more important than in China, where one can see masses of them on the streets in every city. Virtually everyone seems to ride—well-dressed businessmen with their briefcases strapped to the frame; a husband with his wife riding behind him and their child on the handlebars; women of all ages, some even in long, narrow dresses; and college students carrying their books on their backs. The newly arrived American cyclist, however, would be astonished to see how many other uses, besides simply riding, the Chinese have been able to figure out for bicycles.

You'll often have to cut this deeply to make your prose work. Most good writers do. (See Chapter 5 for a detailed discussion of revising and editing.)

EXERCISE 13.5 Streamline and strengthen this paragraph from a student's first draft by cutting unnecessary generalizations or explanations and trimming in places that seem wordy. You may need to cut or revise words, phrases, or whole sentences. Compare and contrast your revised version with a classmate's version.

> There are many different scholarly views concerning Alexander the Great's ultimate goal in relation to his military pursuits. Some historians consider Alexander to have been a power-hungry tyrant without whom the world would have been better off. Others see Alexander as the great unifier of humankind, one who attempted to bring together many cultures in one coherent empire. Others view him as the ultimate pragmatist—not necessarily having any preplanned goals and aspirations of conquering the world, but merely a king who made the very best of his existing circumstances. Some believe that Alexander's accomplishments were not great at all, but that most of what was written concerning Alexander is basically just a mixture of legend and myth. Others feel his achievements stand as monuments in human history to the enormous capability of the human spirit and will.

13d How can you improve paragraph appearance?

As we point out in Chapters 19 and 20 on document design, printed matter has its own body language—that's why writers need to think about how their work is going to look in print. The look of a Web page, an essay, or a brochure affects potential readers' attitudes before they read a word. When they see a long stretch of print unbroken by paragraphs, white space, headings, dialogue, or graphics, most readers assume the material will be hard to read.

That's why, no matter what kind of project you're working on, you should consider breaking up long paragraphs. Your readers are much more likely to take a friendly attitude toward a piece when they can see that your paragraphs are fairly short. How short is a "fairly short" paragraph? Probably no more than seven or eight sentences—and in many cases, even fewer.

◼ 1 Break up long paragraph blocks that look hard to read. You shouldn't chop up paragraphs arbitrarily just to make your paper look inviting; a paragraph is supposed to develop an idea, and it usually takes several sentences to do that. But often after you write a paragraph and reread it, you can spot places where you can divide it. Here are junctures where you can begin new paragraphs.

13d
¶

Checklist 13.1

Places to Break Up a Long Paragraph

* **Shifts in time.** Look for spots where you have written words such as *at that time, then,* or *afterward* or have given other time signals.

* **Shifts in place.** Look for spots where you have written *another place* or *on the other side* or have used words that point to places.

* **Shifts in direction.** Look for spots where you have written *on the other hand, nevertheless,* or *however* or have otherwise indicated contrast.

* **Shifts in emphasis or focus.** Look for spots where you have shifted to a new point, perhaps using words such as *another, in addition,* or *not only.*

But don't break an entire paper into one- or two-sentence paragraphs. It's true that long paragraphs intimidate readers; however, too many short ones can distract them or make them feel the material is trivial. Extremely short paragraphs are best saved for special effects, as the following section explains.

◼ 2 Use short paragraphs for effect. Sometimes one-sentence paragraphs work well, particularly when you want to give some point special emphasis. Here, in its original context, is a very brief paragraph—a single sentence fragment—from a well-regarded professional science writer:

Ah, romance. Can any sight be as sweet as a pair of mallard ducks gliding gracefully across a pond, male by female, seemingly inseparable? Or, better yet, two trumpeter swans, the legendary symbols of eternal love, each ivory neck one half of a single heart, souls of a feather staying coupled together for life?

Coupled for life—with just a bit of adultery, cuckoldry, and gang rape on the side.

Alas for sentiment and the greeting card industry, it turns out that, in the animal kingdom, there is almost no such thing as monogamy. As a wealth of recent findings makes clear as a crocodile tear, even creatures long assumed to have faithful tendencies and to need a strong pair bond to rear their young are in fact perfidious brutes.

—Natalie Angier, "Mating for Life?"

13d
¶

Don't be afraid to use one- or two-sentence paragraphs occasionally, but do so deliberately and to achieve a specific effect. Sometimes you may want to insert a very short paragraph to make a transition between two longer paragraphs. At other times you can use brevity for dramatic emphasis, as Angier has done in the passage above.

3 Adapt paragraph length to your writing situation.
Finally, then, how long should a paragraph be? The answer, as you might expect, depends on your writing situation.

- **Consider your purpose.** If you're laying out a complex argument in your senior thesis project, your paragraphs might be fairly long. If you're writing an editorial for the student or local newspaper, they need to be short because the columns are narrow and newspaper readers don't expect long paragraphs. If you're writing a business report for a supervisor, you'll want to seem efficient and businesslike; keep the paragraphs short so the content can be skimmed quickly.

- **Consider your audience.** Are they experienced readers who are used to reading history or biography or technical articles? Then long paragraphs probably won't bother them. Are they more likely to be casual readers who pick up a newspaper or a magazine and peruse it quickly? Then you'll do well to keep your paragraphs short.

- **Consider your medium.** Are you writing something that will be read from a computer screen? If so, it's especially important to write short paragraphs. People tire more quickly when they read material online, so content needs to be organized in compact units that can be absorbed easily. Also, if a reader misses a point while she is reading online, she has to scroll back to pick it up, and finding that point will be much harder when paragraphs are long.

Following are some guidelines for determining paragraph length.

SUMMARY **Guidelines for Paragraph Length**

Consider long paragraphs if . . .

- You are developing complicated ideas in detail.
- Readers are experienced and skillful.
- Readers are patient and seeking information.

Choose short paragraphs if . . .

- Readers are impatient and reading for diversion.
- Readers are skimming for content.
- Readers are young or inexperienced.
- Readers are reading online.

13d
¶

CHAPTER 14

How Do You Manage Opening and Closing Paragraphs?

14a What makes an opening paragraph effective?

Newspaper editors talk about the *lead* for a news story, the opening that has to catch the readers' attention and give them a strong signal about what to expect. The opening paragraph for whatever you write is also a lead—the introduction to your paper that gets you off to a good or a bad start with readers. Like the opening of a front-page news story, any first paragraph should do the following things:

- Get your readers' attention and interest them in reading more.
- Make a *commitment* to readers—that is, introduce your main idea in a way that promises to follow up with more information.
- Signal to readers what direction your project will take.
- Set the tone of your project.

These are important functions, and that's why first paragraphs can be difficult to write—but it's also why they're worth your time and attention.

Different kinds of writing call for different opening paragraphs. For certain kinds of writing—laboratory reports, grant proposals, business letters—readers expect specific kinds of opening paragraphs. In such cases, find out what the typical pattern is and use it. In other kinds of writing, such as newspaper articles, critical analyses, personal experience papers, and opinion pieces, you have more freedom and can try various approaches.

The following sections illustrate types of opening paragraphs that you may find useful.

■ **1 Begin with a narrative.** Many professional authors begin a piece with an attention-getting narrative or anecdote that catches their readers' attention and sparks their interest in the topic. The following opening narrative, taken from a magazine article, pulls readers into a terrifying experience and makes us want to know more about what caused it.

Like most Peace Corps volunteers, Martin Giannini embarked on his mission full of high hopes and enthusiasm. His assignment in Togo promised to be the adventure of a lifetime. It certainly was—but not the kind he expected. Giannini's African adventure ended in a padded room in a Chicago psych ward. "I was totally loony," admits Giannini. "It felt like I was in some 'X-Files' episode with instructions being planted in my brain. I tried to escape, but couldn't get past the four guards." What led Giannini, a healthy young man with no history of mental illness, to take on a battalion of guards in a psychiatric hospital? A drug, say his doctors. An antimalaria drug the Peace Corps recommended.

—Dennis Lewon, "Malaria's Not-So-Magic Bullet"

14a
¶

You may occasionally want to begin a paper with two or three short anecdotes rather than a single, longer one. This variation works well to show that your topic touches upon several issues or situations.

■ **2 Begin with a description that establishes tone and forecasts content.** Here is an example taken from an article on exotic Southern cuisine. John T. Edge's opening description creates a vivid picture of the region he's writing about and sets a tone of cautious fascination.

It's just past four on a Thursday afternoon in June at Jesse's Place, a country juke seventeen miles south of the Mississippi line and three miles west of Amite, Louisiana. The air conditioner hacks and spits forth torrents of arctic air, but the heat of summer can't be kept at bay. It seeps around the splintered doorjambs and settles in, transforming the squat particleboard-plastered roadhouse into a sauna. Slowly, the dank barroom fills with grease-smeared mechanics from the truck stop up the road and farmers straight from the fields, the soles of their brogans thick with dirt clods. A few weary souls make their way over from the nearby sawmill, the kind of place where more than one worker has muscled a log into the chipper and drawn back a nub. I sit alone at the bar, one empty bottle of Bud in front of me, a second bottle in my hand. I drain the beer, order a third, and stare down at the pink juice spreading outward from a crumpled foil pouch and onto the dull, black vinyl bar.

I'm not leaving until I eat this thing, I tell myself.

—John T. Edge, "I'm Not Leaving Until I Eat This Thing"

■ **3 Begin with a question or a series of questions that relate to your topic.** Diane Ackerman begins one of the essays in her book *A Natural History of the Senses* with a series of provocative questions.

What would the flutterings of courtship be without a meal? As the deliciously sensual and ribald tavern scene in Fielding's *Tom Jones* reminds us, a meal can be the perfect arena for foreplay. Why is food so sexy? Why does a woman refer to a handsome man as a real dish? Or a French girl call her lover *mon petit chou* (my little cabbage)? Or an American man call his girl cookie? Or a British man describe a sexy woman as a bit of crumpet [. . .]? Sexual hunger and physical hunger have always been allies. Rapacious needs, they have coaxed and driven us through famine and war, to bloodshed and serenity, since our earliest days.

—Diane Ackerman, "Food and Sex"

14a
¶

4 Begin by quoting a key source. Have you come across in your research a statement from an expert, an interview subject, or another source that expresses a key issue more vividly than you could in your own words? If so, don't hesitate to begin your opening paragraph with a quote. Here is an example taken from an article analyzing why Y2K—the inability of many computer systems to register the year 2000—posed so many problems for U.S. businesses and government agencies.

Seventy years ago, W. I. Thomas and Dorothy Swaine Thomas proclaimed one of sociology's most influential ideas: "If men define situations as real, they are real in their consequences." Their case in point was a prisoner who attacked people he heard mumbling absent-mindedly to themselves. To the deranged inmate, these lip movements were curses or insults. No matter that they weren't; the results were the same. The Thomas Theorem, as it is called, now has a corollary. In a microprocessor-controlled society, if machines register a disordered state, they are likely to create it. For example, if an automatic railroad switching system mistakenly detects another train stalled on the tracks ahead and halts the engine, there really will be a train stalled on the tracks.

—Edward Tenner, "Chronologically Incorrect"

5 Start with your thesis. Sometimes you will do best to open your essay by simply telling your readers exactly what you are going to write about. Such openings work well for many papers you write in college courses, for reports you might have to write on the job, and for many other kinds of factual, informative prose. Here's a good example from an article about animal rights. Joseph Hart announces the topic directly and forecasts the main points the paper will cover.

In the eyes of the law, animals are the private property of humans. So long as we obey the handful of statutes designed to protect creatures from cruelty, humans have the legal right to imprison, kill, eat, and experiment upon other species with impunity. But a growing number of "animal law" specialists and animal rights activists have joined forces to break down these legal barriers between species, and assisting them is our closest animal cousin: the chimpanzee.

—Joseph Hart, "Chimps Are People Too"

See Section 3a for more on constructing a thesis statement and incorporating it into a writing project.

14a
¶

Going Public   *Using a Narrative to Revise an Opening Paragraph* _____

When she began to write a course paper on saving local wetlands, student writer Katie Wegner started with the following thesis.

> Our neighborhood is one of many in the Myrtle Beach area that is built on a wetland. Burroughs and Chapin, the largest and most powerful developer on the coast, is among the companies who are building on these natural sponges. Wetlands are crucial to maintaining balance in our ecological system, but there is such weak legislation to prevent developers from building on these crucial areas that they are quickly disappearing.

This is a useful paragraph for getting started, but Katie knew she wanted a more vivid opening that would help readers feel a personal connection to the issue. Her final draft uses a rhetorical question and a narrative to introduce her thesis:

> When a hard rain falls, do you find it relaxing to cuddle up and listen to the rhythmic drumming of raindrops on your roof? Must be nice. I can't relax because I, like many other Myrtle Beach residents, am too busy worrying about how much my neighborhood will flood after the drumming stops. This is because our

neighborhood is one of many in the area built on a
wetland. Burroughs and Chapin, the largest and most
powerful developer on the coast, is principal among
the companies who are building on these natural
sponges. Wetlands are crucial to maintaining balance
in our ecological system, but because there is such
weak legislation to prevent developers from building
on these critical areas, they are quickly
disappearing. Now Burroughs and Chapin is stretching
its tentacles inland toward our capital city.
Something must be done before it's too late.

14b
¶

EXERCISE 14.1 Choose from the strategies discussed above and write two versions of an opening paragraph for one of the following essay titles. Then join with classmates who have chosen to write on the same title and read your paragraphs aloud. Discuss which ones seem to work well and why.

1. The American Legal System as Seen through *Judging Amy, Law and Order,* and *Ally McBeal*

2. What It Means to Live Below the Poverty Level: A Case Study

3. Why You Should Vote in the Next Election

4. Random Drug Testing in Schools: Safety Measure or Civil Rights Violation?

14b What makes a closing paragraph effective?

Closing paragraphs can be hard to write because it's often difficult to come to a satisfying conclusion that doesn't fall back on clichés. The only direct advice we can give is that your closing paragraph should wind up your paper in a way that makes readers feel that you have left no loose ends—that you have fulfilled the commitment you made in the opening paragraph. You don't want your readers asking "And so?" when they finish, or looking on the back of the page for something they may have missed.

There are no simple prescriptions for achieving that important goal. However, we suggest five general strategies you can use, alone or in combination, as seems appropriate for your rhetorical situation.

■ **1 Summarize the main points you have made.** Often you'll want to bring your paper to a close by reemphasizing your main points. (But don't repeat the very same words you have already used, or your ending may sound redundant or forced.)

Here is the conclusion of a paper in which the student writer has argued convincingly that spanking children is an ineffective form of discipline.

> It is unfortunate that the new spanking advocates get so much attention in the popular press, since their arguments are so poorly supported. These crusaders draw on personal anecdotes and "experts" of dubious credibility to glorify physical punishment and to blame non-spanking parents for everything from school shootings to violent rap lyrics. Yet even a cursory look at the scientific research in this area confirms that kids who are spanked are more—not less—likely to misbehave, turn to criminal behavior, or suffer from addiction and other mental problems. How we choose to treat our nation's children is a serious matter. We all have the responsibility to make these decisions based on the best information available—not on the dire predictions of a few extremists.

■ **2 Make a recommendation when one is appropriate.** Such a recommendation should grow out of the issue you have been discussing. This strategy brings a paper to a positive ending and closes the topic. Here is a conclusion from a student paper on nutrition.

> But even if you are an athlete who wants quick results, you should not go to extremes in trying to improve your overall nutrition. When you decide to change your eating habits, your motto should be "Eat better," not "Eat perfectly." By increasing carbohydrates and reducing fat in the diet—that is, by eating more fruits, vegetables, and whole grains and cutting down on whole milk and meat—you can improve your energy level rather quickly. You will also feel better, play better, and look better than you ever imagined.

■ **3 Link the end to the beginning.** One excellent way to end a writing project is to tie your conclusion back to your beginning, framing and unifying your paper. Notice how skillfully the author of an editorial from *Wired* has used this strategy.

OPENING PARAGRAPH

Any significant social phenomenon creates a backlash. The Net is no exception. It is, however, odd that the loudest complaints are shouts of "Get a life!"—suggesting that online living will dehumanize us, insulate us, and create a world of people who won't smell flowers, watch sunsets, or engage in face-to-face experiences. Out of this backlash comes a warning to parents that their children will "cocoon" and metamorphose into social invalids.

CLOSING PARAGRAPH

But the current sweep of digital living is doing exactly the opposite [of isolating people]. Parents of young children find exciting self-employment from home. The "virtual corporation" is an opportunity for tiny companies (with employees spread across the world) to work together in a global market and set up base wherever they choose. If you don't like centralist thinking, big companies, or job automation, what better place to go than the Net? Work for yourself *and* get a life.

14b
¶

—Nicholas Negroponte, "Get a Life?"

4 Place your argument in a larger context. When readers reach the end of a piece, they may want to know how what you've told them is relevant to larger issues or conversations: Does your analysis of a problem have implications for the community or for others studying your topic? Concluding paragraphs that suggest these sorts of connections are especially common in academic research projects.

In this example, Jan Brunvand ends a research article documenting feminist themes in popular "spooky stories" by suggesting directions for future research.

One might not expect to find women's liberation messages embedded in the spooky stories told by teenagers, but Beverly Crane's case is plausible and well argued. [. . .] What needs to be done to analyze this finding is to collect what Alan Dundes calls "oral-literary criticism," the informants' own comments about their lore. How clearly would the girls who tell these stories perceive—or even accept—the messages extrapolated by scholars? And a related question: Have any stories with clear liberationist themes replaced older ones cautioning young women to stay home, be good, and—next best—be careful, and call a man if they need help?

—Jan Brunvand, "'The Hook' and Other Teenage Horrors"

■ **5 Stop when you're finished.** Probably the most important thing to remember about closing a paper or essay is not to overdo your conclusion. If you have covered all your points and are reasonably well satisfied with what you've said, quit. Don't bore your reader by tacking on a needless recapitulation or adding a paragraph of platitudes.

14b
¶

EXERCISE 14.2 Read the following closing paragraphs from professional articles. What features do you find in them that give the reader a sense that the author has brought his or her essay to a satisfactory close?

1. Our new understanding of the impact of environmental challenges tends to blur some of the hard and fast distinctions between traditional definitions of security and more ambitious modern ones. Helping a Haiti or a Sierra Leone may not yield an immediately identifiable payoff in averting a particular conflict, yet it does aid the cause of peace and tranquility. In the future, a definition of security that leans exclusively on conflict and its prevention will be too cramped to accommodate the reality of a world in which renewable resources will be ever scarcer and in which it will be increasingly difficult to seal ourselves off— morally, emotionally, and physically—from poverty, disease, and environmental degradation in the less developed nations.
—Geoffrey Dabelko, "The Environmental Factor"

2. No one could wish for a more advantageous heritage than that bequeathed to the black writer in the South: a compassion for the earth, a trust in humanity beyond our knowledge of evil, and an abiding love of justice. We inherit a great responsibility as well, for we must give voice to centuries not only of silent bitterness and hate but also of neighborly kindness and sustaining love.
—Alice Walker, "The Black Writer and the Southern Experience"

3. Investing in and educating all American children is an urgent moral and practical imperative. If our democracy is to remain vibrant in the dawning new century and millennium and our economy is to remain on the cutting edge in a global economy, then we must make America's promise of fair opportunities and safe environments real right now to our children right here at home. We must take responsibility for putting into place the resources and bipartisan political support to get our priorities straight, whether we're talking about education, health care, child care, or violence prevention. There are millions of children who are de-

pending on us. [. . .] Before one more child is lost, we must muster the necessary will to make sure all of our children receive the healthy and fair and safe start in life they require and deserve.
—Marian Wright Edelman, "A Voice for Children"

EXERCISE 14.3 Exchange drafts with two or three other students who are working on the same assignment. Each person should read the closing paragraphs from the other papers. Discuss what features each writer used to bring his or her paper to a conclusion. Discuss how those strategies work and which others might also be helpful.

14b
¶

CHAPTER 15

How Do You Manage Transitions?

Skilled writers work hard to help their readers move easily through a piece of writing. They know that people who are reading by choice won't stick around long if they have trouble following an argument or the thread of a narrative. The best unifying device for any piece of writing is *organizational;* that is, it comes from an underlying pattern that moves the reader along smoothly. You'll find examples of such patterns in Sections 3b (for whole papers) and 13b (for paragraphs).

But even when you have a clear organizational pattern, you sometimes need to tighten your writing by using *transitions,* those words and phrases that act like hooks, links, and directional signals to keep readers moving from point to point within a paragraph, and from one paragraph to another. The first section of this chapter helps you identify places where readers might have trouble following your writing; the second section offers strategies for incorporating transitions into a writing project.

15a How do you spot problems with transitions?

When you're revising, learn to check for places where your readers might find your writing choppy or abrupt, and revise accordingly. Here are trouble spots to look for.

▌1 Check for paragraphs made up of short, simple sentences that seem disconnected. Good paragraphs follow what writing experts call the "old-new contract"—they advance an argument or idea by linking each piece of new information to something that's gone before, so that the connections are immediately clear to readers. When a writer neglects to link old and new information, a paragraph may read more like a random series of observations than a coherent discussion. For example:

WEAK TRANSITIONS

Antonio Diaz is the senior sports columnist for the *Sunday Tribune.* He is an avid amateur painter. He devotes all of his spare time to his hobby. Whenever he has a free day, he sets up his easel in the Botanic Garden. His favorite subject there is the water lily pond. His work also furnishes him with subjects. He often brings a sketchbook to the games he covers. He finds his rapid sketches of the athletes useful. They help him reconstruct the excitement of a game for his column.

Here is a revised version, with some sentences combined and others connected (transitional words are boldfaced). Note how much more readable this version is.

15a

trans

BETTER

The senior sports columnist for the *Sunday Tribune,* Antonio Diaz, is **also** an avid amateur painter **who** devotes all his spare time to his hobby. Whenever he has a free day, he sets up his easel in the Botanic Garden, **where** his favorite subject is the water lily pond. Mr. Diaz's work also furnishes him with subjects, **and** he often brings a sketchbook to the games he covers. He finds his rapid sketches of the athletes useful **when** reconstructing the excitement of a game for his column.

2 Check for sentences that begin with vague references like *it is*, *there are*, and *there is*. Often sentences that begin with these phrases (called *expletives*) are poorly connected to each other because it's hard to tell who or what the subject is. For example:

WEAK TRANSITIONS

It is a truism that good manners are like skeleton keys. There are few doors they will not open. Some people think that good manners are pretentious. They are a way of condescending to people. That is a misunderstanding. The real purpose of manners is to make social situations comfortable and to put the people you are with at ease. Manners are also practical to have. There are many companies that insist that their executives have good manners. Some business schools include a course on manners in their curricula.

A reader gets little sense of the relationship between these sentences—there's no clear link between new and old information—and the repetitive patterns are boring. Here is the paragraph reworked with better sentence openings and stronger connections. Transitional terms are boldfaced.

BETTER

Good manners, like skeleton keys, will open almost any door. **While** some people think that good manners are pretentious and condescending, that's a misunderstanding. **On the contrary,** manners exist to make social situations comfortable by putting everyone at ease. **Moreover,** manners are a practical asset in the job market. Many companies insist on well-mannered executives, **which** has prompted some business schools to include a course on manners in their curricula.

For suggestions on revising to eliminate expletive phrases, see Section 18c-6.

15a
trans

■ **3 Check for gaps between paragraphs.** Sometimes major gaps appear between paragraphs, and readers get lost temporarily. Suppose that you encountered the following two paragraphs in an article on Sumo wrestling. You'd probably have trouble figuring out how the second paragraph relates to the first:

The sheer excitement of tight sumo wrestling matches and the colorful hoopla surrounding each day's bouts help account for sumo's popularity. The sport-cum-ritual of sumo also reflects values that Japan holds dear.

The world of sumo places enormous importance on rank and hierarchy.

Here's the original passage as it appeared in a magazine article. The writer T. R. Reid successfully links the paragraphs by making a point in the last sentence of the first paragraph and expanding on it in the first line of the second. The phrases and words that link the two paragraphs are boldfaced.

The sheer excitement of tight matches and the colorful hoopla surrounding each day's bouts help account for sumo's popularity, of course, but I think there's a further explanation as well. The sport-cum-ritual of sumo is dear to the Japanese because it reflects, in microcosm, many of the **values that Japan holds dear.**

Japanese society places enormous importance on rank and hierarchy—and the world of sumo does the same.

—T. R. Reid, "Sumo"

Links between paragraphs can take several forms; the next section explains in more detail.

15b How can you strengthen transitions?

If you want to use transitions effectively, remember the old-new contract: Each sentence or paragraph should contain a seed out of which the next sentence or paragraph can grow. Always include a hint, a reference, a hook, or a repetition that helps the reader link what you're saying with what has come before and what lies ahead. This section explains how to incorporate common kinds of transitions into your writing.

1 Use common transition words to connect ideas. You can make your paragraphs tighter and more focused by using transition words to tie sentences together:

- **Use pointer words.** Set up a path for your readers to follow by putting in words such as *first, second, next,* and *last* to indicate shifts in time or place.

  One student, a nonsmoker, argued eloquently before the committee that there are many reasons to oppose a campus-wide ban on smoking. **First,** such a policy unduly penalizes an activity that, though obnoxious, is not illegal. **Second,** enforcement of the policy might encourage insidious intrusions on the privacy of students in their dormitory rooms and faculty in their offices. **Last,** a ban on smoking might set an unfortunate precedent, leading to the elimination of other habits and activities certain groups regard as similarly offensive or harmful: drinking alcohol, eating fatty foods, dancing, listening to rock music, or even driving a car.

- **Use relationship words.** Connect sentences by using words such as *however, therefore, nevertheless,* and *yet* to show similarity, opposition, addition, or other connections between ideas.

  Opinion at the hearing had generally favored the proposal to abolish smoking on campus. **However,** the student's arguments made some proponents waver as they considered the wider implications of their actions. What would happen, **for example,** if one group on campus, citing statistics on heart disease, demanded a campus-wide ban on fast foods? The ban on smoking would provide grounds for such a restriction.

As these examples show, transition words are not neutral; each one gives readers a different signal about where your argument is going. When you're in doubt about which term to choose, check Chart 15.1 on page 224.

Chart 15.1

Common Transition Words and Phrases

TO SHOW SIMILARITY:
likewise
like
similarly
in the same way
just as

TO SHOW CONTRAST:
however
instead
nevertheless
although
in spite of
on the other hand
not only
but
rather

TO SHOW ACCUMULATION:
moreover
in addition to
for example
and
for instance

TO SHOW CONSEQUENCE:
hence
consequently
so
therefore
as a result of
thus

TO SHOW CAUSATION:
because
since

TO SHOW A SEQUENCE:
next
subsequently
after
finally
first, second, third

15b
trans

2 Repeat a key term throughout a paragraph to establish a central idea. Using one or two key words or phrases several times in a paragraph can tie it together effectively.

The new black middle class came of age in the 1960s during an unprecedented American **economic boom** and in the hub of a thriving **mass culture**. The **economic boom** made luxury goods and convenient services available to large numbers of hard-working Americans for the first time. American **mass culture** presented models of the good life principally in terms of conspicuous consumption and hedonistic indulgence. It is important to note that even the intensely political struggles of the sixties presupposed a perennial **economic boom** and posited models of the good life projected by U.S. **mass culture**. Long-term financial self-denial and sexual asceticism was never at the center of a political agenda in the sixties.   —Cornel West, *Race Matters*

3 Use the demonstrative pronouns *this, that, these, those,* **and** *such* **to tie ideas together.** Each boldfaced word in the following example hooks directly into the previous sentence.

> DEMONSTRATIVE TERMS BOLDFACED
>
> Making a movie is a collaborative endeavor, and scriptwriters point **this** out frequently. Occasionally a screenplay will survive the transfer from paper to film intact, but **that** is the exception rather than the rule. Typically, producers, directors, actors, and agents all have a say in the final product. Coping with **such** high-handed meddling is often difficult for young writers, and **those** who cannot compromise rarely stay in the business for long.

4 Use relative pronouns to show links between ideas. *Who, which, where,* and *that* are powerful words that link a descriptive or informative statement to something that has preceded it. Relative pronouns can be especially helpful when you need to combine several short, choppy sentences into one. Notice how the boldfaced pronouns in the following paragraph serve as links to previous ideas.

15b
trans

> RELATIVE PRONOUNS BOLDFACED
>
> Miranda's first few weeks at the conservatory were exhausting but exhilarating. It was a place **that** challenged her, one **where** she could meet talented people **who** shared her passion for dance. The competition among the students was friendly but intense, **which** only increased her determination to practice and learn.

5 Use parallelism to link ideas. You can create tightly focused paragraphs by writing a series of sentences that incorporate parallel phrases.

 I spent my two days at Disneyland taking rides. **I took** a bobsled through the Matterhorn and a submarine under the Polar Ice Cap and a rocket jet to the Cosmic Vapor Curtain. **I took** Peter Pan's Flight, Mr. Toad's Wild Ride, Alice's Scary Adventures, and Pinocchio's Daring Journey. **I took** a steamboat and a jungle boat. **I took** the Big Thunder Mountain Railroad to coyote country and the Splash Mountain roller coaster to Critter Country. **I took** a "Pirates of the Caribbean" ride (black cats and buried treasure) and a "Haunted Mansion" ride (creaking hinges and ghostly laughter). **I took** monorails and Skyways and Autopias and People Movers. More precisely, those rides **took** me: up and down and around sudden corners and over rooftops, and all I had to do was sit back and let whatever conveyance I was sitting in do the driving. I had no desire to be at the wheel myself. In Disneyland that primal American urge—the urge to drive—gets suspended, replaced by the still more primal urge to be eternally transported to timeless lands of enchantment.

—William Zinsser, *American Places*

Not only does Zinsser hold the details of his paragraph together by using a parallel pattern that begins every sentence with the phrase "I took," but by repeating the phrase he captures the flavor of Disneyland as a place where the visitor travels through fantasy lands. And when he reverses the phrase to "More precisely, those rides **took** me," he wraps up his paragraph with a final unifying touch.

6 Use a semicolon to link two closely related statements. Although some writers may ignore this useful piece of punctuation, the semicolon signals a tight connection that says, "These groups of words go together." Often a semicolon can connect parts of a sentence more effectively than *and* or *also*. For more details about the semicolon, see Section 37a.

CONNECTING SEMICOLONS BOLDFACED

The sculptor Ilya Karensky no longer has to endure his neighbors' contempt for his work**;** now he has to put up with their insincere and inept praise. Ilya knows perfectly well that what his neighbors admire most about his work is the amount of money for which it now sells**;** they like the sculptures themselves no better than they did before.

7 Consider using headings or other visual markers as transitions. In some kinds of documents, writers may use visual signals as well as—or sometimes instead of—words to help readers follow an argument.

Business reports and scientific writing commonly separate sections by using headings and subheadings so that readers can see where one idea ends and another begins. Résumés often use headings such as "education," "experience," "awards," and "references" so that readers can locate relevant information. Brochures, flyers, and instructional manuals employ graphics, images, and color to mark divisions or to tie together related information. On the Web, writers create hyperlinks to connect documents.

But use common sense when you incorporate visual transitions into a writing project. Ask yourself whether the particular strategy is appropriate for the situation. Graphics and color fonts aren't always welcome in academic papers, and a flyer or short essay might not need headings. If you're not sure, look at models to see the kinds of transitions other writers have used in similar situations.

Also be sure that a particular transition gives readers the right signal. For example, a heading indicates a new topic, but it doesn't necessarily show readers how one topic relates to another. You'll often need to supplement visual devices with traditional linking words and phrases.

For more information about integrating visual elements into a text, see Chapter 20. For examples of documents that incorporate visual elements, see the model documents in Chapter 21.

Going Public *Using Transitions to Strengthen an Argument*

In a research paper proposing that in-school health clinics might help keep at-risk students in school, student writer Jason Hatfield wanted to emphasize the problems high school dropouts face. The following paragraph, however, doesn't achieve the effect he hoped for; the choppy, disconnected sentences make it hard for readers to follow his argument.

> As Americans it is our duty to do whatever is necessary to keep our children in school. When a student drops out before graduation, it is a tragedy. He or she does not receive an education. The lack of a diploma will keep them out of high-paying jobs. They may end up poor or on the streets. Too often, they may go to jail. These dropouts are lost along with their thoughts, dreams, and creativity. They cannot contribute to their families and community. What can be done to stop this?

In his revised version, Jason uses parallelism and transition words to unify his argument. Note that although the content and the organization remain nearly the same, the new paragraph is much more readable and more persuasive. Parallel phrases are boldfaced and transition words are italicized.

> As Americans it is our duty to do whatever is necessary to keep our children in school. When a student drops out before graduation, it is a tragedy. He or she will go through life without an education

and without access to high-paying jobs. He or she may end up poor, on the streets, or, too often, in jail. Not only are our dropouts lost, but their thoughts, dreams, and creativity are lost. Everything that makes them valuable to themselves and their communities is lost. What can be done to stop this?

EXERCISE 15.1 Working with a small group of classmates, read the following two paragraphs and diagnose the transition problems you find between the paragraphs and within each one. Where do you have trouble following the writer's line of thought? Why? Then revise the paragraphs to improve the transitions, drawing on at least two of the strategies described in this section.

The dangers of exercise are not only that one might injure one's back or pull a hamstring. People new to exercise need to guard against such injuries. No one wants to be a fallen weekend athlete, crippled on Monday morning from running a ten-kilometer race or biking up a mountain on Sunday. The newcomer to exercise can become a fanatic. This is in some ways encouraged by the environment at a health and fitness club. At 6:00 a.m. the hard-core weightlifters and triathlon competitors are there sweating and puffing, enjoying every minute of it. They seem to have their priorities straight—workouts come before work.

Fitness can take over one's life. It is easy to use up three hours a day before you know it. What happens to earning a living or to studying if one is a student? What happens to one's social life? Exercisers have to go to bed early. When they start to preach, non-exercising friends quickly disappear.

EXERCISE 15.2 Use one or more of the transitional devices discussed in this section to strengthen connections between new and old information in a writing project you're currently working on.

CHAPTER 16

What Kinds of Language Can You Use?

Many people assume that *what* we say is more important than *how* we say it. "Just get to the point," we often hear, "Say what you mean." But experts know that the language choices writers make—nuances in tone, vocabulary, formality, and connotation—can powerfully affect readers. This chapter will introduce you to the repertoire of language choices at your disposal, so that you can recognize them and understand the effects they may have. Among other things, we'll discuss how language can make readers feel excluded or included, how dialect and other language varieties affect writing, and how to avoid stereotyped language that may offend readers.

16a How formal should your writing be?

What's the difference between "a red sweater with shiny buttons" and "a 100%-silk cardigan in vermilion with imported pearl fastenings"? Nothing but the language used to describe it. Language ranges from very informal—slang and casual conversation—to very formal—the language of legal documents, sermons, and expensive clothing catalogs.

Choosing the right degree of formality is an important skill for any writer. The illustration on page 230 puts different kinds of writing on a scale ranging from stiffly formal at one extreme to highly colloquial at the other. This section discusses the levels of formality you're most likely to use when you write for college courses, in the workplace, or for community or campus organizations.

1 Recognize that different writing situations call for different levels of formality. Imagine what would happen if you responded to a casual party invitation with a formal memo, or if you opened a graduation speech with a rendition of your favorite rap song. In either case, you'd be using a level of formality inappropriate to the situation—and your audience would quickly let you know it.

LEVELS OF LANGUAGE
Very formal

Legal documents
Technical reports, case studies
Scientific magazine articles (*Science*)
Grant proposals
Scholarly journals
High-level magazines (*Atlantic Monthly*)
Orations (graduation addresses, dedications)
Sermons
Academic reports, term papers
Prestigious newspapers (*New York Times, Christian Science Monitor*)
Popular magazines (*Vanity Fair, GQ, Newsweek*)
Mass market magazines (*People, TV Digest*)
Personal experience papers
Short story using dialect and slang
Casual conversation

Very informal—colloquial

16a
lang

When you begin a writing project, you need to ask yourself, "How formal do I want this to be?" Your answer will depend on how you respond to these questions.

- What is my **purpose**? Do I hope to provide information, entertain readers, and/or persuade them to adopt a viewpoint?
- Who is my **audience**? How well do I know them? How much distance from them do I want to establish?
- What **impression** do I hope to create? Do I want to come across as dignified and serious, straightforward and friendly, or casual and hip?

When you know your audience well, the answers may come almost intuitively; when you don't, do an analysis so that you can make good language choices. See Sections 1d to 1g for advice on analyzing a writing situation.

2 Choose formal language when you don't know your audience well and want to be serious and dignified. If you are asked to give the opening address at a regional conference on environmental issues, you will probably be speaking to strangers on an important topic and will want to appear thoughtful, well informed, and dignified. Under those circumstances you'll choose moderately formal language. Here is an excerpt from a well-regarded environmental writer whose style might serve as a model for such a talk.

> Sustainability is a hopeful concept not only because it is a present necessity, but because it has a history. We know, for example, that some agricultural soils have been preserved in continuous use for several thousand years. We know, moreover, that it is possible to improve soil in use. And it is clear that a forest can be used in such a way that it remains a forest, with its biological community intact and its soil undamaged, while producing a yield of timber. But the methods by which exhaustible resources are extracted and used have set the pattern also for the use of sustainable resources, with the result that soils and forests are not merely being used but are being used up, exactly as coal seams are used up.
> —Wendell Berry, "Conservation Is Good Work"

16a
lang

Berry's writing is authoritative and his tone is serious. His image is that of a concerned and knowledgeable environmental advocate, but he maintains some distance from his audience. His choice of language reflects these characteristics that are typical of formal writing.

Checklist 16.1

Characteristics of Formal Style

* Considerable distance between reader and writer

* Serious, impersonal tone

* Moderately long sentences

* Frequent use of abstract language and high-level vocabulary

* Few contractions or personal references

* Few action verbs

In most college courses, instructors will expect you to write in a relatively formal style, unless the assignment designates a writing situation in which informality is appropriate— for instance, a reading response journal or an op-ed piece. When you're not sure what level of formality your instructor expects, ask.

3 Choose informal language when you feel comfortable with your audience and want a more relaxed image.

Writers use an informal tone in many different writing situations. We'll give just two examples here.

The first is from an article on high school football published in the popular magazine *Texas Monthly*. It's moderately informal.

> But even if change is afoot, Texas high school football re-
> mains one of the few institutions that distinguishes us from the rest
> of the universe. We have more players, coaches, band members,
> cheerleaders, and pep squads than anyone else. We send more of
> our boys to college and the pros than any other state (more than
> three hundred signed letters of intent to play for Division I schools
> last year alone). Our fans are more fanatical. Our parents are more
> passionate. So believe the hype: we're Number One.
> —Joe Nick Patoski et al., "Three Cheers
> for High School Football"

In this vividly descriptive paragraph, Patoski and his co-authors mix high-level and low-level vocabulary: *distinguishes, institution,* and *fanatical* contrast with the colloquial *our boys* and *hype*. They also mix concrete and abstract language, vary the sentence length, and maintain a moderate distance from readers.

The second example, taken from a book of personal essays, is even more informal.

> Nowadays, some of my city-bred friends muse about moving
> to a small town for the sake of their children. What's missing from
> their romantic picture of Grover's Corners is the frightening im-
> pact of insulation upon a child who's not dead center in the main-
> stream. In a place such as my hometown, you file in and sit down
> to day one of kindergarten with the exact pool of boys who will be
> your potential dates for the prom. If you wet your pants a lot, your
> social life ten years later will be—as they say in government re-
> ports—impacted. I was sterling on bladder control, but somehow
> could never shake my sixth-grade stigma.
> At age seventeen, I was free at last to hightail it for new social
> pastures, and you'd better believe I did.
> —Barbara Kingsolver, "In Case You Ever
> Want to Go Home Again"

In this account Kingsolver is very close to her readers, writing in the first person and using personal details to make her point. The image she projects is that of someone reminiscing in conversation.

Checklist 16.2

Characteristics of Informal Style

- Variety of topics, from serious to casual
- Little distance between reader and writer
- Variety of sentence lengths
- Mix of abstract and concrete language
- Mix of action and non-action verbs
- Occasional personal references and contractions

16a
lang

Writers who choose an informal style usually do so because, although their topics may be serious, they don't want to sound solemn or impersonal. They want their readers to feel as if they're in a conversation.

4 Choose casual language when you want to assume the persona of someone who's relaxed and open. Although it's unlikely you'd choose this style for an academic assignment, you might want to use it if you were writing something for the World Wide Web or for a small group of friends or insiders.

This example came off the Internet, from an article from *Byte* magazine.

 Not to get too Internet on you, but I just downloaded Napster, which lets me cruise the Net for tunes of every stripe, and play them right there on my computer. Well, anything that keeps me from actual work. But think of the vast variety of music out there, and the weird demand for it—Napster, a shareware application, proved so popular at Indiana University's Bloomington campus, for example, according to the *San Francisco Chronicle*, that students were taking up as much as 50 percent of the school's bandwidth downloading tunes instead of chemistry notes.

—Ian Shoales, "Napster"

Shoales's fast-paced, slangy style suits *Byte*, a magazine that pitches its articles to insiders in the computer world.

Writers also choose casual language for intensely personal writing like autobiographical essays, letters, or journals. This example comes from a published diary written by a first-year teacher.

October 5, my birthday. Terrible thing. Somebody stole the Columbus comic book. I said, "Whoever did it, just put it back," but nobody did. So after school I took the whole library down and shoved it in the closet and locked it. The kids noticed right away the next morning.

"I told you if you stole from me, I'd take it all back. I'm not a liar."

"That's not fair," one girl complained. "We didn't all steal the book!" [. . .] I passed out the reading textbooks. The children complained noisily. "You're getting what the rest of the school gets," I reminded them. "I don't see what's the problem."

God, kid! Give me back the stupid book and let me teach you the best way I know how!

—Esme Raji Codell, *Educating Esme*

16a
lang

Codell's choppy sentences, emotional language, and realistic dialogue create a sense of immediacy that draws readers in. While such a colloquial account wouldn't be appropriate for a research article or an academic paper, it's effective here.

Checklist 16.3

Characteristics of Casual Style

* Almost no distance between writer and reader

* Relaxed, casual tone

* Short- to medium-length sentences, short paragraphs

* Concrete and vivid language

* Frequent personal references and contractions

* Lively action verbs

* Frequent slang and colloquial language

EXERCISE 16.1 Working in a small group, decide how you would classify the levels of formality in these passages from two professional writers. Discuss the reasons for any differences.

1. Reading opened up the world. There I was, a skinny bookworm drawing the attention of street kids who, in any other circumstances, would have had me for breakfast. Like an epic tale-teller, I developed the stories as I went along, relying on a flexible plot line and a repository of historical events. I had a great time. I sketched

out trajectories with my finger on Frank's dusty truck bed. And I stretched out each story's climax, creating cliffhangers like the ones I saw in the Saturday serials. These stories created for me a temporary community.

—Mike Rose, *Lives on the Boundary*

2. The women who assembled as delegates at Seneca Falls had demanded equality of opportunity for men and women in affairs of state, church, and family. Elizabeth Cady Stanton, the organizing force and intelligence behind this historic conclave, was an advanced and innovative thinker on women's issues, who understood the complex sources of sexual subordination and, in addition to the vote for women, advocated domestic reforms including the right of women to affirm their sexuality if they chose to do so, or contrarily, to refuse sexual relations altogether when necessary to avoid pregnancy. Stanton also supported cooperative child rearing, rights to property, child custody, and divorce. Though venerated within her own small circle, she came to be viewed by more traditional supporters as a source of potential controversy and embarrassment.

—Ellen Chesler, *Woman of Valor*

16b
lang

EXERCISE 16.2 What level of formality do you think would be appropriate for writing in these situations? In each case, consider what impression you might want to make and how much distance you would want to maintain from readers. Give reasons for your choice.

1. A letter to a representative or senator asking to be considered for a summer internship in his or her office.

2. A brochure recruiting people to work on a house being constructed by Habitat for Humanity.

3. A column in your weekly church newsletter that recounts noteworthy activities by members of the church.

4. A biographical sketch for your World Wide Web home page.

16b How emotionally charged should your language be?

Words affect people strongly, and even subtle differences in meaning can have big effects. If they didn't, it would make no difference whether a teacher called your six-year-old "a highly imaginative child" or "a big liar." And we wouldn't see national debates over hate speech legislation and "political correctness" on college campuses.

It's simply because words are so powerful that writers must understand the kinds of emotional associations words carry and then use them appropriately. And what's appropriate will depend on your writing situation. In some situations, like academic writing and much business writing, strongly charged language may offend readers. In others, including some argumentative and political writing, you may need vehement words to get your point across. This section will help you make these kinds of decisions.

16b
lang

1 Understand how denotation and connotation work.

When writing experts talk about emotionally charged language, they distinguish between two kinds of meaning. **Denotation** is the literal meaning of a word, the object or concept that it refers to. For example, the denotative meaning of *puppy* is "a young dog"—nothing more.

Connotation refers to the emotional associations that go along with a word. For example, connotatively, *puppy* suggests cuteness, playfulness, innocence, and warmth. For many people, it conjures up childhood memories of a favorite pet. Contrast these associations with the ones evoked by *half-grown mongrel*. While this phrase's **denotation** is almost identical to that of *puppy*, its **connotations** are much more negative, suggesting a scruffy cur who knocks over garbage cans and probably bites.

This example shows that even when words share similar denotations, their connotations may range from strongly positive ("puppy") to more neutral ("young dog") to strongly negative ("little mongrel"). Here are a few more examples.

HIGHLIGHT *Similar Denotation, Different Connotations*

VERY POSITIVE ──────▶ NEUTRAL ──────▶ VERY NEGATIVE

urge	remind	nag		browbeat	drive insane
lithe	slender	thin	skinny	scrawny	emaciated
free spirit	nomad	wanderer	homeless person	loafer	bum

Writers need to be concerned about denotation—that is, you should choose words that precisely convey the idea you're trying to express (don't use "puppy" when you really mean "wolf cub"). But for most writers, choosing words with appropriate connotations is a problem. Connotative meanings elicit stronger responses from readers. And because they have to do with the contexts in which particular words are used, they also shift more frequently and vary more from audience to audience. The following sections offer guidelines for choosing the right level of connotation in common writing situations.

2 Choose mostly neutral language for informative research, term papers, case studies, and reports. When you're writing a piece that's primarily informative, your readers usually expect you to give them a neutral report on the topic. They'll probably be put off by strongly emotional language or descriptions designed to evoke pity or outrage. In the following example, the anthropologist Michael Moffett introduces the thesis of his study examining how undergraduate students at Rutgers University chose their majors.

16b
lang

> The top ten majors and all the rest [. . .] fell into a gradient of status in general student opinion, one that was based on three criteria. First, how good was the occupation to which a given subject presumably led? Second, and closely related, how difficult was that subject at Rutgers? And third, much less important, how much social good did the occupation or profession in question accomplish?
> —Michael Moffett, "How College Students Choose Their Majors"

Although Moffett probably holds opinions about what criteria students should use to pick a major, and perhaps even about which majors provide the best educational experience, his purpose here is to report what the students he interviewed for this study thought about the issue. He thus uses neutral, descriptive language, focusing not on his feelings about the topic but on data from his research.

3 Avoid strongly connotative language when you are writing newsletters, press releases, or informative brochures. The audience for these documents might expect a writer to put a positive spin on the information he or she is presenting, but they don't want to be showered with emotional language. They want to draw their own conclusions. Consider this paragraph from a brochure describing a student tutoring program called Helping One Student To Succeed (HOSTS).

> At Zavala Elementary School, teachers select second- and third-grade students to attend the HOSTS program for four half-hour periods each week. Mentors come once a week to meet with students in a cheerful, book-lined classroom for 30 minutes. The students and their mentors read together, talk about books, learn study skills, and practice writing. They also become friends.

This is not strictly neutral language: "a cheerful, book-lined classroom" has positive overtones, as does the last sentence. But the connotation is restrained; it doesn't distract from the information.

Be particularly careful to use such restraint when you're writing a press release or a memo for circulation. You want to avoid giving the impression that you're selling something.

4 Use connotative language appropriately in arguments, reviews, editorials, and opinion pieces. Connotative language sometimes works well when you want to express strong feelings of approval or disapproval. Here are two examples, one that uses language with moderately strong connotations, and one that's more emotionally charged.

The first example is from the conclusion of Roger Ebert's review of the movie classic *Casablanca*. It comes from his Web page, "The Great Movies," at <http://www.suntimes.com/ebert/greatmovies/casablanca.html>.

Stylistically, the film is not so much brilliant as absolutely sound, rock-solid in its use of Hollywood studio craftsmanship. [. . .] Seeing the film over and over again, year after year, I find it never grows over-familiar. It plays like a favorite musical album; the more I know it, the more I like it. The black-and-white cinematography has not aged as color would. The dialogue is so spare and cynical it has not grown old-fashioned. Much of the emotional effect of "Casablanca" is achieved by indirection; as we leave the theater, we are absolutely convinced that the only thing keeping the world from going crazy is that the problems of three little people do after all amount to more than a hill of beans.

—Roger Ebert, *Casablanca*

Ebert uses connotative language effectively here. His praise is restrained but warm, and he supports his claims with details from the film. Such a review is a suitable model for an evaluative piece you might write for a class or a local paper.

Our second passage, taken from a syndicated newspaper column, uses much stronger language.

When hoopla and hype raged over the $368 billion deal with Big Tobacco [in 1997], one unasked question kept nagging. Why are we negotiating with drug pushers?

Why the haggling with an industry that lies about its product, jokes about restrictions and makes a fortune off a drug that kills 300,000 Americans a year? Why treat with kid gloves tobacco companies that sneakily aim advertising gimmicks so every day 3,000 more teenagers are hooked on coffin nails?

—Sandy Grady, "Tobacco Deal Reduced to Ashes"

One encounters this kind of heavy-handed language fairly often on the editorial pages of newspapers and in political campaign literature. Vehement language is sometimes appropriate in these settings, where writers voice strong positions on important questions. Vigorous public debate is a value our culture holds dear—democracy can't thrive without it.

Yet writers take risks when they choose such charged language. Grady's piece is so laden with extreme terms ("drug pushers," "hooked on coffin nails") that it's likely to turn many readers off. As we point out in Section 16c-4, overly sharp language can alienate readers who don't initially agree with your position. Thus, emotionally charged writing is best left for audiences you know well or for settings where readers expect it. This means that it's rarely appropriate for academic writing. (See Section 7a for detailed advice about what instructors expect in academic papers.)

■ 5 Be alert to the connotations in your own language and that of others. As we point out in Section 9b-7, cultivating the ability to recognize connotation plays an important role in becoming a critical thinker. For example, if you encounter a business proposal that's full of phrases like *expand in a robust way, exciting opportunity,* and *meaningful change,* you need to make a careful analysis before you accept the claims. Whose words are these, and what specifics underlie these glowing phrases?

In your own writing, particularly in academic papers, be aware of the connotations your words evoke, both positive and negative. Highly charged words like *unparalleled, superlative, unregenerate, immoral,* and *depraved* are usually too extreme for reports, research papers, and oral presentations. If you do use such terms, give explicit examples that elaborate on them.

16b
lang

EXERCISE 16.3 Working with a group of classmates, list all the synonyms you can think of for one of the following words. Then arrange the words from those with the most positive to those with the most negative connotations. In what writing situations might each be appropriately used, and why?

large luxury car	politician	cry	disorganized
open-minded	single parent	child	strict

EXERCISE 16.4 Find and copy a syndicated newspaper column such as those written by George Will, William Safire, Molly Ivins, or William Raspberry. Underline words and phrases with strong negative or positive connotations. Then copy a news story from the same paper and do the same. Discuss the differences in how the two pieces handle connotative language.

16c How do you choose reader-friendly language?

16c
lang

Have you ever suffered through a lecture that went completely over your head? Or stopped reading an editorial halfway through because the writer made assumptions that insulted you? Or fallen asleep while reading a particularly dull textbook? If so, you know what it's like to try to read a text that's not reader-friendly.

Language is a powerful instrument. Writers use it to voice new ideas, to draw people together, to encourage deliberation, and to effect change. But writers who are careless about word choices or who don't think sufficiently about their audiences may find that their language alienates the readers they want to reach. This is why, when you want to engage readers, it's important that you choose your words carefully. Draw readers into your discussion; don't shut them out.

1 Choose language familiar to your readers. When you're drafting or revising a piece of writing, ask yourself whether your readers will be comfortable with the vocabulary you're using. There are times when a difficult or technical term *is* appropriate—when it draws a subtle distinction or describes a complex phenomenon that simpler words can't capture. But writers sometimes wrongly assume that they need to impress readers by choosing formal and highly complicated language. The result is more likely to seem stuffy and difficult to read than smart and sophisticated. Here's an example from an academic paper:

UNNECESSARILY DIFFICULT LANGUAGE
Scholarly authorities hold a myriad of viewpoints with regard to the ongoing disputation involving the major prescription drug companies' ethical obligation to manufacture minimally profitable pharmaceuticals that ameliorate the world's major diseases.

REVISED

Scholars disagree on whether big drug companies have a moral obligation to manufacture low-profit drugs to treat the world's major diseases.

See how much more readable the second sentence is? Our point is that even when you're writing in a relatively formal style, you'll reach more readers by choosing familiar words when you can. Usually that's not hard to do; you can find good substitutes for most high-level words. See Section 18c for more tips on reworking inflated sentences.

2 Balance abstract and concrete language. Abstract words are general; they refer to ideas, concepts, and categories that we can't perceive directly through our five senses—words like *justice, charm, culture, life*. Concrete words do just the opposite; they name specific people and things that we can see, hear, taste, smell, or touch—*Judge Joe Brown, grin, turquoise bracelet, my pet poodle*. Of course, most words are neither wholly abstract nor concrete. They exist on a continuum between the two extremes, and writers must decide what level of specificity seems most appropriate for their purpose. For example:

16c
lang

HIGHLIGHT *The Continuum from Abstract to Concrete*

MOST ABSTRACT			MOST CONCRETE
publication	➤ book	➤ 19th-century British novel	➤ dogeared copy of *Oliver Twist*
food	➤ vegetable	➤ lettuce	➤ fresh-picked Romaine leaves from my garden
vehicle	➤ car	➤ convertible	➤ red 1960 Corvair

Passages laden with too many abstractions can be intimidating and hard to follow. Yet writing that contains nothing but specifics gives readers too little guidance; readers may not see the main point amid all the details. That's why skilled writers strive for an effective mix of both. They use abstract terms to help readers grasp big ideas and connections but provide plenty of vivid and concrete images to illustrate those ideas and to hold readers' interest. Exactly what ratio of abstract to concrete language you use in a particular text will depend on your writing situation. For more on balancing concrete and abstract language, see Sections 18b-1 (sentences) and 13c-1 (paragraphs).

■ **3 Limit your use of jargon.** Jargon comes in two forms. The specialized insider language of professional groups is one kind of jargon. Physicians, for instance, use the terms *hypertension* and *ideopathic* among themselves; lawyers use the terms *tort* and *indemnify;* graphic artists use the terms *pixel* and *color separation.* When you're writing for a group of specialists, these technical terms are a necessary part of your vocabulary. But you'll shut out readers if you use this kind of jargon when you're writing for an audience that includes nonspecialists.

When you need to use a specialized term, define it the first time you use it and then give an example. For example, using the term *endorphin* in an article about exercise, you could explain that an endorphin is a chemical in the brain that raises an individual's pain threshold, and then you might give as an example of the chemical's effect the sense of well-being that many people claim to feel after strenuous exercise.

16c
lang

A second kind of jargon is abstract, impersonal writing full of long sentences and nominalizations (see Section 18c-2). Writing that contains this sort of jargon is especially common in academic and bureaucratic settings. Here is an example.

> When systems of institutional control are working without significant challenge, the authority of the knowledge embodied in the institutions seems similarly potent. When the institutions are attacked and then fragment, however, problems about knowledge and its legitimacy come to the fore.
> —Stephen Shapin, *The Scientific Revolution*

This isn't *bad* writing; it's clear enough to someone practiced in reading this level of language and willing to make the effort to understand it. But this kind of noun-laden, abstract writing can intimidate general readers and thus lose them. If you find you've lapsed into this style for an opinion piece, a book review, or an important report, you'll do well to revise, to use more concrete and personal language.

■ **4 Use a civil, fair-minded tone for public writing.** Striking the right tone in your writing is crucial. When you want to build common ground with your readers and convince them to consider your ideas, try to come across as an open-minded person who doesn't feel she has all the answers. Treat your audience—even those whom you suspect may disagree with you—with respect.

Most readers will be put off by an author who sounds arrogant and contemptuous. Consider the following passage.

The existence of a literature presupposes a literate and coherent public that has both the time to read and a need to take seriously the works of the literary imagination. I'm not sure whether the United States ever had such a public; certainly it hasn't had one for the last thirty years. What we have instead is an opening-night crowd, astonished by celebrity and opulent spectacle, tolerating only those authors who present themselves as freaks and wonders and offer the scandal of their lives as proof of their art.

—Lewis Lapham, "Notebook"

Lapham is a longtime social critic who has been writing his grumpy column for *Harper's* for years. Undoubtedly the caustic tone—characterized by put-downs, name-calling, sarcasm, and sweeping condemnations—appeals to some people, particularly those who already agree with the author. But readers who are looking for information or enlightenment will usually feel insulted and quit reading.

16c
lang

If you want readers to pay attention to your concerns, begin with the assumption that your readers are intelligent and that each of you is able to understand the other's point of view. Avoid name-calling and blanket generalizations. Instead of making pronouncements, qualify your claims using words and phrases such as *It's possible that . . . , One solution is . . . , in many cases, often, usually.* Such terms suggest and

Humor is not always civil. Satirical items like those posted regularly on The Onion *(at <http:www.theonion.com>) push the envelope, hoping to amuse and, sometimes, even offend readers.*

speculate rather than dictate. For more on constructing a credible image in your writing, see Section 1g. For advice on handling different viewpoints, consult Section 11c.

5 Build common ground by referring to experiences readers can identify with. One of the joys of language is that it allows us to tell stories, and through stories we build community. For example, if you're writing an appeal for volunteers to work in your local Habitat for Humanity program, you can tell of the satisfaction you got from working with two young women carpenters to build a house. You could also give colorful details about the family who put in their own "sweat equity" so they could move into the house.

In an article on alcoholism, you could describe one family's struggle with it over three generations, the kind of story that former Senator George McGovern recounts in his 1996 book about his daughter, *Terry: My Daughter's Life-and-Death Struggle with Alcoholism*. The plague of alcoholism touches so many lives that such accounts strike a chord with large numbers of readers. Because McGovern based his book on excerpts from his daughter's diary, his stories are particularly effective.

EXERCISE 16.5 Revise one of the passages below to achieve a more effective balance between abstract and concrete language. You may need to add sentences and revise existing sentences. Discuss your revisions with a group of classmates.

1. Never buy a pet from a pet shop without first checking to see where the establishment gets its animals. Many stores buy their stock from unregulated "puppy mills," where large numbers of animals are raised in terrible conditions. Buyers may end up with a sick or mentally damaged pet.

2. During the month of February, twelve students were mugged at knifepoint in the main student parking garage. In April, a woman barricaded herself in the garage elevator to escape an assailant. In June, two cars parked on the top level of the garage had their windshields smashed. My roommate is even afraid to park her car on campus.

EXERCISE 16.6 Revise the following paragraph to create a more civil and appropriate tone. Assume that you're writing to readers of your campus newspaper.

Apparently the university "doesn't have the funds" this year to renovate the dorms on campus. Yeah, right. It's tough for me to believe that there's a money shortage when every time I pass by the president's house he's having another fancy party for his rich donor friends. Everyone knows that all the administrators do is go to parties, make a speech every now and then, and draw fat salaries. What a scam! They don't care about the students; they just care about lining their wallets. If they had to live in our dorms, I bet we'd see some upgrades pretty fast.

16d How do you avoid stereotyped language?

Biased language isn't always bad. Slanted but colorful writing regularly enlivens articles in popular books and magazines and the editorial pages of any newspaper. Consider this passage about Internet users.

 Certain early users of the Net (bless them!) are now whining about its vulgarization, warning people of its hazards as if it were a cigarette. If only these whiners were more honest, they'd admit that it was they who didn't have much of a life and found solace on the Net, they who woke up one day in midlife crisis and discovered there was more to living than what was waiting in their e-mail boxes. So, what took you guys so long? Of course there's more to life than e-mail, but don't project your empty existence onto others and suggest "being digital" is a form of virtual leprosy for which total abstinence is the only immunization.
                              —Nicholas Negroponte, "Get a Life?"

The example comes from *Wired* magazine, a publication written and read by computer buffs who would freely admit they're far from objective about the Internet. And Negroponte makes no pretense to objectivity. He uses vigorous, colorful language to poke fun at attitudes held by certain members of his audience. Yet because he's written for these readers so often, and because his humor targets insiders who feel comfortable in the computer world, his exaggerated complaints entertain rather than offend his audience.

When you write papers in college, in business, or in most community settings, however, you have a different kind of audience. Now you're writing to inform or persuade readers whom you don't know well, and you don't want to offend them by lapsing into language that excludes a part of your audience or suggests that you think in stereotypes.

No matter who their audience may be, responsible writers will avoid language that stigmatizes or demeans particular groups. Language that attributes to individuals negative associations based on gender, race or ethnicity, religion, profession, or class is always out of place in public writing.

This section suggests ways of eliminating offensive stereotypes in your writing.

■ 1 Avoid sexist language.

1 Avoid sexist language. Activists in the women's movement of the last four decades have made most of us more aware of how profoundly language shapes attitudes and reinforces traditional gender roles. Twenty-five years ago, when the typical writer consistently referred to doctors, scientists, inventors, and artists as "he" and to secretaries, nurses, teachers, and receptionists as "she," youngsters got strong messages about which professions they were expected to choose.

You seldom see such ingrained bias in today's newspapers, books, and magazines, although occasionally a quotation reveals a person's biased attitudes. For instance, a 1990 *New York Times* article quoted a federal appeals judge as saying (emphasis added):

> Whatever the philosophy of the particular judge, and whether **he** views **his** proper role as broad or narrow, **his** decisions—some of them at least—necessarily resolve issues previously unsettled and thus will declare law.

Most readers today will find this language sexist and offensive.

To keep sexist blunders out of your writing, keep these guidelines in mind.

- **Avoid using *he* and *him* as all-purpose pronouns to refer to people in general.** Don't write "Everyone should remember *he* is a student."

WHY WRITE . . .	WHEN YOU COULD WRITE . . .
Every executive expects *his* bonus.	Every executive expects *a* bonus. Executives expect *their* bonuses. Every executive expects *his or her* bonus.

- **Guard against using the word *man* as a catchall term to refer to all people or all members of a group.** Don't write "All *men* are subject to disappointment" or "The company merger threw thousands of *men* out of work." Instead use *people* as a general term, or refer to a specific occupation or role: *worker, parent, voter.*

WHY WRITE . . .	WHEN YOU COULD WRITE . . .
the *man* who wants to be an astronaut	*anyone* who wants to be an astronaut
men who make their own auto repairs	*car owners* who make their own repairs

- **Watch out for assumptions that professions or roles are primarily for men or for women.** Don't write "Any senator will improve *his* chances of election by going back home frequently" or "A nurse usually starts *her* profession when *she* is in *her* twenties." Also be careful not to slip into hidden assumptions by writing "woman doctor" or "woman engineer," thereby suggesting one wouldn't expect to find women in those professions.

WHY WRITE . . .	WHEN YOU COULD WRITE . . .
men who hope to become scholarship athletes	*young people* who hope to become scholarship athletes
housewives who like to cook	*people* who like to cook
policeman	police officer
mailman	mail carrier/letter carrier
cleaning woman	custodian/janitor
businessmen	business executives

- **When possible, find out what name a married woman wants to go by and honor that choice.** Here are the possibilities:

woman's first and last names	Olga Perez
woman's first and last names + husband's last name	Olga Perez Marciano
woman's first name + hyphenated last name	Olga Perez-Marciano
woman's first name + husband's last name	Olga Marciano
title + husband's full name	Mrs. Ralph Marciano

Some traditionalists may find this array of choices complicated and unnecessary; to many women, however, the distinctions are important. Many women, single or married, prefer the title *Ms.* to *Miss* or *Mrs.* When you're not sure, *Ms.* is the best choice.

- **Watch out for between-the-lines implications that men and women behave in stereotypical ways.** Don't suggest that women are generally talkative and overly emotional or that most men are sports-minded and sloppy. Avoid sexist descriptions such as "a slim blonde" or "a petite brunette" unless you make the same kind of comments about men. Finally, the generic term *woman* (or *women*) is more appropriate than *lady* or *girl*, which many women find patronizing.

EXERCISE 16.7 Rewrite the following sentences to eliminate sexist language or implications. If necessary, refer to Chapter 29 for strategies.

1. Women who want to look their best in their forties and fifties often consider cosmetic surgery.

2. Today even a high school physics teacher should know his astrophysics, or he'll look out of date to his students.

3. The hospital's new series of nutrition workshops appeals to mothers concerned about their children's health.

4. Businesswomen often worry about leaving their children in day care while they work long hours to get ahead.

5. The lady running for Congress in my district has been a county judge for many years.

2 Avoid ethnic, racial, and religious stereotypes. In many writing situations you simply don't need to mention race or national origin—it's not relevant. In writing about general topics—business or the media or education, for example—the race or nationality of individuals is often unimportant. At other times, however, issues of race or nationality may be central to your discussion. In such cases, these guidelines may be helpful.

- **Be as accurate as possible.** For example, the term *Asian* (now widely preferred to *Oriental*) is so broad as to be almost useless. There are dozens of countries in Asia, and their cultures and the physical characteristics of their people vary greatly. You'll do much better to use *Filipino, Japanese, Chinese, Korean, Indian,* and so on. When you refer to individuals whose forebears came from one of these countries but who are themselves American-born, combine the term with *American: Japanese American, Korean American,* and so on.

  Many people of Spanish descent in the Americas no longer like the term *Hispanic*—again, it's extremely broad and suggests that all such people share similar traits and cultures. You'll do better to be specific: *Cuban, Puerto Rican, Mexican, Brazilian,* and so on. When appropriate, combine the name with *American—Mexican American, Cuban American,* and so on. The term *Latino* (or

Latina), used to refer broadly to people of Latin American descent, is widely accepted.

American Indian and *Native American* are both acceptable when you're writing about the people who originally populated North America. But many of the North American natives whom we have traditionally thought of as *Eskimos* have come to prefer the designation *Inuit,* and that term is now official with the Canadian government. *Eskimo* remains appropriate, however, in an archaeological or cultural context, such as speaking of *Eskimo carvings*.

When you're writing about individuals' religious affiliations, be similarly specific; generalizations such as *Eastern sects* and *Christian conservatives* are vague and inaccurate. It's better to specify a particular religion or denomination—*Sikh Muslims, Orthodox Jews, Southern Baptists*—or to name a particular religious group—*Promise Keepers, Campus Crusade for Christ.*

16d
lang

- **Use terminology preferred by the people you're writing about, insofar as you know their preferences.** When you're not sure, adopt the terminology you see in respected newspapers and magazines or hear on major television or radio news shows (but not call-in talk shows). Most media editors are careful about their language.

  The term currently favored by individuals whose forebears came from Africa seems to have shifted to *African American,* although *black* is still widely used. *The New York Times,* a dependable source for up-to-date usage, shifts back and forth between the terms. The terms *Negro* and *colored people* are no longer appropriate for public writing. The term *people of color,* popular with many writers concerned about choosing unbiased language, seems too vague to be useful for identifying African Americans and probably should be reserved for broadly designating nonwhite groups.

- **Be careful not to allow ethnic, national, or religious stereotypes to seep into your writing.** Might one infer from your language that you think of Jews as rich financiers? Is there a hint that someone with an Italian surname has underworld connections? Or an innuendo suggesting that a person of Middle-Eastern origin might sympathize with anti-American terrorists? Check your writing for such biases.

EXERCISE 16.8 Almost everyone has had some experience with the difficult issue of ethnic labels and names. Working with fellow students, make a list of all the ethnic groups represented in your composition class, writing on the board the terms preferred by members of each definable group. Discuss those preferences and a writer's responsibility to know and use them.

EXERCISE 16.9 Consider which of these sentences might be inappropriate in an academic paper. Which seem acceptable? Why? Write an alternative for those that aren't appropriate.

1. Jewish director-producer Steven Spielberg traces his interest in filmmaking back to his childhood, when he recorded family occasions with his parents' movie camera.

2. Negro baseball players formed their own leagues in the early 1900s.

3. Indians, Eskimos, and other primitive groups are often portrayed sympathetically in the movies.

4. Unlike most American teenagers, Asian students are typically hardworking, academically oriented, and respectful of authority figures.

16d
lang

3 Avoid stereotypes about age, physical condition, and sexual orientation. If you were born in the United States, part of your heritage is the assertion in the Declaration of Independence that all of us are created equal. Of course, we haven't always done a good job of living up to it. Slavery, the Chinese Exclusion Act, the disenfranchisement of women and African Americans, and many other instances testify to that. But most of us still want to work toward the ideal of just treatment, and in language such treatment means not demeaning or patronizing people based on traits they cannot control. These guidelines may be helpful.

- **Consider that many persons over age 60 don't like being called** *elderly, senior citizens,* **or** *old people.* Most seem to prefer *older people* or, better, a specific designation such as *people in their sixties* (or *late seventies,* and so on). Don't slip into patronizing remarks such as "For a 70-year-old, he's remarkably alert."
- **Reserve the terms** *boys, girls,* **and** *kids* **for people under eighteen.** Young working adults just out of high school deserve to be called men and women. So do college students, whether they are first-year students or graduate students. The phrase *college kids,* which many people use unthinkingly, is rather patronizing. It's also inaccurate: almost half of all U.S. college students now are over 25, and a great many of them have families and major responsibilities. When you refer to people under age 18, *child* or *adolescent* is widely preferred to *kid.*

- **When referring to individuals or groups with disabilities or illnesses, be as specific as possible and avoid language that implies pity**—for example, *crippled* and *victim.* The phrases *visually handicapped* and *hearing impaired* are descriptive and objective; so are *a person with multiple sclerosis* and *a paraplegic.* In general, it works well to mention the individual first and his or her handicap or disease second—"a person with AIDS" or "my cousin who is autistic." Terms such as *disabled veteran* and *a person with muscular disability* seem generally acceptable. Once again, it's useful to know with what terms the individuals themselves feel comfortable.
- **Mention a person's sexual orientation only when it is relevant to the issue under discussion, and then use specific, nonjudgmental terminology.** Many people whose sexual orientation is toward their own gender seem comfortable with the adjective *homosexual* to refer to both men and women but less comfortable with the noun, *a homosexual.* They choose the terms *gay* and *lesbian* when they want to be specific about an individual's sexual orientation. Although some groups of gay rights activists use the word *queer* in their literature, that term is clearly offensive coming from someone outside such a group.

16d
lang

EXERCISE 16.10 Working in a group, decide which of these sentences have hints of offensive bias (some of them are certainly arguable). Which might be acceptable in some circumstances? How could you change those that are not?

1. The chemistry professor was impressed to see that most of the girls in his advanced course had scored high marks on the exam.

2. Barney Frank, who is almost the only open homosexual in the U.S. Congress, represents a district in Massachusetts.

3. Although Betty Friedan is over 70, she still writes extensively and travels widely.

4. The hospice is looking for volunteers to help AIDS victims with household tasks and grocery shopping.

5. Many Americans were unaware that President Franklin Delano Roosevelt was crippled, since he was rarely photographed in his wheelchair during public appearances.

4 Avoid language that reflects flippant or derisive attitudes toward some professions or implies unflattering class distinctions. When you're writing at a formal level, it's better to avoid occupational labels that carry a tinge of contempt. *Shrink* for psychiatrist is one; so is *cop* for police officer. *Prof* for professor doesn't go over well, nor does *computer nerd* or *techie* for computer technician. On the other hand, calling a medical doctor a *physician* or a lawyer an *attorney* conveys respect for those individuals, as does the word *journalist* instead of *reporter*.

Be careful, too, about using terms that may have negative class connotations. The phrases *yuppie, fraternity guy, soccer mom,* and *dotcom millionaire* may be literally accurate, but they have accusatory overtones that suggest shallowness and snobbery. Many social work professionals have come to feel that the label *lower-class* is demeaning; they prefer *disadvantaged*. The term *inner city* is preferable to *slum* or *ghetto,* which suggest squalor. Other class markers to avoid are *welfare mother, dropout,* and *redneck.*

16d
lang

EXERCISE 16.11   Which of these sentences might alienate a reader sensitive to bias? Which ones should be changed? Why or why not? What changes would you suggest?

1. The cops used poor judgment about gathering evidence at the crime scene.

2. Welfare mothers have become the target of budget-conscious legislators who believe that taxpayers shouldn't have to support people who don't work.

3. That organization is known for attracting sorority girls and fraternity guys.

4. It's amazing that Jason became a successful lawyer, since he grew up in the inner-city ghetto, surrounded by poverty and despair.

■ 5 **Use your good judgment and keep your sense of humor when you write.** Don't sanitize your writing to the point that it becomes deadly dull. Every day we read columnists or listen to commentators who use biased language to spoof, satirize, persuade, or praise, and they do it very well. Consider this example from the syndicated columnist and humorist Dave Barry.

If the psychology community needs further proof of the difference between genders, I invite it to attend the party held by my neighborhood each Halloween. This party is attended by several hundred children, who are experiencing stress because their bloodstreams [. . .] contain roughly the same sugar content as Cuba. Here's how the various genders respond: The females, 97 percent of whom are dressed as either a ballerina or a princess, sit in little social groups and exchange candy. The males, 97 percent of whom are dressed as either Batman or a Power Ranger, run around making martial-arts noises and bouncing violently off each other like crazed subatomic particles.   —Dave Barry, "Neither Man nor Rat Can Properly Fold the Laundry"

Exaggerated images? Of course. Gender and age stereotypes? Definitely. Biased language? Certainly. But fun? Absolutely. Insulting to Barry's readers? Almost certainly not; they probably loved it.

It's unrealistic to say you should never use biased or exaggerated language to convey a mood, create an image, or make sardonic comments. Like a professional writer, however, you should make it your goal to be so attuned to your readers that you can write for them with respect, awareness, and good taste—and still have fun with language.

16e
lang

16e How do you handle language varieties?

Do you speak differently in different settings? Do you use language in different ways depending on whether you're at home with your family, hanging out with friends, working, or writing a paper for a course? If you're like most people in the United States, you know several varieties of English, each shaped by your cultural heritage, your region, and your exposure to other languages. Linguists call these varieties of English **dialects**. Dialects of English—which include southern dialect, northeastern dialect, African American Vernacular English, and many others—differ from each other in vocabulary, pronunciation, and grammar. Their features can be quite distinctive.

One dialect of English, sometimes referred to as **edited American English**, or standard English, is the language used in most academic, business, and public writing. It's the variety taught in most schools and emphasized in this book. If a dialect you use in other settings differs from this "standard," you may have difficulties when some of its features appear in your writing. You can use this handbook and other resources, such as your campus writing center, to edit out those features.

Learning to use a standard dialect for certain writing situations doesn't mean that you have to abandon all others. It means only that you have to cultivate some flexibility so that you can switch back and forth among different ways of speaking as the situation demands. But all educated people need to be able to use the standard written dialect of the United States, edited American English, so they can communicate on an equal footing with the millions of others who use it.

In addition to the various dialects of English, many languages are spoken in the United States. If you speak English as your second language (ESL), you'll find information in Chapters 31 to 33 to help you with the challenges of writing in a new language.

This section offers suggestions for dealing with dialects and languages in your writing.

1 Recognize the uses and importance of dialects. Dialects are important and useful to the groups that speak them. A dialect helps to hold a group together and to give it a sense of community and identity. Those who belong to a dialect group feel comfortable with each other because it's reassuring to be around other people who "talk your language." Thus dialects act as a major source of strength within a group and, as such, should be appreciated and protected for private communication between individuals within a particular community. Usually such communication is spoken.

Here is how the writer James Lee Burke represents the Cajun dialect of southern Louisiana in a novel.

> She had put my three-legged raccoon, Tripod, on his chain. [. . .] She pulled him up in the air by his chain. His body danced and curled as if he were being garroted.
> "Clarise, don't do that."
> "Ask him what he done, him," she said. "Go look my wash basket. Go look your shirts. They blue yesterday. They brown now. So smell, you."
> "I'll take him down to the dock."
> "Tell Batiste not to bring him back, no. [. . .] He come in my house again, you gonna see him cooking with the sweet potato."
> —James Lee Burke, *Black Cherry Blues*

2 Acknowledge the limitations of dialect. When dialects show up in *public writing*—and that is what most of the writing you do in college and your profession will be—they can be misunderstood and misinterpreted. Some vocabulary within a dialect may not be understood by those outside it. Certain grammatical forms that are completely natural and logical within a community may be regarded as nonstandard by other users of the language.

In this passage from the novel *The Bluest Eye,* Toni Morrison represents the dialect known as Black English or African American Vernacular English (AAVE).

The onliest time I be happy seem like was when I was in the picture show. Everytime I got, I went. I'd go early, before the show started. They'd cut off the lights, and everything be black. Then the screen would light up, and I'd move right in on them pictures. [. . .] Them pictures give me a lot of pleasure, but it made coming home hard, and looking at Cholly hard.

—Toni Morrison, *The Bluest Eye*

The passage reveals the character Pauline's most private kind of communication, inner speech to herself.

This conversation between two characters in a novel of the early West, *Zeke and Ned,* offers another example of private dialect.

16e
lang

"Jewel's not a talker," Ned admitted. "That don't mean she's easy to live with, though."

"Why, where'd you get the notion that women are easy to live with," Tuxie asked. "Women are a passel of trouble, though I need my Dale."

"I wish Jewel would let up about my leaving," Ned said. "I need to go to town once in a while. It's boresome, getting drunk at home."

—Larry McMurtry and Dianna Ossana, *Zeke and Ned*

Here the private language of two articulate men carries the flavor of their personalities, but "passel of trouble" and "It's boresome" would sound out of place and colloquial in a written communication.

Letting a private dialect intrude into your public writing, then, is not so much "wrong" as it is inappropriate. When your readers find the marks of your personal language in writing that is directed to a group of readers who don't share that dialect, they'll be jarred by the mismatch.

3 Use dialect when appropriate. When can you use dialect in your writing? First, you can use it in your private life among friends or others who share the dialect, either in conversation or in letters or email. Second, you might use it in a first, discovery draft when you're trying to get your ideas down and don't want to slow your thinking by worrying about the conventions of standard English. (You can edit out or translate inappropriate dialect features in a future draft.) Finally, you might use dialect in an anecdote you are adding to a paper to illustrate a point, or you could incorporate it into dialogue that is an essential part of a personal narrative. Here's an example from a professional writer:

Two years ago, when I started writing this paper, trying to bring order out of chaos, my ten-year-old daughter was suffering from an acute attack of boredom. [. . .] Patiently I explained that I was working on something special and needed peace and quiet, and I suggested that she paint, read, or work with her computer. None of these interested her. Finally, she pulled up a chair to my desk and watched me, now and then heaving long, loud sighs. [. . .] I lost my patience. "Looka here, Allie," I said, "you too old for this kinda carryin' on. I done told you this is important. You wronger than dirt to be in here haggin' me like this and you know it."

—Barbara Mellix, "From Outside, In"

16e
lang

Except for these instances, however, spoken dialect generally doesn't fit into the kind of public writing you'll be doing in college, in business, or in community work.

4 Use languages other than English when appropriate.

If you speak a language other than English, you might use it in your writing for the same reasons that you'd use varieties of English. You might use it in your private life to communicate among friends or family or to explore and develop ideas before beginning a writing project.

You might also use another langauge to reproduce a speaker's exact words or to create an authentic atmosphere in a description or narrative. Finally, it's appropriate to include non-English words that can't easily be translated into English, as the essayist Judith Ortiz Cofer does in the following example.

Even the home movie cannot fill in the sensory details such a gathering [a family New Year's Eve party] left imprinted in a child's brain. The thick sweetness of women's perfumes mixing with the ever-present smells of food cooking in the kitchen: meat and plantain *pasteles*, as well as the ubiquitous rice dish made special with pigeon peas—*gandules*—and seasoned with previous *sofrito* sent up from the Island by somebody's mother or smuggled in by a recent traveler.

—Judith Ortiz Cofer, "Silent Dancing"

As with dialect, words and phrases from different languages should be used in public writing only to achieve a particular effect—otherwise you'll risk confusing readers. And if the meaning of a word or phrase isn't apparent from the context, it's wise to provide an English translation, as Cofer does above.

CHAPTER 17

How Do You Construct Effective Sentences?

17a How are sentences structured?

Traditional terms used to describe the architecture of sentences— *clauses, phrases, subordination, coordination, parallelism*—can make writing sentences seem complicated. But even the most complex sentences are based on a few comprehensible structures and principles. We cover these elements in this chapter.

We know, of course, that you'll rarely think about particular sentence structures when you compose. Few writers—if any—work that way. But even while dashing off a draft, you'll be more confident when you've developed a feel for the way sentences function, an instinct for how the parts fit together.

1 Understand sentence patterns. Sentences are tough to define. A sentence can be described as a group of words that expresses an idea and that is punctuated as an independent unit. All sentences have a **subject** (the doer of an action) and a **predicate** (the action done). Beginning with this assumption, you'll find that just five patterns can describe the framework of many sentences you write. In recognizing these patterns and their variations, you take a step toward controlling the shape of your sentences. The patterns may also remind you of key sentence concepts and elements, such as transitive and intransitive verbs, direct objects, indirect objects, and complements.

1. **Subject + verb (intransitive).** This is the simplest sentence pattern, the one with the fewest parts. Like all sentences, it includes a *subject*, the doer of an action; and a *verb*, the action performed. But in this pattern the verb is *intransitive*—that is, it doesn't need an object to complete its meaning.

Subject	Verb (intransitive)
The lawyer	fainted.
The floodwaters	receded.
All the children	smiled at once.

EXERCISE 17.1 Compose three sentences that follow the subject–intransitive verb pattern. Underline the intransitive verb in each sentence.

2. **Subject + verb (transitive) + direct object.** This sentence pattern adds a third element to the subject and verb: an *object*, which identifies to what or to whom an action has been done. Objects can be words, phrases, or clauses. The pattern requires a transitive verb that conveys its action to an object.

Subject	Verb (transitive)	Object
The lawyer	accepted	the case.
The heavy rains	destroyed	the levee.
Some of the children	were reading	books.

Note that the subject–verb–object pattern illustrates the *active voice*, in which the subject performs the action described by the transitive verb. But when that action is performed by the object, you have a *passive construction* (see Section 23e).

The case was accepted by the lawyer.
The levee was destroyed by heavy rains.
The books were being read by some of the children.

Only transitive verbs can be involved in passive constructions because they require an object that can become a subject. Intransitive verbs don't take objects.

It is important that a transitive verb and its object fit together logically. In the following example, the verb *intimidate* cannot logically convey its action to the object *enthusiasm*. *Enthusiasm* might be *undermined, dampened,* or *eroded,* but we don't usually speak of it as *intimidated.*

FAULTY The negative attitudes of the senior staff *intimidated* the **enthusiasm** of the volunteers.

REVISED The negative attitudes of the senior staff *dampened* the **enthusiasm** of the volunteers.

EXERCISE 17.2 Write three sentences that follow the subject–verb–object pattern. Underline the object. Be sure the verb is in the active voice.

EXERCISE 17.3 Revise any of the following sentences in which the boldfaced verb cannot logically convey its action to its object. First try to explain the problem with the original verb; then change the verb, not the object.

1. At her parents' request, Margery **interrogated** her sister Kyla's low grades at college.

2. Kyla **blasphemed** her instructor's methods of teaching history.

3. Her psychology instructor **jaded** her with long lectures about statistics and methods.

4. Her chemistry teacher **obliged** difficult lab reports every week.

5. Worst of all, her English teacher persistently **admonished** the clarity of her writing.

17a
sent

3. **Subject + verb (linking) + subject complement.** Linking verbs, which are often forms of *to be*, connect a subject to a **subject complement**, that is, to a word or phrase that extends or completes the meaning of a subject or renames it in some way. Among the common linking verbs are *to seem, to appear, to feel,* and *to become.*

Subject	Linking verb	Subject complement
The lawyer	became	a federal judge.
The storms	seemed	endless.
The children	are	happy.

A complement should be compatible with its subject. When it is not, the sentence is illogical, sometimes subtly so.

FAULTY COMPLEMENT   **Prejudice** is unacceptable **behavior** in this club.

The problem is that *prejudice* is not behavior; it's an attitude. So the sentence has to be modified to reflect this difference.

REVISED   **Prejudiced behavior** is unacceptable in this club.

For the same reason, it's wrong to use *when* as a complement.

> WRONG   **Plagiarism** is **when** a writer doesn't credit her source.

When is an adverb; *plagiarism* is a noun. *Plagiarism* has to be a concept or an idea, so it cannot be *when*.

> RIGHT   **Plagiarism** is the **failure** to credit a source.

EXERCISE 17.4 In the following sentences, indicate whether the bold-faced words are objects or complements.

1. Halloween may be the oddest **holiday** of the year.

2. The roots of Halloween are deeply **religious.**

3. But Halloween celebrations today seem quite **secular.**

4. Children and adults wear **costumes** and pull **pranks.**

5. For all its images of ghosts and goblins, Halloween now seems less **scary.**

EXERCISE 17.5 Write three sentences that follow the subject–verb–subject complement pattern. Underline the subject complement. Try to vary your linking verbs.

EXERCISE 17.6 Revise any of the following sentences in which the subject complement cannot work logically with its subject. First explain the problem with the original complement; then change the complement, not the subject. The complement is boldfaced.

1. Photography is an excellent **fun.**

2. Revising every paper in this class four times seems **exorbitant.**

3. Gerald felt **unconscionable** after arriving too late to say farewell.

4. Philosophy is **when** you read Plato and Aristotle.

5. Wearing baggy jeans quickly became **free and easy** among youngsters.

4. **Subject + verb (transitive) + indirect object + direct object.** An **indirect object** explains for whom or what an action is done or directed. As you can see in this pattern, indirect objects ordinarily precede direct objects.

Subject	Verb (transitive)	Indirect object	Direct object
The lawyer	found	the clerk	a job.
The storms	brought	local farmers	needed rain.
The children	told	their parents	stories.

If you have trouble understanding what an indirect object does in a sentence, turn it into the object of a prepositional phrase.

> The lawyer found a job **for the clerk.**
> The storms brought needed rain **to local farmers.**
> The children told stories **to their parents.**

17a
sent

EXERCISE 17.7 In the following sentences, circle the indirect objects and underline the objects.

1. The IRS agent asked the auditor three tough questions.

2. The placement office finds students jobs after college.

3. Did you send Rosa, Peg, Lester, and Davida the same email message?

4. Give Daisy more cookies.

5. The distinguished senator gives proponents of the National Endowment for the Arts headaches.

EXERCISE 17.8 Write three sentences that follow the subject–verb–indirect object–direct object pattern. Circle the indirect object and underline the direct object.

5. **Subject + verb (transitive) + direct object + object complement.** Just as a subject complement modifies or explains a subject, an **object complement** does the same for the object of a sentence.

Subject	Verb (transitive)	Direct object	Object complement
The lawyer	called	the verdict	surprising.
The flood	caught	the town	napping.
The children	found	their spinach	vile.

EXERCISE 17.9 In the following sentences, underline the direct objects and circle the object complements.

1. Most men find football entertaining.
2. Thoroughbred horses often turn their wealthy owners poor.
3. Our careful preparation makes us lucky.
4. The mayor called the federal court decision against the city ordinance unfortunate.
5. The justices considered the mayor's appeal frivolous.

17a
sent

EXERCISE 17.10 Write three sentences that follow the subject–verb–direct object–object complement pattern. Underline the direct object and circle the subject complement.

2 Understand compound subjects, verbs, and objects.

You can develop sentences simply by expanding their subjects, verbs, or objects to include all the ideas you need to express. Such modifications are usually routine, but some writers do have problems punctuating the resulting sentences.

Compound subjects. Two subjects attached to the same verb are usually connected by the conjunction *and* or *or*. No comma is needed between these compound subjects.

> **Lawyers and judges** attended the seminar.
> **Storms or fires** ravage California each year.

When a third subject is added, the items are separated by commas (see Section 36c-3).

> **Storms, fires, and earthquakes** ravage California each year.

Subjects can also be expanded by expressions such as *neither . . . nor* and *either . . . or*, which are called **correlatives**.

> **Neither the judge nor the lawyer** attended the seminar.
> **Either fires or earthquakes** strike California each year.

Compound verbs. Single subjects can perform more than one action. When they do, the verbs attached to them are compound. Like nouns, verbs can be joined by *and*, *or*, or correlatives such as *either . . . or*. No comma should be used between two verbs that form a compound verb.

> The judge **confused and angered** the prosecutor.
> The earthquake **damaged or destroyed** many homes.
> Children **either like or hate** spinach.

When a third verb is added, the items are separated by commas.

> The judge **confused, angered, and embarrassed** the prosecutor.

Compound verbs can each take separate objects, expanding the sentence structure even more.

> The judge **confused** *the jury* and **angered** *the prosecutor.*
> The earthquake **damaged** *roads* and **destroyed** *homes.*

Compound objects. A verb may also have more than one object. Two objects attached to the same verb are usually connected by the conjunction *and* or *or.* No comma is needed between two objects; commas are required for three or more objects.

> Lawyers attended **the seminar and the dinner.**
>
> Forest fires ravage **California, Arizona, New Mexico, or Colorado every year.**

Objects can also be connected with correlatives.

> Forest fires ravage **either California or New Mexico every year.**

Many variations of these elements are possible. But don't pile up more compound expressions than readers can handle easily. Sentences should always be readable.

TOO MANY COMPOUNDS
> Both lawyers and judges attended the after-lunch seminars and discussion groups; broke for drinks, cocktails, and coffee in the late afternoon; returned for a film, a professional roundtable, and a business session; and then either went out to dinner or retired to their hotels.

REVISED FOR CLARITY
> Both lawyers and judges attended the after-lunch seminars and discussion groups. **They** broke for drinks, cocktails, and coffee in the late afternoon **and then** returned for a film, a professional roundtable, and a business session. **Afterward,** they either went out to dinner or retired to their hotels.

17b What do modifiers do?

Modifiers are words, phrases, or clauses that expand what we know about subjects, verbs, or other sentence elements, including other modifiers and complete sentences. Although modifiers can cause problems, most writers use them routinely without difficulty (see Chapter 30). In fact, it would be hard to compose sentences without them. Even simple modifiers change the texture of sentences, while more complex modifiers increase your options for shaping sentences.

■ **1 Use adjectives to modify nouns and pronouns.** Adjectives describe and help to explain nouns and pronouns by specifying *how many, which size, what color, what condition, which one,* and so on. Single adjectives are usually placed before the terms they modify.

> The **angry** judge scowled at the **nervous** witness.

But adjectives often work in groups. Adjectives in a group are called **coordinate adjectives** when each one works on its own, describing different and unrelated aspects of a noun or pronoun.

> the **undistinguished, tired-looking** lawyer
> our cat, **shedding and overweight**

Placed before a noun or pronoun, coordinate adjectives can be linked either by conjunctions (usually *and*) or by commas. The order of the adjectives doesn't affect their meaning.

> The **angry, perspiring** judge scowled at the **balding and nervous** witness.

> The **perspiring, angry** judge scowled at the **nervous and balding** witness.

> The **tired and underpaid** jurors listened to a **tedious and awkward** interrogation.

> The **underpaid and tired** jurors listened to an **awkward and tedious** interrogation.

Coordinate adjectives may also follow the words they modify, giving variety to sentence rhythms.

> The judge, **angry and perspiring,** scowled at the witness, **balding and nervous.**

For a stylish variation, you can also move coordinate adjectives ahead of an article (*the*) at the beginning of a sentence.

> **Tired, bored, and underpaid,** the jurors listened to an endless interrogation.

Not all clusters of adjectives are coordinate. Often, groups of adjectives must follow a specific sequence to make sense. Changing their sequence produces expressions that are not *idiomatic;* that is, they don't sound right to a native English speaker.

NOT IDIOMATIC	the wooden heavy gavel
IDIOMATIC	the heavy wooden gavel
NOT IDIOMATIC	a woolen green sweater
IDIOMATIC	a green woolen sweater
NOT IDIOMATIC	the American first satellite
IDIOMATIC	the first American satellite

Adjectives in such groupings—which often include numbers—are not separated by commas.

The judge wielded a **heavy wooden** gavel.
The **first American** satellite was Explorer I.
The police rescued **two lucky** kayakers.

Adjectives (along with adverbs and nouns) can also form *compound* or *unit modifiers*, groups of words linked by hyphens that modify a noun (see Section 40b-5). The individual words in compound modifiers need each other; they often wouldn't make sense standing alone in front of a noun.

A **well-known** case would provide a **high-impact** precedent.
The **wine-dark** sea surged in the moonlight.

Finally, adjectives play an important role as subject complements and object complements (see Section 17a-1), modifying words to which they are joined by linking verbs.

The judge's decision seemed **eccentric.**
The children were **sleepy.**
The press called the jury **inept.**

EXERCISE 17.11 Rewrite each of the following sentences so that the adjectives in parentheses modify an appropriate noun or pronoun. Place the adjectives before or after the word they modify, and punctuate them correctly (for example, be sure to add hyphens to unit modifiers and to separate coordinate adjectives with commas or *and* as necessary).

1. The elm trees once common throughout North America have disappeared, victims of disease. (*towering; graceful; Dutch elm*)

2. This infection destroys the vascular system of the elm, causing trees to become husks in a few short weeks. (*fungal; relentless; mature; thriving; leafless*)

3. Few parks in the United States can match the diversity of New York's Central Park, with its zoo, gardens and fields, ponds and lakes, and museum. (*great urban; sizable; pleasant; glistening; world class*)

4. The city seems to stop at the edge of the park where New Yorkers can stroll quietly under a canopy of shade trees or strap on roller blades and buzz tourists. (*noisy; crowded; sprawling; business suited or casual; cool; green; curious; delighted*)

5. Bankers, show people, and street people alike jostle shoulders and shopping bags in this oasis. (*wealthy; glittering; down on their luck; refreshing; urban*)

17b
modif

■**2 Use adverbs to modify verbs, adjectives, and other adverbs.** Adverbs in sentences explain *how, when, where,* and *to what degree* things happen.

ADVERBS THAT MODIFY VERBS
The prosecutor *spoke* **eloquently** to the jury.
Immediately, the defense attorney *replied.*
The jury *tried* **hard** to follow their summaries.

ADVERBS THAT MODIFY ADJECTIVES
Tornadoes seem **freakishly** *unpredictable.*
Tornado chasing remains **quite** *popular.*

ADVERBS THAT MODIFY OTHER ADVERBS
The reading program has improved **very** *considerably.*
Less *easily* appreciated is a new interest in music at the school.

Adverbs increase your options in constructing sentences because they typically can be put in more places than adjectives, enabling you to experiment with sentence structure and rhythm. All three versions of the following sentence convey the same information, but they do so in subtly different ways.

The news reporter **passionately and repeatedly** defended the integrity of her story.

Passionately and repeatedly, the news reporter defended the integrity of her story.

The news reporter defended the integrity of her story **passionately and repeatedly.**

But this very flexibility causes significant problems. Be sure to review Section 30f on the appropriate placement of adverbs, especially *only.*

EXERCISE 17.12 Rewrite the following sentences so that each adverb in parentheses modifies an appropriate verb, adjective, or adverb. Notice which adverbs work best in one position only and which can be relocated more freely in a sentence.

1. The elm trees once common throughout North America have disappeared, victims of disease. (*sadly; quite; almost; completely*)

2. This lethal infection destroys the vascular system of the elm, causing trees to become husks in a few short weeks. (*nearly; always; completely*)

3. The delicate paintings had not been packed, so they arrived damaged. (*extremely; well; severely*)

4. Annoyed, the senator replied to the reporter in an angry tone. (*visibly; unusually*)

5. We left the photo shop poorer but better equipped for difficult telephoto shots. (*considerably; much; extremely*)

17b
modif

■ **3 Understand that nouns can operate as modifiers.** In some sentences you may find words that look like nouns but act like adjectives, modifying other words. Don't be confused: nouns often work as modifiers.

> We ordered the **sausage** plate and a **vegetable** sampler.
> The **instrument** cluster glowed red at night.

Proper nouns can serve as modifiers too.

> The choir was preparing for the **Christmas** service.
> We ordered a **New York** strip steak.

EXERCISE 17.13 In the following sentences, underline any nouns that function as modifiers. Discuss disputed cases with colleagues.

1. The Atlanta Braves, Washington Redskins, and Cleveland Indians are sports teams whose names occasionally stir controversy among Native American political interest groups.

2. Car insurance is getting so expensive in urban areas that many college students have to rely on the city bus.

3. Ike signed up for two computer courses even though he couldn't explain the difference between an Apple Macintosh and a McIntosh apple.

4. At Martha's Fourth of July party, the Vienna sausage didn't sit well with the Boston cream pie and strawberry ice cream.

5. I'm not sure which television station carries *The Drew Carey Show*.

4 Understand that verbals can operate as modifiers. Especially common as modifiers are participles—words like *dazzling, frightening, broken*. Because participles are based on verbs, they give energy and snap to sentences.

The waiter brought a **sizzling** steak on a **steaming** bed of rice.
The margaritas arrived **frozen**, not on the rocks.
The officer, **smiling**, wrote us a $100 ticket.
Trembling, I opened the **creaking** door.

For more about participle and infinitive phrases, see Section 17c-2.

17c
phrase

EXERCISE 17.14 In the following sentences, underline any participles that function as modifiers. Discuss disputed cases with colleagues.

1. I. M. Pei is one of America's most original and inspiring architects.

2. Born in Guangzhou, China, in 1917, Pei came to the United States in 1935 and became a naturalized citizen in 1954.

3. Pei is responsible for some of the most startling and admired buildings of our era.

4. Pei's work includes the glittering and much debated pyramid that now serves as the main entrance to the Louvre, one of the leading museums in the world.

5. Yet Pei can also count among his commissions Cleveland's Rock and Roll Hall of Fame, a daring work poised on the shores of Lake Erie.

17c What are phrases?

Technically, a **phrase** is a group of related words without a subject and a finite verb, but this definition is hard to follow. It's probably more helpful to appreciate phrases in action, doing their part to give shape to sentences.

1 Understand prepositional phrases. Among the more mundane of sentence elements, a *prepositional phrase* consists of a preposition and its object, either a noun or a pronoun. The object can be modified.

Preposition	Modifier (optional)	Object(s)
to		Jeff and me
in	your own	words
beyond	the farthest	mountain

It's easy to generate examples of prepositional phrases: *off the sofa, on the hard drive, across the miles, under the spreading chestnut tree, over the far horizon, from me, for her.* Just try writing a paragraph without using a prepositional phrase and you'll appreciate how essential they are to establishing relationships within sentences. Don't, however, mistake prepositional phrases with *to* (*to Starbucks, to Lila*) for infinitives or infinitive phrases, which include a verb form (*to see, to watch the stars, to be happy*). For more on prepositions and infinitives see Sections 28b and 24a-1.

17c
phrase

The power of prepositional phrases resides in their flexibility and simplicity. Moving a prepositional phrase into an unexpected slot gets it noticed. Consider what happens to the first sentence in this paragraph when its prepositional phrase is repositioned.

| ORIGINAL | The power of prepositional phrases resides in their flexibility and simplicity. |
| PREPOSITIONAL PHRASE MOVED | In their flexibility and simplicity, the power of prepositional phrases resides. |

The sentence sounds just different (some might say awkward) enough to cause readers to pause—which may or may not be the effect you wish to achieve. And that's the point: where you put prepositional phrases can influence readers enough to make a difference. For additional discussion, see Section 18c-7.

EXERCISE 17.15 Study the following passages and discuss the effect of relocating the boldfaced prepositional phrases within the speeches. How would the style of the passage be changed—if at all?

1. **Upon this battle** depends the survival of Christian civilization. **Upon it** depends our own British life, and the long continuity of our institutions and our Empire. The whole fury and might of the enemy must very soon be turned **on us**. Hitler knows he will have to break us in this island or lose the war.   —Winston Churchill

2. **With malice toward none, with charity for all, with firmness in the right,** let us strive on to finish the work we are in, to bind up the nation's wounds, to care for him who shall have borne the battle and for his widow and his orphan, to do all which may achieve and cherish a just and lasting peace among ourselves and with all nations. —Abraham Lincoln

■ **2 Appreciate the versatility of verbals and verbal phrases.** Verbals are verb forms that can act as nouns, adjectives, or adverbs (see Chapter 24). Verbals can stand alone, or they can form phrases by taking objects, complements, or modifiers.

17c
phrase

	Verbal	Verbal phrase
Infinitive	to serve	to serve the sick
	to prevent	to prevent forest fires
Gerund	serving	serving the sick [is]
	preventing	preventing forest fires [is]
Participle	serving	serving without complaint,
	prevented	prevented from helping,

Verbals and verb phrases that act as nouns can serve as subjects or direct objects. As modifiers, verbals can function as adverbs or adjectives. Although verbals may seem complicated, you'll recognize the roles they play in sentences.

Verbals as subjects. Both infinitives and gerunds can act as subjects in sentences. On their own, they don't look much different from other subjects.

INFINITIVE AS SUBJECT
To serve was the doctor's ambition.

GERUND AS SUBJECT
Serving was the doctor's ambition.

But when they expand into phrases, they can be harder to recognize. Yet they remain subjects and can be either simple or compound.

INFINITIVE PHRASES AS SUBJECTS
To serve the sick was the doctor's ambition.

To serve the sick and to comfort the afflicted were the doctor's ambitions.

GERUND PHRASES AS SUBJECTS

Serving the sick was the doctor's ambition.

Serving the sick and comforting the afflicted were the doctor's ambitions.

Verbals as objects. Both infinitives and gerunds can act as objects in sentences. On their own, they don't look much different from other objects.

INFINITIVE AS DIRECT OBJECT

The lawyer loved **to object.**

GERUND AS DIRECT OBJECT

The lawyer loved **objecting.**

As phrases, verbals can seem complicated in their role as direct objects. Yet they play that role like any other noun, simple or compound.

INFINITIVE PHRASES AS DIRECT OBJECTS

The lawyer chose **to object to the motion.**

The lawyer chose **to object to the motion and to move for a mistrial.**

GERUND PHRASES AS DIRECT OBJECTS

The lawyer loved **objecting to the prosecutor's motions.**

The lawyer loved **objecting to the prosecutor's motions and winning concessions from the judge.**

Verbals as complements. Both infinitives and gerunds can act as complements in sentences.

INFINITIVE AS SUBJECT COMPLEMENT

To know Rebecca was **to love her.**

GERUND AS OBJECT COMPLEMENT

The IRS caught Elmo **cheating on his taxes.**

Verbals as adjectives. You'll frequently want to use participles and participle phrases to modify nouns and pronouns in your sentences.

PARTICIPLES AS ADJECTIVES

Frowning, the instructor stopped her lecture.

The **suspended** fraternity appealed to the dean.

PARTICIPLE PHRASES AS ADJECTIVES

Frowning at us, the instructor stopped her lecture.

The fraternity, **suspended for underage drinking,** appealed to the dean.

We kept close to the trail, **not knowing the terrain well.**

17c
phrase

Notice the freedom you have in placing participle phrases. You do want to be certain, however, that readers can have no doubt what a particular phrase modifies.

Infinitives, too, can function as adjectives, although it can be difficult to perceive the infinitive in this role as a modifier, providing details.

INFINITIVES AS ADJECTIVES
The manager had many items **to purchase.** modifies *items*
Reasons **to stay** were few. modifies *reasons*

INFINITIVE PHRASES AS ADJECTIVES
The manager had many items **to purchase for the grand opening.**
modifies *items*

Reasons **to stay calm** were few. modifies *reasons*

17c
phrase

Verbals as adverbs. Infinitives and infinitive phrases can act like adverbs, answering such questions as *why, how, to what degree,* and so on.

INFINITIVES AS ADVERBS
Difficult **to please,** Martha rarely enjoyed movies. modifies *difficult*
The sedan seemed built **to last.** modifies *built*

INFINITIVE PHRASES AS ADVERBS
The gardener dug a trench **to stop the spread of oak wilt.**
modifies *dug*

The Senate recessed **to give its members a summer vacation.**
modifies *recessed*

The pilot found it impossible **to see the runway in the fog.**
modifies *impossible*

EXERCISE 17.16 Underline all verbals in the following sentences and then indicate whether they function as subjects, objects, complements, adjectives, or adverbs.

1. Waving at the crowd, the winner of the marathon took a victory lap.

2. The waiter certainly seemed eager to please us.

3. The salesperson enjoyed demonstrating the self-closing door on the minivan.

4. Harriet bought an awning to reduce the light streaming through her bay windows.

5. To cherish the weak and the dying was Mother Theresa's mission in life.

6. Reasons to applaud during the candidate's speech were few.

7. Finding an appealing painting at a reasonable price was impossible.

8. The clerk caught Liza sampling the produce.

9. Surprised by the storm front's ferocity, weather forecasters revised their predictions.

10. We decided we finally had sufficient reason to object.

3 Understand absolute phrases. **Absolutes** are versatile phrases that modify whole sentences rather than individual words. They are constructed from participles or infinitives. When absolute phrases are based on participles, they always include a subject and may include modifiers and other elements.

17c
phrase

> Our representatives will, **time permitting,** read the entire petition to the city council.
>
> **The supply craft having docked,** the astronauts on the *International Space Station* were ready for their space walk.
>
> Our plane arrived early, **the winds having been favorable.**

When the participle is a form of *to be*, it can often be omitted for a more economical or elegant expression.

> **The winds [being] favorable,** our plane arrived early.

Absolutes based on infinitives don't require a noun or pronoun.

> **To speak frankly**, we are facing the gravest crisis in the history of this company.
>
> Your buzz cut, **to be honest**, would look better on a coconut.

Because absolutes are not attached to particular words, you can place them exactly where they work best in a sentence. Absolutes can add sophistication to your sentences. They are worth trying.

EXERCISE 17.17 Turn the phrases in parentheses into absolutes and incorporate them into the full sentences preceding them.

EXAMPLE The senator's amendment to the tax bill would fund a worthless pork barrel project. (*to put it bluntly*)

REVISION The senator's amendment to the tax bill would, to put it bluntly, fund a worthless pork barrel project.

1. Many newspaper reporters don't know beans about their beats. (*to speak candidly*)

2. We should be able to take the launch to the island. (*the weather having cleared*)

3. Johnson became a viable candidate for governor again. (*the tide of public opinion having turned*)

4. Work in the electronic classrooms had to stop for the day. (*the entire network down*)

5. We hurried from exhibit to exhibit at the art museum. (*the time being late*)

4 Appreciate appositive phrases. An **appositive** is a noun or noun phrase that restates or expands the meaning of the words it modifies. Think of appositives as variations on a theme, a second way of naming nouns and giving them more texture. Appositives are placed immediately after the words they modify and are usually surrounded by commas (see Section 36b-2).

Napoleon, the **Emperor of France**, crowned himself.

Death Valley, **the largest national park in the continental United States**, blooms with wildflowers in the spring.

Gerund phrases can stand as appositives too.

Alchemy, **changing base metals into more precious ones**, is discredited medieval lore.

Appositives are also routinely introduced by words or phrases such as *or, as, for example, such as,* and *in other words.*

Dachshunds, **or wiener dogs**, are growing in popularity.

Katharine Hepburn's best movies, **including** *The African Queen* **and** *The Philadelphia Story*, are classics of American cinema.

The test actually measures college survival skills, **that is, the ability to pass multiple-choice examinations.**

Most appositives are interchangeable with the words they modify: delete those modified terms and the sentence still makes sense.

APPOSITIVES AS MODIFIERS

Abraham Lincoln, **the first Republican President**, presided over the Civil War.

Halloween, **All Hallows' Eve**, comes two days before All Souls' Day, **also known as the Day of the Dead.**

MODIFIED TERMS REPLACED BY APPOSITIVES
The first Republican President presided over the Civil War.
All Hallows' Eve comes two days before **the Day of the Dead**.

Some appositives—often proper nouns—can't be deleted without blurring the meaning of a sentence. These appositives are not surrounded by commas (see Section 36d-5).

Bob Dylan's masterpiece *Blonde on Blonde* is a double album.

Nixon **the diplomat** is more respected by historians than Nixon **the politician**.

Like absolutes, appositive phrases can give your prose depth and grace.

17d
clause

EXERCISE 17.18 Turn the phrase(s) in parentheses into appositives and incorporate them into the full sentences preceding them. Be sure to use the right punctuation.

> EXAMPLE   Sally Ride served on the presidential commission that investigated the 1986 explosion of the space shuttle. (*America's first woman astronaut;* Challenger)
>
> REVISION   Sally Ride, America's first woman astronaut, served on the presidential commission that investigated the explosion of the space shuttle *Challenger.*

1. Rudolph Giuliani first gained prominence as a federal prosecutor. (*107th mayor of New York City*)

2. In Anasazi architecture, a prominent feature is the kiva. (*a covered circular enclosure sunk in the ground and used for religious ceremonies and community meetings*)

3. The technique called pure fresco produces enduring images such as those on the ceiling of the Sistine Chapel. (*painting with plaster stained with pigment; Michelangelo's masterpiece*)

4. The gizzard of a bird is thick with muscles for grinding food. (*a part of the digestive system*)

5. Shakespeare's masterpiece includes three witches. (Macbeth; *the Weird Sisters*)

17d What do clauses do in sentences?

Clauses are groups of related words that have subjects and verbs. As such, they are the framework for most sentences, the parts to which other modifying words and phrases are attached. The four basic sentence types (*simple, compound, complex,* and *compound-complex*) are based on some combination of independent and dependent clauses (see Section 17e). Writers who don't understand clauses often have problems with sentence boundaries (see Sections 35a-2 and 35a-3) or with composing longer sentences.

■ 1 Understand independent clauses. An **independent clause** can stand alone as a complete sentence. Most independent clauses have an identifiable subject and a predicate (that is, a verb plus its auxiliaries and modifiers). Sometimes a subject is understood and is not stated in the clause.

Subject	Predicate
The house	burned.
The dreams we had	came true today.
The children	caught colds.
[You]	Come here at once.

EXERCISE 17.19 Circle the subject and underline the predicate in the following independent clauses. If the subject is understood, write the word *understood* as the subject in parentheses after the sentence.

1. The wood on the deck warped after only one summer.

2. Jeremy has been trying to reach you all day.

3. Attend the rally this afternoon.

4. Keeping focused on schoolwork is hard on weekends.

5. Be careful.

■ 2 Understand dependent clauses. A **dependent clause** is one that cannot stand alone as a complete sentence. Many dependent clauses that have identifiable subjects and predicates are introduced by subordinating conjunctions—words such as *although, because, if, until, when, whenever, while*—that place the dependent clause in relationship to another independent clause.

Subordinating conjunction	Subject	Predicate
When	the house	burned . . .
If	the dreams we had	came true today . . .
Because	the children	caught colds . . .

Dependent clauses can have various functions in a sentence. Easiest to understand are those that act as adjectives or adverbs. Slightly more intricate are dependent clauses that act as nouns (and serve as subjects, objects, or complements). Note that all dependent clauses must work with independent clauses to create complete sentences.

17d
clause

Adjective clauses. Adjective clauses, also known as *relative clauses*, attach themselves to nouns or pronouns using one of the relative pronouns: *who, whom, whomever, whose, that, which.*

> Former President Clinton, **who was born in Hope, Arkansas**, actually grew up in Hot Springs.

> Venus is the planet **that shines brightest in the sky.**

> The new engine, **which is Mercedes-Benz's first V-6**, has a dozen spark plugs and three valves per cylinder.

The adverbs *when* and *where* can introduce adjective clauses when the resulting clauses modify nouns, not verbs.

> The immigrants settled in those California cities **where jobs were plentiful.** clause modifies the noun *cities*, not the verb *settled*

> We enjoy the winter **when the snow falls.**
> clause modifies the noun *winter*, not the verb *enjoy*

Adjective clauses are surrounded by commas when they are considered nonessential—that is, when they can be removed from a sentence without destroying its coherence. When clauses are essential to the meaning of a sentence, they are not surrounded by commas (see Section 36d-5).

One caution about adjective clauses: sentences sometimes derail when a writer mistakes an adjective clause for a main clause.

> INCORRECT   Talks with North Korea **which** may create a situation favorable to the emergence of a middle class that will push for democratization.

> REVISED   Talks with North Korea may create a situation favorable to the emergence of a middle class that will push for democratization.

EXERCISE 17.20 Add an adjective clause to each of the following sentences at the point indicated. Remember that adjective clauses are usually introduced by *who, whom, whomever, whose, that,* or *which.* An adjective clause may also begin with *where* or *when* if it modifies a noun, not a verb.

1. All the students in class who . . . said they supported President Bush.

2. But everyone in the class who . . . opposed the President's policies.

3. Companies that . . . are prospering more today than firms that . . . .

4. The original *Star Wars* trilogy, which . . . , will soon be joined by a new series of films in the saga.

5. Teens prefer to congregate in places where . . . .

6. A person whose . . . is unlikely to find a job quickly.

7. Tom Cruise, who . . . , has been an Oscar nominee several times.

8. Tom Cruise, whom . . . , remains a top box-office draw.

9. Many youngsters dislike September when . . . .

10. The Rolling Stones remain the rock band that . . . .

Adverb clauses. Adverb clauses work just like adverbs, modifying verbs, adjectives, and other adverbs. They are easy to spot since they are introduced by one of the many subordinating conjunctions, words such as *after, although, as, before, if, since, though, until, when,* and *while.*

> Lilian left **before the hail fell.** modifies the verb *left*
>
> The bookcase was not as heavy **as we had expected.**
> modifies the adjective *heavy*
>
> Hubert spoke haltingly **whenever a girl looked him in the eye.**
> modifies the adverb *haltingly*

Sometimes an adverb or subordinate clause seems to modify an entire sentence or a group of words.

> **Although the stock market plunged**, investors had high hopes for a quick recovery.

As subordinate clauses, adverb clauses play a notable role in crafting powerful sentences. For much more about subordination, see Section 17g.

EXERCISE 17.21 Add an adverb clause to each of the following sentences at the point indicated. Remember that adverb clauses are introduced by subordinating conjunctions such as *although, before, since, unless,* and many others.

1. Even though . . . , Americans vote in record low numbers.

2. Many young people put little faith in the social security system since . . . .

3. Because . . . , many students come to college knowing how to operate computers.

4. If . . . , the polar ice caps will melt and the level of the oceans will rise.

5. Although they . . . , surprising numbers of children still smoke.

17d
clause

Noun clauses. Whole clauses that act as nouns are quite common. Such clauses act as subjects or objects, not as modifiers.

> **How a computer works** is beyond my understanding.
> noun clause as subject

> The FAA report did not explain **why the jets collided.**
> noun clause as direct object

> The employment agency found **whoever applied** a job.
> noun clause as indirect object

> You may speak to **whomever you wish.**
> noun clause as an object of a preposition

Because noun clauses are distinctive structures, they can work beautifully in parallel constructions (see Section 17h).

> The world will little note, nor long remember, **what we say here;** but it can never forget **what they did here.**

EXERCISE 17.22 Underline all the noun clauses in the following sentences. Then explain the function of each clause, as either a subject or an object.

1. What politicians say often matters much less than how they say it.

2. Whoever sent a letter of condolence should receive a prompt reply from us.

3. Why so many people care so much about celebrities is beyond my comprehension.

4. Someone had better explain how the dogs got loose.

5. Where you go for a vacation reveals a great deal about who you are.

17e What types of sentences can you write?

17e
sent

While you'll rarely revise sentences just to make a *simple* sentence *compound* or a *compound* sentence *complex*, recognizing these terms will make it easier for you to diagnose problems in your sentences and to talk about them with peer editors. The most familiar sentence types are all built from just two basic components: independent clauses and subordinate clauses (see Section 17d).

	one independent clause
SIMPLE SENTENCE	**Windows rattled.**
	independent clause + independent clause
COMPOUND SENTENCE	**Windows rattled** and **doors shook.**
	dependent clause(s) + one independent clause
COMPLEX SENTENCE	*As the storm blew,* **windows rattled.**
	dependent clause(s) + two or more independent clauses
COMPOUND-COMPLEX SENTENCE	*As the storm blew,* **windows rattled** and **doors shook.**

■ **1 Use simple sentences to express ideas clearly and directly.** Simple sentences can attract the attention of readers with the power of their single independent clauses.

Jesus wept.
I come to bury Caesar, not to praise him.

But don't assume that simple sentences will necessarily be short or without ornament.

NASA, the federal agency in charge of space exploration, has no current plans for a moon base or for human missions to Mars and Venus, the planets closest to earth in both size and distance.

As you can see, simple sentences can be expanded by compounding or modifying their subjects, verbs, or objects.

ORIGINAL SENTENCE	Extreme sports worry parents.
VERB EXPANDED	Extreme sports **have captured the attention of a fascinated media but worry many parents.**

OBJECT EXPANDED   Extreme sports worry **police, health-care workers, and many parents.**

EXPANDED SENTENCE   Increasingly popular among teenagers, extreme sports such as BMX biking, bungee jumping, and skateboarding have captured the attention of a fascinated media but worry police, health-care workers, and many parents.

Despite its increased length, the final sentence still has only one independent clause and no dependent clauses, so it remains a simple sentence.

EXERCISE 17.23 Working in small groups, expand the following simple sentences by compounding subjects, objects, and verbs and adding modifying words and phrases as necessary. You may replace a general term (*aircraft*) with particular examples (*helicopters, jets, gliders*). But do not add either full independent or dependent clauses. Make sure the final versions remain simple sentences.

17e
sent

EXAMPLE   Bugs scare people.

EXPANDED   Tiny spiders, harmless caterpillars, and frail mantises sometimes terrify or even paralyze full-grown adults, from Ph.D.'s in physics to NFL linebackers.

1. Pets enrich our lives.

2. The sciences challenge our assumptions.

3. Many activities can damage our health.

■2 Use compound and complex sentences to express relationships between clauses. These relationships involve *coordination* when independent clauses are joined to other independent clauses.

The rain fell for days, **but** the city's reservoirs were not filled.
Our fuel pump failed, **so** we were stranded on the expressway.

They involve *subordination* when dependent clauses are joined to independent clauses.

Although the rain fell for days, the city's reservoirs were not filled.
Because our fuel pump failed, we were stranded on the expressway.

To write effective sentences, you need to handle both coordination (see Section 17f) and subordination (see Section 17g) confidently.

17f How does coordination build sentences?

When you coordinate two or more independent clauses, you connect or associate ideas. Independent clauses can stand on their own grammatically, but they grow richer when they enter into coordinate relationships. These relationships can be established in several ways: with *coordinating conjunctions;* with various *correlative constructions;* with semicolons, colons, and dashes; and with *conjunctive adverbs.*

■ **1 Use coordinating conjunctions to join independent clauses.** The **coordinating conjunctions** are *and, or, nor, for, but, yet,* and *so.* They express fundamental relationships between ideas: similarity, addition, or sequence (*and*); exception, difference, or contrast (*or, nor, but, yet*); and process or causality (*for, so*). Commas ordinarily precede coordinating conjunctions (see Section 36c-1).

The solemn service ended, **and** we went home immediately.
sequence
SAT scores in math rose nationally, **but** verbal scores dropped.
contrast
I got a high score on the final examination, **so** I passed geology.
causality

Different coordinating conjunctions give readers different signals, so select them carefully. Many writers habitually choose *and* even when another conjunction might express a relationship more precisely.

VAGUE	The statue's hair is carved in early archaic style, **and** its feet show traits of late archaic sculpture.
MORE PRECISE	The statue's hair is carved in early archaic style, **yet** its feet show traits of late archaic sculpture.
VAGUE	Michelangelo's Sistine Chapel ceiling is among the greatest works of Renaissance art, **and** conservators approached the task of cleaning it with great caution.
MORE PRECISE	Michelangelo's Sistine Chapel ceiling is among the greatest works of Renaissance art, **so** conservators approached the task of cleaning it with great caution.

Coordinating conjunctions are also useful for combining sentences that are short, choppy, or repetitive. Linking sentences this way can produce more readable and mature writing.

CHOPPY AND REPETITIVE	We liked the features of the computer. It was too expensive for our budgets. We thought it looked complicated.
COMBINED	We liked the features of the computer, **but** it was too expensive for our budgets **and** looked complicated.

Relying too much on coordinating conjunctions (especially *and*) to link ideas can be stylistically dangerous. A string of clauses linked by *and*s quickly grows tedious and should be revised, often by making some clauses subordinate (see Section 17g).

17f
coord

TOO MANY *AND*S	The French physician Nostradamus was active in fighting the plague in the sixteenth century **and** he grew so interested in astrology that he wrote a book of prophecies called *Centuries* **and** it has fascinated readers ever since.
REVISED	The French physician Nostradamus, active in fighting the plague in the sixteenth century, grew so interested in astrology that he wrote a book of prophecies called *Centuries* which has fascinated readers ever since.

EXERCISE 17.24 Use coordinating conjunctions (*and, or, nor, for, but, yet, so*) to create compound sentences by linking the following pairs of independent clauses. Be sure to punctuate the sentences correctly.

1. The stock market finally rose. Investors remained nervous.

2. Citizens' groups invest time and money on get-out-the-vote campaigns. Many voters still skip general elections.

3. Vitamin C is good for colds. Vitamin E keeps the skin in good condition.

4. Most Americans get their news from television. News anchors are powerful people.

5. Tough drunk-driving laws are fair. There is no reason to tolerate inebriated drivers on the highway.

■ **2 Use correlative constructions to join independent clauses. Correlatives** are conjunctions that work in pairs, expressions such as *if . . . then, either . . . or, just as . . . so,* and *not only . . . but also.* Like coordinating conjunctions, correlatives can be used to form compound sentences that ask readers to examine two ideas side by side.

> **Just as** Napoleon faced defeat in Russia, **so** Hitler saw his dreams of conquest evaporate at the siege of Leningrad.

> **Not only** is Captain Janeway a better leader than Kirk, **but** she is **also** a more interesting human being.

17f
coord

EXERCISE 17.25 Create compound sentences by finishing the correlative construction begun for you. Be sure that the sentence you produce is a compound sentence, one with two independent clauses. Punctuate the sentence correctly.

1. If I agree to read *War and Peace* by the end of the summer, then you . . .

2. Either the new owners of the former Soviet Union's nuclear weapons will safeguard these deadly stockpiles, or . . .

3. Just as eating too much fat contributes to poor physical health, so . . .

4. Not only does the First Amendment protect speech, but it also . . .

■ **3 Use semicolons, colons, and dashes to link independent clauses.** Semicolons usually join independent clauses roughly balanced in importance and closely associated in meaning.

> We expected chaos; we found catastrophe.

> The eyes of the nation were suddenly on the Supreme Court; the nine justices could not ignore the weight of public opinion.

Colons are more directive than semicolons. They imply that the second independent clause explains, exemplifies, or expands on the first.

> There was a lesson in the indictment: even small acts have consequences.

Like colons, dashes can function as conjunctions, connecting clauses with verve and energy. Some writers and editors, however, object to dashes used this way.

Expect George Ratliff's new film to cause controversy—the theme is bold and provocative.

The cathedral of Notre Dame was restored in the nineteenth century— its facade had suffered damage during the French Revolution.

See Chapters 37 and 40 for more on semicolons, colons, and dashes.

EXERCISE 17.26 Use a semicolon, a colon, or a dash to link the following independent clauses. Be prepared to explain why you chose each form of linkage.

1. Don't feel sorry for the spare and thorny plants you see in a desert. They don't want or need more water.

2. Barren stalks, wicked thorns, and waxy spines are their adaptations to a harsh environment. Such features conserve water or protect the plants from desert animals and birds.

3. Spring rains can create an astonishing desert spectacle. Cacti and other plants explode into colorful bloom.

4. Even the dour prickly pear bears handsome flowers. You've got to see the display to believe it.

5. Many animals call the desert home, too, from tiny lizards to scrawny coyotes. They are just as well adapted as the plants.

17f
coord

4 Use conjunctive adverbs with semicolons to join independent clauses.

Conjunctive adverbs are words such as *consequently, however, moreover, nevertheless, similarly,* and *therefore*. Like any adverb, they can appear at various places in a sentence. But often the adverb follows a semicolon, illuminating the relationship between clauses and holding our attention.

Members of the zoning board appreciated the developer's arguments; **however,** they rejected her rezoning request.

The muffler was leaking dangerous fumes; **moreover,** the brake linings were growing thin.

The comma that typically follows a conjunctive adverb in these constructions also gives weight to the word or phrase.

Note that it is the semicolon, not the adverb, that actually links the independent clauses. That connection becomes more obvious when the conjunctive adverb is moved.

Members of the zoning board appreciated the developer's arguments; they rejected her rezoning request, **however.**

The muffler was leaking dangerous fumes; the brake linings, **moreover,** were growing thin.

The punctuation surrounding conjunctive adverbs can be confusing. See Section 37a-3 for more details.

17f
coord

EXERCISE 17.27 Use a semicolon and the conjunctive adverb in parentheses to link the following independent clauses. To gain practice punctuating this tricky construction, use the form illustrated in the example—with the semicolon followed immediately by the conjunctive adverb, followed by a comma.

> EXAMPLE   The aircraft lost an engine in flight. It landed safely. (*however*)
>
> REVISED   The aircraft lost an engine in flight; **however,** it landed safely.

1. Ordinary books are still more convenient than most computerized texts. They employ a technology that doesn't go out of date as quickly—paper. (*moreover*)

2. Most people would save money by using public transportation. They elect to use their private automobiles for daily commuting. (*nevertheless*)

3. American colonists resented England's interference in their political and commercial lives. The thirteen colonies decided to fight for independence. (*therefore*)

4. German and Japanese automakers discovered that they could build quality products cheaper in North America than at home. Foreign computer manufacturers decided to build silicon-chip plants in the United States. (*similarly*)

5. Many cities have been unable to meet air-quality standards. Tougher air-pollution measures have been imposed on their factories and drivers. (*consequently*)

EXERCISE 17.28 Build coordinate sentences by combining the following independent clauses. You may use coordinating conjunctions, correlatives, conjunctive adverbs, semicolons, or colons. Be sure to get the punctuation right.

EXAMPLE   Pencils were invented in the sixteenth
                 century. Erasers were not added to them
                 until 1858.

COORDINATION   Pencils were invented in the sixteenth
                 century; **however,** erasers were not added to
                 them until 1858.

1. Today, French Impressionist paintings are favorites among art lovers. The public loudly rejected them at their debut in the nineteenth century.

2. Painters such as Renoir and Monet wanted art to depict life. They painted common scenes and ordinary people.

3. Many critics of the time were disturbed by the Impressionists' banal subjects. They thought the Impressionists' paintings themselves looked crude and unfinished.

4. The official Salon refused to hang the Impressionists' works. The painters were forced to exhibit independently.

5. The Impressionists refused to abandon their examination of modern life. They refused to change their style to please the critics.

17g
subord

17g How does subordination build sentences?

Use subordination to create complex or compound-complex sentences. Subordinating conjunctions provide the link between main ideas (independent clauses) and secondary ones (dependent or subordinate clauses). Subordination can be achieved with the aid of relative pronouns or subordinating conjunctions. The relative pronouns are *that, what, whatever, which, who, whom, whomever,* and *whose.*

Subordinating conjunctions are more numerous and suggest a wide variety of relationships; see the chart of subordinating conjunctions on page 288. For more on subordinating conjunctions see Section 17d-2.

Chart 17.1

Subordinating Conjunctions		
after	in order that	unless
although	now that	until
as	once	when
as if	provided	whenever
as though	rather than	where
because	since	whereas
before	so that	wherever
even if	than	whether
even though	that	which
if	though	while
if only	till	

A subordinating conjunction or a relative pronoun turns an independent clause into a dependent clause that cannot stand alone as a sentence.

INDEPENDENT   I wrote the paper.
DEPENDENT   **While** I wrote the paper . . .
DEPENDENT   The paper **that** I wrote . . .

1 Use subordination to clarify relationships between clauses.
Like most tools for building sentences, subordination provides options for stating and clarifying thoughts. So it's probably misleading to regard the independent clause in a subordinate construction as always more important or more weighty than the dependent clause. In fact, the clauses work together to establish a complex relationship—of time, causality, consequence, contigency, contrast, and so on.

USING SUBORDINATION TO EXPLAIN *WHO* OR *WHAT*

VAGUE   The *Morte D'Arthur* includes stories about the knights of the Round Table. It was the work of Sir Thomas Malory.

CLEARER   The *Morte D'Arthur*, **which** was the work of Sir Thomas Malory, includes stories about the knights of the Round Table.

USING SUBORDINATION TO EXPLAIN *UNDER WHAT CONDITIONS*

VAGUE   Many people go into debt. Credit is easy to get.
CLEARER   **If** credit is easy to get, many people go into debt.

USING SUBORDINATION TO CLARIFY *CAUSALITY*

VAGUE   The film enjoyed a brisk summer box office. It won an Academy Award last March.

CLEARER   The film enjoyed a brisk summer box office **because** it won an Academy Award last March.

USING SUBORDINATION TO HIGHLIGHT *CONTRAST*

VAGUE   Members of Congress often campaign for a balanced budget. Most of them jealously protect projects in their own districts from cuts in federal spending.

CLEARER   **Although** members of Congress often campaign for a balanced budget, most of them jealously protect projects in their own districts from cuts in federal spending.

17g
subord

2 Use subordination to shift the emphasis of sentences.
Generally readers will focus on ideas in your independent clauses. Compare the following sentences, both equally good but with slightly different emphases due to changes in subordination.

> **While** the Supreme Court usually declares efforts to limit the First Amendment unconstitutional, Congress regularly acts to ban forms of speech most citizens find offensive.

> The Supreme Court usually declares efforts to limit the First Amendment unconstitutional, **even though** Congress regularly acts to ban forms of speech most people find offensive.

The first sentence directs readers to consider the efforts of Congress to rein in the First Amendment; the second sentence gives more emphasis to the Supreme Court. The differences are small but significant. Notice the same kind of shift in focus in the following pair of sentences.

> Jared had never walked a picket line, **even though** he had been a staunch union member for twenty years.

> **Even though** Jared had never walked a picket line, he had been a staunch union member for twenty years.

3 Use subordination to expand sentences. You can often use subordination to combine simple clauses into more graceful or powerful sentences.

CHOPPY	The running back had an ankle injury. He chalked up a hundred-yard afternoon. He had been laid off for two months too.
SUBORDINATED	**Although** he had endured an ankle injury and a two-month layoff, the running back chalked up a hundred-yard afternoon.
CHOPPY	Spectators at the air show were watching in horror. An ultralight aircraft struggled down the runway. It was built of kevlar and carbon fiber. It hit a stand of trees and disintegrated in a plume of smoke and fire.
SUBORDINATED	**While** spectators at the air show watched in horror, an ultralight aircraft built of kevlar and carbon fiber struggled down the runway **until** it hit a stand of trees and disintegrated in a plume of smoke and fire.

17g
subord

4 Use subordinate clauses sensibly. If you pile more than two or three subordinate clauses into one sentence, you may confuse readers. Be sure readers can keep up with all the relationships you establish between clauses. If you suspect they can't, simplify those relationships, perhaps by breaking one long complex sentence into several simpler sentences.

TOO MUCH SUBORDINATION	**Although** his book *Politically Correct Bedtime Stories,* **which** was a best-seller for over a year, was turned down by 30 publishers **while** he struggled at two jobs **while** he wrote the book, James Finn Garner isn't resentful, **which** suggests the importance of persistence.
REVISED	Persistence counts. James Finn Garner isn't resentful, **even though** his *Politically Correct Bedtime Stories,* a best-seller for over a year, was turned down by 30 publishers. He struggled at two jobs **while** he wrote the book.
TOO MUCH SUBORDINATION	An assumption **that** is held by many people in certain cultures, **that** people **who** have college degrees should never have to work with their hands, is often a deterrent to capable young people in those cultures **who** seek nontraditional careers.

REVISED   Many people in certain cultures assume **that** college-educated people should never work with their hands. This attitude often, however, deters capable young people from seeking nontraditional careers.

EXERCISE 17.29 Join the following pairs of sentences by making one of the independent clauses subordinate.

1. The original books of Babylonia and Assyria were collections of inscribed clay tablets stored in labeled containers too heavy for one person to move. We think of books as portable, bound volumes.

2. Clay tablets had many drawbacks. They remained the most convenient medium for recording information until the Egyptians developed papyrus around 3000 B.C.

3. Egyptian books were lighter than clay tablets but still awkward to carry or read. A single papyrus book comprised several large, unwieldy scrolls.

4. The Greeks developed papyrus leaflets. They folded and bound the leaflets to produce the first modern-looking book.

5. That first book was the Greek Bible. It takes its name from Byblos, the Phoenician city that supplied Greece with papyrus.

EXERCISE 17.30 Join the following pairs of sentences by making one of the independent clauses subordinate.

1. Japan was a powerful and thriving nation early in the seventeenth century. Its leaders pursued a policy of isolation from the rest of the world.

2. This policy lasted for more than two hundred years. Commodore Matthew Perry of the United States forced Japan to open itself to trade in 1854.

3. Many Japanese resented the presence of Europeans and Americans. They attacked both the foreigners and the rulers called shoguns who had yielded to foreign military pressure.

4. A rebellion in 1867 deposed the shogun. The Japanese emperor was restored to power.

5. The emperor wanted his nation to stand on an equal footing technologically and militarily with the West. He supported major reforms in government, trade, and education.

17g
subord

EXERCISE 17.31 Rewrite the following sentences to reduce any undue complexity in subordination and in other modification. If necessary, break longer sentences into shorter ones.

1. Although for many years scientists believed that there might be another planet on the fringes of the solar system whose gravitational pull influenced the orbit of Uranus, there was no concrete evidence that this additional planet existed, even though astronomers spent decades speculating about its mass, distance from Earth, and orbital mechanics.

2. Because the orbit of Uranus seemed oddly influenced by an unseen planetary body, scientists searched for other objects until they actually discovered Neptune and, later, Pluto, which, unfortunately, did not seem to have the mass necessary to explain the orbital disruptions of Uranus that prompted the explorations.

3. If a mysterious Planet X at the fringes of the solar system is an appealing notion, few scientists now take the idea seriously because *Voyager 2* provided data that suggested that the mass of Uranus is exactly what it should be if we calculate its orbit accurately.

4. Some scientists now are debating whether Pluto itself is a real planet because rather than resembling other planets it is more like a group of asteroid-like bodies at the fringe of the solar system, which are much smaller than planets, which have irregular shapes, and which do not have atmospheres.

17h How does parallelism work?

Sentences are easier to read when closely related ideas within them follow similar language patterns. Subjects, objects, verbs, modifiers, phrases, and clauses can be structured to show such a relationship, called **parallelism**.

PARALLEL WORDS	The venerable principal spoke **clearly, eloquently**, and **invariably**.
PARALLEL PHRASES	**Praised by critics, embraced by common readers,** the novel became a best-seller.
PARALLEL CLAUSES	**It was the best of times, it was the worst of times.**

Items are parallel when they share common grammatical structures.

> clearly,
> eloquently,
> invariably

> praised   by   critics,
> embraced   by   common readers,

> It   was   the   best   of   times,
> it   was   the   worst   of   times

The famous opening clauses from Dickens's *A Tale of Two Cities* are exactly parallel. Longer expressions generally show more variation in their parallel terms, especially in the modifiers.

17h
/ /

1 Recognize sentence patterns that require parallel construction.
When words or phrases come in pairs or triplets, they usually need to be parallel. That is, each element must have the same form: a noun or noun phrase, an adjective or adjective phrase, an adverb or adverbial phrase.

NOUNS/NOUN PHRASES	**Optimism in outlook** and **egotism in behavior**—those are essential qualities for a leader.
ADJECTIVES	The best physicians are **patient, thorough,** and **compassionate.**
ADVERBS	The lawyers presented their case **passionately** and **persuasively.**

Items in a list should also be parallel.

LIST ITEMS	The school board's objectives are clear: **to hire** the best teachers, **to create** successful classrooms, **to serve** the needs of all families, and **to prepare** students for the twenty-first century.

2 Use parallelism in comparisons and contrasts.
Sometimes parallelism adds a stylistic touch, as in the following example. The first version, though acceptable, is not as stylish as the revised and parallel version.

NOT PARALLEL	Pope was a poet of the mind; Byron wrote for the heart.
PARALLEL	Pope was a poet of the mind, Byron a bard for the heart.

17h
//

Figure 17.1 *The elements of this Navaho rug in the Chinle style are roughly parallel. The rug is by Irene Harvey.*

Parallelism is required in comparisons following *as* or *than*.

NOT PARALLEL   The city council is *as* likely **to adopt the measure** *as* **vetoing it.**

PARALLEL   The city council is *as* likely **to adopt the measure** *as* **to veto it.**

NOT PARALLEL   **Smiling** takes fewer muscles *than* **to frown.**

PARALLEL   **Smiling** takes fewer muscles *than* **frowning.**

■ 3 **Recognize expressions that signal the need for parallel structure.** These include the following correlative constructions: *not only . . . but also, either . . . or, neither . . . nor, both . . . and, on the one hand . . . on the other hand.*

As Franklin once remarked, *either* **we hang together** *or* **we hang separately.**

A musician's manager sees to it that the performer is *neither* **overworked onstage** *nor* **undervalued in wages.**

We spoke *not only* **to the President** *but also* **to the Speaker of the House.**

On the one hand, **interest rates might be tightened;** *on the other hand,* **prices might be increased.**

■ 4 **Use parallelism to show a progression of ideas.** You can set up parallel structures within sentences or entire paragraphs. These structures make ideas easier to follow.

Jane Brody, the *New York Times* health writer, says, "Regular exercise comes closer to being a fountain of youth than anything modern medicine can offer." **Exercise halves** the risk of heart disease and stroke, **lowers** the chance of colon cancer, and **reduces** the likelihood of osteoporosis. **It lessens** the chances of developing diabetes and **strengthens** the immune system. **Exercise** even **helps** people overcome depression.

5 Use parallelism for emphasis. Readers really take note when patterns are repeated in longer clauses. By using parallelism of this kind, you will get their attention.

17h
/ /

If welfare reform works, **the genuinely needy will** be protected and assisted, **the less conscientious will** be motivated to find work, and **the average taxpayer will** see federal dollars spent more wisely.

You can also use parallelism to express an idea cleverly. Parallelism offers patterns of language perfect for setting up a joke or underscoring sarcasm.

People who serve as their own lawyers in court have *either* **a fool for a client** *or* **a judge for a brother.**

Sentences and paragraphs can be both more economical and more powerful when you set their related ideas in parallel patterns. When revising a passage, look for opportunities to use parallelism.

6 Correct faulty parallelism. It is easy for parallel constructions to go off track. When an item doesn't follow the pattern of language already established in a sentence, it lacks parallelism and disrupts the flow of the sentence. To correct faulty parallelism, first identify the items that ought to be parallel; then choose one of the items (usually the first) as the pattern; and finally revise the remaining items to fit that pattern. Review these examples to see how they have been revised to achieve parallelism.

NOT PARALLEL	Criminals are imprisoned for two reasons: **to punish them** and **for the protection of law-abiding citizens.**
PARALLEL	Criminals are imprisoned for two reasons: **to punish them** and **to protect law-abiding citizens.**

NOT PARALLEL	When you open a new computer pr... easy to feel overwhelmed by the int... trated by the vague documentatio... know what to do next.
PARALLEL	When you open a new computer easy to feel overwhelmed by the interface, frustrated by the vague docum... confused about what to do nex...

Sometimes you'll have to decide how much of a p... to repeat. You may want to reproduce a structure in its ... phasis, or you might omit a repeated item for economy .

EMPHASIS	We expect you to arrive on ti... ID, to have three sharpened pe... low instructions.
ECONOMY	We expect you to arrive on tin... have three sharpened pencil... structions.

The difference can be striking. Consider what... remove the artful repetition from a famous s... Churchill that is a model of parallel structure.

EMPHASIS	We shall fight on the beach... the landing grounds, we sh... and in the streets, we shall... shall never surrender.
ECONOMY	We shall fight on the ... grounds and in the fields... shall never surrender.

No simple style rule can be given for structuring ... you don't want to be inconsistent within a singl... ing and omitting an element that is part of a p...

WRONG	The education bill is ... programs for another ... autonomy in the cl... dozen new charter s... courses more widely a...

The words signaling the parallel structure ... the items must be expressed as infinitives (... *to make*) or only the first item should inclu...

17h
//

Jane Brody, the *New York Times* health writer, says, "Regular exercise comes closer to being a fountain of youth than anything modern medicine can offer." **Exercise halves** the risk of heart disease and stroke, **lowers** the chance of colon cancer, and **reduces** the likelihood of osteoporosis. **It lessens** the chances of developing diabetes and **strengthens** the immune system. **Exercise** even **helps** people overcome depression.

■ **5 Use parallelism for emphasis.** Readers really take note when patterns are repeated in longer clauses. By using parallelism of this kind, you will get their attention.

If welfare reform works, **the genuinely needy will** be protected and assisted, **the less conscientious will** be motivated to find work, and **the average taxpayer will** see federal dollars spent more wisely.

You can also use parallelism to express an idea cleverly. Parallelism offers patterns of language perfect for setting up a joke or underscoring sarcasm.

People who serve as their own lawyers in court have *either* **a fool for a client** *or* **a judge for a brother.**

Sentences and paragraphs can be both more economical and more powerful when you set their related ideas in parallel patterns. When revising a passage, look for opportunities to use parallelism.

■ **6 Correct faulty parallelism.** It is easy for parallel constructions to go off track. When an item doesn't follow the pattern of language already established in a sentence, it lacks parallelism and disrupts the flow of the sentence. To correct faulty parallelism, first identify the items that ought to be parallel; then choose one of the items (usually the first) as the pattern; and finally revise the remaining items to fit that pattern. Review these examples to see how they have been revised to achieve parallelism.

NOT PARALLEL   Criminals are imprisoned for two reasons: **to punish them** and **for the protection of law-abiding citizens.**

PARALLEL   Criminals are imprisoned for two reasons:
to punish them and
to protect law-abiding citizens.

NOT PARALLEL When you open a new computer program, it's easy to **feel overwhelmed by the interface, frustrated by the vague documentation,** and **not know what to do next.**

PARALLEL When you open a new computer program, it's easy to feel
> **overwhelmed by the interface,**
> **frustrated by the vague documentation,** and
> **confused about what to do next.**

17h
//

Sometimes you'll have to decide how much of a parallel structure to repeat. You may want to reproduce a structure in its entirety for emphasis, or you might omit a repeated item for economy.

EMPHASIS We expect you **to** arrive on time, **to** bring an ID, **to** have three sharpened pencils, and **to** follow instructions.

ECONOMY We expect you to arrive on time, present an ID, have three sharpened pencils, and follow instructions.

The difference can be striking. Consider what happens when we remove the artful repetition from a famous speech by Winston Churchill that is a model of parallel structure.

EMPHASIS **We shall fight** on the beaches, **we shall fight** on the landing grounds, **we shall fight** in the fields and in the streets, **we shall fight** in the hills; we shall never surrender.

ECONOMY We shall fight on the beaches and landing grounds and in the fields, streets, and hills; we shall never surrender.

No simple style rule can be given for structuring a parallel sentence. But you don't want to be inconsistent within a single sentence, both including and omitting an element that is part of a parallel structure.

WRONG The education bill is expected **to fund** literacy programs for another year, **give** teachers more autonomy in the classroom, **to authorize** a dozen new charter schools, and **make** honors courses more widely available.

The words signaling the parallel structure are inconsistent. Either all the items must be expressed as infinitives (*to fund, to give, to authorize, to make*) or only the first item should include *to*.

REVISED   The education bill is expected **to fund** literacy programs for another year, **to give** teachers more autonomy in the classroom, **to authorize** a dozen new charter schools, and **to make** honors courses more widely available.

 Tip

Check your sentences regularly for faulty parallelism if in the past you have had your sentences marked for the problem. You might also ask peer editors to point out any examples of faulty parallelism.

17h
//

EXERCISE 17.32 Write a sentence with good parallel structure that incorporates the elements given below. Here is how one example might work.

SUBJECT   A football coach: three actions during a game

SAMPLE SENTENCE   Keeping his temper as best he could, the coach paced the sidelines, gnashed his teeth, and tried not to cry during the 66-to-3 drubbing.

1. A shy guy: three actions before asking for a date

2. A senator: two actions in delivering a speech

3. A teacher: three actions in calming a noisy class

4. A diver: four actions before hitting the water

5. A schnauzer: three actions to get a cookie

EXERCISE 17.33 Read these sentences and decide which ones have faulty parallel structures. Then revise those in which you find inconsistent or faulty patterns.

1. On opening night at the new Tex-Mex restaurant, the manager called the servers together to be sure they understood all the items on the menu, could pronounce *fajitas,* and that they would remember to ask, "Salt or no salt?" when customers ordered margaritas.

2. Two servers had a wager to see whose customers would order the most drinks, devour the most chips, and, of course, leaving the biggest gratuities. *would leave*

3. Offering the best southwestern cuisine and to serve the hottest salsa were the restaurant's two goals. *serving*

4. But customers soon made it clear that they also expected real barbecue on the menu, so the manager added slow-cooked beef ribs smothered in sauce, hefty racks of pork ribs dripping with fat, and there was smoked sausage on the menu too that was juicy and hot.

5. Servers had to explain to tourists that one was supposed to eat beef ribs with one's fingers, wrap one's own fajitas, and to bite into jalapeños very carefully.

17i How do you craft balanced sentences?

Effective balanced sentences merge the best attributes of coordination and parallelism (see Sections 17f and 17h). In a **balanced sentence,** a coordinating conjunction links two or more independent clauses that are roughly parallel in structure. The result is a sentence so intentionally designed and rhythmic that it draws special attention to its subject. For that reason, balanced sentences are often memorable and quotable.

> And so, my fellow Americans, ask not what your country can do for you; ask what you can do for your country.
> —John F. Kennedy, Inaugural Address

> The inherent vice of capitalism is the unequal sharing of blessings; the inherent virtue of socialism is the equal sharing of miseries.
> —Winston Churchill

> We live here and they live there. We black and they white. They got things and we ain't. They do things and we can't. It's just like living in jail.
> —Richard Wright, *Native Son*

In your writing you might find balanced sentences effective for openings and closings, where you want readers to remember a major point. But they may seem out of place in lighter, more colloquial writing.

In crafting a balanced sentence, you'll almost always begin with two independent clauses joined to make a compound sentence (see Section 17f). Then you can sharpen the relationship between the clauses by making them reasonably parallel. You may need to revise both clauses quite heavily.

COMPOUND   New programs to end adult illiteracy may be costly, **but** the alternative is continued support of even more expensive welfare programs.

BALANCED   New adult literacy programs may be costly, **but** current welfare programs are costlier still.

COMPOUND   Most people involved in education and business take computers for granted, **yet** that doesn't mean these people really understand what computers do.

BALANCED   Most people in business and education take computers for granted; few understand what computers do.

EXERCISE 17.34 Complete the following sentences in ways that make them balanced.

1. If Alfred Hitchcock is the master of suspense, then . . .

2. Politics makes strange bedfellows, and . . .

3. If all the world is really a stage, then . . .

4. In theory, college seems the surest pathway to economic security; in practice, . . .

5. When the going gets tough, the tough get going, but when . . .

17j How do you craft cumulative sentences?

The intricate architecture of balanced sentences (see Section 17i) can make them seem formal and even old-fashioned. A structure perhaps better suited to contemporary writing, which tends to be informal, is the **cumulative sentence** in which an independent clause is followed by a series of modifiers, sometimes simple, sometimes quite complex.

The apprehensive mood was shot through with shafts of gaiety, **as a black sky is streaked with lightning.**
—Maya Angelou, "Champion of the World"

The crater spread toward the horizon, **shallow and barren, ringed by flows of volcanic rock, crumbly as dry cake.**

She [Georgia O'Keeffe] is simply hard, **a straight shooter, a woman clean of received wisdom and open to what she sees.**
—Joan Didion, "Georgia O'Keeffe"

In writing a cumulative sentence, you add on to an original thought, expanding and enriching it by attaching modifying words, phrases, and clauses. The effect is artful but also easy and natural. In our daily speech we often state an idea and then explain or embellish it; cumulative sentences can convey the same informality.

> Dusty? Of course, it's dusty—this is Utah. But it's good dust, **good red Utahn dust, rich in iron, rich in irony.**
> —Edward Abbey, *Desert Solitaire*

> But then they danced down the street like dingledodies, and I shambled after as I've been doing all my life after people who interest me, because the only people for me are the mad ones, **the ones who are mad to live, mad to talk, mad to be saved, desirous of everything at the same time, the ones who never yawn or say a commonplace thing, but burn, burn, burn like fabulous roman candles exploding like spiders across the stars and in the middle you see the centerlight pop and everybody goes "Awww!"**
> —Jack Kerouac, *On the Road*

17j
sent

Crafting effective cumulative sentences takes practice, but the habit of addition is easy to acquire and especially useful in writing descriptive and narrative passages. Almost any of the modifying phrases and clauses described in Sections 17b through 17d can be attached gracefully to the ends of clauses.

Attach adjectives and adverbs. Either as individual words or as complete phrases, these modifiers play an important role in shaping cumulative sentences.

> It was a handsome sedan, **black as shimmering oil, deeply chromed, and sleek as a rocket.**

> The storm pounded the coast **so relentlessly that residents wondered whether the skies would ever clear again.**

Attach prepositional phrases. You can place prepositional phrases (see Section 17c-1) at the ends of sentences to describe or modify nouns or pronouns within the sentence.

> The church was all white plaster and gilt, **like a wedding cake in the public square.**

When the object of a closing prepositional phrase is artfully compounded, the effect can be memorable. In the following example, dust is described as settling *upon* a rich variety of plants.

A veil of dust floats above the sneaky, snaky old road from here to the highway, drifting gently downward to settle **upon the blades of the yucca, the mustard yellow rabbitbrush, the petals of the asters and autumn sunflowers, the umbrella-shaped clumps of blooming buckwheat.**

—Edward Abbey, *Desert Solitaire*

Attach appositives and free modifiers. You can conclude cumulative sentences with modifiers that rename someone or something within the body of a sentence. These modifiers act like appositives (see Section 17c-4), but they may be separated in distance from the noun or pronoun they embellish. Here are two such *free modifiers* from Bob Costas's eulogy for baseball legend Mickey Mantle.

17j
sent

And more than that, he [Mickey Mantle] was a presence in our lives—a fragile hero to whom we had an emotional attachment so strong and lasting that it defied logic.

He got love—love for what he had been; love for what he made us feel; love for the humanity and sweetness that was always there mixed in with the flaws and all the pain that wracked his body and his soul.

Notice the way these modifiers are introduced by dashes. Notice, too, that the modifying phrase itself can be quite complex and much longer than the original independent clause.

Attach clauses. You can experiment with both relative and subordinate clauses (see Section 17d) at the ends of sentences, compounding them and keeping them roughly parallel.

Mother Theresa was a woman **who gave her life to the poor and gained the admiration of the world for her service.**

The astronaut argued that Americans need to return to the moon **because our scientific explorations there have only begun and because we need a training ground for more ambitious planetary expeditions.**

As the lengthy example above from Jack Kerouac demonstrates, you can combine different kinds of modifiers to extend a sentence considerably.

The Kennedys had a spark and Jack Kennedy had grown into a handsome man, **a male swan rising out of the Billy the Kid version of an Irish duckling he had been when he was a young senator.**

—Stanley Crouch, "Blues for Jackie"

EXERCISE 17.35 Combine the following short sentences into one longer cumulative sentence.

> EXAMPLE Virginia adopted the dog. It was a friendly pup with skinny legs. It had a silly grin.
>
> COMBINED Virginia adopted the dog, a friendly pup with skinny legs and a silly grin.

17j
sent

1. Caesar was my friend. He had been faithful to me. He had been just to me.

2. Dr. Kalinowski recommended that her patient take up racquetball. It would ease his nerves. It would quicken his reflexes. It would tone his muscles. The muscles had grown flaccid from years of easy living.

3. The members of the jury filed into the courtroom. The members of the jury looked sullen and unhappy. They looked as if they'd eaten cactus for lunch.

4. The reviewer thought the book was a disappointment. It did not summarize the current state of knowledge. It did not advance research in the field.

5. The Constitution provides for a legislative body. It is designed to be coequal with the executive branch of government. It is also designed to be coequal with the judicial branch of government.

6. Winnetka is a suburb of Chicago. It is famous for its tree-lined streets. It is known for its wealthy residents.

7. Prohibition was repealed in 1933. It had caused bootlegging. It had spurred the development of organized crime.

8. Pagodas are pyramidal structures. They are usually octagonal, hexagonal, or square. They may have many stories. Each story has a tile roof. The tile roofs turn upward.

9. Nijinsky (1890–1950) was a dancer and a choreographer. He was considered the greatest dancer of his time. He is the subject of much interest today.

10. Jim Crow laws enacted in states that practiced segregation held African Americans in bondage. They denied African Americans access to public accommodations. They limited the educational opportunities of African Americans. They restricted access to voting. They encouraged job discrimination.

CHAPTER 18

How Do You Write Stylish Sentences?

Good sentences must be carefully and grammatically constructed. But just as there's more to cooking than preparing wholesome meals, there's more to writing than crafting competent sentences. As you revise, you want to compose sentences that are varied, rhythmic, rich in detail, and sometimes even memorable. This chapter focuses on various ways to give your sentences that subtle quality called *style*.

18a What are agent/action sentences?

You can build readable sentences by using an agent/action pattern. In agent/action sentences, clear subjects (agents) perform strong actions.

agent/action   agent / action
The **pilot** *ejected.*   My **grandmother** *makes* hand-sewn quilts.

Agent/action sentences are highly readable because they answer these important questions.

- What's happening?
- Who's doing it (and to what or to whom)?

1 Whenever you can, make persons or things the subjects of your sentences and clauses. Readers will take more interest in what you're writing if people are involved. And they usually are—most issues touch on human lives, one way or another.

WITHOUT PEOPLE   Although the federally funded student loan program has made education accessible to a low-income population, the increasing default rate among that population has had a significant effect on the future of the program.

WITH PEOPLE   Hundreds of thousands of **young people** have been able to go to college because of federally funded student loans, but now **students** who have defaulted on their loans may be jeopardizing the program for **others**.

Starting your sentences with references to people can contribute to sentence variety too. Compare the following pairs of sentences.

DULL	**Strong trepidation** was felt by Alexa about her first college research paper.
LIVELIER	**Alexa** felt strong trepidation about her first college research paper.
DULL	**Access to a steady stream of lively and diverse cultural events** is one of the advantages of attending college in a big city.
LIVELIER	**Students attending college in a big city** can enjoy a steady stream of lively and diverse cultural events.

EXERCISE 18.1 Recast these sentences in agent/action patterns that show more clearly who is doing what to whom. Break the sentences into shorter ones if you like.

1. Raising $3 million to renovate the drama facilities on campus was the goal of Lincoln Brown, the new college president.

2. The experience of playing Horatio in a college production of *Hamlet* had been influential in convincing President Brown of the value of the performing arts.

3. Helping President Brown to convince wealthy donors that restoring and expanding the old theater was a good idea was a small group of actors, all of them alumni of the school.

4. An unexpected donation of $1 million made by a prominent local banker who had once played Hamlet gave the actors and President Brown reason to celebrate.

▪ 2 Don't overload the subjects of sentences. Readers will get lost if you bury subjects under abstract words and phrases. When revising, you may have to recover the central idea of a particularly difficult or murky sentence. Ask yourself, "What is its key word or concept?" If you can locate such a word, see what happens to the sentence when you make that key word the subject. In the following difficult sentence, the main idea is buried in an opening noun phrase 24 words long.

OVERLOADED SUBJECT	**The encouragement of total reliance on the federally sponsored student loan program for medical students from low-income families to pay their way through school** causes many young doctors to begin their careers deeply in debt.

What is this sentence about? Many readers would say "young doctors"; indeed, *doctors* is one of those human subjects we heartily recommend (see Section 18a-1). So let's see what happens when the sentence is revised to focus on them.

REVISED   **Many young doctors from low-income families** begin their careers deeply in debt because they have relied totally on federal student loans to pay their way through medical school.

Better, isn't it?

EXERCISE 18.2 Rewrite the following sentences to simplify their overcrowded openings.

18a
sent

1. Among those who are unhappy about the lack of morality and standards in the television shows coming from Hollywood today and who would like to see pressure on producers for more responsible programming are activists from remarkably different political groups.

2. The elimination of hurtful gender, racial, and ethnic stereotypes, particularly from situation comedies, where they are sometimes a key element of the humor, is a key demand of political groups on the left.

3. TV's almost complete disregard of the role religion plays in the daily lives of most ordinary people, evident in the fact that so few sitcom characters ever go to church or pray, irritates groups on the political right.

4. Raising the specter of censorship and equating every attack on Hollywood to an assault on the First Amendment has been the quick response of many television producers to criticism of their products.

3 Make sure verbs convey real actions. Strung-out verb phrases such as *give consideration to* and *make acknowledgment of* slow down your writing. To get rid of them, read your draft and focus on the action. Ask, "What's happening?" When you find out, try to express that action in a single lively verb.

DULL VERB   Some groups who **are in opposition to** the death penalty **believe that there is doubt about** its morality.

STRONGER VERB   Some groups who **oppose** the death penalty **doubt** its morality.

Identifying the action may also help you spot the real agent in a sentence, as in this example.

DULL VERB   American society **has** long **had** a fascination with celebrities.

STRONGER VERB   Celebrities **have** long **fascinated** Americans.

EXERCISE 18.3 Rewrite the following sentences to pinpoint their centers of action and to make their verbs stronger.

1. The fears of many prospective students over age 30 are understandable to college counselors.

2. Many such students are in a state of confusion when they are confronted by the first textbooks, syllabi, and assignments they have seen in a decade or more.

3. In many schools, counselors have proceeded to establish special groups or programs for older students so that their feelings of dislocation and discomfort will be relieved.

4. The sobering realization among those responsible for demographic studies of college populations is that older students may hold the key to financial solvency for many institutions.

■ 4 Make sure subjects can do what their verbs demand.
Verbs describe actions that subjects perform: *butter melts; scholars read.* In most cases, you know when you've written nonsense: *butter reads; scholars melt.* But as sentences grow longer, you can sometimes lose the logical connection between subjects and predicates, a problem described as **faulty predication.**

FAULTY   The narrative **structure** of Aretha Franklin's
PREDICATION   song **begins** as a child and continues through
                her adult life.

Can *narrative structures begin as children*? Unlikely. The writer is probably thinking either of a character in the song or of Aretha Franklin, the singer. In either case, the sentence has to be revised. Here's a possible revision.

REVISED   In Aretha Franklin's song, the narrative **structure follows** the life of a character from childhood to adulthood.

Notice how heavily the sentence had to be revised to make it work. Just swapping one verb for another often won't solve the problem. Here are two more examples. In the first, an abstract concept, *pleasure*, is asked to take a human action and *yearn*; in the second, *windows* are expected to *concentrate*, an impossibility.

FAULTY PREDICATION	Ellen's **pleasure** in gardening **yearned** for a bigger yard.
REVISED	Ellen's **pleasure** in gardening **made** her yearn for a bigger yard.
FAULTY PREDICATION	The **windows** of the electronics store **concentrate** their attention on audiophiles.
REVISED	The **windows** full of electronic components **attract** the attention of audiophiles.

18a
sent

EXERCISE 18.4 Revise any of the following sentences in which the subject cannot logically perform the action described by the verb. Try to explain what is wrong with the original verb choices, which are bold-faced.

1. Hundreds of miles from any city or large municipal airport, Big Bend National Park in Texas **endeavors** an experience of pristine isolation unlike that of busier parks such as Zion or Yellowstone.

2. The park **comprehends** mountain, desert, and riparian environments.

3. While coyotes, road runners, and javelinas are common, a few lucky visitors every year also **apprehend** mountain lions and bears.

4. Other national parks can **profess** more spectacular landmarks than Big Bend, but few **entertain** a more remarkable outdoor experience.

■ **5 Replace *to be* verbs whenever possible.** Though the verbs *is, are,* and their variants are often unavoidable, they're not as interesting as verbs that do things.

| DULL VERBS | It **is** the tendency of adolescents **to be more concerned** about the opinion of others in their age group than they **are** about the values parents are trying to instill in them. |
| ACTION VERBS | Adolescents **crave** the approval of their peers and often **resist** their parents' values. |

EXERCISE 18.5 Replace the *to be* forms in the following sentences with active and more lively verbs. The original verbs are boldfaced. (It may help if you make the agent a person or a concrete object.)

1. There **was** an inclination to protest among local restaurateurs when the city decided to increase the number of health inspectors.

2. It **had been** the determination of city officials, however, that many restaurants **were** not in a state of compliance with local health ordinances.

3. The occurrence of rodent droppings in pantries and the storage of meat at incorrect temperatures **were** also matters of concern to several TV reporters.

4. It was the hope of both politicians and restaurateurs that there **would be** a quick solution to this embarrassing problem.

18a
sent

6 Reduce the number of passive verbs. Passive verb constructions (see Section 23e) often make sentences harder to read. Readers typically have to work harder to figure out who is doing what to whom. Passive constructions also attract abstract nouns and tedious strings of prepositional phrases. So consider turning passive verbs into active ones.

It's easy to spot a sentence with a passive verb: the subject doesn't perform the action, the action is *done* to the subject. In effect, the object switches to the subject position, as in the following sentences.

       subj.   action
Madison **was selected** by Representative Barton for an appointment to the Air Force Academy.

       subj.   action
The candidate **had been nominated** for the academic honor by several teachers.

Passive verbs are always constructed with some form of *be* plus the past participle. (See Section 23d for an explanation of what a past participle is.)

               be + past participle
The latest budget bill **has been vetoed** by the President.
        be + past participle
The veto **was provoked** by a stubborn House of Representatives.

Notice that not every sentence with a form of the verb *to be* is passive, especially when *be* is used as a linking verb.

The President **was** unhappy that members of the House of Representatives **had seemed** unwilling to fund new government projects.

Nor is every sentence with a past participle passive. Perfect tenses, for example, also use the past participle. (See Section 23a-2 for an explanation of perfect tenses.) Here's an active verb in the past perfect tense.

The Congress **had funded** such projects in previous years.

To identify a passive verb form, look for *both* the past participle and a form of *be*.

The projects **had been supported** by previous Congresses when they **had been proposed** by other presidents.

When you have identified a passive form, locate the word that actually performs the action in the sentence and make it the subject.

18a
sent

	subj.	performer of action
ORIGINAL PASSIVE	*Madison* **was selected** by Representative Barton for an appointment to the Air Force Academy.	

	subj.
REVISED ACTIVE	*Representative Barton* **selected** Madison for an appointment to the Air Force Academy.

Notice that the revised version is shorter than the original.

But not every passive verb can or should be made active. Sometimes you don't know who or what performs an action.

Hazardous road conditions **have been predicted.**
Our flight **has been canceled.**

EXERCISE 18.6 Identify the passive verbs in the following sentences and then rewrite those that might be improved by changing passive verbs to active verbs.

1. The writing of research papers is traditionally dreaded by students everywhere.

2. The negative attitudes can be changed by writers themselves if the assignments are regarded by them as opportunities to explore and improve their communities.

3. When conventional topics are chosen by researchers, apathy is likely to be experienced by them and their readers alike.

4. But if writers are encouraged to choose topics in their communities that can be explored through books, articles, fieldwork, interviews, and online investigations, a better project will be produced.

18b How can you achieve clarity?

When something is well written, a careful reader should be able to move along steadily without backtracking to puzzle over its meaning. You can work toward this goal by using a number of strategies.

■ **1 Use specific details.** Writing that uses a lot of abstract language is often harder to understand and less pleasurable to read than writing that states ideas more specifically. Abstract terms like *health-care provider system, positive learning environment,* and *two-wheeled vehicle* are usually harder to grasp than concrete terms like *hospital, classroom,* and *Harley.* Of course you have to use abstract words sometimes; it's impossible to discuss big ideas without them. But the more you use specific details, the clearer your sentences will be. For example, specialists might understand the following sentence from a scholarly book. But stating its ideas more concretely gives the statement broader appeal.

ABSTRACT It is also important to recognize that just as we can learn from knowledge about the efficacy of alternative bargaining structures, we can also benefit from knowledge of alternative approaches to welfare and employment policies.
—William Julius Wilson, *The Truly Disadvantaged*

REVISED We should recognize that just as it helps us to learn more about how groups bargain in other countries, it would also help us to learn more about how they handle welfare and unemployment.

An especially effective way to add texture to sentences is to *downshift*—that is, to state a general idea and then provide more and more specific details. The resulting sentences will be both clear and interesting.

Toi Soldier was a magnificent black Arabian stallion, **a sculpture in ebony, his eyes large and dark, his graceful head held high on an arched neck.** He was a competitor in any Arabian horse show, **equally poised in equitation classes or under harness.**

Downshifting is the principle behind many cumulative sentences (see Section 17j).

EXERCISE 18.7 Working in a group, develop one of the following sentences into a brief paragraph by downshifting. Each subsequent sentence should add more detail to the original statement.

1. High schools could do more to get students involved in their communities.

2. It's not surprising that so few Americans speak a foreign language.

3. The commercialization of sports has changed more than just professional athletics.

■ 2 **State ideas positively.** Negative statements can be surprisingly hard to read. When you can, turn negative statements into positive ones. Your writing will seem more confident and may be more economical.

DIFFICULT   Do we have the right **not to be victims** of street crime?
CLEARER   Do we have the right **to be safe** from street crime?

DIFFICULT   It is **not unlikely** that I will attend the conference.
CLEARER   **I will probably** attend the conference.

18b
clear

EXERCISE 18.8 Revise the following sentences to restate negative ideas more positively or clearly where such a change makes for a better sentence. Not all sentences may need revision.

1. It would not be awful if you never turn in a paper late.

2. The remark wasn't exactly the kind I would not ever repeat to my mother.

3. Would it ever not be inappropriate not to say "Hello" to an ex-spouse?

4. What do I think of your new leopardskin pillbox hat? Why, it's not unattractive.

■ 3 **"Chunk" your writing.** Consider breaking lengthy sentences into more manageable pieces or creating a list to present unusually complex information. People can comprehend only so much material at one time. Chunking is the principle behind dividing telephone and social security numbers into smaller parts: the breaks make the long strings of numbers easier to recall. It's also a principle operating on many Web pages, where information is constricted to fit relatively small screens.

TOO LONG
Citing an instance in which a 16-year-old student was working 48 hours a week at Burger King in order to pay for a new car and simultaneously trying to attend high school full time, New York educators have recently proposed legislation that prohibits high school students from working more than 3 hours on a school

night, limits the total time they can work in a week to 20 hours when school is in session, and fines employers who violate these regulations as much as $2000.

In many respects this long sentence is admirable. It uses parallelism to keep a complex array of information in order. Yet most readers would probably like to see its wealth of information broken into more digestible chunks.

REVISED

18b
clear

Educators in New York have recently proposed legislation that prohibits high school students from working more than 3 hours on a school night. In support of the proposal, they cite the example of a 16-year-old student working 48 hours a week at Burger King in order to pay for a new car while simultaneously trying to attend high school full time. The proposed law would limit the total time students can work in a week to 20 hours when school is in session and would fine employers who violate these regulations as much as $2000.

Another efficient way to cut very specific or technical information to manageable size is to create a list. Lists give readers a sense of order and direction. Which of the following passages do you find more readable?

To get started with your new computer, unpack it, saving the Styrofoam packing; position it away from sources of heat; plug the keyboard, mouse, and printer into the designated ports on the back of the machine; check that the outlet you'll use is grounded; and, finally, attach the power cord to the computer and plug it in.

To get started with your new computer:
1. **Unpack** it, saving the Styrofoam packing.
2. **Position** your computer away from sources of heat.
3. **Plug** the keyboard, mouse, and printer into the designated ports on the back of the computer.
4. **Check** that the outlet you'll use is grounded.
5. **Attach** the power cord to the computer and plug it in.

Notice that all the items in the list are parallel (see Section 17h).

EXERCISE 18.9 Make the following sentences more readable by breaking them into manageable chunks.

1. The job a young woman has in high school can play an important role in introducing her to new responsibilities, increasing her self-confidence, and getting her accustomed to the expectation that

she will likely have to earn her own way through life and should-
n't anticipate that someone else, usually a man, will shoulder the
burden of providing her security, shelter, or other necessities.

2. Parents are often ambivalent about having their high school–aged
children work because almost inevitably it causes a conflict between the demands of schoolwork and extracurricular activities
(such as sports, civic clubs, debate teams, band) and the expectations of employers, a balance many high schoolers are simply not
mature enough to handle on their own, often choosing the immediate material goods furnished by a job over the less obvious benefits afforded by a good education.

3. Many parents, however, aware of the limitations of their own
training in school, may believe that it is no more important to
learn square roots, the capitals of Asian countries, or the metrics
of Chaucer's poetry than it is to discover how tough it is to deal
with customers, show up on time, manage other workers, or pay
taxes, experiences that an after-school job will quickly give most
teenagers, whose images of work are badly distorted by films and
television.

18c
wordy

**4 Use charts and graphs to present quantitative infor-
mation.** Readers grasp numbers and statistics much more quickly
when they see them presented visually. See Chapter 10 for more on
how charts and graphs work and Chapter 20 for advice on incorporating them into your writing.

18c How can you write more economically?

For those who aspire to be good writers, the war against what the
writer and editor William Zinsser calls "clutter" never ends. Such clutter consists of clichés, strung-out phrases, pointless repetitions, and
overstuffed descriptions.

But wait until you have a first draft before you start trimming your
prose. Many writers overstuff a first draft because they want to get all their
ideas down. That's fine: it *is* easier to cut material than to create more.

1 Condense sprawling phrases. Some long-winded expressions often just slow a reader's way into a sentence, especially at the
beginning.

Figure 18.1 *Like some contemporary architecture, the modern sentence is spare, pragmatic, and a bit playful. This is the Centre Georges Pompidou—a cultural center in Paris—designed by Richard Rogers and Renzo Piano. You can find out more about it at <http://www.greatbuildings.com/buildings/Centre_Pompidou.html>.*

WHY WRITE . . .	WHEN YOU COULD WRITE . . .
in the event that	if
in light of the fact that	since
on the grounds that	because
regardless of the fact that	although
on the occasion of	when
at this point in time	now
it is obvious that	obviously
on an everyday basis	routinely
with regard/respect to	for

We are so accustomed to these familiar but wordy expressions that we don't notice how little they convey.

> WORDY   **Regardless of the fact that** Marisol graduated from the police academy just last year, she has the confidence of a seasoned officer.
>
> REVISED   **Although** Marisol graduated from the police academy just last year, she has the confidence of a seasoned officer.
>
> WORDY   **At this point in time**, the committee hasn't convened.
>
> REVISED   The committee hasn't convened **yet**.

EXERCISE 18.10 Revise the following sentences to eliminate the sprawling, wordy, or clichéd opening phrase.

1. On the occasion of the newspaper's seventy-fifth anniversary, the governor visited the editorial offices.

2. Regardless of the fact that I have revised the speech three times, I still don't like my conclusion.

3. In the modern American society in which we live today, many people still attend church regularly.

4. By virtue of the fact that flood insurance rates are so high, many people go uninsured, risking their property.

■ **2 Cut nominalizations.** Nominalizations are nouns made by adding endings to verbs and adjectives. The resulting words tend to be long and abstract. Worse, nominalizations are often grafted onto terms that are themselves recent coinages of dubious merit.

WORD	NOMINALIZATION
connect	connect**ivity**
customize	customiz**ation**
historicize	historiciz**ation**
knowledge	knowledge**ableness**
merchandise	merchant**ability**
prioritize	prioritiz**ation**
victimize	victimiz**ation**

18c
wordy

Unfortunately, writers in college, business, and government sometimes think that readers will be more impressed by prose laden with these grand abstractions. Here's a parody of a "bureaucratic" style.

> The **utilization** of appropriate **documentation** will achieve a **maximization** of **accountability**, assuring a **prioritization** and ultimate **finalization** of our budgetary requisitions.

Writing larded with nominalizations gives simple thoughts the appearance of complexity and vacuous thinking the cover of darkness. Avoid such sludge.

EXERCISE 18.11 Revise the following sentences to reduce nominalizations that make the prose wordy.

1. The registrar's note is a clarification of the school's admissions policy.

2. It is a matter of substantial disputation among sociologists whether the gentrification of urban neighborhoods is a beneficial process to inner-city residents.

3. The utilization of traditional phonics in more and more elementary reading classes is an indication that many teachers are feeling

dissatisfaction with more contemporary approaches to language instruction.

4. The systems analyst convinced us that the connectivity and interchangeability of our equipment gave our new computer system enhanced potential.

3 Condense long verb phrases to focus on the action.

To show tense and mood, verb phrases need auxiliaries and helping verbs: I *could have* gone; she *will be* writing. But many verb phrases are strung out by unnecessary clutter. Such expressions sap the energy from sentences.

WHY WRITE . . .	WHEN YOU COULD WRITE . . .
give consideration to	consider
make acknowledgment of	acknowledge
have doubts about	doubt
is reflective of	reflects
has an understanding of	understands
put the emphasis on	emphasize

Similarly, don't clutter active verbs with expressions such as *start to*, *manage to*, and *proceed to*.

CLUTTERED VERBS	Malls and markets **always manage to irritate me** when they **start to display** Christmas paraphernalia immediately after Halloween.
REVISED	Malls and markets **irritate me** when they **display** Christmas paraphernalia immediately after Halloween.

EXERCISE 18.12 Revise the following sentences to condense long verb phrases into more active expressions.

1. Many people are of the opinion that the federal government has grown too large.

2. An almost equal number of people hold the conviction that many citizens have need of services provided by federal programs.

3. This difference in public opinion is indicative of the dilemma faced by many politicians today.

4. Their constituents often are not in favor of paying for exactly the services that they have expectations of getting.

■ **4 Eliminate doublings and redundancies.** *Doublings* are expressions in which two words say exactly the same thing. One word can usually be cut.

> trim ~~and slim~~   ~~proper and~~ fitting
> ready ~~and able~~   willing ~~and eager~~

Redundancies are expressions in which a concept is repeated unnecessarily. A redundancy compels a reader to encounter the same idea twice.

> Our entire society has been corrupted by ~~the evil of~~ commercialism.
>
> Mother's holiday feast on the table was surrounded by our family ~~sitting around it.~~

18c
wordy

One might argue, in some cases, that doublings subtly expand the intended meaning. But they usually don't.

> Thanksgiving fosters a sense of belonging ~~and togetherness.~~
> I am of two worlds, which are forever at odds ~~with each other.~~

Many habitual expressions are in fact redundant.

WHY WRITE . . .	WHEN YOU COULD WRITE . . .
trading activity was heavy	trading was heavy
of a confidential nature	confidential
her area of specialization	her specialty
blue in color	blue
round in shape	round

Avoid the repetition of major words in a sentence—unless there are good reasons to emphasize particular terms.

REPETITIOUS   When college **friends come** together, you'll inevitably find some **friends** who **come** from the same background.

REVISED   When college **friends come** together, you'll inevitably find some who share the same background.

REPETITION   Successful diplomats act in the best interests of the nations **for** which they are responsible **for**.

REVISED   Successful diplomats act in the best interests of the nations **for** which they are responsible.

EXERCISE 18.13 Rewrite the following sentences to reduce redundancy and wordiness.

1. I realized that if I were ever to reach law school, I would have to increase my competitiveness in the skill of written prose composition.

2. *Frasier* to me is a situation comedy–type show.

3. Many traits characterize a truly excellent student adviser, and one of the more important qualities, if not the most important quality of an adviser, is a lively personality.

4. I have often wondered if everyone's taste in toothpaste is the same and which brand is the most widely used of those brands of toothpaste that are most widely advertised.

■ **5 Eliminate surplus intensifiers.** An adverb that functions as an **intensifier** should add weight or power to an expression. You waste its energy when you use it carelessly.

WHY WRITE . . .	WHEN YOU COULD WRITE . . .
We're **completely** finished.	We're finished.
It's an **awful** tragedy.	It's a tragedy.
I'm **totally** exhausted.	I'm exhausted.
That's **absolutely** pointless.	That's pointless.
The work is **basically** done.	The work is done.

EXERCISE 18.14 Review the intensifiers in the following passage and cut any words or whole phrases you regard as unnecessary.

The Grand Canyon is a quite unique geological treasure in northwestern Arizona, basically formed by the relentless power of the Colorado River cutting a gorge for many, many eons through solid rock. Standing at the edge of the canyon is a totally awesome experience. The canyon walls drop far into the depths, thousands of feet, a seriously deep drop, exposing very different layers of limestone, sandstone, and volcanic rock. These really magnificent canyons recede into the distance like ancient castles, an absolutely remarkable panorama of color and shadow.

■ **6 Cut down on expletive constructions.** **Expletives** are short expressions such as *it was, there are,* and *this is* that function like starting blocks for pushing into a sentence or clause. For example:

It **was** a dark and stormy night.
There were five of us huddled in the basement.
There are too many gopher holes on this golf course!
It is a proud day for Bluefield State College.

Some expletives are unavoidable. But using them habitually to open your sentences will make your prose tiresome. In many cases, sentences will be stronger without the expletives.

WITH EXPLETIVE   Even though **it is** the oldest manufacturer of automobiles, Mercedes-Benz remains innovative.

EXPLETIVE CUT   The oldest manufacturer of automobiles, Mercedes-Benz still remains innovative.

18c
wordy

WHY WRITE . . .	WHEN YOU COULD WRITE . . .
There is a desire for	We want
There are reasons for	For several reasons
There was an expectation	They expected
It is clear that	Clearly
It is to be hoped	We hope

EXERCISE 18.15 Revise the following sentences to eliminate unnecessary expletive constructions.

1. There are many different ways to fulfill the science requirement at most colleges.

2. It is usually the case that liberal arts majors benefit from science courses that are geared to the history of the field.

3. Taking a course in the hard sciences is a challenge, and it should be taken seriously.

4. This is a point that many science teachers make early in a term, but it is a concept that many students don't grasp until after their first examination.

■ **7 Cut the number of prepositional phrases.** Stylistically, prepositional phrases are capable of dignity and grandeur, thanks to their clarity and simplicity.

In the beginning, God created heaven and earth.

. . . and that government **of the people, by the people, for the people,** shall not perish from the earth.

Never send to know **for whom the bell tolls;** it tolls **for thee.**

But that very simplicity can also grow tedious if you pack too many prepositional phrases of similar length and tempo into a single sentence.

TOO MANY
PREPOSITIONS

In late summer **on** the road **from** our town **into** the country, we expected to find raspberries **in** the fields **near** the highway **by** the recent construction.

REVISED

We expected to find late summer raspberries **on** the country road, **near** the recent construction.

You also want to avoid strings of prepositional phrases that congeal around abstract nouns, making sentences thick and hard to read. In the example, the abstract nouns are boldfaced and prepositional phrases are underlined.

18c
wordy

WORDY

The current **proliferation** of credit cards among college students is the result of extensive **marketing** by banking **institutions** who see college students in terms of their future **affluence**.

Revise a cluttered sentence by looking for the center of action: *who* is doing *what* to *whom*?

REVISED

Banks today are marketing credit cards to college students because they see them as affluent future customers.

For additional discussion of prepositional phrases, see Section 17c-1.

EXERCISE 18.16 Revise the following sentences to reduce the number of prepositional phrases where they make the sentences awkward or monotonous. Some sentences may require extensive revision.

1. Patrick O'Brian was the author of one of the most popular series of novels about the history of the Royal Navy of Britain during the time of the Napoleonic wars.

2. O'Brian's books focus on the lives of a genial captain by the name of Jack Aubrey and a ship's surgeon by the name of Stephen Maturin who is also in the service of the secret intelligence of England.

3. The novels cover a long period of history, focusing on a worldwide struggle for territory and for dominance in the early nineteenth century between the British people and the forces of Napoleon Bonaparte, the emperor of the French nation.

4. In his love of the sea, in his fascination with the languages of the world, and in his professional interest in the world of espionage, O'Brian resembled his much loved heroes.

◼ **8 Cut relative pronouns (*that, which, who, whom*) when you can do it without changing the meaning of a sentence.** Relative pronouns introduce many modifying clauses (see Section 17d-2). You can often cut them for economy.

> WORDY   The book **that I had quoted** was missing.
>
> REVISED   The book **I had quoted** was missing.

You may also want to cut them to avoid having to recall the appropriate pronoun: *who* or *whom; which* or *that?*

> Millie Liam is a woman (**who? whom?**) everyone likes.
> The Cord is an automobile (**which? that?**) collectors cherish.

Cutting the pronoun solves the problem elegantly.

> Millie Liam is a woman everyone likes.
> The Cord is an automobile collectors cherish.

18c
wordy

EXERCISE 18.17 Rewrite these sentences to practice eliminating relative pronouns (*who, whom, that, which*) that might be contributing to wordiness. Retain any such pronouns you regard as necessary for clarity.

1. Some of the people who might be willing to endure a little less environmental consciousness are parents of children whom environmentalists have turned into Green Police.

2. Third graders who used to read Harry Potter novels suddenly can't wait to locate "Tips to Save Our Planet" in the daily newspaper, which carries dozens of slick, unrecyclable inserts.

3. Full of moral superiority, youngsters who can barely read are circulating petitions that condemn industries that are polluting the air.

4. Shrewd are the parents who have outflanked their Green Warriors by asking them to read supermarket labels and to find the items that are marked "Recyclable."

◼ **9 Condense sentences into clauses and clauses into phrases or words.** Often one forceful word can do the work of several. Say more with less.

> ORIGINAL   Queen Elizabeth I was a complex and sensuous woman. She seemed to love many men, yet she never came close to marrying any of her suitors.
>
> CONDENSED   Complex and sensuous, Queen Elizabeth I seemed to love men, yet she never came close to marrying.

ORIGINAL   Thanksgiving is a time for all of us to be together for the simple purpose of enjoying each other's company.

CONDENSED   Thanksgiving is a time for us to be together, enjoying each other's company.

EXERCISE 18.18 Rewrite the following sentences to reduce clutter by substituting single words for wordy phrases. Rearrange the sentences as necessary.

1. In the event that you are in proximity to Greene County this weekend, you should not miss the opportunity to visit the autumn Concours D'Elegance, an annual exhibit of classic cars.

2. There is the possibility that you may have the chance to touch and feel many quite unusual and different vehicles, from dowdy Edsels with gearshift buttons in the middle of their steering wheels to tiny Corvairs with air-cooled engines under louvered deck lids at the back.

3. However, don't expect to make an inspection of the more unique makes and the basically timeless art of such prestigious automakers as Bugatti, Duesenberg, or Hispano-Suiza.

4. Regardless of the fact that Greene County's show is a small show, you can take great satisfaction in examining quite handsome old Hudsons, Nashes, Jaguars, and Corvettes that are tended by owners who are willing and eager to talk about them at great length.

18d How can you achieve sentence variety?

Your readers will quickly be bored if all your sentences are of the same type and pattern. You'll also want to tailor sentence length to the expectations of your audience—for example, experienced readers are typically more comfortable with long sentences than are children. Audience aside, you'll simply want to write sentences that move easily and maturely, conveying readers from point to point with appropriate clarity and emphasis. You can't do this without offering some variety.

1 Vary sentence types. The familiar sentence types discussed in Section 17e offer you a range of possibilities. Simple sentences attract the attention of readers with their economy and punch. Compound sentences put ideas of equal weight side by side. Complex sentences give you a means to state ideas subtly and richly. Varying these sentence types will keep your readers engaged.

■ **2 Vary sentence patterns.** The five standard sentence patterns in English (see Section 17a) are reliable but dull when repeated over and over.

1. Subject + verb
2. Subject + verb + object
3. Subject + verb + complement
4. Subject + verb + indirect object + object
5. Subject + verb + object + complement

18d
varied

Variations can add style. Consider inverting the usual word order.

Gone is the opportunity to win this month's lottery.

Intelligent, cultured, and politically shrewd was Eleanor of Aquitaine, a twelfth-century liberated woman.

Or play with the way a sentence opens.

ORIGINAL	The punk-rock protest songs of the early 1980s were the musicians' way of expressing their criticism of the political establishment.
VARIATION 1	To express their criticism of the political establishment, punk-rock musicians of the early 1980s wrote protest songs.
VARIATION 2	In the early 1980s, punk-rock musicians wrote protest songs as a way of expressing their criticism of the political establishment.

The variations are not necessarily better than the original. They're just different, and they demonstrate the options you have in crafting sentences.
Still another way to vary the shape of sentences is to put interesting details into modifying clauses or phrases at different points in a sentence.

AT THE BEGINNING	**Convinced that he could not master rhetoric until he knew Greek,** Thomas began studying the language when he was 40.
IN THE MIDDLE	Li Po, **one of the greatest of the Chinese poets,** drowned when he fell out of a boat while trying to kiss the reflection of the moon in the water.

AT THE END   Sixteenth-century Aztec youths played a complex game called *ollamalitzli,* **which some anthropologists believe to have been the forerunner of modern basketball.**

EXERCISE 18.19 The following sentences all begin approximately in the same way. Rewrite them to vary the pattern. Treat the four sentences as a single paragraph; you may not need to change all the sentences.

EXAMPLE   Directors and producers have adapted Shakespeare's plays to contemporary tastes in every age and era.

REVISED   In every age and era, directors and producers have adapted Shakespeare's plays to contemporary tastes.

18d
varied

1. Directors and producers have learned to move Shakespeare from the stage to the screen in the twentieth century.

2. Filmmakers first had to adapt dramas to fit the new medium of film; early Shakespeare movies from the silent era looked much like stage plays presented before a camera.

3. Directors quickly realized that actors on the big screen had to restrain their traditional facial expressions and exaggerated stage gestures.

4. Directors and producers have since produced many Shakespeare films that adapt the dress, music, style, and attitudes of particular decades.

EXERCISE 18.20 To each of the following sentences, add at least one modifying phrase or clause. Vary your placement of the modifiers.

1. Three books stand out in my mind as the ones I would recommend to a friend.

2. Lucille Ball is best known for her series *I Love Lucy.*

3. The Super Bowl occurs in January.

4. Reform of the IRS rarely gets far in Congress.

■ **3 Vary sentence length.** Readers like a balance between long and short sentences. If you've produced a cluster of short sentences, your writing may seem choppy. If you write only medium-length sentences, your prose may seem monotonous. Give readers a break; vary the rhythm of your prose.

Here is a paragraph that is tedious chiefly because all the sentences are too nearly of the same moderate length.

ORIGINAL

Our impressions of people are frequently based on our interpretation of their body language. We notice whether or not someone meets our gaze, fidgets constantly, or gestures when speaking. We use our observations to deduce personality traits such as arrogance, submissiveness, or trustworthiness. Most of us are confident of our ability to judge personality by reading body language. We reason that these skills must be highly developed since we rely on them regularly. Recent research confirms that most people can read emotion and gauge social skills from nonverbal signals. However, the same research suggests that they just as consistently fumble or misinterpret cues to more subtle personality traits.

18d
varied

A more lively revised version not only varies the length of sentences but uses varied sentence types, including several questions.

REVISED FOR VARIETY

Our impressions of people are frequently based on our interpretation of their body language. Does someone meet our gaze or turn away? Does he fidget? Does she gesture? From nonverbal cues such as these we draw our conclusions: this person is arrogant, that one is trustworthy. Most of us are confident of our ability to judge personality from nonverbal cues—after all, we've been doing it all our lives. But how accurate are we really? Not very, it turns out. Recent research reveals that while most people can read emotion and gauge social skills correctly, they consistently fumble or misinterpret nonverbal cues to more subtle personality traits.

As the example above suggests, an occasional short sentence works well even in academic and professional writing—where the tendency is to avoid the quick jab. The fact is that short sentences catch the attention of readers. They work well to underscore key points. Mixed with longer sentences, they can mark a writer as direct and confident, able to make a bold claim or a clear statement.

EXERCISE 18.21 The sentences in the following paragraph are monotonously brief. Combine some of these short sentences and edit as necessary to produce a more readable passage. Compare your version to others written by classmates.

The National Air and Space Museum is in Washington, D.C. It is located on the Mall near the Hirshhorn Museum and

Sculpture Garden. The Air and Space Museum is one of the capital's most popular attractions. It presents the artifacts of aviation history. It presents these artifacts in a creative manner. The museum houses a replica of the Wright brothers' first plane. Lindbergh's plane hangs from the ceiling. The plane carried him across the Atlantic to Paris in 1927. It was a solo flight. Also in the museum are planes from World War II and a full-size lunar landing module. Every manner of flying machine is represented in the museum. There are dirigibles and zeppelins. There are fighter planes, passenger planes, and space capsules. There are helicopters and balloons. There is even a remarkable movie projected onto a large screen. The screen towers six stories.

18e How do you use figurative language?

Writers who make an impact on their readers are often those with a gift for finding the image that lasts, the analogy that clarifies, the metaphor that makes a concept come alive. Probably no writer finds it easy to learn to use figurative language. It is a talent developed over time through careful reading and self-conscious experimentation. Stay alert for the way authors use figures of speech such as analogy and metaphor, and have the courage to experiment in your own writing.

1 Look for fresh images that will strike your reader's imagination. Such images can often be found by paying close attention to the world you can see and feel, as this writer did.

> I went to high school at J. W. Sexton in Lansing, Michigan, **a Depression-era brick fortress that sat across the street from a Fisher Body auto assembly plant.** The plant was blocks long on each side and wrapped in **a skin of corrugated steel** painted a **shade of green somewhere between the Statue of Liberty and mold.** It loomed so near the high school that on football Fridays, when the Big Reds butted heads in Memorial Stadium, night-shift workers stood on balconies and watched the game.
> —Ted Kleine, "Living the Lansing Dream"

To create such powerful images, sometimes all you have to do is turn general terms into more particular ones.

GENERAL TERMS   While striking baseball players drove off in their **fancy sports cars**, the **newly created unemployed** at ballparks struggled to **find work.**

SPECIFIC IMAGES   While striking baseball players drove off in **Porsches and Jaguars**, the **peanut vendors and grounds crews** at ballparks found themselves **in unemployment lines.**

2 Use similes and metaphors to dramatize ideas. Similes are comparisons that use *as* or *like*. Here are two examples.

As another fire season approaches, **anxiety about fires in the West is building as inexorably as piles of dead wood** on the forest floor.
—Ted Williams, "Only You Can Postpone Forest Fires"

Life in China was for millennia **like a lethal board game in which a blind destiny threw the dice, and to land on the wrong square at the wrong moment** could mean sudden ruin and repulsive death.
—Dennis Bloodworth, *The Chinese Looking Glass*

Metaphors are direct comparisons, without the use of *as* or *like*. Here are two examples.

Better watch out or **the pendulum of medical dogma** will bash your head in. **It swings back and forth** far more often than most people realize, and with far more velocity.
—Sherwin B. Nuland, "Medical Fads: Bran, Midwives, and Leeches"

The **geological time scale is a layer cake** of odd names, learned by generations of grumbling students with mnemonics either too insipid or too salacious for publication: Cambrian, Ordovician, Silurian, Devonian.
—Stephen Jay Gould, "The Power of Narrative"

A word of advice: don't mix metaphors. What's a mixed metaphor? It's a comparison that is either inconsistent or illogical because it begins with one image and ends with another.

Don't count your **chickens** until the **tide** comes in.

The Internet marketing **ship has sailed,** and companies that have failed to establish a presence on the Web are already **circling the wagons.**

18e
fig lang

EXERCISE 18.22 Complete the following clauses by creating metaphors or similes.

1. The kitchen smelled awful, like a _____ that had _____.

2. Like a _____, the mayor protested over and over that she was innocent of taking illegal campaign contributions.

3. At the end of summer break, I'm usually a _____.

4. My seat in coach for the six-hour flight felt like a _____.

18e
fig lang

Design and Shape of Documents

19 What Is Document Design?

20 How Do You Create Documents and Web Sites?

21 Model Documents

CHAPTER 19

What Is Document Design?

When you want your writing to reach its audience, you need to think not just about what it says, but also about how it looks. Readers expect your writing to be visually inviting and easy to navigate—otherwise they may not bother to read it. Web surfers may avoid your personal home page if its graphics load too slowly. Your employer may ignore a long report if all she needs is an executive summary. And your instructor will cringe if you submit a term paper printed in an ornate font in orange ink. In short, successful writers need to know the basics of *document design*.

Document design might sound intimidating at first—in fact, it can be a sophisticated process—but it includes quite manageable decisions you'll make about a document's format and style: Should you send an email, a letter, or a memo? Would your audience prefer a printed brochure or a Web site? Should you use a playful or a serious font for the main text? Are colors and graphics appropriate? These are just a few of the questions you'll resolve as you turn working drafts into finished documents.

This chapter introduces you to elements of *document format* and *document style* and offers tips on how to address them throughout your writing process.

19a How do documents work?

Documents are the means by which we present writing to an audience. You may think of a document as something people can hold in their hands, like a newspaper, a letter, or some other printed text. But documents also include electronic texts that readers view on computer screens. Email, Web pages, and software formats have expanded the options writers have for reaching an audience. This new flexibility makes it important to understand how different kinds of documents work, so that you can choose the options that best fit your audience and purpose.

Figure 19.1 *Mary Wollstonecraft, one of the first Englishwomen to try to support herself through writing, had few options for spreading her message to a mass audience. In 1792, while composing* A Vindication of the Rights of Women *(at left), she could not have imagined the ease with which writers now publish their thoughts on the WWW, where her works too are available to millions of readers.*

■ 1 Understand document format. *Document format* refers to how writers arrange material on a page or a computer screen. The format of a document tells readers—at a glance—something about its audience and purpose. We recognize a letter by its initial greeting, body of paragraphs, and closing signature, all on an 8½-by-11-inch page. A newsletter we know by the masthead on the front page, by the headlines and articles in the body, and sometimes by the use of multiple columns. The chart on page 332 lists common document formats.

19a
design

By choosing the right format for your project, you set your audience at ease and help them concentrate on your main points. Here are issues to keep in mind:

- **Formats vary in the audiences they reach.** Formats like email and letters allow you to address your writing reliably to a single person or group. Flyers and Web pages, on the other hand, are posted in public spaces for anyone passing by. Whether you choose a personal format over a public one will depend on the subject you're writing about and whom you want to reach.
- **Formats vary in how they announce purpose.** Most formats use headings, titles, or subject lines to focus readers' attention on important points, but the length and style of these features differ. Book covers and pamphlets allow writers to accompany titles with images and decorative typefaces that clue readers into the tone of what's inside. In contrast, email and traditional memos, which are read by busy professionals, state the document's purpose in a single line of text.

Chart 19.1

Document Formats

TRADITIONAL PRINT FORMATS

Letters	Résumés	Papers/Reports	Booklets
Memorandums	Articles	Flyers	Spreadsheets
Pamphlets	Brochures	Books	Newsletters

COMMON ELECTRONIC FORMATS

Email	Web pages (.htm, .html)	Message forums
Word-processing files	Graphics files	Spreadsheets
Help files	Sound files	Animation files
Program scripts	Style sheets	Databases
Rich Text Format (.rtf)	Portable Document Format (.pdf)	

OTHER PRESENTATION FORMATS

Speeches	Slide shows	Video clips
Dramatic performances	Colloquiums	Debates

19a
design

- **Formats vary in how they introduce writers.** Not all formats emphasize the role of the individual writer, as personal letters and academic papers do. Formats such as brochures and pamphlets put a writer's organization first. While a single person may have composed a document, it represents the common purpose of everyone in the group.
- **Formats vary in the kinds of content they allow.** Some material just doesn't work with certain formats. For example, you wouldn't waste space by putting a large photo of yourself on a printed résumé. Often these limitations are technical: for example, some email formats don't support font styles and images.
- **Formats vary in how they guide readers through material.** Most formats allow headers, footers, page numbering, and subsections that help audience members follow a document from beginning to end. In addition, electronic formats often provide hyperlinks and keyword searches to let readers move through material nonsequentially. Which format and features you choose will depend on how you want your audience to read your document: from start to finish? as a reference source? one piece at a time?

2 Consider the different requirements of print and electronic formats. Since print and electronic documents rely on different media, each has special formatting needs. When you create a print document, for instance, you may need to make decisions about paper and binding, as Figure 19.2 demonstrates.

Figure 19.2 *Print formats don't just differ in the quality of their paper and binding; they also differ in size, shape, and color spectrum. Often the format of print documents will depend on cost, not the writer's taste. Thick paper and more colors are usually more expensive—but some projects are worth it.*

Electronic documents have special requirements of their own. You may need particular software to convert a computer file to readable text on a screen. HTML pages require Web browsers; email messages require a mail client; rich text documents require word processors. You can usually identify the kind of software needed to read a document by the icon on your computer desktop representing that file, or by the letters that appear after the final period in a file's name (the file suffix). Fortunately, the latest computer operating systems already know what software to use with each type of file.

19a
design

Electronic and print formats often overlap. On-screen versions of traditional kinds of writing tend to resemble their print counterparts. Web pages, for example, include section titles, running heads, and numbered figures, just like the pages of a print document. But the electronic medium also allows for additional elements like hypertext links and animation. When you convert a print document to an electronic format, try to preserve some traditional visual cues in the new medium, so that the writing will look familiar to readers—whether or not they are computer-savvy.

Name	Type
AustenIndex.htm	HTML Document
DraftNotes.pfl	CoreText Portfolio
PortraitofAuthor.jpg	JPEG Image
Research.doc	Microsoft Word Document

Figure 19.3 *Above is a snapshot from a Windows PC. The icon, the file suffix, and the "Type" description help you determine what kind of viewing software your readers might need.*

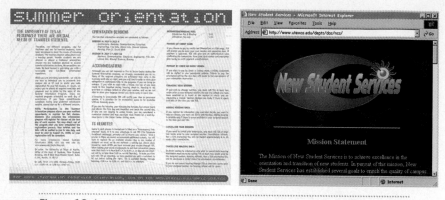

Figure 19.4 *A print brochure can't provide as complete and up-to-date information as a Web site. But only tech-savvy readers may feel comfortable locating material online. A printed WWW address on a brochure helps low-tech readers know exactly where to go.*

■ **3 Know when to combine formats.** Long documents may use several different formats. A firm seeking investors, for example, might publish a packet containing sales statistics, product descriptions, and an introductory cover letter. Each component requires a slightly different format, but it makes sense to combine them into one document with the purpose of persuading readers to invest money.

Sometimes you'll want to combine print and electronic formats. Such combinations are useful when your readers have varying levels of comfort with technology, or when your material can't easily be arranged within a single medium. Suppose your readers use the WWW for locating information but don't typically consult long documents online. Use a short, attractive Web page to get their attention; on that page, provide an email address to which your audience can write to request print versions of longer documents.

■ **4 Understand document style.** Unlike *writing style*, which focuses on the word choices, sentence structures, and figurative language you use in writing, *document style* refers to the ways in which you present your writing through fonts, colors, graphics, images, and various forms of nonvisual media. The decisions you make about document style allow you to influence readers in several ways.

- **Attract readers' attention.** Sometimes a catchy title isn't enough to reel in an audience. On the Web, readers often encounter documents amid a sea of search-engine-identified links. Your page will need something special. Depending on your audience and purpose, that something might be flash, fun, or simple readability.

- **Set a tone.** Images, colors, and fonts convey moods and evoke feelings. You'll want them to set a tone that matches the purpose and audience for your document. In academic writing, you may want a low-key design that strikes a serious tone. For an online memorial, you might use somber colors and fonts to demonstrate respect. Informal documents, on the other hand, might use bright colors, playful fonts, and cartoon images.
- **Make content more meaningful.** Besides creating a mood, the style of your document can add meaning. Typefaces, type styles, and colors can accentuate contrasts among words, phrases, even entire paragraphs. Such effects help you emphasize, downplay, or simply group related material. Graphics, photographs, and diagrams reinforce and illustrate ideas, sometimes revealing in a single image what would take pages to explain.
- **Help readers follow your arguments.** Elaborate page layouts and long documents are sometimes difficult to navigate. Frames, rules, and variations in background color can provide useful visual cues, showing readers where one set of ideas ends and another begins. This book, for example, uses colored tabs in the margins and bold headings in the body of the text to keep readers on track.

19a
design

Colors clearly mark areas of the layout, accentuate text, and set a casual tone.

Fonts give text passages a consistent look and provide special emphasis.

Images attract the eyes to special sections of the page and complement explanatory text.

Lines and **boxes** group related material, making the layout easy to follow.

Figure 19.5 *In this newsletter page you can see the basic elements of document style at work.*

EXERCISE 19.1 Find a print or electronic document that you think is either extremely effective or extremely ineffective in communicating its message to readers. Working with a small group of classmates, identify specific features of document format and document style that make the piece successful or unsuccessful.

19b How do you prepare and plan your design?

Document format and document style are often the last things we consider in the writing process—when we consider them at all. But they are the first things an audience notices. If you think about design issues early in the writing process, you can avoid composing something that readers may pass over or misunderstand.

■ **1 Identify suitable formats for your document.** When you're planning a writing project, start by learning what kinds of formats will best reach your readers. For example, if members of your audience don't regularly check their online accounts, a printed memo will spread the word better than an email message. Choosing an appropriate format, however, is not simply a matter of online or off: There are many print and electronic formats, and audiences expect certain kinds in certain situations. For instance, a prospective employer might skip over job applications not accompanied by a cover letter. Likewise, online readers won't download documents that are incompatible with their viewing software.

As you research the expectations of your audience, you should also look for standard formats—layouts that are regularly used for particular kinds of writing. Standard formats have been tested by time and across audiences, and they provide reliable guidelines for producing effective, readable documents.

E-Tips
Find potential formats by surfing the Web, exploring the library, or surveying your word processor's document templates. These templates adhere to traditional page layouts, so they provide a great starting place for designing a document, even if you will eventually want a customized final product.

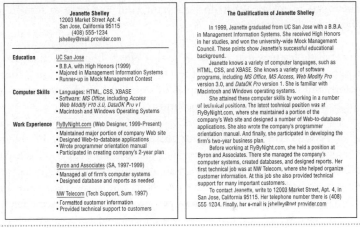

Figure 19.6 *Résumés have evolved to include a section with basic contact information followed by a series of bulleted lists showing achievements. This layout, illustrated at left, showcases the writer's vocational skills. Imagine the disadvantages you would face if you applied for a job with a résumé formatted like an academic essay, like the one on the right.*

The project you're planning may have a number of standard formats—or perhaps none at all. When there isn't a clear choice, weigh the merits of different layouts according to your purpose and message. When you need to make many separate supporting points, for example, opt for a layout that allows multiple subsections. If you have to present a great deal of statistical evidence, you might look for formats with space for supplementary graphics.

2 Explore possible document styles. As part of your planning process, research your audience's expectations about style. Has your instructor requested particular fonts or graphics? Will the readers of your soccer club's newsletter expect colors and photos? If you don't know much about these expectations, aim for a style that reflects the kind of relationship you have with your readers. In a business letter, flashy graphics or colors could distract from a serious message. But a striking design might be appropriate for Web pages and brochures that compete for attention.

Planning your document's style is often more challenging than choosing a format. Unlike format, style evokes different reactions in different individuals, and you may not be able to predict these effects until you've completed and tested a first draft. Still, you can start thinking about style by considering the lasting impression you want your document to make. What do you want your audience to remember about your project?

Once you've thought about the impact you'd like to make, identify stylistic features that will achieve that effect. Look at similar documents others have written: Do they have conventions for using fonts, colors, and images? Which examples do you like best? What features of these documents do you remember most?

■ **3 Assess the design resources available to you.** Producing documents usually requires more than just pen and paper. When you plan a writing project, assess what you already have available, what you might need to acquire to get the job done, and how much time and money you have for procuring new resources. Don't be discouraged if all you have are a word processor and a black-and-white printer—you can still make attractive, professional-looking documents.

Checklist 19.1

Planning a Document

• What formats will reach your audience? Will they accept electronic formats? What software will they use to view and/or print your document?

• Are there standard formats for this kind of project? Will standard formats allow you to present everything you need to include? What adjustments will you need to make to standard layouts?

• What features of document style are conventionally used for this kind of project? What will readers expect or accept? Can you use graphics, colors, or images?

• Do you want to create a certain mood? Do you want your audience to feel comfortable? excited? informed? respected?

• How will you produce your document? Do you have the necessary computer resources? Do you need to hire a professional printer? How much time and money will new resources cost?

19c How do you draft and revise your design?

In drafting a document, you'll need to tinker with it to achieve the best combination of format and style. This experimentation can be frustrating, especially when you're working with new software programs or techniques, but it's an essential part of the design process. In this section we offer guidelines to help you keep the final product in mind, so you can reduce the trial and error required to produce a polished document.

■ **1 Start with standard formats.** Since audiences expect certain layouts for certain kinds of writing, these formats are good starting points. A standard format may even help you shape your first draft. For instance, when a layout includes a section for documenting outside sources, you can assume that you'll need to include research. When a format requires itemized lists of information (a résumé, for example), you know that you probably won't need to develop traditional paragraphs.

For some projects you may want to push the envelope, altering a standard layout or developing an entirely new format. Innovations like these are especially popular when print documents are converted to Web formats, which allow new kinds of content (graphics, images, sound) and new ways of navigating documents (hyperlinks, search engines). But when customized formats don't meet your goals, stick with something more traditional.

19c
design

■ **2 Work with accessible formats.** It's pointless to work with a format or a style that will never reach your audience. Why pour hours into the design of a Web page if you know your readers don't browse the Internet? Why spend money on paper and binding if your instructor has asked you to submit a course project as an email attachment? At this stage of the process you'll save time and frustration by drafting only in formats that you know will reach your readers.

■ **3 Experiment with document style.** After you've selected a workable format, tinker with sets of fonts, colors, and graphics. Consider how these features work together to create an overall tone and direct readers' attention. Here are stylistic features that you should be experimenting with at this stage:

- **The main text.** Try a variety of readable typefaces, sizes, and color schemes; supplement text with images; set aside special material with boxes or frames; emphasize phrases and words with boldface or italics.
- **Headings.** Increase size; adjust type styles; highlight with colors; separate material from main text with horizontal rules.
- **Lists.** Use small images instead of bullets; vary left and right indentation; frame with boxes or background colors.

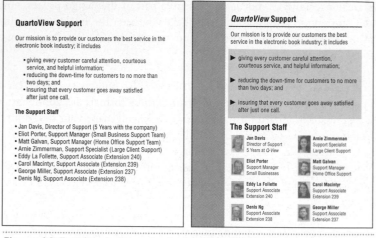

Figure 19.7 *While the formatting in the document on the left is generally effective, the revision on the right has enhanced the layout with colors, images, multiple type styles, and simple graphics. The original would be fine for an internal policy statement; the revision is more appropriate for a customer information packet. Note these changes: (1) Display text has been highlighted with color and changed from all-caps. (2) The first list uses stylized bullets and background color for contrast; the second list has portrait photos instead of bullets, two columns, and boldface emphasizing each name. (3) The margin has been colored and widened to hem in the main content of the page.*

19c
design

- **Tables.** Adjust type size, type style, and color scheme for column and row headings; add background color or shading to groups of cells.
- **Margins.** Offset with color or shading; use vertical rules; insert explanatory images and supplementary text; use decorative images.
- **Headers and footers.** Add navigational icons; use horizontal rules; vary type; use decorative images. (Note: *Headers,* which appear only at the top of each page, differ from *headings,* which appear in the body.)

See Sections 20d and 20e for more on working with fonts, type size, and graphics.

▪ 4 Revise for readability, impact, and flow. When you've created a design draft, evaluate how well format and style work together. Can readers move through the document easily and intuitively? Do its immediate impact and lasting impressions serve your writing goals? Even if your first draft seems relatively successful, chances are you'll need to revise to enhance readability, impact, and flow.

- **Add meaningful contrasts to improve readability.** Imagine the nightmare of reading a twenty-page document with no paragraphing or sentence punctuation to show where ideas begin and end. Readers might have a similar reaction—though not so drastic—to pages that contain a great deal of material in a plain format or style. Variations in color, font size, and font style help readers more clearly identify points of special interest and transitions.

- **Enhance contrasts where appropriate.** If you want to strengthen the effect your document has on readers, increase the contrast among design elements. Bright colors, extra-large fonts, and vivid images all attract readers' eyes. Keep in mind, however, that very striking features can make it difficult for a reader to focus on the surrounding material. You'll need to weigh the importance of making a big splash versus leaving a more subtle impression.

- **Group related material to improve flow.** When readers' eyes dance around the page, they can't easily focus on a single point. Help readers navigate smoothly by grouping related material— explanatory text, graphics, images, tables. You can emphasize groupings by framing material in boxes or using a common background color.

- **Position material strategically for balance.** Too much material in one area makes it difficult for readers to focus. Too much space between material disrupts flow. Use white space strategically to show places where readers might pause as they move toward a new thought—but don't create such a wide gap that they don't know which way to go.

19d
design

19d How do you edit and proof your design?

Once you've decided on a good overall combination of format and style, you can turn your attention to the subtler details that mark the difference between a truly professional-looking document and one that's merely competent. This section discusses ways to add this final polish. For more technical explanations of the design techniques discussed here, see Chapter 20.

■ **1 Fine-tune fonts, colors, and type styles.** Even slight adjustments to typeface, type size, type style, and colors can add meaning and make material easier to read, as Figure 19.8 below illustrates.

■ **2 Add functional graphics and images.** Don't just add graphics and images because you think a plain, black-and-white page looks dull. Make sure these striking design features serve a purpose (see the examples in Figure 19.9). Here are five good reasons to insert graphics and images into your document:

- To attract attention when your document competes with others
- To illustrate a point that can't be better explained with words
- To provide visual cues to the organization of a document
- To set a mood for your reader
- To enliven the discussion of a topic

Keep in mind that not all writing situations and formats allow images. If you think images would help you achieve your purpose, but you aren't using a format that supports them, consider adding supplementary documents—an attachment to an email message, for example. Be sure, though, not to *require* your audience to use a format with which they aren't comfortable.

19d
design

Figure 19.8 *The Web page on the right is clearer and more readable than the original on the left: (1) The heading font is reduced and changed to the same face as the rest of the page. (2) The column headings have a lighter color to contrast with the dark background. (3) The row headings are boldfaced to distinguish them from the numbers in the body of the table. (4) Subtle background coloring added to odd-year rows makes each series of numbers easier to follow. (5) The "Note" text appears in plain style, since an extended text in italics and boldface is difficult to read.*

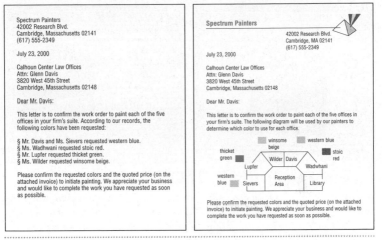

Figure 19.9 *Even a standard business letter (left) can be made more effective with the addition of images (right). (1) A horizontal rule helps distinguish the letterhead from the main content. (2) A graphic logo creates a professional persona. (3) An explanatory diagram helps to clarify written instructions.*

19d
design

3 Adjust alignment, spacing, and positioning. Page layouts need to balance written material and open space. (See Figure 19.10 on p. 344.) After editing your text, altering fonts, and adding images, you may notice that your layout has become cluttered in some areas and empty in others. Another common problem occurs when one or two lines of text are separated from the preceding or following paragraphs by a page break or a graphic. Lines left by themselves are said to be "widowed" or "orphaned." Many word processors now provide features that help you avoid widowed or orphaned lines, but you may need to tinker with the layout on your own. Take a few minutes to adjust the alignment, spacing, and positioning of paragraphs, graphics, and images to give your audience a clear path to follow.

4 Make document style consistent. You don't want your readers to have to adjust to a new style every time they turn a page. Although the content will differ, the layout of each page should give readers reliable cues for navigating material. Professional document designers use a tool called *style sheets* to guarantee consistency across a number of pages. Style sheets, which are now available in many word processors and Web browsers, specify the look of pages and passages in a section or an entire document. If your composing software doesn't provide style sheets, you can check the consistency of your design by skimming the layout of each page.

Figure 19.10 *The Web page on the right has improved the original on the left by making just a few alignment and spacing changes. (1) The page was changed from center alignment to left alignment. (2) The photograph was right-aligned so that the text could wrap around it, eliminating the need for scrolling and preventing an orphaned heading at the top of the page. (3) Extra space was added above and within the navigation bar, reducing the clutter of images and text.*

■ 5 Test a final draft in your audience's viewing environment. Before you deliver your document to an audience, proof the final draft in the same reading environment your audience will use. For print documents, verify that page numbering and section headers are accurate and that the binding of the document does not inhibit reading. For electronic documents, make sure your writing is readable with the version of viewing software your audience will use.

19e How do you copyright your work?

When you have a final product, protect your work by copyrighting it. You don't need to be a professional writer to take advantage of the copyright laws. In fact, you already have exclusive rights to the work you create in a writing class. Be aware, however, that copyrights are not always simple, nor do you always automatically own what you create. When you work for a company, your employer often owns the rights to all writing you compose on the job. And if you're a freelance author, you may be asked to give up your copyright in order to have your work published.

Currently the most complex issues related to copyright involve the Internet and computer software. Who, for example, owns the copyright to an online conversation involving many private participants? Does a software company own any rights to an electronic document created with its program? These questions will probably take many lawyers to resolve. While they wrangle, you can protect yourself and your work by following a few simple guidelines.

■ **1 Copyright your final product.** To protect your work, you need to include four elements somewhere on the document you wish to protect.

- The word *Copyright* or the universal copyright symbol: ©
- The year of publication (that is, printing, posting, or sending, depending on your document format)
- The name of the copyright holder
- A reservation-of-rights statement (optional), wherein you stipulate under what conditions you permit the copying of your document—or that you allow no copying whatsoever

Here are two examples of copyright lines:

© 2001 Dan's Alaskan Sportfishing Ventures, Inc. All rights reserved.

© 2000 by Daniel J. Kurland. All rights reserved. This Web page may be linked to other Web pages. Please inform the author.

Material you copyright is protected during your lifetime plus 50 years.

19e
design

■ **2 Document or credit borrowed images.** With rights come responsibilities. You need to acknowledge all images and graphics you borrow from another author or designer, just as you would cite works consulted or quoted in the body of your writing. Before you publish your work, give credit for images and graphics obtained from outside sources, even when they come from easy-to-access public spaces such as the WWW. Most Web sites that allow people to use their images state clearly the conditions of free use. In other cases, ask the Web developers by email for permission. If you don't have permission for an image, remove it from your design, even if—especially if—it's there simply for decorative purposes.

■ **3 Respect software copyrights.** You'll sometimes need expensive software to design intricate documents, and your audience may need special programs to view them. In both cases you must take care to avoid software pirating. There are legal ways to work around such problems: you can usually rent time with expensive design software at your local printing shop, and readers can usually download trial versions of viewing software.

EXERCISE 19.2 Imagine that you've been asked to create one of the documents described below. Working on your own or with a small group of classmates, draft a plan for designing and composing the document. What format and stylistic features would you incorporate, and why? What software or other resources would you need? How would you tailor the document to suit the audience's needs?

1. A publicity package for your brother's bluegrass band.

2. A report on spending trends among teenagers for your business marketing class. Your instructor has asked you to submit a formal written report to her and to deliver to the class a short oral presentation summarizing your findings.

3. A Web site for a campus organization to which you belong.

4. A campaign flyer supporting a candidate in a local or campus election.

19e
design

CHAPTER 20

How Do You Create Documents and Web Sites?

As Chapter 19 points out, successful writers know how to create the right combination of document format and document style to fit a writing situation. Yet even when you know how you want a document to look, creating that look with your computer is a separate matter. Computers and software programs have different features and capabilities, and they don't always provide obvious instructions. Fortunately, most word-processing and design programs do share a standard language for document design. This chapter will help you build a basic design vocabulary and it offers pointers for working with specific design elements and avoiding common pitfalls. It also presents step-by-step guidelines for creating Web sites.

20a How do you design documents with a computer?

Whether the final product will be printed on paper or viewed on an electronic screen, you'll most likely use a computer when you create a document. People have become so accustomed to composing with word processors that, for most of us, typewriters have been relegated to storage closets and pen and paper serve only for taking notes. But although most writers use computers, few use them to their full advantage. By familiarizing yourself with your computer's capabilities, you can make the design process easier and improve the quality of your final product.

1 Explore the design features of your word processor. Before you decide on a design for your document, make sure you know what choices are available. Word-processing programs are much more than glorified typewriters. Most of them support a variety of print and electronic formats, and they often have sophisticated options for enhancing document style. In recent versions of word processors, you can save in online formats (such as HTML), insert pictures and graphics,

Figure 20.1 *With a personal computer and a color printer, writers can publish on their desktops in minutes what historically has taken elaborate equipment and long hours of labor. The lithograph press illustrated here shows how many hands were once involved in producing a professionally printed document.*

add a table, use multiple columns, enhance text with colors and decorations, and do much, much more.

The only way to find out what you can accomplish with your word-processing program is to explore its features, either through the user's manual or by hands-on experimentation (see Figure 20.2 below).

—Save in different formats; view available templates; change margins, paper size and orientation; preview printed versions.

—Add section and page breaks; insert graphics, footnotes, tables, and other special material.

—Use the extra tools provided by word processors: spell checking, revision tracking, etc.

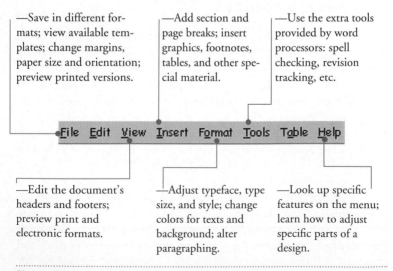

—Edit the document's headers and footers; preview print and electronic formats.

—Adjust typeface, type size, and style; change colors for texts and background; alter paragraphing.

—Look up specific features on the menu; learn how to adjust specific parts of a design.

Figure 20.2 *Learn the basic features of your word processor through its menu.*

2 Consider using other kinds of software. Although you can do a lot with word processors alone, other types of software, like those listed in Chart 20.1 below, offer additional design options. For instance, if you aren't satisfied with your word processor's clip art selection, you may need drawing software to design your own graphics. If you want to include a sophisticated table of numerical data, you'll need spreadsheet software.

Chart 20.1

Design Software

SOFTWARE	WHAT IT CAN CREATE
HTML editors	Web pages of varying complexity
Spreadsheet software	Complex tables, graphs, statistical reports
Image editors	Digitized photos, complex images
Drawing software	Simple images, charts, decorated text
Presentation software	Slide shows and handouts
Sound and video editors	Digitized music and film clips

20b
design

20b How do you organize long documents?

When you're composing a long document or one that combines several formats, you'll need to consider how your audience will digest so much information. Readers can be overwhelmed by large documents that offer little direction and confused by documents that abruptly change formats. This section offers guidelines to help you minimize confusion and manage what might otherwise be an unwieldy project.

1 Divide long documents into sections. When you compose with a word processor, you can divide a document into sections in two ways: you can insert multiple sections into one file or you can generate a new file for each section. One file is more convenient when you need to print the sections in a specific order and when you don't plan to reuse sections in another document. Multiple files, on the other hand, are often used on the WWW. Writers divide their content into several HTML files in order to reduce the amount of scrolling required to read a page and to allow readers to jump from page to page in a non-linear fashion.

Where should you divide your document? Begin by creating a new section each time you change formats. Create a new section, for example, when you switch from one column to two or change the width of your margins. Also consider creating sections when you begin the discussion of a new topic. You might find it helpful to vary subtly the stylistic features of sections divided in this way, thereby providing visual cues to the document's organization.

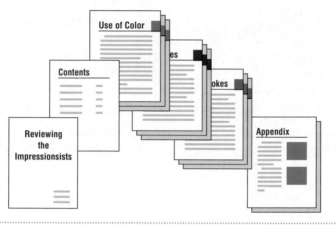

Figure 20.3 *A print essay might be divided into sections according to both topic and format. Breaks would appear between the title page and the table of contents, before major changes in topic, and before supplementary material.*

2 Insert a table of contents. It's hard for readers to gauge what's inside a long document simply by looking at its cover. Provide a comprehensive list of sections early so that your audience will have an overview of what you've written.

Some formats don't allow for a standard table of contents, but there are ways to work around such limitations. Suppose you are preparing a job application that includes a cover letter, a résumé, a list of references, and a sample of your work. List the accompanying pages in the cover letter so that your readers will know they have everything. Web sites often use a *site map*, which functions like a table of contents. (See Section 20g-3 for more on site maps.)

3 Attach appendixes, indexes, and glossaries. If you expect your document to be used as a reference, an index can help readers locate information. Appendixes and glossaries, on the other hand, help you streamline long, complex pieces of writing. These sections appear at the end of a document and contain detailed material (statistics, definitions, graphics, extended technical discussions) that would disrupt the flow of the text if it were included in the body of the document.

20c How do you lay out pages?

Many formats specify rules for page size, margin width, paragraphing, alignment, and so on. When the specifications are rigid, you're best served by following them to the letter. But when you have flexibility, take full advantage of it by shaping your document's layout to suit your purpose. Below you'll find a list of page features you can use to achieve specific effects. Most of these features are available in the latest word processors.

■ **1 Choose a manageable size and orientation.** The size of your pages will affect the amount of material you can put on each. Large pages give you more surface area, but they can be difficult to manipulate: for example, they don't work well for extended passages of text because readers must concentrate on a relatively small area of a wide surface. Large electronic pages may require too much scrolling.

20b
design

Orientation—the direction material faces on the page—also affects readers. The most common orientation is *portfolio,* shown on the left in Figure 20.4. Portfolio orientation works well with most formats because it presents the main text in one medium-size column. *Landscape* orientation is generally reserved for graphic material too wide for portfolio orientation.

Figure 20.4 *Portfolio layouts are longer than they are wide. In landscape layouts, width surpasses length.*

■ **2 Break material into units.** You do this even when you aren't designing a document. Paragraphs and sentences, for example, divide text into digestible chunks. When you take advantage of visual layout techniques, you have even more options for dividing your thoughts into manageable units.

Subsections. Subsections, groups of related paragraphs under a heading, are just a step up from plain paragraphs. By highlighting topics within a larger section, subsections help readers follow your discussion.

Reviews from Center Stage

Lame indeed.
The recent popularity of boy-band parody Wounded Duck isn't all that surprising. What is surprising is the ability of surly fans to endure the tiresome antics for an hour-long set. How many times can you watch the elaborately choreographed dancers flub their moves before it gets old?
Okay, I'll admit to guffawing through the first three songs—but once you get the gist of the show, there isn't much more to see. My advice—should the Duck fly into town opening for another band—show up ten minutes before the headliners, get a few laughs, and then listen to some real music.

How old school is too old school?
Before Friday, I thought I had an answer to this question. DJ Crusty's energetic set showed that digging up musical fossils isn't all about giving rock legends cameos in your music video. There are still treasures to be found—treasures encased in wax. Crusty's ability to synthesize diverse flavors of vinyl into addictive compounds explains why he has crossed over from the club set into the mainstream.

20c
pages

Lists. It's often awkward to form a series of regular, repetitive statements into a paragraph. Try a list instead. Use numbered lists when information needs to be presented in a strict order.

Festival 2000: Survivor's Guide

The spring rains and crowds can sometimes put a damper on your ability to enjoy the music. Never fear! We've provided a list of suggestions to make the best of your aural outing.

♪ Take your own water bottles. You'll have to wait in line for even the basics once inside.
♪ A waterproof mat is also a good idea. The ground gets pretty muddy, especially by the final days.
♪ Bring plenty of your own toilet tissue. Supplies in the portable facilities run low after just a few hours.
♪ If you're planning on attending more than one day, earplugs will keep your hearing from going dull.
♪ A hooded raincoat can keep you dry during the early afternoon showers.
♪ If you plan on heading for the mosh pit, ignore all of the above and just bring elbow pads.

Tables. Tables work well for presenting more structured information, especially (but not exclusively) statistical data, which can also be turned into graphs (see Section 20e-1). You can also use tables to display categories of information and complicated lists. See Section 10a for more on how tables and graphs work.

Festival 2000: Daily Venue Schedules

	Center Stage	East Stage	West Stage	Welcome Stage
Wed.	Classic Rock	World Beat	Punk	Polka
Th.	Funk and Soul	Swing	Reggae and Ska	Metal Mania
Fri.	Rock and Pop	Blues	Hip-hop and R & B	Local Grab Bag
Sat.	Rock and Pop	Jazz	Country	DJ Showcase
Sun.	International Folk	Classical	Gospel	Amateur Contest

Frames. When you want to set material apart from the main text, place it in a frame or a box, which you can create with lines and/or changes in background color.

About the Festival (cont.)

The annual festival began in 1982 as a relatively small, "y'all come" event. There was only one stage in the town square at that time. Those first few years didn't attract much national attention, but the music was rich with a variety of local flavors—from rock to jazz to punk to (we're not ashamed to admit) disco.

1987: Going National
A big break came for the festival in 1987, when national, independent label Snub Pop agreed to host a second stage. Before long, other national labels were seeing the festival as an opportunity to promote otherwise unknown bands.

The menu of bands was interesting enough to attract music lovers from all over the state. Eventually, the small festival grew to include most types of American music, until, last year, we finally added a fourth venue, allowing us to accommodate more and more international genres as well.

---

3 Arrange material according to relevance. Readers of English tend to move from the upper left corner of a page to the lower right. So put important lead-ins, such as titles and informative images, at the top of a page and less interesting but necessary material toward the bottom. Here are specific suggestions:

- Place the most important material in one or more columns spanning the body of the page (but be aware that columns wider than six or seven inches can be difficult for readers to follow).
- Move supplementary material, such as comments and brief notes, toward the side and bottom margins.
- Group related pieces of material (explanatory text and illustrations, for example) near each other.
- Distinguish special material by indenting or framing it.
- In headers, place navigational details such as current section titles (also called *running heads*), page numbers, and information about the writer.
- In footers, place routine but necessary information such as contact addresses, page numbers, organizational information, and credits (in cases where the writer's organization is emphasized more than the writer).

20c
pages

4 Align material to direct readers' eyes down and across the page. Left alignment is usually the most readable layout for extended passages of text, but images and graphics often work well with center or right alignment: Right-aligned images are effective when they are wrapped by left-aligned text, that is, when the lines of text appear on the same horizontal lines used by the image (see Figure 19.10). Center alignment is better for images not wrapped by text, since left or right alignment leaves too much white space in the body of the page.

Rules for Hiking in the Park
Don't go off the trail. The animal habitats in the park are extremely fragile. While we encourage people to enjoy the natural benefits provided inside, in order to maintain the survival of the fauna and flora, visitors must restrict themselves to clearly marked trails.
Don't take anything out of the park. Just as we don't want visitors leaving their marks, we don't want them removing what might be necessary parts of a fragile ecology.
Don't feed the animals. Wild animals can become dependent upon humans, if they expect to be fed. Once in the habit of receiving handouts they can become aggressive when refused—then they must be removed.
Report violations of these rules. It's your park. When other visitors violate these rules, they are destroying public property.

Rules for Hiking in the Park
Don't go off the trail. The animal habitats in the park are extremely fragile. While we encourage people to enjoy the natural benefits provided inside, in order to maintain the survival of the fauna and flora, visitors must restrict themselves to clearly marked trails.
Don't take anything out of the park. Just as we don't want visitors leaving their marks, we don't want them removing what might be necessary parts of a fragile ecology.
Don't feed the animals. Wild animals can become dependent upon humans, if they expect to be fed. Once in the habit of receiving handouts they can become aggressive when refused—then they must be removed.
Report violations of these rules. It's your park. When other visitors violate these rules, they are destroying public property.

Figure 20.5 *While the subsection headings are clearly emphasized in both pages, the center alignment in the page on the right makes them stand out even more. This alignment doesn't lead fluently into the main text—but maybe that's not important.*

20c pages

You can also use alignment to make readers pause at important points. Page designers will use this technique to make section openings stand out by centering or right-aligning headings within a left-aligned body of text. Use this method of emphasis carefully; too many disruptions can make pages seem choppy.

5 Format paragraphs for readability. Layouts with a significant amount of text require extra attention to paragraphing. First, decide on a paragraph format. *Block paragraphs* have no indentation on the first line but are separated by extra spacing between them. Standard *indented paragraphs*, on the other hand, need no extra spacing. Besides paragraph format, you must determine line spacing. Print formats often use indented paragraphs with more than single spacing between lines of type. Web pages and email, on the other hand, are easier to read when they are single-spaced. Not only does the type look lighter on a screen, but single spacing means that readers need not do extra scrolling to get through the document.

6 Use white space to avoid clutter. White space reduces clutter by separating material into readable units. Here are common ways of creating white space:

- Leave ample margins at the top and sides of your pages.
- Surround titles, graphics, and frames with unused space.
- Double-space between paragraphs.
- Indent special blocks of material.
- Allow adequate space between columns in multicolumn documents.

20d How do you choose type?

Typefaces (or *fonts*) and *type styles* have their own personalities; they convey mood, attitude, and tone, and they affect the readability of a document. A thick, heavy typeface like **Arial Black** speaks loudly and commands attention; a script font like *Coronet* conveys a delicate, artistic mood. Type styles, such as **boldface**, *italic*, and SMALL CAPS, serve more practical purposes, enhancing words and phrases to make them stand out. Finally, you can adjust *type size* (usually measured in *points*) to enhance your document's style and readability.

1 Select a suitable typeface. What typeface you choose for a project will depend on a variety of factors, from the tone you want to achieve to your document's format. Some fonts read better in print than on a computer screen. Some fonts serve decorative purposes and are not designed for extended passages of text. Fortunately, fonts have been divided into families that share certain characteristics. Knowing the general characteristics of each family will help you make appropriate choices.

20d
type

- **Serif fonts.** Serifs are the little lines, or "feet," that appear at the bottom or top of the main strokes in a letter. Two common serif fonts are `Courier` and **Bookman**. Serif fonts are highly readable for print documents.
- **Sans serif fonts.** Sans serif fonts—letters without the little feet—have a clean, avant-garde look that appeals to many readers. Two common sans serif fonts are Arial and Helvetica. Sans serif fonts are generally the best choices for display type (see Section 19c-3) and material to be read on an electronic, faxed, or photocopied page.
- **Decorative or ornamental fonts.** Decorative fonts have a lot of personality—they can be elegant, jazzy, authoritative, comical. But they aren't always easy to read, which makes them poor choices for long passages of text. Save these fonts for display text or where you want to create a special effect. When you use a decorative font, explore the options available in your word processor, from **Playbill** to *Charm* *Lariat Handscript* to *Vivaldi*. Only a few will fit the tone you want to convey.
- **Symbol fonts.** Special characters, called *dingbats*, allow you to add simple graphic ornaments to your documents. To find out what you have available, select a font with "symbol" or "ding" in its title and start typing characters, or choose the "Insert Symbol" command in your word processor. You'll see small graphics suitable for various purposes, as shown in Chart 20.2.

Chart 20.2

Symbol Fonts ("Dingbats")	
Stylized bullets	▶ ◇ ☛ ✓ ❶
Explanatory diagrams	🗁 🖫 ⇒ 📄 ↑ 🖃
Business-related text	© ® ™ % ¢ £ ¥
Technical writing	θ ∠ ⊆ π √ Ω Σ ♭ ♯
Informative symbols	♂ ♀ 🔋 🔒 🔓 📱 ☏
Thematic icons	🌍 ⌛ ♦ ♁ ☀ ☞ ∞
Playful imagery	♣ ♥ 🐟 🐾 🎆 👽 ♈

2 Use type styles strategically. Type styles that differ from plain text will draw readers' attention. But use them sparingly, or they'll lose their impact. Here is a chart of common type styles and suggestions for using each.

20d
type

Chart 20.3

Type Styles	
TYPE STYLE	COMMON USES
Boldface	Strong emphasis, headings
Italic	Highlights, special/foreign words, book titles
Underline	Emphasis, headings, book titles
Superscript and subscript	Footnotes, endnotes, technical notation
~~Strikethrough~~	Revisions in drafts
SMALL CAPS	Subtle emphasis, strong highlights, headings
Shadow, Emboss, Wave	Decorative emphasis, highlights, headings

3 Adjust type size for readability. Medium type sizes (usually 10 or 12 points) work best for the main body of text. Extended passages in large type can be difficult to process, since readers can barely digest a few words before they have to jump to a new line. Instead, use larger type to emphasize headings and titles. "Fine print," on the other hand, isn't always bad. Use smaller type to downplay less important material in margins, headers, and footers. You'd rather draw readers' eyes toward the body of a page than toward running titles, contact information, or supplementary comments—material that is useful but not essential to your main points.

Here are a few final cautions:

- Electronic documents may look strange if the fonts you use aren't installed on your readers' computers.
- Changing the font face may change the height and length of lines.

- Serif fonts can be difficult to read on computer screens.
- Certain font styles and colors may have special meaning in Web pages and other hyperlinked documents.

20e How do you use graphics and images?

According to the maxim, a picture is worth a thousand words. Used thoughtfully, it can be worth much more; used poorly, much less. Effective images take a good deal of planning and editing. The tips in this section will help you use images to enhance and complement the text of your document.

1 Present numerical data with graphs. Graphs help readers visualize the significance of statistical information. How better to show a trend in rising prices than a line shooting upward? What more clearly illustrates the allocation of a budget than a simple pie chart? With the help of word-processing or spreadsheet software, you can graph quantitative information clearly and quickly. Below are examples of common types of statistical graphs. For more on understanding and interpreting graphs, see Section 10a.

20e
images

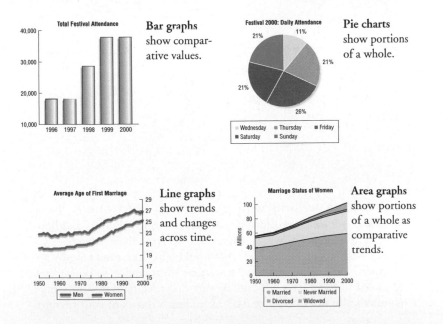

Bar graphs show comparative values.

Pie charts show portions of a whole.

Line graphs show trends and changes across time.

Area graphs show portions of a whole as comparative trends.

■ **2 Clarify details through charts and diagrams.** Statistics aren't the only kind of information you can present visually. Use a chart or a diagram to give readers details about your topic that are difficult to explain in words. Suppose you're making a presentation that touches on the work groups in your organization. You could try to describe the complex intergroup relationships with words alone, or you could simply provide an organizational chart. This strategy allows you to focus your text on the discussion of important policy issues without bogging down in preliminary details.

While charts show connections among related things, diagrams supplement verbal descriptions with instructive images. Without diagrams, how-to manuals would be a nightmare: "Step 7. Connect four-prong plug A into socket B, above panel C. . . ." Such instructions are easier to follow when accompanied by a diagram of the parts involved. Below are examples of common types of charts and diagrams.

20e
images

Organizational charts show hierarchical relationships.

Flow charts show procedural relationships.

Timelines show sequential relationships.

Diagrams illustrate textual descriptions.

■ **3 Enliven writing with photos and illustrations.** Some ideas and emotions are difficult to express in words. Photos and illustrations (cartoons, drawings, engravings) let you show readers—at a glance—aspects of your subject that would otherwise need lengthy description. Because photos and illustrations affect readers so powerfully, you need to use them with care. Be sure that they reinforce important points and do not distract or mislead readers. Viewers of your personal home page might enjoy seeing a photo of your children, but the same photo would distract potential employers from your credentials in an online résumé.

Many options exist for acquiring photos and illustrations to use in a document. You can purchase digitized photos on the Web (some are even free) or on CDs, usually with certain copyright restrictions. You can create your own with a digital camera. You can translate existing photos or illustrations into electronic formats with a scanner.

For a minimal cost, you can buy disks or CD-ROMs that have thousands of clip art images. Clip art collections may not furnish you with sophisticated images, but they can be useful when you need graphics for posters, brochures, newsletters, and other low-cost publications.

■ **4 Separate material with borders and rules.** Borders and rules—horizontal or vertical lines between units of material—provide visual guides to how you have divided material in a document. Create borders around frames, photographs, tables, and graphs to more clearly distinguish them from surrounding paragraphs. Select a line width and color that isn't overwhelming. If you use a thick blue border for a supplementary diagram, you'll end up distracting readers from a more important focal point.

20f
color

Rules often mark the beginning of new sections; they also distinguish marginal material from the central content of a page. You'll often see horizontal rules separating footnotes or running heads from the main text. You might see a vertical rule wherever marginal comments or graphics appear on the sidebar of a page.

20f How do you work with color?

Color complicates design and increases the costs of printing, but it does make documents more vivid. You'll need to match your use of color to your writing situation. Color may not be appropriate in academic papers, but it may be necessary to attract attention to brochures, newsletters, and Web pages. Once you've decided to use color, there are many factors to consider. In Web pages, you need to be aware that tones and hues will look different on different types of screens. Such complications can usually be worked out, especially if you test design drafts before creating your final product.

▌1 Select a readable color scheme. Color schemes assign colors to various elements on a page (headings, rules, frames, borders, graphics). Designers create color schemes to orchestrate the interaction of multiple tones and hues within a layout, all to achieve specific effects, from adding emphasis to setting a mood. The most important decisions in any color scheme are what to use for background and type. To be readable, these colors must contrast but not clash. Bright colors must be used sparingly, since they can tire the eyes. At right you will find a selection of readable color combinations.

dark blue on biege

black on orange

brick red on blue

white on blue-green

light gray on red

black on gold

▌2 Create a mood for your document. Different colors evoke different emotions. Bright colors have a bold effect, even when applied sparingly. Soft colors, on the other hand, may need to cover an entire page to have a noticeable impact. Combinations make a difference too. Some combinations—for example, purple and orange or yellow and black—are bold; they shout for attention. Others—shades of blue combined with ivory—are subtle. Some colors just seem to clash—pink and bright green, for instance, and purple and yellow. But tastes in color vary greatly, and one can't say flatly that certain colors should never be combined.

20f
color

 Bright red always gets attention, dominating other colors.

 Blues, at least in the softer shades, are soothing.

 Greens are often cheerful, associated with nature and good health.

 Yellow is vibrant and attention-getting.

 Browns and grays seem somber and formal.

▌3 Use color to highlight or soften elements of your layout. Colors, because of their wide range of effects, give you more control over the impact created by other features of your layout. Once you've decided to go beyond black and white, you'll have many more options for emphasizing or downplaying text and images. A bold heading can be made less striking, for example, by changing the color from black to a softer blue or gray. Plain text in the body of a paragraph can be made more striking by changing it to red.

20g How do you design Web pages?

If you've never created a Web page (or a Web site consisting of several hyperlinked Web pages), you might find the prospect daunting. Yet college instructors and employers increasingly expect writers to be able to compose documents for this medium. Creating a Web page or site is both simple and difficult. The basic process is relatively easy and requires not much more skill than it takes to operate word-processing software—if a little more patience.

But Web sites have been evolving into more and more challenging forms with enhanced design possibilities. Many combine diverse design elements such as stylized text, graphics, animation, and even sound. Consequently, we cannot offer models and guidelines to suit every possible occasion. (Besides, if you have access to the Internet, you're within a few mouse clicks of any number of examples—albeit of varying quality.) What we can offer here is an outline of the basic processes involved in writing for the Web, which should be enough to get you started. We have outlined the process in Chart 20.4 on page 362, but your work may take different paths, depending on your skills, materials, and work habits.

■ **1 Plan your Web project carefully.** Planning a Web project isn't that different from planning other types of documents (see the flow chart on page 362). You'll need to determine your audience, assess your resources, choose an effective layout, and make decisions about document style. Web projects, however, do have special demands.

First, you'll need to know that Web documents use the HTML (HyperText Markup Language) electronic format. HTML tags or codes (see p. 376) tell WWW browsers how to display words and images and how to hyperlink separate documents to each other—the feature that makes the Web what it is. There are several methods for creating HTML documents, which we explain in Section 20g-2. As you begin your project, think about what method you'll use to create your HTML documents, whether you'll use a single-page or a multi-page format, and how you'll lay out and link individual pages.

Chart 20.4

20g
Web

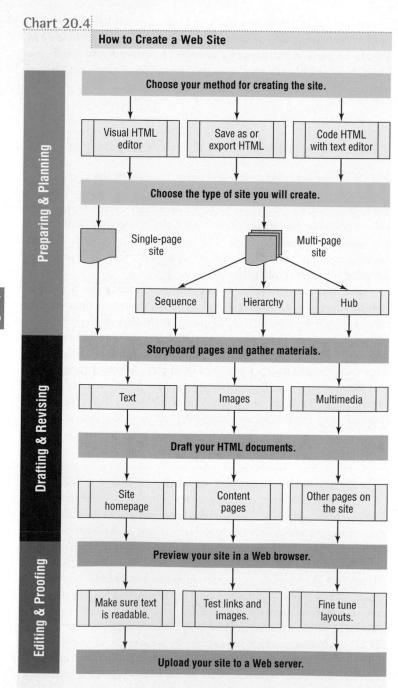

How to Create a Web Site

Preparing & Planning

Choose your method for creating the site.

Visual HTML editor

Save as or export HTML

Code HTML with text editor

Choose the type of site you will create.

Single-page site

Multi-page site

Sequence

Hierarchy

Hub

Drafting & Revising

Storyboard pages and gather materials.

Text

Images

Multimedia

Draft your HTML documents.

Site homepage

Content pages

Other pages on the site

Editing & Proofing

Preview your site in a Web browser.

Make sure text is readable.

Test links and images.

Fine tune layouts.

Upload your site to a Web server.

Besides using HTML format, you'll need to adhere to the publication requirements of the WWW. You'll eventually need to "upload" your documents to a Web server to make them accessible to the world. You can, however, create Web pages without uploading them. Here we focus on the design of Web pages; later we'll discuss uploading (see Section 20g-11).

2 Choose a method for creating HTML pages. Numerous software programs exist to help you create HTML documents. These tools vary in their user interfaces, their sophistication, and their adherence to Web publishing standards. Later in this chapter we will walk you through the process of creating simple Web pages using each of three basic methods.

- **Visual HTML editors,** or WYSIWYG ("wizzy-wig") editors, which stands for "What You See Is What You Get," are especially useful for new Web writers. The design tools they offer allow you to edit materials as they'd look in WWW browsers (in other words, you don't have to edit the HTML codes). But these tools don't always support the latest standards or design features. (See Section 20g-8.)

- **HTML text editors** are the original tools for creating Web pages. In these programs you must enter HTML codes by hand (so you have to understand the codes). Text editors don't have many user-friendly design tools, but they are extremely flexible, since you can always compose with the latest Web standards and features. Use this method if you like to see what's going on "under the hood" of your Web documents. (See Section 20g-7.)

- **"Save as" or "Export" HTML options** in word processors and other kinds of software allow you to work on HTML documents as you would any other format. Once you have a finished product, you'll convert your work to HTML using your program's menu options. This method of creating HTML documents is fast and easy, but the pages generated often need fine-tuning to make them appealing. (See Section 20g-9.)

20g
Web

You can also combine these methods to take advantage of the strengths each has to offer. For example, you might start a page by exporting an existing document to HTML and then add features with a visual editor. (See the examples on p. 364.) Or you might use a visual editor to experiment with page features you're thinking of coding yourself. Even if you begin with a visual editor, you can later tinker with the HTML tags directly.

A PERSONAL HOME PAGE WITH A VISUAL EDITOR

Menus and **toolbars** vary with each visual editor, but all are based on standard Web design features.

The **body** looks almost exactly as it would if you were viewing it in a browser. But the editor allows you to modify text, insert pictures and tables, format fonts, and change colors.

Header information, such as page title and author, does not appear in the main window of visual editors. Instead you edit this information through the menus of your program.

A PERSONAL HOME PAGE WITH AN HTML TEXT EDITOR

Menus and **toolbars** are often much simpler in text editors.

Header information appears like the rest of the document, in coded format.

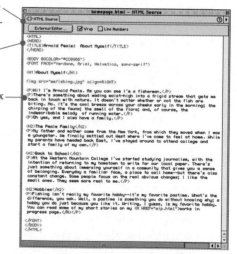

The **body** includes a mix of HTML *tags* (special snippets of text enclosed by angle brackets: < >) and text. Textual styles, images, colors, hypertext links, paragraph breaks, horizontal rules—all are added through standard HTML tags, which won't appear when you look at the page in the browser.

■ **3 Choose a single-page or a multi-page format.** Decide early in your design process how you want to organize your Web page: will you create a single, scrolling page or multiple pages connected by links? If you have a limited amount of information to present—as in a personal home page, a résumé, or a brief report—consider choosing a single, scrolling page. A single page is simple and clear: readers need only move down the page to find information. But most readers online don't like to scroll much beyond a few screens. If you have more than two or three screens of information or if your material breaks easily into sections, consider a set of pages connected by links.

A site that will consist of multiple pages is harder to create than a single-page site. You have to decide how to arrange your information so readers can navigate the pages easily and intuitively. You'll need to create a home page as the entry into the site. But material deeper in the site may be connected to that home page in different ways—again depending on your purpose and subject—to create a **hierarchy**, a **sequence**, or a **hub** (see below).

A **hierarchical** pattern organizes pages into increasingly more specific groupings. Readers find material by starting with general categories (topics, areas, units) and working their way down to more specific information. This structure is regularly used by large organizations. Large organizations (such as colleges) often organize their Web sites this way.

20g
Web

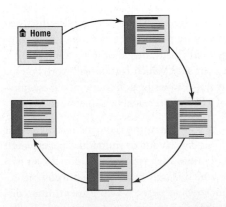

Sequential sites present readers with fewer options. If you are offering a proposal argument, your site might move readers step by step from problem to solution, with each stage of the argument building on material from the preceding screen. Readers are encouraged to click "Next Page" rather than select from a menu of options. Make sure to provide links back to the home page so readers won't reach a dead end.

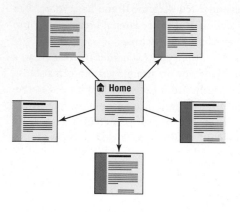

A **hub** structure encourages exploration. Here the home page links to related pages that neither require a specific order of reading nor fit into clear hierarchical groups. You might use a hub design to catalog items—say, all the native plants in a particular wetlands environment. Readers could browse each item, going back and forth from the home page. You might also provide direct links to related pages on the hub.

Besides creating links on your site that reflect the structure of your content, you'll also make links directly between pages or to other sites on the Internet. As you build your site, keep these suggestions in mind:

20g
Web

- Make sure all pages link to your home page.
- Don't create "dead-ends" that require endless clicking on the "Back" button to find new content.
- When you link to Web pages outside your site, make it clear to readers that they are being taken somewhere else.
- As your site grows, consider providing a *site map,* a special page that outlines the organization of your material.
- Use hypertext links to cross-reference material you discuss on a number of pages.
- Gather material you refer to often into a central resource, such as a glossary, to which other pages can easily link.

EXERCISE 20.1 Experiment with the three organizational models discussed in Section 20g-3 as part of the planning process for a Web site you're composing. What are the advantages and disadvantages of using a hierarchy, a sequence, or a hub to organize your site? Which pattern will work best for your project, and why? If you're not composing a Web site, use these questions to evaluate the structure of a Web site created by someone else.

■ **4 Storyboard pages.** As you determine the overall structure of your site, consider also the on-screen layout of individual pages you'll create. For the sake of simplicity, new Web writers should focus on two types of pages: the *home page,* which clearly conveys the purpose of the site and how to navigate it, and *content pages,* which present, in a consistent and readable manner, the site's most important material. The

"Women in Science" Web page on page 403 illustrates basic features of home pages and content pages. (If you're designing a single-page site you might want to think in terms of *areas* on the page—with *home* at the top and *content* below.)

As you prepare your page layouts, you'll no doubt have questions:

- What text is needed for the site to achieve its purpose?
- How will you break up text onto different pages? (See Sections 19c-3, 20b, and 20c.)
- Will you use images or multimedia? (See Sections 19d-2 and 20f.)
- What materials can you gather from outside sources?
- What materials can you create yourself?
- How will you gather all these materials to create your site?

EXERCISE 20.2 Storyboard a home page and a content page for a Web site you're working on, using the guidelines in Section 20g-4. Ask classmates to review your designs and offer suggestions for improvement.

5 Gather materials. Whatever materials you add to your site, you'll need to assemble them in electronic formats accessible to those browsing the Web. Photographs from your last vacation can't go onto a Web site until they have been "digitized" by a scanner and converted to JPEG or GIF files (two graphics formats that are Web-compatible). Although we don't have space here to explain how to digitize photographs, make animations, and record voices—all of which involve an understanding of specific software programs—we can give you guidelines for gathering material already (or easily) converted to Web formats.

20g
Web

- **Create a working folder on your disk.** Place all your materials—HTML files, graphics files, and other media—for the project in this folder. When you're ready to publish your project, all you'll need to do is upload the folder to the Web server. As you're storing files here, follow the WWW naming conventions discussed in Section 20g-11.
- **Write the text that will appear on your site.** Web sites may contain less written matter than you'd find in printed sources. But online prose needs to be just as clear and grammatical as any other professional writing. Remember, too, that what you post on a Web page is very public. So proofread carefully and edit to eliminate wordiness (see Sections 5b and 5c). Because reading on screen is more tiring than reading print, make every word count.
- **Collect images from the Web.** Section 20e provides general suggestions for using images. The same guidelines apply here. In the illus-

TO SAVE AN IMAGE FROM THE WEB:

1. Go to an image gallery, such as <http://gallery.yahoo.com>.
2. Find an image you like.
3. Right-click (Windows) or control-click (Macintosh) to bring up the floating menu.
4. Select "Save Image As . . ." (*Netscape*) or "Save Picture As . . ." (*Internet Explorer*).
5. Choose your Web project folder from the file chooser.
6. Note the online gallery's fair use requirements. If necessary ask for permission by email.

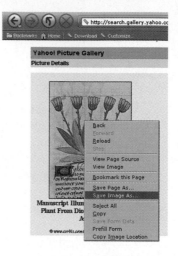

20g
Web

tration above we explain how to collect images from the Web. These images will already be in the proper electronic format for Web writing. But you still need to insure that you have permission, either from a posted copyright statement on the site or through email correspondence. It's a good idea to keep a running list of images you have borrowed and from where. You'll want to cite these locations on a credits page or in the footers of pages where you use images. Sound files and other types of multimedia can sometimes be gathered from Web galleries too. When you use these sources, document them as you would a borrowed image. (See also Section 19e.)

• **Create other media.** You may decide to compose your own media files. For example, you may want to publish on the Web a graph you have drawn. Sometimes graphics and drawing software allow you to convert your file to Web formats, an option that often appears in the program's "File" menu. At other times you will need more advanced or specialized software to achieve the conversion. The same is true for recording voice or sound, digitizing photographs, and creating animations in Web-compatible formats. But before you buy new software, explore what you already have on your computer. You may be surprised at what you can do with software you already own.

EXERCISE 20.3 In a project folder, gather all the materials you will need for a Web site you're composing, including the text you plan to use and at least one image. Refer to the guidelines in Section 20g-5 if you need help. (To draft a Web page from these materials, follow the steps in Exercise 20.4 on page 370.)

■ **6 Draft HTML documents.** What you do to draft your HTML documents will depend on what method of Web page composition you use (see Section 20g-2). But keep in mind the differences between drafting home pages and content pages. Home pages have less rigid layout standards, since you will use that layout only once on your site. But when you revise the layout of one content page, you should revise others to be consistent, a task that can be tedious if you've already created a lot of HTML documents. See Section 21i for tips on creating content pages.

The next few sections take you step by step through the creation of an HTML document, first using a text editor, then a visual editor, and finally the export features of a standard word processor. The instructions will help you compose a simple Web page with a few paragraphs of text, a single image, and a link.

■ **7 Consider drafting with an HTML text editor.** As we've said, this isn't the easiest way for new Web writers to construct HTML documents. We start here, however, because this method shows most clearly the nuts and bolts of all Web pages—no matter how they're created. To see what we mean, go to any location in your Web browser and from the "View" menu choose "Source" or "Page Source" (or see Figure 20.6). You now see a document containing the HTML codes for the page you were just viewing. This document will include the readable text you see in the browser window and a number of HTML tags—those cryptic letters and words that appear between angle brackets.

20g
Web

Depending on the page you're viewing, the HTML tags may seem daunting and difficult to learn. In fact, composing with HTML is relatively easy—if you start with the basics. While these basics won't allow you to make flashy, elaborate sites, they will allow you to publish material on the Web in a clear and organized fashion. Once you feel comfortable with the basics, you can then increase your HTML vocabulary, learning more striking Web design techniques.

- **Choose your editing software.** Both Macintosh and Windows operating systems come with basic text-editing software: *Simple Text* and *Notepad,* respectively. These programs offer all you need to write HTML documents. If, however, you have access to a text editor specialized for HTML documents, such as *BBEdit* on the Macintosh, you will probably want to use it.
- **Create an HTML template.** All HTML documents have a basic structure, a required series of tags that tell browser programs necessary information about the organization of the page. Type the tags that are shown in the following figure into a new document

Figure 20.6 *You can create an HTML template by typing the tags and words into your text editor exactly as shown above. Later, when you start making pages or customized templates, you'll put more personalized information into the areas highlighted above. The area between the <BODY> ... </BODY> tags will contain the main content for each page. (Microsoft ® Notepad is a trademark of Microsoft. Title bar screen shot reprinted by permission of Microsoft Corporation.)*

20g
Web

Figure 20.7 *Preview your template and notice how little of what you typed appears on the final product. Browsers hide all HTML tags or convert them to special kinds of content, such as images or empty lines. You'll need to review what different tags do in order to know how they can help you achieve the layout you want. (Title bar screen shot reprinted by permission of Microsoft Corporation.)*

using your HTML text editor. Save that document in your working folder as *htmltemplate.html*—you will make a copy of this document every time you start composing a new page, knowing that it will have the required structure.

- **Preview your HTML document in a browser.** This is an action you'll repeat again and again as you draft your Web pages. By using a Web browser to open the pages you save in your working folder, you'll be able to see how they will appear once uploaded. To preview your HTML template, open your Web browser, choose "Open" from the "File" menu, and browse for the file you just saved in your working folder. You should then see something like what is shown in Figure 20.7.

EXERCISE 20.4 Using the guidelines on pages 369–70, create and preview an HTML template for a Web site you're composing.

- **Review the basic HTML tags.** Making a simple Web page (as you've just proved) is easy, but the template itself doesn't do

20g
Web

Chart 20.5

Basic HTML Tags	
HTML TAGS	**WHAT THEY DO**
<HTML> </HTML>	Appears as the first and the last tags in an HTML document. These tags tell browser programs to translate codes on the page to a readable format.
<HEAD> </HEAD>	Follows the opening <HTML> tag in a document. Tags between the <HEAD> tags provide information about the document, but this material does not appear in the browser window.
<TITLE> </TITLE>	Identifies the title that will appear in the title bar on the browser when a page opens. The page title appears between the tags.
<META . . . >	Provides extra information about the document, data often used by Web search engines to index the document once it has been uploaded to a Web server.
<BODY> </BODY>	Brackets the material in the body of the page, including the text, images, and any formatting that will appear in the browser window.

much. To achieve the design you want, you'll need to learn more about HTML tags. First let's consider the function of the tags we just used to create the template.

Notice how nearly all tags come in pairs. The first in each pair is the *opening tag;* the second, which always includes a slash before the tag name, is the *closing tag.* All text between the opening and closing tags is formatted in a special manner, depending on the tag. Some tags, such as <BODY>, <HEAD>, and <HTML>, help the browser software identify parts of the document. Other tags, such as those in the list below, add stylistic features to the text they surround.

Some tags, however, don't come in pairs, among them the <META> and <HR> tags (see below). These tags add special content to the page. The <IMG> tag, for example, tells the browser to insert an image; the <HR> tag creates a horizontal rule.

Chart 20.6

More HTML Tags	
HTML TAGS	WHAT THEY DO
<B> </B>	Boldfaces text between the tags.
<I> </I>	Italicizes text between the tags.
<P> </P>	Formats text between the tags as a simple paragraph.
<CENTER> </CENTER>	Centers text between the tags.
<H1> </H1>	Forms a level-one heading—the largest HTML heading size. To vary heading size, choose <H2>, <H3>, <H4>, <H5>, or <H6>. <H6> is smallest.
<A ... > </A>	Hyperlinks the text between the tags. (See p. 375.)
<FONT ... > </FONT>	Sets the font for text between the tags. (See p. 375–76.)
<UL> <LI><LI> <LI> ... </UL>	Creates a bulleted list. Place the <LI> tag before each item in the list.
 	Inserts a line break. All text following the tag appears on the next line.
<HR>	Inserts a horizontal line across the page.
<IMG ... >	Inserts an image onto the page. (See pp. 374–75.)

For more tags, see Kevin Werbach's *The Bare Bones Guide to HTML* at <http://werbach.com/barebones/barebones.html> or *A Beginner's Guide to HTML* at <http://www.ncsa.uiuc.edu/General/Internet/WWW/HTMLPrimer.html>.

Now that you know how to create a template for your Web page and how to use basic HTML tags, the best way to learn to create a Web page using an HTML text editor is to practice. The following exercise guides you step by step through the process of drafting a simple Web page that includes text, an image, a hypertext link, and footer.

EXERCISE 20.5 To begin this exercise, you will need to have created a project folder that contains all the materials you want to include on your Web page (see Exercise 20.3 on p. 368) and an HTML template for your page (see Exercise 20.4 on p. 371). Use these materials as you follow the instructions in steps 1-4 below. When you finish, you'll have a completed Web page that will look something like the example on page 375, which was created by Stella Galvan, a student at the University of Texas at Austin.

20g
Web

Step 1. Create and draft the body of your new Web page.
- Make a copy of the template you created in Exercise 20.4, naming it something appropriate like "homepage.html" or "topic1.html." Store this copy in your project folder.
- Open the new document (the copy of your template) in your HTML text editor and change the words between the opening and closing <TITLE> tags to match the content it will contain.
- Then enter the text you've prepared for the page between the <BODY> . . . <BODY> tags in the new document. If you don't have the text written yet, make up something with which you can experiment.
- Just below the opening <BODY> tag, create a page heading by typing your title between the <H1> . . . </H1> tags.
- Format paragraphs by surrounding them with <P> . . . <P> tags.

Step 2. Change the background color of your page and insert an image.
- Some HTML tags allow you to set *elements,* or special features of document style. All elements appear in the opening tag followed by an equal sign and a value (between quotation marks). The <BODY> tag provides an element—BGCOLOR—that lets you

set the background color of the page. Change the background color for your HTML document by modifying your <BODY> tag:

<BODY BGCOLOR="TAN">

Different tags allow you to modify different elements of your page. Check your HTML guide to learn more about formatting options.

- The <IMG> tag allows you to add pictures to your Web page. Add the following text to your document just below the header, setting the SRC element to match the name of a graphics file in your working folder and the ALIGN element to RIGHT:

<IMG SRC="yourimage.jpg" ALIGN="RIGHT">

When you preview your page in a browser you'll see the image aligned to the right of your text.

Step 3. Add a hypertext link and attach a page footer.

- Using the <*A*> tag (also called the "anchor tag"), link your page to others, either within your Web project or at another location on the WWW. To link to the Internet search engine Google, for example, you would enter this text:

<A HREF="http://www.google.com">Search at Google</A>

The HREF element allows you to specify an Internet address to which the text between the <A> . . . </A> tags will be linked. To link to another page in your project, set the HREF element to match the name of another HTML document in your working project folder.

- Footers on Web pages are useful places to unobtrusively credit yourself and others and to link readers to the site's home page (from content pages). Here is the footer Stella Galvan created for the sample Web page featured above. You can create a simple footer using the same codes:

<CENTER>
<HR>&copy 2000 Stella Galvan
<A HREF="homepage.html">Return to Home</A>
</CENTER>

Review the tags above using the list on page 372. (You won't find *&copy* on the list—this code creates the copyright symbol.) Check your HTML guide for more extensive lists of codes.

Step 4. Fine-tune your text.

- Use HTML tags to change font face and style where it's appropriate. The <FONT> tag includes three important elements:

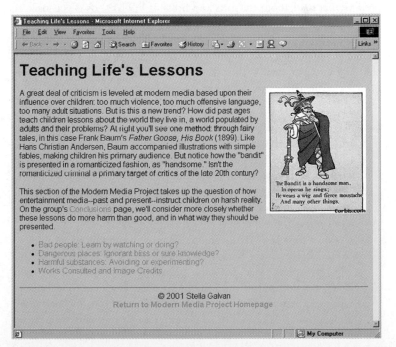

```
lessons.html - Notepad                                                    _ □ ×
File   Edit   Search   Help
<HTML>

<HEAD>
 <TITLE>Teaching Life's Lessons</TITLE>
 <META NAME="Author" CONTENT="Stella Galvan">
 <META NAME="Date of Creation" CONTENT="2000-12-15">
</HEAD>

<BODY BGCOLOR="TAN">

 <H1>Teaching Life's Lessons</H1>

 <IMG SRC="baum-bandit.jpg" ALIGN="RIGHT">

 <P>A great deal of criticism is leveled at modern media based upon their influence over
 children: too much violence, too much offensive language, too many adult situations.
 But is this a new trend? How did past ages teach children lessons about the world
 they live in, a world populated by adults and their problems? At right you'll see one
 method: through fairy tales, in this case Frank Baum's <I>Father Goose, His Book</I>
 (1899). Like Hans Christian Andersen, Baum accompanied illustrations with simple
 fables, making children his primary audience. But notice how the "bandit" is presented
 in a romanticized fashion, as "handsome." Isn't the romanticized criminal a primary
 target of critics of the late 20th century?

 <P>This section of the Modern Media Project takes up the question of how
 entertainment media---past and present--instruct children on harsh reality. On the
 group's <A HREF="conc.html">Conclusions</A> page, we'll consider more closely whether
 these lessons do more harm than good, and in what way they should be presented.

 <UL>
  <LI><A HREF="people.html">Bad people: Learn by watching or doing?</A>
  <LI><A HREF="places.html">Dangerous places: Ignorant bliss or sure knowledge?</A>
  <LI><A HREF="things.html">Harmful substances: Avoiding or experimenting?</A>
  <LI><A HREF="sources.html">Works Consulted and Image Credits</A>
 </UL>

 <CENTER>
 <HR>&copy 2001 Stella Galvan<BR>
 <A HREF="homepage.html"><B>Return to Modern Media Project Homepage</B></A>
 </CENTER>

</BODY>

</HTML>
```

(Microsoft ® Notepad is a trademark of Microsoft. Title bar screen shot reprinted by permission of Microsoft Corporation.)

20g
Web

COLOR, FACE, and SIZE. In combination with the <I> (italics) and <B> (boldface) tags, you can have nearly as much control over the style of your text as you do with a word processor. For example, the text between the <I> . . . </I> tags below will be Helvetica, a size larger than normal, red, and italicized. (Notice that quotation marks surround element values):

<FONT COLOR="RED" SIZE="+1" FACE="Helvetica">
</I . . . </I>
</FONT>

- To adjust the layout of text, use the list tags *<UL>* and *<OL>* and the line break tag *
*. The *
* tag is especially useful for presenting text that doesn't extend a full line but shouldn't be double-spaced (such as lines in poems). The list tags are useful for presenting all kinds of material. You can make a hypertextual table of contents for your site, by creating a list that links each item to a separate page.

20g
Web

Review the list of tags on page 372 as you fine-tune the text on your page. For more advanced options, consult your HTML guide.

8 Consider drafting with a visual HTML editor. If you aren't concerned about the nuts and bolts of HTML, or if you need to produce an attractive Web document quickly, try a visual Web authoring program. The quality of the page you finally produce will depend on the software you have available—but most programs generate suitable layouts. For new Web writers, almost any visual editor will do, even an up-to-date word-processing program that has an HTML editing mode.

- **Choose your editing software.** Visual editors often cost money, but some computers come with them preinstalled. *Netscape*'s suite of Internet applications comes with both a Web browser (*Communicator*) and an editor (*Composer*); Microsoft's *Internet Explorer* often comes with a version of *Frontpage*. Other editors include *Dreamweaver* and *Claris Home Page*. Predictably, the more features offered, the more expensive the program.
- **Create a new HTML document.** In most programs, all you'll need to do is select "New" from the "File" menu, just as you would in a word processor. Save the blank page in your project folder. Note that your editing software might provide predesigned templates. Choose a template for your new document if you find one that's appropriate. Make sure to adjust the template to suit your needs.

- **Set the document title.** Unlike HTML text editors, visual editors allow you to use the program's menus and dialog boxes to make modifications to your document. For this reason you'll need to explore your software for a few minutes, learning the available options. In particular, look for an option that allows you to change the title of your HTML document. This menu item often appears under "Format" and "File" menus. Having found this option, your editor will display a dialog box that allows you to modify various properties of your document, including the name of the author (see Figure 20.8 below). The options will vary with the software you use.

- **Insert the text you have written into the new document.** If you already have the text stored in a word-processed document, you can cut and paste the material using your program's "Edit" menus. Otherwise type your words into the visual editor as you would into any other program. Notice, however, that you'll have less flexibility in the way you format your paragraphs, which will normally appear in single-spaced block style (this is the Web standard). You can change font and alignment by using options found in your program's formatting menus and toolbars. Follow the guidelines in Section 20c for formatting passages of text.

- **Preview your page in a Web browser.** Most visual editors have a preview option among their menus and toolbars. This option will display your page in a Web browser program, allowing you to see how it will appear to readers on the Web. Ideally, your page won't change much from the editor to the browser program—that is,

20g
Web

Page Properties ☒

Location: file:///C|/MyWork/Media/lifelessons.html
Last Modified: Unknown

Title: Teaching Life's Lessons

Author: Stella Galvan

Description: A research project on the effect of media on children

Advanced users:
To edit other contents of the <head> region, use "HTML Source" in the View
Menu or Edit Mode Toolbar.

[OK]   [Cancel]

Figure 20.8 *The Page Properties dialog box from* Netscape Composer *allows you to specify the title (as it will appear in the browser's title bar), the author, and a brief description, which search engines will use to index your page. After filling in the boxes, press the "OK" button.*

Figure 20.9 *Your image-formatting dialog box should also allow you to set properties such as alignment and size (achieved here through the "More Properties" option).*

20g
Web

after all, the claim of WYSIWYG software. If the page does look significantly different, try upgrading either your editor or your browser; the versions you have may not have the latest standards. Most software makers provide free updates on the Web.

- **Insert an image into your page.** Most WYSIWYG editors have an "Insert" menu that allows you to add nontextual content to your page, such as pictures, tables, and horizontal rules. After moving your cursor to the location where you want the picture, select the menu option that allows you to place an image on your page. Select an image you have already saved in your Web project folder. After clicking "OK" in the dialog box, you should see the image on your page, as it will appear to browsers on the Web (see pp. 374–75).

- **Link your page to another.** Set the cursor where you want to add a link to another page. Type the text you would like to be linked, such as "Search at Google" or "Next Page." Select the text you just typed and choose the option to insert a link from your editor's menus. In the dialog box that appears, type the Internet address or page name. To link to a page in your working folder, simply enter the filename, as shown. Some editors allow you to edit other elements of the link, such as the target window. To link to sites outside your folder, use the full Web page URL.

- **Change the page's background color.** One especially useful feature of visual editors is their ability to assign colors according to how they appear on the screen, rather than through codes or names. To change the background color of your page, choose the appropriate menu option, probably "Change Background" or "Format Page." You will then see a dialog box displaying color options. To select your color, click on the box with the desired hue and then select the "OK" button. When you return to the editor's main window, the background will have changed. A similar dialog box is often used to assist in picking colors for fonts, rules, and tables.
- **Add a footer.** Using the knowledge you have so far, try building a footer for your page. Insert a horizontal rule, a copyright symbol followed by the year and your name, and a link to your project's home page. Finally, use your editor's alignment tools to center the footer material.

Your editor window should now look something like it would appear if it were viewed in a Web browser, as in Figure 20.10. What shows up in the browser may differ from the page you created in the program, but the inconsistencies don't usually outweigh the ease of laying out pages with a visual editor. If you wanted to use the visual editor to create an exact image of what your readers will see, you could probably come close, but you might have to do some tweaking with the program's menus and dialog boxes.

We suggest, rather, that you focus on the important parts of your page, namely its ease of reading and navigation. It is often a good idea to leave some control over the layout of a page to your readers, who

20g
Web

may have preferred settings for browsing the Web, such as large type, reduced colors, and text-only. If you make your page so that readers with special needs can't use their preferences, they may prefer not to read your page at all. (Read about accessibility on pp. 381–82.)

▇9 Consider drafting by exporting from your word processor. As we've discussed, this is the fastest and easiest method for creating Web documents. The latest word processors and spread-sheets allow you to open any existing document and convert it to HTML within seconds. The resulting pages may not have the layouts you expect, but they will be Web compatible (which may be all you care about).

- **Open the text you've prepared in your word processor.** To make your text more readable on screen, create block paragraphs (see Section 20c-5). Feel free to use bullets and numbers for lists, and if your word processor allows, set background and font colors. Be aware that some word processors accommodate standard Web lay-

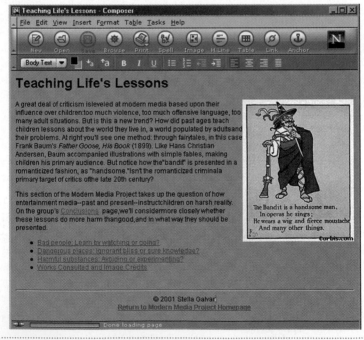

Figure 20.10 *A page in a visual editor looks nearly as it would in a browser. The main differences here are in the menus and toolbars, which allow you to edit material rather than navigate it.*

outs, allowing you to identify different levels of headings to help organize your material.

- **Select the export option.** Some word processors allow you to "Save as" HTML; others permit you to "Export" the document to HTML. After selecting the appropriate option, you'll be prompted to name the file and storage location. Create a name that is compatible with Web standards (see Section 20g-11) and store the document in your project folder. Note that your word processor may generate files besides the HTML document you explicitly name. This often occurs when you have images in your document. When you publish your document on the Web, you'll need to upload to the server all files and folders created by your word processor.
- **View the generated page in a browser.** To see the results created by your word processor, open the new HTML document in a Web browser. If the results aren't satisfactory, return to your word processor, experiment with simpler layouts, and try again. Alternatively, edit the HTML document directly using one of the other two methods discussed in this chapter.

20g
Web

10 Edit and proof your Web page. Although Web pages have many special features, the writing that appears on them requires the same care and attention that you would give to a print document. Besides editing for style and clarity, keep in mind some basic document design concerns. Will readers be able to move through the material in the manner you expect? Are the colors you have chosen readable on-screen? Have you cited your images correctly? Finally, be aware of these common problems for Web pages:

- **Broken links.** These occur whenever linked text goes nowhere. Remember that the URL specified by your link must match exactly the web address or HTML page to which you're linking.
- **Broken images.** If the images you inserted into your page don't appear correctly in Web browsers, check that you've correctly spelled their filenames and that they are in the proper Web folder.
- **Absent closing tags.** If you've entered the HTML codes using a text editor, you have an extra error to look out for. Check your codes to make sure you've provided closing tags for all headings, font styles, and lists. Otherwise your text may be unreadable.
- **Accessibility problems.** A major concern of Web developers is making sure that content on the Internet is available to readers with physical impairments. The visually impaired, for example, can now browse the Web using special programs that convert text to speech. However, these tools don't work if authors fail to

provide textual alternatives to visual content. Most visual editors provide a space to enter a textual description for your image. If you edit the HTML codes yourself, use the ALT element in your image tags to provide an informative description of the graphics you use.

EXERCISE 20.6 Use the guidelines in Section 20g-10 to edit and proof the Web page you drafted in Exercise 20.5 (pp. 373–76) or another Web project you're composing.

■ **11 Upload your page to a Web server.** We are limited in the kind of instruction we can offer for this step, primarily because how you publish your pages will depend on your writing situation. If you are composing a project for class, your instructor should give you uploading instructions. If you are composing pages for yourself or your organization, you'll probably need to establish an account with an Internet service provider, which might be your college or university. In any case, prepare your pages for uploading by making sure they follow Internet filename conventions:

- Use *no* spaces or punctuation in your filenames, except a period before the file suffix. You can separate words with underscore marks (_), rather than spaces.
- Use the appropriate file suffix: ".html" or ".htm" for HTML documents; ".jpg" or ".gif" for graphics; ".txt" for plain text.
- Use all lowercase letters (optional, but suggested).

20g
Web

Checklist 20.1

Creating a Web Site

1. **Choose a method for creating your page.** Will you use an HTML text editor (Section 20g-7) or a visual HTML editor (Section 20g-8), or will you export HTML documents from your word processor (Section 20g-9)?

2. **Decide on an organizational strategy.** Will you arrange your site as a hierarchy, a sequence, or a hub (Section 20g-3)?

3. **Plan page layout(s) and gather your materials in a project folder** (Sections 20g-4 and 5.)

4. **Draft your Web page(s)** (Sections 20g-7, 8, and 9.)

5. **Edit and proof your page(s), being sure to test all hypertext links** (Section 20g-10).

6. **Upload your page(s) to a Web server** (Section 20g-11).

CHAPTER 21

Model Documents

In this chapter you'll find model documents illustrating a variety of print and electronic formats. As explained in Chapter 19, many print formats have corresponding electronic formats. Where possible, we show examples of documents in both media. You may notice that electronic versions vary slightly according to the email or Web browsing software used to display or compose the document. In these model documents, we've tried to represent a variety of software programs on the assumption that you'll see at least a few with which you're familiar. More important, we emphasize in each example those features that regularly appear in most programs.

Each example is accompanied by a discussion of the purpose and the common uses of the format, a checklist alerting you to conventions of that format, and an explanation of its basic parts. Besides seeing a variety of formats, you'll also see applications of document style. Note how each example brings style and format together to present writing effective for specific purposes.

While each of the formats presented in this chapter has its own checklist, Checklists 21.1 and 21.2 provide general guidelines for presenting documents in print and on screen. And of course you should proofread every document carefully.

Checklist 21.1

Typical Print Documents

- Use standard letterhead paper ($8\frac{1}{2}''$ by $11''$).

- Use portfolio orientation unless you plan to fold the document or you need extra room for graphics and images.

- Leave at least a one-inch margin on all sides. If you plan to bind the document, add more space on the bound edge.

- Use double or single-and-a-half spacing unless otherwise specified, especially with small type. Single spacing is used in letters or sometimes in long documents to cut printing costs.

- Use headers and/or footers with running titles and page numbers for multi-page documents.

Checklist 21.2

Typical Onscreen Documents

- Make sure your audience has the right software to view the document format you're using.
- Short, single-spaced block paragraphs are most common for onscreen documents.
- Use sans serif typefaces and avoid long stretches of bold, underlined, or italicized text.
- If you have hypertext links, test them to make sure they work.

21a Email

Over the last few years instructors and employers have come to expect students and workers to conduct business through email. In the classroom, you may be asked to submit assignments as file attachments or to collaborate with fellow students through online messages. In workplaces, email has replaced printed memos (see Section 21e) for everyday correspondence, and it has become an important means of communicating cheaply across long distances.

Although email is used to communicate for many purposes, all email includes a few basic elements. The message on the facing page, composed by Arnold Peale for his English composition class, illustrates the basic parts of an email message. Keep in mind that the onscreen look of messages will differ according to your *email client*, the program you use to read and write messages. Take some time to explore your email client's features.

Checklist 21.3

Email

- Use short block paragraphs; long paragraphs are difficult to read onscreen. Double-space between paragraphs but don't indent.
- Avoid "Reply All" when responding to messages received. Respond to everyone on an email list only when you think all will be interested in your comments.
- Make sure attached files are in a format your audience can view and that you have scanned them for viruses.
- If you use a common signature for all your messages, make sure the text of the signature is suitable for both professional and personal audiences; otherwise edit the signature when the occasion calls for it.
- Use asterisks, dashes, and caps to emphasize text.
- See also the checklists for specialized types of email massages.

EMAIL MESSAGE

The **message header** includes all necessary delivery information. (See below.)

A **salutation** is often optional; use one when addressing an audience you don't know.

The **body** can include block paragraphs, lists, and subsections set off by dashed lines or extra spacing.

The **closing** and **signature** will depend on the formality of the message. For professional messages, include your title and organization.

21a
models

EMAIL HEADER

The **To** line includes one or more email addresses for recipients. Remember that addresses must be completely accurate.

The **From** line will usually be filled out by your email program with your name and address. If you have more than one email account, you may be asked to specify which one will be used to send the message.

```
    To: emilyjackson@mail.um.net
  From: Arnold Peale <apeale@mail.um.net>
Subject: Web project requirements
    Cc: jasonc@mail.um.net; betho@mail.um.net
   Bcc:
X-Attachments:
```

The **Attachments** line will include the filenames of electronic documents you would like to send along with your message. Email clients vary in how they ask you to specify your attachments.

The **Subject** line includes a short phrase about the topic of your message—make sure it is relevant to your recipients.

Cc lines can be used to send other individuals copies of the message. (See also Section 21e.)

21b Business letters

When you write a business letter, remember that it may become part of a permanent file documenting your request or complaint. Make the letter as complete and accurate as possible so that the person(s) receiving it can act on it quickly. The letters that follow were written by a student at Bowling Green State University to the Office of the Registrar asking for action to clear up a bureaucratic mistake. The letter was successful. After receiving the complaint, the registrar sent an email message to the student, promising to watch over his loan account personally for the remainder of his stay at Bowling Green.

Checklist 21.4

Business Letters

- Choose a *block, modified block,* or *indented* letter format.

- Single-space paragraphs and addresses in the letter; double-space between the return address, date, inside address, salutations, body paragraphs, and closing.

- Use one-inch margins on all sides.

- When using letterhead paper, you don't need to repeat the return address as long as it includes all necessary contact information.

- Make the inside address as specific as possible so that the letter will go directly to its intended audience.

- Place a colon after the salutation.

- In the body, be brief but state all pertinent facts, including names and dates. Keep your letter to one page if you can.

- Make your diction and style fairly formal, unless you already have established a casual tone with the addressee.

- Follow your closing with a comma, four blank lines, your name, and your professional title; sign in the space created by the blank lines.

- After the closing and signature, note any copies of the letter you have sent and any attached documents you have enclosed with the letter.

- Proofread your letter carefully and keep a copy for your records.

BUSINESS LETTER IN BLOCK FORMAT

Taverner P. Meyer
122 Main Street
Bowling Green, OH 43403

December 8, 2001

Office of the Registrar
211 Administration Building
Bowling Green State University
Bowling Green, OH 43403

Dear Registrar Representative:

I am writing to you regarding the status of my student loan for the 2001–2002 academic year. In September, I was notified by the student financial aid center that I would not be receiving any funds this year since I was no longer registered as a student here at Bowling Green. Since I am registered full time for both this semester and next, I made several phone calls to offices on campus—including yours—to inquire after my status.

At that time, I learned that your office had accidentally lost the computerized file of my registration for the fall semester (my copy of the paper version of this is enclosed.) Since I was not registered, the student loan was automatically canceled.

The Bursar's Office will not help me pursue the problems, unless I provide proof of registration; meanwhile, your office will not provide me with proof of registration without an Account Paid receipt from the Bursar—which I can't provide without first accessing my student-loan funds.

This is the fourth consecutive semester in which my registration has been electronically lost; you should have copies of letters dealing with the earlier instances in your files.

It is unacceptable that I be expected to pay for an administrative error; without the student-loan money, I am living month to month, struggling to pay rent and buy groceries. Since the situation seems to exist as a vicious circle where each point demands I start somewhere else, I am writing to request your help and suggestions regarding what I can do further.

I am specifically asking that you place the necessary phone calls to the Financial Aid Office to start payment of my student loan. Thank you for your assistance.

Yours truly,

Taverner P. Meyer

Cc: Bursar's Office
    Financial Aid Office
    Chair, Department of Psychology

Enc: Copy of fall registration

The **return address** is used by your audience to respond.

The **date** helps your audience identify this letter in a series of correspondence.

The **inside address** directs your letter to a specific office or person in an organization.

Salutations formally address specific members of the audience, opening the letter.

Body paragraphs are single-spaced, each one separated by double spacing.

The **closing** and **signature** officially end the letter, identifying you, your titles, and your affiliations.

Enclosed documents are declared at the very end.

**21b
models**

BUSINESS LETTER IN MODIFIED BLOCK FORMAT

Taverner P. Meyer
122 Main Street
Bowling Green, OH 43403

December 8, 2001

Office of the Registrar
211 Administration Building
Bowling Green State University
Bowling Green, OH 43403

Dear Registrar Representative:

I am writing to you regarding the status of my student loan for the 2001–2002 academic year. In September, I was notified by the student financial aid center that I would not be receiving any funds this year since I was no longer registered as a student here at Bowling Green. Since I am registered full time for both this semester and next, I made several phone calls to offices on campus—including yours—to inquire after my status.

At that time, I learned that your office had accidentally lost the computerized file of my registration for the fall semester (my copy of the paper version of this is enclosed.) Since I was not registered, the student loan was automatically canceled.

The Bursar's Office will not help me pursue the problems, unless I provide proof of registration; meanwhile, your office will not provide me with proof of registration without an Account Paid receipt from the Bursar—which I can't provide without first accessing my student-loan funds.

This is the fourth consecutive semester in which my registration has been electronically lost; you should have copies of letters dealing with the earlier instances in your files.

It is unacceptable that I be expected to pay for an administrative error; without the student-loan money, I am living month to month, struggling to pay rent and buy groceries. Since the situation seems to exist as a vicious circle where each point demands I start somewhere else, I am writing to request your help and suggestions regarding what I can do further.

I am specifically asking that you place the necessary phone calls to the Financial Aid Office to start payment of my student loan. Thank you for your assistance.

Yours truly,

Taverner P. Meyer

Cc.: Bursar's Office
     Financial Aid Office
     Chair, Department of Psychology

Enc: Copy of fall registration

The **return address** and the **date** are left-justified at the center of the page.

The **inside address** and **salutation** remain left-justified at the left-hand margin.

The **body paragraphs** are either in block or indented style depending on whether you use modified block or indented letter format.

The **closing** and **signature** are left-justified at the middle of the page.

⌐1c Letters of application

A letter of application is an especially important form of business communication. The same advice and guidelines apply to it as to a business letter. In a letter of application, however, you have the extra challenge of presenting yourself favorably without seeming to brag. Use the application letter to draw attention to the reasons an employer should consider you for a job or an interview.

On the facing page you'll find two examples of Chad Polatty's letter of application for a Web programming position, one of them formatted as a printed document, the other as email. The salutation, the body paragraphs, and the closing are the same in both examples. The only major differences between the two are in how Chad reaches the job recruiter, how the recruiter contacts him for further information, and the formatting of attached documents, such as résumés and references.

21c
models

Checklist 21.5

Letter of Application

- Follow the basic formatting guidelines for a business letter (see p. 386) or email (see p. 384), depending on the medium you use to correspond.

- State the position for which you are applying. Follow up with a summary of your qualifications for the position. Focus on those qualifications that best suit the job in question; the résumé will cover the rest.

- Focus on how you might meet the organization's needs and on what you could accomplish *for the organization*—not on what you hope to get from the position.

- Show some knowledge about the organization or company to which you are applying, but offer praise only in order to show why you're interested in working for them.

- Maintain a polite and respectful—but confident—tone.

- Remember that your letter of application may have a long life. If you're hired, it will become part of your personnel record. If you're not hired, it may go into a file of applicants for later consideration.

LETTER OF APPLICATION IN BLOCK FORMAT

September 2, 1999

632 Steadman Rd.
Leesville, SC 29070
(803)657-5501

Management Decisions
Attn: Mike Smith
5 Century Drive, Suite 150
Greenville, SC 29607

Re: Web Database Programmer Position

Dear Mr. Smith:

I am writing in regard to your newspaper ad in the August 29 edition of The State newspaper concerning your need for a Web Database Programmer. I believe that I have the qualifications, experience, and enthusiasm that you are looking for.

I have been employed with 2 organizations over the past 3 years that have drawn on my database programming skills. My work at CMB*LIC Mortgage Corporation involved the setup of new software, training of personnel, and the direct use of AutoCAD on a 10-user LAN. I also worked as an assistant programmer at Hydronic Corporation, doing much of the same design, code, and test work as the regular database programmer/analysts.

In December, I will graduate with a Bachelor of Science degree from the University of South Carolina. In my degree program, I have studied and developed a thorough understanding of the following programming languages: Pascal, Assembler, COBOL, RPG, Perl, and HTML.

I have enclosed a copy of my resume outlining a detailed description of my education and employment history. I would welcome any opportunity to talk with you further about the Web Database Programmer position. Please feel free to contact me any time at (803)657-5501.

Sincerely,

Chad A. Polatty
tpolatty@mail.pbtcomm.net

Encl.: resume

The **return address** should include a telephone number so the recruiter can contact you immediately if more information is needed or an interview is requested.

The **inside address** and **salutation** will match the contact name given in the job listing. When not responding to a listing, locate a contact name at the company's hiring office.

The **closing** and **signature** in a letter of application do not differ from those in standard business letters.

Enclosures will often include a printed résumé and a list of references.

21c
models

LETTER OF APPLICATION IN EMAIL FORMAT

Web Database Programmer Position

File Edit View Insert Format Tools Message Help

From: tpolatty@mail.pbtcomm.net
To: msmith@hightechhiring.com
Cc:
Subject: Web Database Programmer Position
Attach: resume.doc (68.0 KB)

Dear Mr. Smith:

I am writing in regard to your newspaper ad in the August 29 edition of The State newspaper concerning your need for a Web Database Programmer. I believe that I have the qualifications, experience, and enthusiasm that you are looking for.

I have been employed with 2 organizations over the past 3 years that have drawn on my database programming skills. My work at CMB*LIC Mortgage Corporation involved the setup of new software, training of personnel, and the direct use of AutoCAD on a 10-user LAN. I also worked as an assistant programmer at Hydronic Corporation, doing much of the same design, code, and test work as the regular programmer/analysts.

In December, I will graduate with a Bachelor of Science degree from the University of South Carolina. In my degree program, I have studied and developed a thorough understanding of the following programming languages: Pascal, Assembler, COBOL, RPG, Perl, and HTML.

I have attached a copy of my resume outlining a detailed description of my education and employment history. I would welcome any opportunity to talk with you further about the Web Database Programmer position. Please feel free to contact me any time at (803) 555-5501.

Sincerely,

Chad A. Polatty

Email addresses replace postal addresses in the heading of the message. Postal addresses and telephone numbers can appear in the body of the letter if needed.

The **subject line** should announce the position for which you are applying.

File attachments are used instead of enclosures. Make sure to use common or requested electronic formats.

21d Résumés

Your résumé is a concise outline of your academic and employment history, designed to give a prospective employer a quick but thorough overview of your qualifications. Take great care in preparing your résumé. Once in the hands of a recruiter, your list of achievements and skills will be used to decide whether an employer will contact you for an interview.

In your résumé you can enhance your list of qualifications by showing a competency in your field. Learn the language of your profession and use recognizable terms to describe your on-the-job training and coursework. Remember, however, that you need to be familiar and comfortable with the meanings of these terms—chances are you'll be expected to use them in an interview.

Consider recent trends in how employers find job candidates and store information about them: Not only do recruiters search for résumés on the Web, but they also maintain databases of digitized résumés. Most they collect as electronic submissions, but some are scanned versions of print résumés. As a database entry, your résumé will receive a serious look only if it can be found through keyword searches—all the more reason for you to become fluent with the language spoken by others in your profession.

Because résumés are so important, and because they've changed somewhat in recent years, we provide three examples. The first is a printed résumé listing the qualifications of Danny Gomez, a student at the University of Texas at Austin. The second résumé is an email, text-only version of Danny's résumé, as is sometimes requested when recruiters want you to enter the document in a database. Finally, after Checklist 21.6 on page 392, we present a Web résumé created by Jay O'Brien, a student at Shepherd College in West Virginia.

PRINT RÉSUMÉ EMPHASIZING EDUCATION AND EXPERIENCE

Daniel Gomez
danny.gomez@mail.ut.net

Local Address:	**Permanent Address:**
2555 San Jacinto Blvd.	5555 DeAlba Dr.
Austin, TX 78700	El Paso, TX 79955
512-555-5692	915-555-2549

Objective   Seeking a summer internship or co-op in Electrical Engineering

Education   The University of Texas at Austin
- Bachelor of Science, Electrical Engineering
  (expected graduation date: May, 2002)
- GPA (overall/EE): 3.75/4.0

Experience   UT Computer Writing and Research Lab (Sept., 1998 – Present)
Multimedia Specialist
- Monitored computer lab by interacting with students and instructors
- Assisted students and instructors in using MS Office, Internet, FTP, Web page construction (with DreamWeaver and Netscape Composer), and E-mail
- Maintained a safe and clean lab environment

AG Communications Systems (Summer, 1999)
Intern
- Assisted the Problem Isolation & Analysis Department
- Upgraded/converted an Outage DBASE database into MS Access
- Developed user interface for the MS Access database

Other Skills
- Experience using Mac OS, Windows, and MS Office
- Proficient with programming: C++, Turbo Pascal, HTML, and Visual Basic / Visual Basic for Applications
- Fluent in reading, writing, and speaking Spanish

Activities and Awards
- Tau Beta Pi Engineering Honor Society
- Student Engineering Council
- Society of Hispanic Professional Engineers (SHPE):
  - *Special Projects Chair* (1999- Present)
  - *Academic Chair* (1998-1999)
  - *Freshman Rep./ACE* (1997-1998)

References available upon request.

The **header** includes your name and contact information. Most students include a **local address** where they can be contacted at school and a **permanent address**.

The **body** includes a list of your qualifications divided into categories. Use different type styles to highlight information that employers might find most interesting, such as the names of companies you've worked for or your school.

The **footer** will often include the phrase "References available on request."

**21d
models**

RÉSUMÉ FORMATTED AS TEXT-ONLY EMAIL MESSAGE

To: msmith@hightech.jobs.com
From: Danny Gomez <danny.gomez@mail.ut.net>
Subject: Resume

DANNY GOMEZ   (Postal addresses listed at bottom)

OBJECTIVE

Seeking a summer internship or co-op in Electrical Engineering

EDUCATION

The University of Texas at Austin
* Bachelor of Science, Electrical Engineering (expected graduation date: May 2002)
* G.P.A. (overall/EE): 3.75/4.0

EXPERIENCE

UT Computer Writing and Research Lab (Sept 1998 Present)
Multimedia Specialist
* Monitored computer lab by interacting with students and instructors
* Assisted students and instructors in using MS Office, Internet, FTP, Web page construction (with DreamWeaver and Netscape Composer), and E-mail
* Maintained a safe and clean lab environment

AG Communications Systems (Summer 1999)
Intern
* Assisted the Problem Isolation & Analysis Department
* Upgraded/converted an Outage DBASE database into MS Access
* Developed user interface for the MS Access database

OTHER SKILLS
----
* Experience using Mac OS, Windows, and MS Office
* Proficient with programming: C++, Turbo Pascal, HTML, and Visual Basic / Visual Basic for Applications

The **email header** will include the recipient's address, your return address, and a subject line indicating that the message is a résumé.

The **body** of a text-only email does not accept most types of visual formatting. Use asterisks, dashed lines, all caps, and underscores to replace the special type styles and graphics used in print or Web résumés.

Checklist 21.6

Résumés

* At the top of your résumé give your name as you would like to be recognized in a professional setting.

* Provide up-to-date contact information so that a prospective employer can reach you for interviews.

* Before you list your skills, state your objective. This section may be omitted when your employment goals are explained in an accompanying cover letter. Some résumé guides now consider the objective line optional.

* Create a categorized list of your academic degrees and awards, professional certifications, previous jobs, technical skills, and relevant course work.

* Arrange this list according to how effective the categories and qualifications you have listed will be for attaining the desired job.

* Educational achievements usually go first. List year, degree, and institution, as well as scholastic honors won.

* If the prospective job requires specialized skills (computer skills, technical procedures), list those with which you have the most familiarity, assuming an interviewer might ask about them.

* List your work experience. Besides mentioning employers and time periods, state your responsibilities and achievements in succinct but specific terms. Account for all periods longer than a few months.

* List course work only when it explains how you attained skills outside your work experience. List nonwork, nonacademic activities and achievements only if you think an employer might consider them relevant assets.

* You cannot be required to mention age, gender, race, religious or sexual preference, political affiliation, or marital status.

* When requested, include a list of references (all of whom you have checked with beforehand) or indicate a placement service with your complete dossier. This list can usually be submitted as a separate, attached document.

21d
models

ONLINE RÉSUMÉ

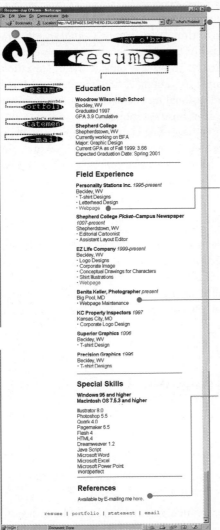

The **page title** includes your name and the word *résumé,* so that the page can be found by WWW search engines.

The **page header** and **footer** do not include postal addresses or telephone numbers. Instead, place a link to your email address clearly on the page; readers will use email to send responses.

Links to other Web pages can help you better demonstrate your goals and qualifications. Jay O'Brien provides a link to an online portfolio of his work—something a print résumé doesn't accommodate.

The **body** can go beyond a single page—but make sure headings are easy to read, so someone browsing your résumé can quickly identify the highlights of your qualifications.

Your **list of references** should never be posted on the Web. Instead, ask interested employers to request references by email.

21d
models

21e Professional memos

Memorandums are used within organizations as a means of communication between members. As a result, memos omit some of the formalities used in business letters to be sent outside the organization: formal salutations and closings, for example, aren't usually required. But memos do maintain a professional tone, and they contain information needed for keeping records of business interactions.

Email (see Section 21a) is the online cousin of the memo. Many people have Internet email (the kind you probably have if you are at an educational institution), which can be used to communicate with people for both personal and professional reasons. Many companies, however, provide internal email systems. These systems operate like Internet email, except that messages can be sent only to other members of the organization, as one would do with a memo.

Opposite you'll find, in print and electronic formats, a memo written by Ryan Starck, a student employee at the University of Texas at Austin. While the topic of the memo is one you'll rarely use—a farewell message to fellow staff members—the format and tone Starck adopts reflect the professional yet collegial nature of most work environments.

21e
models

Checklist 21.7

Memos and Professional Email

* Follow your organization's standard layout, which will usually include a date, a "To" section, a "From" section, and a subject line.

* Use block paragraphing and a one-inch margin (for print memos).

* In the subject line, enter a phrase that will make clear to your recipients the relevance and importance of your message.

* Most printed memos don't have salutations because the intended audience is named in the "To" section. An email message sent to more than one person, however, might require a group salutation.

PRINTED MEMO

Date: 5/12/2000

To: Computer Lab Staff
Division of Housing and Food Service

From: Ryan Starck
Systems Administrator
(Ext. 3442)

Subject: Date of Departure

My plans for this summer have changed recently and as a result I will be leaving my position at Housing much earlier than I originally expected. I had planned to be employed until the beginning of classes in August, but an attractive job offer has convinced me otherwise.

Monday, May 15th will be my official date of notice and my last day of work being Friday, May 26th. I will be leaving Housing to accept a full time Systems Analyst position in the Liberal Arts Computer Labs for the remainder of my student career and possibly longer. Since the position needs to be filled immediately, I had no choice but to end my employment at Housing as soon as possible.

I have begun talking to John Z., who will success me as the PC tech, and am currently working out a training schedule that doesn't interfere with my last day of work being working both jobs to some extent for the next two weeks. Two weeks is a fairly short amount of time to facilitate the necessary training to take over my position, but I will be somewhat available throughout the summer for any questions Eddie C., John Z., or Ryan D. may have.

I would like to thank all of you for the opportunity to work at Housing and with the Computer Labs. I have gained many friends, acquaintances, memories, and a wealth of technical knowledge that will serve me well long after I depart.

Cc: Alyssa Campbell
Eduardo Contreras
Ryan Dionne
Angela Lee

The **date** may be used to refer to the memo in future correspondence.

The **To** section names an individual or group in the organization.

The **From** section should list your name, title, department, and contact information.

The **Subject** line is brief and to the point.

The **body paragraphs** state your business clearly and succinctly.

The **Cc** section lists names of individuals who should receive copies of the memo. This list often includes co-workers who are indirectly involved in the business being discussed.

**21e
models**

EMAIL MEMO

Email addresses replace names and departments in the **To** and **Cc** lines.

A **salutation** is often used in email; when you email a group of people, you may need to state the name of the group, so people will know why they have been copied on the message.

An **email signature** closes the message, providing your name and title (what's in the **From** lines of print memos).

21f Messages to online forums

Besides email, other forms of online communication have recently evolved. Online forums generally consist of dated postings (messages submitted by discussion participants) and threads (lines of discussion focused on a particular topic). Web forums and newsgroups are two formats of online discussion that display threads and postings hierarchically, according to topic. The sample Web forum on the facing page shows a series of threads about an article read for a University of Texas composition class. Email lists, or listservs, are another common type of online forum. Readers and writers participate by subscribing to a listserv, which allows them to receive new postings in their email inbox, and by sending messages to the list's email address. Whichever format you use, keep in mind the common conventions for participating in online discussions—conventions often referred to as "netiquette."

Checklist 21.8

Messages to Online Forums

- Read a number of messages in the forum before you send your own. Try to get a feel for the tone and interests of other participants.

- Avoid posting personal attacks, or *flames*, to authors of messages disagreeing with you. Flame wars make forum participants uneasy and productive discussion nearly impossible.

- Avoid starting off-topic threads—sometimes called *spamming*. Forums differ in how they treat online spam and what members believe constitutes a useless message, but expect some people to become annoyed if you regularly send messages irrelevant to them.

- Don't respond to the entire forum when you really want to respond to just one participant. Avoid this problem by making sure your "To" address doesn't match the address of the forum itself.

- When replying to a thread, remove all text from the previous message that doesn't relate to your response. Don't expect readers to scroll through screens of other people's writing to find your ten-line response.

WEB MESSAGE FORUM

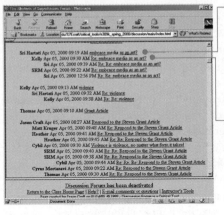

Threads appear as an initial message (starting at the left-hand margin) followed by a series of responses. Each response is attached to the message it most immediately addresses.

Responses are listed as linked text indicated by "Re:" and followed by the subject line of the initial message in the thread. Click on the link to read the message. Some forums allow respondents to create their own subject lines.

WEB FORUM RESPONSE FORM

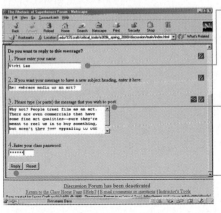

21f
models

Enter the **name** you would like to appear with your posting. Some forums allow anonymous postings; others, such as class forums, require your real name.

Enter your **message** in plain text format. Some forums allow you to use HTML codes to enhance the appearance of the message.

Click the "**Reply**" button (or "Submit") to add your message to the thread. This forum happens to require a password to participate.

21g Newsletters

A newsletter gives an organization an excellent way to keep in touch with its members. With a desktop publishing program or an up-to-date word-processing program, newsletters are relatively easy to create. The model newsletter on the facing page, created by members of an English students' honor society at the Metropolitan State College of Denver, contains six pages, of which we reproduce the first and the third. Although the newsletter includes some enhanced visual features, the students kept production costs down by limiting the layout to two colors and using black-and-white images—a modest but effective decision for print documents having wide circulation. Online newsletters can, without extra expense, include more colors and images, assuming you have the time to put into creating a more elaborate design.

Checklist 21.9

Newsletters

- Select the size of paper and the method of binding, and plan the number of pages you will use. Choose a margin width that allows for binding or folding.

- Determine whether you'll use images and how many colors you want to show. Colorful designs are more costly.

- Decide whether you'll use multi-column pages. More columns usually mean more planning, but when formatted carefully multiple columns make more efficient use of space.

- Map out each page with two goals in mind: (1) showcasing the most important articles and (2) preventing your reader from having to jump from page to page to read a single article.

- For your masthead, use a distinctive font that reflects the spirit of the organization represented by the newsletter.

- Adjust headlines according to their importance, but maintain a consistent font size and style throughout the body of the articles.

- Write short paragraphs to avoid long, unbroken stretches of print, especially when you're using narrow columns.

FRONT PAGE OF A NEWSLETTER

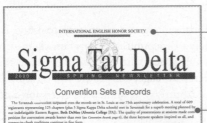

The **masthead** identifies a newsletter with a specific organization, often showing logos or catchphrases members recognize immediately. Mastheads also include publication date and issue number.

Lead articles appear on the front pages of newsletters—they reflect the most important recent events appearing in the issue.

Images are wrapped by text so that the space on each page is used efficiently, and related material is closely grouped.

Borders are *sometimes* used to frame text or decorate the margins.

21g
models

PAGE THREE OF A NEWSLETTER

Running heads often include the same information appearing in the masthead and sometimes page numbering.

Standard articles are introduced with enhanced headlines. This example uses a left-justified block style of paragraphing.

Regular features are columns that appear in each issue; they are often framed or otherwise distinguished from standard articles so they can be easily recognized.

Footers can include page numbering and information appearing in the masthead.

21h Brochures

Brochures can provide information about an organization and its activities easily and inexpensively. Brochures generally answer a few basic questions—who? what? why? when? where?—and they share the common goal of stimulating interest. Ideally, a brochure you create will provide enough information to capture your audience's attention and show readers where to find further details.

Brochures can have relatively high production costs. More expensive brochures are used by organizations that want to project a high-profile image, especially for the purpose of recruiting new members. The brochure shown at right, designed by Brooke Rollins, a student employee at the University of South Carolina's College of Engineering, includes images, colors, stylized fonts, and an unusual square page layout—all features that drive up the costs of production. If your organization doesn't have a high production budget, you might create a simple, elegant brochure that points readers to an organizational Web site—which is cheaper to develop than a printed brochure.

21h
models

Checklist 21.10

Brochures

* Decide on the purpose of the brochure. Is it to introduce your organization? to talk about events or activities? How do you want your audience to respond to the brochure? Choose content accordingly.

* Plan the layout of the brochure carefully, keeping in mind how it will fold and how both sides will look. If the brochure is to be mailed, leave one panel blank for the address.

* Sketch out, or storyboard, each panel to visualize how you'll lay out information in the brochure.

* If possible, make each panel of the brochure a self-contained unit, so that it will still make sense when read in its folded state.

* Limit the amount of information to what readers can absorb in a few minutes, but tell them how they can learn more.

FRONT PANEL OF BROCHURE

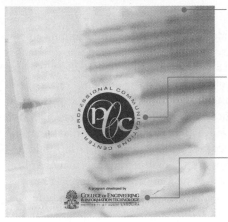

Use **graphics** and **colors** to attract the eyes of readers. Keep in mind that most brochures must compete for attention.

The **logo** for the organization should appear on the front panel. This logo begins building a persona that the following panels will develop.

Show **addresses** and **contact** information so that readers get a clear idea of the organization's affiliations and institutional relationships.

21h
models

INSIDE PANELS OF BROCHURE

Each **panel** includes a main heading with related passages of text. Panels have consistent layouts so readers can easily see the central points.

Headings are set apart from other text using inverted background and foreground colors. Provocative, eye-catching phrases draw readers in.

Contact information and the organizational **logo** reappear on the end panel, reminding readers that further details are available if they are interested.

Images have been carefully selected to portray themes and activities related to the organization. Here the images form a collage extending across all panels.

Paragraphs focus on the highlights of the organization, especially those that will seem most intriguing to the target audience.

21i Web pages

Web pages present a wide variety of visual layouts, often combining diverse design elements such as stylized text, graphics, animation, and sound. Consequently, it's difficult to offer models and guidelines to suit all or even a majority of occasions. There are, however, standard genres of Web pages and sites, ones you'll see regularly as you browse the Web. The model at right, for example, is an organizational Web site created by Women in Science at the University of Texas at Austin. Like all organizational Web sites, this one is designed to introduce the group to a broad audience. Not only does it include explanations of the group's mission, it also provides contact information, listings of events, and the names of members—all useful information for people who might want to join or find out more. See Section 20g on composing and designing Web pages.

21i
models

Checklist 21.11

Common Genres of Web Pages and Sites

• Organizational Web sites

• Personal home pages and online résumés

• Online periodicals and newsletters

• Online essays and reports

• Frequently asked questions (FAQ) pages

• Online directories and informational listings

• Search pages and database listings

ORGANIZATIONAL HOME PAGE

The **title** and **header** include the organization's name.

A **list of contents** links WWW browsers to the main information posted on the Web site.

Images help readers get a feel for what the organization is about.

Brief announcements give browsers the latest news and events.

CONTENT PAGES OF AN ORGANIZATIONAL WEB SITE

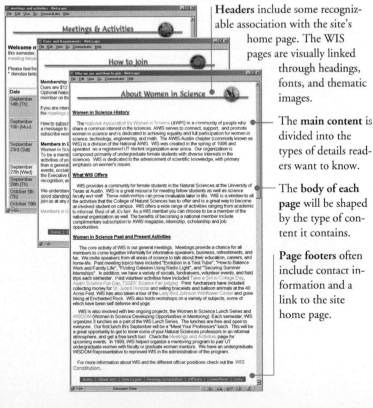

21i
models

Headers include some recognizable association with the site's home page. The WIS pages are visually linked through headings, fonts, and thematic images.

The **main content** is divided into the types of details readers want to know.

The **body of each page** will be shaped by the type of content it contains.

Page footers often include contact information and a link to the site home page.

21j Academic papers

Chart 21.1

Model Academic Documents

Many academic writing projects, including research papers, have design requirements formulated by associations of scholars and professionals in their respective fields. These standards are described in detail in the following chapters.

Modern Language Association (MLA) style, used in the humanities: Chapter 48

American Psychological Association (APA) style, used in the social sciences: Chapter 49

Chicago Manual of Style (CMS) style, used in the humanities: Chapter 50

Council of Biology Editors (CBE) style, used in the sciences: Chapter 51

Columbia Online Style (COS) style, used to cite electronic sources: Chapter 52

Ask your instructor which style you should use.

21j
models

Grammar

22 Questions About Subject-Verb Agreement?

23 Questions About Verb Tense, Voice, and Mood?

24 Questions About Verbals?

25 Questions About Plurals, Possessives, and Articles?

26 Questions About Pronoun Reference?

27 Questions About Pronoun Agreement?

28 Questions About Pronoun Case?

29 Questions About Pronoun Choices?

30 Questions About Modifiers?

31 Are You an ESL Writer?

32 ESL Questions About Verbs?

33 ESL Questions About Gerunds, Infinitives, Articles, or Number?

CHAPTER 22

Questions About Subject-Verb Agreement?

When subjects and verbs don't agree, careful readers notice. So you need to proofread carefully to be sure you've put singular verb forms with singular subjects and plural verb forms with plural subjects. An editor will use the abbreviation *agr* to indicate a problem with agreement.

A rotating wall cloud and hail (indicates) the possibility of a tornado.
agr

22a Agreement: Is the subject singular or plural?

A verb may change its form, depending on whether its subject is singular or plural. The verb is then said to *agree in number* with its subject. Following are guidelines to help you be confident about subject-verb agreement.

1 Understand how subject-verb agreement works. With verbs in the present tense, agreement in number is relatively simple: most subjects take the base form of the verb. The base form is the word produced when *to* is placed before the verb: to *wait;* to *go*.

Subjects and verbs usually agree more readily than politicians.

First person, singular, present tense: I predict.
                                            I go.

Second person, singular, present tense: You predict.
                                            You go.

First person, plural, present tense: We predict.
                                            We go.

Second person, plural, present tense: You predict.
                                            You go.

Third person, plural, present tense: They predict.
                                            They go.

The single notable exception to this pattern occurs with third person singular subjects (for example, *he, she, it, Irene*). A regular verb in the present tense needs an *-s* or *-es* ending.

Third person, singular, present tense: She predicts.
                                            Irene predicts.
                                            He goes.

So to choose a correct verb form in the third person (present tense), you must know whether the subject of a sentence is singular or plural. The choice of the verb form can be fairly easy when a subject is clearly either singular or plural.

> sing. subj.
> *The weather channel* **predicts** storms today.
> plural subj.
> *Meteorologists* **predict** storms today.
> sing. subj.
> *He* **goes** to Oklahoma City today.
> plural subj.
> *The teachers* **go** to Oklahoma City today.

22a
s–v agr

Agreement is also required with irregular verbs such as *to be* and *to have* in a variety of tenses. (See Section 23d.)

SINGULAR SUBJECTS
The weather forecast **is** clear for today.
The weather forecast **was** clear for today.
The weather forecast **has been** accurate for some time.

PLURAL SUBJECTS
The weather forecasts **are** clear for today.
The weather forecasts **were** clear for today.
The weather forecasts **have been** accurate for some time.

EXERCISE 22.1 Decide which verb in boldface is correct.

1. The most violent of all storms, tornadoes (**occur/occurs**) more often in the United States than in any other country.

2. The rotational winds sometimes (**exceed/exceeds**) 500 miles per hour in the vortex of a tornado.

3. Dust devils (**is/are**) less ferocious vortices of warm air.

4. Rising heat currents (**cause/causes**) dust devils.

5. A tornado over water (**has/have**) many of the same characteristics as one over land.

2 **In most cases, treat subjects joined by** *and* **as plural.**
Joining two subjects this way creates a *compound subject* that takes a verb without an *-s* or *-es* ending (in third person, present).

> 1st subj. + 2nd subj.   verb
> *Storm chasers and journalists* alike **want** great videos of destructive storms.
> subj. + subj.   verb
> *The press and storm chasers* alike **risk** their lives in hazardous weather.
> subj. + subj.   verb
> *Meteorologists and the police* **believe** that storm chasers often underestimate the magnitude of tornadoes.

22a
s–v agr

However, a few subjects joined by *and* do describe a single thing or idea. Treat such expressions as singular.

> subj.   verb
> *Peace and quiet* **is** rare on the Texas plains in spring.
> subj.   verb
> *Rock and roll* **is** as noisy as a thunderclap.

Similarly, when a compound subject linked by *and* is modified by *every* or *each,* the verb takes a singular form.

> subj. + subj.   verb
> *Every wall cloud and supercell* **holds** the potential for a tornado.
> subj. + subj.   verb
> *Each spring and each fall* **brings** the danger of more storms.

However, when *each* follows a compound subject, usage varies.

> *The meteorologist and the storm chaser* each **have** their reasons for studying the weather.

> *The meteorologist and the storm chaser* each **has** his or her story to tell.

▨ **3 Understand that subjects joined to other nouns by expressions such as *along with, as well as,* or *together with* are not considered compound.** So the verb agrees only with the subject, which may be either singular or plural.

> sing. subj.　　　　　　　　　　　　　　　　plural noun
> *The National Weather Service,* as well as many *police officers,*
> verb
> **wishes** amateurs wouldn't chase severe storms in their cars.

> plural subj.　　　　　　　　sing. noun　verb
> Many *amateurs,* along with the *press,* **chase** storms in the American heartland.

When subjects linked to expressions such as *as well as, along with,* or *together with* sound awkward with a singular verb, join the subjects with *and* instead.

SLIGHTLY AWKWARD　　　*The National Weather Service,* as well as *local storm chasers,* **considers** tornadoes unlikely today.

BETTER　　　　*The National Weather Service and local storm chasers* **consider** tornadoes unlikely today.

▨ **4 When subjects are joined by *or, neither . . . nor,* or *either . . . or,* be sure the verb (or its auxiliary) agrees with the subject closer to it.** In these examples the arrows point to subjects nearer the verbs.

> plural　　　　　　　　　　　　sing.
> *Neither police officers nor the National Weather Service* **is** able to prevent people from tracking dangerous storms.

> sing.　　　　　　　　plural
> *Either severe lightning or powerful bouts of hail* **mark** the development of a supercell.

> sing.　　　plural
> **Does** *the danger or the thrills of chasing storms* attract people to the "sport"?

> plural　　　　　　　　　　sing.
> **Do** *the thrills of chasing storms or the danger* attract people to the "sport"?

> plural　　　　plural
> *Heavy rains or strong winds* **cause** much damage.

> sing.　　　　　　sing.
> *Heavy rain or baseball-sized hail* usually **causes** the most damage.

22a
s–v agr

The rule holds when one or both of the subjects joined by *or, either . . . or,* or *neither . . . nor* are pronouns: the verb agrees with the nearer subject.

Neither *she* nor *we* **admit** to fear of thunder.

Neither *we* nor *she* **admits** to fear of thunder.

Neither *Jimail* nor *I* **have** any weather predictions today.

Neither *I* nor *Jimail* **has** any weather predictions today.

If a construction seems especially awkward, it can be revised—usually by making the verb plural or rewriting the sentence.

AWKWARD   Neither *you* nor *I* **am** bothered by lightning.

BETTER   Neither *I* nor *you* **are** bothered by lightning.

BETTER   *We* **are** not bothered by lightning.

■ **5 When the subject of a sentence is a phrase or a clause, examine the subject closely.** Many such constructions will be singular, though they may seem plural.

SINGULAR SUBJECTS

Chasing tornadoes **involves** risk.

To calculate all the forces involved in violent storms **requires** a sophisticated knowledge of physics.

That George survived the storms that tore through three Oklahoma counties **is** remarkable.

However, phrases and clauses can form compound subjects, requiring appropriate verb forms.

COMPOUND SUBJECTS

Locating a waterspout and taking photographs of it **are** his chief ambitions.

That the skies are darkening and that the wind is rising **concern** us.

22a
s–v agr

EXERCISE 22.2   Decide which verb in boldface is correct.

1. Storms of all types (**continue/continues**) to intrigue people.

2. The storm chaser, like other thrill seekers, (**learn/learns**) to minimize the dangers of the hunt.

3. It's unlikely that either the dangers or the boredom of storm chasing (**is/are**) going to discourage the dedicated amateur.

4. The meteorologist and the storm chaser (**know/knows**) that neither ferocious tornadoes nor the less violent waterspout (**is/are**) predictable.

5. That the last ten years have seen an increase in the numbers of storm chasers (**is/are**) certain.

22b Agreement: Is the subject an indefinite pronoun?

Words like *each, none, everybody, everyone,* and *any* are called **indefinite pronouns** because they do not refer to a particular person, thing, or group. Sometimes it's hard to tell whether an indefinite pronoun is singular or plural, so you may have trouble choosing a verb that agrees with it in number.

■ 1 Determine whether an indefinite pronoun is singular, plural, or variable. Consult the chart below (or a dictionary) to find out. Then select an appropriate verb form.

Chart 22.1

Indefinite Pronouns		
SINGULAR	VARIABLE (SINGULAR OR PLURAL)	PLURAL
anybody	all	few
anyone	any	many
anything	either	several
each	more	
everybody	most	
everyone	neither	
everything	none	
nobody	some	
no one		
nothing		
somebody		
someone		
something		

22b
s–v agr

The most troublesome indefinite pronouns are *each* and *none. Each* is singular in college writing; *none* varies but is usually singular. Also needing attention are indefinites such as *either* and *neither* because, though plural in informal writing, they are singular in academic work. The following examples show the forms to use in college.

SINGULAR   *Each* **believes** decisive action needs to be taken.

SINGULAR   *Nobody* **knows** what the baseball team will do.

VARIABLE   *None* of the proposals **is** easy to finance.

VARIABLE   *None* but the owners **favor** a big bond issue.

PLURAL   *Many* in sports bars **hope** for a new stadium.

PLURAL   *Few* **want** to pay higher ticket prices.

■ **2 Be careful when indefinite pronouns are modified.**
If a pronoun is always singular, it remains singular even if it is modified by a phrase with a plural noun in it. For example, *each* is usually singular in college usage, even when followed by a prepositional phrase (though this convention is often not observed in casual usage).

> subj.   verb
> *Each* of the whales **makes** unique sounds.
> subj.   verb
> *Each* of the animals **has** a personality.

When the indefinite pronoun varies in number (words such as *all, most, none, some*), the noun in the prepositional phrase determines whether the pronoun (and consequently the verb) is singular or plural.

> NOUN IN PREPOSITIONAL PHRASE IS SINGULAR
>
> *Some* of the research **is** contradictory.

> NOUN IN PREPOSITIONAL PHRASE IS PLURAL
>
> *Some* of the younger whales **are** playful.

If the indefinite pronoun is more clearly plural, so is the verb.

> indef. pron.   verb
> A *few* in the scientific community **wonder** if the whale will survive.
> indef. pron.   verb
> *Many* very much **hope** so.

EXERCISE 22.3 Decide which verb in boldface would be correct in academic writing.

1. Most of New York's immigrants (**is/are**) now non-European.

2. Everybody (**seem/seems**) to have something to contribute.

3. Nobody in the city (**run/runs**) politics anymore.

4. Everybody (**expect/expects**) a piece of the pie.

5. None of the candidates (**is/are**) qualified.

6. All of the groups in the city (**want/wants**) to be heard.

22c Agreement: Is the subject a collective noun?

Nouns that name a group are called **collective:** *team, choir, band, orchestra, jury, committee, faculty, family.* Some collective nouns may be either singular or plural, depending on how you regard them. Here is a sentence with the subject (the collective noun *family*) treated as singular.

> The *Bucci family* **believes** that *its* pizzeria business is helped by the Korean deli around the corner.

Here's the same sentence with the subject taken as plural.

> The *Bucci family* **believe** that *their* pizzeria business is helped by the Korean deli around the corner.

Both versions are acceptable.

To be sure verbs and collective nouns agree, decide whether a collective noun used as a subject acts as a single unit (the *jury*) or as separate individuals or parts (the twelve members of the *jury*). Then be consistent with your usage throughout a paper, making the verb and any pronouns agree in number with the subject.

SINGULAR	The *jury* **expects** its verdict to be controversial.
PLURAL	The *jury* **agree** not to discuss their verdict with the press.
SINGULAR	The *choir* **expects** to choose a variety of hymns and chants.
PLURAL	The *choir* **raise** their voices in song.

22c
s-v agr

Usually your writing will be smoother if you treat collective nouns as singular subjects.

The chart on page 414 should help you manage collective subjects.

EXERCISE 22.4 Decide whether the collective subjects in the following sentences are being treated as singular or plural. Then select the appropriate verb form for academic writing.

1. Lieutenant Data (**reports/report**) to Captain Picard that the data on Klingon encroachments of the neutral zone (**is/are**) not subject to interpretation.

2. The crew of the Federation starship (**is/are**) eager to resolve the conflict.

Chart 22.2

Collective Nouns

SUBJECT	GUIDELINE	EXAMPLES
Measurements	Singular as a unit; plural as individual components.	*Five miles* is quite a long walk. *Five more miles* are ahead of us. *Six months* is the waiting period. *Six months* have passed.
Numbers	Singular in expressions of division and subtraction.	*Four* divided by *two* is two. *Four* minus *two* leaves two.
	Singular or plural in expressions of multiplication and addition.	*Two* times *two* is/are four. *Two* plus *two* is/are four.
Words ending in *-ics*	School subjects are usually singular.	*Physics* is a tough major. *Economics* is a useful minor. *Linguistics* is popular.
	Other *-ics* words vary; check a dictionary.	His *tactics* are shrewd. *Athletics* are expensive. *Ethics* is a noble study. Her *ethics* are questionable. *Politics* is fun. Francie's *politics* are radical.
data	Plural in formal writing; often singular in informal writing.	The *data* are reliable. The *data* is reliable.
number	Singular if preceded by *the;* plural if preceded by *a.*	The *number* has grown. A *number* have left.
public	Singular as a unit; plural as individual people.	The *public* is satisfied. The *public* are here in great numbers.

22c
s-v agr

3. Five years (**has/have**) passed since the last intergalactic crisis.

4. A number of weapons still (**needs/need**) to be brought on line, but the chief engineer reports that the actual number of inoperative systems (**is/are**) small.

5. The jury (**is/are**) still out as to whether a committee of Federation officials (**intends/intend**) to authorize action against the Klingons.

22d Agreement: Is the subject separated from its verb?

A verb agrees with its subject only, not with any nouns in modifying phrases or clauses that come between the subject and verb. So when editing for subject-verb agreement, first identify the subject in a sentence or clause and determine whether it is singular or plural; then choose the appropriate verb form. In the following sentence, for example, a singular subject (*power*) is modified by a prepositional phrase that contains a plural noun (*tornadoes*). But the subject remains singular, and it takes the appropriate verb form (*proves*).

sing. subj.   plural noun   verb
The *power* of Midwestern tornadoes often **proves** deadly.

The principle is the same for plural subjects modified by phrases or clauses with singular nouns. The subject remains plural.

plural subj.   sing. noun   verb
Storms that come late in the spring **are** sometimes unusually violent.

Be especially careful with lengthy or complicated modifiers. In the example that follows, the singular subject and verb are separated by ten words. But the plural nouns *mammals* and *humans* in the modifying phrase have no bearing on subject-verb agreement.

subj.   modifying phrase
The *killer whale,* the most widely distributed of all mammals, ex-
                                   verb
cepting only humans, **demonstrates** highly complex social behavior.

22d
s-v agr

EXERCISE 22.5 Choose the correct verb for academic writing.

1. As the twenty-first century begins, most politicians, regardless of their party or ideology, (**embrace/embraces**) the idea that every child should be able to read by the end of third grade.

2. Almost everyone (**agree/agrees**) with this laudable goal, but trained educators who understand the complex process of learning to read are suspicious of this bandwagon approach.

3. Children's ability to learn how to read (**depend/depends**) on a combination of psychological, physical, and social factors.

4. Moreover, many children from families in low-income neighborhoods, all too common in major cities today, (**need/needs**) intensive tutoring because they are not ready to learn when they arrive in kindergarten.

5. The HOSTS tutoring program, which has had great success in helping children to start reading, (**require/requires**) as many as fifty volunteers in a small elementary school, and such volunteers can be hard to find.

22e Agreement: Is the subject hard to identify?

22e
s-v agr

Occasionally you may simply lose track of a subject because the structure of a sentence is complicated or unusual. Just remember the rule: Keep your eye on the subject.

1 Don't lose track of your subject when a sentence or clause begins with *here* or *there*. In such cases, the verb still agrees with the subject—which usually trails after it.

SINGULAR SUBJECTS
Here **is** a surprising *turn* of events.
There **is** a *reason* for the commotion.

PLURAL SUBJECTS
Here **are** my *tickets.*
There **are** already *calls* for the police chief's resignation.

2 Don't be misled by linking verbs. Common linking verbs are *to be, to seem, to appear, to feel, to taste, to look,* and *to become.* They connect subjects to words that extend or complete their meaning.

The mayor's wife **was** a severe critic.
Many citizens **feel** betrayed.

A linking verb agrees with its subject even when a singular subject is linked to a plural noun.

subj.   l. v.   plural noun
Good *evidence* of the power of television **is** its effects on political careers.

subj.   l. v.   plural noun
The *key* to a candidate's success **is** television appearances.

The same is true when a linking verb connects a plural subject to a singular noun, but such sentences sound normal and don't ordinarily raise questions of agreement.

plural subj.   l. v.   sing. noun
The many new *patrol officers* **are** a tribute to Chief Carey's budget ingenuity.

▇ 3 Don't be misled by inverted sentence order. A sentence is considered inverted when some portion of the verb precedes the subject. Inverted sentence structures occur most often in questions.

verb   subj.   verb
Was their *motive* **to get** revenge?

verb
Among those requesting Chief Carey's resignation **were** many
subj.
citizens.

A verb agrees with its subject, wherever the subject appears in the sentence.

verb   subj.   verb
Have their *fund-raising efforts* **inspired** the critics?
verb   subj.
Also disappointed **is** the *assistant chief.*

22e
s–v agr

▇ 4 Don't mistake singular expressions for plural ones. Singular terms such as *series, segment, portion, fragment,* and *part* usually remain singular even when modified by plural words.

A *series* of questions **is** posed by a reporter.

A substantial *portion* of many political talk shows **is** devoted to forecasting the future.

The word *majority,* however, does not follow this guideline; it can be either singular or plural, depending on its use in a sentence. In this sentence, *majority* is treated as singular.

The *majority* **rules.**

Yet it can also function as a plural noun.

The *majority* of critics **want** Chief Carey's head on a platter.

⬛ *Fine Tuning*

One of the subtlest subject-verb agreement problems occurs within clauses that include the phrase *one of those who.* In college English, the verb in such a clause is plural—even though it looks as if it should be singular.

> Carey is one of those people who never **seem** [not **seems**] dispirited.

The verb is plural because its subject is plural. To understand the situation more clearly, rearrange the sentence this way.

> Of those people *who* never **seem** dispirited, Carey is one.

Now watch what happens if you add the word *only* to the mix.

> Carey is the only one of the city officials who **seems** eternally optimistic.

Why is the verb singular here? The subject of the verb *seems* is still the pronoun *who,* but its antecedent is now the singular pronoun *one,* not the plural *officials.* Again, it helps to rearrange the sentence to see who is doing what to whom.

> Of the city officials, Carey is the only one who **seems** eternally optimistic. ⬛

EXERCISE 22.6 Choose the correct verb.

1. The mayor of the town (**strides/stride**) to the microphone.

2. Among grumbles from the reporters, the crowd (**take/takes**) their seats.

3. (**Does/Do**) the mayor's decision to fire Carey surprise anyone after the last election?

4. The city council president claims that she is one of those people who (**objects/object**) most strongly to politics taking precedence over community unity.

5. But she knows she's not the only one who (**wants/want**) a nationally admired park system.

CHAPTER 23

Questions About Verb Tense, Voice, and Mood?

23a How do you choose verb tenses?

Perhaps you first discovered the complexity of verb tenses when you tried to learn a foreign language. **Tense** is that quality of a verb that expresses time. Tense is expressed through changes in verb forms and verb endings (*see, saw, seeing; work, worked*) and through the use of auxiliaries—what you may know as *helping verbs* (*had* seen, *will have* seen; *had* worked, *had been* working). Most native speakers of English handle basic past, present, and future tenses easily. But as a writer, you'll want to be confident about using all the tenses—for example, the more subtle perfect and progressive tenses.

Editors may simply write *tense* in the margin next to a sentence where some problem with tense is evident.

When she arrived, we will go. *tense?*

1 Know the tenses and what they do. Tense depends, in part, on *voice*. Verbs that take direct objects—that is, transitive verbs—can be either in **active** or in **passive voice**. They are in active voice when the subject in the sentence actually does what the verb describes.

Photographer Eadweard Muybridge (1830–1904) used stop action photography to study the motion of people and animals: The horse will gallop; the horse gallops; the horse is galloping; the horse has galloped. *For more Muybridge images, look for him at <http://www.masters-of-photography.com>.*

subj.   action
Professor Gates **invited** the press to the lecture.

They are in passive voice when the action described by the verb is done *to* the subject.

subj.   action
The press **was invited** by Professor Gates to the lecture.

Below is a chart of English tenses—past, present, and future—in the *active voice*. (See also Section 23e on voice and the more complete Anatomy of a Verb on pp. 432–44.)

Chart 23.1

Verb Tenses in the Active Voice

WHAT IT IS CALLED	WHAT IT LOOKS LIKE	WHAT IT DOES
Past	**I answered** quickly.	Shows what happened at a particular time in the past.
Past progressive	**I was answering** when the alarm went off.	Shows something happening in the past at the same time something else happened in the past.
Present perfect	**I have answered** that question often.	Shows something that has happened one or more times in the past.
Past perfect	**I had answered** the question twice when the alarm went off.	Shows what had already happened before another event, also in a past tense, occurred.
Present	**I answer** when I must.	Shows what happens or can happen now.
Present progressive	**I am answering** now.	Shows what is happening now.
Future	**I will answer** tomorrow.	Shows what may happen in the future.
Future progressive	**I will be answering** the phones all day.	Shows something that will continue to happen in the future.
Future perfect	**I will have answered** all the charges before you see me again.	Shows what will have happened by some particular time in the future.
Future perfect progressive	**I will have been answering** the charges for three hours by the time you arrive at noon.	Shows a continuing future action that precedes some other event also in the future.

23a
tense

Verbs usually look even more complicated when they are in the passive voice, as shown in the following chart.

Chart 23.2
Verb Tenses in the Passive Voice

WHAT IT IS CALLED	WHAT IT LOOKS LIKE
Past	I **was invited** to her party last year.
Past progressive	I **was being invited** by Alicia when the phone went dead.
Present perfect	I **have been invited** to many of her parties.
Past perfect	I **had been invited** to this one too.
Present	I **am invited** to everyone's parties.
Present progressive	I **am being invited** now! That's Alicia calling, I'm sure.
Future	I **will be invited** tomorrow.
Future perfect	I **will have been invited** by this time tomorrow.

As you can see above, many tenses require **auxiliary verbs** such as *will, do, be,* and *have.* These auxiliary or helping verbs combine with other verbs to show relationships of tense, voice, and mood. Two important auxiliaries—*to have* and *to be*—are *irregular. Irregular* means that they show agreement in ways other than just an additional *-s* or *-es* in the third person singular. *To have* is only slightly irregular, forming its third person singular by changing *have* to *has.*

23a
tense

I have	we have
you have	you have
he/she/it has	they have

To be changes more often, in both the present and past tenses.

PRESENT	PAST
I am	I was
you are	you were
he/she/it is	he/she/it was
we are	we were
you are	you were
they are	they were

Other auxiliary verbs, such as *can, could, may, might, should, ought,* and *must,* help to indicate possibility, necessity, permission, desire, capability, and so on. These verbs are called **modal auxiliaries.**

> Rosalind **can** write well.
> Audrey **might** write well.
> Marco **should** write well.

■ **2 Use perfect tenses appropriately.** Some writers seem intimidated by the perfect tense because it looks complicated, so they avoid it in all its forms. But the result can be imprecise sentences.

VAGUE	Audrey could not believe that Kyle actually **asked** her to pay for his lunch. simple past
PRECISE	Audrey could not believe that Kyle **had** actually **asked** her to pay for his lunch. past perfect

Perfect tenses enable you to show exactly how one event stands in relationship to another in time. Learn to use these forms; they make a difference.

SIMPLE PAST	She already **quit** her job even before she knew that she failed the polygraph.
PAST PERFECT	She **had** already **quit** her job even before she knew that she **had failed** the polygraph.

EXERCISE 23.1 Replace the verb forms in parentheses below with appropriate tenses. You may need to use a variety of verb forms (and auxiliaries), including passive and progressive forms. Treat all five sentences as part of a single paragraph. Consult the chart of irregular verbs on pages 427–29 for help with some of the verb forms.

23a
tense

1. Isambard Brunel (**design**) his ship the *Great Eastern* to be the largest vessel on the seas when it (**launch**) in 1857 in London.

2. Almost 700 feet long, the ship—originally named *Leviathan*—(**weigh**) more than 20,000 tons and (**power**) by a screw, paddle wheels, and sails.

3. Designed originally to be a luxurious passenger ship, the *Great Eastern* (**attain**) its greatest fame only after it (**refit**) to stretch the first transatlantic telegraph cable from England to Newfoundland.

4. In the summer of 1865, the *Great Eastern* (**lay**) cable for many difficult days when the thick line (**snap**) two-thirds of the way to Newfoundland. Nine days (**spend**) trying to recover the cable, but it never (**find**).

5. Many people (**be**) skeptical that the *Great Eastern*, a jinxed ship, (**succeed**) in stretching a cable across the Atlantic, but it finally (**do**) so in 1866.

EXERCISE 23.2 For each verb in parentheses, furnish the tense indicated. Use active voice unless passive is specified.

1. In Shakespeare's tragedy *Macbeth*, three witches tell Macbeth that someday he (**rule**—future) Scotland.

2. Macbeth quickly explains to his wife, the ambitious Lady Macbeth, what the witches (**promise**—past perfect) him earlier that day: the Scottish crown.

3. Lady Macbeth, even more ambitious than her husband, immediately (**devise**—present) a plot to murder King Duncan that very night and then (**convince**—present) her husband to do the horrid deed.

4. But even though the plot succeeds and Macbeth becomes king, the new ruler fears that he (**challenge**—future, passive voice) by other ambitious men.

5. Macbeth is finally slain by Macduff, whose wife and children (**slaughter**—past perfect, passive voice) earlier in the play at Macbeth's orders.

23b Questions about tense in parallel constructions?

23b
tense

When verbs that go with the same subject don't share the same verb tense and form, the result is *faulty parallelism.* Parallelism is an arrangement that gives related words, clauses, and phrases a similar pattern, making it easier for readers to see relationships between the parallel expressions. For example: The college's marching band *played* out of tune, *marched* out of step, and yet *maintained* its dignity.

When a sentence has faulty parallelism, an editor will use double slashes to indicate a problem.

The lawyer **explained** the options to her client and **was recommending** a plea of guilty. //

For more on parallelism, see Section 17h.

■ **1 Check to be sure that verbs are alike in form.** Don't shift the tenses or forms of parallel verbs needlessly. In the following example, the verbs describing the lawyer's action shift from past tense to past progressive tense without a good reason. The verbs lack parallelism.

LACK OF PARALLELISM
subj.   verb   verb
The *lawyer* **explained** the options to her client and **was recommending** a plea of guilty.

The sentence reads more smoothly when the verbs are parallel in form.

REVISED FOR PARALLELISM
subj.   verb   verb
The *lawyer* **explained** the options to her client and **recommended** a plea of guilty.

Changes in verb tense within a sentence are appropriate when they indicate obvious shifts in time.

Currently, the lawyer **is defending** an accused murderer and soon **will be defending** a bigamist.

EXERCISE 23.3 Correct any problems with parallelism that the verbs in boldface are causing. Modify the tenses as needed to achieve parallelism.

1. In the middle of the nineteenth century, young French painters **were rejecting** the stilted traditions of academic art, **found** new methods and new subjects, and **would establish** the school of art one critic derided as "Impressionism."

2. The new artists **outraged** all the establishment critics and also **were challenging** all the expectations of Paris gallery owners.

3. Traditionalists thought that painters should **work** indoors, **depict** traditional subjects, and **be using** a balanced style that hid their brushwork.

4. But the youthful Impressionists, including artists like Monet, Degas, and Renoir, soon **were taking** their easels outdoors to the streets of Paris or to public gardens, **laying** on their colors thick and self-consciously, and **had been choosing** scenes from ordinary life to depict.

5. Now these revolutionary artists and their works **are regarded** as classics on their own and **being studied** and **are collected** by an artistic establishment they **are rocking** from its foundation a century ago.

23b
tense

23c Questions about tense consistency in longer passages?

Avoid shifting from tense to tense in longer passages (for instance, from *past* to *present*) unless clarity and good sense require the switch. Choose a time frame and stick with it. The following paragraph shows what can happen when verb forms shift inappropriately.

> At the dawn of the nuclear era, many horror movies **featured** monsters **spawned** by atomic explosions or bizarre scientific experiments. For two decades, audiences **flock** to movies with titles like *Godzilla, Them, Tarantula,* and *The Fly.* Theater screens **come** alive with gigantic lobsters, ants, birds, and lizards, which **spent** their time attacking London, Tokyo, and Washington while scientists **look** for ways to kill them.

The passage sounds confusing because it jumps between two possible time frames. Making the tenses consistent makes the passage more readable. Here it is in the past tense.

> At the dawn of the nuclear era, many horror movies **featured** monsters **spawned** by atomic explosions or bizarre scientific experiments. For two decades, audiences **flocked** to movies with titles like *Godzilla, Them, Tarantula,* and *The Fly.* Theater screens **came** alive with gigantic lobsters, ants, birds, and lizards, which **spent** their time attacking London, Tokyo, and Washington while scientists **looked** for ways to kill them.

23c
tense

It can also be revised to feature the present tense. Notice, however, that this shift does not simply put all verb forms in the present tense. One verb (*spawned*) remains in the past tense.

> At the dawn of the nuclear era, many horror movies **feature** monsters **spawned** by atomic explosions or bizarre scientific experiments. For two decades, audiences **flock** to movies with titles like *Godzilla, Them, Tarantula,* and *The Fly.* Theater screens **come** alive with gigantic lobsters, ants, birds, and lizards, which **spend** their time attacking London, Tokyo, and Washington while scientists **look** for ways to kill them.

EXERCISE 23.4 Revise the following paragraph to make the tenses of the boldfaced verbs more consistent. You may find it helpful to emphasize the present tense throughout the passage—but not every verb ought to be in the present. (Specific events in a literary work are usually described in present tense: After Macbeth *kills* King Duncan, he *seizes* the throne.)

(1) *Macbeth*, one of Shakespeare's shortest plays, **portrays** rebellion, conspiracy, and murder most foul. (2) The smoke of battle **has** barely cleared when Macbeth **encountered** three witches who **promise** him the throne of Scotland. (3) Almost immediately, his wife **persuades** him—against his good conscience—to act, and he quickly **has murdered** King Duncan while the old man **sleeps**. (4) But Macbeth himself **will sleep** no more; his conscience **gives** him no rest for the remainder of the play. (5) Only in the fourth act **did** the pace slow, but then the action **rose** again in the fifth toward a bloody conclusion.

23d Questions about irregular verbs?

Understanding irregular verbs requires a little background information. All verb tenses are built from three basic forms, which are called the *principal parts of a verb.* The three principal parts of the verb are these.

- **Infinitive** (or **present**): This is the base form of a verb, what it looks like when preceded by the word *to: to walk; to go; to choose.*
- **Past:** This is the simplest form of a verb to show action that has already occurred: *walked; went; chose.*
- **Past participle:** This is the form a verb takes when it is accompanied by an auxiliary verb to show a more complicated past tense: *had* **walked**; *will have* **gone**; *would have* **chosen**; *was* **hanged**; *might have* **broken**.

Here are the three principal parts of some regular verbs.

PRESENT	PAST	PAST PARTICIPLE
talk	talked	talked
coincide	coincided	coincided
advertise	advertised	advertised

As you can see, **regular verbs** form their past and past participle forms simply by adding *-d* or *-ed* to the infinitive. **Irregular verbs**, however, change their forms in various ways; a few even have the same form for all three principal parts.

PRESENT	PAST	PAST PARTICIPLE
burst	burst	burst
drink	drank	drunk
arise	arose	arisen
lose	lost	lost

To be sure you're using the correct verb form, consult a dictionary or check the following chart of irregular verbs. The list of troublesome irregular English verbs gives you three forms: (1) the present tense, (2) the simple past tense, and (3) the past participle. (The past participle is used with auxiliary verbs to form verb phrases: *I have ridden, I had ridden, I will have ridden.*)

When in doubt, your safest bet is to check the list, because studies show that errors in verb form irritate readers a great deal.

Chart 23.3

Irregular Verbs

PRESENT	PAST	PAST PARTICIPLE
arise	arose	arisen
bear (carry)	bore	borne
bear (give birth)	bore	borne, born
become	became	become
begin	began	begun
bite	bit	bitten, bit
blow	blew	blown
break	broke	broken
bring	brought	brought
burst	burst	burst
buy	bought	bought
catch	caught	caught
choose	chose	chosen
cling	clung	clung
come	came	come
creep	crept	crept
dig	dug	dug
dive	dived, dove	dived
do	did	done
draw	drew	drawn
dream	dreamed, dreamt	dreamed, dreamt
drink	drank	drunk
drive	drove	driven
eat	ate	eaten

23d
irreg

(Continued)

Irregular Verbs *(Continued)*

PRESENT	PAST	PAST PARTICIPLE
fall	fell	fallen
find	found	found
fly	flew	flown
forget	forgot	forgotten
forgive	forgave	forgiven
freeze	froze	frozen
get	got	got, gotten
give	gave	given
go	went	gone
grow	grew	grown
hang (an object)	hung	hung
hang (a person)	hanged, hung	hanged, hung
know	knew	known
lay (to place)	laid	laid
lead	led	led
leave	left	left
lend	lent	lent
lie (to recline)	lay	lain
light	lit, lighted	lit, lighted
lose	lost	lost
pay	paid	paid
plead	pleaded, pled	pleaded, pled
prove	proved	proved, proven
ride	rode	ridden
ring	rang, rung	rung
rise	rose	risen
run	ran	run
say	said	said
see	saw	seen
set	set	set
shake	shook	shaken
shine	shone, shined	shone, shined
show	showed	shown, showed
shrink	shrank, shrunk	shrunk
sing	sang, sung	sung
sink	sank, sunk	sunk
sit	sat	sat
speak	spoke	spoken
spring	sprang, sprung	sprung
stand	stood	stood
steal	stole	stolen
sting	stung	stung

23d
irreg

PRESENT	PAST	PAST PARTICIPLE
swear	swore	sworn
swim	swam	swum
swing	swung	swung
take	took	taken
tear	tore	torn
throw	threw	thrown
wake	woke, waked	woken, waked
wear	wore	worn
wring	wrung	wrung
write	write	written

The glossary at the end of this handbook treats in greater detail various troublesome verbs, including some listed above. Check the entries for *can/may, get/got/gotten, lie/lay, set/sit,* and so on.

EXERCISE 23.5 Choose the correct verb form from the choices in parentheses. In some cases, you may want to consult the glossary for assistance.

1. Alicia wondered whether the mayor had (**spoke/spoken**) too soon in welcoming everyone to participate in the town meeting.

2. The residents of Oakhill had not (**shown/shone**) much interest in the environmental issue until this meeting.

3. Now the Oakhill representative pulled a petition out of her purse and (**sat/set**) it before the mayor.

4. She claimed that she had (**got/gotten**) more than enough signatures to stop the proposed freeway extension.

5. Alicia had to admit that Oakhill (**chose/chosen**) well, for its representative was an effective activist.

23e
voice

23e Do you understand active and passive voice?

Voice is a characteristic of verbs that is easier to illustrate than to define. Verbs that take objects (called transitive verbs) can be either in **active** or in **passive voice**. They are in active voice when the subject in the sentence actually does what the verb describes.

subj.   action
Kyle **managed** the advertising.

They are in passive voice when the action described by the verb is done *to* the subject.

subj.   action
The *advertising* **was managed** by Kyle.

Passive verbs are useful constructions when *who* did an action is either unknown or less important than *to whom it was done*. A passive verb puts the *victim* (so to speak) right up front in the sentence where it gets attention. Passive verbs also work well in scientific writing when you want to focus on the process itself.

Serena Williams **was featured** on ESPN.
Serena Williams **was interviewed** by several reporters.
The beaker **was heated** for three minutes.

The passive is also customary in many expressions where a writer or speaker chooses to be vague about assigning responsibility.

Flight 107 **has been canceled.**
The check **was lost** in the mail.

When you need passives, use them. But most of the time you can make your sentences livelier by changing passive constructions to active ones. In a sentence with an active verb, it is often easier to tell who is doing what to whom. For advice on revising sentences to eliminate weak passive verbs, see Section 18a-6.

23e
voice

EXERCISE 23.6 Identify all the passive verbs in the following sentences; then revise those passive verbs that might be better stated in the active voice. Some sentences may require no revision.

1. Even opponents of chemical pesticides sometimes use poisons after they have been bitten by fire ants, aggressive and vicious insects spreading throughout the southern United States.

2. These tiny creatures have been given by nature a fierce sting, and they usually attack en masse.

3. Gardeners are hampered in their work by the mounds erected by the ants.

4. By the time a careless gardener discovers a mound, a hand or foot has likely been bitten by numerous ants.

5. The injured appendage feels as if it has been attacked by a swarm of bees.

23f What is the subjunctive mood and how do you use it?

As a grammatical term, **mood** indicates how you intend a statement to be taken. Are you making a direct statement? Then the mood is **indicative** ("I enjoy reading science fiction"). Are you giving a command? If so, the mood becomes **imperative** ("Watch out for flying objects!").

When you express a wish or hope, make a suggestion, or describe a possible situation, you may need to indicate the **subjunctive mood**—which often involves no more than using *were* instead of *was*. For example:

If George **were** [not **was**] in charge, we'd be in good hands.

The minister wished there **were** [not **was**] more young people in her church.

If she **were** [not **was**] to accept their terms, she could sign the contract.

■ 1 Recognize the subjunctive form of the verb. For all verbs, the present subjunctive is simply the base form of the verb—that is, the present infinitive form without *to*.

VERB	PRESENT SUBJUNCTIVE
to be	be
to give	give
to send	send
to bless	bless

The base form is used even in the third person singular, where you might ordinarily expect a verb to take another form.

It is essential that *Buck* **have** [not **has**] his lines memorized by tomorrow.

Carrie insisted that *Travis* **be** [not **is**] on time for their dinner at her mother's.

For all verbs except *be,* the past subjunctive is the same as the simple past tense.

VERB	PAST SUBJUNCTIVE
to give	gave
to send	sent
to bless	blessed

For *be,* the past subjunctive is always *were.* This is true even in the first and third person singular, where you might expect the form to be *was.*

> I wish *I* **were** [not **was**] the director.
> Suppose *you* **were** the director.
> I wish *she* **were** [not **was**] the director.

■ **2 Recognize additional forms of the subjunctive.** The subjunctive is employed in *that* clauses following verbs that make demands, requests, recommendations, or motions. These forms can seem legalistic and formal, but they are traditional in expressions such as these.

> The presiding officer asked that everyone be silent.
> I ask only that you be courteous to the speaker.
> The president asked that everyone **show** respect.

Some common expressions also require the subjunctive.

> **Be** that as it may . . .
> As it **were** . . .
> **Come** what may . . .
> Peace **be** with you.

EXERCISE 23.7 In the following sentences, underline any verbs in the subjunctive mood.

1. It is essential that we be at the airport at 2:00 p.m. today.

2. I wish I were less susceptible to telephone solicitors!

3. Far be it from me to criticize your writing!

4. Come what may, the show must go on.

5. If Avery were to arrive early, what would happen to our plans?

6. It is essential that you take over as the supervisor.

Chart 23.4

Anatomy of a Verb: *to pay*

PRINCIPAL PARTS	
Infinitive:	pay
Past tense:	paid
Past participle:	paid

TENSE
Present:	I pay
Present progressive:	I am paying
Present perfect:	I have paid
Past:	I paid
Past progressive:	I was paying
Past perfect:	I had paid
Future:	I will pay
Future progressive:	I will have been paying
Future perfect:	I will have paid

PERSON/NUMBER
1st person, singular:	I pay
2nd person, singular:	you pay
3rd person, singular:	he pays
	she pays
	it pays
1st person, plural:	we pay
2nd person, plural:	you pay
3rd person, plural:	they pay

MOOD
Indicative:	I pay.
Imperative:	Pay!
Subjunctive:	I suggested that he pay me.

VOICE
Active:	I pay
	you paid
	he will pay
Passive:	I am paid
	you were paid
	he will be paid

23f
mood

NONFINITE FORMS (VERBALS)
Infinitives:	to pay present tense, active voice
	to be paying progressive tense, active voice
	to have paid past tense, active voice
	to have been paying past progressive tense, active voice
	to be paid present tense, passive voice
	to have been paid past tense, passive voice
Participles:	paying present tense, active voice
	having paid past tense, active voice
	being paid present tense, passive voice
	paid, having been paid past tense, passive voice

(Continued)

Anatomy of a Verb: *to pay* *(Continued)*

Gerunds: paying present tense, active voice
                           having paid past tense, active voice
                           being paid present tense, passive voice
                           having been paid past tense, passive voice

23f
mood

CHAPTER 24

Questions About Verbals?

24a What are verbals?

Verbals lead a double life: they look like verb forms but act like other parts of speech: nouns, adjectives, adverbs. Like verbs, verbals can express time (present, past), take objects, and form phrases. Though you may not recognize the three types of verbals by their names—*infinitives, participles,* and *gerunds*—you use them all the time. (See also Section 33a.)

1 Understand infinitives. You can identify an **infinitive** by looking for the word *to* preceding the base form of a verb: *to seek, to find.* Infinitives also take other forms to show time and voice: *to be seeking, to have found, to have been found.* Infinitives sometimes act as nouns, adjectives, and adverbs.

INFINITIVE AS NOUN	**To work** in outer space is not easy. subject of the sentence
INFINITIVE AS ADJECTIVE	Astronauts have many procedures **to learn.** modifies the noun *procedures*
INFINITIVE AS ADVERB	NASA compromised **to fund** the space station. modifies the verb *compromised*

An infinitive can also serve as an *absolute*—that is, a phrase, standing alone, that modifies an entire sentence.

To make a long story short, the current space station is smaller than it might have been.

In some sentence constructions, the characteristic marker of the infinitive, *to,* is deleted.

Space station crews will perform exercises to help them [to] **deal** with the consequences of weightlessness.

2 Understand participles. A **participle** is a verb form that acts as a modifier. The present participle ends with *-ing.* For regular verbs, the past participle ends with -*ed;* for irregular verbs, the form of the past participle varies. Participles take various forms, depending on whether the verb they are derived from is regular or irregular. Following are the participle forms of two verbs.

Chart 24.1

Forms of the Participle	
perform (a regular verb)	PARTICIPLES
Present, active:	performing
Present, passive:	being performed
Past, active:	performed
Past, passive:	having been performed
write (an irregular verb)	PARTICIPLES
Present, active:	writing
Present, passive:	being written
Past, active:	written
Past, passive:	having been written

(For the forms of some irregular past participles, check the list of irregular verbs on pp. 427–29.)

As modifiers, participles may be single words. In the following example, the participle *waving* modifies *astronaut.*

> **Waving,** the astronaut turned a cartwheel in the space station for the television camera.

But participles often take objects, complements, and modifiers to form verbal phrases. Such phrases play an important role in structuring sentences.

> **Clutching** a camera, the astronaut moved toward a galley window.

> The designers of the station, **knowing** they had to work within budget constraints, used their ingenuity to solve many problems.

Like an infinitive, a participle can also serve as an *absolute*—that is, a phrase, standing alone, that modifies an entire sentence.

> All things **considered**, the space station is a remarkable machine.

■ 3 Understand gerunds. A **gerund** is a verb form that acts as a noun: *smiling, flying, walking.* Because most gerunds end in -*ing,* they look exactly like the present participle.

24a
verbal

GERUND	**Daring** is a quality moviegoers admire in heroes.
PARTICIPLE	Almost all airline passengers, however, would prefer not to have a **daring** pilot.

The important difference is that gerunds function as nouns, while participles act as modifiers. Gerunds usually appear in the present tense, but they can take other forms. In the following example, the gerund is in the past tense (and passive voice) and acts as the subject of the sentence.

Having been treated unfairly by the news media has angered directors of the program.

Here the gerund is in the present tense and passive voice.

Being asked to design a space station was an opportunity NASA wouldn't have missed.

Gerunds have many functions.

GERUND AS SUBJECT	**Keeping** within current budget restraints poses a problem for NASA.
GERUND AS OBJECT	Some NASA engineers prefer **flying space missions without crews**.
GERUND AS APPOSITIVE	Others argue that NASA needs to cultivate its great talent, **executing** daring missions.
GERUNDS AS SUBJECT AND COMPLEMENT	subj. comp. **Exploring** the heavens is **fulfilling** the dreams of humankind.

24a
verbal

EXERCISE 24.1 Identify the boldfaced words or phrases as infinitives, participles, or gerunds.

1. **Regretting** compromises in the original design, engineers refined the shuttle after the *Challenger* explosion.

2. At the time, the press questioned both NASA's **engineering** and its **handling** of the shuttle program.

3. **To be** fair, NASA's safety record in the **challenging** task of space exploration has been remarkable.

4. **Costing** even more than the space shuttle, NASA's space station is sure **to stimulate** new controversies.

5. **To make** matters more interesting, NASA has recommended **exploring** the possibility of a human mission to Mars.

24b How do verbals cause sentence fragments?

A verbal phrase that stands alone can create a sentence fragment—that is, a clause without a complete subject or verb. Fragments are considered errors in academic and professional writing.

The Secretary of State declined to be interviewed on CNN. **Having been ambushed in the recent past by an unfriendly reporter.**

Verbals alone cannot act as verbs in sentences. In fact, verbals are even described as **nonfinite** (that is, "unfinished") verbs. A complete sentence requires a **finite** verb, which is a verb that changes form to indicate person, number, and tense.

NONFINITE VERB—INFINITIVE	**To have found** success . . .
FINITE VERB	I **have found** success.
NONFINITE VERB—PARTICIPLE	The comedian **performing** the bit . . .
FINITE VERB	The comedian **performs** the bit.
NONFINITE VERB—GERUND	**Directing** a play . . .
FINITE VERB	She **directed** the play.

Verbal phrases are accepted in much informal writing. You'll see such fragments often in magazine articles and in advertising copy.

Harold loved playing comedy clubs—every bit of it. **Telling political jokes. Making satirical comments.** It made life worthwhile.

But in academic writing, fragments should usually be revised. For help on recasting such fragments, see Section 35a.

24c
sp inf

24c What is a split infinitive?

An infinitive interrupted by an adverb is considered split.

to **boldly** go   to **really** try   to **actually** see

Some writers believe that constructions such as these are incorrect, a point disputed by grammarians. Split infinitives are such common expressions in English that most writers use them without apology. Here are guidelines to help you through this minor, but still touchy, matter.

■ 1 Check whether any words separate the *to* in an infinitive from its verb. If a sentence sounds awkward because a word or phrase splits an infinitive, move the interrupter.

> SPLIT INFINITIVE   Harold's intention as a stand-up comic was **to,** as best he could, **make** people laugh at themselves.
>
> REVISED   Harold's intention as a stand-up comic was **to make** people laugh at themselves, as best he could.

■ 2 Revise any split infinitives that cause modification problems. In the following sentence, for example, *only* seems to modify *mock* when it should refer to *the crudest aspects.*

> CONFUSING   Harold intended **to** only **mock** the crudest aspects of human behavior.
>
> CLEARER   Harold intended **to mock** only the crudest aspects of human behavior.

Consider, too, whether a word dividing an infinitive is needed at all. Where the interrupting word is a weak intensifier that adds nothing to a sentence (*really, actually, basically*), cut it.

24c
sp inf

> WEAK INTENSIFIER   Harold found it especially easy **to** basically **demolish** the pretensions of politicians.
>
> INTENSIFIER CUT   Harold found it especially easy **to demolish** the pretensions of politicians.

■ 3 Consider whether a split infinitive is acceptable. In most situations, split infinitives are neither awkward nor confusing, so revising them won't improve a sentence.

> SPLIT INFINITIVE   Words fail **to** adequately **describe** the cluelessness of some public figures.
>
> REVISED   Words fail **to describe** adequately the cluelessness of some public figures.

In academic and business writing, it's probably best to keep *to* and the verb together because some readers still object strongly to split infinitives.

EXERCISE 24.2 Find the split infinitives in the following sentences and revise them. Decide which revisions are necessary, which optional. Be prepared to defend your decisions.

1. In his comic monologue, Harold decided to candidly describe his own inept campaign for city council.

2. Harold usually didn't allow his personal life to too much color his comedy routines.

3. But to really appreciate how absurd politics could be, a person had to basically run for office himself.

4. Harold quickly discovered that it wasn't easy to persuade contributors to only support the best candidate.

5. To actually succeed in politics, Harold learned that a candidate had to really understand human nature.

24c
sp inf

CHAPTER 25

Questions About Plurals, Possessives, and Articles?

25a Questions about plurals of nouns?

Plurals can be tricky. Most plurals in English are formed by adding -*s* or -*es* to the singular forms of nouns.

demonstration → demonstration**s**
picture → picture**s**
dish → dish**es**

However, substantial numbers of words are simply irregular. You could not reliably predict what their plurals would be if you didn't know them.

IRREGULAR
man → m**e**n
ox → ox**en**
mouse → m**ice**
goose → g**ee**se
child → child**ren**
fungus → fung**i** (or fung**uses**)

Plurals may vary, too, according to your usage of terms. You might find maple *leaves* on your driveway but several Toronto Maple *Leafs* on the cover of *Sports Illustrated.*

There are other complications. Some collective nouns can be understood as either singular or plural (*trout*), yet they may still have "s" forms. Compare the following sentences.

The *trout* is delicious. singular

We spotted several *trout* in the stream. plural

The *trouts* depicted in James Prosek's collection include the Mexican golden trout and the Colorado River cutthroat trout. plural

Also troublesome are the plurals of compound words and of numerals. For instance, no one has yet decided whether Sony manufactures *Walkmans* or *Walkmen*. Plurals merit your careful attention, and you should always check the latest dictionaries when you have any doubt about a standard form.

An editor may indicate a faulty plural by circling the problem and writing *pl* in the margin. Or the error may be marked as a misspelling.

> We rented two videoes. *pl*
> Two sentrys stood guard. *sp*

■ **1 Check the dictionary for the plural form of a noun.** Most up-to-date college dictionaries provide the plurals of all troublesome words. If your dictionary does not give a plural for a particular noun, assume that it forms its plural with *-s* or *-es*.

You may eliminate some trips to the dictionary by referring to the following guidelines for forming plurals. But the list is complicated and full of exceptions, so keep that dictionary handy.

■ **2 Add *-es* when the plural adds a syllable to the pronunciation of the noun.** This is usually the case when a word ends in a soft *ch, sh, s, ss, x,* or *zz.* (If the noun already ends in *-e,* you add only *-s.*)

> dish → dishes
> glass → glasses
> bus → buses or busses
> buzz → buzzes
> choice → choices

■ **3 Add *-s* to form a plural when a noun ends in *-o* and a vowel precedes the *-o;* add *-es* when a noun ends in *-o* and a consonant precedes the *-o.*** This guideline has exceptions. A few words ending in *-o* have two acceptable plural forms.

VOWEL BEFORE -*O* (ADD -*S*)	CONSONANT BEFORE -*O* (ADD -*ES*)
video → videos	hero → heroes
rodeo → rodeos	tomato → tomatoes
studio → studios	veto → vetoes

■ **4 Add *-s* to form a plural when a noun ends in *-y* and a vowel precedes the *y.*** When a consonant precedes the *y,* change the *y* to an *i* and add *-es.*

VOWEL PRECEDES -*Y* (ADD -*S*)	CONSONANT PRECEDES -*Y* (CHANGE -*Y* TO *IES*)
attorney → attorneys	foundry → foundries
Monday → Mondays	candy → candies
boy → boys	sentry → sentries

An exception to this rule occurs with proper nouns. They usually retain the *y* and simply add *-s*.

PROPER NAMES ENDING IN *-Y*	EXCEPTIONS TO THE EXCEPTION (ADD *-s*)
Gary → Garys	Rocky Mountains → Rockies
Nestrosky → Nestroskys	Smoky Mountains → Smokies
Germany → Germanys	

5 Check the plural of nouns ending in *-f* or *-fe*. Some form plurals by adding *-s,* some change *-f* to *-ves,* and some have two acceptable plural forms.

ADD *-S* TO FORM PLURAL	CHANGE *-F* TO *-VES* IN PLURAL
chief → chiefs	leaf → leaves
belief → beliefs	wolf → wolves
roof → roofs	knife → knives

TWO ACCEPTABLE FORMS
elf → elfs/elves
hoof → hoofs/hooves
scarf → scarfs/scarves

6 Check the plural of certain nouns that derive from other languages.

analysis → analyses	medium → media
criterion → criteria	phenomenon → phenomena
curriculum → curricula	syllabus → syllabi

25a
plural

7 Check the plural of compound words. The last word in most compounds is pluralized.

dishcloth → dishcloths
bill collector → bill collectors
housewife → housewives

However, the first word in a compound is pluralized when it is the important term. This is often the case in hyphenated expressions.

attorney general → attorneys general
father-in-law → fathers-in-law
hole-in-the-wall → holes-in-the-wall
man-of-war → men-of-war
passerby → passersby

Words that end with *-ful* add *-s* to the end of the whole word, not to the syllable before *-ful.*

> handfuls [not hand*s*ful]
> tablespoonfuls [not tablespoon*s*ful]
> cupfuls [not cup*s*ful]

■ **8 Check the plural of letters, abbreviations, acronyms, and numbers.** These constructions usually form their plurals by adding *-s.*

> the SAT**s**
> all CEO**s**
> the 2000**s**
> four Ph.D. **s**

Use *-'s* only where adding *-s* without the apostrophe might cause a mis-reading.

> three *e*'s and two *y*'s
> several of the *I*'s in the paper

For more on apostrophes see Sections 25b and 28g.

■ **9 Use plurals consistently within a passage.** For example, if the subject of a clause is plural, be sure that words related to it are appropriately plural. In the following example, *mind* and *job* should be plural because the subject *leaders* is plural—and it's likely that the leaders have individual minds and different jobs.

25a
plural

INCONSISTENT	**Leaders** able to make up their **mind** usually hold on to their **job.**
REVISED	**Leaders** able to make up their **minds** usually hold on to their **jobs.**

EXERCISE 25.1 Form the plurals of the following words. Use the guidelines above or a dictionary as necessary.

basis	gas	soliloquy
duo	loaf	zero
tooth	alkali	mongoose
alumnus	datum	heir apparent
moose	Oreo	court-martial

EXERCISE 25.2 Form the plurals of the boldfaced words in the passage below. Use the guidelines on plurals above or a dictionary as necessary.

1. The Corner Café sold typical coffeehouse beverages, including several different **espresso.**

2. On the walls of the café were **photo** of the local soccer team and their moms.

3. The decor reflected the late **1990,** sleek and jazzy.

4. With its sports **trophy** and open doors, the place reflected the **focus** of the neighborhood.

5. No one knows how many **cupful** of coffee have been served there.

6. Many of yesterday's soccer heroes think of themselves as **alumnus** of the Corner Café.

25b Questions about possessives?

A noun or pronoun takes a possessive form to show ownership or some similar relationship: *Rita's, the students', the governor's approval, the day's labor, the city's destruction, hers, his, theirs.* Possession can also be signaled by the pronoun *of: the pride of Brooklyn, the flagship of the company, the signature of the author.*

An editor might signal problems with possessives in several ways. An error might be circled and *poss* written in the margin.

Al lived a dog's life.   *poss*

Or the editor may simply use a caret to insert an apostrophe where one is required. Omitting the apostrophe in a possessive form is a common mechanical error.

The teacher listened to his students' opinions.

1 Add an apostrophe + -s to most singular nouns and to plural nouns that do not end in -s.

SINGULAR NOUNS	PLURALS NOT ENDING IN -S
dog's life	geese's behavior
that man's opinion	women's attitude
the NCAA's ruling	children's imaginations

Singular nouns that end in -s or -z may take either an apostrophe + -s or the apostrophe alone. Use one form or the other consistently throughout a paper.

Ross's handball or Ross' handball
Goetz's play or Goetz' play

The apostrophe alone is used with singular words ending in -s when the possessive does not add a syllable to the pronunciation of the word.

Texas' first settlement
Jesus' words

Although you may occasionally see the apostrophe omitted in signs—*mens room, Macys*—in academic writing you cannot omit an apostrophe that indicates the possessive.

2 Add an apostrophe (but not an *s*) to plural nouns that end in -*s*.

hostesses' job   senators' chambers
students' opinion   Smiths' home

3 Indicate possession only at the end of compound or hyphenated words.

president-elect's decision
fathers-in-law's Cadillacs
the United States Post Office's efficiency

4 Indicate possession only once when two nouns share ownership.

Marge and Homer's family
Evans and Luu's project

But when ownership is separate, each noun shows possession.

Marge's and Homer's educations
Evans' and Luu's offices

5 Use an apostrophe + -*s* to form the possessive of living things and titled works; use *of* with nonliving things.
This guideline should be followed sensibly. Many common expressions violate the convention, and many writers simply ignore it.

TAKE APOSTROPHE + -*S*	TAKE *OF*
the dog's bone	the weight of the bone
Professor Granchi's taxes	the bite of taxes
Time's cover	the attractiveness of the cover

Use *of* whenever an apostrophe + *-s* seems awkward or ridiculous.

> RIDICULOUS The **student** sitting next to Peg's opinion was radical.
>
> REVISED The opinion **of the student** sitting next to Peg was radical.

In a few situations, English allows a double possessive, consisting of both *-'s* and *of.*

> That idea **of Mariah's** didn't win support, although an earlier one did.
>
> An opinion **of Lane's** soon spurred another argument.

6 Do not use an apostrophe with personal pronouns.

Personal pronouns don't take an apostrophe to show ownership: *my, your, her, his, our, their, its.* The forms *it's* and *who's* are contractions for *it is* and *who is* and shouldn't be confused with the possessive pronouns *its* and *whose* (see Section 28g).

> **It's** an idea that has **its** opponents alarmed.
> **Who's** to say **whose** opinion is right?

Indefinite pronouns—such as *anybody, each one, everybody*—do form their possessives regularly: *anybody's, each one's, everybody's.* For more about possessive pronouns, see Section 28f.

25b
poss

EXERCISE 25.3 Decide whether the forms boldfaced in the sentences below are correct. Revise any that you believe are faulty.

1. That claim **of her's** may be right.

2. **Moufida's** belief was that the main concern **of most citizens'** was a thriving economy.

3. **Society's** problems today are not as great as they were in the **1900s'**; each generation benefits from its **parent's** sacrifices while tackling **it's** own problems.

4. **Its** a shame that people forget how much they have benefited from **someone elses** labor.

5. Children are notorious for ignoring their **elders** generosity; ingratitude is even one of the major themes of *King Lear's* plot.

25c Are possessives needed before gerunds?

Gerunds (see Section 24a-3) are verb forms that function like nouns: *eating, biking, walking.* Nouns or pronouns often precede gerunds. When they do, you must decide whether the noun or pronoun will be possessive or not.

A few guidelines may help you decide when the noun or pronoun should be possessive.

Chart 25.1

Possessives Before Gerunds

ACADEMIC WRITING	INFORMAL WRITING
Possessive + gerund	*Regular + gerund*
the *student's* **arguing**	the *student* **arguing**
the *owner's* **complaining**	the *owner* **complaining**
the *baby's* **crying**	the *baby* **crying**
the *siren's* **wailing**	the *siren* **wailing**

25c
poss

■ 1 **Use the possessive form of the noun in formal or academic writing; use the common (nonpossessive) form in informal situations.** This first guideline does not apply to proper nouns or to pronouns.

FORMAL   The woman was startled by the *shelf's* **collapsing** in the shoe store.
[poss. noun / gerund]

INFORMAL   The woman was startled by the *shelf* **collapsing** in the shoe store.
[noun / gerund]

■ 2 **Use the possessive form in *both* formal and informal writing when the word preceding the gerund is a proper noun or a pronoun.**

The editor had little patience with *Libertarians'* **whining** about how wonderful the good old days were in Boston.
[proper noun / gerund]

She ridiculed *their* **glorifying** a time in which many citizens had few rights.
[pronoun / gerund]

■ **3 Use the common form of the noun even in formal writing when the subject of the gerund is modified by other words.**

The complainers admitted they had forgotten about the *Irish* **being** discriminated against in nineteenth-century Boston.

EXERCISE 25.4 Select the appropriate form for the nouns or pronouns used before gerunds in the sentences below. Gerunds are boldfaced. Assume that the passage is written for an academic audience.

1. The same discussions had been going on at the (*art commission/art commission's*) **gatherings** for the past several years.

2. The question was always this: should the commission sponsor local (*artists/artists'*) **painting** or should it seek work from nationally famous figures?

3. Unfortunately, whatever the members of the commission decided, they could count on (*someone/someone's*) **being** unhappy.

4. Mayor Casterbridge and City Councilwoman Meredith decided the (*local artists/local artists'*) **contributing** was the most important concern.

5. Both also knew the council could always count on (*them/their*) **understanding** local tastes.

25d
a(n)

25d Is it *a* or *an?*

Some writers think that they should simply use *a* before all words that begin with consonants and *an* before all words that begin with vowels. In fact, usage is just a bit more complicated, as a few examples show: *an* argument, *a* European, *a* house, *an* honorable person. (See also Section 33b.)

Use *a* when the word following it begins with a consonant *sound;* use *an* when the word following it begins with a vowel *sound.* In most cases, it works out that *a* actually comes before words beginning with consonants, *an* before words with vowels.

INITIAL CONSONANTS	INITIAL VOWELS
a boat	an aardvark
a class	an Egyptian monument
a duck	an igloo

a final opinion	an odd event
a house	an Oedipus complex
a Xerox product	an utter disaster

But *an* is used before words beginning with a consonant when the consonant is silent, as is sometimes the case with *h*. It is also used when a consonant itself is pronounced with an initial vowel sound (*f* → *ef; n* → *en; s* → *es*), as often happens in acronyms.

SILENT CONSONANT	CONSONANT WITH A VOWEL SOUND
an heir	an SAT score
an honest man	an HMO
an hors d'oeuvre	an X-ray star
an hour	an *F* in this course

Similarly, *a* is used before words beginning with a vowel when the vowel is pronounced like a consonant. Certain vowels, for example, sound like the consonant *y*, and in a few cases, an initial *o* sounds like the consonant *w*.

VOWEL WITH A CONSONANT SOUND
a European vacation (**eu** sounds like **y**)
a unique painting (**u** sounds like **y**)
a one-sided argument (**o** sounds like **w**)
a U-joint (**u** sounds like **y**)

EXERCISE 25.5 Decide whether *a* or *an* should be used before each of the following words or phrases.

1. L-shaped room

2. hyperthyroid condition

3. zygote

4. X-rated movie

5. Euclidean principle

6. evasive answer

7. jalapeño pepper

8. unwritten rule

9. unit of measure

10. veneer of oak

CHAPTER 26

Questions About Pronoun Reference?

26a Do pronouns lack antecedents?

Pronouns stand in for and act like nouns, but they don't name a specific person, place, or thing—*I, you, he, she, it, they, whom, this, that, one,* and so on. The person, place, or thing a pronoun stands in for is called the **antecedent,** the word you would have to repeat in a sentence if you couldn't use a pronoun. This connection between a pronoun and antecedent is called *pronoun reference.*

Jill demanded that the clerk speak directly to **her.**

ANTECEDENT	PRONOUN
Jill	*her*
Number: singular	*Number:* singular
Gender: feminine	*Gender:* feminine

Workers denied that **they** intended to strike.

ANTECEDENT	PRONOUN
Workers	*they*
Number: plural	*Number:* plural
Gender: neuter	*Gender:* neuter

You have a problem with pronoun reference if readers can't find a specific word in your sentence that could logically serve as an antecedent, the word the pronoun replaces.

VAGUE   We compared SUVs to minivans, but our budget was so tight we couldn't afford **one.**

In this example, the antecedent of *one* cannot be either *SUVs* or *minivans* because both are plural nouns. To make the sentence clearer, you could replace the pronoun with a noun.

REVISED   We compared SUVs to minivans, but our budget was so tight we couldn't afford **any new vehicle.**

An editor will usually indicate a problem with pronoun reference by circling or underlining the troublesome pronoun and writing *ref* in the margin.

> Passengers had been searched for weapons, but (it) did not prevent the hijacking.   *ref?*

Revise a sentence or passage to eliminate pronouns without clear antecedents. When you aren't sure that the pronoun has an antecedent, ask yourself whether another word in the sentence could substitute for the pronoun. If none can, replace the vague pronoun with a word or phrase that explains precisely what it is.

> VAGUE   The pollsters choose participants scientifically, but **it** did not prevent a faulty prediction.
>
> REVISED The pollsters choose participants scientifically, but **their random sampling** did not prevent a faulty prediction.

When a word that might stand in for the pronoun is possessive, you need to look at the potential antecedent carefully. In the sentence below, *they* seems to refer to *pundits'*, but that word doesn't act as a noun in the sentence.

> VAGUE   As for the television **pundits'** coverage, they either mock third-party candidates or ignore them.

Pundits' is a possessive form. But since *they* can't refer to *pundits'* (or to *coverage*), the sentence has to be revised.

26a
pro ref

> REVISED As for the television **pundits, they** either mock third-party candidates or ignore them.

EXERCISE 26.1 Revise or rewrite the following sentences to eliminate vague pronouns. Treat the sentences as a continuous passage.

1. Leah read avidly about gardening, although she had never planted one herself.

2. Her fondness for the convenience of apartment living left Leah without a place for one.

3. Leah found herself buying garden tools, seeds, and catalogs, but it did not make much sense.

4. Leah's friends suggested building planters on her deck or installing a window garden, but Leah doubted that the landlord would permit it.

5. As for her parents' idea that she invest in a condominium, they overestimated her bank account.

26b Are pronoun references ambiguous?

You have a problem with pronoun reference when a pronoun could refer to more than one antecedent.

AMBIGUOUS   When Ms. Walker talked to Mrs. Mendoza that noon, **she** did not realize that **she** might be resigning before the end of the day.

AMBIGUOUS   As soon as the FDA approves the revolutionary antibiotic, the drug company will begin production in a new plant. **It** will make a major difference when **it** happens.

In the first sentence, who is resigning is not clear; in the second, *it* might be the approval of the drug or the opening of a plant. You can usually eliminate such confusion by replacing the ambiguous pronouns with more specific words or by recasting the sentence. Sometimes you have to do both.

REVISED   When **they** talked to each other at noon, **Ms. Walker** did not realize that **Mrs. Mendoza** might be resigning before the end of the day.

REVISED   As soon as the FDA approves the revolutionary antibiotic, the drug company will begin production in a new plant. **The drug** will make a major difference **as soon as it becomes available.**

**26b
pro ref**

EXERCISE 26.2 Revise the following sentences to eliminate ambiguous pronoun references. Treat the sentences as a continuous passage. Several versions of each sentence may be possible.

1. Amanda could hardly believe that the representatives from Habitat for Humanity would visit wintry Madison, Wisconsin, when it was so bad.

2. When she met them at their hotel, the winds were howling, the visitors were hungry, and it was predicted that they would get worse.

3. But the two women were bundled up and ready to brave the elements, so she figured this wasn't a problem.

4. Later Amanda learned that one of the visitors, Sarah Severson, had been born in Wisconsin, and she told her she knew a great deal about northern winters.

5. The three of them took off through the blizzard in Amanda's lumbering SUV, but it didn't slow them down a bit.

26c Questions about *this, that, which,* and *it?*

Readers may be confused if you use the pronouns *this, that, which,* or *it* to refer to ideas you haven't named specifically in your writing. Vague pronouns of this kind are a problem not just because readers can't locate a clear antecedent, but because writers sometimes resort to vague pronouns when they aren't sure themselves what they mean in a sentence or paragraph. So unpacking a vague "this" or "that" may at times help you get a firmer grip on your ideas.

CONFUSING   In Act III, Hamlet has a chance to avenge his dead father by stabbing his murderous uncle while the man is alone at prayer. But **it** bothers him. [What bothers him?]

REVISED   In Act III, Hamlet has a chance to avenge his dead father by stabbing his murderous uncle while the man is alone at prayer. But **killing a man in cold blood** bothers Hamlet.

1 Revise a sentence or passage to make it clear what *this, that, which,* **or** *it* **means.** Constructions such as the following can be confusing or imprecise.

CONFUSING   The minutes of the committee are usually filled with data, charts, and vivid accounts of the dialogue. I especially like **this.**

Readers can't tell whether you like data, charts, or dialogue—or all three. You can usually clear up such confusion by putting a space after the pronoun (*this____?* or *that____?*) and filling it in with a word or phrase that explains what *this* or *that* is.

CONFUSING   The minutes of the committee are usually filled with data, charts, and vivid accounts of the dialogue. I especially like **this____?**

Now fill in the blank.

REVISED   I especially like **this detailed reporting of informa-tion.**

When the unclear pronoun is *which* or *it,* you ought either to revise the sentence or supply a clear and direct antecedent. Here's an example with *it* as the vague pronoun.

VAGUE   While atomic waste products are hard to dispose of safely, **it** remains a reasonable alternative to burning fossil fuels to produce electricity.

What is the alternative to burning fossil fuels? Surely not *atomic waste products.* The *it* needs to be replaced by a more specific term.

REVISED   While atomic waste products are hard to dispose of safely, **nuclear power** remains a reasonable alternative to burning fossil fuels to produce electricity.

Here's an example with *which* as the vague pronoun.

VAGUE   The house has a tiny kitchen and a slate roof, **which** Mario and Paula intend to remodel.

The *which* seems to refer to the roof, but it's more likely that Mario and Paula plan to remodel their tiny kitchen. Here is an obvious revision.

REVISED   The house has a slate roof and a tiny **kitchen, which** Mario and Paula intend to remodel.

26c
pro ref

■ **2 Avoid using *they* or *it* without antecedents to describe people or things in general.**

VAGUE   In Houston, **they** drive worse than in Dallas.
REVISED   In Houston, **people** drive worse than in Dallas.

■ **3 Avoid sentences in which a pronoun merely repeats the obvious subject.** Such constructions are unacceptable in writing.

INCORRECT   The **mayor,** a Democrat, **he** lost the election.
REVISED   The **mayor,** a Democrat, lost the election.

■ **4 Don't let a nonpossessive pronoun refer to a word that is possessive.**

INACCURATE   Supporting **Senator Jackson's** motion, Senator Kerr applauded **him.**
REVISED   Supporting Senator Jackson's **motion,** Senator Kerr applauded **it.**

EXERCISE 26.3 Decide whether a reader might find the pronouns in boldface unclear. Revise the sentences as necessary.

1. Even tourists just visiting the building soon noticed the aging state capitol's sagging floors, unreliable plumbing, and exposed electrical conduits. **This** was embarrassing.

2. When an electrical fire in the office of the Speaker of the House was soon followed by another in the Senate chamber, it was clear **it** was a problem.

3. Old paintings and sculptures were grimy and cracked, **which** had been donated by citizens over the decades.

4. The governor's proposal for reconstructing the state capitol, the legislators endorsed **it** almost unanimously.

5. **This** was passed by a voice vote.

26c
pro ref

CHAPTER 27

Questions About Pronoun Agreement?

27a Are pronoun antecedents lost?

Pronouns and nouns are either singular or plural. Singular pronouns (such as *she, it, this, that, her, him, my, his, her, its*) refer to something singular; plural pronouns (such as *they, these, them, their*) refer to plural nouns. This connection is called **agreement in number.**

The soccer **players** gathered **their** equipment.

ANTECEDENT	PRONOUN
players	*their*
Number: plural	*Number:* plural

The **coach** searched for **her** car.

ANTECEDENT	PRONOUN
coach	*her*
Number: singular	*Number:* singular

Problems with *pronoun agreement* occur when you use a singular pronoun to stand in for a plural noun (or its *antecedent*) or a plural pronoun to substitute for a singular noun (or its *antecedent*). You're apt to

Like wax figures, pronouns stand in for the nouns they replace. This head is being prepared for the Wax Museum at Fisherman's Wharf. See <http://www.waxmuseum.com>.

make the error when words and phrases come between a pronoun and its antecedent, causing a kind of "misdirection." You lose track of the actual antecedent.

                                 sing.

AGREEMENT ERROR   A typical **voter** today expects all sorts of

                                 plural

                   governmental services, but **they** often don't

                   want to pay for them.

The plural pronoun *they* refers inconsistently to a singular noun, *voter.* The simplest way to be sure that pronouns and antecedents agree in this sentence is to make *voter* plural.

                               plural

REVISED   Typical **voters** today expect all sorts of gov-

                               plural

                   ernmental services, but **they** often don't

                   want to pay for them.

Some editors will mark an agreement error by placing *agr* in the margin next to a problem sentence.

    Everyone believes that they are fair. *agr?*

27a

pro agr

■ **1 Be sure that singular pronouns refer to singular antecedents and plural pronouns to plural antecedents.** Here's an example.

                             sing.

AGREEMENT ERROR   An **American** always takes it for granted

                                 plural

                   that government agencies will help **them**

                   when trouble strikes.

Since *American* is singular and *them* is plural, revision is necessary to make pronoun and antecedent either consistently plural or consistently singular.

                             plural

REVISED   **Americans** always take it for granted that

                               plural

                   government agencies will help **them** when

                   trouble strikes.

                             sing.

REVISED   An **American** always takes it for granted

                   that   government   agencies   will   help

                          sing.

                   him or her when trouble strikes.

Note that words such as *student, individual,* and *person* are singular, not plural. Don't use *they* to refer to them.

> AGREEMENT ERROR If a **person** watches too much television,
> **they** may become a couch potato.
>
> REVISED If a **person** watches too much television, **he
> or she** may become a couch potato.

■ 2 Keep pronouns consistent in number throughout a passage.

Don't switch back and forth from singular to plural forms of pronouns and antecedents. The following paragraph—with pronouns and antecedents boldfaced—shows this common error.

> One reason some **teenagers** [**pl.**] quit school is to work to support **their** [**pl.**] families. If **he or she** [**sing.**] is the eldest child, the **teen** [**sing.**] may feel an obligation to provide for the family. So **they** [**pl.**] look for a minimum wage job. Unfortunately, the **student** [**sing.**] often must work so many hours per week that **they** [**pl.**] cannot give much attention to schoolwork. As a result, **he or she** [**sing.**] grows discouraged and drops out.

To correct such a tendency, be consistent. Treat the troublesome key term—in the passage above it is *teenager*—as either singular or plural, but not both. Notice that making such a change may require adjustments throughout the passage.

> One reason some **teenagers** [**pl.**] quit school is to work to support **their** [**pl.**] families. If **they** [**pl.**] are the eldest children, such **teens** [**pl.**] may feel an obligation to provide for **their** [**pl.**] families. So **they** [**pl.**] look for minimum wage jobs. Unfortunately, these **students** [**pl.**] often must work so many hours per week that **they** [**pl.**] cannot give much attention to schoolwork. As a result, **they** [**pl.**] grow discouraged and drop out.

**27a
pro agr**

EXERCISE 27.1 Revise the following sentences wherever pronouns and antecedents do not agree in number. You may change either the pronouns or the antecedents.

1. Many a college class is conducted using the Socratic method, but they aren't always successful.

2. In the Socratic method, a teacher leads a student through a series of questions to conclusions that they believe they've reached without the instructor's prompting.

3. Yet when instructors ask leading questions, the cleverer students sometimes answer it in unexpected ways.

4. However, no instructor, except perhaps for Socrates himself, can foresee all the questions and answers eager students might have for them.

5. But an instructor should be as open as students to accepting new ideas when lively debates lead them to question their beliefs.

27b Questions about agreement with indefinite pronouns?

A troublesome and common agreement problem involves references to pronouns described as indefinite. Common indefinite pronouns include *everyone, anybody, anyone, somebody, all, some, none, each, few,* and *most.* It is not always easy to tell whether one of these indefinite words is singular or plural.

Everyone should keep (**his? their?**) temper.
No one has a right to more than (**his or her? their?**) share.

Yet a decision usually has to be made before a pronoun can be selected.

▓ 1 Use the chart below or a dictionary to determine whether an indefinite pronoun or noun in your sentence is singular, variable, or plural. The chart, which is not exhaustive, reflects formal and college usage.

27b
pro agr

Chart 27.1

Indefinite Pronouns		
SINGULAR	VARIABLE (SINGULAR OR PLURAL)	PLURAL
anybody	all	few
anyone	any	many
anything	either	several
each	more	
everybody	most	
everyone	neither	
everything	none	
nobody	some	
no one		
nothing		
somebody		
someone		
something		

▪ 2 If the indefinite word is regarded as singular, make any pronouns that refer to it singular.

sing.   sing.
Did **anybody** misplace **her** notes?
sing.   sing.
Everyone should keep **his** temper.
sing.   sing.
No one has a right to more than **his or her** share.

Using singular pronouns in these cases may seem odd at times because the plural forms occur so often in speech and informal writing.

INFORMAL	**Each** of the candidates has **their** own ideas.
INFORMAL	We discovered that **everyone** had kept **their** notes.
REVISED—FORMAL	**Each** of the candidates has **his or her** own ideas.
REVISED—FORMAL	We discovered that **everyone** had kept **her** notes.

In a few situations, however, the singular indefinite pronoun does take a plural referent, even in formal and college writing.

sing.   plural
Because **each** of the players arrived late, the coach gave **them** a stern lecture on punctuality.

sing.   plural
Nobody was late, were **they?**

sing.   plural
Everybody has plenty of money, and **they** are willing to spend it.

27b
pro agr

▪ Point of Difference

Some grammarians and linguists now support these informal constructions. They point out that, in effect, indefinite pronouns like *everyone* or expressions like *each of the legislators* describe groups, not individuals. That's why most speakers of English intuitively consider them as plurals. Moreover, treating such indefinites as plurals avoids the need to use a clumsy *his or her* to avoid sexist language.

Everyone is entitled to **his or her** opinion.

Nonetheless, most editors and professional writers do not accept these forms—yet.▪

▪ 3 If the indefinite word is usually plural, make any pronouns that refer to it plural.

plural   plural
Several of the jet fighters had to have **their** wings stiffened.
plural   plural
Few, however, had given **their** pilots trouble.

4 If the indefinite word is variable, use your judgment to determine which pronoun suits the sentence better. In many cases, words or phrases modifying the pronoun determine its number.

var.   plural   var.
All of the portraits had yellowed in **their** frames. **Some** will be re-
plural
stored to **their** original condition.
var.   sing.   var.
All of the wine is still in **its** casks. **Some** of the vintage is certain to
sing.
have **its** quality evaluated.

None is considered variable because it is often accepted as a plural form. However, in formal writing, you should usually treat *none* as singular. Think of *none* as meaning *not one*.

> **None** of the women is reluctant to speak **her** mind.
> **None** of the churches has **its** doors locked.

EXERCISE 27.2 Select the word or phrase in parentheses that would be correct in formal and college writing.

1. Anybody can learn to drive an automobile with a manual transmission if (**they are/he or she is**) coordinated.

2. But not everyone will risk (**his or her/their**) (**life/lives**) trying.

3. Few today seem eager to take (**his or her/their**) driver's tests in a five-speed.

4. Everyone learning to drive a manual car expects (**his or her/their**) car to stall at the most inopportune moment.

5. Most of all, nobody wants to stop (**his or her/their**) manual-shift car on a steep hill.

27c
pro agr

27c Questions about agreement with collective nouns?

Questions about agreement occur frequently when pronouns refer to collective nouns, that is, to nouns that describe groups of things: *class, team, band, government, jury*. Collective nouns like these can be either singular or plural, depending on how they are used in a sentence.

> The **chorus** sang **its** heart out.
> The **chorus** arrived and took **their** seats.
>
> The **team** looks sharp today.
> The **team** lost their luggage.

A pronoun that refers to a collective noun should be consistently either singular or plural.

Identify any collective noun in a sentence to which a pronoun refers. Choose whether to treat that noun as a single body (the *jury*) or as a group of more than one person or object (the twelve members of the *jury*). Then be consistent. If you decide to treat the word as singular, be sure that pronouns referring to it are singular. If you decide it is plural, all pronoun references should be plural.

> The **jury** rendered **its** decision.
> The **jury** had **their** pictures taken.

In most cases, your sentences will sound more natural if you treat collective nouns as single objects. Notice how awkward the following sentence seems because the collective noun is treated as plural.

> AWKWARD   The **band** are unhappy with **their** latest recordings.

27c
pro agr

EXERCISE 27.3 In the following sentences, select the appropriate words in parentheses. Be prepared to defend your answers.

1. The **class** entered the lecture hall and took (**its/their**) seats, eager to hear from the architect after (**its/their**) field trip to several of his buildings.

2. He belonged to a revitalized **school** of design that had enjoyed (**its/their**) best days four decades ago.

3. The aging architect was accompanied by several **members of his firm,** carrying (**its/their**) designs in huge portfolios.

4. Students hoped that the **board of directors** of the college might give (**its/their**) blessing to a commission by the architect.

5. Any **panel of experts** was likely to cast (**its/their**) vote in favor of such a project.

27d Questions about agreement with *or, nor, either . . . or, neither . . . nor?*

When the antecedents for a pronoun are nouns joined by *or, nor, either . . . or,* or *neither . . . nor,* the choice of a pronoun can be puzzling.

■ 1 When two nouns joined by *or, nor, either . . . or,* or *neither . . . nor* are singular, be sure any pronoun referring to them is singular.

sing.
Neither Brazil nor Mexico will raise **its** oil prices today.

■ 2 When two nouns joined by *and* or *or* are plural, be sure any pronoun referring to them is plural.

plural
Players or managers may file **their** grievances with the commissioner.

■ 3 When a singular noun is joined to a plural noun by *or, nor, either . . . or,* or *neither . . . nor,* any pronoun should agree in number (and gender) with the noun nearer to it.

sing.   plural
Either poor diet or long, stress-filled **hours** in the office will take
plural
their toll on the business executive.
plural   sing.
Either long, stress-filled **hours** in the office or poor **diet** will take
sing.
its toll on the business executive.

Pronouns also agree in gender with the nearer antecedent when two nouns are joined by *or.*

masc.   fem.   fem.
Either a **priest** or a **nun** will escort you to **her** office.
fem.   masc.   masc.
Either a **nun** or a **priest** will escort you to **his** office.

EXERCISE 27.4 In the sentences below, select the appropriate words in parentheses.

1. Neither the tour guide nor any of his customers had bothered to confirm (**his/their**) flight from Chicago's O'Hare Airport back to Toledo.

27d
pro agr

2. Either the ticket agents or a flight attendant working the check-in desk had misread **(their/her)** computer terminal and accidentally canceled the group's reservations.

3. Either the tourists or their guide had to make up **(their/his)** **(minds/mind)** quickly about arranging transportation back to Toledo.

4. Neither the guide nor his wife relished the thought of spending **(his/her/their)** hard-earned money on yet another expensive ticket.

5. Wandering about the vast terminal, the guide located a commuter airline willing to fly either the group or its bags to **(its/their)** destination cheaply.

27d
pro agr

CHAPTER 28

Questions About Pronoun Case?

28a Do you understand case: subjective/objective/ possessive?

Some personal pronouns (and *who*) change their form according to how they are used in a sentence. These different forms are called **case**. **Subjective** (or **nominative**) **case** is the form a pronoun takes when it is the subject of a sentence or a clause: *I, you, she, he, it, we, they, who*. A pronoun is also in the subjective case when it follows a linking verb as a **predicate nominative**.

> It is **I**.
> It was **they** who cast the deciding votes.

Objective case is the form a pronoun takes when something is done to it: Elena broke *them;* Buck loved *her*. This is also the form a pronoun takes after a preposition: (to) *me, her, him, us, them, whom*. The subjective and objective forms of the pronouns *you* and *it* are identical.

The **possessive case** is the form a pronoun takes when it shows ownership: *my, mine, your, yours, her, hers, his, its, our, ours, their, theirs, whose*.

In most situations, writers are able to select the appropriate form (or *case*) without thinking much about their choices.

> **Whose** book did **she** give to **him**?
> **They** were more confident of **their** position than **we** were of **ours**.

But at other times, selecting the right case is no easy matter. The correct pronoun choice may even look or sound wrong.

An editor will ordinarily circle an error in case and write *case* in the margin next to a sentence with such a problem.

> To (who) did you write? *case*

■ **1 Use the appropriate case.** Choose subjective forms when pronouns act as subjects, objective forms when pronouns act as objects (especially in prepositional phrases), and possessive forms when pronouns show ownership. Use the chart below to select the appropriate forms.

Chart 28.1

Pronoun Case		
SUBJECTIVE FORMS	OBJECTIVE FORMS	POSSESSIVE FORMS
I	me	my, mine
we	us	our, ours
you	you	your, yours
he	him	his
she	her	her, hers
it	it	its, of it
they	them	their, theirs
who	whom	whose

You are most likely to have a problem selecting the correct case when faced with a pair of pronouns. The second pronoun is usually the troublesome one.

> **You** and (**I? me?**) need to review the grant proposal.

The pronouns here are both part of the subject. So you should select the subjective form of the *I/me* pair—which is *I.*

But even if you didn't recognize the need for a subjective form, you could still make the right choice by imagining how the sentence would read if you dropped the first pronoun. With only one pronoun in the sentence, you can usually tell immediately what the correct form should be.

> WRONG   **Me** need to review the grant proposal.
>
> RIGHT   **I** need to review the grant proposal.

Given this choice, most people will select the correct pronoun: *I.*

> REVISED   **You** and **I** need to review the grant proposal.

This simple but effective technique works with many confusing pairs of pronouns or nouns and pronouns.

■ **2 When a pronoun is followed by an appositive, the pronoun and noun share the same case.** An *appositive* is a noun or noun phrase that describes or explains another noun.

28a
case

SUBJECT   **We** *lucky sailors* missed the storm.
OBJECT   The storm missed **us** *lucky sailors.*

You may run into a problem when a pronoun in a prepositional phrase is followed by an appositive noun. The proper form for the pronoun is the objective case, even though it may sound odd to the ear.

For **us** engineers, the job market looks promising.

We engineers may sound more correct, but *we* is the subjective form and should not be used after the preposition *for.*

28b Questions about pronoun case in prepositional phrases?

Prepositions are words that link nouns or pronouns to the rest of sentences; they point out many basic relationships: *on, above, to, for, between, beyond,* and so on. When you join a preposition and a pronoun, you create a *prepositional phrase: above it, to him, of whom.* Pronouns in such phrases are the objects of the prepositions and are almost always in the objective case. Difficulties with case are rare when a single pronoun closely follows its preposition.

28b
case

Come *with* **me** now.
Wait *for* **us.**

You would never say *Come with I now* or *Wait for we.*

But add another pronoun or noun after the preposition, and you may suddenly have questions about the correct form.

Come *with* Josh and (**I? me?**) now.
Wait *for* (**he? him?**) and (**I? me?**).

Just remember to use the objective case when pronouns are the objects of prepositional phrases.

    prep. obj.   obj.
Come *with* **Josh** and (**I? me?**) now.

    prep.   obj.   obj.
Wait *for* (**he? him?**) and (**I? me?**).

      prep.   obj.   obj.
Just *between* you and (**I? me?**), the answer is "Yes."

A glance at the chart on page 467 shows that the forms needed in these sentences are the objective ones: *me* and *him.*

Come with Josh and **me** now.
Wait for him and **me**.
Just between you and **me**, the answer is "Yes."

In some cases, you can reach the same conclusion by deleting the words causing problems and considering the alternatives.

FIRST VERSION   Come *with* I now.
SECOND VERSION   Come *with* me now.

In this case, the deletion makes it clearer that the second version is correct, and so the full sentence can be restored.

REVISED   Come *with* Josh and **me** now.

EXERCISE 28.1 Select the correct pronoun from the choices offered in parentheses.

1. In the reporter's opinion, neither (**she/her**) nor her competitors had done a good job in covering the city's financial crisis.

2. It was likely that both political parties would now accuse (**she/her**) and (**they/them**) of media bias.

3. Knowing her colleagues at the competing TV stations, the reporter was convinced that both she and (**they/them**) had rushed their stories.

4. She had assumed that the city manager's staff had been honest about the financial problems, but now she wasn't sure they had been truthful with (**she/her**).

5. "You and (**I/me**) will just have to accept the criticism," the reporter told a professional colleague, who just frowned at (**she/her**).

28c
case

28c Questions about pronoun case in comparisons?

You may have questions about pronoun case when you're writing a comparison that includes *than* or *as* followed by a pronoun. You'll recognize this familiar difficulty immediately.

I am taller *than* (**him? he?**).
Politics does not interest me as much *as* (**she? her?**).

■**1 Expand the comparison into a complete clause.** For example, you might be puzzling over a choice like this.

I am taller *than* (**him? he?**).

To expand the comparison—*than* (*him? he?*)—into a clause, you need to add a verb, in this case *is.*

I am taller *than* (**him? he?**) *is.*

■**2 Now choose the appropriate form of the pronoun.** The correct pronoun form will usually be more obvious once a verb is in place.

REVISED   I am taller *than* **he** (is).

To work as the subject of the verb *is,* the pronoun (*him/he*) must take its subjective form (*he*). However, you don't have to write the verb *is* into the sentence; it can remain implied.

Here is another example, with *as.*

Politics does not interest me as much *as* (**she? her?**).

Notice, however, that the comparison can be expanded in two different ways.

Politics does not interest me as much *as* it interests (**she? her?**).
Politics does not interest me as much *as* (**she? her?**) does.

As a result, the pronoun you select will determine what the sentence means. Select the subjective pronoun *she,* and this is the result.

REVISED   Politics does not interest me as much *as* **she** (does).

Choose the objective pronoun *her,* and the sentence has a different meaning.

REVISED   Politics does not interest me as much *as* (it interests) **her.**

For the sake of clarity, it often makes sense to write out the implied verbs in such situations.

Here's a second example.

Sean likes Keesha better *than* (**I? me?**).

FIRST VERSION   Sean likes Keesha better *than* **I** do.
SECOND VERSION   Sean likes Keesha better *than* he likes **me.**

EXERCISE 28.2 Select the correct pronoun from the choices offered in parentheses.

1. Although the Cowardly Lion needed the Wizard's help as much as Dorothy did, the King of the Jungle was less determined than (**she/her**) to hike to Oz.

2. Dorothy probably felt more confident than (**he/him**) that she could deal with the wonderful Wizard.

3. Perhaps Dorothy could relate more easily to (**he/him**) than a lion could.

4. Although more cautious in his appraisal of the Wizard than Dorothy, the Scarecrow was no less eager for guidance than (**she/her**).

5. Perhaps the Scarecrow even feared that Dorothy would like the Wizard more than (**he/him**).

28d Questions about pronoun case after linking verbs?

Linking verbs, such as *to be, to seem, to appear, to feel,* and *to become,* connect a subject to a word or phrase that extends or completes its meaning—the **subject complement.** When complements are pronouns, they are in the subjective case.

      subj. l.v.   subj. comp.
The *culprits* are obviously **they.**
               subj.   l.v. subj. comp.
The *commander in chief* will be **he.**
      subj.   l.v. subj. comp.
The *one* who will prevail is **I.**

Yet complements can be puzzling. Many writers would have a tough time deciding which of the following pairs of sentences is correct.

It is **I.**   It is **me.**
That is **she.**   That is **her.**
This is **he.**   This is **him.**

In college English, the left-hand column is considered correct. The pronouns after the verb are all subject complements in the subjective case: *I, she, he.* But exceptions are allowed: *It is me* is acceptable too.

    So in most academic writing, use the subjective case of a pronoun when it is the complement of a linking verb.

28d
case

> The next CEO of the corporation will be **she**.
> The director was **he**.

But do use the objective case of a pronoun when it sounds more natural. You'd certainly use these forms when writing dialogue, for example.

> It is **me**.
> That's **her**.

Or work around the problem. Rather than write "The director was he," reverse the order and try "He was the director."

EXERCISE 28.3 Review Sections 28a through 28d. Select the correct pronoun from the choices in parentheses below.

1. That is (**he/him**) in the office there.

2. The guilty party certainly was not (**she/her**).

3. Spying three men in uniform, we assumed that the pilots were (**they/them**).

4. They are (**who/whom**)?

5. We were surprised that the person who had complained was (**she/her**).

28e Is it *who* or *whom?*

In informal spoken English, the distinction between *who* and *whom* (or *whoever/whomever*) is usually ignored. In written English, however, many readers still expect the convention to be honored.

1 Choose between the subjective and objective forms of *who.* Select the subjective form (*who*) when pronouns act as subjects, the objective form (*whom*) when pronouns act as objects. The appropriate choice is especially important in prepositional phrases.

SUBJECTIVE FORM	**Who** wrote this report?
OBJECTIVE FORM	You addressed **whom?**
OBJECTIVE FORM	To **whom** did you write?

The problem, of course, with *who/whom* is figuring out whether the word is acting as a subject or an object. Which is right?

Who did you address?
Whom did you address?

To select the appropriate form, you need to identify the subject and the object.

APPROPRIATE   obj.   subj.
Whom did you address?

If you can locate the verb, you can usually figure out who is doing what to whom.

(**Who? Whom?**) are you taking on the tour?

The verb is *are taking.* The doer of the action is clearly *you: you are taking.* The person receiving the action, then, is the objective form of *who/whom: whom.*

APPROPRIATE   **Whom** are you taking on the tour?

Be careful with sentences containing passive verbs, where the subject remains in the subjective case (*who*) even though it does not actually perform the action described by the verb.

APPROPRIATE   **Who** was accused of cheating?

When you can't recall all the fine points of *who/whom,* play it safe by using *who* in most situations—except immediately after a preposition. After a preposition, use *whom: to whom, for whom, with whom.* Using *who* in all other circumstances will mean you are technically incorrect whenever the word is acting as an object. But *who* misused as an object usually sounds less awkward than *whom* misused as a subject.

28e
who(m)

WHO MISUSED   You addressed **who?**
AS AN OBJECT

WHOM MISUSED   **Whom** wrote this report?
AS A SUBJECT

2 Take care with *who/whom* in dependent clauses.

When *who/whom* (or *whoever/whomever*) is part of a dependent clause, *who/whom* takes the form it would have in the dependent clause, not in the sentence as a whole. Constructions of this kind are quite common. The phrases underlined in the following examples are clauses within full sentences.

The system rewards <u>**whoever** works hard</u>. [subjective]

The surplus will increase no matter <u>**whom** we elect president</u>. [objective]

<u>**Whomever** we nominate</u> is likely to be elected. [objective]

EXERCISE 28.4 Decide which of the pronoun forms in parentheses is correct in each of the following sentences.

1. Sam Donaldson looks like a man (**whom/who**) wouldn't trust a nun with a prayer.

2. (**Whom/Who**) wouldn't like to win the state lottery?

3. To (**who/whom**) would you go for sound financial advice?

4. Are these the young children (**who/whom**) you took by bus to Santa Fe?

5. Officials couldn't determine (**who/whom**) rigged the club elections.

28f Questions about possessive pronouns?

28f
poss

The most common way of showing ownership in English is to add an apostrophe + -*s* to a noun: *Sarah's book*, the *dog's owner*. The familiar -'*s* is not, however, used with **personal pronouns** (or *who*)—and this exception confuses some writers who are inclined to add -'*s* to personal pronouns that don't require it.

The possessive forms of **indefinite pronouns** can be troublesome as well. Some indefinite pronouns take the apostrophe + -*s* to indicate ownership, but others do not.

1 Remember that personal pronouns don't need apostrophes to show ownership. This is true whether the possessive pronoun comes before or after a noun.

BEFORE THE NOUN	AFTER THE NOUN
That is **my** *book*.	The *book* is **mine**.
That is **your** *book*.	The *book* is **yours**.
That is **her** *book*.	The *book* is **hers**.
That is **his** *book*.	The *book* is **his**.
That is **our** *book*.	The *book* is **ours**.
That is **their** *book*.	The *book* is **theirs**.
Whose *book* is this?	The *book* is **whose**?

2 Remember that while some indefinite pronouns can form the possessive by adding -'*s*, others cannot. Among the indefinite pronouns that cannot add -'*s* to show possession are these.

Chart 28.2

Possessive Forms of Indefinite Pronouns

INDEFINITE PRONOUN	FORM OF THE POSSESSIVE
all	the opinion **of all**
any	the sight **of any**
each	the price **of each**
few	the judgment **of few**
most	the dream **of most**
none	the choice **of none**
some	the expectation **of some**

Indefinite pronouns ending in *-body* or *-one* can form the possessive with *-'s* or with *of.*

INDEFINITE PRONOUN	FORMS OF THE POSSESSIVE
anybody	**anybody**'s opinion
	the opinion of **anybody**
someone	**someone**'s hope
	the hope of **someone**

28g Special problems: *its/it's* and *whose/who's*

Don't mistake the possessive pronoun *its* for the contraction *it's* (which means *it is* or *it has*). This error is both very common and easy to fix. A related error is mistaking *whose* for *who's.*

1 Remember that *its* is a possessive form; *it's* is a contraction of *it is.*

WRONG   The school lost it's charter because of low test scores.

RIGHT   The school lost its charter because of low test scores.

WRONG   Its a fact that property crimes in the neighborhood have decreased.

RIGHT   It's a fact that property crimes in the neighborhood have decreased.

WRONG   Its unlikely that the aircraft will lose it's way in the dark. Its equipped with radar.

RIGHT   It's unlikely that the aircraft will lose its way in the dark. It's equipped with radar.

The apostrophe makes the contracted form—*it's*—look suspiciously like a possessive. And the possessive form—*its*—sounds like a contraction. But don't be fooled. The possessive forms of a personal pronoun never take an apostrophe, while contractions always require one.

POSSESSIVE FORM   The iron left its grim outline on the silk shirt.
CONTRACTION   It's a stupid proposal.

If you consistently misuse *its/it's,* circle these words whenever they appear in your work and then check them. It may help if you always read *it's* as *it is.* Eventually you will eliminate this error.

2 Remember that the possessive of *who* is *whose*. Don't mistake *whose,* the possessive, for *who's,* which is the contraction for *who is* or *who has.*

POSSESSIVE FORM   **Whose** teammate is on first base?
CONTRACTION   **Who's** on first?

28g
its/it's

EXERCISE 28.5 Circle all occurrences of *its/it's* in the following passage and correct any errors.

1. Its been decades since Americans have felt as comfortable traveling in Eastern Europe as they do now.

2. Its likely that tourism will remain a major industry in Hungary, Poland, and the Czech Republic.

3. Each of these countries has much to attract tourists to its cities.

4. Yet its the small towns of Eastern Europe that many Americans may find most appealing.

5. In rural areas, sensitive travelers often get a better feel for a country and its people.

EXERCISE 28.6 Review Sections 28f and 28g. Identify and correct any pronoun-related errors in the sentences below.

1. There is usually not much doubt about whose responsible for enormous environmental disasters.

2. Its not hard to spot a capsized oil tanker.

3. Yet anybodys home or yard can contribute to environmental pollution.

4. The earth is our's to protect or despoil.

5. Ecology has to be everyone's responsibility.

28g
its/it's

CHAPTER 29

Questions About Pronoun Choices?

29a Questions about reflexive and intensive pronouns?

Reflexive and **intensive pronouns** are created when *-self* is added to singular personal pronouns and *-selves* to plural personal pronouns: *myself, yourself, herself, himself, itself, oneself, ourselves, yourselves, themselves.* These words are *reflexive* in sentences like the following, where both the subject and the object of an action are the same person or thing.

> subj.   obj.
> *They* took **themselves** too seriously.

They are *intensive* when they modify a noun or another pronoun to add emphasis.

> noun
> *Warren* **himself** admitted he was responsible.
> pron.
> *I* never vote **myself.**

Some writers use reflexive pronouns—especially *myself*—inappropriately because they think that intensive forms are more formal than simple personal pronouns. Other writers use the nonstandard forms *hisself* or *theirselves.* Both issues are addressed in this section.

There are no specific proofreading symbols for problems with reflexive and intensive pronouns. An editor is likely just to circle a doubtful form and mark *pron.* in the margin.

> Jack ⟨hisself⟩ appeared at the meeting. *pron.*

▊ 1 Don't use reflexive pronouns to make sentences sound more formal. The basic pronoun form is adequate.

> NONSTANDARD   The memo is for Ms. Matthews and **yourself.**
>
> REVISED   The memo is for Ms. Matthews and **you.**

Use the pronoun reflexively only when the subject and object in a sentence refer to the same person or thing.

subj.   obj.
Maggie rediscovered **herself** in her paintings.
subj.   obj.
Jones had only **himself** to blame.

Similarly, don't use *myself* in place of a more suitable *I* or *me*.

NONSTANDARD   *Collins and myself* wrote the lab **report.**

REVISED   *Collins and I* wrote the lab **report.**

Compare the sentence above to a similar one using *myself* correctly as an intensive pronoun.

I wrote the lab report **myself.**

2 Use intensive pronouns for emphasis.

The gift is for *you* **yourself.**
The *residents* did all the plumbing and wiring **themselves.**

3 Never use *hisself* or *theirselves.*
Although you may hear these expressions—especially *theirselves*—in speech, the correct forms in writing are always *himself* and *themselves.*

WRONG   Lincoln wrote the letter **hisself.**

CORRECT   Lincoln wrote the letter **himself.**

WRONG   They saw **theirselves** on television.

CORRECT   They saw **themselves** on television.

29a
pron

EXERCISE 29.1 Correct any problems with reflexive or intensive pronouns in the sentences below.

1. "God helps them who help themselves" is an adage credited to Benjamin Franklin.

2. The delegates to the Constitutional Convention in 1787 were not sure they could agree among theirselves on a new form of government.

3. George Washington hisself presided over the convention.

4. Aaron and myself wrote a paper on Madison's contribution to the Constitution.

5. You might want to read about the topic yourself.

29b Questions about *that, which,* and *who?*

The puzzler here is when to use the pronouns *that* and *which.* You may have learned a rule that requires *that* as the lead-in for essential or restrictive modifiers (that is, for clauses that strictly limit the meaning of the word modified).

ESSENTIAL CLAUSE   The car **that hit me** rolled into the shallow ditch.

The same rule insists that *which* be used with nonessential or nonrestrictive clauses (that is, with modifiers that add information not crucial to the meaning of a sentence).

NONESSENTIAL CLAUSE   My vehicle, **which is a sport utility,** sustained little damage.

Yet in reading you may have noticed that some writers use *which* interchangeably.

ESSENTIAL CLAUSE   The car **which hit me** rolled into the shallow ditch.

What form is correct? And when is *who* a better alternative to *which* and *that?*

■ **1 Use *that* to introduce essential (restrictive) clauses.** A clause introduced by *that* will almost always be essential. No commas are used around such clauses.

The concept **that** intrigued the shareholders most involved profit sharing.

Only the report **that** I wrote recommended that concept.

■ **2 Use *which* to introduce nonessential (nonrestrictive) clauses.** Such clauses are ordinarily surrounded by commas.

NONESSENTIAL CLAUSE   The Web site, **which** is not on the university's server, contains controversial advice about plagiarism.

NONESSENTIAL CLAUSE   The agency, **which** was created in 1978, helps businesses use energy more efficiently.

But understand that many writers use *which* to introduce essential clauses as well. In these clauses, context and punctuation may determine whether a *which* clause is essential or not. If the clause is essential, no commas separate it from the rest of the sentence; if nonessential, commas enclose the clause.

| ESSENTIAL CLAUSE | The business plan **which** intrigued the shareholders was the simplest one. |
| NONESSENTIAL CLAUSE | The business plan, **which** intrigued the shareholders, was quite simple. |

Some readers still prefer to distinguish between *that* and *which* even though the distinction is disappearing in general usage. For more about this issue, see Section 30i.

3 Use *who* rather than *that* or *which* when modifying a person.

INAPPROPRIATE	The woman **that** was promoted is my boss.
BETTER	The woman **who** was promoted is my boss.
INAPPROPRIATE	The delegates, **which** represented all regions of the country, met in Philadelphia for their convention.
BETTER	The delegates, **who** represented all regions of the country, met in Philadelphia for their convention.

29b
pron

EXERCISE 29.2 Decide among *that/which/who* in the following sentences. Add commas where needed.

1. Charlie Chaplin's tramp (**that/which/who**) wore a derby, baggy trousers, and a mustache may still be the most recognized character on film.

2. The popularity (**that/which/who**) Chaplin had in the early days of film may never be equaled either.

3. His graceful gestures and matchless acrobatics (**that/which/who**) some critics likened to ballet were perfectly suited to the silent screen.

4. A flaw (**that/which/who**) weakens many of Chaplin's films is sentimentality.

5. Chaplin's tramp made a last appearance in *The Great Dictator* (1940) (**that/which/who**) satirized Hitler's regime.

29c When to use *I, we, you,* or *one?*

Pronouns change the distance between writers and readers. Choosing *I* or *you* puts you closer to readers; using *one* creates distance.

■1 **Use *I* when you or your opinions belong in what you're writing.** In general, avoid the first person *I* in scientific reports and expository essays.

WITH *I*	**I learned** through a survey **I did** that students who drive a car on campus are more likely to have jobs than those who do not.
REVISED	**A survey showed** that students who drive a car on campus are likely to have jobs.

However, when you find that avoiding *I* makes you resort to an awkward passive verb, use *I* instead.

WORDY	**It is believed** that procedures for voting in campus elections are too complex.
REVISED	**I believe** that procedures for voting in campus elections are too complex.

You can often eliminate an awkward passive without using *I*.

REVISED WITHOUT *I*	Procedures for voting in campus elections are too complex.

The same advice—to use *I* sensibly—applies when you find yourself cobbling clumsy phrases just to avoid the pronoun.

WORDY	**In the opinion of this writer,** federal taxes should be lowered.
REVISED	**I believe** federal taxes should be lowered.
REVISED WITHOUT *I*	Federal taxes should be lowered.

🍎 *Point of Difference*

You should know that some instructors and editors simply will not allow *I* in college, professional, or scientific prose. When writing for them, respect their rules. However, most writers today recognize that using *I* is both natural and sensible even in relatively formal work. Not using *I* or *we* (when more than one author is involved) can even lead to questions about who is taking responsibility for a statement.🍎

■ **2 Use *we* whenever two or more writers are involved in a project or when you are writing to express the opinion of a group.**

> When **we** compared our surveys, **we** discovered the conflicting evidence.
>
> **We** believe that the city council has an obligation to reconsider its zoning action.

Or use the first person *we* to indicate a general condition when it is appropriate to comment editorially.

> **We** need better control of our medical care systems in the United States.

Avoid *we* or *us* as a chummy way of addressing your reader. In most college writing, *we* used this way sounds pompous.

■ **3 Use *you* to address readers personally or to give orders or directions.** *You* sounds direct, cordial, and personal. So be sure you really want your readers included when using the second person in college writing. The following sentence, for example, may be too personal. It seems to implicate readers directly in scholastic dishonesty.

> INAPPROPRIATE   A recent student government survey suggested that **you** will cheat in two courses during **your** college career.
>
> REVISED   A recent student government survey suggested that **most students** will cheat in two courses during **their** college careers.

29c
pron

Because *you* is both vague and potentially personal, it is a pronoun to avoid in most academic writing, especially reports and research projects. *You* may be more appropriate in persuasive writing, however, where your goal is to move people to act.

■ **4 Use *one* to express a general thought.** *One* is often useful for conveying moral sentiments or sweeping claims.

> Consider the anxiety of not knowing where **one's** next meal is coming from.
>
> **One** learns a great deal about old Russia from reading Dostoevsky.

Notice that *one* makes the sentence more formal than it would be if *one* were replaced by *I* or *you*.

Sentences with too many *ones,* however, may seem like the butlers of British comedy—sneering and superior.

> POMPOUS   **One** can never be too careful about maintaining **one's** good reputation, can **one?**

In most cases, *you* or an appropriate noun sounds less stiff than *one,* especially when giving directions.

> WORDY   If **one** is uncertain about the authority of **one's** sources, **one** should consult a librarian in the reference room.

> REVISED   If **you** are uncertain about the authority of **your** sources, consult a librarian in the reference room.

5 Whatever pronouns you choose, be consistent. Don't switch pronoun forms in the middle of a sentence or paragraph. Problems are most likely to occur with the indefinite pronoun *one.*

> NONSTANDARD   **One** cannot know what **their** future holds.

Here the pronoun shifts incorrectly from *one* to the plural form *their.* Several revisions are possible.

> REVISED   **One** cannot know what **his or her** future holds.
> REVISED   **People** cannot know what **their** futures hold.
> REVISED   **One** cannot know what the future holds.

You may shift between *one* and *he* or *she,* as the example above demonstrates.

29c
pron

EXERCISE 29.3   Revise the sentences below to create a passage appropriate for a college report. Pay particular attention to the words and phrases in boldface.

1. **I was amazed to learn that** the Chinese speak a variety of dialects of a language **they** describe as Han.

2. Although there are only eight major varieties of Han, **you would find them** as different from each other as one Romance language is from another.

3. **One finds,** moreover, that each of the eight versions of Han occurs in a great many dialects, adding to **your** linguistic confusion.

4. **You will be glad to know,** however, that the Chinese use only one system of writing—a set of common ideographs—for expressing all **their** dialects.

5. As **you** might expect, there have been efforts to reform the Chinese language to make it easier **for you** to communicate between one region and another in the vast and populous country.

29d Do your pronouns treat both sexes fairly?

What happens when you need to use a pronoun but don't know whether it should refer to a man or a woman?

Each of the engineers we hire will earn (**his? her?**) job.

Until just a few years ago, most writers would use a masculine pronoun (**he, him, his**) in any such situation—on the grounds that someone talking about *man*kind is also thinking about *woman*kind.

> SEXIST Each of the engineers we hire will earn **his** job.
>
> SEXIST An experienced **pilot** can sense when **his** plane has a problem.

In fact, such male-only constructions can exclude women from more than just grammar. (See also Section 16d.)

Today members of either sex may belong to almost every profession or group—students, athletes, coal miners, truckers, secretaries, nurses. Let your language reflect that diversity. Obviously, you should acknowledge the inevitable exceptions.

> Each of the nuns received an award for **her** service to the community.
>
> None of the NFL quarterbacks received a payment for **his** appearance at the benefit.

But in situations where you cannot assume that members of a group will all be male or female, be sure your language accommodates both sexes. You can do that in a variety of ways.

1 Use the expressions *he or she, him or her,* or *his or her* instead of the pronoun of either sex alone.

> SEXIST Every secretary may invite **her husband.**
>
> REVISED Every secretary may invite **his or her spouse.**

Unfortunately, variations of *he or she* grow tiresome when they occur more than once in a sentence. Other expressions have been created to express gender diversity including *he/she, s/he,* and *(s)he.* But many readers and editors don't like these inventions. So when the widely accepted *he or she* seems clumsy, try another strategy to avoid sexist usage.

■2 Make singular pronoun references plural. Because plural pronouns do not have a specific gender in English, you can often avoid the choice between *he* and *she* simply by turning singular references into plural ones.

> SEXIST   **Every** secretary may invite **her husband.**
>
> REVISED   **All** secretaries may invite **their spouses.**

> TIRESOME   Before **he or she** leaves, **each** band member should be sure **he or she** has **his or her** music.
>
> REVISED   Before leaving, **all** band members should be sure **they** have **their** music.

Notice that these revisions eliminate *he or she* entirely.

■3 Cut any troublesome pronouns. Here are more examples.

> ORIGINAL   *Anybody* may bring **his or her** favorite CD.
>
> REVISED   *Anybody* may bring a favorite CD.

> ORIGINAL   *Nobody* should leave until **he or she** has signed the guest book.
>
> REVISED   *Nobody* should leave without **signing** the guest book.

> ORIGINAL   *Each* should keep a record of **his or her** losses and gains in weight.
>
> REVISED   *Each* should keep a personal record of losses and gains in weight.

These options are useful, but they are not always available.

■4 Alternate between *he* and *she.*

In most cases, you can vary the pronouns sensibly and naturally within chunks of prose—between paragraphs, for example, or between the examples in a series. Handled skillfully, the shift between masculine and feminine references need not attract a reader's attention.

> The dean of students knew that any student could purchase term papers through mail-order term paper services. If **he** could af-

ford the scam, a student might construct **his** entire college career around papers **he** had purchased.

Yet the dean also acknowledged that the typical plagiarist was rarely so grossly dishonest and calculating. **She** tended to resort to such highly unethical behavior only when **she** believed an assignment was beyond **her** capabilities or **her** workload was excessive.

Avoid varying pronoun gender within individual sentences.

EXERCISE 29.4 Revise the following sentences to make them read better and to eliminate exclusionary pronouns. Treat the sentences as part of one paragraph.

1. Earlier this century, a laborer might fear that heavy equipment would mangle his limbs or that pollutants might damage his lungs.

2. Today a worker has to be concerned with new threats to her health.

3. Anybody who faces a computer terminal eight hours a day must worry about his exposure to radiation and wonder whether his muscles and joints are being damaged by the repetitive limb motions required by his job.

4. Frankly, the typical worker is often so concerned with her job performance that she may not consider that her workplace poses risks.

5. Of course, every worker wants their job to be safe.

29d
pron

CHAPTER 30

Questions About Modifiers?

Much of the work in sentences is handled by words and phrases that expand what we know about subjects, verbs, and other sentence elements—especially adjectives and adverbs (see Section 17b). In this chapter, we look at some of the issues writers face when dealing with modifiers, including familiar problems such as misplaced modifiers and double negatives, and the challenge of distinguishing between essential (restrictive) and nonessential (nonrestrictive) clauses. If you are unsure when such clauses need to be surrounded by commas, see Section 36b. If you are unsure whether to introduce these clauses with a *that, which,* or *who,* see Section 29b.

30a Questions about misplaced or dangling modifiers?

Adjectives and adverbs can cause confusion if they become detached from the words they are supposed to modify in a sentence. Two forms of this common problem are **misplaced modifying phrases** and

Modifiers, like fashion accessories, should be selected carefully.

dangling modifiers. A modifier is considered misplaced when it hooks up with the wrong word or phrase, sometimes with comic effect.

MISPLACED MODIFYING PHRASE	**Carved from solid oak,** the angry matriarch could not break down the door.
CORRECTED	The angry matriarch could not break down the door **carved from solid oak.**

A modifier dangles when it doesn't have a word or phrase to connect with in a sentence. As a result, it doesn't make a logical connection.

DANGLING MODIFIER	**Before sending out the invitations,** a date for their wedding has to be chosen. The boldfaced phrase doesn't apply to anything in the main part of the sentence. The sentence needs people to carry out the action.
CORRECTED	**Before sending out the invitations,** the couple will have to choose a date for their wedding.

An editor who spots a dangling modifier in your work will write *dm*, *dang*, or *dang mod* in the margin next to the offending phrase or clause.

⟨Angered by the crowd's booing,⟩ the concert was canceled.
dang mod

▊ 1 Be sure that an introductory modifying phrase is followed by the word it modifies.

30a
mm/dm

Sometimes you will have to supply a word that the introductory phrase can modify. In other cases, the whole sentence may have to be rearranged.

MISPLACED MODIFIER	**Never having had children,** rising college costs do not concern Mirella. The boldfaced phrase doesn't describe *costs,* the closest noun to it; it describes *Mirella.*
REVISION	**Never having had children,** Mirella is unconcerned about rising college costs.
MISPLACED MODIFIER	**Insulting and predictable,** fewer and fewer television viewers are attracted to the comedian's monologues. The boldfaced phrase doesn't describe *viewers;* it describes *monologues.*
REVISION	**Insulting and predictable,** the comedian's monologues attracted fewer and fewer television viewers.

2 Supply a word for a dangling modifier to modify. This often means rewriting the entire sentence, since you must usually add a word or phrase that the sentence alludes to but doesn't actually include. For example:

DANGLING   **On returning to the office,** the furniture had
MODIFIER   been rearranged.

There is nothing in the sentence for *On returning to the office* to modify. The sentence has to be revised to include a subject to which the modifier will relate.

ONE POSSIBLE   **On returning to the office,** the staff found that
REVISION   the furniture had been rearranged.

3 Distinguish between absolute phrases and dangling modifiers. Some modifying phrases may look like dangling modifiers but are actually **absolute phrases;** that is, they are complete in themselves, serving only to give additional information about the sentence of which they are a part.

absolute
Given the fiasco at dinner, the guests weren't surprised when Perri pushed her husband into the pool.

absolute
To be quite honest, Robert is a whining nerd and we would prefer that you leave him at home.

For more on absolute phrases, see Section 17c-3.

30a
mm/dm

EXERCISE 30.1 Rewrite or rearrange these sentences, placing modifiers in appropriate positions. You may need to add a noun for the modifier to modify. Not all of the sentences need to be revised.

1. Although they are among the most famous of reptiles, biologists have only recently begun to study rattlesnakes.

2. The deadly snakes, which take their name from the two characteristic pits on their snouts, belong to the family of pit vipers.

3. After studying the habits of pit vipers, the pits, which serve as infrared sensors and enable the snakes to seek heat, evolved to detect danger rather than to hunt prey.

4. Given their lethal capabilities, it is not surprising that pit vipers are universally loathed.

5. Despite their fearful reputation, however, people are seldom bitten by the snakes unless they are provoked.

30b How do you place adjectives effectively?

Adjectives are words that modify nouns or pronouns. They explain how many, which color, which one, and so on. All the words in boldface here function as adjectives.

A **successful** mayor is **rare** these days.
The **darkest** nights are **moonless.**
German beers pour slowly.
The truck, **tall** and **ungainly,** rolled down the hill.
Pale and **redheaded,** she looked **Irish.**

Most, but not all, adjectives come before the nouns or pronouns they modify: *red* Viper; *outstanding* athlete.

But you must take care to place adjectives carefully to avoid ambiguity and pileups. An adjective becomes ambiguous when readers can't tell which word it modifies. For example:

AMBIGUOUS   Adam had his **enthusiastic parents' support.**
            Enthusiastic attaches itself to parents *instead of to* support.

CLARIFIED   Adam had his **parents' enthusiastic support.**

Adjectives pile up when writers place one modifier after another until readers get confused or bored. For example:

TEDIOUS   **Recent, controversial, divisive** anti-gun legislation met defeat in the state legislature.

REVISED   **Recent** anti-gun legislation, **controversial and divisive,** met defeat in the state legislature.

1 Relocate adjectives that are potentially confusing or ambiguous. You may have to read your sentences carefully to appreciate how they might be misread. Better still, ask a friend to read your work and point out where readers might get confused.

AMBIGUOUS   The **long-lost diplomats's memoirs** were revealing.
            Does *long-lost* go with *diplomat* or *memoirs?*

CLARIFIED   The **diplomat's long-lost memoirs** were revealing.

AMBIGUOUS   The **ingenious Web site's designer** resigned. Does *ingenious* go with *Web site* or *designer?*

CLARIFIED   The **ingenious designer** of the **Web site** resigned.

30b
adj

■ 2 Consider placing adjectives after the words or phrases they modify. You can avoid tedious strings of adjectives this way and make sentences more graceful.

TEDIOUS   A **new, powerful, quick,** and **easy-to-use** database was installed today.

REVISED   A new database, **powerful, quick,** and **easy to use,** was installed today.

EXERCISE 30.2 Rearrange the adjectives to make each of these sentences clearer or more effective. Several options are possible.

1. Lisa and Julia wanted to find a politically sophisticated women's group that could help them plan their lobbying strategy.

2. Professional children's care in the workplace of employed parents was one of their goals.

3. They viewed the negative board members' attitudes as a challenge to their persuasive abilities.

4. Before explaining their plan, Lisa asked for the undivided employees' attention.

5. Obtaining an endorsement was essential if they were to overcome the stubborn management's resistance.

30c
adj

30c How do you handle predicate adjectives?

Many people have problems selecting the right term to follow linking verbs such as *seem, become, look, appear, feel, smell.* An adjective that follows a linking verb is called a **predicate adjective.**

> I *feel* **bad.**
> You *seem* **uneasy.**
> The lawyer *became* **angry.**
> The perfume *smells* **vile.**
> Dick *appears* **calm.**

■ 1 Remember that only adjectives, not adverbs, can modify a noun. So after a linking verb you need an adjective—not an adverb—to modify a noun. In the following examples, the first version of the sentence shows the incorrect *adverb* modifier; the second version shows the correct *adjective* form.

INCORRECT   The accountant feels **badly** about underestimating our quarterly taxes.
The modifier *badly* completes the linking verb *feels* and describes *accountant*, a noun, so it should be the adjective *bad*.

CORRECT   The accountant feels **bad** about underestimating our quarterly taxes.

INCORRECT   Lillian appears **pessimistically** about her chances for getting into the graduate program.
The term modifies *Lillian*, a noun, so it must be an adjective.

CORRECT   Lillian appears **pessimistic** about her chances for getting into the graduate program.

The same principle applies when you modify a noun that acts as the object in a sentence, as in the following example.

INCORRECT   The tenant kept the woodwork in his apartment **flawlessly**.
To describe *woodwork* (a noun), the writer should use the adjective form (*flawless*) rather than the adverb (*flawlessly*).

CORRECT   The tenant kept the woodwork in his apartment **flawless**.

30c
adj

■ **2 Learn to manage *good* and *well*.** Among the modifiers most often confused are *good* and *well*. Remember that *good* is always an adjective and that *well* is usually an adverb. But *well* can also be an adjective that describes someone's physical condition. Use *good* after a linking verb when you want to give information about the subject. For example:

Jasper Hayes looks **good**.
His scholastic record is **good**.
He feels **good** about being a father.

But when you are referring to someone's state of health, use *well* to finish the linking verb. In this case, *well* functions as an adjective.

Most college students feel **well** in spite of their eating habits.
Despite five hours of heart surgery, Mr. Seltzer looks remarkably **well**.

In academic and professional writing, don't use *good* as an adverb.

NO   The system doesn't run **good**.

NO   Most jobs in child care don't pay **good**.

In such cases, use *well* to describe the action of the verb. *Well* functions as an adverb in these sentences.

YES   The system doesn't run **well**.

YES   Most jobs in child care don't pay **well**.

EXERCISE 30.3 In these sentences, replace the boldfaced modifier with a better one.

1. In the United States, most people feel **confidently** that their drinking water is safe.

2. In many parts of the world, however, even water that looks **well** can be full of bacteria and pollution.

3. Some major relief organizations, such as the International Rescue Committee, feel **optimistically** that they can bring clean water to the rural areas of Africa and India.

4. They teach villagers what must be done to keep a sanitation system running **good**.

5. Parents who know that their children's drinking water should be boiled feel **badly** because often they cannot afford the fuel to boil it.

30d
adj

30d Questions about absolute adjectives?

Some words called *absolute adjectives* cannot be compared or qualified—at least not logically. For example, since *equal* means "exactly the same," you shouldn't write that something is *more equal* any more than you'd say it is *more empty*. Similarly either a thing is *perfect* or it's flawed. An object is either *unique* or there are others like it.

In practice, writers and speakers do qualify absolute expressions all the time, often meaningfully. Even the preamble of the Constitution describes "a more perfect union," and the pigs in George Orwell's satire *Animal Farm* are famously *more equal* than other animals. But in most cases you should avoid using qualifiers (such as *less, more, most, least, very*) with the following absolute words: *unique, perfect, singular, empty, equal, full, definite, complete, absolute*, and, of course, *pregnant*.

Consider these examples.

ILLOGICAL   We doubted that the new operating system was **absolutely perfect.**

REVISED   We doubted that the new operating system was **perfected yet.**

ILLOGICAL   Jack's story is **more unique** than Jane's.

REVISED   Jack's story is **unique;** Jane's is not.

EXERCISE 30.4 Working with other students in a group, read over these sentences and decide which ones have faulty modifiers. Confer to decide how any problems with modifiers might be solved.

1. Ms. Oliveras was disappointed with the grant proposals she had read—she thought the projects proposed should have been more unique.

2. She was looking for a very singular plan in which to invest the foundation's money.

3. The board of trustees had most definite opinions about what constituted "community values," a situation that made her a little nervous.

4. But because her knowledge of the community was more complete than theirs, she felt she better understood what was important.

5. When she finally came across the B'nai B'rith proposal for a preschool learning center, she decided it was the most perfect to meet the needs of the town.

30e
adv

30e Questions about adverb form?

Adverbs are words that modify verbs, adjectives, or other adverbs, explaining where, when, and how. Many adverbs end in *-ly.*

The Secretary of State spoke **angrily** to the press.
The water was **extremely** cold.
The candidate spoke **evasively.**

Some adverbs have both short and long forms.

slow/slowly   fair/fairly   rough/roughly
quick/quickly   tight/tightly   deep/deeply

The problem for many writers is that the short adverb forms look suspiciously like adjectives. Is it correct then to say "drive slow" or "tie it tight" instead of "drive slowly" and "tie it tightly"? The answer is yes—but you have to consider your audience.

In most cases, the short form of the adverb sounds more casual than the long form. Consequently, in most academic and business situations, you'll do better to use the *-ly* form.

COLLOQUIAL	The computer booted **quick.**
STANDARD	The computer booted **quickly.**
COLLOQUIAL	The employees expected to be treated **fair.**
STANDARD	The employees expected to be treated **fairly.**

EXERCISE 30.5 Working with a group of other students, discuss the following sentences and decide what the problems are. Then replace nonstandard adverb forms with appropriate ones.

1. Max was real surprised when he got a response from the IRS to his initial suggestion for clearer tax forms.

2. The local IRS director seemed to take his suggestion very serious.

3. She had written back prompt to Max, and that made him think good of her.

4. Max sat down quick and designed a handsome template for IRS consideration.

5. But Max reacted bad when the IRS rejected his design.

30f
adv

30f Where do you place adverbs?

Adverbs are usually easier to work with than adjectives because they're flexible and can take various positions in a sentence. For example:

George daydreamed **endlessly** about his vacation, **thoroughly** reviewing each travel brochure.

George daydreamed about his vacation **endlessly,** reviewing **thoroughly** each travel brochure.

Endlessly George daydreamed about his vacation, reviewing each travel brochure **thoroughly.**

But because adverbs are so flexible, it's also easy to drop them in inappropriate spots, particularly when a sentence has two verbs and the adverb might modify either one of them. The result may be a confusing or ambiguous sentence.

ADVERB MISPLACED	Analyzing an argument **effectively** improves it.
	Does *effectively* go with *analyzing* or *improves?*

1 Place adverbs so it is clear which words they modify.

ADVERB MISPLACED	Before the Battle of Agincourt, King Henry V encourages his troops to fight **eloquently.**
ADVERB REPOSITIONED	Before the Battle of Agincourt, King Henry V **eloquently** encouraged his troops to fight.
ADVERB MISPLACED	Hearing the guard's footsteps approach **quickly** Mark emptied the safe.
	The reader doesn't know whether *quickly* goes with *footsteps* or *Mark.*
ADVERB REPOSITIONED	Hearing the guard's footsteps approach Mark **quickly** emptied the safe.

A comma after *approach* in either sentence would also clarify the meaning.

2 Place the adverbs *almost* and *even* next to the words they modify. Notice the ambiguities these words cause in the following sentences because they are misplaced.

ADVERB MISPLACED	Much to his dismay, Hugo realized he had **almost** dated every woman at the party.
	Putting *almost* next to *dated* instead of *every* confuses the meaning.
ADVERB BETTER PLACED	Much to his dismay, Hugo realized he had dated **almost** every woman at the party.
ADVERB MISPLACED	A true workaholic, Jen **even** thought time spent driving to the office could be used productively.
	Even could modify *thought* here, but it really goes with *time.*
ADVERB BETTER PLACED	A true workaholic, Jen thought **even** time spent driving to the office could be used productively.

30f
adv

■ 3 **Place the adverb** *only* **directly ahead of the word you want it to modify.** The word *only* means "this one and no other." In the wrong place, *only* can lead to a misreading.

CONFUSING   Verna **only** knew of one person who opposed her marriage plans.
Could be misinterpreted to mean that Verna was the only person who knew of someone opposed to her marriage.

CLEARER   Verna knew of **only** one person who opposed her marriage plans.

CONFUSING   Her parents **only** worried about how much the elaborate affair would set them back.
Could be misinterpreted to mean that Verna's parents never did anything but worry about the cost of their daughter's wedding.

CLEARER   Her parents worried **only** about how much the elaborate affair would set them back.

EXERCISE 30.6 Rewrite the sentences to clarify them.

1. People who attend the theater regularly complain that the manners of the average audience member are in severe decline.

2. Far from listening in respectful if not attentive silence, he broadcasts a running commentary frequently modeled, no doubt, on his behavior in front of the television at home.

3. Sitting next to a woman who spends most of the evening unwrapping cellophane-covered candies slowly can provoke even the most saintly theatergoer to violence.

4. Cellular phones, beepers, and wristwatch alarms even go off intermittently causing an evening in the theater to resemble a trip to an electronics store.

5. For their part, actors marvel at how audiences today only manage to cough during the quietest moments of a play.

30g
neg

30g Questions about double negatives?

Sentences that say *no* in two different ways are emphatic and usually very colloquial.

Ain't no way I'm revising this paper again!

They make their point, but you need to avoid them in academic and professional writing.

■ 1 Check that you don't have two *no* words (a *double negative*) in the same sentence or independent clause. In addition to *no,* look for such words as *not, nothing, nobody,* and *never.* If you've doubled them, you can usually just drop or alter a single word.

DOUBLE NEGATIVE   That modem will **not** work **never.**

CORRECTED   That modem will **never** work.

DOUBLE NEGATIVE   The child does **not** want **no** help tying his shoes.

CORRECTED   The child does **not** want help tying his shoes.

■ 2 Don't mix the adverbs *hardly, scarcely,* or *barely* with another negative word or phrase. Such pairings create double negatives, which should be edited.

DOUBLE NEGATIVE   The morning was so cool and clear that the hikers **couldn't hardly** wait to get started.

CORRECTED   The morning was so cool and clear that the hikers **could hardly** wait to get started.

DOUBLE NEGATIVE   They figured there **wouldn't be scarcely** any other groups on the trail.

CORRECTED   They figured there **would be scarcely** any other groups on the trail.

30g
neg

Double negatives shouldn't be confused with negative statements that express ideas indirectly—and perhaps with ironic twists. Consider the difference in tone between these simple sentences, framed negatively and positively.

NEGATIVE   The proposal was not unintelligent.
POSITIVE   The proposal was intelligent.

NEGATIVE   Sean was hardly unattractive.
POSITIVE   Sean was attractive.

EXERCISE 30.7 Rewrite sentences that contain double negatives to eliminate the problem. Not every sentence is faulty.

1. Some critics claim that in this age of videos, computers, and the Internet, young people don't hardly read anymore.

2. Yet cities, like Madison, Wisconsin, which are centers of education and technology, haven't never had so many bookstores.

3. Many bookstores aren't no longer just places to buy books.

4. They serve as community centers where people can buy coffee, go to poetry seminars, and get on the Internet without never buying any books.

5. But bookstore owners know that scarcely any browsers leave the store empty-handed.

30h Questions about comparatives and superlatives?

The comparative and superlative forms of most adjectives and a few adverbs can be expressed two ways.

ugly (an adjective)

Comparative	uglier	more ugly
Superlative	ugliest	most ugly

slowly (an adverb)

Comparative	slower	more slowly
Superlative	slowest	most slowly

You can usually trust your ear when selecting the forms. As a general rule, you add *-er* and *-est* endings to one-syllable adjectives and adverbs but use the terms *more* and *most* (or *less* and *least*) before words of two or more syllables.

Curtis likes **brighter** colors than Kyle.
Kyle wears **more conservative** clothes than Curtis.
Kyle's white Oxford is the **most conspicuous** shirt he owns.
Camille talks **faster** than Susi.
Susi usually speaks **more deliberately**.

Two problems typically arise with comparatives and superlatives. The first is using a superlative form when comparing only two objects.

FAULTY COMPARISON   Jason was the **tallest** of the two men.
                    should be *taller*

FAULTY COMPARISON   Martina was the **most talented** of the two
                    gymnasts. should be *more talented*

A less frequent error involves doubling the comparative and superlative forms, using both the ending *-er* or *-est* and *more* or *most.*

> FAULTY COMPARISON   That was the **most ugliest** dog of all.
> should be *most ugly* or *ugliest*

▦ 1 Be sure to use the comparative form, not the superlative, when comparing two items.
That means using an adverb or adjective with an *-er* ending or modified by *more* or *less.*

> FAULTY COMPARISON   Marta was the **smartest** of the two children.
> *Smartest* is the superlative, not the comparative, form.
>
> REVISED   Marta was the **smarter** of the two children.
>
> FAULTY COMPARISON   Celeste, her twin, was the **most imaginative.** *Most imaginative* is the superlative, not the comparative, form.
>
> REVISED   Celeste, her twin, was the **more imaginative.**

▦ 2 Use the superlative form when comparing more than two objects or qualities.
In most cases when you compare three or more things or qualities, you need to use *-est* adjectives or adverbs or preface the modifiers with *most* or *least.* For example:

> Given the choice of several toys, Celeste would choose the one that was the **most** challenging.
>
> Of all the children in her kindergarten class, Marta was the **liveliest.**

30h modif

▦ 3 Avoid doubling the comparative or superlative forms.
You'll confuse your reader if you use the two comparative forms in the same phrase. For example:

> CONFUSING   Jasper was **more stricter** as a parent than Janice was.
>
> CLEAR   Jasper was **stricter** as a parent than Janice was.
>
> CONFUSING   Of all the members of the archery team, Diana was the **most angriest** about the stolen targets.
>
> CLEAR   Of all the members of the archery team, Diana was the **angriest** about the stolen targets.

EXERCISE 30.8 Write sentences in which you use the appropriate forms of comparison for the situation given.

1. Today community librarians are constantly trying to decide what is (**more/most**) important: expanding computer facilities or buying more books.

2. These librarians consider who among their clients has the (**greater/greatest**) need—schoolchildren, working adults, or retired people.

3. In general, librarians enjoy the reputation of being among the (**most helpful/helpfullest**) of city employees.

4. In good libraries, librarians are also likely to be among the (**most bright/brightest**) city employees.

5. Well-trained librarians, or information specialists as they are often called today, will find their (**better/best**) job prospects in medium-sized cities with a growing population.

30i
modif

30i Questions about nonessential and essential modifiers?

Writers sometimes puzzle over how to introduce (Section 29b) or how to punctuate (Section 36b) nonessential and essential modifiers. In either case, you first have to understand and reliably identify these structures. (Although many texts use only the terms *nonrestrictive* and *restrictive* modifiers, we prefer the terms *nonessential* and *essential* because they are more descriptive.)

1 Understand nonessential modifiers. A modifier is **nonessential** when it adds information to a sentence but can be cut without a loss of sense. Observe what happens when nonessential modifiers are removed from these sentences.

WITH NONESSENTIAL MODIFIER	The police officers, **who were wearing their dress uniforms,** marched in front of the mayor's car.
MODIFIER REMOVED	The police officers marched in front of the mayor's car.

WITH NONESSENTIAL   The chemistry building, **which had been**
MODIFIER   **erected in 1928 and badly needed repairs,**
                      was scheduled for demolition.

MODIFIER REMOVED   The chemistry building was scheduled for
                      demolition.

Useful information is sacrificed when the nonessential modifiers are
cut, but the sentences still make good sense.

■ 2 Understand essential modifiers. When you can't remove a
modifying expression from a sentence without affecting its meaning,
you have an *essential modifier*—which is not surrounded by commas.
Watch what happens when essential modifiers are removed from sentences.

ESSENTIAL MODIFIER   Diamonds **that are synthetically produced**
                          are more perfect than natural diamonds.

ESSENTIAL MODIFIER   Diamonds are more perfect than natural
REMOVED   diamonds. The sentence now makes little sense.

ESSENTIAL MODIFIER   We missed the only speaker **whose work**
                          dealt with business ethics.

ESSENTIAL MODIFIER   We missed the only speaker.
REMOVED   Removing the modifier changes the sentence significantly.

ESSENTIAL MODIFIERS   The fruit basket **that we received** was not
                          the one **we ordered.**

ESSENTIAL MODIFIERS   The fruit basket was not the one.
REMOVED   The sentence makes no sense with the essential modi-
                          fiers removed.

30i
modif

Understand, however, that context will often determine whether a
modifier is essential. Remember this sentence?

NONESSENTIAL   The police officers, **who were wearing**
                      their dress uniforms, marched in front of
                      the mayor's car.

We can make its nonessential modifier essential just by pairing the sentence with another that affects its overall meaning.

ESSENTIAL   The police officers **who were wearing**
                      their dress uniforms marched in front of
                      the mayor's car. The officers **who were in**
                      plain clothes mingled with the crowd as
                      part of a security detail.

Notice that the punctuation changes too, with the modifiers no longer surrounded by commas.

When in doubt whether a phrase or clause is essential, imagine the sentence with the modifier in parentheses. If the sentence no longer makes sense, the modifier is essential and no commas should surround it. If the parentheses work, the modifier is nonessential and should be enclosed by commas. Of course, you should always read any sentences in context.

PARENTHESES DON'T WORK	The stocks **(we bought last year)** declined in value.
MODIFIER IS ESSENTIAL	The stocks we bought last year declined in value.
PARENTHESES WORK	The oil stocks **(which luckily are only a small part of our portfolio)** declined in value last year.
MODIFIER IS NOT ESSENTIAL	The oil stocks**,** **which luckily are only a small part of our portfolio,** declined in value last year.

Any clause introduced by *that* will be essential (restrictive) and should not be surrounded by commas. (See Section 29b.)

WRONG	The committee, that I chair, meets every Monday.
RIGHT	The committee that I chair meets every Monday.

30i
modif

EXERCISE 30.9 Following the model provided, first write a sentence with a nonessential modifier. Then add a second sentence that would make the modifier in the first sentence essential. Be sure that your version shows the same changes in punctuation that occur in the model.

NONESSENTIAL	The students, who had stood for hours in line, applauded when the ticket window opened.
ESSENTIAL	The students **who had stood for hours in line** applauded when the ticket window opened. Those **who had only just arrived** despaired at ever getting seats for the game.

CHAPTER 31

Are You
an ESL Writer?

Jocelyn Steer and Carol Rhoades

As a writer whose first language is not English, you already have many skills that will help you become a more proficient and expressive writer in English. Because you have studied the grammatical systems and word usage of two or more languages, you know that ideas can be expressed in a variety of ways. You also understand that the grammatical rules and word meanings in each language limit the ways in which a writer can say something. One of the most valuable skills you will have learned by studying a second or more languages is flexibility. If you can't remember the precise word for something in another language, you quickly learn how to describe what you mean or use synonyms. You probably also know and understand words in another language which you can't quite express in your own language.

Writing in your own language is not always simple, and writing in a second language can be even harder. It's easy to become discouraged and to feel that you can't express your ideas as well as you would like. When that happens, remind yourself that the language skills you have developed have enabled you to reach college-level classes in English.

Remember, too, that this book is designed to help you learn new skills and further develop your abilities to write well in English.

This chapter offers an overview of some common problem areas for ESL (English as a Second Language) writers. We list common errors you need to be aware of as you proofread your own writing, so that you can pinpoint particular problems you have and then work to correct them. We end by identifying reference books and other resources to which you can turn for more detailed information and help. For help with grammatical and mechanical elements that can be especially tricky for ESL writers, see Chapters 32 and 33. These chapters give you detailed guidelines for choosing the proper forms of verbs, for distinguishing between count and noncount nouns, and for making many other grammatical choices. See Chapters 22 to 30 for more general discussions of grammar and mechanics. (Chart 31.2 on p. 510 lists the most relevant sections of these chapters.)

31a Common problem areas for ESL writers

It's always a good idea to proofread your papers for grammar and punctuation errors before handing in the final copy. (See Section 5c.) Reading your work aloud can help you find errors that you may not otherwise spot. You'll find that the mistakes you notice when you are proofreading are usually mistakes you know how to correct. Check your work several times before you hand it in. Many errors that instructors mark on your final drafts could probably have been corrected by more thorough proofreading.

If you know what your most common errors are, check for them first and then look for other problems. Also, make sure that you haven't unconsciously typed some words or word endings in your own language rather than English. This can happen even if you are thinking in English as you write.

In this section you'll find a series of common problems for ESL writers—and their solutions. Why not make a list of your own common mistakes, using these suggestions?

1 Be sure each clause has a subject. Every clause in English must have a subject, except for imperative sentences ("Sit down").

The subject is missing.

> INCORRECT ⌃Is difficult to write in English.
>
> CORRECT **It** is difficult to write in English.
> You must have *it* before the verb *is*.

2 Be sure a main or an auxiliary verb isn't missing from your sentence.

The main verb is missing.

> INCORRECT The teacher⌃extremely helpful. *verb missing*
> CORRECT The teacher **is** extremely helpful.

The auxiliary verb is missing.

> INCORRECT Hurry! The plane⌃leaving right now. *verb missing*
> CORRECT Hurry! The plane **is** leaving right now.

3 Don't forget the -s on verbs used with third person singular nouns and pronouns (*he, she, it*). It is easy to forget the -s on present tense verbs used with the third person singular. If this is a problem for you, check all present tense verbs in a paper to make sure you haven't forgotten an -*s*.

INCORRECT	The library close at 5:00 today. *3rd person sing. -s*
CORRECT	The library closes at 5:00 today.

When you have the auxiliary *do* or *does* in a sentence, add -*s* to the auxiliary, not to the main verb.

INCORRECT	He don't knows the answer to the question.
	3rd person sing. -s
CORRECT	He **doesn't** know the answer to the question.

4 Don't forget -*ed* endings on past participles. Check

your papers to be sure that you use the past participle (-*ed* ending) for verbs in the following cases. (See Section 23d for a list of the three parts of a verb.)

In passive voice (see Section 23e).

INCORRECT	The amenities were **provide** by the hotel.
CORRECT	The amenities were **provided** by the hotel.
INCORRECT	The documents were **alter** by the thief.
CORRECT	The documents were **altered** by the thief.

In the past perfect tense (see Section 32a-3).

INCORRECT	Juan had **finish** the race before Fred came.
CORRECT	Juan had **finished** the race before Fred came.

In participle adjectives (see Section 17c-2).

INCORRECT	She was **frighten** by the dark.
CORRECT	She was **frightened** by the dark.

Be sure that you *don't* add endings to infinitives.

INCORRECT	George started to **prepared** dinner.
CORRECT	George started to **prepare** dinner.

5 Don't confuse adjective pairs like *bored* and *boring*.

The following sentences are very different in meaning, although they look similar.

John is bored. This means that John is bored by *something*—maybe his class or his homework; it is a feeling he has as a result of something.

John is boring. This means that John has a personality that is not interesting; he is a boring person.

31a
ESL

The ending of the adjective, *-ed* or *-ing,* is what creates a difference in meaning. Adjectives ending in *-ed* have a passive meaning. Adjectives ending in *-ing* have an active meaning. (See Section 23e for an explanation of passive voice.)

The English spelling system often confuses Jorge.

-ED ENDING   Jorge is **confused** by the English spelling system. passive

The **confused** student looked up words in his spelling dictionary. passive

-ING ENDING   English spelling is **confusing**. active

It is a **confusing** system. active

Joan's work satisfies her.

-ED ENDING   She is **satisfied** by her work. passive

She is a **satisfied** employee. passive

-ING ENDING   Her work is **satisfying**. active

Joan does **satisfying** work. active

Here are some common pairs of adjectives that confuse students, along with the preposition that is used after the *-ed* adjectives.

31a
ESL

Chart 31.1

Adjective Pairs

amusing	amused by	exciting	excited by/about
annoying	annoyed by	frightening	frightened by
boring	bored by	interesting	interested in
confusing	confused by	irritating	irritated by
embarrassing	embarrassed by	satisfying	satisfied with

6 Avoid repeating sentence elements. You may find that you repeat unnecessary words in your sentences. Be on your guard for the three types of repetition shown in these examples.

In adjective clauses.

The store that I told you about ~~it~~ closed down.
It is not necessary because *that* replaces *it.*

The man whom I met ~~him~~ yesterday was kind.
Whom replaces *him.*

The school where I go ~~there~~ is very expensive.
Where replaces *there.*

In the subject of the sentence.

My brother he is the director of the hospital.

Because *my brother* and *he* refer to the same person, the *he* is unnecessary repetition.

Multiple connectors.

Although the employee was diligent, but she was fired.

Although and *but* both express contrast. You don't need two connectors in one sentence with the same meaning. You must take out one of them.

Because she fell asleep after eating a big lunch, so she missed her class.

So and *because* both express cause. Cut one of them.

7 Place adverbs correctly in the sentence.

Adverbs can appear in many different places in a sentence—at the beginning, in the middle, at the end. However, there are a few positions where adverbs *can't* be placed. Here are some guidelines. (For more help with adverb placement, see Section 30f.)

Don't put an adverb between the verb and its object.

	verb	adverb	obj.
INCORRECT	She answered (slowly) the question.		

	verb	obj.	adverb
CORRECT	She answered the question **slowly**.		

Don't place adverbs of frequency before the verb *be*.

INCORRECT   Louise (regularly) is late for class.

CORRECT   Louise is **regularly** late for class.

Don't place adverbs of frequency after other verbs.

INCORRECT   Juan arrives (often) late to class.

CORRECT   Juan **often** arrives late to class.

31a
ESL

EXERCISE 31.1 Review Section 31a. Then read the following paragraph and proofread it for the mistakes described in that section. In some cases you will need to add something and in others you will delete an element. (There are seven errors. For answers, see p. 511.)

> There are long lines at the cashier's office
> because students signing up for financial aid. Is
> extremely frustrating to spend the entire day in
> line. Because some students they have other jobs and
> classes, so they can't wait very long. Then you very
> tired when you finally arrive at the desk where you

can talk to the clerk there. The clerk usually give
you a form to fill out, and then you have to wait in
another line!

31b Finding other ESL resources

You may have questions about grammar or punctuation that aren't covered in Chapters 31–33, which deal specifically with the concerns of ESL writers. This section points you to additional resources in this book and in other publications that you can consult.

■ **1 Consult relevant material in other chapters of this book.** Many questions you have about grammar and mechanics are not specific to ESL writers. Native speakers of English will have many of these questions too. The chart below lists possible questions, each with the chapter or section in the handbook that covers that problem.

Chart 31.2

Where to Find More Help with ESL Grammar Questions

IF YOU HAVE A QUESTION ABOUT . . .	EXAMPLES	GO TO THIS CHAPTER/ SECTION
Abbreviations	Dr., APA, Ms.	42a
Adjective clauses	clauses beginning with *who, which, that*	17d, 29b, 34b
Capitalization	English, Japanese	41b-c
Comparatives/ superlatives	more interesting/the most interesting	30h
Dangling modifiers	Reading the paper, the phone rang.	30a
Irregular verbs	*sit, sat, sat*	23d
Parallelism	I like swimming and fishing	17h, 23b
Passive voice	I was hit by a car.	23e
Plural nouns	child: children	25a
Possessives	the teacher's book	25b-c
Pronouns	his gain; their loss	26–29
Punctuation	commas, periods	34–40
Sentence problems:		
Run-ons	I am a student I come from Mexico.	35d
Fragments	Because it is my house.	35a-b
Subject-verb agreement		22

If you have several areas of difficulty with grammar, focus on one at a time. Study the examples in this chapter and those in the other grammar chapters in this handbook. Also, look for examples of correct usage in your daily reading in English.

■ **2 Consult reference books especially designed for ESL writers.** Of course, a general writer's handbook like *The Scott, Foresman Handbook for Writers* cannot possibly cover all the ESL information you need. We suggest, therefore, that you refer regularly to ESL reference books for help with grammar and usage. ESL grammar textbooks can give you more detailed grammatical explanations. Some ESL dictionaries provide useful spelling and usage information. See the following list of ESL reference books.

HIGHLIGHT *References for ESL Students*

We suggest the following reference books and Web sites for ESL students who have questions about grammar and usage.

• Betty S. Azar. *Basic English Grammar (English as a Second Language).* 2nd ed. New York: Prentice Hall, 1995.

• Jocelyn Steer and Karen Carlisi. *The Advanced Grammar Book.* 2nd ed. New York: Newbury, 1997.

• *Dave's ESL Café* at <http://www.eslcafe.com/>.

• ESL Resources at OWL—the Online Writing Lab at Purdue University at <http://owl.english.purdue.edu/handouts/esl/eslstudent.html>.

• *The ESL Study Hall* at the George Washington University at <http://gwis2.circ.gwu.edu/~gwvcusas/>.

We also recommend the following dictionary written for the ESL student.

• *Longman Dictionary of American English.* 2nd ed. New York: Longman, 1997.

31b
ESL

ANSWER KEY

EXERCISE 31.1

There are long lines at the cashier's office because students **are** signing up for financial aid. **It** is extremely frustrating to spend the entire day in line. Because some students they have other jobs and classes, so they can't wait very long. Then you **are** very tired when you finally arrive at the desk where you can talk to the clerk there The clerk usually **gives** you a form to fill out, and then you have to wait in another line!

CHAPTER 32

ESL Questions About Verbs?

Jocelyn Steer and Carol Rhoades

English verbs are complicated. If you are a nonnative speaker, you will probably still have questions about them, even after many years of studying English. For example, do you have difficulty deciding between "I have lived in the United States for a year" and "I lived in the United States for a year"? Should you write "She is liking the class very much" or "She likes the class very much"? Are you still confused about transitive and intransitive verbs? This section will answer some of your verb questions.

32a Which verb tense should you use?

A verb's tense expresses time. Chart 32.1 shows the twelve most commonly used verb tenses, along with a list of common adverbs and expressions that accompany them. These words and phrases are the signposts that help you choose the best verb tense. A diagram illustrates the timeline for each tense; in the diagram, **X** indicates an action and a curved line indicates an action in progress.

The remainder of this section explains how to use these tenses appropriately. For more information on verbs, see Chapter 23.

Chart 32.1

Verb Tenses			
WHAT IT IS CALLED	WHAT IT LOOKS LIKE	WHAT IT DESCRIBES	TIME WORDS USED WITH IT
Simple present	• I *sleep* eight hours every day.	Habits, regular activities	• every day • often • regularly • always
——X——	• Water *freezes* at 0°C.	Facts, general truths	• usually • habitually

WHAT IT IS CALLED	WHAT IT LOOKS LIKE	WHAT IT DESCRIBES	TIME WORDS USED WITH IT
Simple past	• I *slept* only four hours yesterday. • He *went* to sleep three hours ago.	A finished action in the past	• yesterday • last year • ago
Simple future	• I *will* try to sleep more. • I *am going to sleep* early tonight.	A single action in the future A planned action in the future (use *be going to*)	• tomorrow • in *x* days • next year
Present perfect	• I *have* already *written* my paper. • I *have lived* here for three months.	A past action that occurred at an unspecified time in the past An action that started in the past and continues to the present	• already • yet • before • recently • so far • for + time period • since + date
Past perfect	• She *had* already *slept* three hours when the burglar broke into the house.	One action in the past that occurs before another action in the past	• when • after • before • by the time
Future perfect	• I *will have finished* the paper when you stop by tonight.	One action in the future that will be completed before another action in the future	• by the time • when
Present progressive	• He *is sleeping* now.	A continuous activity in progress now	• right now • at this time • this week/year

32a
ESL verb

(Continued)

Verb Tenses *(Continued)*

WHAT IT IS CALLED	WHAT IT LOOKS LIKE	WHAT IT DESCRIBES	TIME WORDS USED WITH IT
Past progressive	• While he *was sleeping*, the telephone rang. • He *was sleeping* at 10 a.m.	A continuous activity in progress in the past; often interrupted by another time or action	• while • during that time • between *x* and *y*
Future progressive	• I *will be sleeping* all day.	A continuous activity happening in the future	• all the while • during that time • between *x* and *y*
Present perfect progressive	• The woman *has been waiting* for many hours. • He *has been sleeping* since eight o'clock.	A continuous activity that began in the past and continues to the present; emphasis is on the duration	• for + time period • since + exact date
Past perfect progressive	• She *had been waiting* for three hours before he arrived. • He *had been sleeping* an hour when the train crashed.	A continuous activity in the past that is finished before another action in the past	• for • since
Future perfect progressive	• I *will have been sleeping* for twelve hours by the time you arrive.	A continuing future activity which started before another future event	• by • when

32a
ESL verb

1 Review the difference between the simple present tense and the present progressive tense. You may be confused because the simple present tense doesn't really refer to an action going on in the present; rather, it is used to talk about repeated and habitual actions. You should use the simple present tense when you want to talk about *regular, repeated* activity.

SIMPLE PRESENT	The mail carrier usually **arrives** at 10 a.m. This is an activity that is repeated daily.
PRESENT PROGRESSIVE	Look! She **is putting** the mail in the box now. This is an activity occurring at the moment of speaking—now.
PRESENT PROGRESSIVE	She **is delivering** mail for John this month. This is an activity that is in progress over a period of time. Use the progressive tense with the expression *this + time period.*

2 Review nonaction verbs and the present tense. Some verbs in English can't be used in a progressive form because they express a state and not an activity. Nonaction verbs include verbs of existence, of thought, of emotions, and of sense perceptions. Chart 32.2 lists some of these verbs. To use one of these nonaction verbs, you must use a simple form of the verb even though the time intended is *now.*

INCORRECT	I can't study because I **am hearing** my roommate's singing.
CORRECT	I can't study because I **hear** my roommate's singing.
INCORRECT	Maria **is preferring** Carlos's apartment to her own.
CORRECT	Maria **prefers** Carlos's apartment to her own.

32a
ESL verb

Chart 32.2

Nonaction Verbs*

appear	forget	owe	seem
be	hate	own	smell
belong	have	possess	sound
consist	hear	prefer	surprise
contain	know	recognize	taste
deserve	like	remember	think
desire	love	require	understand
dislike	mean	resemble	want
feel	need	see	wish

*There are exceptions to the nonaction rule ("I **am thinking** about getting a job"; "He **is seeing** a doctor about his insomnia"). These exceptions can usually be paraphrased using other verbs ("He **is seeing** a doctor about his insomnia" means "He **is consulting** a doctor about his insomnia"). You will need to keep a list of these exceptions as you come across them.

■ **3 Review the difference between the simple past tense and the present perfect tense.** If an action happened in the past and is finished, you can always use the simple past tense to describe it. (See Chapter 23 on how to form the past tense and for a list of irregular verbs.) Often you will also use a time word like *ago* or *yesterday* to show the specific time of the past action.

> SIMPLE PAST   My brother **saw** that movie three days ago.
> We know exactly when the brother saw the movie—three days ago. You *must* use the simple past in this sentence.

Use the **past tense** to show that something is completed, and use the **present perfect tense** to indicate that the action may continue or that it still has the possibility of occurring in the future. Compare these sentences to see how the two tenses express different ideas.

> SIMPLE PAST   My grandmother never **used** a computer.
> This implies that the grandmother may no longer be alive.
>
> PRESENT   My mother **has** never **used** a computer.
> PERFECT   This sentence indicates that the mother is still alive and may use a computer in the future.

When you don't know or you don't want to state the exact time or date of a past action, use the present perfect tense.

> PRESENT   Sarah **has seen** that movie before.
> PERFECT   We don't know when Sarah saw the movie; she saw it at an unspecified time in the past.

You must use the present perfect for an action that began in the past and continues up to the present moment, especially when you use the time words *for* and *since*.

> PRESENT   This theater **has shown** the same film for
> PERFECT   three months! I hope they change it soon.
> The action started in the past—three months ago—and continues to the present. The film is still playing.

■ **4 Review the difference between the present perfect tense and the present perfect progressive tense.** You can use a **present perfect progressive** tense to show that an action is still in progress.

> PRESENT PERFECT   Catherine **has been writing** that letter since
> PROGRESSIVE   this morning. She hasn't finished; she's still writing.

In general, when the statement emphasizes *duration* (length of time), you need to use a present perfect progressive tense.

> PRESENT PERFECT My best friend **has been writing** her novel for
> PROGRESSIVE five years.
> This tells us how long the friend has been writing; the emphasis is on duration, or length of time.

However, when the statement emphasizes *quantity* (how much), you will use a **present perfect tense.**

> PRESENT PERFECT Toni Morrison **has written** several well-received novels.
> This tells us how many books; it talks about quantity.

EXERCISE 32.1 Review Sections 32a-1 and 32a-2. Choose the correct tense—simple present or present progressive. (For answers, see p. 528.)

1. Many people have bizarre dreams, but I usually (**dream/am dreaming**) about something that (**happens/is happening**) during the day.

2. I often (**remember/am remembering**) my dreams right after I (**wake/am waking**) up.

3. Sometimes when I (**hear/am hearing**) a noise while I (**dream/am dreaming**), I will incorporate that into my dream.

4. I (**know/am knowing**) a lot about dreams because I (**write/am writing**) a paper about them this semester.

5. To prepare for the paper, I (**research/am researching**) many psychological explanations for various dream symbols, such as snakes, bodies of water, and people.

6. I'm not sure that I (**believe/am believing**) those explanations, but they are very interesting.

EXERCISE 32.2 Review Section 32a-3. Choose the best verb tense—simple past or present perfect. Use the present perfect whenever possible. (For answers, see p. 528.)

1. This month the newspapers (**had/have had**) many articles about a phenomenon called the glass ceiling.

2. This refers to an unofficial limitation on promotion for women who (**worked/have worked**) in a corporation for several years and who cannot advance beyond middle management.

32a
ESL verb

3. Last year my mother (**applied/has applied**) for the position of vice president of the company she works for, but they (**did not promote/have not promoted**) her.

4. She (**had/has had**) the most experience of all the candidates for the job, but a man was chosen instead.

5. She (**was/has been**) with that company for ten years. Now she doesn't know how much longer she will stay there.

EXERCISE 32.3 Review Section 32a. Fill in the blanks with the most precise and appropriate tense of the verb *talk*. Pay special attention to time words. Incorporate the adverbs in parentheses into your answers. (For answers, see p. 528.)

1. They _____ about the issue since yesterday.

2. Some employees _____ about it when we arrived at work.

3. They _____ (**probably**) about the issue when they leave work.

4. We _____ about it many times in the past.

5. I never _____ about this topic last week.

6. We _____ about this problem for two hours by the time the president visited our office.

7. Workers _____ about this issue quite often these days.

8. They _____ about the subject right now.

9. After they _____ about it for many weeks, they reached a consensus.

10. They _____ (**never**) about this issue again.

32b How do you use transitive and intransitive verbs?

A **transitive verb** is a verb that has a direct object. This means that the verb has an effect on, or does something to, that object. The verb *raise* in the sentence "She raised her children" is transitive because the subject of the sentence (*she*) is acting on someone else (*her children*). Without the direct object (*her children*), this sentence would be incomplete; it would not make sense.

INCORRECT	She raised.
	This thought is incomplete; we need to know *what* she raised.
CORRECT	She raised **her children** on a farm.

There are two types of transitive verbs. (See Chart 32.3 on page 520 for a list of them.) One type—verb + direct object—*must* be followed directly by a noun or pronoun.

VERB + DIRECT OBJECT (trans. v. = transitive verb)

subj.   trans. v.   noun
This university **needs** more parking lots.

subj.   trans. v.   pronoun
The trustees **discussed** it at the last meeting.

The second type—verb + (indirect object) + direct object—*can* be followed by an indirect object (a person receiving the action) before the direct object. When you use *to* or *for* in front of the indirect object, the position changes, as you can see in the following examples.

VERB + (INDIRECT OBJECT) + DIRECT OBJECT

dir. obj.
Ron bought **a rose.**

indir. obj.   dir. obj.
Ron bought his wife **a rose.**

or

dir. obj. + *for/to* + dir. obj.
Ron bought **a rose** *for his wife.*

An **intransitive verb** is complete without a direct object. In fact, you cannot put a direct object after an intransitive verb.

INCORRECT	She grew up **her children.** *Her children* cannot come after the verb *grew up* because *her children* is an object; objects cannot come after intransitive verbs.

However, other words can come after intransitive verbs.

CORRECT	She grew up **quickly.** *Quickly* is an adverb. You can put an adverb after this verb. This sentence means that she matured at a very fast rate.
CORRECT	She grew up **on a farm.** *On a farm* is a prepositional phrase, not a direct object.

There are two kinds of intransitive verbs—linking verbs and action verbs. (See Chart 32.3 on p. 520 for a list of these verbs.)

	subj. l.v. comp.
LINKING	This book **seems** very old. l.v. = linking verb
VERBS	subj. l.v. comp.
	Your professor **is** an expert in law.

32b
ESL verb

subj.   a.v.
ACTION VERBS   Jacqueline **complained.** a.v. = action verb

subj.   a.v.   prep. phrase
Jacqueline **complained** to me before breakfast.

(For more information on transitive and intransitive verbs, see Section 23e.)

Chart 32.3

Transitive and Intransitive Verbs

TRANSITIVE VERBS*

• **Verb + direct object:** attend, bring up, choose, do, have, hit, hold, keep, lay, need, raise, say, spend, use, want, watch, wear

• **Verb + (indirect object) + direct object:** bring, buy, get, give, make, pay, send, take, tell

INTRANSITIVE VERBS*

• **Linking verbs:** appear, be, become, seem, look

• **Action verbs:** arrive, come, get dressed, go, grow up, laugh, lie, listen, live, rise, run, sit, sleep, walk, work

---

*These lists are not complete. You can always consult your dictionary to find out whether a verb is transitive or intransitive.

32c
ESL verb

32c How do you use two-word and three-word verbs?

Some verbs in English consist of two or three words, usually a main verb and a preposition. These verbs are **idioms** because you can't understand the meaning of the verb simply by knowing the separate meaning of each of the two or three words. For example, the verb *put* has a completely different meaning from the verb *put off* ("to postpone"), and the verb *put up with* ("to tolerate") has yet another distinct meaning. There are many two- and three-word verbs in English. Since it would be difficult to memorize all of them, it's best for you to learn them as you hear them and to keep a list of them for reference. Chart 32.4 on pages 521–22 lists common two- and three-word verbs.

Two-word verbs that are transitive—which means they can have a direct object—are divided into two groups: **separable** and **inseparable.** (See Section 32b for an explanation of transitive verbs.)

■ **1 Separable verbs.** You can place the object *before* or *after* the preposition.

CORRECT   Lee checked **the book** *out* from the library.
The object (*the book*) is placed *before* the preposition (*out*).

CORRECT   Lee checked *out* **the book** from the library.
The object comes *after* the preposition.

However, whenever the object is a *pronoun* (such as *it* in the following example), the pronoun *must* come *before* the preposition.

INCORRECT   Gary checked out **it** from the library.
CORRECT   Gary checked **it** out from the library.

■ **2 Inseparable verbs.** You cannot separate the verb and the preposition.

INCORRECT   My sister **majored** history **in.**
CORRECT   My sister **majored in** history.

INCORRECT   The frantic student **stayed** all night **up** to study.
CORRECT   The frantic student **stayed up** all night to study.

INCORRECT   Please **after** your brother **look.**
CORRECT   Please **look after** your brother.

INCORRECT   The detective **looked** the case **into.**
CORRECT   The detective **looked into** the case.

32c
ESL verb

Chart 32.4

Common Two-Word and Three-Word Verbs

Here are some common two-word and three-word verbs. Such verbs have two parts: the main verb and one (or more) prepositions. This list is not complete; there are many more such verbs. An asterisk (*) indicates an *inseparable* verb: the verb and the preposition cannot be separated by an object. A cross (+) indicates verbs that have additional meanings not given here.

VERB	DEFINITION
break down*	stop functioning
bring on	cause something to happen
call off	cancel
catch up with*+	attain the same position, place
check into*	explore, investigate
come across*	encounter unintentionally
cut down on*	reduce the amount of

(Continued)

Common Two-Word and Three-Word Verbs *(Continued)*

VERB	DEFINITION
do over	repeat
figure out	solve a problem, dilemma
find out	discover
get along with*	have harmonious relations
get in* +	enter a car
get off* +	exit from (a bus, a train, a plane)
get on*	enter (a bus, a train, a plane)
get over*	recover from (a sickness, a relationship)
give up	stop trying
go over*	review
grow up*	mature, become an adult
keep up with*	maintain the same level
look after*	take care of
look into*	explore, investigate
make up+	invent
pass away*	die
pick out	make a selection
put off	postpone
put up with*	tolerate
run into* +	meet by chance
show up*	appear, arrive
stand up for*	defend, support
sum up	summarize, conclude
take after*	resemble, look alike
touch on*	discuss briefly

EXERCISE 32.4 Review Sections 32a, 32b, and 32c. Each of the following sentences contains errors related to verb tense, transitive/intransitive verbs, and two-word verbs. Identify the errors and correct them. (For answers, see p. 528.)

1. Before I study psychology, I thought it was an easy subject.

2. Now I am knowing that it isn't easy.

3. It has had a lot of statistics.

4. I am studying psychology since April, and I only begin to learn some of the concepts.

5. I have been tried to learn more of the concepts every day.

6. Last night I have studied from 9:00 to midnight.

7. I went my adviser last Monday.

8. She told to me to see her after class.

9. But when I went to see her after class, she already left.

10. It's January. By the middle of June, I have studied psychology for six months.

32d Which modal should you use?

You already know that a verb's tense expresses time. A *modal,* which is an auxiliary or helping verb, expresses an attitude about a situation. For example, if you want to be polite, you can say, "Open the door, please." To be even more polite, you can add a modal auxiliary verb: "*Would* you open the door, please?" Modals are used to express necessity, obligation, regret, and formality. Modals can be used to express ideas about the past, present, or future.

> PAST I **could** speak Japanese as a child.
> PRESENT My brother **can** speak Japanese now.
> FUTURE I **might** learn another language next semester.

You probably already know the common modals, such as *should, must,* and *have to.* However, you may have questions about others, such as *had better,* or perhaps you are uncertain about the difference between, for example, *have to* and *ought to.* In this section we list the modals by their uses or functions and provide a list of common modal errors to avoid.

32d
ESL verb

1 Choose the modal that best expresses your idea.
Chart 32.5 (pp. 524–25) summarizes the functions of modals. It also lists the past form of the modals. Modals in the present are followed by the base form of the verb—for example, "Kim **may** win the prize" (subject + modal + base form of the verb). The form of modals in the past varies. (See Section 32d-3 for more details.)

2 Use the correct form of the modal auxiliary and the main verb that follows it.
Modals that express present and future time have this form.

> SUBJECT + MODAL + BASE FORM OF VERB
> Clarissa **had better** register for classes soon.

Chart 32.5

Modals

WHAT IT MEANS	PRESENT OR FUTURE FORM	PAST FORM
Permission		
(*Informal → Formal*)		
can	**Can** I be excused?	He **could have**
could	**Could** I be excused?	**been** excused, but
may	**May** I be excused?	he didn't ask.
would you mind*	**Would you mind** if I *brought* my dog?	**Would you have minded** if I *had brought* my dog?
Ability		
can	Joe **can** drive a car.	He **couldn't** drive a car last year.
be able to	Carl **is able to** study and listen to music at the same time.	Celia **was never able to** play the Mozart concertos.
Advice		
should	You **should** quit.	He **should have**
ought to	You **ought to** quit.	quit last year.
had better	You **had better** quit.	He didn't quit; this sentence shows regret.
Necessity		
have to	He **has to** pay a fine.	He **had to** pay a fine last week.
must	She **must** pay her taxes.	No past form; use *had to*.
Lack of necessity		
not have to	You **don't have to** attend school in summer.	He **didn't have to** take the final exam last year.
not need to	You **don't need to** pay in advance.	You **didn't need to** pay in advance.

Would you mind is followed by *if* + the past tense of the verb.

WHAT IT MEANS	PRESENT OR FUTURE FORM	PAST FORM
Possibility		
(*More sure → Less sure*)		
can	It **can** get cold in May.	No past form.
may	It **may** get cold in June this year.	I'm not sure, but it **may have** just happened.
could	It **could** get cold in July this year.	It **could have** just happened.
might	It **might** get cold in July this year.	It **might have** just happened.
Conclusion		
must	Your eyes are all red; you **must have** allergies. I'm almost certain that this is true.	You got an *A* on your test. You **must have studied** hard! I'm certain that you did this in the past.
Expectation		
should/ ought to	Your keys **should be** on the desk where I left them. I expect them to be there.	John **should have been** elected. He didn't get elected, but I expected him to.
Polite requests		
(*Informal → Formal*)		
can	**Can** you give me a hand?	No past forms.
will	**Will** you give me a hand?	
could	**Could** you give me a hand?	
would you mind + present participle	**Would you mind giving** me a hand?	

32d
ESL verb

Here are specific tips to help you with modal formation.

- Don't use *to* or a present participle (*-ing* form of a verb) after the modal.

INCORRECT   Jacquie **can** t~~o~~ play the guitar very well.
CORRECT   Jacquie **can** play the guitar very well.

INCORRECT   **Must** I t~~o~~ hand in this paper tomorrow?
CORRECT   **Must** I hand in this paper tomorrow?

EXCEPT   We **have to** write a ten-page paper.

INCORRECT   They **should** readi~~ng~~ before class.
CORRECT   They **should read** before class.

- There is no *-s* on the third person singular of a modal.

INCORRECT   Kwang **might**~~s~~ go to graduate school.
CORRECT   Kwang **might** go to graduate school.

- Never use two modals together.

INCORRECT   They **might** co~~uld~~ drive all night.
CORRECT   They **might** drive all night.

- *Do, does,* and *did* are not used in questions with modals, except for the modal *have to.*

32d
ESL verb

INCORRECT   **Do** I **must** answer all the questions?
CORRECT   **Must** I answer all the questions?

EXCEPT   **Do** I **have to** answer all the questions?

- *Do, does,* and *did* are not used in negative statements with modals; use *not* instead, placed after the modal.

INCORRECT   They **do not can** enter the test room.
CORRECT   They **cannot** enter the test room.

INCORRECT   Jorge **did not could** have worked any harder.
CORRECT   Jorge **could not have** worked any harder.

3 Use the perfect form to express past time.

As you can see from the chart of modals on pages 524–25, many modals have a past form. The past of modals that give advice or express possibility, expectation, and conclusion have a *perfect* verb form (modal + *have* + past participle), as you can see in the following examples.

ADVICE   Gail **should have taken** that marketing job last year. Gail didn't take the job.

POSSIBILITY   Although he chose not to, Bob **could have gone** to Mexico over spring break. Bob didn't go to Mexico.

EXPECTATION   Where is Sue? She **should have been** here by now. Sue hasn't arrived yet.

CONCLUSION   Ted finished; he **must have worked** all night.

EXERCISE 32.5 Review Section 32d-1. Fill in the blanks with a modal from the list below. More than one answer is possible for each blank. Try to use each modal only once. (For answers, see p. 528.)

would	must	have to	ought to	should have
should	can	might	had better	must have

1. Can you believe the line waiting to see the movie *Gladiator?* That _____ be a good movie!

2. Where is my purse, Mom? It _____ be on the table where you put it last night.

3. I'm sorry, Professor Jones, but I _____ not take the test tomorrow because I _____ go to Immigration about my visa.

4. Jason, you _____ eat your vegetables or you won't get any dessert.

32d
ESL verb

EXERCISE 32.6 Review Section 32d. Each of the following sentences contains errors related to modal auxiliaries. Identify the errors and correct them. (For answers, see p. 528.)

1. Megan's boss told her, "You had better to improve your attitude, or we will have to take disciplinary action."

2. Megan was very distressed by this news; she did not could understand the basis for her boss's complaints.

3. She tried to think of things that she had done wrong. She knew that she should had been more enthusiastic at the last meeting, but she felt she couldn't be hypocritical. She simply didn't agree with her boss.

4. Megan was really worried. Her boss mights send her a "pink slip," which would mean that she had been fired.

·· ANSWER KEY ···

EXERCISE 32.1
1. dream; happens
2. remember; wake
3. hear; am dreaming
4. know; am writing
5. am researching
6. believe

EXERCISE 32.2
1. have had
2. have worked
3. applied; did not promote
4. had
5. has been

EXERCISE 32.3
1. have been talking
2. were talking
3. will probably be talking
4. have talked
5. talked
6. had been talking
7. are talking (or talk)
8. are talking
9. had talked
10. will never talk

EXERCISE 32.4
1. Before I **studied** psychology, I **(had) thought** it was an easy subject.
2. Now I **know** that it isn't easy.
3. It **has** a lot of statistics.
4. I **have been studying** psychology since April, and I **have only begun** to learn some of the concepts.
5. I **have been trying** to learn more of the concepts every day.

6. Last night I **was studying** from 9:00 to midnight.
or
Last night I **studied** from 9:00 to midnight.
7. I went **to** my adviser last Monday.
8. She told ~to~ me to see her after class.
9. But when I went to see her after class, she **had** already **left**.
10. It's January. By the middle of June, I **will have studied** psychology for six months.

EXERCISE 32.5
1. must; should
2. should; ought to; must; had better
3. cannot/might have to; might/should
4. had better; must; should; ought to

EXERCISE 32.6
1. Megan's boss told her, "You had better ~to~ improve your attitude, or we will have to take disciplinary action."
2. Megan was very distressed by this news; she **could not** (*or* **did not**) understand the basis for her boss's complaints.
3. She tried to think of things that she had done wrong. She knew that she **should have been** more enthusiastic at the last meeting, but she felt she couldn't be hypocritical. She simply didn't agree with her boss.
4. Megan was really worried. Her boss **might** ~to~ send her a "pink slip," which would mean that she had been fired.

CHAPTER 33

ESL Questions About Gerunds, Infinitives, Articles, or Number?

Jocelyn Steer and Carol Rhoades

This chapter offers guidelines for handling several grammatical concepts that many ESL writers find confusing: gerunds, infinitives, articles, and number agreement. If you have learned British English but will now be writing American English, you should pay special attention to the material in Section 33b on articles and count/noncount nouns, for there are differences between the British and American rules.

33a How do you use gerunds and infinitives?

The many functions of gerunds and infinitives in English may be confusing to you. (See Section 24a for definitions of *gerund* and *infinitive*.)

Gerunds can function as subject, object, complement, and object of a preposition. (See Sections 17a-1 and 28b for explanations of *complement* and *object of a preposition*.)

subj.
Finding a parking space is impossible here!
obj.
George enjoys **reading** for half an hour before bed.
comp.
His favorite hobby is **cooking.**
obj. prep.
She is afraid of **flying.**

An **infinitive** can be the subject of a sentence, and it can be the object of a verb.

subj.
To find a parking space here is impossible!
obj.
My sister hopes **to be** a marine biologist.

ESL writers often have difficulty with gerunds and infinitives that act as objects in a sentence. This section will focus on the problem.

1 Review which form—gerund or infinitive—to use. You already know that some verbs in English are followed by gerunds and other verbs are followed by infinitives.

INFINITIVE (*TO* + BASE FORM OF VERB)
I want **to go** with you.

GERUND (BASE FORM OF VERB + *-ING*)
He enjoys **jogging** in the park.

Other verbs, however, can have *either* a gerund or an infinitive after them without a difference in meaning.

GERUND OR INFINITIVE (NO CHANGE IN MEANING)
gerund
The dog began **barking** at midnight.
infinitive
The dog began **to bark** at midnight.
These two sentences have exactly the same meaning.

Finally, some verbs in English (including *forget, regret, remember, stop, try*) can be followed by *either* a gerund or an infinitive, but with a change in meaning.

GERUND OR INFINITIVE (CHANGE IN MEANING)
Paul stopped **working** in the cafeteria. Paul *no longer* works in the cafeteria.

Paul stopped his tennis game early **to work** on his homework.
Paul stopped his game *in order to* work on his homework.

Paul forgot **to visit** his cousin while he was in Mexico.
He did *not* visit his cousin.

Paul will never forget **visiting** Mexico.
Paul visited Mexico and he will always remember the trip.

Native speakers know intuitively whether to use a gerund or an infinitive after a verb, but this is not usually true for ESL students.

Chart 33.1 on page 531 and Chart 33.2 on pages 531–32 can help you; be sure to keep these charts handy for reference when you are writing.

2 Review when a verb must be followed by a noun or a pronoun. As we've seen, some verbs in English (called *transitive verbs*) need to have a noun or pronoun after them. For example, when you use *tell* in a sentence, you need a direct object (*What did you tell?*) or an indirect object (*Whom did you tell?*) to complete the sentence.

33a
ESL

Chart 33.1
Verbs Followed by Gerunds or Infinitives

VERB + INFINITIVE
These verbs are followed by **infinitives**.

afford	consent	intend	pretend
agree	decide	learn	promise
appear	deserve	manage	refuse
arrange	expect	mean	seem
ask	fail	need	threaten
beg	hesitate	offer	wait
claim	hope	plan	wish

VERB + GERUND
These verbs are followed by **gerunds**.

admit	deny	mention	recommend
anticipate	discuss	miss	resent
appreciate	dislike	postpone	resist
avoid	enjoy	practice	risk
complete	finish	quit	suggest
consider	can't help	recall	tolerate
delay	keep	recollect	understand

VERB + GERUND OR INFINITIVE
These verbs can be followed by either a **gerund** or an **infinitive**, with no change in meaning.

begin	can't stand	hate	prefer
can't bear	continue	like	start

33a
ESL

Chart 33.2
Verbs Followed by Gerunds or Infinitives with a Change in Meaning

VERB + GERUND OR INFINITIVE
These verbs can be followed by either a **gerund** or an **infinitive**, but the meaning of the sentence will change depending on which one you use.

VERB	MEANING
try (to be)	make an attempt to be
try (being)	do an experiment
regret (to be)	feel sorry about
regret (being)	feel sorry about *past* action

(Continued)

Verbs Followed by Gerunds or Infinitives with a Change *(Continued)*

remember (to be)	not forget
remember (being)	recall, bring to mind
forget (to be)	not remember
(never) forget (being)	always remember
stop (to be)	stop in order to be
stop (being)	interrupt an action

> INCORRECT   I told₌to write me a letter.
> The object is missing; the sentence is incomplete.

> CORRECT   I told **my son** to write me a letter.
> *My son* is the indirect object; this sentence is complete.

Remember that an *infinitive verb* comes after transitive verb + noun or pronoun constructions. The chart below lists the verbs that follow this pattern.

Chart 33.3

Verbs Followed by Nouns, Pronouns, or Infinitives

VERB + (NOUN OR PRONOUN) + INFINITIVE
These verbs must be followed by a **noun** or a **pronoun** + an **infinitive**.

advise	forbid	persuade
allow	force	remind
cause	hire	require
challenge	instruct	tell
convince	invite	urge
encourage	order	warn

33a
ESL

3 Instead of being followed by an infinitive, the verbs *have, make,* and *let* are followed by a noun or pronoun and the base form of the verb. This means that you omit *to* before the verb.

> HAVE   I **had** my mother *cut* my hair.
> Here *had* means to cause someone to do something.

> MAKE   The teacher **made** him *leave* the class.
> Here *made* means to force someone to do something; it is stronger than *had*.

> LET   Professor Betts **let** the class *leave* early.
> Here *let* means to allow someone to do something.

■ **4 Use a gerund after a preposition.** Many verbs are followed by prepositions. Sometimes adjectives are followed by prepositions. Always remember to use a gerund, not an infinitive, after prepositions. Here are two common sentence patterns with prepositions followed by gerunds.

>   verb   adj.   prep.   gerund
> Carla has been very worried **about passing** her statistics class.
>   verb   prep.   gerund
> Mrs. Short apologized **for interrupting** our conversation.

The chart below lists common preposition combinations with verbs and adjectives.

Chart 33.4

Common Verb (+ Adjective) + Preposition Constructions

be accustomed to	be faithful to	pray for
be afraid of	be familiar with	prevent from
approve of	be fond of	prohibit from
be aware of	be good at	protect from
believe in	be grateful to	be proud of
be capable of	be guilty of	rely on
be committed to	hope for	be responsible for
complain about	insist on	be satisfied with
be composed of	be interested in	be scared of
consist of	be jealous of	stop from
depend on	look forward to	succeed in
be disappointed in	be made of	take advantage of
be divorced from	be married to	take care of
dream of/about	object to	be tired of
be envious of	be opposed to	be worried about
be excited about	be patient with	

33a
ESL

EXERCISE 33.1 Fill in the blanks with the infinitive, gerund, or base form of the verbs in parentheses. (For answers, see p. 540.)

1. Women who have not wanted (**work**) _____ because of health threats can now relax.

2. A recent study completed in Rancho Bernardo, California, shows that women who work outside the home seem (**have**) _____ fewer health problems than those who work inside the home.

3. Another federal study reports that women employed outside the home do not risk (**have**) _____ more "stress-induced" heart attacks than women working inside the home.

4. In fact, this study appears (**support**) _____ the benefits of working outside the home for women.

5. In general, working women are found (**be**) _____ both physically and mentally healthier than women who stay at home.

6. Many working women will appreciate (**hear**) _____ that their
chances for depression actually increase if they decide (**drop**)
_____ out of the work force.

7. These studies do not pretend (**decide**) _____ for women what is
best for them.

8. However, the studies might help some women (**make**) _____ a
decision about (**go**) _____ back to work outside the home or
about (**quit**) _____ their jobs because they have children at home.

33b Questions about articles and number agreement?

Are you sometimes confused about which article to use—*a, an,* or
the? Do you know when no article should be used? Are you still uncertain about whether to use *a few* or *a little* before some nouns? If so, you
are certainly not alone; many ESL students ask these questions. This
section gives you general guidelines about articles and expressions of
quantity. For the finer points about article use that are not covered
here, we suggest that you consult one of the ESL grammar references
listed on page 511.

1 Decide whether the noun is count or noncount. Before
you can know which article to use, you will need to determine whether
the noun in question is *count* or *noncount.* A **count noun** refers to
something that you can count or that you can divide easily.

COUNT NOUNS   There are sixty **seconds** in one **minute.**
Joan bought six **books** for her class.

When there is more than one of the noun (*seconds*), the count noun
must be plural. (See Section 25a for a discussion of plural nouns.) If
there is only one (e.g., *one minute*), the count noun is singular.

A **noncount noun** generally refers to something that cannot usually be counted or divided. Noncount nouns include **mass nouns** such
as materials (*wood, plastic, wool*), food items (*cheese, rice, meat*) and liq-
uids (*water, milk*), and **abstract nouns** (*beauty, knowledge, glory*).

NONCOUNT NOUNS   Joe drank a lot of **milk** as a teenager.
"Give me **liberty** or give me **death!**"

Some nouns that are noncount in English may seem like things that you can count, such as *money*. Many other noncount nouns in English can confuse ESL students: *furniture, hair, traffic, information, advice*. It is always a good idea to consult an ESL dictionary or grammar book when you are unsure whether a noun is count or noncount.

Unlike count nouns, which can be singular or plural, noncount nouns have only the singular form. In addition, since you can't count these nouns, you can't use numbers or words that express number (*several, many*) to describe them. You will use other types of expressions to indicate quantity for noncount nouns; these expressions, called *quantifiers*, are discussed in Section 33b-5.

Most nouns are either count or noncount. However, some noncount nouns can change to have a count meaning. Using a noncount noun as a count noun usually limits the noncount noun in some way. For example, imagine you are at a restaurant and your English-speaking friend asks the waiter, "Can we have three waters, please?" You are confused because you learned that *water* is a noncount noun, but your friend has used it in the plural form, with a number. In this case, *three waters* means *three glasses of water,* and it is acceptable to say that. Other instances in which a noncount noun changes to a count noun include when you mean *an instance of, a serving of,* or *a type of* the noncount noun.

> count noun
> I Iis grandmother started a **business.**   one instance of business
> count noun
> I'd like two **coffees** to go, please.   two servings of coffee
> count noun
> There are three new **wines** on the menu.   three kinds of wine

33b
ESL

■ **2 Decide whether the count noun requires a definite article (*the*) or an indefinite article (*a/an*).** When the count noun is singular, you'll need an article, either *a/an* or *the,* in front of it. How do you know which article to use? Generally, when you introduce the noun, without having referred to it before, then you will use the *indefinite* article, *a* or *an*. (See Section 25d for the difference between *a* and *an*.)

INDEFINITE MEANING
Bob: I just signed up for a literature class.
Ted: Oh, really? I didn't know you were interested in that.
This is the first time Bob has mentioned the class to Ted.

After that, when both of them know what is being discussed, Bob will use the *definite* article, *the*.

DEFINITE MEANING
Bob: Can you believe **the** class meets on Friday evenings?
Both Bob and Ted now share the same information.

Note how the same guidelines apply to written English in the following sentences on homelessness.

There are several reasons why **a** person may end up homeless. Perhaps **the** person lost his or her job and could not pay for **an** apartment. Or perhaps **the** apartment was sold to **a** new owner who raised the rent. **The** new owner may not realize how expensive the rent is for that person.

Certain other situations also require the definite article, *the*.

* When there is only one of the noun.

  The earth is round.   There is only one earth.

* When the noun is superlative.

  This is **the best** brand you can buy.
  There can only be one brand that is the best.

* When the noun is limited. You will usually use *the* before a noun that has been limited in some way to show that you are referring to a *specific* example of the noun.

  The book **that I read** is informative.
  That I read limits the book to a specific one.

  The book **on George W. Bush** is out.   *On George W. Bush* limits the book.

If you are making a *generalization,* however, *the* is not always used.

  A book **on plants** can make a nice gift.
  On plants limits the noun, but the sentence does not refer to a specific book on plants—it refers to *any or all books on plants*. The definite article, *the,* would not be correct here.

▇3 **Choose articles before general nouns carefully.** When you want to make generalizations, choosing the correct article can be tricky. As a rule, use *a/an* or *the* with most *singular count nouns* to make generalizations.

  A dog can be good company for **a** lonely person.
  Use *a/an* to mean any dog, one of many dogs.

The computer has changed the banking industry dramatically.
Use *the* to mean *the computer in general.*

The spotted owl is an endangered species.

The capitalist believes in free enterprise.
Use *the* to make general statements about specific species of animals (*spotted owl*) or groups of people (*capitalists*).

He was ill and went to **the** hospital.
American English uses the definite article with *hospital* even when we do not refer to a specific hospital; British English does not use the article with *hospital.*

Use a *plural count noun* to make general statements, without *the.*

Capitalists believe in free enterprise.
Computers have changed the banking industry dramatically.

Finally, *noncount nouns* in general statements do not have an article in front of them.

Sugar is a major cause of tooth decay.

Many educators question whether **intelligence** can be measured.

Consumed in moderate amounts, **red wine** is thought by some researchers to reduce chances of heart disease.

4 Be aware of two possible article problems with non-count nouns. First make sure that you don't use *a/an* with noncount nouns.

33b ESL

> INCORRECT   I need ₳ work.
> CORRECT   I need work.

Second, keep in mind that a noncount noun can never be plural.

> INCORRECT   Joe needs some information₧ about the class.
> CORRECT   Joe needs some information about the class.

And remember that sometimes noncount nouns can change to have a count meaning (see Section 33b-1).

5 Pay careful attention to quantifiers. The words that come before nouns and tell you *how much* or *how many* are called **quantifiers.** Quantifiers are not always the same for both count and noncount nouns. See Chart 33.5 on page 538 for a list of quantifiers.

Chart 33.5

Quantifiers		
USE THESE WITH COUNT AND NON-COUNT NOUNS ONLY	USE THESE WITH COUNT NOUNS ONLY	USE THESE WITH NONCOUNT NOUNS
some books/money	**several** books	**a good deal of** money
a lot of books/money	**many** books	**a great deal of** money
plenty of books/money	**a couple of** books	**(not) much** money*
a lack of books/money	**a few** books	**a little** money
most of the books/money	**few** books	**little** money

Much is ordinarily used only in questions and in negative statements: "Do you have *much* milk left?" "No, there isn't *much* milk."

A few/a little and *few/little.*   It may not seem like a big difference, but the article *a* in front of the quantifiers *few* and *little* changes the meaning. *A few* or *a little* means "not a lot, but enough of the item."

> There are **a few books** in the library on capital punishment.
> Use *a few* with count nouns.

> There is **a little information** in the library on capital punishment.
> Use *a little* with noncount nouns.

33b
ESL

Few or *little* (without *a*) means that there is *not enough* of something. These quantifiers have a negative meaning.

> There are **few** female leaders in the world.
> not enough of them

> My mother has **little** hope that this will change.
> not much hope

Most and *most of.*   Using *most of* can be tricky. You can use *most of* before either a count or a noncount noun, but if you do, don't forget to put *the* before the noun.

> *MOST OF* + *THE* + SPECIFIC PLURAL NOUN
> **Most of the** *women* in the class were married.   Not: *most of women*

> *MOST OF* + *THE* + SPECIFIC NONCOUNT NOUN
> **Most of the** *jewelry* in the house was stolen.   Not: *most of jewelry*

> *MOST* + GENERAL PLURAL NOUN
> **Most** *cars* have seat belts.   Not: *most of cars*

EXERCISE 33.2 In the list of nouns below, write *C* after the count nouns and *NC* after the noncount nouns. If you are not sure, consult an ESL dictionary. Then make a note of the nouns you had to check. (For answers, see p. 540.)

1. furniture
2. work
3. dollar
4. job
5. advice

6. people
7. equipment
8. money
9. newspaper
10. traffic

EXERCISE 33.3 Review all of Section 33b. Each of the following sentences has at least one error in the use of articles or quantifiers. Circle the error and correct it. (For answers, see p. 540.)

1. Much people have visited the new restaurant downtown called Rock-and-Roll Hamburger Haven.

2. Most of customers are young people because music in restaurant is very loud.

3. The restaurant serves the usual food—hamburgers, pizza, and pasta. It is not expensive; in fact, most expensive item on the menu is only $8.

4. Food is not very good, but the atmosphere is very appealing to these young men and women.

5. There are much posters on the walls of famous rock star. There is even authentic motorcycle of one star on a platform.

6. Some of regular customers say they have seen some stars eating there.

7. These "regulars" give these advices to anyone who wants to spot a star there: look for dark glasses and a leather coat.

EXERCISE 33.4 Write a descriptive paragraph about ordering and eating a meal at your favorite restaurant. Refer to Chart 33.5 on page 538, which lists quantifiers used with count and noncount nouns, and use at least four words from this list in your paragraph. Underline all the nouns in your paragraph and write *C* (for count nouns) and *NC* (for noncount nouns) above them. Then check your use of articles. (For help, refer to Sections 33b-2 through 33b-4.) Make sure your subject-verb agreement is correct.

33b
ESL

ANSWER KEY

EXERCISE 33.1
1. to work
2. to have
3. having
4. to support
5. to be
6. hearing; to drop
7. to decide
8. to make; going; quitting

EXERCISE 33.2
1. NC
2. NC
3. C
4. C
5. NC
6. C
7. NC
8. NC
9. C
10. NC

EXERCISE 33.3
1. **Many** people have visited the new restaurant downtown called Rock-and-Roll Hamburger Haven.

2. Most of **the** customers are young people because **the** music in **the** restaurant is very loud.
3. The restaurant serves the usual food—hamburgers, pizza, and pasta. It is not expensive; in fact, **the** most expensive item on the menu is only $8.
4. **The** food is not very good, but the atmosphere is very appealing to these young men and women.
5. There are **many** posters on the walls of famous rock stars. There is even **an** authentic motorcycle of one star on a platform.
6. Some of **the** regular customers say they have seen some stars eating there.
7. These "regulars" give **this advice** to anyone who wants to spot a star there: look for dark glasses and a leather coat.

EXERCISE 33.4
Answers will vary.

33b
ESL

PART
VI

Punctuation and Mechanics

34 How Do You Punctuate Sentence Endings?

35 Questions About Sentence Boundaries: Fragments, Comma Splices, and Run-ons?

36 Questions About Commas?

37 Questions About Semicolons and Colons?

38 Questions About Quotation Marks and Ellipses?

39 Questions About Parentheses and Brackets?

40 Questions About Dashes, Hyphens, and Slashes?

41 Questions About Italics and Capitalization?

42 Questions About Abbreviations and Numbers?

CHAPTER 34

How Do You Punctuate Sentence Endings?

34a When do you use periods?

Sentences and some abbreviations end with periods. Periods say, "That's all there is." Although periods cause few problems, writers occasionally put them in the wrong place or forget them entirely.

An editor will use a caret and a circled period to show where a period has been omitted.

He told me, "Yes‸" But he lied.   ⊙

1 Use periods at the end of statements.

Hannibal, a Carthaginian general, was a brilliant military strategist.

2 Use periods at the end of indirect questions and mild commands.

Military theorists wonder whether any battle plan has been more tactically perfect than Hannibal's at Cannae (216 B.C.E.).

On the map, locate the Roman and Carthaginian positions.

Strong commands may also be punctuated with exclamation points.

3 Use periods to punctuate some abbreviations.

Cong.	natl.
sing., pl.	pp.

When a statement ends with an abbreviation, the period at the end of the sentence is not doubled.

We visited the Folger Library in Washington, D.C.

The period at the end of the abbreviation is retained when the sentence is a question or an exclamation.

Have you ever been to Washington, D.C.?
Our flight departs at 6 a.m.!

When an abbreviation occurs in the middle of a sentence, it retains its period. The period may even be followed by another punctuation mark.

Though she had not yet earned her Ph.D ., Zora had two job offers.

Abbreviations for institutions, corporations, networks, or government agencies usually don't require periods; neither do words shortened by common use.

NFL	GM	HBO	FEMA
lab	auto	dorm	co-op

Similarly, acronyms—first-letter abbreviations pronounced as words—don't take periods.

CARE   NATO   NOW

When in doubt about punctuating abbreviations, check a dictionary.

■ **4 Use periods in conventional ways.** Not all periods mark the ends of sentences. They are also used, for example, to indicate decimals, to mark chapter and verse in biblical citations, and to separate parts of email addresses and URLs.

0.01 $189.00   75.47

Matthew 3.1
sugarbear@mail.utexas.edu
http://www.google.com

34b When do you use question marks?

Question marks terminate questions; they can also be used to suggest doubt or uncertainty.

An editor will use a caret and a question mark (or sometimes a question mark alone) to show where this piece of punctuation is needed. Unnecessary question marks are indicated by *No?*

To whom did you speak/ ?
I asked Sue if she were angry? *noP*

■ **1 Use question marks to end direct questions.**

Have you ever heard of the Battle of Cannae?
Who fought in the battle?
Do you know that Hannibal defeated the Roman legions?
How?

■ **2 Use question marks to indicate that a name, date, or fact cannot be established with certainty.** Such a question mark should not be used to indicate that a writer is unsure of facts that might be available with more research.

> Hannibal (247**?**–183 B.C.E.) was a Carthaginian general and military tactician.

■ **3 Do not use question marks to terminate indirect questions.** **Indirect questions** are statements that seem to have questions within them. Compare these examples to see the difference.

INDIRECT QUESTION	Varro wondered whether Hannibal's strategy would succeed.
DIRECT QUESTION	Will Hannibal's strategy succeed?
QUESTION WITHIN A STATEMENT	Varro wondered, "Will Hannibal's strategy succeed?"
INDIRECT QUESTION	The reporter asked how the new agency would be funded.
DIRECT QUESTION	How will the new agency be funded?
QUESTION WITHIN A STATEMENT	"How will the new agency be funded?" the reporter asked.

■ **4 Punctuate as questions any compound sentences that begin with statements but end with questions.**

> The strategy seemed reasonable, but would it work on the battlefield**?**

Don't confuse these constructions with indirect questions.

34b
?

■ **5 Place question marks after direct questions that appear in the middle of sentences.** Such questions will usually be surrounded by parentheses, quotation marks, or dashes.

> Skeptical of their tour guide's claim—"Would Hannibal really position his cavalry here**?**"—the scholars in the group consulted a map.

■ **6 Place question marks outside quotation marks except when they are part of the quoted material itself.**

> Was it Terence who wrote "Fortune helps the brave"**?**
> The teacher asked, "Have you read any Cicero**?**"

For a more detailed explanation of quotation marks, see Section 38a.

■ 7 Do not allow question marks to bump against other punctuation marks. For instance, you wouldn't place a comma, colon, or semicolon after a question mark.

> WRONG "Where did the battle begin ?," the tourist asked.
> RIGHT "Where did the battle begin ?" the tourist asked.

Don't multiply question marks to add emphasis. One mark is sufficient.

> WRONG Are you serious ???
> RIGHT Are you serious ?

34c When do you use exclamation marks?

Exclamations give emphasis to statements. They are vigorous punctuation marks with the subtlety of a Ferrari F-60. In academic writing, they should be about as rare too.

An editor will use a caret and an exclamation point (or sometimes an exclamation alone) to show where this piece of punctuation is needed or should be omitted.

> I won the $90 million lottery/ ∧!
> Columbus wasn't the first European in America/ no!

■ 1 Use exclamation marks to express strong reactions or commands.

> They are retreating!
> Our time has come at last!

Save exclamations for those occasions—rare in college and business writing—when your words really deserve emphasis. Too many exclamations can make a passage seem juvenile.

> OVERDONE The Roman forces at the Battle of Cannae outnumbered Hannibal's forces roughly two to one! Yet Roman casualties would be ten times higher than those suffered by Hannibal's army!
>
> TEMPERED The Roman forces at the Battle of Cannae outnumbered Hannibal's forces roughly two to one. Yet Roman casualties would be ten times higher than those suffered by Hannibal's army.

34c
!

■ **2 Do not allow exclamation marks to bump against other punctuation marks.** For instance, you wouldn't place a comma, colon, or semicolon after an exclamation mark.

> WRONG   "Please check your records again!," the caller demanded.

> RIGHT   "Please check your records again!" the caller demanded.

Don't multiply exclamation marks to add emphasis. One mark is sufficient.

> WRONG   Don't shout!!
> RIGHT   Don't shout!

EXERCISE 34.1 Edit the following passage, adding, replacing, and deleting periods, question marks, exclamation points, and any other marks of punctuation that need to be changed.

1. Hannibal simply outfoxed the Roman general Varro at Cannae!!!

2. Hannibal placed his numerically smaller army where the Aufidius River would protect his flank—could the hotheaded Varro appreciate such a move—and arrayed his forces to make the Roman numbers work against themselves!

3. It must have seemed obvious to Hannibal where Varro would concentrate his forces?

4. "Advance!," Hannibal ordered!

5. Is it likely that Varro and the Romans noticed how thin the Carthaginian forces were at the center of the battle line?

6. Predictably, the Romans pressed their attack on the weakened Carthaginian center. But in the meantime, Hannibal's cavalry had destroyed its Roman counterpart!

7. You might be wondering, "Why didn't Hannibal use his cavalry to strengthen his weak center"?

8. It was because he wanted it behind the Roman lines to attack from the rear!

9. Hannibal expected the troops at the ends of his battle line to outflank the Romans, but would such a strategy work.

10. It did! The Romans found themselves surrounded and defeated!

34c
!

CHAPTER 35

Questions About Sentence Boundaries: Fragments, Comma Splices, and Run-ons?

Three of the most troublesome and common punctuation problems are the fragment, the comma splice, and the run-on. All three problems arise from confusion about sentence boundaries. Once you get a feel for those boundaries and the signals writers use to mark them, you are less likely to have these problems.

35a How do you repair sentence fragments?

Sentence fragments are phrases or clauses that look like complete sentences, but either they lack subjects or verbs (see Section 17a-1) or they are subordinate constructions (see Section 17g).

NO SUBJECT	Fits perfectly!
NO VERB	The gold ring.
SUBORDINATE	That I found on the subway.
COMPLETE SENTENCE	The gold ring that I found on the subway fits perfectly.

An editor or instructor will usually mark such constructions with the abbreviation for sentence fragment, *frag*.

The bill died. Because the President vetoed it. *frag*

1 Check that all sentences have complete subjects and verbs, either stated or implied. To avoid a fragment, you need a subject and verb that can stand alone; don't be fooled by subjects or verbs in subordinate clauses (see the next section). Subject and verb pairings can be as simple as *It is* or *They were*. Sometimes, too, subjects may be understood rather than stated—for example, in commands. But complete sentences always need subjects and verbs.

The sun rose. subject is *sun;* verb is *rose*

When we arrived at the canyon, the sun, hidden beneath a thick blanket of clouds, had already risen.
subject is *sun;* verb is *had risen*

It was a beautiful morning. subject is *it;* verb is *was*

Keep quiet. subject *you* is understood; verb is *keep*

■ **2 Check that you have not allowed a dependent or subordinate clause to stand alone as a sentence.** Subordinate clauses—that is, clauses that begin with words such as *although, because, if, since, unless, when, while*—won't work as sentences by themselves even though they have a subject and a verb (see Section 17d-2).

FRAGMENT	It will be a miracle. **If the mail comes on time.**
FRAGMENT	The town decided to ration water. **Since there had been no rain for months.**

Standing alone, these fragments can leave readers wondering what's missing. Usually, such fragments can be repaired by attaching them to surrounding sentences.

COMPLETE SENTENCE	If the mail comes on time, it will be a miracle.
COMPLETE SENTENCE	The town decided to ration water since there had been no rain for months.

Here is another sentence fragment resulting from a dependent clause not linked to a complete sentence.

35a
frag

FRAGMENT	Rainbows can be observed only in the morning or late afternoon. **When the sun is less than forty degrees above the horizon.**
FRAGMENT ELIMINATED	Rainbows can be observed only in the morning or late afternoon when the sun is less than forty degrees above the horizon.

■ **3 Check that you have not allowed a relative clause or appositive to stand alone as a sentence.** Words like *who, which, that,* and *where* typically signal the beginning of a relative clause that must be connected to a sentence to make a complete thought (see Section 17d-2). If the clause is left unattached, a fragment results.

FRAGMENT   The Capitol is on Congress Avenue. **Which is the widest street in the city.**

CORRECTED   The Capitol is on Congress Avenue, which is the widest street in the city.

The appositive, a group of words that gives more information about a noun, is another construction that produces fragments when allowed to stand alone (see Section 17c-4).

FRAGMENT   Anderson resigned her professorship. **A position she had held for twenty years.**
The phrase starting with *A position* is punctuated as a sentence, but it doesn't express a full idea by itself.

CORRECTED   Anderson resigned her professorship, a position she had held for twenty years.

4 Check that you have not substituted a verbal for the verb in a sentence.
If you have, the result will be a fragment. Verbals (see Sections 24a and 24b) are tricky constructions because they look like verbs, but they act as nouns, adjectives, or adverbs. For instance, in the phrase "to look at something," *to look* is the infinitive of a verb, but it doesn't act as a verb. In the phrase "running for office," *running* is a gerund, not a verb. In the phrase "recognizing his weakness," *recognizing* acts as a noun, not a verb (see Section 17c-2). To eliminate fragments caused by verbals, it helps to remember the following:

- An *-ing* word by itself can never act as the verb of a sentence. To qualify as a verb, the *-ing* word must have an auxiliary such as *have been, is,* or *were.*
- An infinitive, such as *to run* or *to go,* can never act as the verb of a sentence.

Here are examples of verbals causing sentence fragments. The fragments are boldfaced.

35a
frag

FRAGMENT   The reporter from Reuters asked the senator probing questions. **Suspecting a coverup.**
The boldfaced portion is a verbal phrase modifying *reporter* that cannot act as a sentence.

FRAGMENT
ELIMINATED   Suspecting a coverup, the reporter from Reuters asked the senator probing questions.

FRAGMENT   **To break the story.** That was the reporter's goal.
The boldfaced portion is an infinitive phrase acting as a noun and shouldn't be punctuated as a sentence.

FRAGMENT
ELIMINATED   To break the story was the reporter's goal.

▮ 5 Check that you have not treated a disconnected phrase as a sentence. Turning a disconnected phrase into a full sentence usually means adding a subject or a verb (sometimes both), depending on what has been left out of the phrase. Here the disconnected phrases that are sentence fragments are boldfaced.

FRAGMENTS   David cleaned his glasses. **Absentmindedly. With the hem of his lamb's-wool sweater.**

The prepositional phrase—*with the hem of his lamb's-wool sweater*—can be joined to the end of the sentence. *Absentmindedly* needs to be attached to the word it modifies: *David.*

FRAGMENTS   Absentmindedly, David cleaned his glasses with the
ELIMINATED   hem of his lamb's-wool sweater.

▮ 6 Check that you have not treated a list as an independent sentence. Sometimes a list gets detached from the sentence that introduced or explained it. The result can be a sentence fragment that needs to be revised either by connecting it to the preceding sentence or by making it stand as a sentence on its own.

FRAGMENT   Bucking a Washington tradition, some politicians have left office willingly to pursue new interests. **Pat Schroeder and Sam Nunn among them.**

FRAGMENT   Bucking a Washington tradition, some politicians
ELIMINATED   have left office willingly to pursue new interests, among them Pat Schroeder and Sam Nunn.

35a
frag

Lists are often introduced by words or phrases such as *especially, for example, for instance, such as,* and *namely.* If a fragment follows such an expression, be sure to correct it—usually by attaching the fragment to the preceding sentence.

FRAGMENT   People suffer from many peculiar phobias. **For example, ailurophobia (fear of cats), aviophobia (fear of flying), ombrophobia (fear of rain), and vestiphobia (fear of clothes).**

FRAGMENT   People suffer from many peculiar phobias—for ex-
ELIMINATED   ample, ailurophobia (fear of cats), aviophobia (fear of flying), ombrophobia (fear of rain), and vestiphobia (fear of clothes).

EXERCISE 35.1 Rewrite the following sentences to eliminate any sentence fragments.

1. Although most movie stars are human and created by the usual birds-and-bees process. One of the most popular movie stars in recent memory, the liquid metal cyborg in *Terminator 2,* was created by a computer.

2. The technology of computer animation has developed rapidly over the past decade. Making a spectacular range of special effects possible.

3. Industrial Light and Magic was responsible for the astonishing cyborg. A special-effects company owned by director George Lucas.

4. The company was founded to create the special effects for *Star Wars.* Subsequently creating the special effects for a string of hits, including *E.T.: The Extra-Terrestrial* and *Who Framed Roger Rabbit?* Also the special effects for *Ghost.*

5. While the cyborg appears in *Terminator 2* for only about five minutes, creating the footage cost millions of dollars. Keeping thirty-five computer animators busy for ten months.

35b Do you understand intentional fragments?

Writers concerned to avoid fragments in their own work may sometimes wonder why incomplete sentences occur in newspapers, popular magazines, and fiction, as well as in much electronic communication. For example, in a passage from *Men's Journal* (January 2000) evaluating the classic film *The Big Sleep,* the first sentence is a fragment.

35b frag

> Bogart, Bacall, and Raymond Chandler rewritten by William Faulkner: hard-boiled heaven. Scene for scene, the private-eye movie doesn't get any better than this.

Are sentence fragments considered wrong at some times but not at others? The answer is yes, depending on a writer's purpose and audience.

1 Understand what intentional fragments are. Intentional fragments are groups of words that convey complete ideas even though they may lack subjects, verbs, or both. Presented and punctuated as sentences, such constructions enable writers to set a quick pace, present vivid images, convey information quickly, or establish a casual tone in their informal work. Fragments make writing sound like conversation, direct and personal. You can hear that tone in a passage from a road test in *Bicycling*, in which the first and third sentences are obvious fragments.

> **Glitches?** We noticed an undercut in the weld between the top and seat tubes, which the bright yellow paint showed in stark relief when the light was right. **Too bad, as the rest of the welds were just first rate.**

■ 2 Use intentional fragments cautiously. The problem is that intentional fragments can look just like the fragments many readers consider major errors. They should not appear regularly in any formal or academic writing, and certainly not in a research paper, report, job application letter, or literary analysis. You might use them judiciously in email, listservs, memos, narratives, journal pieces, and other informal writing. For readers conservative about grammar, avoid fragments entirely.

EXERCISE 35.2 Bring to class some advertisements that use intentional fragments or locate a Web site or listserv that routinely includes fragments. Working with other students in a small group, identify these fragments; then join forces to rewrite them and eliminate all incomplete sentences. Assess the difference between the original material and the revised versions. Why do you think the writers may have used fragments?

35c
cs

35c How do you avoid comma splices?

A comma splice occurs when you try to join two independent clauses with a comma only. The error is common and considered serious in academic and professional writing—but it is easy to identify and fix. Look at this example of a comma splice.

COMMA SPLICE
Local shopkeepers were concerned about a recent outbreak of graffiti, they feared that it indicated the arrival of troublesome gangs in the neighborhood.

Notice that the groups of words on each side of the comma could stand alone as complete sentences. When that happens, you ordinarily have a comma splice.

An editor or instructor will usually mark a comma splice with the abbreviation *cs*.

> Yellowstone is the oldest of America's national parks, it is located in Wyoming.   *cs*

■ 1 Remember that commas can't link complete sentences.

When two independent clauses are joined, they require a linkage stronger than a comma alone to show their relationship. Using a comma where a semicolon or conjunction is needed will usually blur the meaning of a sentence: readers may not know if a writer wants to show a connection between the clauses, a subordination of ideas, or a contrast. Consider how confusing these sentences are.

COMMA SPLICE	The report is highly critical of the media, it has received little press coverage.
COMMA SPLICE	Shawna is an outstanding orator, she has no formal training in speech.

Although the independent clauses are obviously connected, the comma splices do not explain how. Inserting conjunctions relieves the confusion.

COMMA SPLICE ELIMINATED	The report is highly critical of the media, **so** it has received little press coverage.
COMMA SPLICE ELIMINATED	Shawna is an outstanding orator, **although** she has no formal training in speech.

Here are more examples of typical kinds of comma splices.

COMMA SPLICE	A technician carefully measured the chemicals for the experiment, she made sure all weights were exact.
COMMA SPLICE ELIMINATED	A technician carefully measured the chemicals for the experiment, **and** she made sure all weights were exact.
COMMA SPLICE	Maria was supposed to be on stage in five minutes, however, she was still donning her costume. This illustrates a frequent mistake: using a comma before *nevertheless* or *however* in a compound sentence. You need a semicolon.
COMMA SPLICE ELIMINATED	Maria was supposed to be on stage in five minutes; however, she was still donning her costume.

35c
cs

Very short sentences, usually in threes, may be joined by commas. These constructions are rare.

> I came, I saw, I conquered.
> He ate, I paid, we left.

▪2 Eliminate a comma splice by replacing the faulty comma with a semicolon.

COMMA SPLICE   When David detailed his Mustang, every brush, sponge, and swab was arranged in one neat row, he laid out each towel, chamois, and duster in another.
The separation between these two closely related independent ideas gets lost among the commas that are separating items in the series.

COMMA SPLICE
ELIMINATED   When David detailed his Mustang, every brush, sponge, and swab was arranged in one neat row; he laid out each towel, chamois, and duster in another.

▪3 Eliminate a comma splice by replacing the faulty comma with a period.

COMMA SPLICE   David polished a square inch of his car at a time, by the end of the day he had finished the hood and one fender.
These two independent clauses should have a stronger separation to emphasize their difference.

COMMA SPLICE
ELIMINATED   David polished a square inch of his car at a time. By the end of the day, he had finished the hood and one fender.

35c
cs

▪4 Eliminate a comma splice by inserting a coordinating conjunction after the comma. The coordinating conjunctions are *and, or, nor, for, but, yet,* and *so.*

COMMA SPLICE   His progress was slow because he did every step by hand, it wasn't easy work.
These two independent clauses need a strong separation to stress that they are in a sequence. The comma doesn't provide that separation.

COMMA SPLICE
ELIMINATED   His progress was slow because he did every step by hand, **and** it wasn't easy work.

▪5 Eliminate a comma splice by subordinating one of the independent clauses. You can do that by introducing one of the

independent clauses with a subordinating word such as *although, because, since,* or *when.* For more on subordination, see Section 17g.

COMMA SPLICE Detailing a vehicle requires skill, learning to do it can pay off in a profitable career.

The two clauses of the sentence are not equally important, so the first one should be changed to a subordinate clause and the comma retained.

COMMA SPLICE **Although** detailing a vehicle requires skill,
ELIMINATED   learning to do it can pay off in a profitable career.

🍎 *Point of Difference*

Although comma splices are nonstandard in academic writing, alert readers will notice them in contemporary fiction. In that genre, authors often feel less bound by strict conventions. So don't be surprised if you spot a comma splice now and then in the novels of respected writers. Here are two instances.

The first is from *The Desert Rose* by the Pulitzer Prize–winning novelist Larry McMurtry.

If she needed money she could always just steal it out of Billy's billfold, she had done that a few times and he hadn't even noticed.

The second is from *Monk's Hood,* a medieval mystery by the English historian Edith Pargeter, who wrote mysteries under the name of Ellis Peters.

Brother Mark had done his part, the habit was there, rolled up beneath Brother Cadfael's bed.🍎

35c
cs

EXERCISE 35.3 Identify the sentences that have comma splices and correct them.

1. At one time the walls in many Philadelphia neighborhoods were covered with graffiti, however they are covered with murals today.

2. Since 1984 a city-sponsored program has been teaming young graffiti writers with professional artists, the result is the creation of over a thousand works of public art.

3. The murals are large, they are colorful, they are 99 percent graffiti-free.

4. A forty-foot-tall mural of Julius ("Dr. J.") Erving has become a local landmark, even Dr. J. himself brings friends by to see it.

5. The theory behind the program is that graffiti writers, being inherently artistic, will not deface a work of art they respect, so far the theory holds.

35d Do you have questions about run-on sentences?

A *run-on* occurs when no punctuation at all separates two independent clauses (see Section 17d-1). The reader is left to figure out where one sentence ends and a second begins.

> RUN-ON   We were surprised by the package quickly we tore it open.

You need to provide a boundary strong enough to separate the independent clauses clearly. You usually have several options for repairing a run-on.

> RUN-ON   We were surprised by the package; quickly, we tore
> ELIMINATED   it open.

> RUN-ON   We were surprised by the package. Quickly, we tore
> ELIMINATED   it open.

An editor or instructor will usually write *run-on* (or *r-o*) next to a sentence with such a problem.

The Taj Mahal is one of the world's most beautiful buildings it is located near Agra in India. *run-on*

1 Eliminate a run-on by separating independent clauses with a period.

> RUN-ON   Politicians were once fearful of reforming the social
>   security system now they are scrambling to prevent
>   its bankruptcy.
>   The sentence needs to be punctuated after *system* so as not to confuse readers. Adding a period makes a natural separation.

> RUN-ON   Politicians were once fearful of reforming the social
> ELIMINATED   security system. Now they are scrambling to prevent
>   its bankruptcy.

A run-on is a grammatical train wreck, two clauses colliding like these locomotives in a staged exhibition near Waco, Texas, on September 15, 1896. As many as 40,000 people witnessed this notorious run-on. For more information, see <http://www.discovery.com/area/ wayback/wayback970224/ wayback1.html>.

2 Eliminate a run-on by inserting a semicolon between independent clauses. A semicolon suggests that the ideas in the two sentences are closely related.

RUN-ON   Emily's entire life revolves around ecological prob-
            lems she can speak of little else.
            The two clauses are closely related but need to be separated to
            show they are separate ideas. A semicolon separates the sentences
            but preserves a relationship between them.

RUN-ON   Emily's entire life revolves around ecological prob-
ELIMINATED lems; she can speak of little else.

For more on semicolons, see Section 37a.

3 Eliminate a run-on by joining independent clauses with a comma and a coordinating conjunction. The coordinating conjunctions are *and, or, nor, for, but, yet,* and *so.*

35d
run-on

RUN-ON   Poisonous giant toads were introduced to Australia
            in the 1930s to control beetles they have since be-
            come an ecological menace.

RUN-ON   Poisonous giant toads were introduced to Australia
ELIMINATED in the 1930s to control beetles, **but** they have since
            become an ecological menace.

RUN-ON   The manager suggested a cut in our hourly wages
            then I walked out of the negotiations.

RUN-ON   The manager suggested a cut in our hourly wages,
ELIMINATED **so** then I walked out of the negotiations.

4 Eliminate a run-on by subordinating one of the independent clauses to the other.

RUN-ON   Albert had to finish the financial report by himself his irresponsible co-author had lost interest in the cause.

RUN-ON
ELIMINATED   Albert had to finish the financial report by himself **because** his irresponsible co-author had lost interest in the cause.

EXERCISE 35.4 Rewrite these sentences to eliminate punctuation problems that create run-on sentences.

1. Centuries of superstition and ignorance have given bats a bad reputation millions of the flying mammals are killed each year in a misguided effort to protect livestock, crops, and people.

2. Entire species of bats are being wiped out at an alarming rate: for example, in the 1960s a new species of fruit-eating bat was discovered in the Philippines by the 1980s it was extinct.

3. In truth, bats are industrious and invaluable members of the natural order, they spread the seeds of hundreds of species of plants.

4. Strange as it may sound, bats are essential to the economies of many countries, the plants they pollinate or seed include such cash crops as bananas, figs, dates, vanilla beans, and avocados.

5. Many plants essential to such delicate ecosystems as the African savanna and the South American rain forest rely solely on bats for propagating, should the bats disappear, the entire system could collapse.

35d
run-on

CHAPTER 36

Questions About Commas?

Commas are interrupters or signals to pause. As signals, they aren't as strong as semicolons, which typically appear at major intersections between clauses. And they are certainly not as forceful as periods, which mark the ends of sentences. Instead, commas make a reader slow down and pay attention to the words and ideas they set off. For this reason, it's just as important to omit commas where they aren't needed as it is to include them where they are.

Rules may help you manage commas, but ultimately you have to develop a *feel* for them. One way to develop good comma sense is to observe writers using the mark. So the next time you read an enjoyable article or story, notice how commas make it clearer and easier to read.

An editor will usually suggest where a comma is needed with a comma and caret.

The garden, which had been neglected for years now ˆ,
flourished under the rabbi's care.

Where you need to delete a comma, an editor may draw a slash through the mark and write *no comma (no,)* in the margin.

The painting/ that I bought appreciated in value.   *no,*

36a Do you understand commas that separate?

Some commas keep words, phrases, and clauses from colliding. But you may have to rely on both some rules and your instincts to place them appropriately. Use too many commas, and your writing will seem plodding and fussy; use too few, and your readers may be confused.

■ 1 Use commas after introductory phrases of more than three or four words. Pauses at these points can make sentences easier to read.

In some situations, commas have the message of a yield sign—slow down, but don't quite stop.

> To appreciate the pleasures of driving in snow, you have to live in Michigan or Wisconsin.
>
> Over the loud objections of all the Jeep's occupants, I turned off the main road.

An introductory comma isn't necessary when an introductory phrase is only two or three words long and the sentence is clear without the punctuation.

> For now I'll abstain from voting.
> On Tuesday we'll be in New Mexico.

However, in these situations commas aren't wrong either. Use a comma whenever it helps to avoid confusion or to clarify a sentence, as it might after an introductory prepositional phrase or verbal.

36a
^
,

> In Louisiana, state laws are still influenced by the Napoleonic Code.
> Stranded, the hikers headed due south.
> To write better, she read the best magazines and novels carefully.

2 Use commas after introductory subordinate clauses.
Subordinate clauses are signaled by words such as *although, if, when, because, as, after, before, since, unless, while.* (See Section 17d-2.)

> **Although** the vote was close, we passed the motion.
> **While** the military band played taps, the flag was lowered.
> **When** the police officers arrived, they found the window broken.

3 Use commas before sentence elements or clauses that follow a main clause when the additional thought is incidental, additional, or contrasting. Such clauses may be signaled by words such as *although, though, if, when, because, as, after, before, since, unless, while, that is.*

> We will attend the judge's lecture, which is scheduled to last an hour.
>
> The orientation adviser urged us to be sensitive to our neighbors, implying that we might offend someone verbally.
>
> The restaurant was second-rate, though its prices were steep.

Commas are not used, however, when the additional clause is closely related to the main idea of the sentence.

> We drove on to Detroit **even though** the roads were crowded.
>
> The flag was lowered **while** the military band played taps.
>
> The police officers found the window broken **when** they arrived.

Deciding whether a modifying clause is closely related to a main clause is often a judgment call; writers won't agree in every case. Notice, however, that if these sentences started with the subordinate clauses, most writers would put a comma after them. For instance, "While the band played taps, the flag was lowered."

4 Use commas after conjunctive adverbs at the beginning of sentences or clauses. Commas are needed because words of this kind—*consequently, nevertheless, however, therefore*—are interrupters that mark a shift or contrast in a sentence. For a chart of conjunctive adverbs, see page 579.

> Mr. Howard reviewed the testimony carefully. **However,** he found no evidence of perjury.
>
> Althea studied hard; **therefore,** she passed the examination easily.

36a
^
,

Putting a comma after these words sets them off and draws attention to them (but see also Section 37a-3).

5 Use commas to set off absolute phrases. Absolutes are phrases made up of nouns and participles. You are most likely to recognize them through examples.

> **His head shaved,** Martin was in the Marines now.
>
> The pioneers pressed forward across the desert, **their water almost gone.**

Absolutes like these are always separated from the rest of the sentence by commas. See Section 17c-3 for more about absolutes.

6 Use commas to mark contrasts or transitions.

Owning a car in most cities is a necessity, not a luxury.

On the other hand, a car in a place like New York City is not practical.

Ollie had seen many celestial events, but never an eclipse.

Kelly's chief requirement in clothes is not style, but low price.

7 Use commas to separate words where verbs or predicates have been deleted to avoid repetition. Constructions of this kind are fairly common.

Appollonia is the patron saint of toothaches; Blaise, of throat infections; Vitus, of epilepsy.

Brad Pitt once worked as a giant chicken; Rod Stewart, as a gravedigger; Whoopi Goldberg, as a makeup artist in a mortuary.

8 Use commas to keep ideas clear and distinct.

The motto of some critics seems to be whatever is, is wrong.
People who must, can operate cars with hand controls only.
Those who can, do; those who can't, complain.

9 Use commas to separate conversational expressions from the main body of a sentence. Such expressions are probably more common in speech than in writing, but here's how they are punctuated.

No, I am sure the door was locked.
The dancers are full of themselves, aren't they?
"Well, I'm not sure I recall," said the former governor.

36a

⌃
,

EXERCISE 36.1 Insert commas in these sentences where needed.

1. When Mount Saint Helens erupted in 1980 the north slope collapsed sending torrents of mud and rock down into the Toutle River valley.

2. Stripped of all vegetation for fifteen miles the valley was left virtually lifeless; whatever trees there were were dead.

3. In an effort to prevent erosion and speed the valley's recovery ecologists planted grasses and ground covers.

4. However the species they planted were not native but alien or exotic.

5. All things considered the scientists probably should have left nature to take its course since the alien plants are now inhibiting the regrowth of native species.

36b Do you understand commas that enclose?

Enclosing some words and phrases with commas makes sentences more readable; the commas help to chunk information into manageable segments. But it's important to place commas only around expressions that really need to be separated. Remember, too, that it usually takes two commas to bracket material in the middle of a sentence; it's easy to forget that second comma. Of course, only one comma is needed before a modifier at the end of a sentence.

1 Use commas to mark nonessential (nonrestrictive) modifiers. A **nonessential modifier** adds information to a sentence that can be removed without radically altering the basic meaning of the sentence. (For a detailed discussion of essential and nonessential modifiers, see Section 30i.)

> Authentic Navajo rugs, **which can take months to weave,** come in several distinctive styles.

> Neil Armstrong, **who was born in a small Ohio town,** was the first human to walk on the moon.

2 Use commas to enclose nonessential (nonrestrictive) appositives. An **appositive** is a noun or noun equivalent that follows a noun and gives additional information about it. Appositives are usually nonessential modifiers.

> Colleen O'Brien, **our neighborhood-watch coordinator,** was arrested last week for shoplifting.

> George Washington, **the first President of the United States,** served two full terms.

Some appositives are essential modifiers, giving information that can't be removed from a sentence. Such modifiers should not be

36b
^
,

enclosed by commas. Because *the psychiatrist* and *the father* in the following example are essential to the meaning of the sentence, setting them off with commas would confuse readers.

> Sue Ellen reflected that Dr. Rizzo **the psychiatrist** was quite a different person from Dr. Rizzo **the father.**

Deciding whether modifiers are essential or nonessential can be especially tricky when the appositives involved are titles. Use commas around titles when they can be deleted from a sentence, no commas when they cannot. Compare the following examples.

ESSENTIAL	Shakespeare's tragedy *Hamlet* is one of his longest plays.
	Cut *Hamlet* here and the sentence is meaningless.
NONESSENTIAL	Shakespeare's longest tragedy**,** *Hamlet***,** lasts more than four hours.
	The sentence would still make sense with *Hamlet* cut.
ESSENTIAL	The Beatles' song "**Yesterday**" remains one of the most popular tunes of all time.
NONESSENTIAL	The Beatles' final album**,** *Let It Be***,** remains my favorite.

■ 3 Use commas to enclose various interrupting words, phrases, and clauses. It is important to use commas in pairs when the interruptions come in the middle of sentences.

> The President intends**, predictably,** to veto the bill in its current form.
>
> The first landmark we recognized**, well before the plane landed,** was the Washington Monument.
>
> The senators**, it seemed,** were eager for a filibuster.
>
> Tell me**, Mr. Reuter,** what is your opinion?
>
> She could not**, in good conscience,** ignore the clamor for passage of the measure.
>
> He could**, of course,** make a strong case in the media.
>
> The student government voted to cut**, not eliminate,** the art society's grant.

Be especially careful with words such as *however, nevertheless, moreover, therefore,* and *consequently.* They should appear between commas when they fall in the middle of a sentence because they're strong interrupters.

Popular opinion, **however,** began to move toward the President's position.

 Point of Difference

Contemporary editors are moving toward using fewer commas around words such as *however* and *therefore*. In many newspapers and magazines—even the august *New York Times*—you will often find no commas around *of course* when it appears in the middle of a sentence.

EXERCISE 36.2 Discuss the following sentences to decide which modifiers are essential and which are not; then fix the sentences that need to be changed.

1. Carter a salesclerk with a passion for Native American art urged Iona his manager at a gallery in Alpine to increase her stock of Navajo rugs.

2. On a sales trip, Carter had met with several art dealers who specialized in Native American crafts; the dealer Carter met in Tuba City had offered rugs produced by several well-known artists.

3. The rugs that he showed Carter included examples of all the classic Navajo designs produced from wool which the weavers had shorn, carded, and dyed themselves.

4. Iona who had managed the store for ten years was uncertain that her regular customers would buy the premium rugs which cost as much as $6000.

5. But because Iona the lover of art was more speculative than Iona the businesswoman, the gallery soon featured a selection of Navajo rugs which quickly increased sales traffic.

36c

36c Do you understand commas that link?

Though commas often mark separations, they can also inform readers that certain ideas belong together. When commas come before linking words, they let readers know that the ideas will continue; the stop isn't as full as it would be if it were marked by a semicolon or period. Similarly, commas that mark off the items in a series help readers understand that those items belong together.

1 Use commas before the coordinating conjunctions *and, or, nor, for, but, yet,* and *so* when those words link independent clauses to form compound sentences. Clauses are described as **independent** when they can stand on their own as sentences (see Section 17d-1). Joining two independent clauses with a comma and a coordinating conjunction produces a compound sentence (see Sections 17e and 17f).

> Texas is larger in land area than California, **and** its history is different too.

> Some people find California more appealing, **but** such persons often have not spent much time in Texas.

> West Texas can seem empty at times, **yet** the vastness of its deserts and high plains is part of its appeal.

> Desert plants are fully adapted to their harsh terrain, **so** they wouldn't survive in more hospitable climates.

A comma is especially important when the two clauses separated by the conjunction are lengthy. In the following example, the comma emphasizes the break between the two clauses and prevents any misreading.

> Experts have tried to explain why dogs wag their tails, but they have not come up with a satisfactory reason for this attention-grabbing behavior.

Be especially careful not to place the comma after a conjunction that joins independent clauses. This is a common error.

> WRONG   My friends shared my opinion but, they were afraid to say so.

> RIGHT   My friends shared my opinion, but they were afraid to say so.

> WRONG   Bart's father remembers his first sports car fondly so, he knows how Bart feels behind the wheel of his Boxster S.

> RIGHT   Bart's father remembers his first sports car fondly, so he knows how Bart feels behind the wheel of his Boxster S.

2 Don't use commas alone to link independent clauses.

Doing so produces the error called a *comma splice.* For much more about comma splices, see Section 35c.

COMMA SPLICE   The plane to Atlanta was late, we missed our connecting flight to Indianapolis.

COMMA SPLICE   The plane to Atlanta was late; we missed our
ELIMINATED   connecting flight to Indianapolis.

3 Use commas to link more than two items in a series.

Commas are needed to mark pauses for readers and to keep the items in a series from colliding.

The mapmaker had omitted the capital cities of Idaho, New York, and Delaware!

Maggie found traces of spaghetti sauce on the floor, in the cabinets, under the rug, and on the ceiling.

The tabloid exposé failed to explain who had seen the aliens, where exactly they had landed, or why they had decided to visit New Orleans.

Point of Difference

Most English teachers and editors of books recommend that you use a comma before the conjunction (usually *and* or *or*) that signals the end of a series.

. . . for tax cuts, job security, and pay equity.
. . . the Indians, White Sox, or Yankees.

But this guideline is not followed by journalists, who usually omit what they regard as an unnecessary comma.

. . . for tax cuts, job security and pay equity.
. . . the Indians, White Sox or Yankees.

Leaving out the final comma can occasionally cause confusion, which is why many editors think it should be used.

. . . chicken, peas, and pork and beans.
. . . by coach, wagon, and horse and buggy.

36c
^
,

4 Use commas to link coordinate adjectives in series.

Coordinate adjectives modify the noun they precede, not each other (see Section 17b-1).

Drew is a **hapless, flustered, underappreciated** manager.
It was an **intriguing, careful, and lengthy** report.
Mimi is a **sarcastic, vindictive, and slightly** frazzled secretary.

When adjectives are coordinate, they can be switched around without affecting the sense of a phrase much. The examples above could just as easily and accurately read like this:

> Drew is a **flustered, underappreciated, hapless** manager.
> It was a **lengthy, careful, and intriguing** report.
> Mimi is a **vindictive, slightly frazzled, and sarcastic** secretary.

■ **5 Do not use commas to mark off noncoordinate modifiers in series.** Noncoordinate adjectives or adjectivals work together to modify a noun or pronoun (see Section 17b-1). The order of the modifiers is either essential to their meaning or idiomatic—as a result, they cannot be switched around.

> the **best supporting** actor
> a **new Mustang** convertible
> his **customary good** humor
> a **long fly** ball
> in **large cardboard** boxes

To determine whether a series of modifiers is coordinate or noncoordinate, try inserting *and* between them. Coordinate modifiers will still make good sense separated by *and.* Noncoordinate modifiers will not.

> COORDINATE   a hapless and flustered and underappreciated manager
>
> NONCOORDINATE   a new and Mustang convertible

36c
^
,

EXERCISE 36.3 Rewrite the following sentences, adding commas where they are needed to link ideas, moving commas that are misplaced, and correcting comma splices. Some sentences may be correct.

1. The mower cut its final swath across the deep green grass, the long golden rays of the setting sun toyed listlessly with the dancing grasshoppers in its wake.

2. Although all of the day's daylilies had already closed up shop the night-blooming flowers were starting to offer their perfumes to the hushed expectant air.

3. An orchestra of crickets tree frogs and, whippoorwills warmed up for the evening's concert; fireflies silently urgently signaled their ardor in the undergrowth.

4. Overhead, the moon's bright silver slipper held court with an audience of stars: Orion the Pleiades Pegasus Cassiopeia.

5. Wafting romantically out of the gazebo and across the lawn, Heather slipped on a lone red roller skate and pitched headlong into the pool.

36d Do you put commas where they aren't needed?

A comma where none is needed disrupts the flow of meaning in a sentence. Every comma in a sentence should be placed for a reason: to mark a pause, to set off a unit, to keep words from running together. Cut those that don't serve any such purpose.

1 Eliminate commas that interrupt the flow of a sentence. Sentences with commas inserted where they are not needed can be more confusing to a reader than those with a few commas omitted. Sometimes a comma interrupts what would otherwise be a clear statement.

UNNECESSARY COMMA	Five years into graduate school, Frida found herself, without a degree or prospects for a job.

The writer doesn't mean "Frida found herself," but "Frida found herself without. . . ." Revision is necessary.

COMMA CUT	Five years into graduate school, Frida found herself without a degree or prospects for a job.

36d

At other times, unneeded commas seem to fit a guideline, but really don't. In the following example, the writer may recall that commas often follow introductory words, phrases, and clauses and so places a comma after what looks like an introductory word.

UNNECESSARY COMMA	Although, Frida is 51 years old, she has decided to pursue a new career.

In this case *although* introduces a subordinate clause: *Although Frida is 51 years old. Although* can't be separated from the rest of the clause and still make sense. The comma must be cut.

COMMA CUT   Although Frida is 51 years old, she has decided to pursue a new career.

Here's a second example of a subordinating word incorrectly separated from the remainder of its subordinate clause.

UNNECESSARY COMMA   However, cold it gets, the train arrives on time.

COMMA CUT   However cold it gets, the train arrives on time.

▒ 2 Don't use a comma to separate a subject from a verb.
This common error usually occurs when the full subject of a sentence is more complex than usual—perhaps a noun clause or a verb phrase.

UNNECESSARY COMMA   What happened to the team since last season, isn't clear.

What happened to the team is the subject of the sentence, so it shouldn't be separated from the verb *is* with a comma. The comma must be cut.

COMMA CUT   What happened to the team since last season isn't clear.

Here are additional illustrations of the problem.

WRONG   Fighting for the championship, means playing hard.

RIGHT   Fighting for the championship means playing hard.

WRONG   To keep the team's spirit up, won't be easy.

RIGHT   To keep the team's spirit up won't be easy.

36d
^
i

Of course, when modifiers separate subjects from verbs, commas are used to set off the modifying expressions (see Section 36b). Compare these sentences.

NO MODIFIER/   Frida is determined to complete her edu-
NO COMMAS   cation.

MODIFIERS/COMMAS   Frida, who just turned 51 years old, is determined to complete her education.

In rare cases, a comma may be required between subject and verb to assure clarity.

Those who hope, thrive; those who despair, fail.

▉ 3 Don't use commas to separate compound subjects, predicates, or objects.

WRONG   The Mississippi/ and the Missouri are two of the United States' great rivers.

RIGHT   The Mississippi and the Missouri are two of the United States' great rivers.

WRONG   We toured the museum/ and then explored the monument.

RIGHT   We toured the museum and then explored the monument.

WRONG   Alexander broke his promise to his agent/ and his contract with his publisher.

RIGHT   Alexander broke his promise to his agent and his contract with his publisher.

WRONG   I tried to contact the company by posting an email to its Web site/ and by sending a certified letter to its Denver office.

RIGHT   I tried to contact the company by posting an email to its Web site and by sending a certified letter to its Denver office.

Of course, commas are used to separate full independent clauses joined by conjunctions. Compare the following sentences, both punctuated correctly.

RIGHT   We toured the museum and then explored the monument.

RIGHT   We toured the museum, and then we explored the monument.

36d
^
,

▉ 4 Don't use commas to introduce a series. Usually no punctuation mark is needed. When one is called for, it will usually be a colon, not a comma.

WRONG   States with impressive national parks include/ California, Utah, Arizona, and New Mexico.

RIGHT   States with impressive national parks include California, Utah, Arizona, and New Mexico.

Commas can be used to enclose lists that function as nonessential modifiers.

RIGHT   States with impressive national parks, California, Utah, Arizona, and New Mexico among them, benefit from tourists' dollars.

In such cases, however, all the commas can be confusing. The modifier might be better enclosed by dashes (see Section 40a).

RIGHT   States with impressive national parks—California, Utah, Arizona, and New Mexico among them—benefit from tourists' dollars.

▊ 5 Don't use commas around modifiers that are essential to the meaning of a sentence. When a modifying phrase is essential, it should *not* be set off with commas (see Section 30i).

WRONG   What Asha observed, as a civic volunteer, changed her opinion of journalists.

RIGHT   What Asha observed as a civic volunteer changed her opinion of journalists.

WRONG   Journalists, who say they are dedicated to community service, often have political agendas of their own.

RIGHT   Journalists who say they are dedicated to community service often have political agendas of their own.

EXERCISE 36.4 Working in a group, analyze these sentences to see if all the commas are needed. Then work together to rewrite sentences to get rid of commas that cause awkward interruptions. Notice that some of the commas are necessary.

36d

1. Psychologists, who have studied moods, say that such emotional states are contagious, and compare them to social viruses.

2. Moreover, some people are emotionally expressive, and likely to transmit moods; others, seem to be more inclined to "catch" moods.

3. Trying to pinpoint the exact means by which moods are transmitted, is difficult, since the process happens almost instantaneously.

4. One transmission mechanism is imitation: by unconsciously imitating facial expressions, people produce, in themselves a mood that goes with the expression.

5. People who get along well with others, generally, synchronize their moods, by making a series of changes in their body language.

36e Do you understand the conventional uses of commas?

Aside from the important role commas play within sentences both in linking and separating ideas, commas have many conventional uses you simply have to know to get right.

1 Use commas to introduce quotations or to follow them. For proper placement of these commas and more about punctuating quotations, see Section 38a.

> The lawyer insisted, "He can't be held responsible."
>
> "Don't tell me he can't be held responsible," bellowed Judge Carver.
>
> Ms. Rice said, "I'm not sure about the motion on the floor."
>
> She then asked, "Would the secretary read the motion?"
>
> "Speak up," she added.

No commas are needed when a quotation fits right into a sentence without an introductory phrase or frame. Compare the following examples.

COMMAS NEEDED

"Experience," said Oscar Wilde, "is the name everyone gives to their mistakes."

Said P. G. Wodehouse, "I always advise people never to give advice."

NO COMMAS NEEDED

Oscar Wilde defined experience as "the name everyone gives to their mistakes."

P. G. Wodehouse advised people "never to give advice."

36e
^
,

2 Use commas correctly to separate units of three within numbers. Commas are optional in four-digit numbers.

> 4,110 or 4110
> 99,890
> 1,235,470
> 10,000,000,000

Do not use commas in decimals, social security numbers, street addresses, or zip codes.

■ **3 Use commas correctly in dates.** In American usage, commas separate the day from the year. Note that a year is enclosed by commas when it appears in the middle of a sentence.

World War II began on September 1, 1939.

Germany expanded the war on June 22, 1941, when its armies invaded Russia.

Commas aren't required when only the month and year are given.

World War II began in September 1939.

Commas are not used when dates are given in British form, with the day preceding the month.

World War II began on 1 September 1939.

■ **4 Use commas correctly in addresses.** Commas ordinarily separate street addresses, cities, states, and countries. When these items occur in the middle of a sentence, they are enclosed by commas.

Miami University is in Oxford, Ohio.

Though born in London, England, Denise Levertov is considered an American writer.

The prime minister lives at No. 10 Downing Street, Westminster, London, England.

Commas aren't used between states and zip codes.

Austin, Texas 78712

■ **5 Use commas correctly to separate proper names from titles and degrees that follow.**

Tonya Galvin, Ph.D., has been chosen to replace Howard Brill, M.D.

■ **6 Use commas to follow the salutation in personal letters.**

Dear Dr. Camero,
Dear Ms. Daniel,

36e
^
i

EXERCISE 36.5 Review the following sentences and add commas where necessary.

1. In the autumn of 1863, Abraham Lincoln President of the United States traveled to Gettysburg Pennsylvania to speak at the dedication of a cemetery there.

2. The cemetery was for the soldiers who had fallen at the Battle of Gettysburg, and Lincoln's speech—now known as the Gettysburg Address—opened with the famous words "Fourscore and seven years ago."

3. The Battle of Gettysburg had started on July 1 1863 and had raged for three days.

4. The Civil War would not end until April 1865.

5. The bloodiest battle of the war took place near Sharpsburg Maryland along the banks of Antietam Creek, where a single day of fighting produced over 23000 casualties.

36e
^
ꭵ

CHAPTER 37

Questions About Semicolons and Colons?

Do you have questions about semicolons?

In a sentence, a semicolon marks a stronger pause than a comma, but a weaker pause than a period. Many writers find semicolons confusing. So they avoid them and place commas where semicolons are needed. Or they misuse them, using semicolons where commas work better. In your papers, an editor will use a caret and a semicolon to indicate where a semicolon should be inserted.

> Give Matthew the book, it belongs to him. ⌄

1 Use semicolons to separate items of equal grammatical weight. Semicolons can be used to separate one independent clause from another, one phrase from another, one item in a list from another.

> independent clause; independent clause

> Director John Ford released *Stagecoach* in 1939; a year later, he made *The Grapes of Wrath.*

> phrase; phrase

> My course in cinema taught the basics of movie production, including how to write treatments, outlines, and scripts; how to audition and cast actors; and how to edit 16-mm film.

> item in a list; item in a list; item in a list

> We rented cassettes of *Planes, Trains and Automobiles; Star Trek: Insurrection;* and *Blade Runner—The Director's Cut.*

Because semicolons work only between comparable items, it would be wrong to place a semicolon between an independent clause and a prepositional phrase. Also incorrect would be a semicolon separating a dependent clause and an independent clause. Commas are usually the correct punctuation in such cases.

independent clause, prepositional phrase

WRONG   Many young filmmakers regularly exceed their budgets; in the tradition of the finest Hollywood directors.

RIGHT   Many young filmmakers regularly exceed their budgets, in the tradition of the finest Hollywood directors.

dependent clause, independent clause

WRONG   Although director Alfred Hitchcock once said that actors should be treated like cattle; he won fine performances from many of them.

RIGHT   Although director Alfred Hitchcock once said that actors should be treated like cattle, he won fine performances from many of them.

2 Use semicolons to join independent clauses closely related in thought. Coordinating conjunctions (such as *and, or, nor, for, but, yet, so*) aren't needed when clauses are linked by semicolons.

The history of British cinema is uneven; the best British films come from the period just before and during World War II.

Italian cinema blossomed after World War II; directors like De Sica, Fellini, and Antonioni won critical acclaim.

Omitting the semicolons in the examples above would create run-on sentences (see Section 35d). Replacing the semicolons with commas would produce comma splices (see Section 35c). Both run-ons and comma splices are major sentence errors. Sometimes, however, placing semicolons between very short independent clauses can seem like punctuation overkill.

WITH SEMICOLONS   For best director, Norman picked Alfred Hitchcock; Ryan nominated François Truffaut; and Cleo chose Agnes Varda.

When such clauses are short and closely related, they can be separated by commas.

37a

;

WITH COMMAS   For best director, Norman picked Alfred Hitchcock, Ryan nominated François Truffaut, and
Cleo chose Agnes Varda.

▇ 3 Use semicolons between independent clauses joined by words such as *however, therefore, nevertheless, nonetheless, moreover,* and *consequently*. These words are called *conjunctive adverbs*, but by themselves they cannot link sentences. They require a semicolon.

> Bob Hope started his career in vaudeville; **however,** he made his major mark as a film star and television comic.
>
> The original *Rocky* was an Oscar-winning movie; **unfortunately,** its many sequels have exhausted the original idea.
>
> Films about British spy 007 have been in decline for years; **nevertheless,** new James Bond films continue to appear.

In sentences like those above, using a comma instead of a semicolon before the conjunctive adverb produces a comma splice. This is a common punctuation error (see Section 35c-2).

But here's an important point: when a word like *however* or *therefore* occurs in the middle of an independent clause, it *is* preceded and followed by commas. In the following pair of sentences, note carefully where the boldfaced words appear and how the shifts in their location change the punctuation required.

> *Casablanca* is now admired as a film classic; **however,** its producers and stars regarded it as an average spy thriller.
>
> *Casablanca* is now admired as a film classic; its producers and stars, **however,** regarded it as an average spy thriller.

37a
;

▇ 4 Use semicolons to join independent clauses connected by words or phrases such as *indeed, in fact, at any rate, for example,* and *on the other hand*. These expressions, like conjunctive adverbs, ordinarily require a semicolon before them and a comma after.

> Box office receipts for *The Blair Witch Project*'s opening week were spectacular; **in fact,** the film broke records for an independent film.
>
> The film's directors did not have a major studio promoting the project; **on the other hand,** a brilliant Internet campaign created huge prerelease buzz.

A period could be used instead of the semicolon in these situations.

> Naturally, *The Blair Witch Project* spawned many imitators and parodies. However, none of these works succeeded in the market.

Chart 37.1

Frequently Used Conjunctive Adverbs		
consequently	meanwhile	rather
furthermore	moreover	then
hence	nonetheless	therefore
however	otherwise	thus

5 Use semicolons to separate clauses, phrases, or items in a series that might be confusing if commas alone were used to mark boundaries. Semicolons are especially helpful when complicated phrases or items in a list already contain commas or other punctuation.

> The sound track for the film included the Supremes' "Stop in the Name of Love!"; Bob Dylan's "Rainy Day Women #12 & 35"; and Rodgers and Hart's "Glad to Be Unhappy."

> Matt Damon's filmography includes *School Ties*, which is set in an upper-class prep school; *Saving Private Ryan*, a Steven Spielberg movie in which Damon plays the title character; and *Good Will Hunting*, a drama which earned him an Oscar for best screenplay.

6 Do not use semicolons to introduce quotations. Direct quotations can be introduced by commas or colons.

> WRONG   Wasn't it Mae West who said; "When I'm good I'm very good, but when I'm bad, I'm better"?

> RIGHT   Wasn't it Mae West who said, "When I'm good I'm very good, but when I'm bad, I'm better"?

7 Do not use semicolons to introduce lists.

> WRONG   Paul Robeson performed in several classic films; *Show Boat, Song of Freedom, King Solomon's Mines.*

> RIGHT   Paul Robeson performed in several classic films: *Show Boat, Song of Freedom, King Solomon's Mines.*

Semicolons may separate items *within* a list (see Section 37a-1).

37a
;

■ 8 Use semicolons correctly with quotation marks. Semicolons ordinarily fall outside quotation marks (see Section 38a-6).

> The first Edgar Allan Poe work filmed was "The Raven"; movies based on the poem appeared in 1912, 1915, and 1935.

EXERCISE 37.1 Revise the following sentences, adding or deleting semicolons as needed. Not all semicolons below are incorrect. You may have to substitute other punctuation marks for some semicolons.

1. For many years, biblical spectacles were a staple of the Hollywood film industry, however, in recent years, few such films have been produced.

2. Cecil B. DeMille made the grandest epics; he is quoted as saying; "Give me any couple of pages of the Bible and I'll give you a picture."

3. He made *The Ten Commandments* twice, the 1956 version starred Charlton Heston as Moses.

4. The most famous scene in *The Ten Commandments* is the parting of the Red Sea; the waters opening to enable the Israelites to escape the pursuing army of Pharaoh.

5. DeMille made many nonbiblical movies, some of them, however, were also epic productions with casts of thousands and spectacular settings.

EXERCISE 37.2 Use semicolons to arrange the following clauses, phrases, and bits of information into complete sentences. You will have to add words and ideas.

1. The action in mad-killer movies like *Scream.* A masked killer dispatches random teenagers and even an occasional high school principal. A masked killer attacks the annoying reporter, Gale Weathers. A masked killer attacks and, maybe, kills Dewey, the bumbling cop.

2. Strange titles of Bob Dylan songs from the 1960s. "Subterranean Homesick Blues" "It's Alright, Ma (I'm Only Bleeding)" "Love Minus Zero/No Limit" "Don't Think Twice, It's All Right" "I Shall Be Free—No. 10."

3. Items in E. D. Hirsch's list of everything Americans should know. Carbon-14 dating. "*Veni, vidi, vici.*" "Doctor Livingstone, I presume?" "Yes, Virginia, there is a Santa Claus."

37a
;

4. Exceptionally long movie titles. *Alice Doesn't Live Here Anymore. They Shoot Horses, Don't They? Jo Jo Dancer, Your Life Is Calling. The Effect of Gamma Rays on Man-in-the-Moon Marigolds. Close Encounters of the Third Kind: The Special Edition.*

37b Do you have questions about colons?

Colons are strong directional signals. They show movement in a sentence, pointing your reader's attention to precisely what you wish to highlight, whether it is an idea, a list, a quotation, or even another independent clause. Colons require your attention because their functions are limited and quite specific. In your papers, an editor may use a caret and a colon to indicate where a colon should be used rather than another mark of punctuation.

He spoke just one word, "Rosebud."   ⌃

1 Use colons to direct readers to examples, explanations, or significant words and phrases.

Orson Welles's greatest problem may also have been his greatest achievement: the brilliance of his first film, *Citizen Kane.*

Citizen Kane turns on the meaning of one word uttered by a dying man: "Rosebud."

A colon that highlights an item in this way ordinarily follows a complete sentence. In fact, many readers object strongly to colons placed after linking verbs.

WRONG   America's most bankable film star is: Tom Hanks.
RIGHT   America's most bankable film star is Tom Hanks.

**37b
:**

2 Use colons to direct readers to lists.

Besides *Citizen Kane,* Welles directed, produced, or acted in many movies: *The Magnificent Ambersons, Journey into Fear, The Lady from Shanghai,* and *Macbeth,* to name a few.

Colons that introduce lists ordinarily follow complete sentences. Here is a pair of sentences—both correct—demonstrating your options.

VERSION 1—WITH A COLON	The filmmakers the professor admired most were a diverse group: Alain Robbe-Grillet, François Truffaut, Spike Lee, and Penny Marshall.
VERSION 2—WITHOUT A COLON	The filmmakers the professor admired most were Alain Robbe-Grillet, François Truffaut, Spike Lee, and Penny Marshall—a diverse group.

Colons are omitted after expressions such as *like, for example, such as,* and *that is.* In fact, colons are intended to replace these terms.

WRONG	Shoestring budgets have produced many artistically successful films, such as: *Plutonium Circus, Breaking Away,* and *Slackers.*
RIGHT	Shoestring budgets have produced many artistically successful films, such as *Plutonium Circus, Breaking Away,* and *Slackers.*

Never introduce a list with a colon that separates a preposition from its objects(s).

WRONG	Katharine Hepburn starred in: *Little Women, The Philadelphia Story,* and *The African Queen.*
RIGHT	Katharine Hepburn starred in *Little Women, The Philadelphia Story,* and *The African Queen.*

37b : Colons are used, however, after phrases that specifically announce a list, expressions such as *including these, as follows,* and *such as the following.* Compare the following sentences to understand the difference.

VERSION 1—WITH A COLON	The producer trimmed her budget by cutting out some **frills:** special lighting, rental costumes for the cast, and crew lunches.
VERSION 2—WITHOUT A COLON	The producer trimmed her budget by cutting out **frills, such as** special lighting, rental costumes for the cast, and crew lunches.
VERSION 3—WITH A COLON	The producer trimmed her budget by cutting out **frills such as these:** special lighting, rental costumes for the cast, and crew lunches.

3 Use colons to direct readers to quotations or dialogue.

> Orson Welles commented poignantly on his own career: "I started at the top and worked down."

Don't introduce short quotations with colons. A comma or no punctuation mark at all will suffice. Compare the following sentences.

> Dirty Harry said "Make my day!"
> As Dirty Harry said, "Make my day!"
> We recalled Dirty Harry's memorable phrase: "Make my day!"

In the last example, the colon *is* appropriate because it directs attention to a particular comment.

4 Use colons to join two complete sentences when the second sentence illustrates or explains the first.

> Making a film is like writing a paper: it absorbs all the time you'll give it.

Don't use more than one colon in a sentence. A dash can usually replace one of the colons.

> PROBLEM   Most critics agree on this point: Orson Welles made one of the greatest of films: *Citizen Kane.*
>
> SOLUTION   Most critics agree on this point: Orson Welles made one of the greatest of films—*Citizen Kane.*

Colons and semicolons are not interchangeable, but you can use both marks in the same sentence. A colon, for example, might introduce a list of items separated by semicolons.

> Alfred Hitchcock's quips were often as sharp as his films: "There is no terror in a bang, only in the anticipation of it"; "Drama is life with the dull bits left out"; "Actors are cattle."

5 Use colons to separate titles from subtitles.

> *Nightmare on Elm Street 3: Dream Warriors*
> "Darkest Night: Conscience in *Macbeth*"

6 Use colons in conventional situations. Colons separate numbers when indicating time or citing Bible passages—though MLA style uses a period in biblical citations.

> 12:35 p.m.   Matthew 3:1 (or Matthew 3.1)

37b
:

Colons traditionally follow salutations in business letters.

Dear Ms. Kael: Dear Mr. Ebert:

Colons separate place of publication from publisher and separate date from page numbers in various MLA bibliography entries.

Glenview: Scott, 1961   14 August 1991: 154–63

Colons appear in Web addresses, with no space left after the mark.

<http://google.com/>

EXERCISE 37.3 Revise the following sentences by adding colons or making sure colons are used correctly. Don't assume that every sentence contains an error.

1. No one ever forgets the conclusion of Hitchcock's *Psycho;* the discovery of Norman's mother in the rocking chair.

2. Hitchcock liked to use memorable settings in his films, including: Mt. Rushmore in *North by Northwest,* Radio City Music Hall in *Saboteur,* and the British Museum in *Blackmail.*

3. One actor appears in every Hitchcock film Hitchcock himself.

4. *Rear Window* is a cinematic tour de force: all the action focuses on what Jimmy Stewart sees from his window.

5. Hitchcock probably summed up his own technique best; "There is no terror in a bang, only in the anticipation of it."

37b
:

CHAPTER 38

Questions About Quotation Marks and Ellipses?

38a When do you use quotation marks?

Quotation marks, which always occur in pairs, highlight whatever appears between them. Use double marks (" ") around most quoted material and around titles. Use single quotation marks (' ') to mark quotations (or titles) that fall within quotations.

An editor will use a quotation mark within an inverted caret to indicate that a quotation mark has been omitted.

> "She stole everything but the cameras,ˬGeorge Raft ˇ̈
> once said of Mae West.

1 Use quotation marks around material you are borrowing word for word from sources.

> Emerson reminds us that "nothing great was ever achieved without enthusiasm."
>
> "Next to the originator of a good sentence is the first quoter of it," writes Emerson.

E-Tips

Your email program probably does not use quotation marks to distinguish between your current message and a message you may be responding to. Instead, it usually marks the copied material with a vertical line or other typographical device, typically in the left margin. If the copied material goes back and forth several times, additional lines or characters may appear in the margin. So email has its own way of signaling borrowed material.

---

2 Use quotation marks to set off dialogue. When writing a passage with several speakers, start a new paragraph each time the speaker changes.

Mrs. Bennet deigned not to make any reply; but unable to contain herself, she began scolding one of her daughters.

"Don't keep coughing so, Kitty, for heaven's sake! Have a little compassion on my nerves. You tear them to pieces."

"Kitty has no discretion in her coughs," said her father; "she times them ill."

"I do not cough for my own amusement," replied Kitty fretfully.   —Jane Austen, *Pride and Prejudice*

When dialogue is provided not for its own sake but to make some other point, the words of several speakers may appear within a single paragraph.

Professor Norman was confident that his colleagues would eventually see his point. "They'll come around," he predicted. "They always do." And Professor Brown, for one, was beginning to soften. "I've supported many proposals not half so intelligent."

3 Use quotation marks to cite the titles of short works.

These include titles of songs, essays, magazine and newspaper articles, TV episodes, unpublished speeches, chapters of books, and short poems. Titles of longer works appear in *italics* (see Section 41a-1).

"Love Is Just a Four-Letter Word" song
"Love Is a Fallacy" title of an essay

4 Use quotation marks to draw attention to specific words.

Italics can also be used in these situations (see Section 41a-3).

People clearly mean different things when they write about "democracy."

You might also use quotation marks to signal that you are using a word ironically, sarcastically, or derisively.

The clerk at the desk directed the tourists to their "suites"—bare rooms crowded with cots. A bathroom down the hall would serve as the "spa."

But don't overdo it. Highlighting a tired phrase or cliché just makes it seem more fatigued.

Working around electrical fixtures makes me more nervous than "a cat on a hot tin roof."

■ **5 Surround quotation marks with appropriate punctuation.** A quotation introduced or followed by *said, remarked, observed,* or a similar expression takes a comma.

> Benjamin Disraeli *observed*, "It is much easier to be critical than to be correct."

Commas are used, too, when a single sentence quotation is broken up by an interrupting expression such as *he asked* or *she noted.*

> "If the world were a logical place," Rita Mae Brown *notes*, "men would ride sidesaddle."

When such an expression comes between two successive sentences quoted from a single source, a comma and a period are required.

> "There is no such thing as a moral or an immoral book," *says* Oscar Wilde. "Books are well written, or badly written. That is all."

No additional punctuation is required when a quotation runs smoothly into a sentence you have written.

> Abraham Lincoln observed that "in giving freedom to the slave we assure freedom to the free."

See Section 46c for guidelines on introducing and framing quotations.

■ **6 Use quotation marks correctly with other pieces of punctuation.** Commas and periods ordinarily go *inside* closing quotation marks.

> "This must be what the sixties were like," I thought.

> Down a hotel corridor lined with antiwar posters, I heard someone humming "Blowin' in the Wind."

However, when a sentence ends with a citation in parentheses, the period follows the parenthesis.

> Mike Rose argues that we hurt education if we think of it "in limited or limiting ways" (3).

In American usage, colons and semicolons go *outside* closing quotation marks.

> Riley claimed to be "a human calculator": he did quadratic equations in his head.

> The young Cassius Clay bragged about being "the greatest"; his opponents in the ring soon learned he wasn't boasting.

38a
" "

Question marks, exclamation points, and dashes can fall either inside or outside quotation marks. They fall *inside* when they apply only to the quotation.

> When Mrs. Rattle saw her hotel room, she muttered, "Good grief!"
>
> She turned to her husband and said, "Do you really expect me to stay here?"

They fall *outside* the closing quotation mark when they apply to the complete sentence.

> Who was it who said, "Truth is always the strongest argument"?

E-Tips

Word processors usually give you the option of choosing to print either straight quotes (" ") or left- and right-hand quotation marks (" "). The latter, sometimes called "smart quotes," resemble quotation marks seen in printed items. If you are preparing an HTML document for posting to a Web site, be sure to turn off smart quotes because they will be misconstrued in the HTML document and might appear as an unreadable symbol.

38a
" "

EXERCISE 38.1 Rework the following passage by adding or deleting quotation marks, moving punctuation as necessary, and indenting paragraphs where you think appropriate.

Much to the tourists' surprise, their "uproar" over conditions at their so-called "luxury resort" attracted the attention of a local television station. (In fact, Mrs. Rattle had read "the riot act" to a consumer advocate who worked for the station.) A reporter interviewed Mrs. Rattle, who claimed that she had been promised luxury accommodations. This place smells like old fish she fumed. Even the roaches look unwell. Didn't you check out the accommodations before paying? the reporter asked, turning to Mr. Rattle. He replied that unfortunately they had prepaid the entire vacation. But Mrs. Rattle interrupted. I knew we should have gone to Paris. You never said that! Mr. Rattle objected. As I was trying to say, Mrs. Rattle continued, I'd even rather be in Philadelphia.

EXERCISE 38.2 Write a passage extending the reporter's interview in Exercise 38.1. Or create a dialogue on a subject of your own.

 Point of Difference
The guidelines in this section on quotation marks apply in the United States. Conventions for marking quotations differ significantly from language to language and country to country. French quotation marks, called *guillemets,* look like this: « ». Guillemets are also employed as quotation marks in Spanish, which uses dashes to indicate dialogue. In books published in Britain, you'll find single quotation marks (' ') where American publishers use double marks (" "), and vice versa.

> AMERICAN   Carla said, "I haven't read 'The Raven.'"
>
> BRITISH   Carla said, 'I haven't read "The Raven".'

American and British practices differ, too, on the placement of punctuation marks within quotation marks. In general, British usage tends to locate more punctuation marks (commas especially) outside quotation marks than does American usage.

> AMERICAN   To be proper, say "I *shall* go," not "*will.*"
>
> BRITISH   To be proper, say 'I *shall* go', not '*will*'.

In the United States, follow American practice.

38b When do you use ellipses?

In a sentence an ellipsis mark (sometimes called a "dot, dot, dot") indicates that words or even whole sentences have been cut from a passage or quotation. In MLA style, ellipses added to a quoted passage are now enclosed by brackets: [. . .]. We show MLA-style ellipses in Section 46c-4 and in the sample MLA paper.

38b
. . .

1 Place ellipses where material has been omitted from a direct quotation. This material may be a word, a phrase, a complete sentence, or more.

COMPLETE PASSAGE

Abraham Lincoln closed his First Inaugural Address (March 4, 1861) with these words: "We are not enemies, but friends. We must not be enemies. Though passion may have strained it must not break our bonds of affection. The mystic chords of memory, stretching from every battlefield and patriot grave to every living heart and hearthstone all over this broad land, will yet swell the chorus of the Union, when again touched, as surely they will be, by the better angels of our nature."

PASSAGE WITH ELLIPSES

Abraham Lincoln closed his First Inaugural Address (March 4, 1861) with these words: "We are not enemies, but friends. ... The mystic chords of memory ... will yet swell the chorus of the Union, when again touched, as surely they will be, by the better angels of our nature."

2 Use ellipses to indicate pauses of any kind or to suggest that an action is incomplete or continuing.

We were certain we would finish the report on time ... until the computer crashed and wouldn't reboot.

The rocket rumbled on its launch pad as the countdown ended, "four, three, two, one. ..."

3 Use the correct spacing and punctuation before and after ellipsis marks. An ellipsis is typed as three spaced periods (. . . not ...). When an ellipsis mark appears in the middle of a quoted sentence, leave a space before the first and after the last period.

    mystic chords of memory ... will yet swell

In MLA style, leave a space before the first and after the closing bracket.

    mystic chords of memory, [. . .] will yet swell

If punctuation occurs before the ellipsis, include the mark when it makes your sentence easier to read. The punctuation mark is followed by a space, then the ellipsis mark or (in MLA style) the brackets.

    The mystic chords of memory, ... all over this broad

    land, will yet swell the chorus of the Union.

(See Section 46c-4 on ellipses at the end of a quotation.) When an ellipsis occurs at the end of a complete sentence from a quoted passage or when you delete a full sentence or more, place a period at the end of the sentence, followed by a space and then the ellipsis.

    We must not be enemies. ... The mystic chords

When a parenthetical reference follows a sentence that ends with an ellipsis, leave a space between the last word in the sentence and the ellipsis. Then provide the parenthetical reference, followed by the closing punctuation mark.

    passion may have strained it ... " (102).

4 Keep ellipses to a minimum at the beginning and end of sentences. When you quote from a passage, most readers will understand that you are using only part of a longer work; as a consequence, you don't need ellipses at the beginning and end of most quotations.

UNNECESSARY ELLIPSES
Abraham Lincoln spoke of hope for the Union in his First Inaugural Address (March 4, 1861): ". . . We are not enemies, but friends. . . ."

ELLIPSES REMOVED
Abraham Lincoln spoke of hope for the Union in his First Inaugural Address (March 4, 1861): "We are not enemies, but friends."

5 Use a full line of spaced dots when you delete more than a line of verse. MLA places these dots in brackets.

```
For Mercy has a human heart,

Pity a human face,

[. . . . . . . . . . . . .]

And Peace, the human dress.
```
—William Blake, "The Divine Image" (1789)

EXERCISE 38.3 Abridge the following passage, using at least three ellipses. Be sure the passage is still readable after you have made your cuts.

Within a week, the neglected Victorian-style house being repaired by volunteers began to look livable again, its gables repaired, its gutters rehung, its roof reshingled. Even the grand staircase, rickety and worm-eaten, had been rebuilt. The amateur artisans made numerous mistakes during the project, including painting several windows shut, papering over a heating register, and hanging a door upside down, but no one doubted their commitment to restoring the historic structure. Some spent hours sanding away layers of varnish accumulated over almost six decades to reveal beautiful hardwood floors. Others contributed their organizational talents—many were managers or paperpushers in their day jobs—to keep other workers supplied with raw materials, equipment, and inspiration. The volunteers worked from seven in the morning to seven at night, occasionally

38b
. . .

pausing to talk with neighbors from the area who stopped by with snacks and lunches, but laboring like mules until there was too little light to continue. They all felt the effort was worth it every time they saw the great house standing on the corner in all its former glory.

38b
. . .

CHAPTER 39

Questions About Parentheses and Brackets?

39a When do you use parentheses?

Parentheses are enclosures for comments, asides, or extra information added to sentences; the marks also enclose in-text notes for MLA and APA documentation (see Chapters 48–49). Parentheses are much more common than brackets, which are used in a few specific situations (see Section 39b). An editor will indicate a need for parentheses with carets and symbols in the margin.

> During his first term ∧1969–1973∧ as President, Richard   (/)
> Nixon visited both Moscow and Beijing.

■ 1 Use parentheses to separate material from the main body of a sentence or paragraph. This material may be a word, a phrase, a list, even a complete sentence.

> The airplane flight to Colorado was quick **(only about ninety minutes)** and uneventful.
>
> The emergency kit contained all the expected items **(jumper cables, tire inflator, roadside flares)**.
>
> The buses arrived early, and by noon the stagehands were working at the stadium. **(One of the vans carried a portable stage.)** Preparations for the concert were on schedule.

■ 2 Use parentheses to insert examples, directions, or other details into a sentence.

> The call to the police included an address **(107 West St.)**.
>
> If the children get lost, have them call the school **(346-1317)** or the church office **(471-6109)**.

■ 3 Use parentheses to highlight numbers or letters used in listing items.

> The labor negotiators realized they could **(1)** concede on all issues

immediately, **(2)** stonewall until the public demanded a settlement, or **(3)** hammer out a compromise.

▇ 4 Use the correct punctuation with or around parentheses.

When a complete sentence standing alone is surrounded by parentheses, place its end punctuation inside the parentheses.

The neighborhood was run-down and littered. (Some houses looked as if they hadn't been painted in decades **.)**

However, when a sentence concludes with a parenthesis, the end punctuation for the complete sentence falls outside the final parenthesis mark.

On the corner was a small church (actually a converted store **).**

When parentheses enclose a very short sentence within another sentence, the enclosed sentence ordinarily begins without capitalization and ends without punctuation.

The editor pointed out a misplaced modifier (**the writer glared at her)**, crossed out three paragraphs (**the writer grumbled)**, and then demanded a complete rewrite.

Punctuation may be used, however, when an enclosed sentence is a question or exclamation.

The coup ended (**who would have guessed it?)** almost as quickly as it began.

▇ 5 Don't use punctuation before a parenthesis in the middle of sentences.

A comma before a parenthesis is incorrect; if necessary, a parenthesis may be followed by a comma.

WRONG   Although the Crusades failed in their announced objective, (**Jerusalem still remained in Muslim hands afterward)** the expeditions changed the West dramatically.

RIGHT   Although the Crusades failed in their announced objective (**Jerusalem still remained in Muslim hands afterward),** the expeditions changed the West dramatically.

EXERCISE 39.1 Add parentheses as needed to the following sentences.

1. Native Americans inhabited almost every region of North America, from the peoples farthest north the Inuit to those in the Southwest the Hopi, the Zuni.

2. In parts of what are now New Mexico and Colorado, during the thirteenth century, some ancient tribes moved off the mesas no one knows exactly why to live in cliff dwellings.

3. One cliff dwelling at Mesa Verde covers an area of 66 meters 217 feet by 27 meters 89 feet.

4. Spectacular as they are, the cliff dwellings served the tribes known as the Anasazi for only a short time.

5. The Anasazi left their cliff dwellings, possibly because of a prolonged drought A.D. 1276–1299 in the entire region.

39b When do you use brackets?

Like parentheses, brackets are enclosures. But brackets have fewer and more specialized uses. Brackets and parentheses are usually *not* interchangeable.

An editor will indicate a need for brackets with carets and symbols in the margin.

"She͏͏Aretha Franklin͏is almost as gifted a pianist as she is   [/]
a singer," the reviewer commented.

1 Use brackets to insert comments or explanations into direct quotations. Although you cannot change the words of a direct quotation, you can add information between brackets.

"He [George Lucas] reminded me a little of Walt Disney's version of a mad scientist."   —Steven Spielberg

In other cases, you can insert bracketed material to make the grammar of a quotation fit smoothly into your own syntax. But use this strategy sparingly, taking care not to change the meaning of the original.

Any change you make in an original text, even if only from an uppercase to a lowercase letter or vice versa, should be signaled with brackets.

In *The Dinosaur Heresies,* Bakker rejects " [o] rthodox theory." Dinosaurs, he argues, are not just big reptiles with a "metabolism [that is] pitifully low compared to mammals'."

Brackets around the letter *o* indicate that you have changed Bakker's original capital letter to lowercase.

39b
[ ]

▪ **2 Use brackets to avoid one set of parentheses falling within another.** Turn the inner pair of parentheses into brackets.

The Web site included a full text of the resolution (expressing the sense of Congress on the calculation of the consumer price index **[H.RES.99]**).

▪ **3 Use brackets to acknowledge or highlight errors that originate in quoted materials.** In such cases the Latin word *sic* ("thus") is enclosed in brackets immediately after the error. See Section 46c-6 for details.

The sign over the cash register read "We don't except **[sic]** personal checks for payment."

▪ **4 In MLA style, use brackets around ellipses to show where material has been cut from a quotation.** Without the brackets, readers might think that the ellipses were in the original quotation.

"Poor naked wretches, [. . .] that bide the pelting of this pitiless storm [. . .]."

39b
[ ]

CHAPTER 40
Questions About Dashes, Hyphens, and Slashes?

40a When do you use dashes?

Dashes can either link or separate ideas in sentences. They are bold marks of punctuation to be used with care and a little flair.

Professional editors will use a caret and the symbol $\frac{/}{m}$ to indicate where a dash is needed.

> They were brave soldiers‸ men and women the country $\frac{/}{m}$ could cheer for.

1 Use dashes to add illustrations, examples, or summaries to the ends of sentences. A dash gives emphasis to any addition.

> Dvorak's *New World* Symphony reflects musical themes the composer heard in the United States—including Native American melodies and black spirituals.

> Beethoven's Ninth Symphony was a great accomplishment for an artist in bad health—and completely deaf.

2 Use pairs of dashes to insert information into the middle of a sentence. Information between dashes gets noticed.

> The giants of nineteenth-century Italian opera—Rossini, Donizetti, Bellini, Verdi—worked for demanding and sensitive audiences.

> Many regard Verdi's *Otello*—based on Shakespeare's story of a marriage ruined by jealousy—as the greatest of Italian tragic operas.

3 Use dashes to highlight interruptions, especially in dialogue. The interruption can even be punctuated.

> Candice sputtered, "The opera lasted—I can hardly believe it—five hours!"

> "When—perhaps I should say if?—I ever sit through Wagner's *Ring,* I expect to be paid for it," Joshua remarked.

598   Questions About Dashes, Hyphens, and Slashes?

■ **4 Use dashes to set off items, phrases, or credit lines.**

Charles Ives, William Grant Still, Aaron Copland, George Gershwin—these composers sought to create an American musical idiom.

Members of the audience are asked
—to withhold applause between movements
—to stifle all coughing and sneezing
—to refrain from popping gum.

"Music is the universal language."   —Henry Wadsworth Longfellow

■ **5 Don't use a hyphen when a dash is required.** Keyboarded dashes are made up of two unspaced hyphens:--. No space is left before or after a dash.

WRONG
Beethoven's music-unlike Mozart's-uses emphatic rhythms.

RIGHT
Beethoven's music--unlike Mozart's--uses emphatic rhythms.

You should also be able to create an actual long dash ("em dash") on your word processor by selecting an option that automatically turns - into —. Or you may be able to create the em dash with a key command.

■ **6 Don't use too many dashes.** They can clutter a passage. One pair per sentence is the limit.

WRONG   Mozart—recognized as a genius while still a child—produced more than 600 compositions during his life—including symphonies, operas, and concertos.

RIGHT   Mozart, recognized as a genius while still a child, produced more than 600 compositions during his life—including symphonies, operas, and concertos.

40a

EXERCISE 40.1 Add and delete dashes as necessary to improve the sentences below.

1. Legend has it that Beethoven's Third Symphony was dedicated to Napoleon Bonaparte the champion of French revolutionary ideals until he declared himself emperor.

2. Scholars believe—though they can't be sure—that the symphony was initially called *Bonaparte*—testimony to just how much the idealistic Beethoven admired the French leader.

3. The Third Symphony a revolutionary work itself is now known by the title *Eroica*.

4. The Third, the Fifth, the Sixth, the Seventh, the Ninth Symphonies, they all contain musical passages that most people recognize immediately.

5. The opening four notes of Beethoven's Fifth, da, da, da, dum, may be the most famous in all of music.

40b When do you use hyphens?

Hyphens either join words or divide them between syllables. They should not be confused with dashes, which have an entirely different function (see the preceding section). An editor will usually place carets within the line to indicate missing hyphens.

My mother‸in‸law will retire in June. ‑

1 Learn common hyphenation patterns.

Hyphenate words beginning with the prefixes *all-*, *self-*, and *ex-* or ending with the suffix *-elect*.

all-encompassing	**ex-**hockey player
self-contained	mayor-**elect**

Hyphenate most words beginning with *well-*, *ill-*, and *heavy-*.

well-dressed	**ill-**suited	**heavy-**handed

Most common nouns beginning with *un-*, *non-*, *anti-*, *pro-*, *co-*, and *pre-* are not hyphenated.

uncertain	**anti**slavery	**co**ordinate
nonviolent	**pro**democracy	**pre**recorded

Unabridged dictionaries provide extensive lists of combinations formed with these troublesome prefixes.

40b
-

2 Follow the conventional uses of hyphens.

Use hyphens to write out numbers from twenty-one to ninety-nine. Fractions also take hyphens, but use only one hyphen per fraction.

twenty-nine	one forty-seventh of a mile
one-quarter inch	two hundred forty-six

Use hyphens to indicate double titles, elements, functions, or attributes.

> the secretary-treasurer of our club
> members of the AFL-CIO
> a city-state such as Sparta
> in the space-time continuum

Use hyphens in some technical expressions:

> uranium-235   A-bomb

Use hyphens to link prefixes to proper nouns and their corresponding adjectives.

> **pre-**Columbian   **anti-**American
> **mid-**Victorian   **neo-**Darwinism

Use hyphens to prevent words from being misread.

> a recreation area   the re-creation of an event
> a chicken coop   a student co-op

■ 3 Use hyphens to link some compound nouns and verbs. The conventions for hyphenating words are complicated and inconsistent. Here are some expressions that do take hyphens.

> brother-in-law   great-grandmother
> two-step   walkie-talkie
> water-skier   hit-and-run
> hocus-pocus   president-elect
> cold-shoulder   double-talk
> strong-arm   off-Broadway

Here are some compounds that aren't hyphenated. Some can be written as either single words or separate words.

> cabdriver   best man   sea dog
> cab owner   blockhouse

When in doubt whether to hyphenate, check a dictionary or a reference tool such as the Government Printing Office's *Manual of Style*.

■ 4 Use hyphens to create compound phrases and expressions.

> Some classmates resented her **holier-than-thou** attitude.

> Product innovation suffered because of a **not-invented-here** bias.

■ 5 Use hyphens to link compound modifiers before a noun. The hyphen makes the modification easier to read and understand.

> an **up-or-down** vote
> an **English-speaking** country
> a **sharp-looking** suit
> a **stop-motion** sequence
> a **seventeenth-century** vase

How can you tell when you are dealing with a compound modifier? Try removing one of the modifiers, placing a comma between them, or inserting *and*. If the expression changes in meaning or becomes difficult to understand, it may require a hyphen (but see also Sections 36c-4 and 36c-5).

> a stop, action camera? → a **stop-action** camera
> a well, known artist? → a **well-known** artist
> a bone and chilling scream? → a **bone-chilling** scream

Do not use hyphens with adverbs that end in *-ly*. Nor should you use hyphens with *very*.

> a **sharply honed** knife   a **quickly written** note
> a **bitterly cold** morning   a **very hot** day

When compound modifiers follow a noun, omit the hyphen.

> The artist was **well known.**
> The scream was **bone chilling.**

■ 6 Handle suspended modifiers correctly. Sometimes a word or phrase may have more than a single hyphenated modifier. These **suspended modifiers** should look like the following.

> Anne planned her vacation wardrobe to accommodate **cold-**, **cool-**, and **wet-**weather days.

> Whether the math class should be a **first-** or **second-**semester course was the one thing we couldn't determine.

■ 7 Do not hyphenate words at the end of lines. Most style manuals advise against such divisions when typing. On a computer, word wrap automatically eliminates end-of-line divisions.

If you must divide a word, break it only at a syllable. Check a dictionary for accurate syllable breaks. Don't guess.

> fu/se/lage   vin/e/gary
> lo/qua/cious   cam/ou/flage

**40b
–**

Never hyphenate contractions, numbers, abbreviations, acronyms, or one-syllable words at the end of lines. The following divisions would be inappropriate.

would- n't	250,- 000,000
NA- TO	U.S.- M.C.
Ph.- D.	NB- C

EXERCISE 40.2 In the following sentences, indicate which form of the words in parentheses is preferable. Use a dictionary if you are not familiar with the terms.

1. Local citizens have a (once in a lifetime/once-in-a-lifetime) opportunity to preserve an (old-growth/oldgrowth) forest.

2. A large, wooded parcel of land is about to be turned into a shopping mall by (real-estate/realestate) speculators and (pinstripe suited/pinstripe-suited) investors.

3. The forest provides a haven for (wild-life/wildlife) of all varieties, from (great horned owls/great-horned owls) to (ruby throated/ruby-throated) hummingbirds.

4. Does any community need (video stores/video-stores), (T shirt/T-shirt) shops, and (over priced/overpriced) boutiques more than acres of natural habitat?

5. This (recently-proposed/recently proposed) development can be stopped by petitioning the (city-council/city council).

40c When do you use slashes?

Slashes are used to indicate divisions. They are rare pieces of punctuation with a few specific functions. About the only problem slashes pose concerns the spacing before and after the mark. That spacing depends on how the slash is being used.

1 Use slashes to separate expressions that indicate a choice. In these cases, no space is left before or after the slash.

either/or	he/she	yes/no	pass/fail
win/lose	up/down	on/off	right/wrong

Some readers object to these expressions, preferring *he or she,* for example, to *he/she* (sometimes written as *s/he*).

2 Use slashes to indicate fractions. Use a hyphen to attach a whole number and a fraction. Again, no spaces are left between the numbers, slashes, and hyphens.

2/3   2-2/3   5-3/8

3 Use slashes in typing World Wide Web addresses.

<http://nps.gov/glac/press.htm>

Note that no spaces precede or follow slashes in World Wide Web addresses.

4 Use slashes to divide lines of poetry quoted within sentences. When used in this way, a space is left on either side of the slash.

```
Only then does Lear understand that he has been a

failure as a king: "O, I have taken / Too little care

of this!"
```

If you cite more than three lines of verse, set the passage as a block quotation and break the lines as they occur in the poem itself. No slashes are required.

```
Poor naked wretches, wheresoever you are,

That bide the pelting of this pitiless storm,

How shall your houseless heads and unfed sides,

Your looped and windowed raggedness, defend you

From seasons such as these?
```

40c

/

CHAPTER 41

Questions About Italics and Capitalization?

41a When do you use italics?

Italics, like quotation marks, draw attention to a title, word, or phrase. In a printed text, italics are *slanted letters*. In typed or handwritten papers, italics are signaled by <u>underlining the appropriate words</u>. In email systems that don't yet transmit underscoring or italic letters, italics can be signaled by typing _ before and after the emphasized word or expression: _Newsweek_.

If you are using a computer that can print italicized words, ask your instructor or editor whether you should print actual italics in your paper. (They may prefer that you use an underscore.)

An editor will underline a word that needs to be italicized and mark *ital* in the margin.

I was reading Stephen King's <u>Christine</u>.   *ital*

■ **1 Use italics to set off some titles.** Some titles and names are italicized; others appear between quotation marks. Chart 41.1 on page 605 provides guidance.

Neither italics nor quotation marks are used for the names of *types* of trains, ships, aircraft, or spacecraft.

DC-10	Trident submarine
B-1	Boeing 777

Neither italics nor quotation marks are used with titles of major religious texts, books of the Bible, or classic legal documents.

the Bible	the Qur'an
1 Romans	the Magna Carta
the Constitution	the Declaration of Independence

■ **2 Use italics to set off foreign words or phrases.** Italics emphasize scientific names and foreign terms that haven't become accepted into the English vocabulary.

Pierre often described his co-workers as *les bêtes humaines.*

Chart 41.1

Titles *Italicized* or "In Quotes"

TITLES *ITALICIZED*

books	*Misery* or Misery
magazines	*Slate* or Slate
journals	*JAMA* or JAMA
newspapers	*USA Today* or USA Today
films	*Casablanca* or Casablanca
TV shows	*Dawson's Creek* or Dawson's Creek
radio programs	*All Things Considered* or All Things Considered
plays	*Hamlet* or Hamlet
long poems	*Beowulf* or Beowulf
long musical pieces	*The Mikado* or The Mikado
albums	Radiohead's *Kid A* or Kid A
paintings	Schnabel's *Adieu* or Adieu
sculptures	Christo's *Running Fence* or Running Fence
dances	Antonio's *Goya* or Goya
ships	*Titanic* or Titanic
	U.S.S. *Saratoga* or U.S.S. Saratoga
trains	the *Orient Express* or the Orient Express
aircraft	*Enola Gay* or Enola Gay
spacecraft	*Apollo 11* or Apollo 11
software programs	*Microsoft Word* or Microsoft Word

TITLES "IN QUOTES"

chapters of books	"Lessons from the Pros"
articles in magazines	"Is the Stock Market Too High?"
articles in journals	"Vai Script and Literacy"
articles in newspapers	"Inflation Heats Up"
sections in newspapers	"Living in Style"
TV episodes	"Drew's New Car"
radio episodes	"McGee Goes Crackers"
short stories	"Araby"
short poems	"The Red Wheelbarrow"
songs	"God Bless America"

41a
italic

Foreign words absorbed by English over the centuries should not be italicized. To be certain, look them up in a recent dictionary.

crèche   gumbo   gestalt   arroyo

Common abbreviations from Latin appear without italics or underscoring.

etc.   et al.   i.e.   viz.

■ **3 Use italics (or quotation marks) to emphasize or clarify a letter, a word, or a phrase.**

Does that word begin with an *f* or a *ph?*

"That may be how you define *fascist*," she replied.

When some people talk about *school spirit*, they really mean "Let's party."

EXERCISE 41.1 Indicate whether the following titles or names in boldface should be italicized, in quotation marks, or unmarked. If you don't recognize a name below, consult an encyclopedia or another reference work.

1. launching a **Titan III** at Cape Kennedy

2. **My Fair Lady** playing at the **Paramount Theater**

3. watching **I Love Lucy**

4. sunk on the passenger ship **Andrea Doria**

5. returning **A Farewell to Arms** to the public library

6. watching **Casablanca** again on a **Panasonic** DVD player

7. discussing the colors of Picasso's **The Old Guitarist**

8. reading Jackson's **The Lottery** one more time

9. picking up a copy of **The Los Angeles Times**

10. whistling **Here Comes the Sun** from the Beatles' **Abbey Road**

11. The White House Web site is at
    <http://www.whitehouse.gov/>

12. You can write the senator at
    <senator@hutchison.senate.gov>

41b
cap

41b How do you capitalize sentences, titles, and poems?

Capital letters can cause problems simply because you have to remember the conventions guiding their use. Fortunately, you can observe the guidelines for capital letters in almost every sentence you read.

In your papers, an editor may write *cap* in the margin next to a small letter that needs to be changed to uppercase.

> I wrote a letter to president Bush. *cap*

An editor will write *lc* (for "lowercase") in the margin indicating a capital letter that needs to be changed to a small letter.

> We spoke to the Librarian today. *lc*

1 Capitalize the first word in a sentence. You can set most word processors to capitalize sentence beginnings automatically.

> Naomi picked up the tourists at their hotel.
> What a remarkable city Washington is!

2 Capitalize the first word in a direct quotation that is a full sentence.

> Ira asked, "Where's the National Air and Space Museum?"
> "Good idea!" Naomi agreed. "Let's go there."

Use lowercase for quotations that continue after an interruption.

> "It's on the Mall," Naomi explained, "near the Hirschhorn gallery."

3 Don't capitalize the first word of a phrase or clause that follows a colon unless you want to emphasize the word. You may also capitalize the first word after a colon if it is part of a title.

NO CAPS AFTER COLON	They ignored one item while parking the car: a no-parking sign.
CAPS FOR EMPHASIS	The phrase haunted her: Your car has been towed!
CAPS FOR TITLE	*Marilyn: The Untold Story*

41b
cap

4 Don't capitalize the first word of a phrase or sentence enclosed by dashes.

> Audrey's first screenplay—a thriller about industrial espionage—had been picked up by an agent.
>
> Her work—she couldn't believe it—was now in the hands of a studio executive.

5 Capitalize the titles of papers, books, articles, poems, and so on. In MLA style, capitalize the first and last word of the

title. Capitalize all other words *except* articles (*a, an, the*), prepositions, the *to* in infinitives, and coordinating conjunctions—unless they are the first or last words.

> Non-fiction book: *Amusing Ourselves to Death*
> Novel: *With Fire and Sword*
> Magazine article "Confessions of a Sports Car Bolshevik"
> Title of a term paper: "Can Quality Survive the Standardized Test?"

Articles and prepositions are capitalized when they follow a colon, usually as part of a subtitle.

> *A Dream Deferred: The Second Betrayal of Black Freedom in America*

Checklist 41.1

Capitalizing Titles

TO CAPITALIZE A TITLE, FOLLOW THESE THREE STEPS.

• Capitalize the first word.

• Capitalize the last word.

• Capitalize all other words *except*

—articles (*a, an, the*)

—the *to* in infinitives

—prepositions

—coordinating conjunctions

41b
cap

6 Capitalize the first word in lines of quoted poetry unless the poet has used lowercase letters.

Sumer is ycomen in,	Ida,
Loude sing cuckoo!	ho, and Oh,
Groweth reed and bloweth meed,	Io!
And springth the wode now.	spaces
Sing cuckoo!	with places
—"The Cuckoo Song"	tween 'em
	—T. Beckwith, "Travels"

EXERCISE 41.2 Correct the problems in capitalization in the following sentences.

1. The passenger next to me asked, "do you remember when air travel used to be a pleasure?"

2. I couldn't reply immediately: My tray table had just flopped open and hit me on the knees.

3. The plane we were on—A jumbo jet that seated nine or ten across—had been circling Dulles International for hours.

4. "We'll be landing momentarily," the flight attendant mumbled, "If we are lucky."

5. I had seen the film version of this flight: *airplane!*

41c When do you capitalize persons, places, and things?

When you are unsure whether a particular word needs to be capitalized, check a dictionary. Don't guess, especially when you are dealing with proper nouns (nouns that name a particular person, place, or thing—*Geoffrey Chaucer, Ohio, Lincoln Memorial*) or proper adjectives (adjectives formed from proper nouns—*Chaucerian*). The guidelines below move from persons to places to things.

1 Capitalize the names and initials of people and characters.

W. C. Fields	Anzia Yezierska
Cher	Minnie Mouse
I. M. Pei	J. Hector St. Jean Crèvecoeur

A few people prefer that their names not be capitalized. Respect that choice. Similarly, you should follow the capitalization people use in their email addresses—where lowercase letters dominate.

e. e. cummings	bell hooks
sugarbear@mail.utexas.edu	

41c
cap

2 Capitalize titles that precede names.

Commissioner Angela Brown
Vice President Mondale
Justice Sandra Day O'Connor
Auntie Mame

3 Capitalize titles after names when the title describes a specific person. But don't capitalize such a title when the title is more general. Compare:

> Robert King, the Dean of Liberal Arts
> Robert King, a dean at the university

Don't capitalize the titles of relatives that follow names. Compare:

> Anthony Pancioli, Cathy's uncle
> Cathy's Uncle Anthony

EXCEPTION   Capitalize academic titles that follow a name.

> Iris Miller, **Ph.D.**
> Enrique Lopez, Master of Arts

■ 4 Don't capitalize minor titles when they stand alone without names.

> a commissioner in Cuyahoga County
> a lieutenant in the Air Force
> the first president of our club

EXCEPTIONS   Prestigious titles are regularly capitalized even when they stand alone. Lesser titles may be capitalized when they clearly refer to a particular individual or when they describe a position formally.

> President of the United States
> the President
> Secretary of State
> the Chair of the Classics Department argued . . .

■ Point of Difference

Style manuals don't always agree about capitalizing titles. Some recommend, for example, that you not capitalize expressions such as *the president* or *the secretary of state* unless they are followed by a name: *President Carter, former Secretary of State Henry Kissinger.* You should follow whatever manual of style is recommended in your course, field, or office.■

■ 5 Capitalize the names of national, political, and ethnic groups.

Kenyans	Australians	African Americans
Chinese	Chicanos	Croatians
Libertarians	Democrats	Republicans

EXCEPTION   The names of racial groups, economic groups, and social classes are usually not capitalized.

blacks	whites
the proletariat	the knowledge class

■ **6 Capitalize the names of businesses, corporations, organizations, unions, clubs, schools, and trademarked items.**

> Time, Inc.
> Oklahoma State University
> National Rifle Association
> Chemical Workers Union
> Kleenex
> Xerox copy

Note that some companies and institutions capitalize more than just an initial letter in their names or logos.

> DaimlerChrysler
> FedEx
> AOL

■ **7 Capitalize the names of religious figures, religious groups, and sacred books.**

God	the Savior	Buddha
Buddhism	Catholics	Judaism
the Bible	the Qur'an	Talmudic tradition

EXCEPTIONS The terms *god* and *goddess* are not capitalized when used generally. When *God* is capitalized, pronouns referring to God are also capitalized.

> The Greeks had a pantheon of gods and goddesses.
> The Goddess of Liberty appears on our currency.
> The cardinal praised God and all His works.

41c
cap

■ **8 Do not routinely capitalize academic ranks.** Such ranks include the terms *freshman, first-year, sophomore, junior, senior, graduate, postgrad.*

> The college had many fifth-year seniors.
> The freshman dormitory was a dump.
> The teacher was a graduate student.

EXCEPTION Capitalize academic ranks when these groups are referred to as organized bodies or institutions.

> a representative of the Senior Class
> the Freshman Cotillion

█9 Capitalize academic degrees when they are abbreviated. Abbreviated degrees include Ph.D., LL.D., M.A., M.S., B.A., B.S. Do not capitalize those degrees when they are spelled out.

> Maria earned her **Ph.D.** the same day Mark received his **LL.D.**
> Leon Railsback, **M.A.**
> Leon has a **m**aster of **a**rts degree.
> Who conferred the **b**achelor of **s**cience degrees?

EXCEPTION Academic degrees spelled out in full are capitalized when they follow a name.

> Leon Railsback, **M**aster of **A**rts
> Maria Ramos, **D**octor of **P**hilosophy

█10 Capitalize the names of places. Also capitalize words based on place names and the names of specific geographic features such as lakes, rivers, and oceans.

Asia	Old Faithful
Asian	the Amazon
the Bronx	the Gulf of Mexico
Lake Erie	Deaf Smith County
Washington	the Atlantic Ocean

EXCEPTION Don't capitalize compass directions unless they name a specific place or are part of a place name.

north	North America
south	the South
eastern Ohio	the Middle East

41c
cap

Many writers forget to capitalize words that identify nationalities or countries—words such as *English, French,* or *Mexican.*

WRONG	Kyle has three english courses.
RIGHT	Kyle has three English courses.
WRONG	Janet drives only american cars.
RIGHT	Janet drives only American cars.

When proofreading, be sure to capitalize most words derived from the names of countries.

█11 Capitalize abstractions when you want to give them special emphasis. Terms such as *love, truth, mercy,* and *patriotism* (which ordinarily appear in small letters) may be capitalized when you discuss them as concepts or when you wish to give them special emphasis, perhaps as the subject of a paper.

> What is this thing called Love?
> The conflict was between Truth and Falsehood.

There is no need to capitalize abstractions used without special emphasis.

> Byron had fallen in love again.
> Either tell the truth or abandon hope of rescue.

12 **Capitalize the names of buildings, structures, or monuments.**

Yankee Stadium	Hoover Dam
the Alamo	the Golden Gate Bridge
Trump Tower	Indianapolis Speedway

13 **Capitalize the names of particular objects.** They might include ships, planes, automobiles, brand-name products, events, documents, and musical groups.

S.S. *Titanic*	Boeing 777
Ford Focus	Eskimo Pie
Super Bowl XXX	the Constitution
Rolling Stones	Fifth Amendment

14 **Capitalize most periods of time.** Periods of time include days, months, holidays, historical epochs, and historical events. You can set most word processors to capitalize days of the week automatically.

Monday	the Reformation
May	World War II
Middle Ages	Bastille Day
Fourth of July	Pax Romana

EXCEPTION Seasons of the year are usually not capitalized.

| winter | spring | summer | fall |

15 **Capitalize terms ending in *-ism* when they name specific literary, artistic, religious, or cultural movements.** When in doubt, check a dictionary.

Impressionism	Vorticism
Judaism	Catholicism
Buddhism	Romanticism

41c
cap

EXCEPTION Many terms ending in *-ism* are not capitalized.

socialism   capitalism   monetarism

■ **16 Capitalize school subjects and classes only when the subjects themselves are proper nouns.**

biology   chemistry
English   Russian history
French   physics

EXCEPTION Titles of specific courses (such as you might find in a college catalog) are capitalized.

Biology 101   Chemistry Lab 200   English 346K

■ **17 Capitalize all the letters in acronyms and initialisms.**
(See Section 42a for more detail.)

NATO   OPEC   SALT
DNA   GMC   MCAT

EXCEPTION Don't capitalize familiar acronyms that seem like ordinary words. When in doubt, check a dictionary.

radar   sonar   laser

EXERCISE 41.3 Capitalize in the following sentences as necessary.

1. The east asian students visiting the district of columbia were mostly juniors pursuing b.a.'s while the african-american students were predominantly graduate students seeking master's degrees.

2. The constitution and the declaration of independence are on view at the national archives.

3. I heard the doorkeeper at the hilton speaking spanish to the general secretary of the united nations.

4. Visitors to washington, d.c., include people from around the world: russians from moscow, egyptians from cairo, aggies from texas, buckeyes from ohio.

5. At the white house, the president will host a conference on democracy and free enterprise in the spring, probably in april.

41c
cap

CHAPTER 42

Questions About Abbreviations and Numbers?

42a How do you handle abbreviations?

Using abbreviations, acronyms (*NATO, radar*), and initialisms (*HBO, IRS*) can make some writing simpler. Many conventional abbreviations are acceptable in all kinds of papers.

a.m.	p.m.
Mrs.	Mr.
B.C.	A.D.
Ph.D.	M.D.

Other abbreviations are appropriate on forms, reports, and statistics sheets, but not in more formal writing.

Jan.—January
ft.—foot
no.—number
mo.—month

An editor will usually indicate a problem with an abbreviation by circling a word or expression and marking *abbr* in the margin.

The house has more than 2400 ⟨sq. ft. ⟩ *abbr*

An abbreviation is the Mini-Me for a complete word or expression.

█1 Be consistent in punctuating abbreviations and acronyms. Abbreviations of single words usually take periods.

vols.   Jan.   Mr.

Initialisms are usually written without periods. You may still use periods with these terms, but be consistent.

HBO   IRS   AFL-CIO   URL

Acronyms ordinarily do not require periods.

CARE   NATO   NOW

Acronyms that have become accepted words never need periods.

sonar   radar   laser   scuba

Periods are usually omitted after abbreviations in technical writing unless a measurement or other item might be misread without a period—for example, *in.*

Consistently use three periods or none at all in terms such as the following. Current usage generally omits the periods.

m.p.g. *or* mpg   r.p.m. *or* rpm   m.p.h. *or* mph

█2 Be consistent in capitalizing abbreviations, acronyms, and initialisms. Capitalize the abbreviations of words that are capitalized when written out in full.

General Motors—GM   University of Toledo—UT
U.S. Navy—USN   98° Fahrenheit—98°F.

Don't capitalize the abbreviations of words not capitalized when written out in full.

pound—lb.   minutes—min.

Capitalize most initialisms.

IRS   CRT   UCLA   NBC

Always capitalize *B.C.E.* and *A.D.* Printers may set them as small caps: *B.C.E.* and *A.D.*

You may capitalize *A.M.* and *P.M.*, but they often appear in small letters: *a.m.* and *p.m.* Printers may set them as small caps: *A.M.* and *P.M.*

Don't capitalize acronyms that have become accepted words: *sonar, radar, laser, scuba.*

█3 Use the appropriate abbreviations for titles, degrees, and names. Some titles are almost always abbreviated (*Mr., Ms.,*

42a
abbr

Mrs., Jr.). Other titles are normally written out in full, though they may be abbreviated when they precede a first name or initial.

President	President Bush	Pres. George W. Bush
Senator	Senator Clinton	Sen. Hillary Clinton
Professor	Professor Eberly	Prof. Rosa Eberly
Reverend	Reverend Call	Rev. Ann Call
	the Reverend Dr. Call	Rev. Dr. Call
Secretary of State	Secretary Powell	Sec. Colin Powell

Never let abbreviated titles of this kind appear alone in a sentence.

> **WRONG** The **gov.** urged the **sen.** to support the bill.
> **RIGHT** The **governor** urged the **senator** to support the bill.

Give credit for academic degrees either before a name or after—not both. Don't, for example, use both *Dr.* and *Ph.D.* in the same name.

> **WRONG** **Dr.** Katherine Martinich, **Ph.D.**
> **RIGHT** **Dr.** Katherine Martinich
> Katherine Martinich, **Ph.D.**

Abbreviations for academic titles often stand by themselves, without names attached.

> Professor Kim received her **Ph.D.** from Penn State and her **B.S.** from St. Vincent College.

■ **4 Use the appropriate technical abbreviations.** Abbreviations are often used in professional, governmental, scientific, military, and technical writing.

DNA	UHF	EKG	START
SALT	GNP	LEM	kW

When writing for nontechnical audiences, spell out technical terms in full the first time you use them. Then in parentheses give the specialized abbreviation you will use in the rest of the paper.

> The two congressional candidates debated the effects a tax increase might have on the gross national product (GNP).

■ **5 Use the appropriate abbreviations for agencies and organizations.** In some cases, the abbreviation or acronym regularly replaces the full name of a company, agency, or organization.

FBI	IBM	MCI	AT&T
AFL-CIO	GOP	PPG	MGM
A&P	BBC	NCAA	MTV

42a
abbr

■ **6 Use the appropriate abbreviations for dates.** Dates are not abbreviated in most writing. Write out in full the days of the week and months of the year.

> WRONG   They arrived in Washington on a **Wed.** in **Apr.**
> RIGHT   They arrived in Washington on a **Wednesday** in **April.**

Abbreviations of months and days are used primarily in notes, lists, forms, and reference works.

■ **7 Use the appropriate abbreviations for time and temperatures.** Abbreviations that accompany time and temperatures are acceptable in all kinds of writing.

43 B.C.	A.D. 144	1:00 a.m.	98°F
143 B.C.E.	1066 C.E.	4:36 p.m.	13°C

Notice that the abbreviation B.C. appears after a date, A.D. usually before one. Both expressions are always capitalized. You may also see B.C.E. (Before the Common Era) used in place of B.C. and C.E. (Common Era) substituted for A.D.

■ **8 Use the appropriate abbreviations for weights, measures, and times.** Technical terms or measurements are commonly abbreviated when used with numbers, but they are written out in full when they stand alone in sentences. Even when accompanied by numbers, the terms usually look better in sentences when spelled out completely.

28 mpg	3 tsps.	40 km.	450 lbs.
50 min.	30 kg.	2 hrs.	40 mph

Mariah didn't really care how many **miles per hour** her Audi could travel on the autobahn.

The abbreviation for number—*No.* or *no.*—is appropriate in technical writing, but only when immediately followed by a number.

> NOT   The **no.** on the contaminated dish was **073.**
> BUT   The contaminated dish was **no. 073.**

No. also appears in footnotes, endnotes, and citations.

■ **9 Use the appropriate abbreviations for places.** In most writing, place names are not abbreviated except in addresses and in reference tools and lists. However, certain abbreviations are accepted in academic and business writing.

USA   USSR   UK   Washington, D.C.

42a
abbr

In addresses (but not in written text), use the standard postal abbreviations, without periods, for the states.

Alabama	AL	Montana	MT
Alaska	AK	Nebraska	NE
Arizona	AZ	Nevada	NV
Arkansas	AR	New Hampshire	NH
California	CA	New Jersey	NJ
Colorado	CO	New Mexico	NM
Connecticut	CT	New York	NY
Delaware	DE	North Carolina	NC
Florida	FL	North Dakota	ND
Georgia	GA	Ohio	OH
Hawaii	HI	Oklahoma	OK
Idaho	ID	Oregon	OR
Illinois	IL	Pennsylvania	PA
Indiana	IN	Rhode Island	RI
Iowa	IA	South Carolina	SC
Kansas	KS	South Dakota	SD
Kentucky	KY	Tennessee	TN
Louisiana	LA	Texas	TX
Maine	ME	Utah	UT
Maryland	MD	Vermont	VT
Massachusetts	MA	Virginia	VA
Michigan	MI	Washington	WA
Minnesota	MN	West Virginia	WV
Mississippi	MS	Wisconsin	WI
Missouri	MO	Wyoming	WY

All the various terms for *street* are written out in full, except in addresses.

boulevard	road	avenue	parkway
highway	alley	place	circle

42a
abbr

But *Mt.* (for *mount*) and *St.* (for *saint*) are acceptable abbreviations in place names when they precede a proper name.

Mt. Vesuvius   **St.** Charles Street

■ 10 Use the correct abbreviations for certain expressions preserved from Latin.

i.e. (*id est*—that is)
e.g. (*exempli gratia*—for example)
et al. (*et alii*—and others)
etc. (*et cetera*—and so on)

In most writing, it is better to use English versions of these and other Latin abbreviations. Avoid using the abbreviation *etc.* in formal or academic writing. Never write *and etc.*

11 Use the appropriate abbreviations for divisions of books.
The many abbreviations for books and manuscripts (*p., pp., vols., ch., chpts., bk., sect.*) are fine in footnotes or parenthetical citations, but don't use them alone in sentences.

WRONG	Richard stuck the **bk.** in his pocket after reading **ch.** five.
RIGHT	Richard stuck the **book** in his pocket after reading **chapter** five.

12 Use symbols as abbreviations carefully.
Symbols such as %, +, =, ≠, <,> make sense in technical and scientific writing, but in other academic papers, spell out the full words. Most likely to cause a problem is % for *percent.*

ACCEPTABLE	Mariah was shocked to learn that **80%** of the cars towed belong to tourists.
PREFERRED	Mariah was shocked to learn that **80 percent** of the cars towed belong to tourists.

You can use a dollar sign—$—in any writing as long as it is followed by an amount. Don't use both the dollar sign and the word *dollar.*

WRONG	The fine for parking in a towing zone is **$125 dollars.**
RIGHT	The fine for parking in a towing zone is **$125.**
RIGHT	The fine for parking in a towing zone is **one hundred twenty-five dollars.**

42a
abbr

The ampersand (&) is an abbreviation for *and.* Do not use it in formal writing except when it appears in a title or name: *Road & Track.*

EXERCISE 42.5 Correct the sentences below, abbreviating where appropriate or expanding abbreviations that would be incorrect in college or professional writing. Check the punctuation for accuracy and consistency. If you insist on periods with acronyms and initialisms, use them throughout the passage.

1. There's a better than 70% chance of rain today.

2. Irene sent angry ltrs. to a dozen networks, including NBC, A.B.C., ESPN, and CNN.

3. The Emperor Claudius was born in 10 b.c. and died in 54 A.D.

4. Dr. Kovatch, M.D., works for the Federal Department of Agriculture (FDA).

5. I owe the company only $175 dollars, & expect to pay the full amount before the end of the mo.

42b How do you handle numbers?

You can express numbers in writing either through numerals or through words.

1	one
25	twenty-five
100	one hundred
1/4	one-fourth
0.05%	five hundredths of a percent *or*
	five one-hundredths of a percent

You'll likely use numerals in technical, scientific, and business writing. In other kinds of documents, you may combine words and numerals. (For guidelines on using hyphens with numbers that are spelled out, see Section 40b-2.)

▇ 1 Write out numbers from one to nine; use numerals for numbers larger than nine.

42b
num

10	15	39
101	115	220
1001	1021	59,000
101,000	10,000,101	50,306,673,432

In most cases, spell out ordinal numbers (that is, numbers that express a sequence): *first, second, third, fourth,* and so on. Spell out numbers that identify centuries.

in the fifteenth century
twentieth-century philosophers

 Point of Difference

These guidelines have variations and exceptions. The MLA style manual, for example, recommends spelling out any number that can be expressed in one or two words.

thirteen	twenty-one
three hundred	fifteen thousand

The APA style manual suggests using figures for most numbers above ten unless they appear at the beginning of a sentence.

Thirty-three workers were rescued from an oil platform.

Check the style manual in your field to confirm how numbers ought to be presented in your writing.

2 Combine words and figures when you need to express large round numbers.

100 billion	$32 million	103 trillion

Avoid shifting between words and figures. When you need numerals to express some numbers in a sentence, use numbers throughout.

There were over **125,000** people at the protest and **950** police officers, but only **9** arrests.

When one number follows another, alternate words and figures for clarity.

33 fifth graders	12 first-term representatives
2 four-wheel-drive vehicles	five 5-gallon buckets

**42b
num**

3 Use numerals when comparing numbers or suggesting a range. Numerals are easier to spot and compare than words.

A blackboard at the traffic office listed a **$50** fine for jaywalking, **$100** for speeding, and **$125** for parking in a towing zone.

4 Don't begin sentences with numerals. Either spell out the number or rephrase the sentence so that the numeral is not the first word.

WRONG   32 people were standing in line at the parking violation center.

RIGHT   Thirty-two people were standing in line at the parking violation center.

Sentences may, however, begin with dates.

1998 was the year Marla graduated from high school.

■5 **Use numerals for dates, street numbers, page numbers, sums of money, and various ID and call numbers.**

July 4, 1776	1860–1864
6708 Beauford Dr.	1900 East Blvd.
p. 352	pp. 23–24
$2,749.00	43¢
Channel 8	103.5 FM
PR 105.5 R8	SSN 111-00-1111

Don't use an ordinal form in dates.

WRONG   May 2**nd**, 1991

RIGHT   May 2, 1991 *or* 2 May 1991

■6 **Use numerals for measurements, percentages, statistics, and scores.**

35 mph	13°C	Austin, TX 78750
75 percent	0.2 liters	5.5 pupils per teacher
2½ miles	15%	Browns 42—Steelers 7

Use numerals for time with *a.m.* and *p.m.;* use words with *o'clock.*

2:15 p.m.	6:00 a.m.	six o'clock

■7 **Form the plural of numbers by adding** *-s* **or** *-'s.*

five 6s in a row   five 98's

See Section 25a for more on plurals.

42b
num

EXERCISE 42.2 Decide whether numbers used in the following sentences are handled appropriately. Where necessary, change numerals to words and words to numerals. Some expressions may not need revision.

1. 4 people will be honored at the ceremony beginning at nine p.m.

2. The culture contained more than 500,000,000,000 cells.

3. We forgot who won the Nobel Peace Prize in nineteen ninety-one.

4. The examination will include a question about the 1st, the 4th, or the Tenth Amendment.

5. We paid $79.80 for the hotel room and twenty dollars for admission to the park.

PART

VII

Research and Writing

43 How Do You Design a Research Project?

44 How Do You Find Information?

45 How Do You Evaluate and Use Sources?

46 How Do You Acknowledge Sources?

47 How Do You Complete a Project?

CHAPTER 43

How Do You Design a Research Project?

Until recently, most college research projects were designed to introduce students to academic standards for research—that is, to the procedures for gathering, assessing, and reporting information that apply in higher education. The resulting research papers were—and remain—important exercises in handling information responsibly. Not many students, however, wrote such research papers expecting to publish them or share them with anyone except teachers and classmates. Few undergraduates had the time, resources, or incentive to reach deeply into scholarly archives or to develop interesting projects on their own. What's more, there was no audience for such work and no easy way for a writer to reach a public intrigued by the questions a college student might pursue.

But times have changed. Students in college courses can now find tools, media, and audiences to support their serious academic writing and research—which may include service projects designed for specific local or national communities. At some schools, college researchers can seek funding for their work and then present their findings at annual

The Library of Congress in Washington, D.C., is one of the world's greatest storehouses of knowledge. Visit its Web site at <http://lcweb.loc.gov> to tour its online collections. You'll have to visit in person to study the main reading room, depicted here.

conferences that focus on undergraduate research. Thanks to the Internet, students and instructors anywhere in the world can explore each other's online courses and Web sites. And anyone with modest computer skills can do things with technology that skilled technicians couldn't imagine a decade ago, including earning a degree from an online university.

So where just a few years ago, a research paper was typically a ten-page effort with a dozen sources—six books and six articles—a research project today can be that very same paper, or that paper moved to a Web site, or a Web site itself, or a hypertext, a multimedia project, a MOO, a CD-ROM, a listserv, or any combination of these forms. College researchers, often working collaboratively, now can address readers beyond the walls of their classrooms, "publishing" their work themselves and reaching audiences potentially vaster than those claimed by most printed journals.

Of course, the electronic tools that make all this possible do not supplant the need for clear, powerful, and responsible writing. Though you may be entering a brave, new electronically mediated world of learning and writing, you'll still need to know how to find a topic for a project, how to establish a research methodology, how to use research tools, and how to evaluate, organize, and document information. Even if we can't anticipate the kinds of work you'll do in college, we can offer reliable methods for managing research, whether you are preparing a traditional paper, an electronic project, or something in between. That's what this and subsequent chapters are about; what we suggest here, you'll be able to adapt to your assignments and interests. But don't permit our advice to restrict your creativity: the point of research is not to limit horizons, but to expand them.

E-Tips

For more about research opportunities, see The Council on Undergraduate Research at <http://www.cur.org/> and the National Conferences for Undergraduate Research at <http://www.union.edu/NCUR/>. For undergraduate funding opportunities in the sciences, explore the Community of Science (COS) database at <http://fundingopps2.cos.com/> or the list of Research Sponsors maintained at the University of Virginia <http://www.cs.virginia.edu/research/sponsors.html>. In the Arts, check out "Grants and Applications" at the Web site of the National Endowment for the Humanities <http://www.neh.gov/grants/index.html>. For general advice about grants, see The Foundation Center at <http://www.fdncenter.org/>.

43

43a How do you claim a topic?

In college, your exploration of a subject should evolve through both research and dialogue. The research should bring important information to your attention, and the dialogue may help transform that material into knowledge.

Because of developments in information technology, we're more aware than ever that intellectual conversations never cease—and that's why many research paths are consciously open-ended. College projects can start dialogues that last a lifetime; many students find themselves changing their majors and redirecting their careers as a result of work they began in a paper or a service project. That's normal and wonderful. So if you think of research as an active process of creating knowledge rather than a passive one of reporting information, you'll be more comfortable with the notion that almost every college project should be supported by research.

■ 1 **Size up an assignment carefully.** In most cases, a college research project assignment will be explained in an assignment sheet. Go over the sheet carefully, as if it were a contract, annotating and highlighting its key features. Consider issues such as the following.

- **Scope.** An instructor may give you options for presenting a project—as a conventional paper, an oral report, a Web project, a community service project. Understand the range of those options in terms of what you must do and at what length. Look for word, page, or time limits at both ends (*no less than; no more than*).
- **Due dates.** There may be separate due dates for different stages of the project: topic proposal, annotated bibliography, outline, first draft or prototype, final version.
- **Presentation.** Note exactly what your project must include. The instructor may require items such as a research journal, transcripts of interviews, cover sheet, abstract, appendices, bibliographies, illustrations, charts, links, and so on. Gather important materials into a folder or portfolio from the start of the project.
- **Format.** Note any specific requirements for margins, placement of page numbers, line-spacing, titles, headings, illustrations, graphics, and so on. If an instructor doesn't give specific format instructions for a paper, model it on one of the professional styles explained in this book: MLA—for papers in English and the humanities; APA—for papers in psychology and the social sciences; CMS—for work in the humanities and other fields; CBE—

43a
research

for papers in the natural sciences; COS—for projects using many electronic sources.

- **Documentation.** Follow your instructor's preferences for documenting a project. Some may specify MLA, APA, or COS documentation; others may give you the option of choosing any system, providing that you handle it consistently.

- **Collaboration.** Instructors may encourage or require collaboration on research projects. If that's the case with your project, read the ground rules carefully to see how the work may be divided and what reports and self-assessments may be required from project participants. Pay attention, too, to how the project itself will be evaluated.

- **Key words.** Take notice of key words in the assignment. Are you being asked to analyze, classify, define, discuss, evaluate, review, explain, compare, contrast, prove, disprove, persuade, survey? Each of these words means something different. (For a discussion of such terms, see pp. 112–13.)

2 Browse your topic area. When you can choose the topic for a project, look for a subject, cause, or concern about which you can honestly say, "I'd love to learn or do much more about it." The enthusiasm you bring to a project will show in the product you eventually produce. Of course, not all subjects work equally well. You'll want to avoid stale controversies that have been on the national docket without resolution for a generation. Don't be one of a half dozen students turning in projects on gun control, capital punishment, abortion, or legalization of marijuana. You'll find plenty of material on such subjects, but it's unlikely you'll add much to the debate.

Get closer to your subject by spending a few hours browsing, first in your library and then on the Web.

Checklist 43.1

Your Browsing and Background Reading Should . . .

- confirm whether you are, in fact, interested in your topic.

- survey your subject so you can identify key issues and begin narrowing the scope of your project, as appropriate.

- determine whether enough resources exist to support your project in the time available.

One shrewd way to begin exploring an academic topic is to read a specialized encyclopedia, one that deals specifically with your subject. The more technical the encyclopedia, the better its coverage of a subject area is going to be. Library reference rooms have dozens of specialized encyclopedias covering many fields, most of which are not yet available online. See the checklist below and ask reference librarians for their help.

Checklist 43.2

Specialized Encyclopedias

DOING A PAPER ON . . . ?	BEGIN BY CHECKING . . .
American history	*Encyclopedia of American History*
Anthropology, economics, sociology	*International Encyclopedia of the Social Sciences*
Art	*Encyclopedia of World Art*
Astronomy	*Encyclopedia of Astronomy*
Communications, mass media	*International Encyclopedia of Communication*
Computers	*Encyclopedia of Computer Science*
Crime	*Encyclopedia of Crime and Justice*
Economics	*Encyclopedia of American Economic History*
Ethical issues in life sciences	*Encyclopedia of Bioethics*
Environment	*Encyclopedia of the Environment*
Film	*International Encyclopedia of Film*
Health/medicine	*Health and Medicine Horizons*
History	*Dictionary of American History; Guide to Historical Literature*
Law	*The Guide to American Law*
Literature	*Cassell's Encyclopedia of World Literature*
Multiculturalism	*Encyclopedia of Multiculturalism*
Music	*The New Grove Dictionary of American Music*
Philosophy	*Dictionary of the History of Ideas; Encyclopedia of Philosophy*
Political science	*Encyclopedia of American Political History; Oxford Companion to Politics of the World*
Psychology, psychiatry	*International Encyclopedia of Psychiatry, Psychology, Psychoanalysis and Neurology*
Religion	*The Encyclopedia of Religion; Encyclopedia Judaica; New Catholic Encyclopedia*
Rhetoric	*Encyclopedia of Rhetoric*
Science	*McGraw-Hill Encyclopedia of Science and Technology*
Social sciences	*International Encyclopedia of the Social Sciences*
Sociology	*Encyclopedia of Sociology*

43a
research

To get a feel for your topic area, examine books or journals in the field. What are the major issues? Who is affected by them? Who is writing on the topic? You can learn more than you might expect from quick but purposeful browsing. Find two or three books on the subject you are researching and compare their bibliographies. Books that appear in more than one bibliography are likely to be key sources on the subject.

Check out your subject on the Internet too, exploring both newsgroups and Web sites. For example, if your subject is related to religion in the United States, you will find dozens of newsgroups under <alt.religion>, <soc.religion>, or <talk.religion>. Not all such sources are equally helpful, but remember that at this point you're simply deciding whether an issue warrants your attention; you aren't seeking research material.

> **E-Tips**
> You can usually access newsgroups from your Web browser and explore them with a search engine. See <http://www.liszt.com> for a directory of electronic mailing lists, newsgroups, and IRC chat groups. To search USENET groups, try <http://groups.google.com>.

43b How do you plan a project?

You can't wait to organize your project. You'll need a plan from the outset to deal with contemporary research resources and technologies or you may be swamped by the demands of the project.

1 Write a research proposal. For some research assignments, you may be asked to prepare a document outlining your project so that an instructor can give you timely help and advice. Such topic proposals will vary in scope. The prospectus for a short project might fit on a single page; that for a senior thesis might run many pages. Any proposal, however, will likely include some of the following elements, all worth considering even if you do not have to prepare a formal document.

- **Identification of a topic or topic area.** Explain your topic area and, if required, provide a rationale for selecting this subject. See Chapter 2 for detailed advice.
- **A hypothesis, research question, or thesis.** State your hypothesis or question clearly. If required, discuss the hypothesis in some detail and establish its significance, relevance, or appropriateness. Be prepared to explain any premises or assumptions supporting your basic claim(s). See Chapter 3 for help in formulating a thesis.

43b
research

- **Background information or review of literature.** Identify the background reading and research that provides preliminary grounds for your research. For major projects, you may need to do a thorough "review of literature," surveying all major work done in your research area.
- **A review of research resources.** Identify the types and availability of materials you expect to review for this project: books, articles, newspapers, documents, manuscripts, recordings, videos, artworks, databases, online sources, and so on. You might list these items in a preliminary bibliography. See Chapter 44 for much more about research resources.
- **A description of your research methodology.** Outline the procedures you will follow in your research and justify your choice of methodology.
- **An assessment of the ethics of your project if it involves experiments on people.** Most universities have strict guidelines for research with human subjects. Your instructor will likely make you aware of these rules, especially in fields where human research is common, such as in psychology and the social sciences.
- **A schedule or timeline.** For more information about scheduling a project, see Section 43c.

E-Tips

For detailed advice about writing a serious proposal in pursuit of a research grant, see Sea Coast Web Design's "Grant Writing Guide" at <http://www.npguides.org/>.

2 Classify the materials you expect to gather. By classifying your research resources, you can decide how and where to record them. If you'll rely chiefly on printed items, you can use a system of note cards, photocopies, and bibliography cards to manage much of the project (see Section 43b-4). You may also want to include charts, graphs, and illustrations in the paper, some of them created on software, some downloaded from electronic sources. So add a computer disk to your research portfolio—two, in fact, one of them for backup.

43b
research

If you're working with electronic sources, you may still need either note cards for bibliographical references or a database program that organizes your sources for you. You may also need a folder for printouts, a disk for electronic files, maybe even a Zip disk for a large Web project.

Other types of work may require different resources. List all you can think of at the beginning of a project, including any software you may need to complete the job. Consider, too, where to keep all the stuff you accumulate. A rugged portfolio with ample pockets and safe storage for papers and disks is a good investment. Be sure it bears your name and a local phone number in case you lose it. And put your name and number on all your computer disks; sooner or later, you'll forget an important disk in a machine at a computer facility.

3 Prepare a working bibliography. It doesn't matter whether you are using print or electronic sources or whether your project will culminate in a paper, a Web site, a slide show, or a brochure—you need to know where your information came from. The best way to keep track of it is to develop a working or annotated bibliography as you move your way through your sources (see pp. 103–04).

Keep track of sources either with an electronic database program or with an accurate set of 3-by-5-inch bibliography cards, one source per card. Typical bibliography cards look like this:

```
1034
C67
1991
PCL Stacks

Corbett, H. Dickson, and Bruce L. Wilson.

    Testing, Reform, and Rebellion. Norwood: Ablex,

    1991.
```

```
CNN Interactive. "Shuttle Atlantis Makes Repair Call

    to Mir." 17 May 1997. 19 May 1997 <http://

    www.cnn.com/TECH/970/16/shuttle/index.html>.
```

43b
research

Eventually you will need a note-taking program or note cards to generate the Works Cited or References pages required of every standard academic paper. Each database record or bibliography card should contain all the information necessary to find a source again later.

The bibliographical information you need will vary considerably for books, articles, newspapers, and electronic sources. For the exact information required, check the MLA, APA, CMS, CBE, and COS Models in Chapters 48–52. When using a Web page, always record the full electronic address and note the date you viewed the site.

In some cases, writers will skip bibliography cards because they can print out a list of potential sources from online library catalogs, electronic databases, and Web search engines. This strategy can be risky because the information on a printout is usually insufficient for preparing a Works Cited or References list. Printouts can also be misplaced easily among the stack of papers a research project typically generates. So if you rely on such printouts for bibliographical information, keep the lists in one place and know what's on them.

4 Make photocopies and note cards for printed sources.

Photocopy or print out passages from sources that you expect to quote from directly and extensively. While a case can be made for taking all notes on cards, the fact is that most researchers—both faculty members and students—now routinely either photocopy or download their major sources when they can. In such cases, be sure your copies are complete and legible (especially any page numbers). When you are copying from a book or magazine, take a moment to duplicate the title page and publication/editorial staff information. You'll be glad you did later.

In all cases, attach basic bibliographical information directly to photocopies and printouts so that you know their source, making sure each document is keyed somehow to a full bibliography card. That way, you'll later be able to connect information and source easily. Use highlighter pens to mark passages in photocopies and printouts that you expect to refer to later, and keep all these materials in a folder. Never highlight material or write comments in margins of library books.

43b
research

Even when you rely heavily on copied material, you may still need to record information on index cards. While 3-by-5-inch cards are fine for bibliographic entries, larger ones work better for notes. Be sure each note card for a source includes the author's last name or a short title so that you can connect the notes with the right bibliography card. For example, a note card recording information from Corbett and Wilson's *Testing, Reform, and Rebellion* might be headed simply "Corbett, *Test-*

ing," since you have a bibliography card with fuller information on the book (see p. 633).

Don't crowd too much information on a single note card; it's more efficient to record only one major point, quotation, or statistic on each. That way, later, you will be able to arrange cards into an outline of your work, with data exactly where you need it. For the same reason, write on only one side of a note card. Information on the flip side of a card is easily ignored.

Double-check bibliographical information, especially the spelling of names, as they may be difficult to recall or guess. Accuracy in transcribing names will help you and your reader.

Electronic programs are also available to help you keep notes. These programs often include helpful features for finding and sorting information.

Checklist 43.3

Information for Note Cards

* Author's last name and a shortened version of the source's title (for accurate reference to the corresponding bibliography card)

* A heading to identify the nature of the information on the card

* The actual data or information, correctly summarized, paraphrased, or quoted

* Page numbers or correct World Wide Web address for locating the source

■ **5 Print or download electronic sources.** How you record data from an electronic source will depend on how you expect to use it. If you're simply looking for facts, you may want to treat it like a printed source, recording the data on note cards or printing out the source itself. Printouts may be essential from sources whose content changes from day to day—such as Web sites, newsgroups, sessions on Interchange, or online conversations. Some of this material may be archived electronically, but it is much safer to print out material you will cite, carefully recording all necessary bibliographical information on the sheets. Also be sure to record when you made the printout, since most documentation for electronic material requires a date of access.

43b
research

It is possible to copy many electronic sources directly to disk. Do back up all such copies, keeping them, for example, on both a disk and your hard drive. Be especially careful that you know where all down-loaded images come from and who owns their copyrights. As you do with printed sources, you will have to document and credit all copy-righted pictures, photographs, and images borrowed from the Web, whether you use the image in a paper or in an electronic project. To use copyrighted material in your own electronic publications, you must get permission from the holder of the copyright.

A particularly efficient way to organize information gathered mainly from the Web is to use your browser's "bookmark" or "fa-vorites" feature. Bookmarking a site simply adds it to a menu list available on the browser so that you can return to the item easily. Web browsers also enable you to organize bookmarked items and even to annotate them. When you begin a project, you may want to create a separate folder for it on the bookmark menu and move all Web sites relevant to your search into the designated slot, annotating each entry to remind you of its relevance to your research. Note, too, that you can save your list of bookmarks to a disk and thus transport it from machine to machine. But because Web addresses and site con-tents change, don't rely on bookmarked addresses alone as storage spaces for information. Take careful notes on the information you find.

For more on doing research, be sure to see the Web site for this handbook at <http://www.ablongman.com/sfhandbooks>.

■ 6 Consider collaborative research. You may be expected or invited to work as part of a team for some college projects. If so, use the occasion to learn how to work productively to achieve a common goal. You'll quickly discover that careful management is an important part of any collaborative effort. In a group you may want to discuss questions such as the following. See Section 4e for more on collabora-tive writing.

43b
research

- What research and writing skills might your project require?
- What qualities and skills should you look for in your colleagues?
- How will you organize your team?
- How will decisions be made?
- Who—if anyone—will be in charge?
- How will you communicate and coordinate your efforts?
- How will you schedule the work and how will you deal with devi-ations from the schedule?
- How will you assess your work and share the credit?

43c How do you schedule a project?

Few projects follow a simple sequence from start to finish, and most projects have to meet tight deadlines. Because projects have to move forward, you may need to envision your overall research process and then to schedule your work carefully.

1 Determine the hard points of your project. *Hard points* are those features of a project you can't change; they are usually described on the assignment sheet. For instance, when an instructor asks for a ten-page paper on genetic engineering using APA style in two weeks, you have four hard points:

1. format: ten-page paper
2. topic: genetic engineering
3. documentation: APA
4. due date: two weeks from today

All four points will shape your planning, but perhaps none more so than the due date. You know that ten pages in two weeks is a lot of work.

Many college assignments will have only one due date: the day the project must be submitted. When that's the case, you'll have to schedule the remainder of the project yourself. But take that final due date seriously; instructors rarely show tolerance for late work.

Some instructors may give you a series of due dates for a major project, asking that you submit items such as the following at specific times:

- project proposal, prospectus, or thesis
- annotated working bibliography
- storyboards (for projects with graphics)
- first draft
- Web site design specifications
- responses to peer editing

When you are given several due dates, they can be arranged in sequence to form a preliminary timeline into which the remaining hard points of your project can be fitted.

43c
research

PROJECT PROPOSAL		ANNOTATED BIBLIOGRAPHY		FIRST DRAFT		FINAL DRAFT
Oct. 2	→	Oct. 16	→	Oct. 23	→	Nov. 6

■ **2 Create a calendar.** Once you have outlined your writing process and established the hard points of your project, you are ready to sketch out a calendar for your work.

You create a calendar by listing the due dates of a project and leaving sufficient space between them for the activities necessary to meet those deadlines. Then you estimate the time necessary and/or available for each step in the project. Here's a calendar for a paper with four major due dates and a variety of support activities. You would have to determine an appropriate completion date for each activity.

CALENDAR: RESEARCH PAPER

_____ Choosing a topic and defining the project
_____ Creating a management plan
_____ Determining campus resources
_____ Drafting the proposal
Topic proposal: Due October 2

_____ Generating a working bibliography
_____ Gathering and evaluating materials
Annotated bibliography: Due October 16

_____ Summarizing and paraphrasing sources
_____ Organizing/designing the paper
_____ Drafting the project
First draft: Due October 23

_____ Getting/responding to feedback on the draft
_____ Refining/rewriting the project
_____ Documenting the project
_____ Preparing the final materials
Final draft: Due November 6

Your initial calendar should not be much more detailed; you'll waste time if you try to account for every movement in what is to some degree an unpredictable process.

43c
research

You can also mark off your research project on an actual calendar—the kind that provides a box for listing each day's appointments and activities. Or record your due dates on a PDA device, using its alarm function to remind you of due dates several days before they arrive. Whatever type of calendar you create, allow some slack toward the end to make up for the time you'll likely lose early in the project.

You can find software programs now to help you design and organize your research projects. These database products typically have a number of integrated features. They help you to outline a project; they keep track of your notes; they format your bibliography items in proper MLA, APA, or other documentation form; they help you upload your notes either to a word-processing program or to an HTML file you can use in building a Web site. Fortunately, these programs (such as *TakeNote!*) are easy to learn and to use. You might look into one at the outset of a major project.

A screen from a software program designed to support research might look like this "Card Editor" from *TakeNote!*

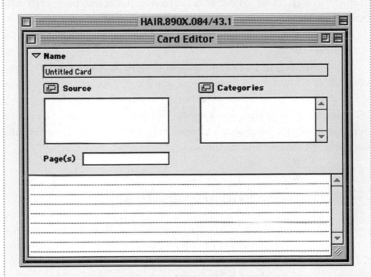

Notice that the software enables you to assign categories to the information you record on the card—a useful way of keeping track of the information in any number of related sources.

Electronic note-taking programs overcome some of the limitations of cards. They will prompt you to provide the information essential to track a source, and they may help you find and rearrange information more ingeniously and quickly. A disadvantage of an electronic database is that it resides on a machine. Unless you have a laptop computer, you may not be able to take the program with you into a library.

43c
research

CHAPTER 44

How Do You Find Information?

As you begin a research paper or project, your goal is to locate potential sources and to prepare a *working bibliography,* that is, a preliminary list of materials relevant to your topic (see pp. 103–04 for an example). Today, more material is accessible to researchers than ever before. By the same token, the enormous range of possibilities can be daunting. In this section we outline strategies to use in navigating the sea of information.

We urge you to be systematic and dogged in your research. Don't close off an investigation just because you haven't located materials you want. And don't be satisfied, either, if your initial searches produce more sources or data than you expect. The first run is liable to be superficial or obvious; always push deeper into the archives, libraries, and networks. Be curious and take risks.

44a How do you use a library?

A first priority for any college student is to learn the physical arrangement of campus libraries and research facilities. Don't be intimidated. Take a tour of these buildings, study the collections, and, above all, get to know the research librarians.

1 Explore your library. Be sure you can locate the following places, features, and services important to your research.

- **Online catalog.** Learn how to use these terminals to examine your library's collection of books, journals, and other materials. In addition, many libraries have comprehensive Web sites that include links to powerful indexes, databases, and online reference tools. Explore the site supported by your own campus library or examine those posted by other colleges and universities. Ask your librarian to direct you to an appropriate site.
- **Card catalog.** Not all libraries have electronic catalogs. And where they do exist, online terminals may not cover materials acquired

before a specific date. Find out if that is the case. And know where the card catalog is located.

- **Reference room.** Study this collection carefully, noting how materials are arranged and where heavily used items (encyclopedias, almanacs, phone books, databases) are located. Notice, too, where the reference librarian is stationed.
- **Bibliographies and databases.** Look for important bibliographies and data terminals in library reference rooms. Print bibliographies in various fields will often be large multi-volume collections. Research databases will be arrayed around terminals, with information either online or accessed via CD-ROM disks.
- **Microforms collections.** Many important materials including documents, newspapers, and periodicals are collected on rolls of film called *microfilm* or rectangular sheets of film called *microfiche*. Know where these collections are, how they are arranged, and how you can gain access to them.
- **Periodical collections.** You'll need to know both where current journals and periodicals are located and where older bound or microfilmed materials are housed.
- **Newspapers.** As with periodicals, current newspapers are usually available in a reading room. Older newspapers will usually be available chiefly on microfilm, and then you are likely to have access to only a limited number of major papers, depending on the size of your library collection. Online archives of newspapers are a recent innovation: you won't be able to search back more than a few years.
- **Special collections.** Libraries will often have rooms or sections that contain rare or special items such as pictures and photographs, maps, government documents, and so on. Learn the location of any important collections in your library.
- **Audio/video collections.** Many libraries now have extensive holdings of audio/video materials as well as facilities for listening to or viewing CDs, DVDs, tapes, and video disks. Learn where these collections are located, where and how they are catalogued, and how to use the playback equipment.
- **Circulation desk/library services.** Learn what circulation desk services are available to a researcher. For instance, you can usually recall materials already on loan if you need them for your project. Most libraries participate in interlibrary loan programs that enable you to acquire materials your library may not own. (These orders take time, so don't wait until the last minute to make such a request.)

44a
library

- **Directories.** Large libraries can be complicated. Look for directories or pamphlets to help you locate collections. Note how the collections are organized, where library call numbers are displayed, how the shelves themselves are arranged, and any other aspects of the physical arrangement.
- **Photocopiers/computers/study areas.** Find out where in the library you can reliably copy information. It's smart to track down two or three copying locations since copiers get heavy use. Also check to see whether computer terminals or plug-ins are available in the library and whether certain areas are reserved for study and research.
- **Study carrels.** Many colleges and university libraries provide carrels in the library for people pursuing serious research. Find out whether you are eligible for such a carrel.

▌2 Use traditional and online library catalogs efficiently.

Most libraries now provide access to their resources via computer terminals or the World Wide Web. But electronic catalogs sometimes cover only a library's more recent acquisitions. To do a thorough job, be prepared to move back and forth from computer terminal to card file during your research.

In traditional card catalogs, books and other materials can usually be located by author, title, and key word. Electronic catalogs can be searched by similar categories, but more quickly and with more powerful options. Electronic catalogs can indicate whether books have been checked out, lost, or recalled. If your library has an electronic catalog, study its screens and learn its basic search techniques and commands. The search menu screen for the online library catalog at the University of Texas at Austin, shown on page 643, can be viewed at <http://dpweb1.dp.utexas.edu/lib/utnetcat/keyword.html>. Notice that the screen supports a variety of keyword combinations and permits a user to specify the location, format, and language of the research material. Librarians find that most people use online catalogs by using keyword searches. For much more about keyword searches, see Section 44d.

44a
library

E-Tips   For a list of online library catalogs, examine the LIBCAT Web site at <http://www.metronet.lib.mn.us/lc/lca.cfm>.

An online catalog offers detailed information about most library holdings. On screen, you'll often be given a short entry first—typically the author, title, publishing information, date, and call number—with an option to select a fuller listing. The full listing describes additional features of the item—whether it is illustrated or has an index or a bibliography.

Be sure to note any new subject headings presented: they are the keywords for additional searches. For instance, if you were exploring "hieroglyphics," a listing on that topic might offer the keywords "Egyptian language—grammar" and "Egyptian language—writing." You might not have considered using those terms in a keyword search of your own.

SUMMARY   *Online Catalogs*

For a book, online catalogs typically list

• Call number and library location

• Author, title, publisher, and date of publication

• The number of pages and the book's physical size

• Whether the book is illustrated

• Whether it contains a bibliography and an index

• The subject headings under which it is listed

44a
library

44b How do you find research materials?

Not long ago, students often worried about finding adequate resources for a research project. Today, resources on almost any topic can seem overwhelming—and that is why it helps to know exactly what kinds of materials provide what types of information. In this section we survey basic research tools and resources.

1 Locate suitable bibliographies. You will save time if you can locate an existing bibliography—preferably an annotated bibliography—on your subject. Bibliographies are lists of books, articles, and other documentary materials that deal with particular subjects or subject areas.

Chart 44.1

Types of Printed Bibliographies

• **Selective bibliographies** usually list the best-known or most respected books and articles in a subject area.

• **Annotated bibliographies** briefly describe the works they list and may evaluate them.

• **Annual bibliographies** catalog the works produced within a field or discipline in a given year.

Consult a reference room librarian to learn whether a bibliography on your specific subject has been compiled. If not, consult one of the more general bibliographies available in almost every field.

44b
info

Although printed bibliographies are losing ground to electronic indexes and databases, they are still available on many subjects. Also be sure to look for bibliographies at the back of scholarly books, articles, and dissertations you consult in your research. Usually compiled by researchers themselves, such bibliographies offer a focused look at a specific topic.

Only a few of the hundreds of bibliographic resources in specific disciplines are listed below.

Checklist 44.1

Bibliographies

DOING A PAPER ON . . . ?	CHECK THIS BIBLIOGRAPHY . . .
American history	*Bibliographies in American History*
Anthropology	*Anthropological Bibliographies: A Selected Guide*
Art	*Guide to the Literature of Art History*
Astronomy	*A Guide to the Literature of Astronomy; Astronomy and Astrophysics: A Bibliographic Guide*
Classics	*Greek and Roman Authors: A Checklist of Criticism*
Communications	*Communication: A Guide to Information Sources*
Engineering	*Science and Engineering Literature*
Literature	*MLA International Bibliography*
Mathematics	*Using the Mathematical Literature*
Music	*Music Reference and Research Materials*
Philosophy	*A Bibliography of Philosophical Bibliographies*
Physics	*Use of Physics Literature*
Psychology	*Harvard List of Books in Psychology*
Social work	*Social Work Education: A Bibliography*

For general subjects, electronic subject guides offered by major public libraries can offer useful lists of print and electronic resources on a vast number of subjects and disciplines, from Art and Architecture to Women's studies. You may find the following Web sites especially helpful.

- New York Public Library Resource Guides
  <http://www.nypl.org/admin/genweb/guides.html>
- Columbia University Library Web "Selected Subject Guides and Resources"
  <http://www.columbia.edu/cu/lweb/eguides/>
- The University of California at Berkeley Libraries
  <http://www.lib.berkeley.edu/>
- The University of Chicago "Libraries, Collections, and Subjects"
  <http://www.lib.uchicago.edu/e/lcs.html>
- The University of Texas at Austin
  <http://www.lib.utexas.edu/subject/>
- The University of Virginia Subject Guides
  <http://www.lib.virginia.edu/resguide.html>

44b
info

■ **2 Locate suitable indexes to search the periodical literature.** Indexes list essential items that cannot be recorded in a library catalog: journal articles, magazine pieces, and stories from newspapers, for instance. Such material is called the *periodical literature* on a subject. You shouldn't undertake any college-level research paper without surveying this extensive body of information. For example, to explore the subject of school vouchers, you'd likely want information from magazines such as *Newsweek* and *U.S. News & World Report* and newspapers such as *The New York Times* and *The Washington Post*. To find such information, you would go to indexes, not traditional library catalogs.

In the past, all periodical indexes were printed works, and you may still have to use these helpful volumes to find older sources. For more recent materials, however, you'll likely use electronic indexes. Many indexes now offer not only the basic bibliographical information on an article—who published it, where, and when—but an abstract of the piece or even the full text. Depending on copyright rules, you can print out the text, download it to your computer, or have it sent to you via email.

You may want to begin periodical searches with general and multidisciplinary indexes such as the following

> *Readers' Guide to Periodical Literature* (print)
> *Readers' Guide Abstracts* (electronic)
> *ArticleFirst* (electronic)
> *CARL Uncover* (electronic)
> *Ethnic NewsWatch* (electronic)
> *Expanded Academic ASAP* (electronic)
> *LEXIS-NEXIS Academic Universe* (electronic)
> *Periodical Abstracts* (electronic)

All major academic fields have individual indexes for their periodical literature, most of them computerized. Because new indexes may be added to a library's collection at any time, check with your reference librarian or your library's Web site about the best sources available for any given subject.

44b
info

Checklist 44.2

Indexes and Databases

DOING A PAPER ON . . . ?	CHECK THIS INDEX . . .
Anthropology	*Anthropological Literature*
Architecture	*Avery Index*
Art	*Art Abstracts*

DOING A PAPER ON . . . ?	CHECK THIS INDEX . . .
Biography	*Biography Index*
Biology	*Biological and Agricultural Abstracts; BIOSIS Previews*
Business	*Business Periodicals Index; ABI/Inform*
Chemistry	*CAS*
Computer science	*Computer Literature Index*
Current affairs	*LEXIS-NEXIS*
Economics	*PAIS (Public Affairs Information Service); EconLit*
Education	*Education Index; ERIC (Educational Resources Information Center)*
Engineering	*INSPEC*
Film	*Film Index International; Art Index*
History	*Historical Abstracts; America: History and Life*
Humanities	*FRANCIS; Humanities Abstracts; Humanities Index*
Law	*LegalTrac*
Literature	*Essay and General Literature Index; MLA Bibliography; Contemporary Authors*
Mathematics	*MathSciNet*
Medicine	*MEDLINE*
Music	*Music Index; RILM Abstracts of Music Literature*
Philosophy	*Philosopher's Index*
Psychology	*Psychological Abstracts; PsycINFO*
Public affairs	*PAIS*
Physics	*INSPEC*
Religion	*ATLA Religion Database*
Science	*General Science Index; General Science Abstracts*
Social sciences	*Social Science & Humanities Index; Social Sciences Index; Social Sciences Abstracts*
Technology	*Applied Science & Technology Abstracts*
Women	*Contemporary Women's Issues*

Ordinarily you can get access to indexes in your library reference room. Electronic tools may also be available via online library catalogs or Web sites. Most indexes, printed or electronic, are relatively easy to manage—provided you read the explanatory information that typically accompanies them.

Electronic indexes usually support title, author, or keyword searches (see Section 44d), but they may also permit searching by other "fields"—that is, categories by which data is entered. For example, a database may be searchable not only by author and title but also by

44b
info

publisher, place of publication, subject heading, accession number, or government document number. Powerful indexes and databases such as *LEXIS-NEXIS* may require special commands and search techniques.

Checklist 44.3

Searching an Electronic Index or Database

* Be sure you are logged onto the right index. A library terminal may provide access to several different databases or indexes. Find the one appropriate for your subject.

* Read the description of the index to find out how to access its information. Not all databases and indexes work the same way.

* When searching by keyword, check whether a list of subject headings is available. To save time, match your search terms to those on the list before you begin.

* Try synonyms if your initial keyword search turns up too few items.

Do anticipate some frustrations with any index. Printed volumes can be clumsy to handle, incorrectly shelved, dusty, and poorly printed. With electronic sources, you may have trouble logging on, finding the right keyword, or narrowing your search. Good research still takes work.

▇ 3 Consult biographical resources. Quite often in preparing a research project, you'll need information about famous people living and dead. Powerful sources are available to help you in the reference room. Good places to start are the *Biography Index: A Cumulative Index to Biographic Material in Books and Magazines, Bio-Base, LEXIS-NEXIS, Current Biography,* and *The McGraw-Hill Encyclopedia of World Biography.*

There are also *Who's Who* volumes for living British, American, and world notables, as well as volumes for African Americans and women. Deceased figures may appear in *Who Was Who.* Probably the two most famous dictionaries of biography are the *Dictionary of National Biography* (British) and the *Dictionary of American Biography.*

On the World Wide Web, you might look at the database maintained by the Arts and Entertainment Network program *Biography* at <http://www.biography.com>. For information about writers and authors, check the Internet Public Library's *Authors Resources* at <http://www.ipl.org/ref/RR/static/hum60.10.00.html>. For the wisdom of famous people, check out the Web version of the 1901 version of *Bartlett's Famil-*

44b
info

iar Quotations at <http://www.columbia.edu/acis/bartleby/bartlett> or, for more recent remarks, *The Quotation Page* at <http://www.starlingtech.com/quotes>. To search for private individuals, you can use features such as *Yahoo!*'s "people search" on the World Wide Web. It provides addresses and phone numbers with almost frightening ease.

Checklist 44.4
Biographical Information

YOUR SUBJECT IS IN . . . ?	CHECK THIS SOURCE . . .
Art	*Index to Artistic Biography*
Education	*Biographical Dictionary of American Educators*
Music	*The New Grove Dictionary of Music and Musicians*
Politics	*Politics in America; Almanac of American Politics*
Psychology	*Biographical Dictionary of Psychology*
Religion	*Dictionary of American Religious Biography*
Science	*Dictionary of Scientific Biography*

YOUR SUBJECT IS . . . ?	CHECK THIS SOURCE . . .
African	*Dictionary of African Biography*
African American	*Dictionary of American Negro Biography*
Asian	*Encyclopedia of Asian History*
Australian	*Australian Dictionary of Biography*
Canadian	*Dictionary of Canadian Biography*
Female	*Index to Women; Notable American Women*
Mexican American	*Mexican American Biographies; Chicano Scholars and Writers: A Bibliographic Directory*

4 Locate statistics. Statistics about every imaginable topic are available in library reference rooms and online. Be sure to find up-to-date and reliable figures.

Checklist 44.5
Statistics

TO FIND . . .	CHECK THIS SOURCE . . .
General statistics	*World Almanac; Current Index to Statistics* (electronic)
Statistics about United States	*Historical Statistics of the United States;* the *Statistical Abstract of the United States;* the *STAT-USA* (electronic); *GPO Access* (electronic)

(Continued)

44b
info

Statistics   *(Continued)*

TO FIND . . .	CHECK THIS SOURCE . . .
World information	*The Statesman's Yearbook; National Intelligence Factbook; UN Demographic Yearbook; UNESCO Statistical Yearbook*
Business facts	*Handbook of Basic Economic Statistics; Survey of Current Business; Dow Jones–Irwin Business Almanac*
Public opinion polls	*Gallup Poll*
Population data	*Population Index* (electronic)

Also consult resources such as *The Internet Public Library* at <http://ipl.sils.umich.edu/ref/RR/>. Even *The Old Farmer's Almanac,* chock full of information, is on the Web at <http://www.almanac.com>.

E-Tips
When you are seeking factual information, check out <iTools.com>. It offers a dictionary, thesaurus, translator, people search, maps, and much more—including an email discussion group search tool. For statistics from more than 70 agencies of the federal government, explore FedStats at <http://www.fedstats.gov/>. The scope of information available at this site is staggering.

5 Check news sources. Sometimes you'll need information from newspapers, particularly when your subject is current and your aim argumentative or persuasive. For information earlier than the mid-1990s you'll have to rely on printed papers or microfilm copies since electronic newspapers and news services are a recent phenomenon. When you know the date of a particular event, however, you can usually locate the information you want. If your subject isn't an event, you may have to trace it through an index or online archive. Only a few printed papers are fully indexed. The one newspaper you are most likely to encounter in most American libraries is *The New York Times,* usually available on microfilm. *The New York Times Index* provides chronological summaries of articles on a given subject.

A useful reference tool for more recent events is *NewsBank,* an index that has been available in electronic format since 1982. An online version is available at <http://www.Newsweek.com>. It covers hundreds of newspapers from across the country. You can use *NewsBank,* which

Search screen from The New York Times *on the Web.*

is keyed to a microfiche collection, to locate a sampling of journalistic coverage and opinion on major issues and notable people. *Facts on File* <www.factsonfile.com> summarizes national and international news weekly; *CQ Researcher* gives background information on major problems and controversies. To report on what editors are thinking, examine *Editorials on File,* a sampling of world and national opinion.

For very current events, you can search the hundreds of newspapers and news services currently online. (The search page from one such newspaper—*The New York Times* on the Web—appears above.) Online news sources differ significantly from their print or video counterparts both in coverage and interactivity. What they offer is immediate information from a wide range of sources. You can consult online news resources from around the globe and with many points of view. As with any source, you must exercise caution when reporting information you find on the Web, making sure that the source is reputable (see Section 45a). The following online news resources are worth consulting.

44b
info

NEWS RESOURCE	ADDRESS
CNN Interactive	<http://www.cnn.com>
C-SPAN Online	<http://www.c-span.org>
Fox News	<http://www.foxnews.com>
London Times	<http://www.the-times.co.uk/news/pages/Times/>

MSNBC	<http://www.msnbc.com/news>
New York Times	<http://www.nytimes.com>
Reuters	<http://www.reuters.com>
Time.com	<http://www.time.com/time/>
USA Today News	<http://www.usatoday.com>
Washington Times	<http://www.washtimes.com/>

A directory such as *Yahoo!* at <http://www.yahoo.com> can point you to hundreds of online newspapers of every sort. Check under its "News & Media" category. You may have to register to use some online newspapers and pay to download archived materials.

Another important online resource is the *Clarinet* news service, which you can find among the newsgroups on Web browsers.

6 Check book and film reviews. To locate reviews of books, see *Book Review Digest* (1905), *Book Review Index* (1965), or *Current Book Review Citations* (1976). *Book Review Digest* lists fewer reviews than the other two collections, but it summarizes those it does include—a useful feature. Many electronic periodical indexes also catalog book reviews. Enter "book reviews" on a search engine or directory, and you will turn up many sites, such as *The New York Times Book Review* at <http://www.nytimes.com/books/yr/mo/day/home/contents.html> and *The New York Review of Books* at <http://www.nybooks.com/nyrev/index.html>.

For film reviews and criticism, see the printed volumes *Film Review Index* (1986) and *Film Criticism: An Index to Critics' Anthologies* (1975) as well as the electronic index *Film Index International.* Numerous Web sites are devoted to films and film reviews; *Yahoo!* alone lists more than 500 sites (of sharply varying quality) under "movie reviews."

7 Write or email professional organizations. Almost every subject, cause, concept, or idea is represented by a professional organization, society, bureau, office, or lobby. It makes good sense to write or email an appropriate organization for information on your topic; ask for pamphlets, leaflets, reports, and so on. Many such groups offer detailed information on their Web sites. For mailing addresses of organizations, consult the *Encyclopedia of Associations,* published by Gale Research. Use a search engine to find Web sites.

Also remember that the U.S. government publishes huge amounts of information on just about every subject of public interest. Check the *Index to U.S. Government Periodicals* or the *Monthly Catalog of United States Government Publications* for listings. Or use a Web site such as

44b
info

Fedworld Information Network at <http://www.fedworld.gov> to look for the material you need.

■ **8 Consult collections of images.** Online resources make it possible to locate images you may need for your research projects. Some search engines—especially *AltaVista*—look for images (as well as audio and video clips). Among the numerous collections of images and clip art on the Web are the following.

IMAGE SITE	ADDRESS
About.com	<http://webclipart.about.com>

(Surveys clipart and graphic sites on the Web)

GraphicMaps.com	<http://www.graphicmaps.com/graphic_maps.html>

(Provides information about maps on the Web)

Image Finder	<http://sunsite.berkeley.edu/ImageFinder/>

(Searches various collections of images)

The Picture Collection	<http://www.thepicturecollection.com/>

(Presents images from Time, Inc. collection)

Webseek	<http://www.ctr.columbia.edu/webseek/>

(Searches a database of Web images)

Note that you may have to pay to acquire or use some images. You'll also need to document any borrowed images you include in your finished project, just as you cite and document other research sources. See Section 19e-2 for more details

44c How do you choose electronic resources?

44c
online

Systematic research is particularly challenging today because you have to deal with an explosion of electronic sources, many of which were not designed with researchers and scholars in mind. For example, the very strength of the World Wide Web—its robust connection of millions of computers, files, and databases—is also its scholarly weakness. It presents a jumble of information, leaving users to screen nuggets of gold from mountains of slag. So it's essential that your searches be more efficient and knowledgeable than ever.

In this section we explain the basic tools and resources you should use when sorting through stacks of electronic information.

■ **1 Check the World Wide Web.** The World Wide Web is a hypertext pathway into the vast resources of the Internet. Web browser software such as *Netscape Navigator* or *Microsoft Internet Explorer* presents information via "pages" that can contain text, graphics, and sound as well as hypertext links. Browsers also support email, Usenet groups, and other forms of electronic communication. The Web can distribute just about any information that fits on a screen, including photo archives, artwork, maps, film clips, charts, magazines—and even audio clips. Web users move through different "sites" by selecting words or graphics linked to other related resources.

Understand, however, that the Web is not a library designed to support research. Online information is not (like library resources) systematically cataloged, edited, or reviewed. So you can't treat the Web like a library or assume that information you find there is routinely reliable. Approach the Web with caution when you use it as a tool for research, applying your best critical reading skills. (See Section 45a for advice about evaluating all types of sources.)

You'll usually locate information on the Internet using search engines and directories—tools that help you cull information from the hundreds of millions of Web pages now online. Such guides, constantly being refined and upgraded, are readily available; just click the "search" button on your Web browser. But you have to use them properly. Among the best known are the following (with indications of whether they are searchable by keyword and/or categories—and some of their many special features). "Metasearch" means that the engine searches several other search engines.

SEARCH TOOLS	ADDRESS
About.com	<http://home.about.com>
(Keywords; categories; news; stock quotes)	
AltaVista	<http://www.altavista.com/>
(Keywords; categories; news; shopping)	
AOL Anywhere	<http://www.aol.com>
(Keywords; categories)	
AlltheWeb	<http://www.alltheweb.com>
(Keywords)	

Ask Jeeves   <http://www.askjeeves.com/>
(Keywords; takes questions; metasearch)

Dogpile   <http://www.dogpile.com/>
(Keywords; categories; metasearch)

Excite   <http://www.excite.com/>
(Keywords; categories; news; stock quotes; weather)

Go   <http://www.go.com>
(Keywords; images)

Google   <http://www.google.com/>
(Keywords; powerful search logic)

HotBot   <http://hotbot.lycos.com/>
(Keywords; categories; advanced searches; news; shopping)

Looksmart   <http://www.looksmart.com/>
(Keywords; categories; news; shopping)

Lycos   <http://www.lycos.com/>
(Keywords; categories; news; shopping)

NorthernLight.com   <http://www.northernlight.com/>
(Keywords; search folders; news; shopping)

Profusion   <http://www.profusion.com/>
(Keywords; metasearch; simple interface)

WebCrawler   <http://webcrawler.com/>
(Keywords; categories; metasearch; news)

Yahoo!   <http://www.yahoo.com/>
(Keywords; categories; news; shopping)

The basic tool of most search engines is the keyword search. For keyword search strategies, see Section 44d. However, many Web directories such as *Yahoo!* also enable you to search the Web by categories. The *Yahoo!* opening screen, shown on page 656, presents a series of general categories that may narrow the topic you hope to explore.

    Commercial Web search engines aren't the only resource for finding information and links on the Web. Hundreds of reference sites with more scholarly intentions have been created by libraries, universities, and government institutions. Here are just a few places to look. (Be aware that Web addresses change frequently for many sources.)

44c
online

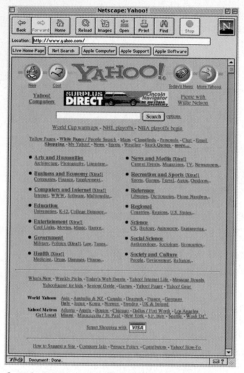

Opening screen for Yahoo! (Reproduced with permission of Yahoo! Inc. © 1998 by Yahoo! Inc. YAHOO! and the YAHOO! logo are trademarks of Yahoo! Inc.)

REFERENCE SITE	ADDRESS
Argus Clearinghouse	<http://www.clearinghouse.net/>
Books on the Internet	<http://www.lib.utexas.edu/Libs/ PCL/Etext.html>
Eserver	<http://eserver.org>
Infomine	<http://infomine.ucr.edu/>
InfoSurf	<http://www.library.ucsb.edu/subj/ resource.html>
Librarians' Index to the Internet	<http://lii.org>
Library of Congress Subject Guide to Internet Resources	<http://lcweb.loc.gov/global/ subject.html>

44c
online

Note that some search engine sites include online guides to both basic and advanced search techniques. Take a few minutes to read such "help" files to discover the remarkable and changing features of these highly competitive tools.

Help screen for searching on AltaVista. (Reproduced with the permission of AltaVista Company. All rights reserved.)

Two points to consider: (1) Web engines and directories all work a little differently and have different strengths. (2) No single search engine covers everything on the Internet. So always use several search engines to explore a subject to be sure you get adequate coverage. Don't be satisfied with your initial searches, even when they supply lots of information. Another combination of keywords or a different search path might provide still better material. If you get an unexpected response from a search, ask why. Look for clues in the results you receive (or don't receive). Check spellings and try synonyms. Don't give up.

E-Tips

For advice on evaluating Web search engines (and more tips on Web searching techniques), see "Search Engine Watch" at <http://searchenginewatch.internet.com/> or click "reviews" at <http://www.zdnet.com>. To see the kinds of subjects people are researching, check out *Webcrawler SearchVoyeur* at <http://webcrawler.com/SearchTicker.html>. It provides the actual (anonymous) searches of people using *Webcrawler*.

44c
online

2 Enter electronic conversations. Some online resources represent ongoing discussions about ideas or work in progress. You will find such resources on the Internet's Usenet newsgroups and listserv discussion groups. You may have interactions in electronic forums as well. In MOOs you can interact within imaginary environments, and with local networking software such as Daedalus's *Interchange* you can become part of a class discussion held online.

Chart 44.2

Listservs and Usenet Newsgroups

LISTSERVS

A listserv is a type of email program that maintains lists of subscribers interested in discussing a specific topic. Users must subscribe to the listserv in order to read or post messages on it.

Major characteristics: Lists are run on large computers; subscribers tend to be active experts working in fields related to the list topic. Lists are often moderated to screen out irrelevant material or "noise." Old text may be archived.

Use for: Excellent window on current issues. Good for listening in on practitioners' conversations, discovering opinions, noting solutions to common problems.

Searching: When you subscribe, check the welcome message for instructions for searching the archives.

USENET NEWSGROUPS

A Usenet newsgroup works like a listserv except that you need not subscribe to the list either to read its messages or to participate in the discussion.

Major characteristics: Thousands of groups focus on a wide range of topics. There is great variation in the expertise of contributors. Anyone may read or post messages.

Use for: Conversations about popular topics and about little-known, obscure subjects. Almost every political group, social interest, religion, activity, hobby, and fantasy has a Usenet group. Just browsing the list of Usenet groups can suggest topic ideas.

Searching: Check the welcome messages and the FAQs (frequently asked questions) for information on how to search. Many lists have archives of older discussions.

44c
online

Usenet newsgroups, listservs, and similar tools can furnish you with interactive and up-to-the-second information on a topic seen from many points of view. These electronic conversations may introduce you to experts and amateurs from all over the world who are knowledgeable about your subject—or to people simply blowing off steam. They offer you the chance to question people who are actually doing the research or living the experiences you are writing about. But you must be very careful when you take information from such environments: make it a habit to confirm any statistic, fact, or claim from such a source with information from a second and different type of authority—a book, an article, a reference work.

Some Web search engines now cover Usenet newsgroups so that you can find and even join online conversations on your topic. (To find older, archived newsgroup materials, check out *Google Groups* at <http:// groups.google.com>.) Usenet groups can help you give a dialogic dimension to a project, placing your own work within an existing community of thought.

Interactive sources can provide a close-up view of your subject. But you need to keep the bigger picture in mind, too. Rely on more traditional resources—journals, books, encyclopedias—to keep the full subject in perspective and to balance other individual and idiosyncratic points of view you may find online.

44d How do you search by keywords?

You need to know how to perform efficient keyword searches in order to explore many basic research resources such as online library catalogs, electronic indexes, and the Internet. A keyword search is simply a scan of an electronic text or database that locates each occurrence of a given word or phrase. When you use the "find" feature of a word processor, you are performing a simple keyword search. Increase the power of this technique and apply it to much larger databases and you have a "search engine," one of the fastest-developing of contemporary research tools. Such engines can seek not only the word(s) you've specified, but related terms and phrases as well.

Perhaps the best advice we can give you when performing a keyword search is to read the instructions for the tool you are using, whether it is an electronic catalog, a search engine, or a directory. (A search engine searches Web pages on its own; a directory is a database of Web pages compiled by people.) While keyword searches are all similar in some respects, the rules and "filters" that control any given system will differ. Your ability to focus a search and get the best results depends on knowing how to direct that search. You'll be surprised by the sophistication of some search engines, particularly those on the World Wide Web (see Section 44c-1) which seem, at times, to anticipate your needs. But you can waste gobs of time just because you ignored the information waiting beneath "help," "simple search" or "advanced search" buttons on the screen.

44d
online

> Be sure to type keywords carefully, especially proper nouns. A
> misspelled search term can prevent you from finding available
> information.

■ 1 Understand how a simple keyword search works.

A keyword search identifies the titles in a catalog or database that contain the keyword(s) you have typed into a box or line on the screen. A librarian or instructor may be helpful in guiding you toward appropriate keywords for your searches.

Or you can use the research tools themselves creatively to find powerful keywords. When searching a library catalog, always look for cross-listings for your particular subject—that is, other terms under which your subject is entered—and follow up on those suggestions. For example, if your project on Civil War ironclad ships leads you to search with the term "Monitor" (the name of a famous Union ship), a particular catalog entry might include the cross-listings *Civil War; Merrimac; U.S. Navy, history; Ericsson, John.* You could then probe the catalog using each of these new terms.

You will have to be ingenious and dogged at times in choosing keywords for Web searches. If you need to know whether alcohol is legally considered a drug, for example, you could begin with general keywords such as "alcohol" or "drugs." But you'd be swamped by the number of responses, and you might never find the particular information you need. Here is where a little preliminary reading should pay off (see Section 43a-2). Once you learn that drugs are regulated by the Federal Drug Administration, you can try searching that term or, even better, its familiar acronym: FDA. When you locate the FDA's official site on the Web, you can then search it for "alcohol" to find the information you seek. "FDA" might not have been the first term to come to mind when you began your exploration, but it is a logical keyword, given the information you are seeking.

So the keywords you choose—whether names, places, titles, concepts, or people—will shape your search. A comparatively small database, such as an online library catalog, may ask you to indicate whether a word you are searching is a title (t), author (a), subject (s), or some other term the system recognizes. In such cases, typing the name of an author (Stephen Carter), a title (*Integrity*), or a narrow subject keyword (ethics) will often produce manageable numbers of items to examine and read.

44d
online

SEARCH ...	KEYWORD ...	FINDS ...
A (author)	Stephen Carter	40 items
T (title)	*Integrity*	25 items
S (subject)	ethics	50 items

You could easily look at all the items found in this simple search. And a simple search may be adequate when the database you are exploring is relatively small or the keyword you are using is distinctive.

However, a simple search using similar terms on the World Wide Web, a huge database, might initially produce useless results (although improvements in search logic are occurring all the time).

KEYWORD ...	FINDS ...
Stephen Carter	2,291,000 items
Integrity	173,000 items
Ethics in America	2,902,000 items

Similarly, typing a general subject keyword into a local online library catalog may provide a substantial number of items.

KEYWORD ...	FINDS ...
Ethics	13,400 items

In these situations, more sophisticated search techniques are obviously required. One such technique is called Boolean searching.

2 Understand the principles of Boolean searching. A Boolean search uses specific terms (or symbols) to give you more control over what you are seeking. Most search engines in online catalogs, databases, or Web sites use some form of Boolean search.

In a Boolean search, by linking keywords with the term AND, you can search for more than one term at a time, identifying only those items in which the individual terms intersect. It may help to visualize these items in terms of sets.

You initiate a Boolean search in different ways. One way is to insert AND between terms you wish to search.

Stephen AND Carter
miniature AND schnauzer AND training
Washington AND Jefferson AND Constitution

44d
online

Another way to initiate a Boolean search is to select an appropriate command from a search engine menu, such as an "all the words" option. Narrowing your search to look for only those items in which occur *all* the words you specify usually reduces the information glut.

Other Boolean operators allow you to direct database searches in different ways.

OR   Using OR between keywords directs the search engine to find any examples of either keyword. Using OR might widen a search, but it would also allow you to locate all documents that cover related concepts.

           dog OR puppy
           Congress OR Senate

NOT   Using NOT between terms permits you to search for sites that include one term but not another. This may be useful when you want to exclude certain meanings of a term irrelevant to your search.

           Indians NOT Cleveland
           apple NOT computer
           republican NOT party

( )   Putting items in parentheses allows for additional fine tuning of a search. In the first example below, you could locate documents that mention either Senator Gramm or Senator Hutchison but not Senator Kennedy or Senator Hatch.

           Senator AND (Gramm OR Hutchison)
           church NOT (Mormon OR Catholic)
           pickup NOT (Ford OR Dodge)

Some search engines use + and − to select the same functions.

+   Putting + (plus sign) immediately before an item, without a space, indicates that the word following it *must* be in the document being sought. Let's say, for example, you are looking on the Web for definitions of certain terms. You might format the request this way:

           +wetlands+definition
           +"sports car" +"definition of"

44d
online

−   Putting − (minus sign) immediately before an item, without a space, indicates that the word following it *must not* be in the document being sought. Let's say you want to search for documents about Richard Nixon that don't discuss Watergate or China. You could format the request like this:

           +Nixon −Watergate −China

▒ **3 Search by exact phrase.** To narrow a search even more, you can search for a specific and distinctive phrase either by placing it between quotation marks or selecting the "exact phrase" option on a search screen. This technique is essential for Web research and can produce dramatically different results. For example, placing quotations marks around "ethics in America" produces just 1,000 hits on *AltaVista* instead of the 2,902,000 hits produced without the exact-phrase specification. Similarly, an *AltaVista* search of the exact phrase "*Integrity* by Stephen L. Carter" produces just 13 items, most of them useful, including reviews of the book.

You can use exact-phrase searches creatively in many ways. When you can't recall who is responsible for a particular expression or quotation—for example, "defining deviancy down"—you can make it the subject of an exact phrase search. Do so on a Web search engine and you may find the expression attributed to former Senator Daniel Patrick Moynihan.

You can also combine exact phrase searches with various Boolean commands to find precisely what you need if you identify appropriate keywords.

"Ten Commandments" AND ("Charlton Heston" OR "Yul Brynner")
"pickup truck" NOT (Ford OR Dodge)

The potential of such searches is limited only by your cleverness.

▒ **4 Focus your search.** Search tools ordinarily give you considerable flexibility in selecting how to search information and how to report it.

Where to search. Many search engines allow you to limit a keyword search to a specific place or "domain" on the Internet. For example, the search engine *Excite* allows you to make any of the following choices under its "Advanced Web Search" option.

- Choose search terms
- Choose display
- Search in a specific language
- Choose country/domain

44d
online

Be sure to look at the results of your search to see if the search engine has returned suggestions for additional searches. You may see links marked "More like this."

When to search. Many keyword searches can be limited to specific periods of time, ranging from years to just one day. Clearly, you can reduce the number of "hits" for a given search this way, making your work more efficient.

You can also use searches limited by time to discover who was thinking what, when. How often were the terms *multiculturalism* and *partial birth abortion* being used ten years ago? How often are they being used today? You could find out on a database such as *LEXIS-NEXIS.*

How to report information. With online library catalogs and electronic indexes, you can usually print out the information you see on screen. Sometimes you have to select individual items to get full bibliographic data.

On the World Wide Web, you can usually see how many "hits" a search has found, and you can decide how many of them to view. It often makes sense to look at the abstracts for the sites first; then you can get full listings for sites that interest you.

E-Tips

To learn more about using Web search engines, see Ellen Chamberlain's "Bare Bones 101," a site that includes detailed descriptions of important search engines, at <http://www.sc.edu/beaufort/library/bones.html>.

44e How do you do field research?

While much college research occurs in the library or online, some of your works—especially in service learning projects—may lead you to seek information on your own through interviews, surveys, and close observation. Such *field work* is particularly common in disciplines such as psychology, anthropology, and education; if you are pursuing degrees in these areas, you'll likely learn formal techniques for field research. But informal field work can be useful in other, less formal research situations provided that you describe your procedures accurately and properly qualify your conclusions. Here we'll look briefly at conducting interviews, using questionnaires, and making observations.

44e
research

■ **1 Conduct interviews.** Sometimes people are the best sources of authoritative or firsthand information. When you can discuss your subject with experts or learn from people in a community, you add credibility, authenticity, and immediacy to a research report or service project. If you are writing a paper about an aspect of medical care, talk to a medical professional or patients affected by a problem. If you're exploring the financial dilemmas of community theaters, try to interview a local producer or theater manager. If you're writing about problems in the building industry, find a builder or banker with thirty minutes to spare.

It is often possible to consult with knowledgeable people via email, newsgroups, or listservs. Although online communications tend to be less formal than face-to-face conversations, they still require appropriate preparation and courtesy. For a directory of experts willing to consult via email, see *Pitsco's Ask an Expert* at <http://www.askanexpert.com>.

Checklist 44.6

Conducting a One-on-One Interview

* Write or telephone your subject for an appointment, and make it clear why you want the interview.

* Confirm your appointment the day before, and be on time for your appointment.

* Be prepared for the meeting. If possible, learn all you can about your subject's professional background, education, work history, and publications.

* Have a list of questions and possible follow-ups ready in your notebook. Establish the basic facts: Who? What? Where? When? How? Why? Then, when appropriate, pose questions that require more than one-word answers.

* Focus your queries on your research question: don't wander from the subject.

* Take careful notes, especially if you intend to quote your source.

* Double-check direct quotations, and be sure your source is willing to be cited "on the record."

* If you plan to tape the interview, get your subject's approval before turning the machine on.

* Promise to send your subject a copy of your completed project.

* Send a thank-you note to an authority who has been especially helpful.

44e
research

■ **2 Conduct surveys.** Research projects that focus on your local community may require surveys of public opinion and attitudes not available from other sources. So you may have to supply the information yourself by preparing questionnaires and conducting studies. Yet polling is demanding, and even the creating of a useful questionnaire requires ingenuity. You'll have to work hard to produce research results that readers will respect. Still, the principles behind effective polls and surveys are not inscrutable.

To begin with, you should have a clear idea about the information you are seeking. You distribute questionnaires not to see what turns up, but to obtain answers to specific research questions you have formulated: *Do people on my dormitory floor feel personally secure in their rooms? Would people in my neighborhood support the presence of a halfway house for juvenile offenders? Are people willing to pay additional taxes for improved public transportation?*

You have to formulate good questions, whether you are gathering factual information or sampling public opinion. Asking the right question isn't easy. You don't want to skew the answers you get by posing vague, leading, or biased questions.

VAGUE	What do you think about dorm security?
REVISED	Do you have any concerns about personal security in Aurelius Hall?
LEADING	Are you in favor of the city's building a halfway house for juvenile criminals right in the middle of our peaceful Enfield neighborhood?
REVISED	Do you favor the city's plan to build a halfway house for juvenile offenders in the Enfield neighborhood?
BIASED	Would you support yet another tax increase to fund a scheme for light rail in the city?
REVISED	Would you support a one-cent increase in the current sales tax to fund a light rail system for the city?

To make responses easy to tabulate, you will often want to provide readers with a range of options for answering your questions.

44e
research

How do you feel about the following statements? Respond using the appropriate number:
1. I disagree totally.
2. I disagree somewhat.
3. I neither agree nor disagree.
4. I agree somewhat.
5. I agree totally.

Our bus system serves the whole community.   _____
Our bus system operates efficiently.   _____
Our bus system runs on time.   _____

Bus fares are too high.   _____
A sales tax increase for buses makes sense.   _____

In addition to exploring your specific issues, you may want to gather demographic data on the people you are surveying; this information may be useful later in interpreting your findings. You must be able to protect the privacy of the people you survey and offer reasonable assurances that any information they volunteer will not be used against them in any way. But personal data can reveal surprising patterns, particularly when you are asking questions on political and social topics.

About you. Knowing a little about respondents to this survey will make interpretation of the data more significant. Please answer the following questions as best you can. Leave off any information you would rather not offer.

1. What is your gender?
   ___M ___F
2. What is your marital status?
   ___Married
   ___Single, divorced/separated/widowed
   ___Single, never married
3. What is your age? ___
4. What is your race? ethnicity?
   ___Asian
   ___Black/African American
   ___Hispanic
   ___White
   ___Other
5. What is the highest level of your education?
   ___elementary school or less
   ___high school graduate
   ___some college
   ___college graduate
   ___post-graduate or professional school
   ___other

44e
research

Try to anticipate the questions your queries might raise in a respondent's mind. For example, the list of educational achievement might be puzzling to someone who went to a technical or trade school out of high school. The category "other" often helps in doubtful cases.

Be sure you survey enough people from your target group so that readers will find your sample adequate. You ordinarily need to choose people at random for your survey, yet those polled should represent a cross-section of the whole population. Surveying just your friends, just people who agree with you, or only people like yourself will almost certainly produce inadequate research. You may have to provide an incentive to get people to cooperate with your survey. In most cases, this may mean suggesting that their responses may help to solve a problem or serve others in some way. J. D. Powers, the company famous for surveying new car owners, sends a crisp dollar bill with its surveys to thank potential respondents. You may not be able to go that far, but you do need to consider whether you can offer some incentive for a response, particularly when your survey is lengthy (as the J. D. Powers survey is).

Finally, you'll have to tabulate your findings accurately, present the results in a fashion that makes sense to readers, let readers know the techniques you used to gather your information, and, most important, report the limits of your study. Those limits provide the qualifications for any conclusions you draw. Don't overstate the results.

Checklist 44.7

Conducting a Survey

- Understand the purpose of your survey or questionnaire before you create it. What information do you want to gather?

- Prepare clear, fair, and unbiased questions. Test your questions on others to be sure participants in your actual survey will understand them.

- Consider the type of responses you need from respondents. Should they respond to a scale? To a list of options you provide? Should they fill in blanks?

- Consider how much space might be adequate for responses and how much space might be too much.

- Create questionnaires that are easy to read, easy to fill out, and easy to tabulate.

- Create questionnaires that are convenient to return. If necessary, provide properly addressed envelopes and return postage.

- Give respondents appropriate assurances about the confidentiality of their responses, and then abide by your commitment.

- Keep track of all your sampling procedures so you can report them accurately in your research paper.

44e
research

■ **3 Make systematic observations.** Some of the best field research you can do may come simply from the careful study of a phenomenon. The techniques of observation you use for a college research or service project may not be so rigorous as those of professional ethnographers who make a science of such studies, but you do need to take the process seriously. On their own, people are notoriously unreliable in recounting what they have seen; their observations are often colored by their prior expectations, experiences, and assumptions. (Not surprisingly, the sworn testimonies of eyewitnesses to events are often conflicting.) So in making research observations—whether about the behavior of sports fans at a football game or the interactions between infants and staff at a day-care center—you want to employ techniques that counteract your biases and ensure the reliability of your claims.

In recording your observations, you could do worse than to begin with a double-column spiral notebook to separate actual observations of a phenomenon from your immediate reactions to it. Your written notes should be quite detailed about matters such as time, place, duration of the study, conditions of the observation, and so on. You may have to summarize such information later.

Of course, you need not rely on notebooks alone for your records. To assure an accurate account of what you are studying, use any appropriate recording methods: photography, tape or video recordings, transcriptions of online conversations, and so on. If you make multiple observations over a period of time, follow the same procedures each time and note any changes that might affect your results. For example, a group of students conducting a traffic count of the patrons entering a major campus facility would want to perform the counts on typical days, not during spring break or on days when the weather is unusually bad.

Checklist 44.8

Making Observations

• Understand the purpose of your observation. What information do you hope to gather? In what forms can that data be gathered and reported?

• Study any literature on your subject and become familiar with the issues/subjects you are studying. What background information do you need to have on your subject(s) to make informed and perceptive observations?

• Plan the method of your observation. How can you gather the information you need? How can you minimize your own impact on the situation you are observing?

• Practice techniques of observation. Determine what methods work best.

• Work with others to confirm the reliability of your observations. Cross-check your field notes with those of fellow researchers.

44e
research

CHAPTER 45

How Do You Evaluate and Use Sources?

Finding research materials, as described in Chapter 44, doesn't come to a halt when you begin developing a project. Throughout the research process you'll find yourself gathering additional information to address new questions or plug gaps in what you've learned. At the same time, you'll be working with the sources you've gathered—reading them, evaluating them, and deciding how they can best support the claims you wish to make. This chapter describes how to handle research materials.

45a How do you evaluate research sources?

Writers have always had to be careful about the sources they cited in research projects, but at least they could be confident that the library materials they used had been reviewed by publishers, editors, and librarians. Today, however, some materials—for example, pages from the Web and messages from listservs—may come to you almost directly from their authors, unreviewed and unrefereed. It falls to you, then, to judge their authority, quality, and credibility. You can learn to make sound judgments if you remember a few basic principles. (For detailed advice on reading critically, see Chapter 9.)

1 Consider the purpose of a source. Sources aren't simply *good* or *bad*. Their value will depend, in part, on how you intend to use them. For example, if you were writing a report on the positions taken by a candidate in a long-past presidential campaign, you'd probably depend on scholarly works published by reputable writers or you'd look up newspaper accounts on microfilm in the library. But if you were developing a project about a political campaign today, you might use less scholarly materials, such as campaign literature, recent articles in newspapers and popular magazines, and even Web sites. These sources might lack the authority and perspective of more scholarly works, but they could still provide a valid snapshot of current political attitudes.

Ultimately, you have to decide which research materials will suit your topic best and then be prepared to defend their relevance, especially when readers are apt to resist them—as they might when you quote from personal home pages or Usenet discussions.

Even if sources can't be described as simply good or bad without considering their purposes, they do have strengths and weaknesses to weigh. We've summarized some of those qualities in the table on pages 672–73, but our guidelines should be taken with caution. Any single source might differ from our characterizations.

In researching a subject, the best sources for you are likely to be those just a step or two above your current level of knowledge. Push yourself to learn more without exceeding your depth.

■ **2 Consider the authority and reputation of a source.** As you accumulate materials for a project, you may find that certain books, articles, and reference tools are cited more often than others. These are likely to be essential materials that people in the field assume most other researchers know. If you haven't already consulted these materials in your own collection of data, go to the library and review them. Don't hesitate to ask librarians or instructors about the authority of books, articles, or other sources that you expect to use. They will often be able to direct you to reliable materials. Do the same with electronic sources: track down the best items so far as you can determine. Inevitably, the most valuable sites will appear on many "favorites" lists.

> **E-Tips**
>
> There are a growing number of guides to online materials. You might begin with *The Argus Clearinghouse* at <http://www.clearinghouse.net/>; be sure to check out its detailed criteria for evaluating Web resources. Also potentially helpful are *Librarians Index to the Internet* at <http://lii.org/> and *ICYouSee* at <http://www.ithaca.edu/library/Training/ICYouSee.html>, a site aimed specifically at college researchers.

45a
evaluate

■ **3 Consider the credentials of authors and sponsoring agencies.** This advice might not seem practical when you are exploring a subject new to you. But you'll quickly pick up the names of people mentioned frequently as experts or authorities—people whose work has had lasting or significant influence. (You may also hear your in-

ASSESSING SOURCES

Source	Purpose	Authors	Audience/ Language
Scholarly books	Advance or report new knowledge	Experts	Academic/ Technical
Scholarly articles	Advance or report new knowledge	Experts	Academic/ Technical
Serious books & articles	Report or summarize information	Experts or professional writers	Educated public/ Formal
Popular magazines	Report or summarize information	Professional writers or journalists	General public/ Informal
Newspapers, news services	Report current information	Journalists	Popular/ Informal
Sponsored Web sites	Varies from report information to advertise	Varies, usually Web expert	Varies/ Usually informal
Individual Web sites	Varies	Expert to novice	Varies/ Casual to slang
Interviews	Consult with experts	Experts	Varies/Technical to colloquial
Listservs	Discuss specific subjects	Experts to interested amateurs	Varies/Technical to colloquial
Usenet newsgroups	Discuss specific subjects	Open to everyone	Varies/Technical to colloquial

Publisher or Medium	Reviewed/ Documented?	Current/ Stable?	Dialogic/ Interactive?
University Press	Yes/Yes	No/Yes	No/No
Scholarly or professional journal	Yes/Yes	Usually no/Yes	No/ No (unless online)
Commercial publishers	Yes/No	Depends on subject/Yes	No/ No (unless online)
Commercial publishers	Yes/No	Yes/Yes	No/ No (unless online)
Commercial press or online	Yes/No	Yes/Yes	No/ No (unless online)
Online WWW	Sometimes/ Links to other sites	Regularly updated/ sometimes	Sometimes/ Often
Online WWW	Usually no/ Links to other sites	Varies/Varies	Sometimes/ Sometimes
Notes, recordings, email	No/No	Yes/No	Yes/Yes
Online email	No/No	Yes/Sometimes	Yes/Yes
Online email	No/No	Yes/No	Yes/Yes

structors mention writers who deal with your topic.) When scanning a lengthy printout of potential sources, look for these familiar authors. But don't be drawn in by celebrity alone, particularly when the names of famous people are attached to subjects about which they may have no special expertise.

With Web sites, listservs, and other online sources, you may find yourself clueless about the credentials of your "authors." All you might know about participants in a discussion group is a name and an email address. When you report factual information from such sources, confirm it when possible through second, more familiar sources. (Reporting opinion is a different matter.) On personal Web sites, check to see what expertise the authors claim for themselves, then try to verify their credentials. If they offer email addresses, write them and ask about the sources they used to support the claims on their pages. Be both open-minded and skeptical.

You can be more confident about electronic information when the sponsoring agency of the source is one you would trust in a print environment. Acquiring information online from *Reuters News Service* or *USA Today* is equivalent to seeing the same information in print. But don't hesitate even in these cases to raise questions about fairness, bias, and completeness.

■ 4 Consider the timeliness and stability of a source.

Timeliness is relative. For some projects, you might need sources that are both immediate and interactive like the conversations in chat rooms and MOOs. For other projects, you may turn to the more professional discussion of current issues you'll find in newspapers, magazines, and popular journals. For still other academic work, you'll want sources that offer the kind of thoughtful commentary or observation that requires time, research, and study.

With books and articles, then, the date of publication is crucial. In general, you want to support your projects with the most current and reputable information in a field. But your instructors and librarians may refer you to classic pieces, too, writings that have shaped thinking in your topic area. For many college papers, you should have a mix of sources, some from the past, some quite recent. While books and articles may sometimes be difficult to acquire, important books and printed articles don't disappear the way electronic sources sometimes do.

Timeliness is a different matter in newer electronic environments where you may not always be able to determine how current a given source is. Few conventions govern the millions of Web pages, so not every site you visit will provide a date for its original posting or its most recent update. You'll want to check for both since the Web is full of sites posted and largely forgotten by their authors. Currency is less a factor in listservs, Usenet newsgroups, and other email postings, since the turnover of material is very rapid, changing from day to day. But this also means that something you read today may be gone tomorrow—or sooner. Obviously, you need to print out or download relevant postings from such sources. You can also check whether the source you are using archives its materials.

Web sites pose similar problems. Some sponsored sites allow you to search their archives for past stories or postings. But those archives may not be complete, and they may not go back many years. Electronic sources are not yet as stable, comprehensive, and dependable over the long run as printed books and articles—though the situation is improving. Scholarly e-journals are increasing in number and prestige, and the archives of significant newspapers and periodicals are growing. Still, the instability of electronic sources is a matter to consider, especially when you are planning a long-term research project.

5 Consider the biases of a source. You'll especially need to consider political, social, and religious leanings when you deal with controversial subjects. In deciding which items to read from a lengthy list, it may help to select opinions from across the spectrum. Otherwise you could write a whole paper unaware that important perspectives were being ignored. (See also Sections 9b-5 and 9b-7.)

It is important to understand that almost all sources have biases and points of view that shape the information they contain (and determine what they exclude). Sometimes those leanings are apparent. You do not have to read much to realize, for example, that the editorial page of *The New York Times* tends to be "liberal" in its politics and that of *The Wall Street Journal* "conservative" (although even these generalizations won't describe particular pieces you find on the pages). It may be harder to detect biases in scholarly journals, popular magazines, and news services on the Web, but be assured that they are there. When you are in doubt about the representativeness of the sources you have selected, consult with instructors or librarians—being aware that they, too, have points of view and may try to influence your selection.

45a
evaluate

E-Tips

Two points on the political spectrum offer thought-provoking online assessments of media bias. See FAIR at <http://www.fair.org/fair.org> for a left-wing take on issues of balance and fairness in the news. See Media Research Center at <http://www.mediaresearch.org/> for a conservative perspective.

■ **6 Consider how well a source presents key information.** The design of a source is probably of greater concern with Web sites than with printed books and articles, for which the conventions were established years ago. Still evolving as an information tool, Web sites bring together the complex resources of print, visual, and audio media, sometimes brilliantly, sometimes garishly. A successful Web site identifies its purpose clearly, arranges information logically, gives access to its materials without exhausting the capacity of its users' technology, furnishes relevant and selective links to other responsible resources, and provides basic bibliographical information: identity and email of author/sponsor, date of posting, date of most recent update, and so on. You may not wish to rely on a site that does not meet these standards.

E-Tips

For an amusing discussion of bad Web design, take a look at Vince Flander's *Web Pages that Suck.com* at <http://www .webpagesthatsuck.com/>. Jakob Nielsen has a fascinating archive of his columns on Web design at <http://www.useit.com/alertbox/>.

■ **7 Consider commercial intrusions into a source.** Books today rarely have advertising, and we often just ignore ads in printed magazines. But commercial intrusions into Web sites are persistent enough to warrant concern. Sponsored Web sites—especially search engines—are often so thick with commercial appeals that they can be difficult to use. Moreover, your search itself may bring up specific advertising messages in an effort to direct you to a sponsor's material. No library catalog ever exerted this kind of pressure.

Sponsored sites may also reflect the commercial connections of their owners, especially when news organizations are in fact owned by larger companies with entertainment or other commercial interests. What appears—or doesn't appear—on a site may be determined by who is supporting the message. Be aware of attempts to influence your judgment, and make it a point to visit many different sites when exploring a subject. Use a variety of search engines, too, to find your materials.

45a
evaluate

Checklist 45.1

Evaluating a World Wide Web Site

• Is the site sponsored by a reputable group you can identify?

• Do the authors of the site give evidence of their credentials?

• Is the site conveniently searchable?

• Is information in the site logically arranged?

• Is the site easy to navigate?

• Does the site provide an email address where you might send questions?

• Is the site updated regularly or properly maintained?

• Does the site archive older information?

• Is the content of the site affected by commercial sponsorship?

For additional advice on evaluating Web sites, see <http://www.library.cornell.edu/okuref/research/webeval.html> and <http://www.library.ucla.edu/libraries/college/help/critical/index.htm>. For an exercise on evaluating a Web site, see <http://www.lib.vt.edu/research/evaluate/evaluating.html>.

45b How do you use research materials?

Once you have found the best sources for your project, you must make use of the information in them. How you treat research materials will vary, but certain techniques make sense for getting the most out of them: positioning, annotating, and summarizing and paraphrasing. Then you must find ways to relate your source materials, to bring them together to form coherent and complex discussions of your topic.

■ 1 Position your sources. Before you begin annotating (see Section 45b-2) or summarizing or paraphrasing a source (Section 45b-3), you may want to set it into an appropriate context—what we call "positioning a source." This technique will encourage you to approach all research materials actively and somewhat skeptically, thinking deeply about their implications and connections.

You position a source by identifying its point of view, biases, strengths, and limitations. Of course, not all sources can be used the same way. Sometimes you'll cite materials because they offer the most balanced treatment of a subject. At other times you'll choose

45b
position

sources that exemplify distinct perspectives and points of view. And at still other times you might select sources you know are "off the wall" but which nonetheless make revealing points about culture and society. Positioning a source helps you make these decisions with your eyes open and aware of the contexts that can shape and influence sources. When you position a source, you simply identify such perspectives so that you do not misrepresent information when you report it.

Sources do reflect different political, social, economic, even generational biases. Differences of religion, gender, or worldview may similarly shape the materials you gather in ways that bear on your research. Even the methods used in creating the source materials will influence how you present them: Was a survey scientific? Was a study sponsored by a group with a stake in its outcome? Does a document you cite represent a person's carefully considered judgment, or is it a paid endorsement, a political screed, even a parody? You need to know before you go public with it.

The answers to such questions do not automatically disqualify sources; instead, they help you to determine how to use them responsibly. You owe it to readers to be honest and forthright with information and to share what you learn about your sources when that information affects your conclusions. Occasionally you might even have to research your sources to be sure they are reliable. If a source providing statistics in support of nationalized health care is a liberal think tank, you and readers should know; when a columnist you quote in supporting a flat tax proposal is wealthy enough to benefit significantly from the policy change, that's relevant information.

The following examples are attempts to position two short articles that appear later in this chapter on pages 683 and 685. Your own efforts to position a source might be much less formal than these: positioning is not so much a written assignment as a mental exercise you should perform with all your research materials. Yet the examples may help you determine the kinds of questions to ask in order to appreciate what a source is and does.

45b
position

EXAMPLE 1	*Journal/Magazine Article, "The Nikes Jumped Over the Moon" by Robert Shrum*

POSITIONING   This short article analyzes a television
                            spot for Nike shoes titled "Cow,"

produced by Jim Riswold, Alice Chevalier,
and John Jay of the Wieden & Kennedy
advertising agency. Shrum's analysis
appeared in the computer journal <u>Slate</u> on
December 13, 1996, as part of the
"Varnish Remover" series. <u>Slate</u> is a
magazine created by Microsoft founder
Bill Gates and edited by liberal
political commentator Michael Kinsley,
former editor of <u>The New Republic</u>. <u>Slate</u>
describes Robert Shrum as "a leading
Democratic political consultant." One
might expect the review of Nike's ad to
reflect the similar political interests
and concerns of the author and the
magazine. The analysis, available at
<http://www.slate.com/Ad/96-12-13/
Ad.asp>, was accessed on July 5, 1997,
for a project investigating Nike's
involvement in contemporary social
causes.

EXAMPLE 2   *An Editorial, "Leave the People Home"*
by Alex Roland

POSITIONING

"Leave the People Home" is an editorial
that appeared in <u>USA Today</u> on July 7,
1997, following the successful landing
on Mars of a research robot. The piece,
written by Alex Roland, appears as a
rebuttal to the paper's official
editorial position endorsing exploration
of Mars by human explorers. Owned by
Gannett, <u>USA Today</u> is a daily newspaper

45b
position

available throughout the country with a
predominantly liberal editorial page. It
routinely publishes counterpoints to its
editorials. USA Today notes that Alex
Roland, "chair of the history department
at Duke University, teaches technology
history and is a former NASA historian."
Roland's academic credentials and work
with the American space agency would
seem to give him authority on this
subject. The editorial was accessed
online on July 7, 1997, for a Web
project exploring the pros and cons of a
human mission to Mars.

Checklist 45.2

Positioning a Source

• What are the background and interests of the author(s)?
• What are the interests and biases of the publisher?
• How much authority does the source claim?
• Are the assertions of authority justified?
• Does the source purport to be objective and/or scientific?
• Does the source present itself as subjective and/or personal?
• Whose interests does the source represent?
• Whose interests does the source seem to ignore?
• To what audience(s) is the source directed?
• What do readers need to know about the source?
• Where do links in the source lead? Who advertises in the source?
• What role should the source play in my project: Authority? Opinion? Illustration?

45b
position

Utne Reader at <http://www.utne.com/> appeals to a predominantly left-of-center readership concerned with issues of culture, earth, body, spirit, and politics. You might discover its point of view most readily by studying its links to other sources.

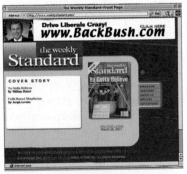

The titles of articles in *The Weekly Standard* at <http://www.weeklystandard.com/> might suggest its right-of-center politics. Or you might recognize the names of some of its authors. Better yet, check the revealing "About Us" link.

The American Institute of Physics publishes a dozen specialized journals, described at <http://www.aip.org/pjs/service.html>. The titles of articles such as *Chaos* or *Physics of Fluids* will quickly reveal the journals' academic orientation. (Reprinted with permission. Copyright 2001, American Institute of Physics (AIP).)

45b
position

■ **2 Annotate your research materials.** Once you have positioned a source, you can begin mining it for information. One way to do that is to annotate the material you've gathered—that is, to attach comments, questions, and reactions to it directly. The point of annotation is to identify ideas and information worth returning to and, more important, to engage in a dialogue with the authors and sources you are encountering.

Annotation is not an easy option when you are reading library books and materials; in these cases, you'll have to record your reactions in notes, summaries, and paraphrases (see Section 45b-3). But much research material today is photocopied, downloaded, or read online—and these media support different forms of annotation.

Many researchers working with photocopied materials will use highlighting pens to tag important passages. But marking material in this way is only part of an effective annotation process. Each section you highlight should be accompanied by a marginal comment that explains the importance of the passage or states your reaction to it. Be sure to highlight any passages worthy of direct quotation.

You can use the annotation features of word-processing programs to record your reactions to files you download from your computer. But once again your comments are the essential element. These annotations can later be incorporated into the paper or project itself if they are thoughtful and entirely in your own words.

Even pages from the World Wide Web can be marked with comments and, in some cases, annotated as part of an ongoing online discussion. For instance, you can use a browser's "bookmark" feature to gather together all Web sites or pages relevant to your project, arranging the items in folders that reflect its overall structure, one folder for each major section or theme. It is even possible to annotate each bookmark to remind yourself why the site or page is important.

You can and probably should take conventional notes on all your important sources, online or off. (See Section 9a-4 for advice about preparing *content, context,* and *response* notes.)

On page 683 is an example of a source that has been annotated in its margins. (To see this source positioned, see Section 45b-1.)

45b
annotate

E-Tips

For a detailed online guide to *Microsoft Word*'s commenting features, see <http://wwwnt.cwrl.utexas.edu/web/teaching. cfm?page=commenting>. The tutorial explains how to either edit or comment on any document you can download in *Word*.

ANNOTATED TEXT

"The Nikes Jumped Over the Moon"

by Robert Shrum

Cow is an animated fairy tale that targets the subteen who still responds to the child within. But it is just as likely to engage the old folks of the athletic shoe market—Gen-Xers and the thirtysomethings. (As far as Nike is concerned, anyone past these demographics is a retired consumer.)

Tone here suggests Shrum is suspicious of Nike?

Naturally, we never see a real shoe in this animated spot—that would break its tone. It opens, instead, with a cow grazing in a bucolic field. Out of shape and shoeless, this one is an eater, not an exerciser. Reponding to the whistles and taunts of Old Man Moon, she attempts to re-enact the fairy tale and "jump over the moon." Leaping, then falling ("Ooh," says the moon), she lies splayed on the feeding ground.

Shrum describes the Nike ad.

The fallen creature now responds to the strains of "Destination Moon" on the soundtrack: "Come and take a trip in my rocket ship." And what is the rocket? A Nike "swoosh" logo appears in a thought balloon over the animal's head. The brand doesn't have to be mentioned: In the age of the advertised image where television often seems more real than real-life, the Nike swoosh is ubiquitous. The cow squeezes into the barn, then races outside wearing Nikes. "We'll travel fast and light," the song goes—as the animal soars over Old Man Moon, punching him so hard that he sees stars.

"Image is everything"

Cow's message isn't that Nikes are a substitute for working out. Rather, the spot tells you that if you wear the shoes and just do the rest, you'll soar, whether your moon be the NBA, a three-mile jogging path, or a playground. The high-jumping bovine also reinforces Nike's core identification with basketball and the Bulls' Michael Jordan. And, because the spot uses an animal, excluding all references to race, gender, or a particular sport, soccer kids in Beverly Hills are as likely to embrace it—and the product—as hoop shooters in Harlem.

Shrum's thesis—or a summary of the Nike ad?

Did Nike eliminate race/class issues deliberately? Or is Shrum reading into the ad something not there?

The spot ends with the Nike slogan that is now as familiar as the swoosh. Evoking freedom, a safe rebellion, "Just Do It" is the life-affirming bookend to Nancy Reagan's "Just Say No." *Cow* recruits the next generation of Nike wearers by building a bridge between young people's innate sense of play and the next stage—competition. Shoes signify more than sports these days. They stand for self-image. If young people do it now, Nike knows they'll keep doing it later. The fairy tale goes on: Buy the shoes, and jump the moon. And it doesn't matter if it's all bull.

Has Shrum proved that the shoes = self image?

Confirms my original suspicions about Shrum & Nike.

45b
annotat

■ **3 Decide whether a given source should be summarized or paraphrased.** Your choice will be determined by both the source and the use you intend to make of it.

A *summary* captures the gist of a source or some portion of it, boiling it down to a few words or sentences. Summaries tend to be short, extracting only what is immediately relevant from a source. Summarize those materials that support your thesis but do not provide an extended argument or idea that you need to share in detail with readers.

When summarizing a source, identify its key facts or ideas and put them in your own words. When an article is quite long, you might look for topic ideas in each major section. If you have a photocopy of the source, highlight any sentences that state or emphasize its key themes. Then assemble these ideas into a short, coherent statement about the whole piece, one detailed enough to stand on its own and make sense several weeks after you examine the material. The summary should be entirely in your own words.

A *paraphrase* usually reviews a complete source in much greater detail than does a summary. When paraphrasing a work, you report its key information or restate its core arguments point by point *in your own words*. You will typically want to paraphrase any materials that provide detailed facts or ideas your readers will need. Predictably, paraphrases run much longer than summaries.

Prepare a paraphrase by working through the original source more systematically than you would with a summary. An effective paraphrase will meet the following conditions.

- The paraphrase reflects the structure of the original piece.
- The paraphrase reflects the ideas of the original author, not your reflections on them.
- Each important fact or direct quotation is accompanied by a specific page number from the source when possible.
- The material you record is relevant to your theme. (Don't waste time paraphrasing parts of the source that are of no use to your project.)
- The material is entirely in your own words—except for clearly marked quotations.

Practically speaking, the distinction between summaries and paraphrases is often less important than that you simply take the notes you need for a project. In gathering information, you'll often find yourself switching between summary and paraphrase, depending on what you are reading.

Now let's look at a source first summarized and then paraphrased. Following is the complete text of an editorial that originally appeared in *USA Today* on July 7, 1997, shortly after the successful landing on Mars of a research robot called *Pathfinder* and an onslaught of problems on the Russian space station *Mir*. Written by Alex Roland, chair of the history department at Duke University, the piece rebutted *USA Today*'s editorial position in favor of the human exploration of Mars.

To prepare the editorial for either a summary or a paraphrase, you might first highlight and annotate the information most relevant to your project. In this case, we've focused on the research question "Should humans explore Mars?"

ANNOTATED TEXT

"Leave the People Home"

by Alex Roland

The debacle currently unfolding aboard the *Mir* space station argues against sending people to Mars any time soon. To think about a manned Mars mission now is like planning your next cruise during an abandon-ship exercise.

The problem is putting people in space. All the really useful things done in space have been achieved with automated spacecraft controlled by people on Earth. The record is long and impressive—scientific probes to the planets and beyond, communications satellites, weather satellites, reconnaissance satellites, the global positioning system.

Two bad things happen when humans come aboard. First, cost increases by an order of magnitude, mostly to pay for life-support equipment and safety precautions. Second, the spacecraft becomes a lifeboat. Whatever mission it was intended to conduct—research, exploration, commerce—takes second place to saving the crew and returning them to Earth. The people, supposedly a means to some end, become the end themselves.

The *Pathfinder* spacecraft, due to touch down on Mars July 4th, is a case in point. At a tiny fraction of what a manned mission would cost (indeed, at a small fraction of the cost of a single shuttle mission), this resourceful spacecraft, and the roving *Sojourner* vehicle it carries, will do more and better research than astronauts could do. Machines can reach more places, stay longer, and take more risks.

But machines, you say, are not as dramatic, not as interesting as people. It is not the practicality of a manned Mars mission that appeals, but the romance. Sending people to Mars is a feel-good mission that speaks to the basic human longing to explore.

Well, our next feel-good mission is already booked. 1997

Later this year, components of the international space station are scheduled to rocket into orbit. In 1999, three years before construction is complete, people will begin to inhabit it permanently. If it proves useful, more durable and safer than *Mir*, there will be plenty of time and a better argument for sending people to Mars.

For now, however, we have all we can do to find a reason, a budget, and a technology to keep people in orbit.

Find out what was happening on Mir.
↳ check
→ newspaper
indexes?

True? Look for opposite view.

Connect to Apollo 13 moonshot?

}—Crucial point

Robots work harder than people?
↓
possible quotation

Yes. We can't ignore why people explore.

To prepare a summary, assemble the key claim and supporting elements into a concise restatement of the overall argument. The summary should make sense on its own, forming a complete statement you might use later in the project itself. But don't be surprised if you go through several versions of that sentence before you come up with one that satisfies you.

EFFECTIVE
SUMMARY

```
Alex Roland, chair of history at Duke
University and a former historian at
NASA, argues in USA Today (7 July 1997)
that using automated spacecraft to ex-
plore planets such as Mars makes better
sense than sending people on such mis-
sions because humans in space increase
costs and risks and reduce the potential
for long-term, productive science.
```

How can something as simple as a summary go wrong? There are a number of ways. You might, for example, make the summary too succinct and leave out crucial details. Such a summary scribbled on a note card might be useless when, days later, you try to make sense of it.

INEFFECTIVE
SUMMARY

```
He argues that using people increases
costs and reduces the science.
International space station, 1997. Better
reason to send after? Budget and
technology.
```

Or your summary might fail because it misses the central point of a piece by focusing on details not relevant to the argument. Useful in a different context, these facts are misleading if they don't capture the essence of what the author wrote.

45b
sources

INACCURATE
SUMMARY

```
Alex Roland, chair of history at Duke
University and a former historian at
NASA, argues in USA Today (7 July 1997)
that the Pathfinder mission to Mars was
very inexpensive and that, very soon, we
will be launching an international space
station.
```

Yet another danger lies in using the actual words of the original author
in your summary. If these unacknowledged borrowings make their way
into your project itself without both quotation marks and documentation, you are guilty of plagiarism (see Section 46b). In the example following, language taken directly and inappropriately from Roland's editorial is underlined.

PLAGIARIZED   Alex Roland, chair of history at Duke

SUMMARY   University and a former historian at

                NASA, argues in USA Today (7 July 1997)

                that all the really useful things done in

                space have been achieved with automated

                spacecraft controlled by people on Earth.

                Machines can reach more places, stay

                longer, and take more risks.

From this "plagiarized summary" you can appreciate how tempting it
might be to slip these words into the body of a paper, forgetting that
you didn't write them yourself. To avoid plagiarism, the safest practice
is *always* to use your own words in summaries.

      A paraphrase of "Leave the People Home" would be appreciably
longer than a summary because a researcher would expect to use the information differently, probably referring to the source in much greater
detail. Here's one possible paraphrase of the editorial.

EFFECTIVE   Recent problems on the Russian space

PARAPHRASE   station Mir, Alex Roland argues in a USA

                Today editorial (7 July 1997), make it

                clear why a human mission to Mars may not

                be a good idea: people in space cause

                problems that robots don't. Automated

                spacecraft perform almost all the really

                important work in space (communications,

                weather satellites, global positioning).

                Spacecraft that carry astronauts must

                also take along everything that keeps

                them alive, adding tremendously to the

                weight and complexity of missions. When

                something goes wrong, the whole project

45b
sources

```
is jeopardized by the need to preserve

the lives of astronauts. The Mars

Pathfinder expedition, in contrast, was

accomplished far more cheaply than even a

routine space shuttle launch and yet can

do more science over the long term than a

human expedition because it isn't as

vulnerable. We may like the adventure and

romance that comes along with human space

exploration, and we'll have that

experience with the international space

station. But humans in space are an

expensive and possibly unnecessary luxury.
```

You'll notice that this paraphrase reviews all the major points in the editorial in the same order as the original. It also borrows none of the author's language. With proper documentation, any part of the paraphrase could become part of the final research project without a need for quotation marks. (See Section 46b-2.)

How can paraphrases go wrong? Various problems can make the paraphrase inaccurate or unusable. A paraphrase should accurately reflect the thinking of the original author. Reserve your comments and asides for annotations or other, separate notes so that you don't confuse your ideas with those of your sources. Consider how the following paraphrase might misreport the views of Alex Roland if the researcher later forgets that the underlined comments in the example should have been personal notes or annotations.

INACCURATE
PARAPHRASE
```
Recent problems on the Russian space

station Mir, Alex Roland argues in a USA

Today editorial (7 July 1997), make it

clear why a human mission to Mars may not

be a good idea: people in space cause

problems that robots don't. You could

argue, though, that people can fix problems

robots can't: one reason Mir was in space

so long is that cosmonauts could repair the
```

45b
sources

station. True, automated spacecraft perform
almost all the really important work in
space (communications, weather satellites,
global positioning)--if you ignore the more
complicated experiments performed by
astronauts. No robot could have fixed the
Hubble Space Telescope, for example.
Spacecraft that carry astronauts must also
take along everything that keeps them
alive, adding tremendously to the weight
and complexity of missions. . . .

You get the point. The reactions to the editorial are valid, but they
don't represent an accurate paraphrase of the original article.

A paraphrase also should not reorganize or improve on the structure or argument of the original piece. For example, the following paraphrase doesn't actually add material to Roland's editorial, but it rearranges its information radically.

INACCURATE
PARAPHRASE

Americans may like the adventure and
romance that comes along with human space
exploration, and we'll have that
experience again soon with the
international space station to be launched
in 1999. But humans in space are an
expensive and possibly unnecessary luxury,
argues Alex Roland in a USA Today
editorial (7 July 1997). Spacecraft that
carry astronauts must also take along
everything that keeps them alive, adding
tremendously to the weight and complexity
of missions. When something goes wrong,
the whole project is jeopardized by the
need to preserve the lives of astronauts.
That's the lesson we should have learned
from problems on the Russian space station
Mir. The Mars Pathfinder expedition, in

45b
sources

contrast, was accomplished far more
cheaply than even a routine space shuttle
launch and yet can do more science over
the long term than a human expedition
because it isn't as vulnerable. So a human
mission to Mars may not be a good idea:
people in space cause problems that robots
don't. Unpeopled, automated spacecraft
perform almost all the really important
work in space (communications, weather
satellites, global positioning).

The most dangerous and academically dishonest sort of paraphrase is one in which a researcher borrows the ideas, structure, and details of a source wholesale, changing a few words here and there in order to claim originality. This sort of paraphrase is plagiarism even if the material is documented in the research project; writers can't just change a few words in their sources and claim the resulting material as their own work. (See Section 46b-2.)

PLAGIARIZED   The catastrophe now unfolding aboard the
PARAPHRASE   <u>Mir</u> space station argues against
launching people to Mars any time soon.
To consider a manned Mars mission now is
like planning your next airflight during
a midair crisis.

    The difficulty is sending people into
outer space.

    Most of the really useful things
achieved in space have been done with
automated spaceships controlled by
technicians on Earth. The record is quite
impressive--scientific probes to the
planets and beyond, communications
satellites, weather satellites,
reconnaissance satellites, the global
positioning system. . . .

You'll see the fault very readily if you compare these plagiarized paragraphs with the opening paragraphs in Roland's original editorial.

E-Tips

Be especially careful to paraphrase or summarize accurately when you record your notes in a research program such as *TakeNote*. Because you can export these notes directly from the program into your word processor or onto a Web site, you want to be certain that the words are your own and that quoted material is in quotation marks. Otherwise, you may find yourself inadvertently plagiarizing your sources when you transfer notes into your project itself.

4 Relate and connect your research materials. Even without prompting, you'll likely find yourself examining each new source in terms of other materials you've gathered for a project. This correlation of materials is a key to good research. Think of your project as a conversation among authors discussing ideas: no single voice should go unchallenged or be allowed to dominate the exchange.

Sometimes you'll want to locate sources that reinforce each other, especially when you're trying to build a persuasive case (see Section 11c-1). In other situations, you'll find authoritative sources that differ notably; then you have to decide which to endorse or, perhaps, to leave that choice to readers. When sources have pronounced biases (political or otherwise), read them "against" pieces with alternative views to keep your own perspectives broad. And when you borrow material from online discussion groups, always find other, more conventional sources to confirm specific facts, figures, or claims you find there. Examine the sources you have selected, reading them as both believer and doubter (see Section 9b-1) and posing these practical questions.

- What information represents "fact" and what "opinion"?
- What have I actually learned from my sources?
- What do I still have to discover?
- What conflicts in the evidence do I need to address?
- What position(s) will I take?

45b
sources

When you actually begin to write, build your project from a variety of sources, drawing on different voices to create a coherent whole. Don't allow whole paragraphs or pages to depend on just one or two sources. If you do, your research project may begin to sound like a report that merely parrots what others have already written, a patchwork of quotations or borrowings held together by a few words or sentences of your own. Your responsibility as a writer is (ideally) to take a discussion farther than it has progressed so far. To do that, you must combine what you learn from many different sources into a coherent argument of your own.

Going Public   *Using Sources*

Following is an exemplary paragraph from a research paper by first-year composition student Andres Romay on the rising homicide rate among juveniles. It makes its case by synthesizing five different sources—as indicated by the parenthetical notes highlighted in orange. The sources furnish the information, but Andres Romay provides the logic that leads from data to conclusion.

> A second factor contributing to the increasing
> rate of homicides committed by juveniles is easier
> access to firearms among adolescents. According to the
> Justice Information Center, between 1984 and 1994,
> guns became much more available to teens than in
> earlier decades ("Partnership"). Additionally, there
> was a 156 percent increase in weapons offenses for
> juveniles within the same decade (Butts).
> Approximately one in every eight suburban youth and
> two in every five inner-city youth carried a gun at
> some time (Osofsky 3-4). Since juveniles have had this
> increased access to guns, juvenile killings with
> firearms have quadrupled (Gest 36). Instead of teens
> settling their disputes by fist-fighting or stabbing,
> they now resort to shooting. Since gunshots are more
> likely to be fatal than other kinds of injuries, it is
> easy to see why the rate of homicides would increase
> as guns become more available. A pilot program in
> Boston launched in 1984 to reduce the availability of
> guns to adolescents through stiffer penalties and
> advanced systems of gun tracing has, predictably,
> reduced the number of juvenile killings in the city
> (Kennedy). Clearly, the availability of guns has a
> causal relationship to the juvenile homicide rate.

45b
sources

CHAPTER 46

How Do You Acknowledge Sources?

In your research project you will create a dialogue among the sources you have assembled. But your voice—and that of any colleagues working on the paper or project—will ultimately shape the final product. So readers will want to know which ideas and claims are your own and which should be attributed to your sources. For that reason, you need to acknowledge your sources in academic or professional projects conscientiously, honestly, and gracefully. That's what this chapter covers.

46a How do you document a research project?

You use documentation in a project so readers can track the sources you have used to make and support your claims. Your notes and bibliography tell readers *who* wrote or discovered *what* and *when*. Documentation typically leads readers to printed sources of information: books, articles, volumes of statistics and research. But documentation may also point to Web pages, interviews, software, films, television programs, databases, images, audio files, and online conversations. Various systems for managing sources and documentation have been devised. Presented in this handbook are systems of the Modern Language Association (MLA), the American Psychological Association (APA), the *Chicago Manual of Style* (CMS), the Council of Biology Editors (CBE), and the *Columbia Guide to Online Style* (COS). Specific guidelines for formal documentation appear in Chapters 48 through 52. This section examines the general principles for acknowledging and using sources.

■ **1 Provide a source for every direct quotation.** A *direct quotation* is any material repeated word for word from a source. Direct quotations in college papers typically require some form of parenthetical documentation—that is, a citation of author and page number (MLA) or author, date, and page number (APA).

> **MLA** It is possible to define literature as simply "that text which the community insists on having repeated from time to time intact" (Joos 51-52).
>
> **APA** Hashimoto (1986) questions the value of attention-getting essay openings that "presuppose passive, uninterested (probably uninteresting) readers" (p. 126).

You are similarly expected to identify the sources for any diagrams, statistics, charts, or pictures in your paper. You need not document famous sayings, proverbs, or biblical citations.

In less formal writing, you should still identify the author, speaker, or work from which you borrow any passage and indicate why the words you are quoting are significant. Many phrases of introduction or attribution are available (see Section 46c-2). Here are just a few.

> One noted astronomer **reported** that . . .
> Marva Collins **agrees** that . . .
> **According to** the GAO, the figures . . .

2 Document all ideas, opinions, facts, and information that cannot be considered common knowledge. *Common knowledge* includes the facts, dates, events, information, and concepts that an educated person can be assumed to know. You may need to check an encyclopedia to find out that the Battle of Waterloo was fought on June 18, 1815, but that fact belongs to common knowledge, and for that reason you don't have to document it.

You may also make assumptions about common knowledge within a field. When you find that a given piece of information or an idea is shared among several of the sources you are using, you need not document it. (For example, if in writing a paper on anorexia nervosa you discover that most authorities define it in the same way, you probably don't have to document that definition.) What experts know collectively constitutes the common knowledge within a field; what they claim individually—their opinions, studies, theories, research projects, hypotheses—is the material you *must* document in a paper.

3 Document materials that readers might question or wish to explore further. If your subject is controversial, you may want to document even those facts or ideas considered common knowledge. When in doubt, document. Suppose that in writing about witchcraft you make a historical assertion well known by scholars within a field but liable to surprise nonspecialists. Writing for nonspecialists, you should certainly document the assertion. Writing for experts, you would probably skip the note.

4 Furnish dates, credentials, and other information to assist readers. Provide dates for important events, major figures, and works of literature and art. Identify any person readers might not recognize.

> After the great fire of London (**1666**), the city was . . .
>
> Henry Highland Garnet (**1815–82**), American abolitionist and radical, . . .
>
> *Pearl* (**c.** 1400), an elegy about . . .

In the last example, the *c.* before the date stands for *circa,* which means "about."

When quoting from literary works, help readers locate the passages you are citing. For novels, identify page numbers; for plays, give act/scene/line information; for long poems, provide line numbers and, when appropriate, division numbers (book, canto, or other divisions).

5 Use links to document electronic sources. Links in hypertexts (such as Web pages) can function as a type of documentation: they can take readers directly to supporting material or sources. But it's important that readers of hypertexts understand where a highlighted passage is leading them. Hyperlinks should be used judiciously to provide real information. Don't overwhelm a Web page with links; they can seem as fussy as a page with too many footnotes.

6 Use computer programs to document your project. Many software programs are available to help you document a paper or create a bibliography. Even most word processors have automatic footnote or endnote features. If you choose to use such a feature, be sure it supports the documentation style—for example, MLA, APA, CBE—required for your project. Also be certain that the program is up to date. The latest software, for example, can properly format footnotes or endnotes for material found on CD-ROMs and Web pages or in email communications. Typically, a bibliography entry will be generated from information you provide—usually in a box or table such as that found on page 696. Be sure to read the instructions for such software carefully and to proofread the output to be sure you have entered your data accurately.

46a
research

Figure 46.1   *Here is a Source screen from the program* TakeNote! *designed to help writers organize notes and information. After providing author, title, year, and publication information, you will get a properly formatted entry for a Works Cited or References page*

46b Do you understand academic responsibility?

Most students understand that it is wrong to buy or download a paper, to let someone heavily edit a paper for them, or to submit someone else's work as their own. This kind of activity is dishonest, and most institutions have procedures for handling scholastic dishonesty when it occurs.

But many students do not realize that taking notes carelessly or documenting sources inadequately may also raise doubts about the integrity of a paper. Representing as your own the words or ideas you found in a source constitutes *plagiarism*. Instructors take this seriously and assume their legitimate right to discipline students who do not. Plagiarism is easily avoided if you take good notes (see Section 45b-3) and follow the guidelines discussed in this section.

46b
plag

■ **1 For conventional sources, acknowledge all direct uses of anyone else's work.** Suppose, for example, that in preparing a research paper on mountain biking, you come across the following passage from *The Mountain Bike Book* by Rob van der Plas.

106

In fact, access and right-of-way are the two intangibles in trail cycling these days. The sport is getting too popular too fast, and in defense, or out of fear, authorities have banned cyclists from many potentially suitable areas.

You will probably use forest service or fire roads and trails intended for hikers most of the time. Don't stray off these trails, since this may cause damage, both to the environment and to our reputation. As long as you stay on the trails and do it with a modicum of consideration for others, you have nothing to fear and should not risk being banned from them by public agencies.

In many areas a distinction is made between single-track trails and wider ones. Single tracks are often considered off-limits to mountain bikers, although in most cases they are perfectly suitable and there are not enough hikers and other trail users to worry about potential conflicts. In fact, single trails naturally limit the biker's speed to an acceptable level.

If you decide to quote all or part of the selection above in your essay, you must use quotation marks (or indention) to indicate that you are borrowing the writer's exact words. You must also identify the author, work, publisher, date, and location of the passage through documentation. If you are using MLA documentation (see Chapter 48), the parenthetical note and corresponding Works Cited entry would look like this.

> As Rob van der Plas reminds bikers, they need
> only use common sense in riding public trails: "As
> long as you stay on the trails and do it with a
> modicum of consideration for others, you have nothing
> to fear and should not risk being banned from them by
> public agencies" (106).

> Works Cited
> van der Plas, Rob. The Mountain Bike Book: Choosing,
>
>   Riding and Maintaining the Off-Road Bicycle.
>
> 3rd ed. San Francisco: Bicycle, 1993.

46b
plag

You must use *both* quotation marks and the parenthetical note when you quote directly. Quotation marks alone would not tell your readers what your source was. A note alone would acknowledge that you are using a source, but it would not explain that the words in a specific portion of your paper are not entirely your own. (By the way, the author in this case spells his last name exactly as shown, so *van der* is not capitalized in the Works Cited entry—though most last names, of course, are capitalized.)

2 Summarize and paraphrase carefully. Quite often you will not quote directly from your sources but report the information you find in them in a summary or paraphrase (see Section 45b-3). A proper summary or paraphrase of a source must be entirely in your own words. Some writers mistakenly believe that they can avoid a charge of plagiarism just by rearranging the elements or changing a few words in a source they are using. They are flat wrong.

For example, you may want to discuss the ideas raised in the selection from *The Mountain Bike Book* on page 697, borrowing the information in van der Plas's paragraphs but not his words. Here are two acceptable summaries of the passage on mountain biking that report its facts appropriately and honestly. Notice that both versions include a parenthetical note acknowledging van der Plas's *The Mountain Bike Book* as the source of information.

> Rob van der Plas asserts that mountain bikers
> need not fear limitation of their right-of-ways if
> they ride trails responsibly (106).

> Though using so-called single-track trails might
> put mountain bikers in conflict with the hikers, such
> tracks are often empty and underutilized (van der
> Plas 106).

Without those parenthetical notes, both versions above might be considered plagiarized even though only van der Plas's ideas—not his actual words—are borrowed. That's because you *must give credit even to ideas* you take from your sources unless you are dealing with common knowledge (see Section 46a-2). Review Section 45b-3 for detailed advice on how to write effective summaries and paraphrases and how to avoid plagiarizing in the process.

46b
plag

3 Appreciate the unique features of electronic discourse. The authorship and source problems of collaborative projects done on paper pale when compared with the intellectual property rights issues raised by electronic documents. To create a hypertext or Web site, for example, writers might link words and images from dozens of authors and artists and various sources and media. Every part of the resulting collage might be borrowed, but the arrangement of the hypertext itself will be unique. Who then deserves credit as the *author* of the project? Similar problems can arise with listserv and Usenet conversations. Such sources cannot be documented in conventional ways.

Over the next decade, as hypertexts and online materials become more common, standards for documenting electronic sources will evolve. For ways to cite Web pages, email, MUDs, MOOs, and other electronic forms, consult Chapter 52, which explains a documentation style— Columbia Online Style or COS—designed expressly for such material.

That said, you must also understand that the basic rules of scholastic honesty still apply in electronic environments. Tempting as it may be, you may *not* copy and paste information from a Web site, listserv, newsgroup, or other electronic source to your own project without fully documenting that material. Nor may you call it your own just because you have altered it in some minor way—changed a few words, reordered the ideas, or reshaped an image.

Going Public *Copying and Pasting* _____

It can be tempting to copy and paste sentences directly from online sources into a project. Here, for example, are two paragraphs from a research essay by Chad Briggs of Wartburg College titled "The Relationship Between Test Anxiety, Sleep Habits, and Self-perceived Academic Competency." It was originally published in the online journal *Psych-E: An Electronic Psychology Journal for Undergraduates* (vol. 1) <http://www.siu.edu/departments/cola/psycho/journal/archives/vol1/briggs.html>.

ORIGINAL SOURCE

Quality of sleep habits was found to be a factor in self-perceived academic competence. If college students experience REM sleep deprivation more than the average population, then the findings of this study need to be passed on to college students. The findings in this study suggest that college students with poor sleep habits may perceive themselves as having lower academic competency. The study also showed that self-perceived academic competency was positively correlated to academic performance. Thus, according to Hobson (1989), Webb & Bonnet (1979), and this study, those college students who do have poor sleep habits will negatively affect their academic performance.

46b
plag

It was also found that test anxiety and grade point average are negatively correlated, and that quality of sleep and grade point average are positively correlated. This, and the fact that quality of sleep and test anxiety are negatively related, suggest interrelationships among the variables test anxiety, sleep habits, self-perceived academic competency and academic performance. This highlights the fact that professors need to instruct their students on how to manage test anxiety. Students also need to be aware of the effects that poor sleep and low self-perceived academic competency have on academic performance. Thus, the phrase, "I think I can, I think I can . . ." may be beneficial only if students reduce their test anxiety and develop better sleep habits. More research needs to be done to find other variables that affect self-perceived academic competence.

Following are two paragraphs based much too closely on material from Chad Briggs's essay, now archived on the Web. This reformulation of the material amounts to plagiarism, even though the author of the plagiarized paragraphs credits Briggs as the source. The boldfaced material looks like it was copied and pasted directly from the online original.

PLAGIARIZED PARAGRAPHS

Getting a good night's sleep before an examination makes sense psychologically. According to Briggs (1999), **quality of sleep habits was found to be a factor in self-perceived academic competence.** That is to say that college students with poor sleep habits may perceive themselves as having lower academic competency. **Those college students who do have poor sleep habits will negatively affect their academic performance.**

There also seems to be a connection between self-perceived academic competency and academic performance. **This highlights the fact that professors need to instruct their students on how to manage test anxiety. Students also need to be aware of the effects that poor sleep and low self-perceived academic competency have on academic performance. Thus, the phrase, "I think I can, I think I can . . ." may be beneficial only if students reduce their test**

anxiety and develop better sleep habits. So a student really can improve performance in college courses by making more time for sleep.

■ **4 Understand the special nature of collaborative projects.** Whether working with writers in your own classroom or with students in other locations across a network, you'll find that in truly collaborative projects it can be tough to remember who wrote what. And that's good. So long as everyone understands the ground rules an instructor sets for a project, joint authorship ought not to be a problem. But legitimate questions do arise.

- Must we write the whole project together?
- Can we break the project into separately authored sections?
- Can one person research a section, another write it, a third edit and proofread?
- What do we do if someone's not pulling his or her weight?
- Do we all get the same grade?

The time to ask such questions is at the beginning of a collaborative effort. First, determine what your instructor's guidelines are. Then sit down with the members of your group and hammer out the rules. (Also see Sections 4e and 43b-6.)

E-Tips

The Web offers a great deal of information on *plagiarism, collusion,* and *cheating.* Use these words as search terms in a search engine and you will discover many academic sites (they end in *.edu*) that discuss the definition and terms of scholastic dishonesty. Or you might use the search engine at the Center for Academic Integrity at <http://www.academicintegrity.org/> to explore more than 7000 Web pages dealing with these issues. An unusually comprehensive site on scholastic integrity is maintained by the University of Texas at Austin at <http://www.utexas.edu/depts/dos/sjs/academicintegrity.html>.

46c
research

46c How do you handle quotations?

Some writers want to treat direct quotations like electronic modules: plug them in at the appropriate spots in the circuit board, and the device should operate. Unfortunately, quotations don't work that way.

You have to select them strategically and then fit them seamlessly into the paper or project. No stylistic touch makes a research project work quite so well as quotations deftly handled.

1 Select direct quotations strategically. Every quotation in an article should contribute something your own words cannot. Use quotations for various reasons.

- To focus on a particularly well stated key idea in a source
- To show what others think about a subject—either experts, people involved with the issue, or the general public
- To give credence to important facts or concepts
- To add color, power, or character to your argument or report
- To show a range of opinion
- To clarify a difficult or contested point
- To demonstrate the complexity of an issue
- To emphasize a point

Never use quotations to avoid putting ideas in your own words or to pad your work.

2 Introduce all direct and indirect borrowings in some way. Short introductions, attributions, or commentaries are needed to introduce readers to materials you've gathered from sources. To be sure readers pay attention, give all borrowed words and ideas a context or *frame*. Such frames can be relatively simple, and they can *precede, follow,* or *interrupt* the borrowed words or ideas. The frame need not even be in the same sentence as the quotation; it may be part of the surrounding paragraph. Here are examples of ways that material can be introduced.

- *Frame precedes borrowed material:*
  In 1896, Woodrow Wilson, who would become Princeton's president in 1902, declared, "It is not learning but the spirit of service that will give a college a place in the public annals of the nation."
  —Ernest L. Boyer

- *Frame follows borrowed material:*
  "One reason you may have more colds if you hold back tears is that, when you're under stress, your body puts out steroids which affect your immune system and reduce your resistance to disease," **Dr. Broomfield comments.**　　—Barbara Lang Stern

- *Frame interrupts borrowed material:*
  "Whatever happens," **he [Karl Marx] wrote grimly to Engels,** "I hope the bourgeoisie as long as they exist will have cause to remember my carbuncles."　　—Paul Johnson

46c
research

Chart 46.1
Verbs of Attribution

accept	allege	deny	mention	say
add	argue	disagree	posit	state
admit	believe	emphasize	propose	think
affirm	confirm	insist	reveal	verify

- *Surrounding sentences frame borrowed material:*
  In the meantime, [Luis] Jimenez was experimenting with three-dimensional form. "Perhaps because of the experience of working in the sign shop, I realized early on that I wanted to do it all— paint, draw, work with wood, metal, clay." **His images were those of 1960s pop culture, chosen for their familiarity and shock value.**

  —Chiori Santiago

- *Borrowed material integrated with passage:*
  The study concludes that a faulty work ethic is not responsible for the decline in our productivity; quite the contrary, the study identifies "a widespread commitment among U.S. workers to improve productivity" **and suggests that** "there are large reservoirs of potential upon which management can draw to improve performance and increase productivity."

  —Daniel Yankelovich

Most borrowings in your research paper should be attributed in similar fashion. Either name (directly or indirectly) the author, the speaker, or the work the passage is from, or explain why the words you are quoting are significant. Many phrases of introduction or attribution are available. Note that the verb of attribution you choose can shape the way readers perceive the quotation that follows. Compare your reactions to the following statements that differ only in their verb of attribution.

Benson **reports** that "high school test scores have dropped again."
Benson **laments** that "high school test scores have dropped again."
Benson **complains** that "high school test scores have dropped again."

President Bush **claimed** that ". . .
One expert **stated** that ". . .
The members of the board **declared** that ". . .
Representatives of the airline industry **contend** that ". . .
Senator Clinton **was quoted** as saying that ". . .

46c
research

■ 3 Tailor your language so that direct quotations fit into the grammar of your sentences. You may have to tinker with your introduction or modify the quotation itself by careful selections, ellipses (see Section 46c-4), or bracketed additions (see Section 46c-5).

> CLUMSY   The chemical capsaicin that makes chili hot:
>   "it is so hot it is used to make antidog and
>   antimugger sprays" (Bork 184).
>
> REVISED   Capsaicin, the chemical that makes chili hot,
>   is so strong "it is used to make antidog and
>   antimugger sprays" (Bork 184).
>
> CLUMSY   Computers have not succeeded as translators
>   of language because, says Douglas Hofstadter,
>   "nor is the difficulty caused by a lack of
>   knowledge of idiomatic phrases. The fact is
>   that translation involves having a mental
>   model of the world being discussed, and
>   manipulating symbols in the model" (603).
>
> REVISED   "A lack of knowledge of idiomatic phrases" is
>   not the reason computers have failed as
>   translators of languages. "The fact is," says
>   Douglas Hofstadter, "that translation
>   involves having a mental model of the world
>   being discussed, and manipulating symbols in
>   the model" (603).

■ 4 Use ellipses (three *spaced* periods: . . .) to indicate where you have cut material from direct quotations. For example, ellipses might be used to trim the lengthy passage below to focus on the oldest portions of the biblical text. The ellipses will tell readers where words, phrases, and even whole sentences have been cut.

46c
research

> ORIGINAL PASSAGE
>   The text of the Old Testament is in places the stuff of schol-
> arly nightmares. Whereas the entire New Testament was written
> within fifty to a hundred years, the books of the Old Testament
> were composed and edited over a period of about a thousand. The
> youngest book is Daniel, from the second century B.C. The oldest

portions of the Old Testament (if we limit ourselves to the present form of the literature and exclude from consideration the streams of oral tradition that fed it) are probably a group of poems that appear, on the basis of linguistic features and historical allusions contained in them, to date from roughly the twelfth and eleventh centuries B.C. . . .   —Barry Hoberman, "Translating the Bible"

PASSAGE AS CUT FOR USE IN AN ESSAY

```
     Although working with any part of an original
scripture text is difficult, Hoberman describes the
text of the Old Testament as "the stuff of scholarly
nightmares." He explains in "Translating the Bible"
that while "the entire New Testament was written
within fifty to a hundred years, the books of the Old
Testament were composed and edited over a period of
about a thousand. . . . The oldest portions of the
Old Testament . . . are probably a group of poems
that appear . . . to date from roughly the twelfth
and eleventh centuries B.C."
```

When an ellipsis occurs in the middle of a sentence, leave a space before the first period and after the third one. In MLA style, shown below, any ellipsis you add to a passage should appear between brackets.

```
"We the people of the United States [. . .] do ordain
and establish this Constitution for the United States
of America."
```

When an ellipsis occurs at the end of a sentence or passage, it also appears between brackets in MLA style. The final punctuation mark follows the closing bracket.

```
"These are the times that try men's souls. The summer
soldiers and the sunshine patriot will, in this
crisis, shrink from the service of his
country [. . .]."                    —Thomas Paine
```

46c
research

The same form (an ellipsis in brackets) is employed in MLA style when entire sentences or paragraphs are omitted.

You don't need ellipses, however, every time you break into a sentence. If your quoted material begins with a capital letter, readers will know you are quoting a complete sentence.

```
According to Richard Bernstein, "The plain and
inescapable fact is that the derived Western European
culture of American life [has] produced the highest
degree of prosperity in the conditions of the
greatest freedom ever known on planet Earth" (11).
```

If the quoted material begins with a small letter, readers can assume introductory words have been cut, so no ellipses are needed.

```
According to Richard Bernstein, the United States has
"produced the highest degree of prosperity in the
conditions of the greatest freedom ever known on
planet Earth" (11).
```

Similarly, if your quoted material begins with a capital letter in brackets, readers should understand that you've added that capital because the quoted material is not from the beginning of a sentence. No ellipses are required.

```
"[T]he derived Western European culture of American
life," according to Richard Bernstein, has "produced
the highest degree of prosperity" (11).
```

You need ellipses at the beginning of a quotation only when a capital letter in a proper noun (or the pronoun I) might lead readers to believe that you're quoting a complete sentence when, in fact, you are not.

```
According to Richard Bernstein, "[. . .] American
life [has] produced the highest degree of prosperity
in the conditions of greatest freedom ever know on
planet Earth" (11).
```

Occasionally ellipses are wanted at the beginning of quoted sentences when they occur *within extended quotations*. Then the ellipses indicate that an opening clause or phrase has been omitted. In such cases, three spaced periods precede the sentence, with a space left between the third period and the first letter of the sentence. Any punctuation occurring at the end of the clause or sentence preceding the quotation is retained.

```
"The text of the Old Testament is in places the stuff
of scholarly nightmares. [. . .] [T]he books of the
Old Testament were composed and edited over a period
of about a thousand [years]."
```
—Barry Hoberman, "Translating the Bible"

Whenever you use an ellipsis, be sure your shortened quotation accurately reflects the meaning of the uncut passage.

5 Use square brackets [ ]—to add necessary information to a quotation. You may want to explain who or what a pronoun refers to, or you may have to provide a short explanation, furnish a date, and explain or translate a puzzling word.

> Some critics clearly prefer Wagner's Tannhäuser to
> Lohengrin: "The well-written choruses [of Tannhäuser]
> are combined with solo singing and orchestral
> background into long, unified musical scenes"
> (Grout 629).

But don't overdo it. Readers will resent the explanation of obvious details.

6 Use [sic] to indicate an obvious error copied faithfully from a source. Quotations must be copied accurately, word by word, from your source—errors and all. To show that you have copied a passage faithfully, place the expression *sic* (the Latin word for "thus" or "so") in brackets one space after any mistake.

> Mr. Vincent's letter went on: "I would have preferred
> a younger bride, but I decided to marry the old
> window [sic] anyway."

If *sic* can be placed outside the quotation itself, it appears between parentheses, not brackets.

> Molly's paper was titled "King Leer" (sic).

7 Place prose quotations shorter than four typed lines (MLA) or forty words (APA) between quotation marks.

> In Utilitarianism (1863), John Stuart Mill declares,
> "It is better to be Socrates dissatisfied than a pig
> satisfied."

46c
research

8 Indent more than three lines of poetry (MLA). Up to three lines of poetry may be handled just like a prose passage, with slashes marking the separate lines. Quotation marks are used.

> As death approaches, Cleopatra grows in grandeur and
> dignity: "Husband, I come! / Now to that name my

```
courage prove my title! / I am fire and air"
(5.2.287-89).
```

More than three lines of poetry are indented 10 spaces and quotation marks are not used. (If the lines of poetry are unusually long, you may indent fewer than 10 spaces.) Be sure to copy the poetry accurately, right down to the punctuation.

```
Among the most famous lines in English literature are
those that open William Blake's "The Tyger":
        Tyger tyger, burning bright,
        In the forests of the night;
        What immortal hand or eye,
        Could frame thy fearful symmetry? (1-4)
```

9 Indent any prose quotation longer than four typed lines (MLA) or forty words (APA). MLA form recommends an indention of one inch, or ten spaces if you are using a typewriter; APA form requires five spaces. Quotation marks are *not* used around the indented material. If the quotation extends beyond a single paragraph, the first lines of subsequent paragraphs are indented an additional quarter inch, or three typed spaces (MLA) or five spaces (APA). In typed papers, the indented material—like the rest of the essay—is double spaced.

You may indent passages of fewer than four lines when you want them to have special emphasis. But don't do this with every short quotation or your paper will look choppy.

10 Refer to events in works of fiction, poems, plays, movies, and television shows in the present tense. When quoting passages from novels, describing scenes from a movie or events in a play, think about the actions as performances that occur over and over again.

```
In his last speech, Othello orders those around him
to "Speak of me as I am. Nothing extenuate, / Nor set
down aught in malice" (V.ii.338-39). Then he stabs
himself and dies, falling on the bed of the innocent
wife he has murdered only moments before: "I kissed
thee ere I killed thee. No way but this, / Killing
myself, to die upon a kiss" (354-55).
```

CHAPTER 47

How Do You Complete
a Project?

Since academic research projects represent a first level of serious professional work, they must usually meet exacting standards as you bring them to completion. These requirements vary from discipline to discipline, but the principles examined in this section apply to most papers and projects. (See also Chapter 5.)

47a Is the organization solid?

In many cases, you'll want to narrow the scope of your project during the writing process and give it a design that reinforces clear, though not necessarily simple, points. Some projects will support specific thesis statements or arguments. Others, including much service learning work, may examine alternatives to the status quo or offer proposals to solve problems. Still other projects might invite readers to join in a conversation.

Your role is to create a framework that will make your project an effective response to the original assignment. This shaping must be deliberate and strategic. In a research project, you usually can't rely on chance to bring all the parts together.

1 Narrow or qualify your claim. The more you learn about a subject or problem, the more careful you'll be in making claims or offering solutions. That's why a final thesis statement will almost certainly be more specific, restrictive, and informative than an initial research question or hypothesis. If nothing else, the thesis should address questions such as Who? What? When? Where? Under what conditions? With what limits? With what scope? And the topic sentences of paragraphs throughout the project (or other guideposts, such as the headings of Web pages) should relate clearly to this claim and be equally specific.

The shape you give your project will depend on what your thesis promises. One way to understand that commitment is to recall the purpose of your research study. For example, does the project ultimately make a claim of *fact*, a claim of *definition*, a claim of *value*, or a claim of *policy* or *proposal?* You'll want to refine your thesis to make a distinct and limited claim, then follow through with the appropriate support and evidence.

ORIGINAL CLAIM OF *FACT*
AIDS is the greatest killer of the young.

CLAIM SPECIFIED AND LIMITED BY RESEARCH
In the United States, AIDS has replaced automobile accidents as the leading cause of death among teenagers.

COMMITMENTS
- Examine American teenagers as a demographic group.
- Present figures on mortality rates among young people.
- Find figures on deaths from auto accidents.
- Find figures on deaths from AIDS.
- Ponder the mortality rate trends.
- Draw out the implications of the study for AIDS prevention.

ORIGINAL CLAIM OF *DEFINITION*
Zoos promote cruelty to animals.

CLAIM SPECIFIED AND LIMITED BY RESEARCH
Confining large marine mammals in sea parks for public amusement is, arguably, a form of cruelty to animals.

COMMITMENTS
- Find legal/popular definitions for "cruelty to animals."
- Define specific criteria for "cruelty."
- Examine what experts say about the condition of animals in marine parks. Or do fieldwork in such a park.
- Find statistics on animal health in marine parks.
- Find expert opinion on both sides of the issue.
- Show that conditions in marine parks meet (or do not meet) criteria for "cruelty to animals."

ORIGINAL CLAIM OF *VALUE*
The EPA is ruining America.

CLAIM SPECIFIED AND LIMITED BY RESEARCH
Air-quality standards first proposed by the U.S. Environmental Protection Agency (EPA) in 1997 may damage the industrial economies of many northern and western states that depend heavily on coal.

COMMITMENTS
- Acquire the actual EPA standards.
- Determine what states may have to do in order to comply with the standards. Interview experts in local/state government.
- Explain the possible consequences of compliance.
- Present arguments of experts who favor the standards.
- Present arguments of those who oppose the standards.

ORIGINAL CLAIM OF *POLICY*
Increases in student fees on campus should be prohibited.

CLAIM SPECIFIED AND LIMITED BY RESEARCH
Additional increases in student fees on campus should be capped at a level not to exceed the national rate of inflation unless students vote in a public referendum to approve higher fees.

COMMITMENTS
- Explain how/why fees are increasing on campus.
- Use interviews to show that students want change.
- Examine the procedure by which fees are raised.
- Detail the problems with the current procedure.
- Offer an alternative proposal.
- Defend the advantages and feasibility of the proposal.

E-Tips   You can find more information about topic sentences and research questions at the Purdue University Writing Center at <http://owl.english.purdue.edu>. Just do a search for "topic" or "research paper."

2 Test your organization. Organizing a sizable paper or project is rarely an easy job. For the draft of a long paper, you may want to check the structure using a method such as the following.

- **Underline the topic idea, or thesis, in your draft.** It should be clearly stated somewhere in the first few paragraphs.
- **Underline just the first sentence in each subsequent paragraph.** If the first sentence is very short or closely tied to the second, underline the first two sentences.
- **Read the underlined sentences straight through as if they formed an essay in themselves.** Ask whether each sentence advances or explains the main point or thesis statement. If the sen-

47a
research

tences—taken together—read coherently, chances are good that
the paper is well organized.

- **If the underlined sentences don't make sense, reexamine those
  paragraphs not clearly related to the topic idea.** If the ideas really
  are not related, delete the whole paragraph. If the ideas are
  related, consider how to revise the paragraph to make the connection
  clearer. A new lead sentence for the paragraph will often
  solve the problem of incoherence. Pay attention to transitions,
  too—those places in a paper where you can give readers helpful
  directions: *first of all, on the other hand, to summarize.* (See Section
  15b.)

- **Test your conclusion against your introduction.** Sometimes the
  conclusions of essays contradict their openings because of changes
  that occurred as the paper developed. When you've completed a
  draft, set it aside for a time and then reread the entire piece. Does
  it hang together? If not, revise it.

Test the structure of other projects similarly. For example, if
you've prepared a brochure, make sure the headings are in the right order,
the various sections follow in correct sequence when the brochure
is folded, and the panels contain all pertinent information, especially
phone numbers and addresses.

In a Web site, try to imagine how a reader encountering it for the
first time might search for information: will users find what they are
seeking by following only a short sequence of links? Check that all the
links work in both directions. Make sure there are no dead ends and
that every page on your site provides a way to return to your home page
or another helpful location in the site. (See Section 20g for more on
composing a Web site.)

47b Is the format correct?

Whether you are reporting your research in a conventional paper,
on a Web site, or through some other less traditional vehicle, you want
the presentation to be effective. Here we focus chiefly on research papers,
but you can find advice about crafting other types of projects in
Part IV, Design and Shape of Documents.

1 Pay attention to the format of work you submit. Be
sure a paper is submitted on good-quality white paper. Print on only

one side of the pages, double-spacing the body of your essay and the notes. Keep fonts simple and use boldface rarely, perhaps to highlight important headings.

Specifications for MLA and APA papers are given in Sections 48d and 49c, respectively. These guidelines, which explain where page numbers go, the width of margins, and the placement of headings, can be applied even to papers that don't need to follow a specific professional style.

In distance learning courses, you may be asked to submit your work as an email attachment or as an html document readable on the Web. In either case, be sure you understand your instructor's requirements for submitting the work. For example, if you are expected to send written work as word-processing files, be sure you use software compatible with your instructor's. Take care with any visual items in your documents (including charts and tables)—be sure they will transfer accurately. Follow your instructor's directions for naming files. Consider that an instructor may receive a great many files in a distance learning course, and you don't want your work to get lost.

2 Insert tables and figures as needed. Use graphics whenever they help readers understand your ideas better than words alone can. Pie charts (Section 10a-1), graphs (Sections 10a-2 and 10a-3), and tables (Section 10a-4) can make information easier to interpret. So learn to use the graphics tools available in word-processing or data management programs. In the latter, you can usually choose how you want your information presented (tables, bar graphs, pie charts); the program itself produces the actual image, which you can modify to suit your needs.

If you have access to the World Wide Web, you can download pictures and other visual items for your projects, but you must document the borrowings and you must get permission to use them from the authors/owners of the material. Be careful, too, not to clutter your work with what one design expert calls "chartjunk." Just because you have easy access to graphics doesn't mean you must illustrate every page. Develop an eye for clean and attractive presentations on paper or on screen. (See Chapter 19 on document design.)

MLA form requires that you label tables (columns of data) and figures (pictures or illustrations), number them, and briefly identify what they illustrate. Spell out the word *Table,* and position the heading above the table, aligned with the left margin.

47b
research

Table 1
First-Year Student Applications by Region

	Fall 1995	Fall 1994	Difference	Percent Change
Texas	12,022	11,590	432	+4
Out of state	2,121	2,058	63	+3
Foreign	756	673	83	+11

Figure, which is usually abbreviated in the caption as *Fig.*, appears below the illustration, flush left.

Fig. 7. Mountain bike.

When preparing an APA paper, you may want to check the detailed coverage of figures and tables in the *Publication Manual of the American Psychological Association*. For APA-style student papers, figures (including graphs, illustrations, and photos) and tables may appear in the body of the essay itself, placed on separate pages, immediately following their mention in the text.

Chromosomes consist of four different nucleotides or
bases--adenine, guanine, thymine, and cytosine--
which, working together, provide the code for
different genes (see Figure 1).

Short tables may even appear on the same page as text material.

Figures and tables are numbered consecutively. Captions for figures appear below the item. If the illustration is borrowed from a source, you must get permission to reproduce it and acknowledge the borrowing as shown.

Figure 1. The four bases of the genetic code: adenine
(A), guanine (G), thymine (T), and cytosine (C). Note.
From Your Genes, Your Choice, by. C. Baker, 1997.
Copyright 1997 by the American Association for the
Advancement of Science. Reprinted with permission.

Titles for tables appear above the item.

Table 2

Errors by Levels of Difficulty

3 Be consistent with headings. You can use headings to give shape to any project. A short research paper (five to six pages) ordinarily needs only a title. In longer papers, however, readers will appreciate headings that explain the content of major sections. All such heads should be brief, parallel in phrasing, and consistent in format like the items in a formal outline (see Section 3c-3). For most academic papers, you probably won't use more than one level of heading after the title.

MLA style (described in detail in Chapter 48) provides fairly loose standards for headings. Titles of MLA papers are ordinarily centered on the first page of an essay while headings appear in the text, flush with the left-hand margin. If you descend to a second level, you'll have to distinguish second-level heads by numbering or lettering them or by setting them off typographically (usually by variations in capitalization

47b
research

or underlining). MLA style leaves you to decide how you will handle such choices, but in all cases, you must keep the headings clean and unobtrusive. Here are two ways of handling headings as they might appear in a moderately long MLA-style paper on mountain biking.

Mountain Biking and the Environment	Title
The Mountain Bike	1st level
History of Mountain Biking	1st level
Mountain Bikes and the Environment	1st level
Trail Damage	2nd level
Conflicts with Hikers	2nd level
Mountain Bikes and Responsible Riding	1st level

Mountain Biking and the Environment	Title
1. The Mountain Bike	1st level
2. History of Mountain Biking	1st level
3. Mountain Bikes and the Environment	1st level
3.1. Trail Damage	2nd level
3.2. Conflicts with Hikers	2nd level
4. Mountain Bikes and Responsible Riding	1st level

APA style (described in detail in Chapter 49) defines five levels of headings for professional articles—more than you'll probably use in a college paper. Here's how to handle two levels of headings.

- First-level heads are centered, using both uppercase and lowercase letters as shown on the next page.
- Second-level heads are capitalized like titles, but also underlined and placed flush with the left-hand margin.

Here's how those APA guidelines look in operation.

Differences in Reading Habits of College Sophomores	Title
Abstract	1st level
Method	1st level
Participants	2nd level
Materials	2nd level
Design and Procedure	2nd level
Results	1st level
Discussion	1st level

Any Web pages you create also need accurate, well-focused headings and titles so readers quickly grasp the point of your projects. Succinct and descriptive titles are important, too, if your pages are to be located by Web search engines and directories. Finally, you want titles that will still make sense if they get shortened when added to a Web browser's list of bookmarks or favorites: the first few words of the title should include all important keywords. A heading such as "The Beauty and Mystery of Anasazi Cliff Dwellings" might be clipped back to the not very helpful "The Beauty and Mystery." Instead, title the Web page "Anasazi Cliff Dwellings: Beauty and Mystery" so that a shortened title will highlight pertinent information.

47c Are the details correct?

Give the final version of your project a careful review. By this point in your work, you've been close to the project for a long time, so you may need to put some distance between it and you before you do the final check. Even a few days, if you can afford them, can be enough to help you see features that need to be polished. Don't skip this step.

1 Include all the components your project requires. Before you submit a project, reread the specifications of either the instructor or the professional society whose guidelines you are following. Must you, for instance, include an abstract or an outline? Check to see what leeway (if any) you have in arranging the title page, notes, bibliography, and other features. A research paper typically follows a specific order.

- Title page (not recommended in MLA; required in APA)
- Outline (optional; begins on its own page; requires separate title page)
- Abstract (optional, but common in APA; usually on its own page)
- Body of the essay (Arabic pagination begins with body of the essay in MLA; in APA, Arabic pagination begins with title page)
- Content or bibliographic notes
- Works Cited/References (begins on its own page separate from the body of the essay and any content or bibliographic notes)

The sample research essay on pages 759–72 illustrates MLA style, and the essay on pages 788–802 illustrates APA style. For a more complex

47c
research

paper such as a master's thesis or a doctoral dissertation, follow the order recommended in a volume such as *The MLA Style Manual* (MLA) or the *Publication Manual of the American Psychological Association* (APA). Many schools publish their own guidelines for submitting graduate-level theses.

2 Follow the rules for documentation right down to the punctuation and spacing.
Accurate documentation is a part of professional research. Instructors and editors notice even minor variations in documentation form. Perhaps the two most common errors in handling the MLA format, for example, are forgetting to put a period at the end of entries in the Works Cited list and placing a comma where none is needed in parenthetical documentation.

WRONG	Pluto, Terry. The Curse of Rocky Colavito. New York: Simon, 1994
RIGHT	Pluto, Terry. The Curse of Rocky Colavito. New York: Simon, 1994.
WRONG	(Pluto, 132-36)
RIGHT	(Pluto 132-36)

You will survive both errors, but they are easy to avoid.

3 Submit your project professionally.
Whether you've written a paper, designed a brochure, or created a Web site, be sure the work meets appropriate standards. Examine what you've produced to see that everything looks "detailed": the writing is sharp and correct, the images are crisp and labeled, the pagination is right, the links are operative, the documentation is solid.

Don't overdo it. For an electronic project, keep the bells and whistles (and gaudy colors) to a functional minimum. For a paper, bind the pages modestly with a paper clip. Nothing more elaborate is needed, unless an instructor asks you to place the essay (still clipped) in a folder along with all materials you used in developing it.

When you submit an article for publication, be sure to follow all instructions for submission provided by the editors. Note in particular how many clean copies they require of your work, to whom those copies should be sent, and whether they expect you to furnish a self-addressed, stamped envelope for return of your work.

47c
esearch

Checklist 47.1

Research Project Requirements

• Have you placed your name, your instructor's name, the date, and the course name on the first or title page?

• Is the title centered? Are only the major words capitalized? (Your title should not be underlined or appear between quotation marks.)

• Did you number the pages? Are they in the right order?

• Have you used quotation marks and parentheses correctly and in pairs? (The closing quotation mark and parenthesis are often forgotten.)

• Have you placed quotation marks around all direct quotations that are shorter than four lines?

• Have you indented all direct quotations of more than four typed lines (MLA) or of forty words or more (APA)?

• Have you remembered that indented quotations are not placed between quotation marks?

• Did you introduce all direct quotations with some identification of their author, source, or significance?

• Did you use the correct form for parenthetical notes?

• Have you handled titles correctly, italicizing books and putting the titles of articles between quotation marks?

• Did you include a Works Cited or References list? Is your list of works cited alphabetized? Did you indent the entries correctly?

For more on doing research, be sure to see the Web site for this handbook at <http://www.ablongman.com/sfhandbooks>.

part VIII

Documentation

48 Modern Language Association (MLA)
    Documentation

49 American Psychological Association (APA)
    Documentation

50 Chicago Manual of Style (CMS)
    Documentation

51 Council of Biology Editors (CBE)
    Documentation

52 Columbia Online Style (COS)
    Documentation

CHAPTER 48

How Do You Use
MLA Documentation?

In many professional fields in the humanities, writers follow the conventions of documentation and format recommended by the Modern Language Association (MLA). The basic procedures for MLA documentation are spelled out in this chapter. If you run into documentation problems not discussed here, refer to the *MLA Handbook for Writers of Research Papers,* fifth edition (1999), by Joseph Gibaldi. Style updates are also available at the MLA Web site at <http://www.mla.org/.

48a How to use MLA documentation

MLA documentation usually involves just two steps: creating an in-text note for every source as you use it in a paper or project (Section 48a-1); creating an entry on a Works Cited page for each source used in the project (Section 48a-2). That's all there is to it.

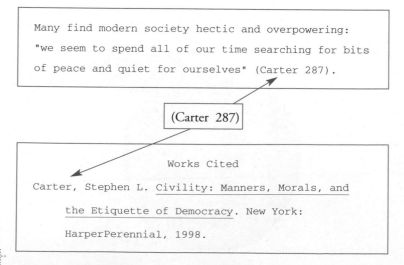

Many find modern society hectic and overpowering:
"we seem to spend all of our time searching for bits
of peace and quiet for ourselves" (Carter 287).

(Carter 287)

Works Cited

Carter, Stephen L. Civility: Manners, Morals, and

    the Etiquette of Democracy. New York:

    HarperPerennial, 1998.

In some disciplines, instructors still prefer footnotes at the bottom of a page or endnotes gathered in a single list at the end of the paper. We provide examples of these footnote forms in Section 48c.

■ 1 (Step 1) In the body of your paper, note each source as you use it.

Until recently, most sources used in a project had authors and page numbers, so you could cite them with a simple note in parentheses placed after the material borrowed. But many online sources, especially Web sources, no longer have authors or page numbers, so you must treat them differently.

For conventional sources with authors and page numbers, enclose the author's last name and the relevant page number(s) within parentheses. Here's how you would cite a passage from *Civility* by Stephen L. Carter.

```
Many find modern society hectic and overpowering: "we
seem to spend all of our time searching for bits of
peace and quiet for ourselves" (Carter 287).
```

The note in parentheses tells readers to look for a work by Carter on the Works Cited page of the project; they will find the quoted sentence on page 287 of Carter's book. Notice that a single typed space separates the author's name and the page number, that the note itself falls *outside* the quotation marks, and that it is *followed* by the punctuation mark. In MLA documentation, page numbers are *not* preceded by *p.* or *pp.* or by a comma.

```
(Carter 287)

(Bly 253-54)
```

You can shorten a parenthetical note by naming the author of the source in the body of the essay; then the parenthetical note consists of a page number only.

```
Stephen L. Carter, professor of law at Yale, notes
that "we seem to spend all of our time searching
for bits of peace and quiet for ourselves"
(287).
```

This is a common and readable form, one you should use regularly, especially when you build an entire paragraph from material in a single source. As a general rule, make all parenthetical notes as brief and inconspicuous as possible.

48a
MLA

For sources without conventional authors or page numbers, the note will be a little more complicated. Ordinarily, you cite such a source just by naming it or describing it within the paper or project itself:

```
Included in the "When Nixon Met Elvis" exhibit at the
National Archives Online Exhibit Hall is . . .

The Arkansas State Highway Map indicates . . .

Software such as Microsoft's FoxPro . . .
```

You would also use this form when citing a complete book, article, or Web site rather than just a specific chapter, section, or passage:

```
The Media Research Center Web site offers . . .

In "Hamlet's Encounter with the Pirates," Wentersdorf
argues . . .

Under "Northwest Passage" in Collier's
Encyclopedia . . .
```

One principle remains the same: readers must be able to connect any source you cite in the project to a corresponding item on the Works Cited page. That means that the name you use to identify a source in the paper has to be the same name by which you list the item on the Works Cited page—where readers can find more information about the source (for instance, its electronic address).

On the rare occasions when an electronic source has paragraph numbers, screen numbers, or titles for the Web pages you are citing, you can put this helpful information in parentheses. (To handle complex parenthetical notes, see either Chart 48.2 on pages 726–28 or the MLA Models in Section 48b, where we illustrate parenthetical notes for every type of source listed.)

■ **2 (Step 2) On a separate page at the end of your project, list alphabetically every source you cited.** This list of sources is titled "Works Cited." The Works Cited entry for Stephen Carter's book mentioned above would look like this.

```
Carter, Stephen L. Civility: Manners, Morals, and
      the Etiquette of Democracy. New York:
      HarperPerennial, 1998.
```

48a
MLA

Appropriate forms for dozens of Works Cited items appear in the list of MLA Models in Section 48b.

The Works Cited page is placed after the body of the essay (and the endnotes, if there are any). You include only sources you actually mention in the body of the project itself, not all that you might have examined in preparing the work. For a sample Works Cited list, see pages 770–72. A checklist for setting up your own Works Cited list appears on page 771. The first entries on a Works Cited page might look like this.

Subsequent lines indented one-half inch or five spaces   "Works Cited" centered   All items double spaced

```
                      Works Cited

     Arni, Sherry. "I Can Live with It." English

         Journal 79 (Nov. 1990): 76.

     Corbett, H. Dickson, and Bruce L. Wilson. Testing,

         Reform, and Rebellion. Norwood: Ablex, 1991.

     Dinan, John. "Standardized Tests: Multiple Choices

         of the Wrong Kind." English Journal 67 (Oct.

         1978): 54-56.
```

Works published since 1900 include a publisher's name. Publishers' names should be shortened whenever possible. Drop words such as *Company, Inc., LTD, Bro.,* and *Books.* Abbreviate *University* to *U* and *University Press* to *UP.* When possible, shorten a publisher's name to one word.

Chart 48.1

Abbreviations for Publishers in MLA Style

Addison Wesley Longman	Longman
Barnes and Noble Books	Barnes
Charles Scribner's Sons	Scribner's
Columbia University Press	Columbia UP
Doubleday and Co., Inc.	Doubleday
Gale Research	Gale

(Continued)

48a
MLA

Abbreviations for Publishers in MLA Style   *(Continued)*

Harper & Row	Harper
HarperCollins	HarperCollins
Harvard University Press	Harvard UP
Houghton Mifflin	Houghton
W. W. Norton and Co.	Norton
Random House	Random
Simon and Schuster	Simon
University of Chicago Press	U of Chicago P
The Viking Press	Viking

Chart 48.2

Additional Guidelines for Preparing In-text Notes and Works Cited Entries in MLA Style

• **When citing a work without an author** (but with conventional page numbers)—an unsigned article in a magazine or newspaper, for example—list the title, shortened if necessary, and the page number. Shortened titles must always begin with the words used to alphabetize the item on the Works Cited page.

> ("In the Thicket" 18)
>
> ("Students Rally" A6)

> Works Cited
>
> "In the Thicket of Things." Texas Monthly Apr. 1994: 18.
>
> "Students Rally for Academic Freedom." The Chronicle
>
> of Higher Education 28 Sept. 1994: A6.

• **When citing more than a single work in one note**, separate the citations with a semicolon.

> (Polukord 13-16; Ryan and Weber 126)

• **When citing two or more sources within a single sentence**, place the parenthetical notes right after the specific statements they support.

> While the budget cuts might go deeper than originally
>
> reported (Kinsley 42), there is no reason to believe
>
> that "throwing more taxpayers' dollars into a
>
> bottomless pit" (Doggett 62) will do much to reform
>
> "one of the least productive job training programs ever
>
> devised by the federal government" (Will 28).

48a
MLA

Notice that a parenthetical note is always placed outside any quotation marks but before the period that ends the sentence.

• **With a quotation long enough to require indention** (more than four typed lines), place any parenthetical note outside the final punctuation mark. Compare the following examples.

SHORT QUOTATION (NOT INDENTED)

Ralph Bunche never wavered in his belief that the races in America had to learn to live together: "In all of his experience of racial discrimination Bunche never allowed himself to become bitter or to feel racial hatred" (Urquhart 435). He continued to work . . .

The note is placed inside the final punctuation mark.

LONG QUOTATION (INDENTED TEN SPACES)

Winner of the Nobel Peace Prize in 1950, Ralph Bunche, who died in 1971, left an enduring legacy:

> His memory lives on, especially in the long struggle for human dignity and against racial discrimination and bigotry, and in the growing effectiveness of the United Nations in resolving conflicts and keeping the peace.
>
> (Urquhart 458)

The note is placed outside the final punctuation mark.

• **When citing more than one work by a single author in a paper**, a parenthetical note listing only the author's last name could refer to more than one book or article on the Works Cited page. To avoid confusion, place a comma after the author's name and identify the particular work being cited, using a shortened title. For example, a Works Cited page (see Section 48a-2) might list the following four works by Richard D. Altick.

Works Cited

Altick, Richard D. The Art of Literary Research. New York: Norton, 1963.

---. The Shows of London. Cambridge: Belknap-Harvard, 1978.

---. Victorian People and Ideas. New York: Norton, 1973.

---. Victorian Studies in Scarlet. New York: Norton, 1977.

48a
MLA

The first time—and every subsequent time—you refer to a work by Richard Altick, you need to identify it by a shortened title in the parenthetical note.

```
(Altick, Shows 345)

(Altick, Victorian People 190-202)

(Altick, Victorian Studies 59)
```

 Should you underline or italicize the title of a book, play, movie or other major work? Writers working with typewriters did not have a choice; they could only underscore titles that would be italicized in printed works. Now, however, word processors and printers make it possible for writers to produce italics. However, MLA style still favors underlining the titles in material that will be graded or printed. That's because italics can sometimes be hard to read. See the MLA Style section at <http://www.mla.org/www_mla_org/> for MLA's rationale for the policy.

48b MLA models

Below you will find MLA models to follow in creating notes and the corresponding Works Cited entries for more than sixty kinds of sources. Simply locate the type of source you need to cite in either the Models Index or the Alphabetical Index and then locate that item by number in the list that follows.

MLA Models Index

Books/Dissertations

1. Book, generic
2. Book, two or three authors or editors
3. Book, four or more authors or editors
4. Book, revised by a second author
5. Book, edited—focus on the original author
6. Book, edited—focus on the editor
7. Book, edited—focus on the editor, more than one editor
8. Book, written by a group
9. Book with no author
10. Book, focus on a foreword, introduction, preface, or afterword
11. Work of more than one volume

48b
MLA

12. Book, translation—focus on the original author
13. Book, translation—focus on the translator
14. Book in a foreign language
15. Book, republished
16. Book, part of a series
17. Book, a reader or anthology
18. Book, a second, third, or later edition
19. Book, a chapter in
20. Book published before 1900
21. Book, issued by a division of a publisher—a special imprint
22. Dissertation or thesis—published
23. Dissertation or thesis—unpublished
24. Book review, movie review

Articles and Magazine Pieces

25. Article in a scholarly journal, generic
26. Article in a popular magazine, generic
27. Article in a weekly or biweekly magazine
28. Article in a monthly magazine—author named
29. Article or selection from a reader or anthology

Newspapers

30. Article in a newspaper
31. Editorial in a newspaper
32. Letter to the editor
33. Cartoon

Reference Works

34. Reference work or encyclopedia (familiar or online)

35. Reference work (specialized or less familiar)
36. Bulletin or pamphlet
37. Government document

Electronic Sources

38. Computer software
39. WWW page, generic
40. WWW page, online book
41. WWW page, online scholarly journal
42. WWW page, online popular magazine
43. WWW page, online newspaper editorial
44. WWW page, personal home page
45. Listserv/Newsgroup/Usenet newsgroup
46. Synchronous communication (MOOs, MUDs) newsgroup
47. Email
48. CD-ROM/diskette database or publication

Miscellaneous Entries

49. Microfilm or microfiche
50. Biblical citation
51. Videotape / DVD
52. Movie
53. Television program
54. Radio program
55. Personal interview
56. Musical composition
57. Recording/audio clip
58. Speech
59. Lecture
60. Advertisement
61. Letter—published
62. Letter—unpublished
63. Artwork
64. Drama or play

48b
MLA

MLA Alphabetical Index

Advertisement, 60

Afterword, book, 10

Anonymous—book, 9; newspaper editorial, 31

Anthology, 17, 29

Article in a journal or magazine paginated issue by issue, 26, 27, 28

Article in a journal paginated by the year or volume, not issue by issue, 25

Article in a monthly magazine, 28; online, 42

Article in a newspaper, 30; online, 43

Article in a reader or anthology, 29

Article in a scholarly journal, 25

Article in a weekly or biweekly magazine, 27

Article in a collection citing original place of publication, 29

Article on CD-ROM, 48

Article online, 41, 42

Artwork, 63

Audio clip, 57

Biblical citation, 50

Biweekly magazine, 27

Book review, 24

Book, chapter in, 19

Book, collection or anthology, 17

Book, edited—focus on the editor, 6

Book, edited—focus on the editor, more than one editor, 7

Book, edited—focus on the original author, 5

Book, foreign language, 14

Book, foreword, introduction, preface, or afterword, 10

Book, four or more authors or editors, 3

Book, group authorship, 8

Book, multivolume, 11

Book, no author, 9

Book, on CD-ROM, 48

Book, one author, 1

Book, online, 40

Book, published before 1900, 20

Book, republished, 15

Book, revised by a second author, 4

Book, series, 16

Book, special imprint, 21

Book, two or three authors or editors, 2

Bulletin, 36

Cartoon, 33

CD-ROM database, 48

Chapter in a book, 19

Collection, article reprinted in, 29

Collections, 17, 29

Computer—email, 47; Internet or online sources, 39–47; software, 38; World Wide Web (WWW), 39–44

Conference, electronic, 45–46

Congressional Record, 37

Database, 48

Diskette, 48

Dissertation—published, 22; unpublished, 23

Document, government, 37

Drama, 64

DVD, 51

Edited book, 5–7

Edition, second, third, or later, 18

Editorial in a newspaper, 31; online, 43

Email, 47

Encyclopedia, 34; online, 34

Entry—encyclopedia, 34; reference work, 35

Feature film, 52
Foreign language, book in a, 14
Foreword, book, 10
Government document, 37
Group author, 8
Home page, 44
Imprint, publisher's, 21
Internet source, 39–47
Interview, personal, 55
Introduction, book, 10
Journal article, 25
Lecture, 59
Letter to the editor, 32
Letter—published, 61; unpublished, 62
Listserv, 45
Magazine article, 26–28; online, 42
Magazine—monthly, 26, 28; online, 42; weekly, 27
Microfiche, 49
Microfilm, 49
Monthly magazine, 26, 28; online, 42
MOO, 46
Movie, 52
Movie review, 24
MUD, 46
Music, 56, 57
Musical composition, 56
Newsgroup, 45
Newspaper—article, 30; cartoon, 33; editorial, 31; letter to the editor, 32; online, 43
Online encyclopedia, 34
Online source, 39–47
Painting, 63
Pamphlet, 36
Passage, biblical, 50
Personal interview, 55
Play, 64
Preface, book, 10

Program, radio, 54
Program, software, 38
Program—television, 53; radio, 54
Published—dissertation or thesis, 22; letter, 61
Publisher's imprint, 21
Radio program, 54
Reader, 17, 29
Recording, audio, 57
Reference work, 34–35; online, 34
Reprinted book, 15
Republished book, 15
Review of a book or movie, 24
Revision of a book, 4
Sculpture, 63
Series, book in a, 16
Software, 38
Sound clip, 57
Speech, 58
Synchronous communication, 46
Talk, 59
Television program, 53
Thesis—published, 22; unpublished, 23
Translation—focus on the original author, 12; focus on the translator, 13
Unpublished—dissertation or thesis, 23; letter, 62
Usenet, 45
Videotape, 51
Volumes, book in multiple, 11
Weekly magazine, 27
Work of art, 63
Work within a collection or anthology, 29
WWW page—generic, 39; online book, 40; online journal, 41; online magazine, 42; online newspaper, 43; personal home page, 44

48b
MLA

1. **Book, Generic—MLA** Provide author, title, place of publication, publisher, and year of publication. For an online book, see model 40.

   IN-TEXT NOTE: (Prosek 246-47)

   Works Cited

   Prosek, James. <u>The Complete Angler: A Connecticut</u>

   <u>Yankee Follows in the Footsteps of Walton</u>. New

   York: Harper, 1999.

   E-TipS How do you document an electronic book? The technology for these products is still evolving, but since e-books are designed to emulate print volumes, treat them as books—with authors, titles, and so on. However, if the publishing information does not make it clear that you are reading an e-book edition of a work, you might describe the medium right after the title: E-book.

   ---

2. **Book, Two or Three Authors or Editors—MLA**

   IN-TEXT NOTE: (Collier and Horowitz 24)

   Works Cited

   Collier, Peter, and David Horowitz. <u>Destructive</u>

   <u>Generation: Second Thoughts About the '60s</u>. New

   York: Summit, 1989.

   Note that the names of second and third authors are given in their normal order, first names first.

3. **Book, Four or More Authors or Editors—MLA** You have two options. You can name all the authors in both the note and the Works Cited entry.

   IN-TEXT NOTE: (Guth, Rico, Ruszkiewicz, and Bridges 95)

   Works Cited

   Guth, Hans P., Gabriele L. Rico, John Ruszkiewicz,

   and Bill Bridges. <u>The Rhetoric of Laughter: The</u>

Best and Worst of Humor Night. Fort Worth:

Harcourt, 1996.

Alternatively, you can name just the first author given on the title page and use the Latin abbreviation *et al.,* which means "and others."

IN-TEXT NOTE: (Guth et al. 95)

Works Cited

Guth, Hans P., et al. The Rhetoric of Laughter: The

Best and Worst of Humor Night. Fort Worth:

Harcourt, 1996.

4. **Book, Revised by a Second Author—MLA** Sometimes you may need to cite a book by its original author, even when it has been revised. In such a case, place the editor's name after the title of the book.

IN-TEXT NOTE: (Guerber 20)

Works Cited

Guerber, Hélène Adeline. The Myths of Greece and

Rome. Ed. Dorothy Margaret Stuart. 3rd ed.

London: Harrap, 1965.

5. **Book, Edited—Focus on the Original Author—MLA**

IN-TEXT NOTE: (Cor. 3.3.119-35)

Works Cited

Shakespeare, William. The Tragedy of Coriolanus. Ed.

Reuben Brower. New York: Signet, 1966.

Coriolanus is a play by Shakespeare, so the note provides act, scene, and line numbers—not author and page numbers. It must be clear in the paper that the note refers to the Shakespeare play.

6. **Book, Edited—Focus on the Editor—MLA**

IN-TEXT NOTE: (Brower xxiii-1)

48b
MLA

Works Cited

Brower, Reuben, ed. <u>The Tragedy of Coriolanus</u>. By

William Shakespeare. New York: Signet, 1966.

7. Book, Edited—Focus on the Editor, More than One Editor— MLA

IN-TEXT NOTE: (Kittredge and Smith xvi-xvii)

Works Cited

Kittredge, William, and Annick Smith, eds. <u>The Last</u>

<u>Best Place: A Montana Anthology</u>. Seattle: U of

Washington P, 1988.

8. Book, Written by a Group—MLA Treat the group as the author of the work. But to avoid an awkward note, identify the group author in the body of your paper and place only the relevant page numbers in parentheses.

IN-TEXT NOTE: The Reader's Digest <u>Fix-It-Yourself Manual</u>
explains the importance of a UL label (123).

Works Cited

Reader's Digest. <u>Fix-It-Yourself Manual</u>.

Pleasantville: Reader's Digest, 1977.

9. Book with No Author—MLA Cite the book by its title, alphabetized by the first major word (excluding *The, A,* or *An*). Use a shortened title in any note.

IN-TEXT NOTE: (<u>Kodak</u> 56-58)

Works Cited

<u>Kodak Guide to 35mm Photography</u>. 6th ed. Rochester:

Eastman, 1989.

10. Book, Focus on a Foreword, Introduction, Preface, or Afterword—MLA The note below refers to information in O'Rourke's introduction, not to material in the anthology itself.

IN-TEXT NOTE: (O'Rourke 5)

Works Cited

O'Rourke, P. J. Introduction. Road Trips, Head

    Trips, and Other Car-Crazed Writings. Ed. Jean

    Lindamood. New York: Atlantic, 1996. 1-8.

11. **Work of More than One Volume—MLA** When you use only
one volume of a multivolume set, identify both the volume you
have used and the total number of volumes in the set.

IN-TEXT NOTE: (Spindler 17-18)

Works Cited

Spindler, Karlheinz. Abstract Algebra with

    Applications. Vol. 1. New York: Dekker, 1994. 2

    vols.

When you use more than one volume of a set, identify the specific volumes in the notes as you cite them. Then, in the Works
Cited entry, list the total number of volumes in that set.

IN-TEXT NOTES: (Spindler 1: 17-18); (Spindler 2: 369)

Works Cited

Spindler, Karlheinz. Abstract Algebra with

    Applications. 2 vols. New York: Dekker, 1994.

12. **Book, Translation—Focus on the Original Author—MLA**

IN-TEXT NOTE: (Freire 137-38)

Works Cited

Freire, Paulo. Learning to Question: A Pedagogy of

    Liberation. Trans. Tony Coates. New York:

    Continuum, 1989.

13. **Book, Translation—Focus on the Translator—MLA**

IN-TEXT NOTE: (Swanton 17-18)

48b
MLA

Works Cited

Swanton, Michael, trans. <u>Beowulf</u>. New York: Barnes,

1978.

14. **Book in a Foreign Language—MLA** Copy the title of the foreign work exactly as it appears on the title page, paying special attention both to accent marks and capitalization.

IN-TEXT NOTE: (Bablet and Jacquot 59)

Works Cited

Bablet, Denis, and Jean Jacquot. <u>Les Voies de la</u>

<u>création théâtrale</u>. Paris: Editions du Centre

National de la Recherche Scientifique, 1977.

15. **Book, Republished—MLA** Give original publication dates for works of fiction that have been through many editions and reprints.

IN-TEXT NOTE: (Herbert 146)

Works Cited

Herbert, Frank. <u>Dune</u>. 1965. New York: Berkeley,

1977.

16. **Book, Part of a Series—MLA** Give the series name just before the publishing information. Do not underline or italicize a series name.

IN-TEXT NOTE: (Pemberton xii)

Works Cited

Pemberton, Michael, ed. <u>The Ethics of Writing</u>

<u>Instruction: Issues in Theory and Practice</u>.

Perspectives on Writing: Theory, Research,

Practice 4. Stamford: Ablex, 2000.

17. **Book, a Reader or Anthology—MLA** When you quote from the front matter of the collection, the page numbers for a note may

sometimes be Roman numerals. (To cite a selection from within an anthology, see model 29.)

IN-TEXT NOTE: (Lunsford and Ruszkiewicz xxi-xxvi)

Works Cited

Lunsford, Andrea A., and John J. Ruszkiewicz, eds.

The Presence of Others: Voices and Images That

Call for Response. 3rd ed. New York: Bedford,

2000.

18. Book, a Second, Third, or Later Edition—MLA

IN-TEXT NOTE: (Rombauer 480-81)

Works Cited

Rombauer, Marjorie Dick. Legal Problem Solving:

Analysis, Research, and Writing. 5th ed. St.

Paul: West, 1991.

19. Chapter in a Book—MLA

IN-TEXT NOTE: (Shalit 144-60)

Works Cited

Shalit, Wendy. "Male Character." A Return to

Modesty: Discovering the Lost Virtue. New York:

Free, 1999. 144-60.

20. Book Published Before 1900—MLA Omit the name of the publisher in citations of works published prior to 1900.

IN-TEXT NOTE: (Bowdler 2: 47)

Works Cited

Bowdler, Thomas, ed. The Family Shakespeare. 10

vols. London, 1818.

48b
MLA

21. **Book Issued by a Division of a Publisher—a Special Imprint—MLA** Attach the special imprint (Vintage in this case) to the publisher's name with a hyphen.

IN-TEXT NOTE: (Hofstader 192-93)

Works Cited

Hofstader, Douglas. <u>Gödel, Escher, Bach: An Eternal</u>

  <u>Golden Braid</u>. New York: Vintage-Random, 1980.

22. **Dissertation or Thesis—Published (Including Publication by UMI)—MLA** If the dissertation you are citing is published by University Microfilms International (UMI), be sure to provide the order number as the last item in the Works Cited entry.

IN-TEXT NOTE: (Rifkin 234)

Works Cited

Rifkin, Myra Lee. <u>Burial, Funeral and Mourning</u>

  <u>Customs in England, 1558-1662</u>. Diss. Bryn Mawr,

  1977. Ann Arbor: UMI, 1977. DDJ78-01385.

23. **Dissertation or Thesis—Unpublished—MLA** The titles of unpublished dissertations appear between quotation marks. *Diss.* indicates that the source is a dissertation.

IN-TEXT NOTE: (Altman 150)

Works Cited

Altman, Jack, Jr. "The Politics of Health Planning

  and Regulation." Diss. Massachusetts Institute

  of Technology, 1983.

24. **Book Review/Movie Review—Titled or Untitled—MLA** Not all book, film, and arts reviews have titles, so the Works Cited form for a review may vary slightly.

IN-TEXT NOTE: (Keen 39)

Works Cited

Keen, Maurice. "The Knight of Knights." Rev. of

  <u>William Marshall: The Flower of Chivalry</u>, by

48b
MLA

```
Georges Duby. New York Review of Books 16 Jan.

1986: 39-40.
```

A book title (*Uncle Tom's Cabin*) within a book title is not underscored or italicized (Uncle Tom's Cabin *and American Culture*).

IN-TEXT NOTE: (Baym 691-92)

Works Cited

```
Baym, Nina. Rev. of Uncle Tom's Cabin and American

    Culture, by Thomas F. Gossett. Journal of

    American History 72 (1985): 691-92.
```

Here's the form for a film review found online, in this case in the e-zine *Slate*. The citation includes both the date of the review itself and the date it was accessed online.

IN-TEXT NOTE: David Edelstein finds Ben Affleck an unlikely convict in Reindeer Games . . .

Works Cited

```
Edelstein, David. "Parlor Games." Rev. of Reindeer

    Games, dir. John Frankenheimer. Slate 25 Feb.

    2000. 8 Mar. 2000 <http://slate.msn.com/

    MovieReview/00-02-25/MovieReview.asp>.
```

25. **Article in a Scholarly Journal—MLA** Scholarly journals are usually identified by volume number or season (rather than day, week, or month of publication). Such journals are usually paginated year by year, with a year's work treated as one volume. Provide author, title of article, title of journal, volume number, year of publication, and page numbers. For an online journal article, see model 41.

IN-TEXT NOTE: (Smith 301)

Works Cited

```
Smith, Laurajane. "Heritage Management as

    Postprocessual Archaeology?" Antiquity 64

    (1994): 300-09.
```

When a scholarly journal is paginated issue by issue, place a period and an issue number after the volume number.

IN-TEXT NOTE: (Morgenroth 91-92)

Works Cited

Morgenroth, Joyce. "Dressing for the Dance." Wilson

   Quarterly 22.2 (1998): 88-95.

26. **Article in a Popular Magazine—MLA** Magazines are paginated issue by issue and identified by the seasonal, monthly or weekly date of publication (not by volume number). Provide author, title of article, title of magazine, date of publication, and page numbers. Months are abbreviated in MLA style.

IN-TEXT NOTE: (Murray 63)

Works Cited

Murray, Spencer. "Roaming Wyoming." Open Road Spring

   1999: 60-65.

Articles in magazines often don't appear on consecutive pages. When that's the case, list the relevant page number(s) in the note. In the Works Cited entry give the first page on which the article appears, followed by a plus sign.

IN-TEXT NOTE: (Mackay 170)

Works Cited

Mackay, Jordan. "A Murder on Campus." Texas Monthly

   Jan. 2000: 112+.

27. **Article in a Weekly or Biweekly Magazine—MLA** Give both the day and the month of publication as listed on the issue. Note that in MLA form the day precedes the month and no comma is used: 18 July 1994. Months are abbreviated in MLA style.

IN-TEXT NOTE: (Smolowe 20)

Works Cited

Smolowe, Jill. "When Violence Hits Home." Time 18

   July 1994: 18-25.

28. **Article in a Monthly Magazine—MLA** Months are abbreviated in MLA style.

IN-TEXT NOTE: (Bond 90)

Works Cited

Bond, Constance. "If You Can't Bear to Part with It,

Open a New Museum." Smithsonian Apr. 1995:

90-97.

29. **Article or Selection from a Reader or Anthology—MLA** List the item on the Works Cited page by the author of the piece you are actually citing, not the editor(s) of the collection. Then provide the title of the particular selection, the title of the overall collection, the editor(s) of the collection, and publication information. Conclude with the page numbers of the selection.

IN-TEXT NOTE: (King 417-20)

Works Cited

King, Robert. "Should English Be the Law?" The

Presence of Others: Voices and Images That Call

for Response. 3rd ed. Ed. Andrea Lunsford and

John Ruszkiewicz. New York: Bedford, 2000. 409-

21.

When you cite two or more selections from a reader or an anthology, list that collection fully on the Works Cited page.

Works Cited

Lunsford, Andrea, and John Ruszkiewicz, eds. The

Presence of Others: Voices and Images That Call

for Response. 3rd ed. New York: Bedford, 2000.

Then, still in the Works Cited list, identify the authors and titles of all articles you cite from that reader or anthology, followed by the names of the editors and the page numbers of your selections.

IN-TEXT NOTE: (King 417-20)

IN-TEXT NOTE: (Turkle 453)

48b
MLA

Works Cited

King, Robert. "Should English Be the Law?" Lunsford

and Ruszkiewicz 409-21.

Turkle, Shirley. "Who Am We?" Lunsford and

Ruszkiewicz 442-58.

For a scholarly article reprinted in a collection, you should usually give more detail about its original place of publication (when known) and then give the facts about the collection.

IN-TEXT NOTE: (Hartman 101)

Works Cited

Hartman, Geoffrey. "Milton's Counterplot." ELH 25

(1958): 1-12. Rpt. in Milton: A Collection of

Critical Essays. Ed. Louis L. Martz. Twentieth

Century Views. Englewood Cliffs: Prentice-

Spectrum, 1966. 100-08.

30. **Article in a Newspaper—MLA** Provide author, title of article, name of newspaper, date of article, and page numbers. For page numbers, use the form in the newspaper you are citing; many papers are paginated according to sections. For an online newspaper, see model 43.

IN-TEXT NOTE: (Rorty E15)

Works Cited

Rorty, Richard. "The Unpatriotic Academy." New York

Times 13 Feb. 1994: E15.

A plus sign following the page number (for example, 7+) indicates that an article continues beyond the designated page, but not necessarily on consecutive pages.

IN-TEXT NOTE: (Peterson 2A)

Works Cited

Peterson, Karen S. "Turns Out We Are 'Sexually

Conventional.'" USA Today 7 Oct. 1994: 1A+.

31. **Editorial in a Newspaper—Author Not Named—MLA** A short-ened title is used in the note. For accurate reference, the first few words of the shortened title must match the initial words of the title listed on the Works Cited page.

IN-TEXT NOTE: ("Negro College" 28)

Works Cited

"Negro College Fund: Mission Is Still Important on

50th Anniversary." Editorial. Dallas Morning

News 8 Oct. 1994: A28.

32. **Letter to the Editor—MLA**

IN-TEXT NOTE: (Cantu 4)

Works Cited

Cantu, Tony. Letter. San Antonio Light 14 Jan. 1986,

southwest ed.: C4.

33. **Cartoon—MLA** To avoid a confusing note, describe a cartoon in the text of your essay.

IN-TEXT NOTE: In the cartoon "Squib" by Miles Mathis . . .

Works Cited

Mathis, Miles. "Squib." Cartoon. Daily Texan 15 Jan.

1986: 19.

34. **Reference Work or Encyclopedia (Familiar or Online)—MLA** With familiar reference works, especially those revised regularly, identify the edition you are using by its date. You may omit the names of editors and most publishing information. No page number is given in the parenthetical note when a work is arranged alphabetically.

IN-TEXT NOTE: (Benedict)

Works Cited

Benedict, Roger William. "Northwest Passage."

Encyclopaedia Britannica: Macropaedia. 1974 ed.

48b
MLA

A citation for an online encyclopedia article would include a date of access and electronic address. However, the online version might not list an author.

Works Cited

"Northwest Passage." <u>Britannica Online</u>.

    Encyclopaedia Britannica. 8 Feb. 2000 <http://

    search.eb.com/bol/topic?eu=57696&sctn=1>.

35. **Reference Work (Specialized or Less Familiar)—MLA** With less familiar reference tools, a full entry is required. (See model 34 for a comparison with familiar reference works.)

IN-TEXT NOTE: (Kovesi)

Works Cited

Kovesi, Julius. "Hungarian Philosophy." <u>The</u>

    <u>Encyclopedia of Philosophy</u>. Ed. Paul Edwards. 8

    vols. New York: Macmillan, 1967.

36. **Bulletin or Pamphlet—MLA** Treat pamphlets as if they were books.

IN-TEXT NOTE: (Morgan 8-9)

Works Cited

Morgan, Martha G., ed. <u>Campus Guide to Computer &</u>

    <u>Web Services</u>. Austin: U of Texas, 1999.

37. **Government Document—MLA** Give the name of the government (national, state, or local) and the agency issuing the report, the title of the document, and publishing information. If it is a congressional document other than the *Congressional Record,* identify the Congress and, when important, the session (for example, *99th Cong., 1st sess.*) after the title of the document. Avoid a lengthy note by naming the document in the body of your essay and placing only the relevant page numbers between parentheses.

IN-TEXT NOTE: This information is from the <u>1985-86</u>

<u>Official Congressional Directory</u> (182-84).

Works Cited

```
United States. Cong. Joint Committee on Printing.

   1985-86 Official Congressional Directory. 99th

   Cong., 1st sess. Washington: GPO, 1985.
```

To cite the *Congressional Record,* give only the date and page number.

```
Cong. Rec. 8 Feb. 1974: 3942-43.
```

38. **Computer Software—MLA** Give the author if known, the version number if any (for example: *Microsoft Word.* Vers. 7.0), the manufacturer, the date, and (optionally) the system needed to run it. Name the software in your text rather than use a parenthetical note.

IN-TEXT NOTE: `With software such as Connectix's Virtual`
`PC . . .`

Works Cited

```
Virtual PC. Vers. 3.0. San Mateo: Connectix, 1999.
```

39. **WWW Page—Generic—MLA** The variety among Web pages is staggering, so you will have to adapt your documentation to particular sources. A typical MLA Works Cited entry for an electronic source may include the following information, though few items will require all these elements. Provide the creator or author of the site, if any; the title of the complete electronic site, underlined (the title of an individual page might appear between quotation marks); the editor (if any) of the electronic site, database, or text, with role indicated (for example, *Ed.*); the version (if any) of the source; the date of electronic publication or most recent update; the identity of the institution or group (if any) sponsoring the electronic site; the date you accessed the information; the electronic address between angle brackets < > and followed by a period. Quite often you will be citing Web pages without authors or creators named. Here, for example, is a citation to an entire Web site.

IN-TEXT NOTE: `More information on National Parks in the`
`United States can be found at Parknet . . .`

Works Cited

<u>Parknet</u>. National Park Service. 12 Dec. 1999

        <http://www.nps.gov/>.

A citation to a particular page on that Web site would look like the following.

IN-TEXT NOTE: ("New Lease")

Works Cited

"A New Lease on Life: Museum Conservation in the

       National Park Service." <u>Parknet</u>. 7 Dec. 1999.

       National Park Service. 10 Feb. 2000 <http://

       www.cr.nps.gov/csd/exhibits/conservation/>.

E-Tips

For any Web site you document, MLA suggests that you provide the full Web location or Uniform Resource Locator (URL), the familiar address beginning http://www. But you may find that the URLs for some Web pages, especially for materials stored in archives, may be too long to offer as a reference. In such cases, give readers the URL to the home page of the Web site where the material is located: the home page will typically have a shorter Web address. Then offer readers the keyword, links, or directions they can use to locate the particular document(s) on that site. Similarly, if you search for information on meta-search engines such as *Ask Jeeves* that search other search engines, the sites you locate may have inconveniently lengthy URLs. In such cases, you may want to track the material down to its original Web locations and offer those much shorter URLs.

Don't give readers a URL they can't access themselves. For example, an index or Web search tool at your school might bring up information within its own local network, but readers without that service or tool may not be able to access that information. When possible, try to track the information down to a URL available to readers from outside the network. (Ask a librarian for assistance.)

40. **WWW—Online Book—MLA** Since most online books do not have page numbers, avoid parenthetical notes by identifying the site in your paper itself. If available, give an original date of publication, the date of the electronic source, and the date you accessed the information.

48b
MLA

IN-TEXT NOTE: In an online version of Henry Adams's The Education of Henry Adams . . .

Works Cited

Adams, Henry. The Education of Henry Adams: An Autobiography. Boston: Houghton, 1918. The American Studies Group at UVA Hypertext. 1996. The University of Virginia. 6 Mar. 1998 <http://xroads.virginia.edu/~HYPER/hadams/ hahome.html>.

41. **WWW—Online Scholarly Journal—MLA** Since most online articles do not have page numbers, avoid parenthetical notes by identifying the site in your paper itself.

IN-TEXT NOTE: In "Tenure and Technology," Katz, Walker, and Cross argue . . .

Works Cited

Katz, Seth, Janice Walker, and Janet Cross. "Tenure and Technology: New Values, New Guidelines." Kairos 2.1 (1997). 20 July 1997 <http:// english.ttu.edu/kairos/2.1/coverweb/ bridge.html>.

42. **WWW—Online Popular Magazine—MLA** Since most online articles do not have page numbers, avoid parenthetical notes by identifying the site in your paper itself.

IN-TEXT NOTE: Shafer claims in "The New Walter Cronkite" that . . .

Works Cited

Shafer, Jack. "The New Walter Cronkite." Slate 18 Oct. 1996. 12 July 1997 <http://slate.msn.com/ Assessment/96-10-18/Assessment.asp>.

48b
MLA

43. **WWW—Online News Source or Newspaper—MLA** Since most online newspaper stories or editorials do not have page numbers, avoid parenthetical notes by identifying the site in your paper itself.

IN-TEXT NOTE: Sue Ann Pressley suggests that the
movement to teach manners in school is . . .

Works Cited

Pressley, Sue Ann. "Louisiana's Courtesy Call." The

   Washington Post Online 5 Mar. 2000. 6 Mar. 2000

   <http://www.washingtonpost.com/wp-dyn/articles/

   A11177-2000Mar4.html>.

Here's how to cite an online editorial; in this example the date of the editorial and the date of access to it are the same.

IN-TEXT NOTE: In an editorial titled "The Proved and the
Unproved," the New York Times . . .

Works Cited

"The Proved and the Unproved." Editorial. New York

   Times on the Web 13 July 1997. 13 July 1997

   <http://www.nytimes.com/yr/mo/day/editorial/

   13sun1.html>.

E-Tips   The URL you offer for an article or editorial in an online newspaper may not take readers directly to the article. Many newspapers—such as the *New York Times*—charge for access to their archived stories and other materials. So researchers may be directed to the paper's archives for the article you are citing, and then they may have to pay a fee to view the material.

44. **WWW—Personal Home Page—MLA** Since most personal Web sites do not have page numbers, avoid parenthetical notes by identifying the site in your paper itself.

IN-TEXT NOTE: For an example of a digitally enhanced
photograph, see the home page of Brett R. Elliott . . .

Works Cited

Elliott, Brett R. Home page. 4 Nov. 1998. 5 Mar.

2000 <http://www.cwrl.utexas.edu/wcb/

students/belliot5/belliot5.html>.

45. **Listserv/Newsgroup/Usenet Newsgroup—MLA** When citing material from a listserv, identify the author of the document or posting; put the subject line of the posting between quotation marks, followed by the date on which the item was originally posted and the words *Online posting;* give the name of the listserv, followed by the date you accessed the item and the electronic address in angle brackets. Because there will be no page number to cite, avoid a parenthetical note by naming the author in the text of your project.

IN-TEXT NOTE: Cook argues for . . .

Works Cited

Cook, Janice. "Re: What New Day Is Dawning?" 19 June

1997. Online posting. Alliance for Computers

and Writing Listserv. 4 Feb 1998

<acw-l@ttacs6.ttu.edu>.

IN-TEXT NOTE: Christy Heady recommends . . .

Works Cited

Heady, Christy. "Buy or Lease? Depends on How Long

You'll Keep the Car." 7 July 1997. Online

posting. ClariNet. 14 July 1997

<news:clari.biz.industry.automotive>.

Sometimes the name on a listserv may be incomplete or unconventional, but reproduce it just as it appears.

IN-TEXT NOTE: With a high-paying job right out of

college, Knight wonders . . .

Works Cited

Knight. "Will BMW Let Me Test Drive?" 4 Mar. 2000.

Online posting. Bimmer.org Forums:E46. 6 Mar.

2000 <http://www.bimmer.org/3series/messages/>.

48b
MLA

46. **Synchronous Communication (MOOs, MUDs)—MLA** Provide the speaker and/or site, the title of the session or event, the date of the session, the forum for the communication (if specified), the date of access, and the electronic address.

    IN-TEXT NOTE: In LinguaMOO, Inept_Guest observes . . .

    ### Works Cited

    Inept_Guest. Discussion of disciplinary politics in

    rhet/comp. 12 Mar. 1998. LinguaMOO. 12 Mar.

    1998 <telnet:lingua.utdallas.edu 8888>.

47. **Email—MLA** Identifying the communication in the essay itself is preferable to using a parenthetical note. Observe the hyphen in *e-mail.*

    IN-TEXT NOTE: Pacheco makes the case that Al Gore . . .

    ### Works Cited

    Pacheco, Miguel. "Re: Gore or Bush?" E-mail to the

    author. 1 Nov. 2000.

48. **CD-ROM/Diskette Database or Publication—MLA** To cite a CD-ROM or similar electronic database, provide basic information about the source itself—author, title, and publication information. Identify the publication medium (CD-ROM; Diskette; Magnetic tape) and the name of the vendor if available. (The vendor is the company publishing or distributing the database.) Conclude with the date of electronic publication.

    IN-TEXT NOTE: (Bevington 98)

    ### Works Cited

    Bevington, David. "Castles in the Air: The Morality

    Plays." The Theater of Medieval Europe: New

    Research in Early Drama. Ed. Simon Eckchard.

    Cambridge: Cambridge UP, 1993. MLA

    Bibliography. CD-ROM. SilverPlatter. Feb. 1995.

For a CD-ROM database that is often updated (*ProQuest*, for example), you must provide publication dates for the item you are examining and for the data disk itself.

IN-TEXT NOTE: (Alva 407-10)

Works Cited

Alva, Sylvia Alatore. "Differential Patterns of

Achievement Among Asian-American Adolescents."

Journal of Youth and Adolescence 22 (1993):

407-23. Proquest General Periodicals. CD-ROM.

UMI-Proquest. June 1994.

Cite a book, encyclopedia, play, or other item published on CD-ROM or diskette just as if it were a printed source, adding the medium of publication (Diskette or CD-ROM, for example). When page numbers aren't available, use the author's name in the text of the paper to avoid a parenthetical note.

IN-TEXT NOTE: Bolter argues . . .

Works Cited

Bolter, Jay David. Writing Space: A Hypertext.

Diskette. Hillsdale: Erlbaum, 1990.

49. **Microfilm or Microfiche—MLA** Treat material on microfilm exactly as if you had seen its original hard-copy version.

IN-TEXT NOTE: ("How Long?" 434)

Works Cited

"How Long Will the Chemise Last?" Consumer Reports.

Aug. 1958: 434-37.

50. **Biblical Citation—MLA** Titles of sacred works, including all versions of the Bible, are not underlined.

IN-TEXT NOTE: (John 18:37-38)

48b
MLA

Works Cited

```
The Jerusalem Bible. Ed. Alexander Jones. Garden

     City: Doubleday, 1966.
```

51. **Videotape/DVD—MLA** Cite a video entry by title in most cases. You may include information about the producer, designer, performers, and so on. Identify the distributor, and provide a date. Avoid parenthetical notes for items on videocassette or DVD by naming the work in the body of your project.

    IN-TEXT NOTE: `Tae-Bo Workout` offers . . .

    Works Cited

    ```
    Tae-Bo Workout: Instructional and Basic. Perf. Billy

         Blanks. Videocassettes. Ventura, 1998.
    ```

    IN-TEXT NOTE: `The Matrix` DVD includes production notes that . . .

    Works Cited

    ```
    The Matrix (Widescreen Edition). Perf. Keanu Reeves

         and Laurence Fishburne. DVD. Warner, 1999.
    ```

52. **Movie—MLA** In most cases, list a movie by its title unless your emphasis is on the director, producer, or screenwriter. Provide information about actors, producers, cinematographers, set designers, and so on, to suit your readers. Identify the distributor, and give a date of production. Avoid parenthetical notes for films by naming the works in the body of your paper.

    IN-TEXT NOTE: In Lucas's film `American Graffiti` . . .

    Works Cited

    ```
    American Graffiti. Dir. George Lucas. Perf. Richard

         Dreyfuss and Ronny Howard. Universal, 1973.
    ```

53. **Television Program—MLA** List the TV program by episode or name of program. Avoid parenthetical notes for television shows by naming the programs in the body of your paper.

IN-TEXT NOTE: In the episode "No Surrender, No

Retreat" . . .

Works Cited

"No Surrender, No Retreat." Dir. Mike Vejar. Writ.

  Michael Straczynski. Perf. Bruce Boxleitner,

  Claudia Christian, and Mira Furlan. Babylon 5

  KEYE-42, Austin. 28 July 1997.

54. **Radio Program—MLA** Avoid parenthetical notes for radio shows by naming the programs in the body of your paper.

IN-TEXT NOTE: Early episodes of Death Valley Days . . .

Works Cited

Death Valley Days. Created by Ruth Cornwall Woodman.

  NBC Radio. WNBC, New York. 30 Sept. 1930.

55. **Personal Interview—MLA** Refer to the interview in the body of your essay rather than in a parenthetical note.

IN-TEXT NOTE: In an interview, Pete Gomes explains . . .

Works Cited

Gomes, Rev. Peter. Personal interview. 23 Apr. 1997.

56. **Musical Composition—MLA** List the work on the Works Cited page by the name of the composer. If you have sheet music or a score, give complete publication information. If you don't have a score or sheet music, provide a simpler entry. In either case, naming the music in the project itself is preferable to using a parenthetical note.

IN-TEXT NOTE: Scott Joplin published "The Strenuous

Life" at a time . . .

Works Cited

Joplin, Scott. "The Strenuous Life: A Ragtime Two

  Step." St. Louis: Stark, 1902.

48b
MLA

IN-TEXT NOTE: Another Cole Porter song, "Too Darn
Hot" . . .

Works Cited

Porter, Cole. "Too Darn Hot." 1949.

57. **Recording/Audio Clip—MLA** Naming the recording in the essay itself is preferable to using a parenthetical note.

IN-TEXT NOTE: An album such as One Endless Night by
Jimmie Dale Gilmore is a good example of . . .

Works Cited

Gilmore, Jimmie Dale. One Endless Night.
   Windchanger/Rounder, 2000.

Here is how to cite an audio clip from a Web site.

IN-TEXT NOTE: The theme for NPR's Car Talk, "Dawgy
Mountain Breakdown" by David Grisman, is . . .

Works Cited

Grisman, David. "Dawgy Mountain Breakdown." CarTalk
   at Cars.com. Natl. Public Radio. 1990. 28 Feb.
   2000 <http://cartalk.cars.com/Radio/Misc/Audio/
   RA/theme2.ram>.

58. **Speech—MLA** When you have no printed text of the speech, give the location and date of the address. Naming the work in the essay itself is preferable to using a parenthetical note.

IN-TEXT NOTE: Reagan explained his position in an
address to . . .

Works Cited

Reagan, Ronald. "The Geneva Summit Meeting: A
   Measure of Progress." U.S. Congress.
   Washington. 21 Nov. 1985.

48b
MLA

With a printed text, give the speaker, title of the speech, where it was delivered, date, and publication information.

IN-TEXT NOTE: (O'Rourke 20)

Works Cited

O'Rourke, P. J. "Brickbats and Broomsticks." Capital

    Hilton. Washington. 2 Dec. 1992. Rpt. American

    Spectator Feb. 1993: 20-21.

59. **Lecture—MLA** Naming the lecture in the essay itself is preferable to having a parenthetical note.

IN-TEXT NOTE: Addressing a conference of educators in Cincinnati, William W. Cook . . .

Works Cited

Cook, William W. "Writing in the Spaces Left."

    Chair's Address. Conf. on Coll. Composition and

    Communication. Cincinnati. 19 Mar. 1992.

60. **Advertisement—MLA** Provide the name of the product or company sponsoring the item, identify it as an advertisement, and give publication information. Naming the advertisement in the project itself is preferable to having a parenthetical note.

IN-TEXT NOTE: An advertisement for the Subaru Outback sedan includes . . .

Works Cited

Subaru Outback. Advertisement. Brill's Content Feb.

    2000: 37.

List an online advertisement similarly. Provide a date of access and an electronic address.

IN-TEXT NOTE: An Ameritrade Anniversary Offer displays . . .

Works Cited

Ameritrade Anniversary Offer. Advertisement. 15 Mar.

    2000. <http://www.ameritrade.com/

    o.cgi?a=gby&o=rfg&p=/html/a.fhtml>.

48b
MLA

61. Letter—Published—MLA

IN-TEXT NOTE: (Eliot 427)

Works Cited

Eliot, George. "To Thomas Clifford Allbutt." 1 Nov.

1873. In Selections from George Eliot's

Letters. Ed. Gordon S. Haight. New Haven: Yale

UP, 1985. 427.

62. Letter—Unpublished—MLA Identifying the letter communication in the essay itself is preferable to having a parenthetical note.

IN-TEXT NOTE: In a letter to Agnes Weinstein dated 23

May 1917, Albert Newton complains . . .

Works Cited

Newton, Albert. Letter to Agnes Weinstein. 23 May

1917. Albert Newton Papers. Woodhill Lib.,

Cleveland.

63. Artwork/photograph—MLA Naming the artwork in the essay itself is preferable to having a parenthetical note.

IN-TEXT NOTE: The work resembles both the painting Ariel

by Fuseli at the Folger and . . .

Works Cited

Fuseli, Henry. Ariel. Folger Shakespeare Lib.,

Washington, D.C.

64. Drama or Play—MLA Citing a printed text of a play, whether individual or collected, differs from citing a performance. For printed texts, provide the usual Works Cited information, taking special care when citing a collection in which various editors handle different plays. In parenthetical notes, give the act, scene, and line numbers when the work is so divided; give page numbers when it is not.

48b
MLA

IN-TEXT NOTE: (Ham. 5.2.219-24)

Works Cited

Shakespeare, William. The Tragedy of Hamlet, Prince

of Denmark. Ed. Frank Kermode. The Riverside

Shakespeare. 2nd ed. Ed. G. Blakemore Evans and

J. J. M. Tobin. Boston: Houghton, 1997.

1183-1245.

IN-TEXT NOTE: (Stoppard 11-15)

Works Cited

Stoppard, Tom. Rosencrantz and Guildenstern Are

Dead. New York: Grove, 1967.

For performances of plays, give the title of the work, the author, and then any specific information that seems relevant—director, performers, producers, set designer, theater company, and so on. Conclude the entry with a theater, location, and date. Refer to the production directly in the body of your essay to avoid a parenthetical note.

IN-TEXT NOTE: In a rare and memorable performance of
Shakespeare's Timon of Athens . . .

Works Cited

Timon of Athens. By William Shakespeare. Dir.

Michael Benthall. Perf. Ralph Richardson, Paul

Curran, and Margaret Whiting. Old Vic, London.

5 Sept. 1956.

48c How to use footnotes or endnotes

In some fields and majors, an instructor may ask for MLA style endnotes or footnotes to document sources, rather than the in-text notes explained in Sections 48a–48b. When that's the case, use the

48c
MLA

following models as examples for your notes. For endnotes and footnotes, place a raised number in your text after every sentence or passage you wish to document. This number is keyed to a specific end-
note or footnote. Both endnotes and footnotes in MLA style are
numbered consecutively throughout a project. On a computer you
can create the raised numbers for notes by selecting *superscript* as the
font type.

If you use endnotes, list them all on a separate, numbered page at
the end of your project. Center the title *Notes* one inch from the top of
this page. The notes are double-spaced, with the first lines indented
half an inch or five spaces.

If you use footnotes, place them two double spaces (that is, four
lines) below the text on the same page where the citation occurs. Footnotes are single spaced, but leave a double space between notes when
you have more than one on a page.

Notice that endnotes and footnotes differ in indention, arrangement, and punctuation from the style of items on a Works Cited page.

- **Book—MLA endnote/footnote**

    [1]James Prosek, The Complete Angler: A
    Connecticut Yankee Follows in the Footsteps of Walton
    (New York: Harper, 1999) 246-47.

- **Book, Edited—MLA endnote/footnote**

    [2]Reuben Brower, ed., The Tragedy of Coriolanus,
    by William Shakespeare (New York: Signet, 1966).

- **Article in a Scholarly Journal—MLA endnote/footnote**

    [3]Laurajane Smith, "Heritage Management as
    Postprocessual Archaeology?," Antiquity 64 (1994):
    300-09.

- **Article in a Popular Magazine—MLA endnote/footnote**

    [4]Jordan Mackay, "A Murder on Campus," Texas
    Monthly Jan. 2000: 112.

- **Article in a Newspaper—MLA endnote/footnote**

    [5]Richard Rorty, "The Unpatriotic Academy," New
    York Times 13 Feb. 1994: E15.

- **Electronic Source—MLA endnote/footnote**

  [6]Bob Sandberg, Jackie Robinson in Dodgers
  Uniform, 1954, American Memory, Lib. of Congress,
  Washington, 30 Jan. 2000 <http://rs6.loc.gov/pnp/
  ppmsc/00000/00047r.jpg>.

48d Sample MLA paper

The sample paper that follows is accompanied by checklists designed to help you set up a paper correctly in MLA style. When your work meets the specifications on the checklists, it should be in proper form.

Ben Brenneman, a senior English major at the University of Texas at Austin, wrote "Can Quality Survive the Standardized Test?" in Spring 2000 while a student in John Ruszkiewicz's course "Grammar and Style for Writers"—a writing class designed for students thinking about careers in teaching English. Brenneman's classmates, however, came from fields ranging from computer science to journalism, and most of them did not expect to become English teachers.

The assignment that generated this paper asked students to prepare a report of roughly 1500 words on a subject related to language. Suggested topics ranged from the Rosetta Stone to Noam Chomsky. Brenneman asked if he could write about a subject close to his own experiences as a student teacher working in Texas high schools—the effect of standardized testing on students and instructors. As you'll see, the report developed into an argument highly critical of standardized testing. The paper then provided the material for an oral report Brenneman delivered late in the semester to his classmates—who were only too eager to describe their own experiences with standardized tests.

The paper appears here substantially as Brenneman wrote it. But it has been modified in several ways to enhance its value as a model. For example, a table has been added to demonstrate how such an item should be formatted, and a quotation has been extended to provide an example of an indented quotation. It is also worth noting that Brenneman chose to write the paper in APA style—the form he encountered most often in educational research. The paper has been reworked to fit MLA conventions. Note that we have numbered the paragraphs in "Can Quality Survive the Standardized Test?" for easy reference in classroom discussions; do *not* number the paragraphs in a paper unless an instructor or editor instructs you to do so.

48d
MLA

Ben H. Brenneman

Professor Ruszkiewicz

English 379

2 March 2000

           Can Quality Survive the Standardized Test?

¶1   In Seeking Diversity (1992), a book on teaching

middle school language arts, author and teacher Linda

Rief says, "I expect good reading and writing, in which

process and product are woven tightly into literate

tapestries of wonder and awe" (10). Rief thus describes

the Holy Grail of writing instruction: a classroom in

which students learn to write because they care about the

final product and want to do excellent work. Such an

environment would give students the ability to write by

turning them into writers. Unfortunately, the American

education system today is failing to teach many students

even the basic skills they will need to survive.

Statements by teachers that "the greater number of the

young people we teach [. . .] do not know how to read,

spell, write, use correct grammar, do simple math,

remember, use logic" are supported by statistics showing

"that only 55% of the nation's 17-year-olds and 49% of

out-of-school adults are able to write an acceptable

letter ordering a product by mail" (Neill 18). Yet the

dominant response to this problem--competency testing in

our public schools--may be destroying any regard students

may have for language by turning into a formulaic

exercise.

¶2   Many states, in fact, have already responded to

problems in their educational systems by passing laws

mandating the skills that students must learn by a

specified grade. The students' ability to reach the

objectives and the faculty's ability to teach this

Checklist 48.1

Title Page—MLA

MLA does not require a separate cover sheet or title page. If your instructor expects one, center the title of your paper and your name in the upper third of the paper. Center the course title, your instructor's name, and the date of submission on the lower third of the sheet, double-spacing between the elements.

The first page of a paper without a separate title page will look like the facing page. Be sure to check all the items in this list.

• Place your name, your instructor's name, the course title, and the date in the upper left-hand corner, beginning one inch from the top of the page. These items are double spaced.

• Identify your instructor by an appropriate title. When uncertain about academic rank, use *Mr.* or *Ms.*

Dr. James Duban   Professor Rosa Eberly
Ms. Evelyn Westbrook   Mr. John Kinkade

• Center the title a double space under the date. Capitalize the first and last word of the title. Capitalize all other words *except* articles (*a, an, the*), prepositions, the *to* in infinitives, and coordinating conjunctions—unless they are the first or last words.

> **RIGHT**   Can Quality Survive the Standardized Test?

Do not underline or boldface the title of your paper. Do not use all caps, place it between quotation marks, or end it with a period. Titles may, however, end with question marks or include words or phrases that are italicized, underlined, or between quotation marks.

> **RIGHT**   Violence in Shakespeare's <u>Macbeth</u>
> **RIGHT**   Dylan's "Like a Rolling Stone" Revisited

• Begin the body of the essay two lines (a double space) below the title. Double-space the entire essay, including quotations.

• Use one-inch margins at the sides and bottom of this page.

• Number this first page in the upper right-hand corner, one-half inch from the top, one inch from the right margin. Precede the page number with your last name.

48d
MLA

Brenneman 2

"standards-based curriculum" are then measured by statewide standardized tests. Students and schools that fall short of the mark can then be identified for improvement. As Neill explains, "the strongest argument in support of competency requirements is the potential for motivating students, schools, and districts" (8). The results of testing are carefully monitored and publicized to show continuing improvement in the performance of public schools (see Table 1).

Table 1
Percentage of Students Passing All Texas Assessment of
    Academic Skills Exams (TAAS)

	1994	1995	1996	1997	1998	4 Yr. Gain
Grade 3	58	66	70	74	76	18
Grade 4	54	64	67	72	78	24
Grade 5	58	66	73	79	83	25
Grade 6	56	60	69	77	79	23
Grade 7	55	58	67	75	78	23
Grade 8	49	50	59	67	72	23
Grade 10	52	54	60	68	72	20

Source: Texas Business and Education Coalition, School
    Gains. 1999. 27 Feb. 2000. <http://www.tbec.org/
    gains.HTML>.

¶3   In many states this progress has been motivated by attaching increasingly serious consequences to the results of these tests. Students who fail the state aptitude test may be held back a grade, or they may even be denied a high school diploma. Teachers are also under increasing pressure to get test scores up. Jack Kaufhold, a professor of educational psychology, notes that principals have been warned, "If your test scores don't

Checklist 48.2

Body of the Essay—MLA

The body of an MLA research paper continues uninterrupted until the separate Notes page (if any) and the Works Cited page. Be sure to type or handwrite the essay on good-quality paper.

- Use margins of at least one inch all around. Try to keep the right-hand margin reasonably straight. Do not hyphenate words at the end of lines.

- Place page numbers in the upper right-hand corner, one inch from the right edge of the page and one-half inch from the top. Precede the page number with your last name.

- Indent the first line of each paragraph one-half inch, or five spaces if you use a typewriter.

- Indent long quotations one inch, or ten spaces if you use a typewriter. In MLA documentation, long quotations are any that exceed four typed lines in the body of your essay. Double-space these indented quotations. For an example, see page 766.

go up, you may lose your job." He adds, "Teachers also know that if their students' achievement test scores fluctuate too much from year to year, they too could be demoted or dismissed" (14).

¶4   State officials justify these types of high-stakes assessments on the grounds that the skills the tests focus on are those students will need to function in society. They argue, moreover, that students who receive a quality education should have little trouble fulfilling the minimum requirements. For instance, the standards for writing set in Texas, called the "Texas Essential Knowledge and Skills" or TEKS, state that students who graduate high school must "write in a variety of forms using effective word choice, structure, and sentences with an emphasis on organizing logical arguments [. . .]; write in a voice and style appropriate to audience and purpose; and organize in writing to ensure coherence" (Texas Education Agency). In other words, everyone who receives a high school diploma should be able to communicate effectively in writing. Students demonstrate their skill during the Texas Assessment of Academic Skills (TAAS) by composing an essay. As Mary argues on a WWW forum sponsored by Teachers.Net, "The TEKS based TAAS are a reflection of the specific standards the children of our state should meet. That's precisely what we should be teaching." Many teachers, however, find that their curriculums are already adequate. Their response to these requirements is like Sheri Arni's: "My answer has been to leave unchanged most of what happens in my classroom" (76). Rief, for example, gives her students "a two-day crash course [. . .] just before they take the state-mandated achievement tests [. . .] Two days is all I allow" (180).

Brenneman 4

¶5   Unfortunately some schools fall short of the mark.
The administrators in these institutions are then forced
to make changes to the curriculum in order to raise
scores quickly. In Maryland, teachers responded to a
writing test that they felt was too difficult by creating
writing labs, increasing the amount of writing done in
regular English, and cooperating between departments to
focus on writing in all disciplines (Corbett and Wilson).
This is the type of reform the tests were intended to
produce. The instructors at this school improved their
curriculum by finding innovative ways to teach their
students how to write. Anne Shaughnessy, when preparing
her students for the Florida assessment, had them discuss
their responses to a sample prompt. She showed them that
the qualities they felt made an essay successful were the
same criteria that would be used to score their tests.
She then had them use the actual rubric to score their
essays in class. In this way Shaughnessy gave her
students some insight into the logic behind the test,
making it more than simply an arbitrary exercise. She
writes, "Clearly I was teaching to the test, but I was
also introducing activities that extended rather than
displaced the writing curriculum" (56).

¶6   These improvements are certainly commendable. They
occur when schools are blessed with creative teachers who
are willing to take risks. However, many educators, when
faced with the possibility of unemployment, turn to the
tried-and-true method the army uses to train new
recruits: drill, drill, drill. In the Maryland case, for
example, Corbett and Wilson note that "teachers would
stop what they were doing with students [. . .] and inject
an intense period of [. . .] 'drill and review'
specifically related to the test" (124). When preparing

48d
MLA

Brenneman 5

for a writing exam, students spend this period responding
to practice prompts, often from previous tests that have
been released by the state. A teacher in Texas reported
that she "had to give a writing test AND a reading test
every six weeks" (Melissa). In teaching circles this
strategy is known as the "drill-and-kill" approach. In
other words, students are drilled until all genuine
interest in the subject is killed by weeks of prompt
writing.

¶7   Teachers are alarmed by the drill-and-kill
approach to test preparation. They fear that the focus
of their instruction has shifted from producing
excellent writing for a general audience to producing
adequate writing in order to avoid the wrath of the
state. This attitude is communicated to the students
simply by the time spent in practice. As one Texas
teacher laments, "from mid-January through April we are
not teachers, we are masters of how to take a test"
(Linda/tx). In this environment students begin to
believe that mastery of the test is the goal of their
education. They often create, or are even taught, ways
to improve their scores by manipulating the test.
According to Donna Garner, any student who got a high
score on the essay portion of the TAAS could miss most
of the questions on the grammar-oriented part of the
test and still pass. She says that, when students
understand this,

> it's rather hard to get them to see the
> seriousness of correct grammar, spelling,
> punctuation, capitalization, and sentence
> structure. Once the students learn to "play the
> TAAS game" by scripting their essays to a set
> pattern, the accuracy of the content is of
> little importance to them.

Brenneman 6

These students see writing as a task they will have to
perform once in order to graduate, not as a skill they
will need to communicate effectively in the real world.

¶8   Kaufhold describes this mindset as "convergent
thinking." He says that these types of tests emphasize
"the need to search for one right answer. Creative ideas
or divergent thinking is discouraged as students narrow
the scope of their thinking toward what will be on the
test" (14). Ironically, such narrowing is actually
endorsed by A.D. Rison in his 1990 book designed to help
students pass the language arts portion of the TAAS. He
supports the use of a "Rison Design," basically the
typical hourglass shape long used to teach the five-
paragraph theme. He believes that students should use this
design so that "many competing functions, thinking,
writing, vision, and other unnecessary movements are
lessened" (136). And yet for years, many teachers of
composition have complained that such a standard form
"almost inevitably encourages dull, formulaic writing"
(Irmscher 97) and that, when these forms were taught, "all
of the students seemed to write exactly alike" (104). By
focusing on formulaic essays, teachers encourage
convergent thinking by giving students the impression that
there is only one correct way to write. In a 1990 article
in the English Journal, John Dinan says that students
"believe that barren, formulaic writing is what we want
from them. Standardized tests of English cultivate this
belief [. . .] because they implicitly define the writing
process as mechanistic and impersonal" (54). The concept
of writing as a mechanical process is very different from
that advocated in Rief's ideal classroom.

¶9   As dull as these exercises are for teachers to
grade, they are even duller for students to write. Rief

Brenneman 8

makes the comment, "I cannot immerse my students in literature I don't like, anymore than any of us can write effectively on topics in which we have little interest" (19). One of the sample prompts Rison gives for fourth graders consists of a picture of a man sitting in a hole eating a sandwich. Beside him lie a pick and a lunchbox. The caption says, "This is a picture of a construction worker. Look at this picture and describe what you see on two sheets" (143). Is this topic supposed to produce a student's best writing? Are there aspects of a construction worker's life to which fourth graders can relate their own experiences? Why should they care about the construction worker at all? Nothing in this exercise has any application beyond preparation for answering similarly bland test prompts in the future. When confronted with one such prompt, Rief cut it out of the test books for her class and replaced it with "Write about anything you care deeply about. Try to convince the reader how much you care" (121).

¶10   The prompts Rison gives for tenth graders are not much better: "Your school wants to add a new course. Your principal has asked for suggestions. Write a letter to your principal telling what courses you would add and give convincing reasons for your choice" (180). The work can seem mindless. Students in Maryland were forced to sit through drill sessions even after they had passed the state-mandated tests for graduation (Corbett). Imagine, day after day of tedious prompt writing for no purpose whatsoever. No wonder Dinan complains,

> To take such a test is to become bored, to
> become a machine--that is, to take on the
> characteristics of a dull, lifeless writer
> [. . .] most students simply don't <u>like</u> writing

Brenneman 9

> very much, they are apprehensive about it,
> beleaguered by it, inclined to do it only on
> demand. (55)

Drilling students for these tests undermines the writing
teacher's attempts to create an environment in which
students are interested in and feel comfortable with
their writing.

¶11   Under these conditions students learn to hate
writing. They see it as a boring chore, a task they must
complete in order to please a higher authority rather
than a process intended to produce something they
themselves can take pride in. As soon as they learn to
write the type of dry, five-paragraph essay that puts
professors to sleep, their growth as writers ends. The
type of idyllic writing classroom Rief describes is still
possible under the pressure of a high-stakes test, but it
requires creative faculty willing to bet their jobs that
students can pass these tests without drills.
Unfortunately, when superintendents are receiving calls
from angry parents whose children aren't going to
graduate, what is good can take a back seat to what is
expedient. In the rush to raise the scores of those who
can't meet the state objectives, creativity is crushed in
those who can.

48d
MLA

Brenneman 10

Works Cited

Arni, Sherry. "I Can Live With It." English Journal 79
        (Nov. 1990): 76.

Corbett, H. Dickson, and Bruce L. Wilson. Testing,
        Reform, and Rebellion. Norwood: Ablex, 1991.

Dinan, John. "Standardized Tests: Multiple Choices of the
        Wrong Kind." English Journal 79 (Oct. 1990): 54-56.

Garner, Donna. "RE: A Special Note on the TAAS Series."
        29 Jan. 2000. Online posting. EducationNews.org
        Bulletin Board. 13 Feb. 2000 <http://
        www.educationnews.org/cgi/webbbs/article/
        article_list.pl>.

Irmscher, William F. Teaching Expository Writing. New
        York: Holt, 1979.

Kaufhold, Jack. "What's Wrong With Teaching for the Test?"
        The School Administrator 55 (Dec. 1998): 14-16.

Linda/tx. "RE: Teaching to the TAAS Criticism Getting to
        Me." 4 Feb. 2000. Online posting. Texas Teachers
        Chatboard. 13 Feb. 2000 <http://texas.teachers.net/
        chatboard/>.

Mary. "RE: Teaching to the TAAS Criticism Getting to Me."
        4 Feb. 2000. Online posting. Texas Teachers
        Chatboard. 13 Feb. 2000 <http://texas.teachers.net/
        chatboard/>.

Melissa. "RE: Does Your School Give a Released TAAS
        Test?" 14 Jan. 2000. Online posting. Texas Teachers
        Chatboard. 13 Feb. 2000 <http://texas.teachers.net/
        chatboard/>.

Neill, Shirley Boes. The Competency Movement: Problems
        and Solutions. Sacramento: Educational News Service,
        1978.

Rief, Linda. Seeking Diversity. Portsmouth: Heinemann,
        1992.

48d
MLA

Checklist 48.3
The Works Cited Page—MLA

The Works Cited list contains full bibliographical information on all the books, articles, and other resources used in composing the paper. For more information about the purpose and form of this list, see Section 48a-2.

* Center the title "Works Cited" at the top of the page.

* Include in the Works Cited list all the sources actually mentioned in the paper. Do not include materials you examined but did not cite in the body of the paper itself.

* Arrange the items in the Works Cited list alphabetically by the last name of the author. If no author is given for a work, list it according to the first word of its title, excluding articles (*The, A, An*).

* Be sure the first line of each entry touches the left-hand margin. Subsequent lines are indented five spaces.

* Double-space the entire list. Do not quadruple-space between entries unless that is the form your instructor prefers.

* Punctuate items in the list carefully. Don't forget the period at the end of each entry.

* Follow this form if you have two or more entries by the same author:

    van der Plas, Rob. The Mountain Bike Book: Choosing,

        Riding and Maintaining the Off-Road Bicycle. 3rd

        ed. San Francisco: Bicycle, 1993.

    ---. Mountain Bike Magic. Mill Valley: Bicycle, 1991.

48d
MLA

Rison, A. D. A. D. Rison's Teachers' and Parents' Guide to Pass the TAAS Test: Language Arts, Reading and Writing. Austin: Sunbelt, 1990.

Shaughnessy, Anne. "Teaching to the Test: Sometimes a Good Practice." English Journal 83 (Apr. 1994): 54-56.

Texas Education Agency. Texas Education Agency Administrative Rules. Chapters 110 and 128, subchapter C. 1 Sept. 1998. 6 Mar. 2000 <http://www.tea.state.tx.us/rules/tac/ch110_128c.html>.

CHAPTER 49

How Do You Use APA Documentation?

In many social science and related courses (anthropology, education, home economics, linguistics, political science, psychology, sociology), writers are expected to follow the conventions of documentation recommended by the American Psychological Association (APA). The basic procedures for APA documentation are spelled out in this chapter. A full explanation of APA procedures is provided by the *Publication Manual of the American Psychological Association,* fifth edition (2001), available in most college libraries. APA services for students are available at <http://www.apa.org/students/>.

49a How to use APA documentation

APA documentation involves just two basic steps: inserting an in-text note at each point where a paper or project needs documentation (Section 49a-1) and then recording all sources used in these notes in a References list (Section 49a-2).

Tebeaux (1991) argues that technical writing developed in important ways during the English Renaissance.

Tebeaux (1991)

References

Tebeaux, E. (1991). Ramus, visual rhetoric, and the emergence of page design in medical writing of the English Renaissance. *Written Communication, 8,* 411-445.

■ 1 (Step 1) In the body of your paper, note each source as you use it.

In its most common form, this APA note consists of the last name of the source's author, followed immediately by the year the material was published, in parentheses. Here is a sentence derived from information in an article by E. Tebeaux titled "Ramus, Visual Rhetoric, and the Emergence of Page Design in Medical Writing of the English Renaissance," published in 1991.

> Tebeaux (1991) argues that technical writing
> developed in important ways during the English
> Renaissance.

Another basic form of the APA in-text note places both the author's last name and a date between parentheses. This form is used when the author's name is not mentioned in the sentence itself. Notice that a comma follows the author's name within the parentheses.

> Technical writing developed in important ways during
> the English Renaissance (Tebeaux, 1991).

A page number may be given for indirect citations and *must* be given for direct quotations. A comma follows the date when page numbers are given. Page numbers are preceded by *p.* or *pp.*

> During the English Renaissance, writers began to
> employ "various page design strategies to enhance
> visual access" (Tebeaux, 1991, p. 413).

When appropriate, the documentation may be distributed throughout a passage.

> Tebeaux (1991) observes that for writers in the late
> sixteenth century, the philosophical ideas of Peter
> Ramus "provided a significant impetus to major changes
> in page design" (p. 413).

APA parenthetical notes should be as brief and inconspicuous as possible.

Chart 49.1

Additional Guidelines for Preparing In-text Notes in APA Style

- **When you cite more than one work written by an author in a single year,** assign a small letter after the date to distinguish between the author's two works.

(Rosner, 1991a)

(Rosner, 1991b)

The charge is raised by Rosner (1991a), quickly answered by Anderson (1991), and then raised again by Rosner (1991b).

- **When you need to cite more than a single work in a note,** separate the citations with a semicolon and list them in alphabetical order.

(Searle, 1993; Yamibe, 1995)

- **When you are referring to a Web site** (but not a particular Web document), you can give the electronic address directly in the paper. The site does not need to be added to the References list.

More information about psychology as a profession is available on the American Psychological Association's Web site (http://www.apa.org/).

- **When two or more sources are used in a single sentence,** the notes are inserted as needed after the statements they support.

While Porter (1981) suggests that the ecology of the aquifer might be hardier than suspected, "given the size of the drainage area and the nature of the subsurface rock" (p. 62), there is no reason to believe that the county needs another shopping mall in an area described as "one of the last outposts of undisturbed nature in the state" (Martinez, 1982, p. 28).

Notice that a parenthetical note is placed outside quotation marks but before the period ending the sentence.

- **When a single source provides a series of references,** you need not repeat the name of the author until other sources interrupt the series. After the first reference, page numbers are sufficient until another citation intervenes. Even then, you need repeat only the author's last name, not a date, when the reference occurs within a single paragraph.

. . . The council vetoed zoning approval for a mall in an area described by Martinez (1982) as the last outpost of undisturbed nature in the state. The area provides a "unique environment for several endangered

(Continued)

49a
APA

Additional Guidelines for Preparing In-text Notes in APA Style   *(Continued)*

species of birds and plant life" (p. 31). The birds,
especially the endangered vireo, require breeding
spaces free from encroaching development (Harrison &
Cafiero, 1979). Rare plant life is similarly endangered
(Martinez).

▓ **2 (Step 2) On a separate page at the end of your paper,
list alphabetically every source cited in an in-text note.**
This alphabetical list of sources is titled "References." A References
page entry for an article on medical writing in the Renaissance by E.
Tebeaux would look like the following:

Tebeaux, E. (1991). Ramus, visual rhetoric, and the

emergence of page design in medical writing of

the English Renaissance. *Written Communication,*

8, 411-445.

A typical APA References entry includes the following basic information, with many variations.

• Author(s), last name first, followed by a period. Initials are
used instead of first and middle names.

• Date of work in parenthesis, followed by a period. For books
and journal articles, provide just the year of publication. For popular magazines and some Web sites and electronic sources, give
the year first, followed by the month (do not abbreviate it), and
the day if necessary: (2001, September 28).

• Title of the work, followed by a period. Capitalize only the
first word of the title, the first word of a subtitle (if any), and all
proper nouns or adjectives. Book titles are italicized, but titles of
articles are neither italicized nor placed between quotation marks.

• Publication information. This information varies according to
the source. For books, provide place of publication (followed by a
colon) and publisher (followed by a period). For articles, give the title of the journal and volume number (italicizing both items), followed by relevant page numbers and a period. For electronic sources,
provide the date of retrieval and a Web address (URL) or electronic
path. Do not add a period at the end of an entry that concludes with
a URL: Retrieved July 27, 2001, from http://www.drc.utexas.edu

49a
APA

The References page itself appears on its own page following the body of the essay (and an endnotes page if there is one). It lists bibliographical information on all the materials you used in composing an essay. See page 801 for a checklist on setting up a References page.

For more specific advice on writing a student paper, consult pages 321–26 of the APA manual (fifth edition). The APA Web site at <http://www.apa.org/> offers writers software that assists in creating APA style papers.

49b APA models

In this section you will find the APA References page and in-text note forms for a variety of sources. Locate the type of source you need to cite in either the Format Index or the Alphabetical Index and then locate the item by number in the list that follows.

APA Models Index

65. Book, one author
66. Book, two authors
67. Book, three or more authors
68. Book, revised
69. Book, edited
70. Book with no author
71. Book, a collection or anthology
72. Work within a collection, anthology, or reader
73. Chapter in a book
74. Book review
75. Article in a scholarly journal paginated by year or volume, not issue by issue
76. Article in a monthly periodical paginated issue by issue
77. Article in a weekly or biweekly periodical
78. Article in a newsletter
79. Article in a periodical—author not named
80. Newspaper article—author named
81. Newspaper article—author not named
82. Computer software
83. Online source/database
84. WWW page—generic
85. WWW page—online scholarly article
86. WWW page—online newspaper article
87. WWW page—online abstract
88. Email
89. Movie/videotape
90. Musical recording

APA Alphabetical Index

Abstract, online, 87
Anonymous work—book, 70; newspaper, 81; periodical, 79
Anthology, 71; work within an, 72
Article in a periodical, 76–77; anonymous, 79

Article in a newsletter, 78
Article in a newspaper, 80–81; online, 86
Article in a periodical, 76–77, 79; online, 84
Article in a scholarly journal, 75; online, 85
Article, online, 85
Audio recording, 89, 90
Biweekly periodical, 77
Book review, 74
Book with no author, 70
Book, chapter within, 73
Book, collection or anthology, 71
Book, edited, 69
Book, one author, 65
Book, revised, 68
Book, three or more authors, 67
Book, two authors, 66
Chapter in a book, 73
Charts, 89
Collection, 71; work within a, 72
Computer software, 82
Database, 83
Edited book, 69
Electronic correspondence, 88
Electronic sources, 83–88
Email, 88
Film, 89
Journal article, 75, 79; online, 85

Listserv, 83
Magazine, 76; biweekly, 77; monthly, 76; weekly, 77
Movie, 89
Multiple authors, book with, 66, 67
Musical recording, 90
Newsgroup, 83
Newsletter, 78
Newspaper article, author named, 80; author not named, 81
Online sources, 83–88
Periodical, 75, 79; online, 85
Program, computer, 82
Recording, musical, 90
Review of a book, 74
Revised book, 68
Scholarly journal, article in, 75, 79; online, 85
Slides, 89
Software, 82
Song, 90
Usenet newsgroup, 83
Videotape, 89
Weekly periodical, 77
Work within a collection, anthology, or reader, 72
WWW page, generic, 84; online abstract, 87; online journal, 85; online newspaper, 86

65. Book, One Author—APA Cite books by providing author, date, title of book, place of publication, and publisher.

IN-TEXT NOTES:

```
Pearson (1949) found . . .

(Pearson, 1949)

(Pearson, 1949, p. 49)
```

49b
APA

References

Pearson, G. (1949). *Emotional disorders of children.*

Annapolis, MD: Naval Institute Press.

66. **Book, Two Authors—APA** Notice the ampersand (&) between authors' names in the References list and in parenthetical notes. Note, however, that *and* is used when the authors are identified in the text itself.

IN-TEXT NOTES:

Lasswell and Kaplan (1950) found . . .

(Lasswell & Kaplan, 1950)

(Lasswell & Kaplan, 1950, pp. 210-213)

References

Lasswell, H. D., & Kaplan, A. (1950). *Power and*

society: A framework for political inquiry. New

York: Yale University Press.

67. **Book, Three or More Authors—APA**

IN-TEXT NOTES:

FIRST NOTE. Rosenberg, Gerver, and Howton (1971)
found . . .

SUBSEQUENT NOTES. Rosenberg et al. (1971) found . . .

FIRST NOTE. (Rosenberg, Gerver, & Howton, 1971)

SUBSEQUENT NOTES. (Rosenberg et al., 1971)

References

Rosenberg, B., Gerver, I., & Howton, F. W. (1971).

Mass society in crisis: Social problems and

social pathology (2nd ed.). New York: Macmillan.

If a work has six or more authors, use the first author's name followed by *et al.* for all in-text references, including the first. In the References list, however, identify all the authors.

49b
APA

68. Book, Revised—APA

IN-TEXT NOTES:

Edelmann (1969) found . . .

(Edelmann, 1969)

(Edelmann, 1969, p. 62)

References

Edelmann, A. T. (1969). *Latin American government*

and politics (Rev. ed.). Homewood, IL: Dorsey.

69. Book, Edited—APA Notice that APA uses an ampersand (&) to join the names of two editors or authors except when the names are mentioned in the body of a paper.

IN-TEXT NOTES:

Journet and Kling (1984) observe . . .

(Journet & Kling, 1984)

References

Journet, D., & Kling, J. (Eds.). (1984). *Readings*

for technical writers. Glenview, IL: Scott,

Foresman.

70. Book, No Author—APA

IN-TEXT NOTES:

In *Illustrated Atlas* (1985) . . .

(*Illustrated Atlas,* 1985, pp. 88-89)

References

Illustrated atlas of the world. (1985). Chicago:

Rand McNally.

When the author of a work is actually listed as "Anonymous," cite the work that way in the References list and parenthetical note.

49b
APA

(Anonymous, 1995)

71. Book, a Collection or Anthology—APA

IN-TEXT NOTES:

Feinstein (1967) found . . .

(Feinstein, 1967)

References

Feinstein, C. H. (Ed.). (1967). *Socialism,*

capitalism, and economic growth. Cambridge,

England: Cambridge University Press.

72. Work Within a Collection, Anthology, or Reader—APA List the item on the References page by the author of the piece you are actually citing, not the editor(s) of the collection. Then provide the title of the particular selection, its date, the editor(s) of the collection, the title of the collection, pages on which the selection appears, and publication information.

IN-TEXT NOTES:

Patel (1967) found . . .

(Patel, 1967)

References

Patel, S. (1967). World economy in transition (1850-

2060). In C. H. Feinstein (Ed.), *Socialism,*

capitalism, and economic growth (pp. 255-270).

Cambridge, England: Cambridge University Press.

73. Chapter in a Book—APA

IN-TEXT NOTES:

Clark (1969) observes . . .

(Clark, 1969)

References

Clark, K. (1969). Heroic materialism. In

Civilisation (pp. 321-347). New York:

HarperCollins.

49b
APA

74. **Book Review—APA** Brackets surround the description of the item reviewed.

IN-TEXT NOTES:

Max (1999) claims . . .

(Max, 1999)

References

Max, D. T. (1999, December 27). All the world's an

I.P.O.: Shakespeare the profiteer [Review of the

book *Shakespeare's 21st-century economics: The*

morality of love and money]. *The New York*

Observer, p. 35.

If a review is untitled, identify the author and date and describe the item in brackets.

IN-TEXT NOTES:

Farquhar (1987) observes . . .

(Farquhar, 1987)

References

Farquhar, J. (1987). [Review of the book *Medical*

power and social knowledge]. *American Journal*

of Psychology, 94, 256.

75. **Article in a Scholarly Journal—APA** Scholarly journals are usually identified by volume number or season (rather than day, week, or month of publication) and are paginated year by year, with a full year's work gathered and treated as a volume. Cite articles from such scholarly journals by providing author, date, title of article, journal, volume, and page numbers.

IN-TEXT NOTES:

Tebeaux (1991) observes . . .

(Tebeaux, 1991, p. 411)

References

Tebeaux, E. (1991). Ramus, visual rhetoric, and the

emergence of page design in medical writing of

49b
APA

the English Renaissance. *Written Communication,*

8, 411-445.

76. **Article in a Monthly Periodical—APA** To cite a magazine published monthly, give the author's name, date (including month, which is not abbreviated), title of the article, name of the magazine and volume number if available (italicized), and page numbers. In APA style, months are not abbreviated.

IN-TEXT NOTES:

Greenstein (2000) notes . . .

(Greenstein, 2000)

References

Greenstein, J. (2000, February). Snow job. *Brill's*

Content, 3, 70-77.

77. **Article in a Weekly or Biweekly Periodical—APA** To cite a weekly or biweekly periodical or magazine, give the author's name, date (including month and day), title of the article, name of the magazine, and volume number if available (italicized), and page numbers.

IN-TEXT NOTES:

Lasch-Quinn (2000) observes . . .

(Lasch-Quinn, 2000)

(Lasch-Quinn, 2000, p. 37)

References

Lasch-Quinn, E. (2000, March 6). Mothers and mar-

kets. *The New Republic, 222,* 37-44.

78. **Article in a Newsletter—APA** To cite a newsletter, give the author's name, date (months are not abbreviated), title of the article, name of the magazine and volume number if available (italicized), and page numbers. If no volume number is given, give as full a date as possible.

IN-TEXT NOTES:

Piedmont-Marton (1997) argues . . .

(Piedmont-Marton, 1997)

49b
APA

References

Piedmont-Marton, E. (1997, July 20). Schoolmarms or

    language paramedics? *The Writer's Block, 4,* 6.

79. Article in a Periodical, No Author Named—APA Quotation marks are used around shortened titles in the in-text notes.

IN-TEXT NOTES:

In "Aladdin releases" (1993) . . .

("Aladdin releases," 1993)

References

Aladdin releases desktop tools. (1993, October).

    Macworld, 10, 35.

80. Newspaper Article, Author Named—APA If the article does not appear on consecutive pages in the newspaper, give all the page numbers, separated by a comma. Note that abbreviations for *page* (*p.*) and *pages* (*pp.*) are used with newspaper entries.

IN-TEXT NOTES:

Bragg (1994) reports . . .

(Bragg, 1994, p. 7A)

References

Bragg, R. (1994, October 15). Weather gurus going

    high-tech. *San Antonio Express-News,* pp. 1A, 7A.

81. Newspaper Article, No Author Named—APA

IN-TEXT NOTES:

In the article "Scientists find" (1994) . . .

("Scientists find," 1994)

References

Scientists find new dinosaur species in Africa.

    (1994, October 14). *The Daily Texan,* p. 3.

49b
APA

82. Computer Software—APA Do not italicize the titles of software. List authors only when they own the product.

IN-TEXT NOTES:

In Adobe Pagemill (1995) . . .

References

Adobe Pagemill 1.0 [Computer software]. (1995).

Mountain View, CA: Adobe Systems.

83. **Online Source/Database, Archived Listserv, or Usenet Newsgroup—APA** For electronic sources such as listservs or newsgroups, provide the same information you would give for printed sources (author, date, title of article, publication information). Then, if helpful, identify the "medium" of the source in brackets, that is, the kind of material it is. Finally, furnish the date of access and a path statement to guide readers to the material.

IN-TEXT NOTES:

Dubrowski (1994) reports . . .

(Dubrowski, 1994)

References

Dubrowski, J. (1994, October 18). Mixed signals from

Washington leave automakers puzzled [Clarinet

news item]. Retrieved October 20, 1995, from

C-reuters@clarinet.com. Directory: biz/

industry/automotive

For databases, give the basic information followed by the date of retrieval of the material and the identity of the source followed in parentheses by the name of the database and, if an online source, the Web entry address for the source.

IN-TEXT NOTES:

Russell (2000) reports . . .

(Russell, 2000)

References

Russell, T. D. (2000). The shape of the Michigan

River as viewed from the land of Sweatt v.

Painter and Hopwood. *Law and Social Inquiry*,

25, 507-519. Retrieved April 15, 2001, from

49b
APA

```
INFOTRAC database (LegalTrac)

http://infotrac.galegroup.com
```

84. WWW Page—Generic—APA

IN-TEXT NOTES:

```
Johnson (1997) explains . . .

(Johnson, 1997)
```

References

```
Johnson, C. W., Jr. (1997, February 13). How our laws

    are made. Retrieved May 27, 1997, from

    http://thomas.loc.gov/home/lawsmade.toc.html
```

85. WWW Page—Online Scholarly Article—APA Because it is immediately obvious that the source is an article from a scholarly journal, no bracketed explanation of the medium is necessary.

IN-TEXT NOTES:

```
Fine and Kurdek (1993) report . . .

(Fine & Kurdek, 1993)
```

References

```
Fine, M. A., & Kurdek, L. A. (1993). Reflections on

    determining authorship credit and authorship

    order on faculty-student collaborations.

    American Psychologist, 48, 1141-1147. Retrieved

    July 17, 1997, from http://www.apa.org/journals/

    amp/kurdek.html
```

86. WWW Page—Online Newspaper Article—APA

IN-TEXT NOTES:

```
Cohen (1997) asks . . .

(Cohen, 1997)
```

References

```
Cohen, E. (1997, January 17). Shrinks aplenty online

    but are they credible? The New York Times

    [Newspaper, article in archives]. Retrieved May

    5, 1997, from http://search.nytimes.com/
```

87. WWW Page—Online Abstract—APA

IN-TEXT NOTES:

```
Shilkret and Nigrosh (1997) report . . .
(Shilkret & Nigrosh, 1997)
```

References

```
Shilkret, R., & Nigrosh, E. (1997). Assessing
    students' plans for college. Journal of
    Counseling Psychology, 44, 222-231. Abstract
    retrieved July 1, 1997, from http//www.apa.org/
    journals/cou/497ab.html#10
```

88. Email—APA Electronic communications not stored or archived have limited use for researchers. APA style treats such information (as well as email) like personal communication. Because personal communications are not available to other researchers, make no mention of them in the References list. Personal communications should, however, be acknowledged in the body of the essay in parenthetical notes.

IN-TEXT NOTES:

```
According to Rice (personal communication, October
14, 1994) . . .
```

89. Movie/Videotape/DVD—APA This is the basic form for films, DVDs, audiotapes, slides, charts, and other nonprint sources. The specific medium is described between brackets, as shown here for a film. In most cases, APA references are listed by identifying the screenwriter.

IN-TEXT NOTES:

```
McCanlies (1998) features . . .
(McCanlies, 1998)
```

References

```
McCanlies, T. (Screenwriter). (1998). Dancer, Texas
    [Film]. Culver City, CA: TriStar.
```

49b
APA

90. **Musical Recording—APA** Ordinarily, music is listed by the composer.

IN-TEXT NOTES:

```
In the song "What Was It You Wanted?" (Dylan, 1989,
track 10) . . .
```

References

```
Dylan, B. (1989). What was it you wanted? [Recorded
    by Willie Nelson]. On Across the borderline
    [CD]. New York: Columbia.
```

49c Sample APA paper

In the social sciences, articles published in professional journals often follow a form designed to connect new findings to previous research. Your instructor will usually indicate whether you should follow this structure for your paper or report.

The sample APA paper that follows is not a formal social science research report. It does, however, include an abstract, and its headings conform to APA form. The paper by Gerald J. Reuter, an undergraduate at the University of Texas at Austin, has been revised, substantially updated, and expanded to enhance its usefulness as a model, especially in the area of online sources. The paper was written for a course taught by the late James Kinneavy.

The sample paper is accompanied by checklists designed to help you set up a paper correctly in APA style. When your work meets the specifications on the checklists, it should be in proper form.

- DIRECT READERS AS CLOSE AS POSSIBLE TO THE SOURCE
- PROVIDE ADDRESS

ELECTRONIC

HTML   PDF

Checklist 49.1

The Components of a Social Science Report

- **An abstract.** A concise summary of the research article.

- **A review of literature.** A survey of published research that has a bearing on the hypothesis advanced in the research report. The review establishes the context for the research essay.

- **A hypothesis.** An introduction to the paper that identifies the assumption to be tested and provides a rationale for studying it.

- **An explanation of method.** A detailed description of the procedures used in the research. Since the validity of the research depends on how the data were gathered, this is a critical section for readers assessing the report.

- **Results.** A section reporting the data, often given through figures, charts, graphs, and so on. The reliability of the data is explained here, but little comment is made on the implications.

- **Discussion/conclusions.** A section in which the research results are interpreted and analyzed.

- **References.** An alphabetical list of research materials and articles cited in the report.

- **Appendixes.** A section of materials germane to the report, but too lengthy to include in the body of the paper.

E-Tips   For additional examples of research articles in APA style, check out *Psych-E* at <http://www.siu.edu/departments/cola/psycho/journal/>. Published at Southern Illinois University, *Psych-E* is an electronic journal that features papers by undergraduates.

49c
APA

The Genome Project: Opportunities and Ethics

Gerald J. Reuter

The University of Texas at Austin

Checklist 49.2

Title Page for a Paper—APA

APA style requires a separate title page; use the facing page as a model and review the following checklist.

- Type your paper on white bond paper. Preferred typefaces (when you have a choice) include Times Roman, American Typewriter, and Courier.

- Arrange and center the title of your paper, your name, and your school.

- Use the correct form for the title, capitalizing all important words and all words of four letters or more. Articles, conjunctions, and prepositions are not capitalized unless they are four letters or more. Do not underline the title or use all capitals. Do not boldface the title.

- Give your first name, middle initial, and last name.

- Number the title page and all subsequent pages in the upper right-hand corner. Place a short title for the paper on the same line as the page number as shown; the short title consists of the first two or three words of the title.

Abstract

Begun in 1988, the human genome project intends to map the 23 chromosomes that provide the blueprint for the human species. The project has both scientific and ethical goals. The scientific goals underscore the advantages of the genome project, including identifying and curing diseases and enabling people to select the traits of their offspring, among other opportunities. Ethically, however, the project raises serious questions about the morality of genetic engineering. To handle both the medical opportunities and ethical dilemmas posed by the genome project, scientists need to develop a clear set of principles for genetic engineering and to continue educating the public about the genome project.

49c
APA

Checklist 49.3

Abstract for a Paper—APA

Abstracts are common in papers using APA style. (If your instructor does not require an abstract, go on to p. 794.)

• Place the abstract on a separate page, after the title page.

• Center the word *Abstract* at the top of the page.

• Include the short title of the essay and the page number (2) in the upper right-hand corner.

• Double-space the abstract.

• Do not indent the first line of the abstract. Type it in block form.

Strict APA form limits abstracts to 960 characters or fewer.

49c
APA

The Genome Project: Opportunities and Ethics

¶1   If you had the opportunity to rid humanity of the
approximately 4,000 genetic diseases, would you do so?
What if doing so also meant that millions of people might
be deprived of health insurance coverage and that children
who didn't meet the physical ideals of a society might not
be conceived? These are the opportunities and the dangers
we face as a result of the ongoing human genome project.
Although the scientific information provided by the project
should prove of near incalculable benefit to humankind,
some of its consequences may prove disastrous. The project
is already having a major impact on medicine, culture, and
society's thinking about genetics and human life. It is
growing increasingly evident that scientists need to
educate the public better about the genome project to
address the pressing ethical issues it raises.

Goal of the Human Genome Project

¶2   The human genome project began in 1988 when the
Congress of the United States allocated approximately $3
billion to support a 15-year multi-university endeavor
to complete the mapping of the human genome (Caskey,
1994). The project marked a milestone on June 26, 2000,
when President Bill Clinton and Prime Minister Tony
Blair jointly announced the completion of the initial
sequencing of the human genome. According to Clinton,
scientists had created "the most important, most
wondrous map ever produced by humankind" (White House,
2000). A human genome is the DNA that in sequence
determines the makeup of a human being, both what it
looks like and how it works ("Human Genome," 2000). The
human genome is a set of 23 chromosomes and 60,000 to
80,000 genes that provide the blueprint for our bodies.
Chromosomes contain DNA made up of four different
nucleotides or bases--adenine, guanine, thymine, and

49c
APA

Checklist 49.4

The Body of a Research Paper—APA

The body of the APA paper runs uninterrupted until the separate References page. Be sure to type the essay on good-quality bond paper. The first page of an APA paper will look like the facing page.

• Repeat the title of your paper, exactly as it appears on the title page, on the first page of the research essay itself.

• Be sure the title is centered and properly capitalized.

• Begin the body of the essay two lines (a double space) below the title.

• Double-space the body of the essay.

• Center first-level heads; do not underline them.

• Use at least one-inch margins at the sides, top, and bottom of this and all subsequent pages.

• Indent the first line of each paragraph five to seven spaces.

• Indent long quotations (more than forty words) in a block five to seven spaces from the left margin. In student papers, APA permits long quotations to be single spaced.

• Include the short title of the essay and the page number (3) in the upper right-hand corner. Number all subsequent pages the same way.

• Do not hyphenate words at the right-hand margin. Do not justify the right-hand margin.

• Label figures and tables correctly. Be sure to mention them in the body of your text: (see Figure 1).

• Provide copyright/permission data for figures or tables borrowed from other sources.

49c
APA

Genome Project   5

Figure 1. The four bases of the genetic code: adenine
(A), guanine (G), thymine (T), and cytosine (C). *Note.*
From *Your Genes, Your Choice*, by C. Baker, 1997.
Copyright 1997 by the American Association for the
Advancement of Science. Reprinted with permission.

cytosine--which, working together, provide the code for
different genes (see Figure 1). The genes in chromosomes
are arranged in a complex sequence. Mapping these
sequences is a highly technical, time-consuming process.
¶3   From the beginning of the project scientists
recognized that their research on the human genome would
have implications far beyond their laboratories.
Consequently, between 3% and 5% of research expenditures
were dedicated to exploring bioethical issues raised by
the project, making it "the world's largest bioethics
program" ("Ethical, Legal," 2000). By this commitment,
scientists hoped to anticipate some of the key societal
issues in gene research, to address the implications of
the research, and in particular to understand how the new
genetic information might bear on philosophical, ethical,
and theological perspectives ("New Goals," 1998). Early
in the project, Swinbanks (1992) observed, however, that
since many scientists believe that they lack expertise in
discussing ethical and political issues, they generally
avoid them. So while the genome project identifies specific

49c
APA

ethical goals, the scientists involved have sometimes
avoided this dimension of their work.

Advantages of the Genome Project

¶4   Human genome project researchers believe that
mapping the full set of human chromosomes will benefit
society in many ways. Magnus (1996) argues that gene
therapy--curing diseases by manipulating the genetic
code--is likely to revolutionize medicine as much as
antibiotics and vaccinations once did. Matsubara (1993)
anticipates important advances in the treatment of
cancer, circulatory diseases, and even mental conditions,
as well as improvements in testing for diseases and the
development of drugs to combat them. Conversely, Baker
(1997) notes that people may be able to select the
specific physical traits and qualities they prefer, from
youthful looks and a thick head of hair to greater height
or intelligence. It may even be possible to modify DNA in
ways that give human beings new and useful traits.

Ethical Dilemmas of the Genome Project

¶5   Any research effort with the scientific potential
of the genome project will likely raise serious ethical
questions about how and by whom the new knowledge it
creates will be used. Zylke (1992), noting that the
genome project is far from the first attempt to modify and
"improve" the hereditary qualities of human beings,
associates the effort with similar attempts in Nazi
Germany to create a superior race. Even in the United
States, Zylke argues, sterilization of the mentally
retarded was common throughout the nineteenth century and
not ruled unconstitutional until years later.

¶6   Families at risk for hereditary conditions such as
sickle cell disease and cystic fibrosis already fear that
improved genetic screening may lead to discrimination
against them in employment and the loss of health-care

49c
APA

benefits. Insurance companies might deny coverage to individuals with a genetic code that makes them susceptible to an expensive condition. Davis (1990) believes that the genome project might also lead to soaring insurance rates and perhaps to the collapse of the entire medical insurance industry.

¶7   Parents may also be tempted to terminate a pregnancy when an unborn child does not possess desirable genetic traits, some of them completely unrelated to concerns for health or well-being. Baker (1997) notes that some governments already have programs that support births among some groups of people and not among others. Similar processes of selection may occur in the future for children with the "wrong" eye color or body type after parents consult with doctors furnished with the complete map of human chromosomes the human genome project will provide. They may be reluctant to accept a child with markers for any diseases at all, thus demanding an unrealistic perfection in their offspring. Furthermore, attempts to control genetic manipulation through legislation may prove futile; Gardner (1995) argues that limits on genetic improvements would quickly collapse once the ban was violated initially.

Living with the Genome Project

¶8   Anticipating such ethical dilemmas, the National Center for Human Genome Research and the National Institutes of Health have included an Ethical, Legal, and Social Implications program (ELSI) in the funding of the genome project. The ELSI program is intended both to anticipate and prevent any ethical problems that might develop as a result of the genome mapping (Davis, 1990).

¶9   However, potential advances in genetic research have led other scientists to consider the implications of restructuring the very design of human beings.

Independent of the ELSI program, Suzuki and Knudtson
(1989) offered a set of principles more than a decade ago
for all geneticists to consider. First, geneticists must
understand the nature of genes--their origin, their role
in the hereditary processes of cells, the possibilities
of controlling them--to grasp the difficult issues arising
from modern genetics. Second, geneticists must appreciate
that it is dangerous to proclaim simple causal
relationships between so-called defects in human DNA and
human behaviors since human hereditary differences
involve the interplay of many genes. Third, information
about an individual's genetic constitution ought to guide
personal decisions rather than determine them. Fourth,
while genetic manipulation of some human cells may lie in
the realm of personal choice, tinkering with human germ
cells does not. Germ cell therapy ought to be explicitly
forbidden without the consent of all members of society.
Finally, the accumulation of genetic knowledge alone,
however precious it may be, does not guarantee the wisdom
to justify decisions about heredity. If such knowledge
breeds a false sense of mastery over genes, it can lead
to folly. Principles such as these and others articulated
by the ELSI project may move scientists to think more
deeply about ethical questions than they are accustomed
to as the genome project develops.

¶10   But as the furor over the cloning of a mammal in
1997 demonstrated, scientists need to press forward with a
final responsibility: the obligation to educate the press
and public about their work. Clearly, education about
human genetics--both its potential and its limitations--
should begin as early as elementary school since an
informed citizenry will ultimately have to make important
decisions in the future. They should make decisions about
their chromosomes without fear or ignorance.

49c
APA

References

Baker, C. (1997). *Your genes, your choices*. American
    Association for the Advancement of Science [Book on
    line]. Retrieved July 16, 2000, from
    http://www.nextwave.org/ehr/books/index.html

Caskey, T. C. (1994). Human genes: The map takes shape.
    Patient Care, 28, 28-32.

Davis, J. (1990). *Mapping the code: The Human Genome
    Project and the choices of modern science.* New York:
    Wiley.

Ethical, legal, and social issues. (2000, July). *Human
    Genome Project information.* Retrieved July 29, 2000,
    from http://www.ornl.gov/hgmis/elsi/elsi.html

Gardner, W. (1995). Can human genetic enhancement be
    prohibited? *Journal of Medicine and Philosophy, 20,*
    65-84. Abstract retrieved July 29, 2000, from
    http://www.med.upenn.edu/~bioethic/genetics/articles/
    2.gardner.can.human.html

Human genome project frequently asked questions. (2000,
    July). *Human Genome Project information.* Retrieved
    July 5, 2000, from http://www.ornl.gov/hgmis/faq/
    faqs1.html

Magnus, D. (1996). Gene therapy and the concept of
    genetic disease. *Ethics and genetics: A global
    conversation.* Retrieved June 28, 2000, from
    http://www.med.upenn.edu/~bioethic/genetics/
    articles/12.gen.disease.html

Matsubara, K. (1993). Background of human genome
    analysis. *The human genome: Toward understanding
    ourselves.* Retrieved July 29, 2000, from
    http://www.genome.ad.jp/brochure/english/
    Background.html#part4

Checklist 49.5

References Page—APA

Sources contributing directly to the paper are listed alphabetically on a separate sheet immediately after the body of the essay. For more information about the purpose and form of this list, see pages 776–77.

* Center the title (References) at the top of the page.

* All sources mentioned in the text of the paper must appear in the References list, except personal communications; similarly, every source listed in the References list must be mentioned in the paper.

* Arrange the items in the References list alphabetically by the last name of the author. Give initials only for first names. If no author is named for a work, list and alphabetize it by the first word in the title, excluding articles (*A, An, The*).

* The first line of each entry is flush with the left-hand margin. Subsequent lines in an entry are indented five spaces.

* The list is ordinarily double spaced. In student papers, APA style does permit single spacing of individual entries; double spacing is preserved between the single-spaced items.

* Punctuate items in the list carefully. Do not forget the period at the end of each entry, except those that terminate with an electronic address.

* In the References list, capitalize only the first word and any proper names in the title of a book or article. Within a title, capitalize the first word after a colon.

* When you have two or more entries by the same author, list them by year of publication, from earliest to latest. If an author publishes two works in the same year, list them alphabetically by title.

49c
APA

Genome Project   11

New goals for the U.S. Human Genome Project: 1998-2003.

   (1998). *Science, 282,* 682-689.

Suzuki, D., & Knudtson, P. (1989). *Genethics: The clash*

   between the new genetics and human values.

   Cambridge, MA: Harvard University Press.

Swinbanks, D. (1992). When silence isn't golden. *Nature,*

   368, 368-370.

The White House. (2000). Text of remarks on the

   completion of the first survey of the entire Human

   Genome Project. *The White House Office of the Press*

   Secretary. Retrieved July 29, 2000, from

   http://www.whitehouse.gov/WH/New/html/

   genome-20000626.html

Zylke, J. (1992). Examining life's code means

   re-examining society's long-held codes. *Journal of*

   the American Medical Association, 267, 1715-1716.

CHAPTER 50

How Do You Use CMS Documentation?

Writers who prefer full footnotes or endnotes rather than in-text notes often use the "humanities style" of documentation recommended in *The Chicago Manual of Style,* fourteenth edition (1993). Basic procedures for this CMS documentary-note system are spelled out in the following sections. If you encounter documentation problems not discussed below or prefer the author-date style of CMS documentation, refer to the full manual or to *A Manual for Writers of Term Papers, Theses, and Dissertations,* sixth edition (1996).

Because notes in CMS humanities style include full publishing information, separate bibliographies are optional in CMS-style papers. However, both notes and bibliographies are covered below, in separate sections.

 E-Tips Do you have specific questions about Chicago style or more general queries about editing? Check out the lively FAQ page supported by the manuscript editing department at the University of Chicago Press. It is at <http://www.press.uchicago.edu/Misc/Chicago/cmosfaq.html>.

50a CMS notes

1 In the text of your paper, place a raised number after any sentence or clause you need to document. These note numbers follow any punctuation mark except dashes, and they run consecutively throughout a paper. A direct quotation from Brian Urquhart's *Ralph Bunche: An American Life* is followed here by a raised note number.

Ralph Bunche never wavered in his belief that the
races in America had to learn to live together: "In

```
all of his experience of racial discrimination Bunche
never allowed himself to become bitter or to feel
racial hatred."¹
```

The number is keyed to the first note (see Section 50a-2). To create such a raised, or "superscript," number, select "superscript" from your word-processing font options or, on a typewriter, roll the carriage down slightly and type the figure.

▉ 2 Link every note number to a footnote or endnote.

The basic CMS note itself consists of a note number, the author's name (in normal order), the title of the work, full publication information within parentheses, and appropriate page numbers. The first line of the note is indented like a paragraph.

```
    1. Brian Urquhart, Ralph Bunche: An American
Life (New York: Norton, 1993), 435.
```

To document particular types of sources, including books, articles, magazines, and electronic sources, see the CMS models in Section 50c.

CMS style allows you to choose whether to place your notes at the bottom of each page (footnotes) or in a single list titled "Notes" at the end of your paper (endnotes). Endnotes are more common now than footnotes and easier to manage—though some word processors can arrange footnotes at the bottom of pages automatically. Individual footnotes are single spaced, with double spaces between them.

Chart 50.1

Additional Guidelines for Preparing Notes and Works Cited Entries in CMS Style

• **When two or more sources are cited within a single sentence**, the note numbers appear right after the statements they support.

```
While some in the humanities fear that electronic
technologies may make the "notion of wisdom" obsolete,²
others suggest that technology must be the subject of
serious study even in elementary and secondary school.³
```

The notes for this sentence would appear as follows.

```
    2. Sven Birkerts, The Gutenberg Elegies: The
Fate of Reading in an Electronic Age (Boston: Faber and
Faber, 1994), 139.

    3. Neil Postman, "The Word Weavers/The World
Makers," in The End of Education: Redefining the Value
of School (New York: Alfred A. Knopf, 1995), 172-93.
```

50a
CMS

Observe that note 2 documents a particular quotation while note 3 refers to a full book chapter.

• **When you cite a work several times in a paper,** the first note gives full information about author(s), title, and publication.

> 1. Helen Wilkinson, "It's Just a Matter of Time," *Utne Reader* (May/June 1995): 66-67.

Then, in shorter papers, any subsequent citations require only the last name of the author(s) and page number(s).

> 3. Wilkinson, 66.

In longer papers, the entry may also include a shortened title to make references from page to page clearer.

> 3. Wilkinson, "Matter of Time," 66.

If you cite the same work again immediately after a full note, you may use the Latin abbreviation *Ibid.* (meaning "in the same place"), followed by the page number(s) of the citation.

> 4. James Morgan, "Blue Highways," in *The Distance to the Moon* (New York: Riverhead, 1999), 93.
>
> 5. Ibid., 89.

To avoid using *Ibid.* when documenting the same source in succession, simply use a page reference—for example, (*89*)—within the text itself. When successive citations are to exactly the same page, *Ibid.* alone can be used.

> 4. James Morgan, "Blue Highways," in *The Distance to the Moon* (New York: Riverhead, 1999), 93.
>
> 5. Ibid.

Here's how a set of notes using several different sources and subsequent short references might look.

> Notes
>
> 1. Helen Wilkinson, "It's Just a Matter of Time," *Utne Reader* (May/June 1995): 66-67.
>
> 2. Paul Osterman, "Getting Started," *Wilson Quarterly* 18 (autumn 1994): 46-55.
>
> 3. James Morgan, "Blue Highways," in *The Distance to the Moon* (New York: Riverhead, 1999), 87-101.
>
> 4. Ibid., 97.
>
> 5. Wilkinson, 66.
>
> 6. Ibid.
>
> 7. Ibid., 67.
>
> 8. Osterman, 48-49.
>
> 9. Morgan, 96.

Notice that note 4 refers to the Morgan chapter and notes 6 and 7 refer to Wilkinson's article.

50a
CMS

50b CMS bibliographies

At the end of your paper, list alphabetically every source cited or used in the paper. This list is usually titled "Works Cited" when it includes only works actually mentioned in the essay; it is titled "Bibliography" if it also includes works consulted in preparing the paper but not actually cited. Because CMS notes are quite thorough, a Works Cited or Bibliography page may be optional, depending on the assignment: check with your instructor or editor about including such a page. Individual items on a Works Cited or Bibliography page are single spaced, with a double space between each item (see sample CMS paper, p. 812).

When an author has more than one work on the list, those works are listed alphabetically under the author's name using this form.

```
Altick, Richard D. The Shows of London. Cambridge:
     Belknap-Harvard University Press, 1978.

---. Victorian People and Ideas. New York: Norton,
     1973.

---. Victorian Studies in Scarlet. New York: Norton,
     1977.
```

For the correct format for books, articles, newspapers, and other sources, including electronic items, check the CMS Models below.

50c CMS models

In this section you will find the CMS notes and bibliography forms for more than twenty types of sources. The numbered items in the list are the sample note forms, often showing specific page numbers as would be the case when you were preparing actual notes; the matching bibliography entries appear immediately after.

CMS Models Index

91. Book, one author
92. Book, two or three authors or editors
93. Book, four or more authors or editors
94. Book, edited—focus on the editor
95. Book, edited—focus on the original author
96. Book written by a group
97. Book with no author

98. Work of more than one volume
99. Work in a series
100. Chapter in a book
101. Article in a scholarly journal
102. Article in a popular magazine
103. Article or selection from a reader or anthology
104. Article in a newspaper
105. Encyclopedia
106. Biblical citation
107. Computer software
108. Electronic sources
109. WWW—book online
110. WWW—article online
111. Email

91. **Book, One Author—CMS** Provide author(s), title of the work (underlined or italicized), place of publication, publisher, and date of publication.

> 1. Steven Weinberg, *Dreams of a Final Theory* (New York: Pantheon Books, 1992), 38.
>
> Weinberg, Steven. *Dreams of a Final Theory*. New York: Pantheon Books, 1992.

92. **Book, Two or Three Authors or Editors—CMS**

> 2. Peter Collier and David Horowitz, *Destructive Generation: Second Thoughts about the '60s* (New York: Summit, 1989), 24.
>
> Collier, Peter, and David Horowitz. *Destructive Generation: Second Thoughts about the '60s*. New York: Summit, 1989.

93. **Book, Four or More Authors or Editors—CMS** Use *et al.* or *and others* after naming the first author in the notes, but list all authors in the bibliography when that is convenient.

> 3. Philip Curtin and others, eds., *African History* (Boston: Little, Brown, 1978), 77.
>
> Curtin, Philip, Steve Feierman, Leonard Thompson, and Jan Vansina, eds. *African History*. Boston: Little, Brown, 1978.

94. **Book, Edited—Focus on the Editor—CMS** If you cite an edited work by the editor's name, identify the original author after the title of the work.

50c
CMS

    4. Scott Elledge, ed., *Paradise Lost*, by John Milton (New York: Norton, 1975).

Elledge, Scott, ed. *Paradise Lost*, by John Milton. New York: Norton, 1975.

95. Book, Edited—Focus on the Original Author—CMS

    5. William Shakespeare, *The Complete Works of Shakespeare*, 4th ed., ed. David Bevington (New York: Longman, 1997).

Shakespeare, William. *The Complete Works of Shakespeare*. 4th ed. Edited by David Bevington. New York: Longman, 1997.

96. Book Written by a Group—CMS

    6. Council of Biology Editors, *Scientific Style and Format: The CBE Manual for Authors, Editors, and Publishers*, 6th ed. (Cambridge: Cambridge University Press, 1994).

Council of Biology Editors. *Scientific Style and Format: The CBE Manual for Authors, Editors, and Publishers*. 6th ed. Cambridge: Cambridge University Press, 1994.

97. Book with No Author—CMS List it by its title, alphabetized by the first major word (excluding *The*, *A*, or *An*).

    7. *Webster's Collegiate Thesaurus* (Springfield: Merriam, 1976).

Webster's Collegiate Thesaurus. Springfield: Merriam, 1976.

98. Work of More Than One Volume—CMS

    8. Karlheinz Spindler, *Abstract Algebra with Applications* (New York: Dekker, 1994), 1:17-18.

Spindler, Karlheinz. *Abstract Algebra with Applications*. Vol. 1. New York: Dekker, 1994.

99. Work in a Series—CMS Do not underline or italicize a series name.

    9. Grayson Kirk and Nils H. Wessell, eds., *The Soviet Threat: Myths and Realities*, Proceedings of the Academy of Political Science, no. 33 (New York: Academy of Political Science, 1978), 62.

Kirk, Grayson, and Nils H. Wessell, eds. *The Soviet Threat: Myths and Realities*. Proceedings of the Academy of Political Science, no. 33. New York: Academy of Political Science, 1978.

50c
CMS

100. Chapter in a Book—CMS

> 10. Delia Owens and Mark Owens, "Home to the Dunes," in *The Eye of the Elephant: An Epic Adventure in the African Wilderness* (Boston: Houghton Mifflin, 1992), 11-27.

> Owens, Delia, and Mark Owens. "Home to the Dunes." In *The Eye of the Elephant: An Epic Adventure in the African Wilderness*. Boston: Houghton Mifflin, 1992.

101. Article in a Scholarly Journal—CMS

Scholarly journals are usually identified by volume number or season (rather than day, week, or month of publication). Such journals are usually paginated year by year, with a year's work treated as a volume. Provide author(s), title of the work (between quotation marks), name of periodical (underlined or italicized), volume number, date of publication, and page numbers.

> 11. Karl P. Wentersdorf, "Hamlet's Encounter with the Pirates," *Shakespeare Quarterly* 34 (1983): 434-40.

> Wentersdorf, Karl P. "Hamlet's Encounter with the Pirates." *Shakespeare Quarterly* 34 (1983): 434-40.

102. Article in a Popular Magazine—CMS

Magazines are paginated issue by issue and identified by monthly or weekly dates of publication (instead of by volume number). When an article does not appear on consecutive pages (as in the example below), omit page numbers in the bibliography entry. Provide author(s), title of the work (between quotation marks), name of magazine (underlined or italicized), date of publication, and page numbers.

> 12. Don Graham, "Wayne's World," *Texas Monthly*, March 2000, 110-11.

> Graham, Don. "Wayne's World." *Texas Monthly*, March 2000.

103. Article or Selection from a Reader or Anthology—CMS

> 13. Pamela Samuelson, "The Digital Rights War," in *The Presence of Others*, 3d ed., ed. Andrea Lunsford and John Ruszkiewicz (New York: St. Martin's Press, 2000), 315-20.

> Samuelson, Pamela. "The Digital Rights War." In *The Presence of Others*. 3d ed. Edited by Andrea Lunsford and John Ruszkiewicz. New York: St. Martin's Press, 2000, 315-20.

50c
CMS

104. **Article in a Newspaper—CMS** Identify the edition of the paper cited (*final edition, home edition, Western edition*), except when citing editorials or features that appear in all editions. Since an individual story may move in location from edition to edition, page numbers are not ordinarily provided. Section numbers are given for papers so divided. Individual news stories are usually not listed in a bibliography.

> 14. Celestine Bohlen, "A Stunned Venice Surveys the Ruins of a Beloved Hall," *New York Times*, 31 January 1995, national edition, sec. B.

105. **Encyclopedia—CMS** When a reference work is familiar (encyclopedias, dictionaries, thesauruses), omit the names of authors and editors and most publishing information. No page number is given when a work is arranged alphabetically; instead the item referenced is named, following the abbreviation *s.v.* (*sub verbo*, meaning "under the word"). Familiar reference works are not listed in the bibliography.

> 15. *The Oxford Companion to English Literature*, 4th ed., s.v. "Locke, John."

106. **Biblical Citation—CMS** Biblical citations appear in notes but not in the bibliography. If important, you may mention the version of the Bible cited.

> 16. John 18.37-38 Jerusalem Bible.

107. **Computer Software—CMS**

> 17. FoxPro Ver. 2.5, Microsoft, Seattle, Wash.

FoxPro Ver. 2.5. Microsoft, Seattle, Wash.

108. **Electronic Sources—CMS** The standards for electronic documentation are in flux. CMS follows the style recommended by the International Standards Organization (ISO). But many issues remain unresolved as new sources and formats evolve. In *The Chicago Manual of Style*, fourteenth edition, the examples of notes for electronic sources generally include three features: a description of the computer source in brackets, such as [*electronic bulletin board*] or [*Web site*]; the date the material was accessed, updated, or cited [*cited 28 May 1996*]; and an electronic address, following the words *available from*. Models 108 through 111 below follow these recommendations as modified in Kate L. Turabian's *A Manual*

for Writers of Term Papers, Theses, and Dissertations, sixth edition (1996). The resulting citations are quite complex. Some simplification may be in order, or you may wish to consult the chapter on Columbia style for online sources (see pp. 826–55).

18. Sylvia Atore Alva, "Differential Patterns of Achievement Among Asian-American Adolescents," *Journal of Youth and Adolescence* 22 (1993): 407-23, *ProQuest General Periodicals* [CD-ROM], UMI-ProQuest, June 1994.

Alva, Sylvia Atore. "Differential Patterns of Achievement Among Asian-American Adolescents." *Journal of Youth and Adolescence* 22 (1993): 407-23. *ProQuest General Periodicals.* CD-ROM UMI-ProQuest, June 1994.

109. WWW—Book Online—CMS

19. Amelia E. Barr, *Remember the Alamo* [book online] (New York: Dodd, Mead, 1888); available from http://etext.lib.virginia.edu/cgibin/browse-mixed?id=BarReme&tag=public&images=images/modeng&data=/lv1/Archive/eng-parsed; Internet; cited 12 May 1997.

Barr, Amelia E. *Remember the Alamo.* Book online. New York: Dodd, Mead, 1888. Available from http://etext.lib.virginia.edu/cgibin/browse-mixed?id=BarReme&tag=public&images=images/modeng&data=/lv1/Archive/eng-parsed; Internet; cited 12 May 1997.

110. WWW—Article Online—CMS

20. Paul Skowronek, "Left and Right for Rights," *Trincoll Journal,* 13 March 1997 [journal online]; available from http://www.trincoll.edu/~tj/tj03.13.97/articles/comm2.html; Internet; accessed 23 July 1997.

Skowronek, Paul. "Left and Right for Rights." *Trincoll Journal,* 13 March 1997. Journal online. Available from http://www.trincoll.edu/~tj/tj03.13.97/articles/comm2.html; Internet; accessed 23 July 1997.

111. Email—CMS

21. Robert D. Royer, "Re: Are We in a State of NOMAIL?" Email to author, 22 July 1997.

Royer, Robert D. "Re: Are We in a State of NOMAIL?" Email to author, 22 July 1997.

50c
CMS

50d Sample CMS paper

The sample CMS paper was written in spring 1996 by Jeremy A. Corley, a student in Joi Chevalier's course "The Rhetoric of Epic Narratives." The paper provides an example of the sort of literary analysis that might be done for a classics or English course. The paper has been lightly edited for style and revised to incorporate CMS-style endnotes and a Works Cited page.

The sample paper demonstrates how to use both endnotes and a Works Cited page. However, the Works Cited page is optional in CMS style because the endnotes themselves include full bibliographical information. Following the sample paper, we provide a single page reformatted to demonstrate the use of CMS-style footnotes. If you choose to use footnotes, do not also include endnotes. You may, however, present a Works Cited or Bibliography page. (A Works Cited page lists only those works mentioned in the paper itself; a Bibliography page includes all the works cited in the paper as well as sources you consulted but did not mention in the paper.)

The sample paper shows all titles italicized. You may either italicize or underline titles in CMS style, but be consistent. Do not mix italicized and underlined titles within the same paper. In numbering the pages of CMS papers, count the title page as part of the front matter, but do not actually number it. Any front matter, such as a preface or table of contents, is numbered in lowercase roman numerals centered at the bottom of the page (i, ii, iii, iv, v . . .). The first regular page of the text is numbered in the upper righthand corner using arabic numerals beginning with 1. Note that footnotes are single spaced. Any indented quotations are also single spaced. (For more on presenting student papers in CMS style, see Kate L. Turabian, *A Manual for Writers of Term Papers, Theses, and Dissertations,* sixth edition, 1996.)

[New Page]

THE UNIVERSITY OF TEXAS AT AUSTIN

DIOMEDES AS HERO OF *THE ILIAD*

E 309K--TOPICS IN WRITING

DIVISION OF RHETORIC AND COMPOSITION

BY

JEREMY A. CORLEY

28 FEBRUARY 1996

[New Page]

DIOMEDES AS HERO OF *THE ILIAD*

¶1   Achilles is the central character of *The Iliad*,
but is his prominence alone enough to make him the
story's hero? There are many examples that would say
otherwise. One of the most interesting aspects of the
epic is its use of a lesser character, rather than the
technical protagonist, as the tale's benchmark for
heroism. This lesser character is Diomedes, and his
leadership skills and maturity prove to be far superior
to those of Achilles. Book V of *The Iliad* is devoted
almost entirely to Diomedes' feats, and there are many
scenes in which he is presented as a leader and hero
throughout the rest of the text. While Diomedes is
singled out for his gallantry, Achilles is, by contrast,
noted for his immaturity and selfishness. Homer depicts
Diomedes in a much more positive light than Achilles,
despite the latter's obvious natural superiority as a
soldier. It seems evident that Homer is emphasizing the
total use of one's abilities, rather than just the

50d
CMS

presence of those abilities, as the basis of heroism. Diomedes, therefore, is the actual hero of *The Iliad*.

¶2   Achilles is immediately placed at the focal point of the story, and his pride and immaturity surface almost instantaneously. In Book I, Agamemnon embarrasses Achilles publicly with an outward display of his power as the Achaians' commander: "Since Apollo robs me of Chryseis . . . I will take your beautiful Briseis . . . to show you how much stronger I am than you are."[1] Achilles can hardly be faulted for taking offense at this incident, as it "threatened to invalidate . . . the whole meaning of his life."[2] Achilles' refusal to fight afterward must be looked at from more than one perspective. This is the first example of Achilles' acting according to his pride, as proven by his regard for himself as "the best man of all."[3] While it is understandable for a soldier such as Achilles, who "towers above all the other characters of *The Iliad*," to be hesitant to fight for and under the man who embarrassed him, Agamemnon, it is also folly for a soldier to stop fighting because of anything as relatively unimportant as an insult, even a public one.[4] A soldier's duty is to defend his homeland and fight in its wars, and Achilles misses this greater duty for his own selfishness. This refusal to fight is compounded by his request to his mother, Thetis, to "see if he [Zeus] will help the Trojans and drive the Achaians back to their ships with slaughter!"[5] This is wholly selfish. Achilles is willing to put the fate of the entire Greek army in peril to feed his own wounded ego. Achilles is acting nothing like the leader that his divine gifts give him the power to be. Homer clearly leaves his central character open for some significant character development.

50d
CMS

¶3   In contrast to Achilles' infantile behavior, which
is consistent throughout most of the story, Diomedes is
cast in a different light. Athena gives Diomedes "courage
and boldness, to make him come to the front and cover
himself with glory."[6] While not Achilles' equal as a
soldier, "Diomedes was extremely fierce" and proved to be
a terrific leader for the Achaians.[7] Diomedes kills off
many Trojan warriors in Book V, acting as many hoped
Achilles would, and even fighting through an injury
suffered from the bow of Pandaros.[8] Rather than back
down, Diomedes prayed to Athena for aid and joined the
battle even more fiercely than before, slaying even more
Trojan soldiers.[9] It is clear at this point that Diomedes
is "obviously a paradigm of heroic behavior in Achilles'
absence."[10] Diomedes represents a well-behaved, properly
subservient soldier in the Achaian army who uses his
courage and his honor to accomplish feats that are beyond
his natural abilities. Diomedes exhibits self-control
above all else, which is the element most wanting in
Achilles' character.[11] His courage is further proven when
he speaks against Agamemnon at the beginning of Book IX
when the Achaian commander is advocating a Greek retreat:
"Two of us will go on fighting, Sthenelos and I, until we
make our goal!"[12] This is the moment when Diomedes is
confirmed as one of the Greeks' greatest leaders, as even
in a time when the army was "possessed by Panic,"[13] we
see that "all cheered bold Diomedes in admiration."[14] The
scene underscores Diomedes' rise to greatness in the
Achaian army.

¶4   Achilles and Diomedes finally come into direct
conflict with one another in Book IX, after Agamemnon has
decided to make a peace offering to Achilles in hopes of
the latter's return to battle. Agamemnon makes an offer
to Achilles that is outrageously generous in exchange for

50d
CMS

Achilles' return to battle. Achilles' response is far from heroic and borders on cowardly: "If I go home to my native land, there will be no great fame for me, but I shall live long and not die an early death."[15] These words show utter selfishness on the part of the man who is supposedly the greatest warrior in Greek history, and Achilles is certainly not, at this point, living up to his reputation or his potential. Observing that Achilles "shall appear in battle once more whenever he feels inclined or when God makes him go," Diomedes speaks against Achilles for the first time, effectively casting himself as something of an adversary to Achilles in the hopes of bringing him back into the battle, an action that serves the overall good of the Achaians.[16] Once more, Diomedes is doing what is best for his people and his army while Achilles thinks only of himself. Peter Toohey observes that "Homer likes to juxtapose," and here he uses that device to highlight the stark contrast between the protagonist of the story and the true hero of the story.[17]

¶5   Homer centers *The Iliad* on Achilles, whose actions are notably selfish and immature. Homer then uses Diomedes, at first a lesser character, as a dramatic foil. Diomedes comes across as an example of the ideal young Greek soldier. Achilles' capacities as a warrior are far superior to those of any man alive, yet Diomedes betters him in both words and actions throughout most of the story. Achilles is finally brought to realize his supreme military prowess, but it is the death of his friend Patroclos that spurs his fighting spirit, still another example of Achilles' penchant for acting on emotion rather than judgment. Achilles is finally reconciled to Diomedes' example when he meets Priam at the end of the story and responds honorably: "I mean myself to set your Hector free," agreeing to return the corpse of Priam's son for a proper burial.[18] Achilles at last achieves a measure of respect that his abilities could have earned him long before. It is in that time, however, when Achilles was still selfish and immature, that Diomedes shone as the example of leadership and valor. Diomedes is, at least in a measure of consistency, the true hero of *The Iliad*.

[New Page]

NOTES

1. Homer, *The Iliad*, trans. Robert Fitzgerald (New York: Anchor Press, 1974), 14.

2. R. M. Frazer, *A Reading of "The Iliad"* (Lanham, Md.: University Press of America, 1993), 12.

3. Homer, 15.

4. Frazer, 11.

5. Homer, 18.

6. Ibid., 58.

7. Scott Richardson, *The Homeric Narrator* (Nashville: Vanderbilt University Press, 1990), 159.

8. Homer, 59.

9. Ibid., 60-61.

10. W. Thomas MacCary, *Childlike Achilles: Ontogeny and Philogeny in "The Iliad"* (New York: Columbia University Press, 1982), 95.

11. G. S. Kirk, *"The Iliad": A Commentary,* vol. 2 (New York: Cambridge University Press, 1990), 34.

12. Homer, 103.

13. Ibid., 102.

14. Ibid., 103.

15. Ibid., 110.

16. Ibid., 115.

17. Peter Toohey, "Epic and Rhetoric: Speech-making and Persuasion in Homer and Apollonius," *Arachnion: A Journal of Ancient Literature and History on the Web* 1 (1995) [journal online]; available from http://www.cisi.unito.it/arachne/num1/toohey.html; Internet; accessed 21 February 1996.

18. Homer, 293.

50d
CMS

[New Page]

WORKS CITED

Frazer, R. M. *A Reading of "The Iliad."* Lanham, Md.:
University Press of America, 1993.

Homer. *The Iliad.* Translated by Robert Fitzgerald. New
York: Anchor Press, 1974.

Kirk, G. S. *"The Iliad": A Commentary.* Vol. 2. New York:
Cambridge University Press, 1990.

MacCary, W. Thomas. *Childlike Achilles: Ontogeny and
Philogeny in "The Iliad."* New York: Columbia
University Press, 1982.

Richardson, Scott. *The Homeric Narrator.* Nashville:
Vanderbilt University Press, 1990.

Toohey, Peter. "Epic and Rhetoric: Speech-making and
Persuasion in Homer and Apollonius." *Arachnion: A
Journal of Ancient Literature and History on the Web*
1 (1995). Journal online. Available from
http://www.cisi.unito.it/arachne/num1/toohey.html;
Internet; accessed 21 February 1996.

Interested in classical Greek and Roman culture? You can find
out more about Homer, *The Iliad,* and related topics at *The
Perseus Project* at <http://www.perseus.tufts.edu/>.

Sample CMS page with footnotes. In CMS style, you have the option of placing all your notes on pages following the body of a paper (see the sample CMS paper above), or you may locate them at the bottom of each page as demonstrated on the facing page.

3

Book I, Agamemnon embarrasses Achilles publicly
with an outward display of his power as the
Achaians' commander: "since Apollo robs me of
Chryseis . . . I will take your beautiful Briseis
. . . to show you how much stronger I am than you
are."[1] Achilles can hardly be faulted for taking
offense at this incident, as it "threatened to
invalidate . . . the whole meaning of his life."[2]
Achilles' refusal to fight afterward must be
looked at from more than one perspective. This is
the first example of Achilles' acting according
to his pride, as proven by his regard for himself
as "the best man of all."[3] While it is
understandable for a soldier such as Achilles,
who "towers above all the other characters of *The
Iliad*," to be hesitant to fight for and under the
man who embarrassed him, Agamemnon, it is also
folly for a soldier to stop fighting because of
anything as relatively unimportant as an insult,
even a public one.[4] A soldier's duty is to defend
his homeland and fight in its wars, and Achilles

---

1. Homer, *The Iliad*, trans. Robert
Fitzgerald (New York: Anchor Press, 1974), 14.

2. R. M. Frazer, *A Reading of "The Iliad"*
(Lanham, Md.: University Press of America, 1993),
12.

3. Homer, 15.

4. Frazer, 11.

50d
CMS

CHAPTER 51

How Do You Use CBE Documentation?

Disciplines that study the physical world—physics, chemistry, biology—are called the natural sciences; disciplines that examine (and produce) technologies are described as the applied sciences. Writing in these fields is specialized, and no survey of all forms of documentation can be provided here. For more information about writing in the following fields, we suggest that you consult one of these style manuals.

- **Chemistry:** *The ACS Style Guide: A Manual for Authors and Editors,* second edition (1998)—American Chemical Society
- **Geology:** *Suggestions to Authors of Reports of the United States Geological Survey,* seventh edition (1991)—U.S. Geological Survey
- **Mathematics:** *A Manual for Authors of Mathematical Papers,* revised edition (1990)—American Mathematical Society
- **Medicine:** *American Medical Association Manual of Style,* ninth edition (1997)
- **Physics:** *AIP Style Manual,* fourth edition (1990)—American Institute of Physics

A highly influential manual for scientific writing is *Scientific Style and Format: The CBE Manual for Authors, Editors, and Publishers,* sixth edition (1994). In this latest edition of *The CBE Manual,* the Council of Biology Editors (recently renamed the Council of Science Editors—CSE) advocates a common style for international science but also recognizes important differences between disciplines and even countries.

CBE style itself includes the choice of two major methods of documenting sources used in research: a *name-year* system that resembles APA style and a *citation-sequence* system that lists sources in the order of their use. In this chapter, we briefly describe this second system.

▌1 (Step 1) Where a citation is needed in the text of a paper, insert either a raised number (the preferred form) or a number in parentheses. Citations should appear immediately after the word or phrase to which they are related, and they are numbered in the order you use them.

```
Oncologists¹ are aware of trends in cancer
mortality².
```
```
Oncologists (1) are aware of trends in cancer
mortality (2).
```

Source 1 thus becomes the first item listed on the References page, source 2 the second item, and so on.

```
1. Devesa SS, Silverman DT. Cancer incidence and mor-
   tality trends in the United States: 1935-74. J
   Natl Cancer Inst 1978; 60:545-71.
2. Goodfield J. The siege of cancer. New York: Dell;
   1978. 240 p.
```

You can refer to more than one source in a single note, with the numbers separated by a dash if they are in sequence and by commas if out of sequence.

IN SEQUENCE
```
Cancer treatment²⁻³ has changed over the decades. But
Rettig⁴ shows that the politics of cancer research
remains constant.
```

OUT OF SEQUENCE
```
Cancer treatment²'⁵ has changed over the decades. But
Rettig⁴ shows that the politics of cancer research
remains constant.
```

If you cite a source again later in the paper, you refer to it by its original number.

```
Great strides have occurred in epidemiological
methods⁵ despite the political problems in
maintaining research support and funding described by
Rettig⁴.
```

■ **2 (Step 2) On a separate page at the end of the text of your paper, list the sources you used in the order they occurred.** These sources are numbered: source 1 in the paper would be the first source listed on the References page, source 2 the second item, and so on. Notice, then, that this References list is *not* alphabetical. The first few entries on a CBE list might look like this.

Subsequent lines begin under first words of first line   "References" centered   All items double spaced

References

1. Devesa SS, Silverman DT. Cancer incidence and

   → mortality trends in the United States: 1935-

   74. J Natl Cancer Inst 1978;60:545-71.

2. Goodfield J. The siege of cancer. New York:

   → Dell; 1978. 240 p.

3. Loeb LA, Ernster VL, Warner KE, Abbotts J,

   → Laszo J. Smoking and lung cancer: an

   overview. Cancer Res 1984;44:5940-58.

4. Rettig RA. Cancer crusade: the story of the

   → National Cancer Act of 1971. Princeton:

   Princeton Univ Pr; 1977. 382 p.

5. Craddock VM. Nitrosamines and human cancer:

   → proof of an association? Nature 1983 Dec

   15:638.

A typical **CBE citation-sequence style References entry for a book** includes the following basic information.

- Number assigned to the source.
- Name of author(s), last name first, followed by a period. Initials are used in place of full first or middle names. Commas ordinarily separate the names of multiple authors.
- Title of work, followed by a period. Only the first word and any proper nouns in a title are capitalized. The title is not underlined.
- Place of publication, followed by a colon.
- Publisher, followed by a semicolon. Titles of presses can be abbreviated.
- Date, followed by a period.
- Number of pages, followed by a period.

**51
CBE**

Reference
number   Author   Title of book   Place

2. Goodfield J. The siege of cancer. New York:

Dell; 1978. 240 p.

Publisher Date Pages Period

A typical **CBE citation-sequence style References entry for an article in a scholarly journal** (where the pagination is continuous through a year) includes the following basic information.

- Number assigned to the source.
- Name of author(s), last name first, followed by a period. Initials are used in place of full first or middle names. Commas ordinarily separate the names of multiple authors.
- Title of article, followed by a period. Only the first word and any proper nouns in a title are capitalized. The title does not appear between quotation marks.
- Name of the journal. All major words are capitalized, but the journal title is not underlined. A space (but no punctuation) separates the journal title from the date. Journal titles of more than one word can be abbreviated following the recommendations in *American National Standard Z39.5-1985: Abbreviations of Titles of Publications.*
- Year (and month for journals not continuously paginated; date for weekly journals), followed immediately by a semicolon.
- Volume number, followed by a colon, and the page numbers of the article. No spaces separate these items. A period follows the page numbers.

Reference
number   Author(s)   Title of article

1. Devesa SS, Silverman DT. Cancer incidence and

mortality trends in the United States: 1935-74.

J Natl Cancer Inst 1978;60:545-71.

Name of periodical   Year Volume Pages Period

51
CBE

A typical **CBE citation-sequence style References entry for an article in a popular magazine** includes the following basic information.

- Number assigned to the source.
- Name of author(s), last name first, followed by a period. Initials are substituted for first names unless two authors mentioned in the paper have identical last names and first initials.
- Title of article, followed by a period. Only the first word and any proper nouns in a title are capitalized. The title does not appear between quotation marks. (Where quotation marks are needed, CBE recommends British style. See *CBE Manual,* pp. 180–81.)
- Name of magazine, abbreviated. All major words are capitalized, but the journal title is not underlined. A space (but no punctuation) separates the magazine title from the year and month.
- Year, month (abbreviated), and day (for a weekly magazine). The year is separated from the month by a space. A colon follows immediately after the date, followed by page number(s). The entry ends with a period.

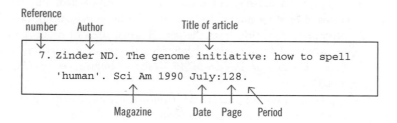

A typical **CBE citation-sequence style References entry for an electronic item** includes the basic information provided for a print document (author, title, publication information, page numbers) with the following additions.

- Electronic medium, identified between brackets. For books and monographs, this information comes after the title [*monograph online*]; for periodicals, it follows the name of the journal [*serial online*].
- Availability statement, following the publication information or page numbers.
- Date of access, if helpful in identifying what version of an electronic text was consulted.

Electronic medium

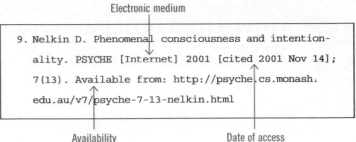

9. Nelkin D. Phenomenal consciousness and intention-
ality. PSYCHE [Internet] 2001 [cited 2001 Nov 14];
7(13). Available from: http://psyche.cs.monash.
edu.au/v7/psyche-7-13-nelkin.html

Availability
statement

Date of access

There are so many variations to these basic entries, however, that you will certainly want to check the *CBE Manual* when you do a major CBE-style paper.

Checklist 51.1

CBE Style

- CBE style normally requires a separate title page. The title of the essay can be centered about a third of the way from the top of the page, followed by *by* on a separate line and the writer's name, also on a separate line. Other information such as instructor's name, course title, and date can be included on the bottom third of the page.

- CBE style normally requires an abstract of about 250 words on a separate sheet immediately following the title page. The title "Abstract" is centered on the page.

- Double-space the body of a CBE paper. Avoid hyphenating words at the end of the line.

- Number pages consecutively in the upper right-hand corner, counting the title page as the first page.

- Take special care with figures and tables. They should be numbered in separate sequences. The *CBE Manual* includes an entire chapter on handling illustrative material.

- The References page follows the text of the CBE essay on a new page. Remember that the items on this page are *not* listed alphabetically. References pages can also be titled "Literature Cited" or "References Cited."

- All works listed on the References page should be cited at least once in the body of your paper.

- Entries on the References page are single spaced, with a space left between the entries.

51
CBE

CHAPTER 52

How Do You Use
COS Documentation?

In preparing a college research project, you may use a wide variety of electronic sources and services—Web sites, listservs, and email. When the time comes to document these items, however, conventional citation systems may prove inadequate. Either they don't mention the types of sources you are using, or the guidelines for documenting them are cumbersome and intricate. That's not surprising; most citation systems were originally designed for printed documents, so they wobble as they try to accommodate sources without authors, titles, or even page numbers.

An exception is the system of documentation presented in *The Columbia Guide to Online Style* (1998) by Janice R. Walker and Todd Taylor. Columbia Online Style (COS), designed expressly for electronic environments, acknowledges that online and computer sources differ from printed ones and yet have a logic of their own that makes reliable citation possible. To help you deal effectively with computer resources, we offer an authoritative version of Columbia Online Style.

52a How to use COS documentation

Fortunately, you don't have to forget what you have learned about other documentation systems to use COS—it doesn't replace MLA, APA, CMS, or CBE style. Instead, COS is designed to work with all of them so that writers can document electronic sources consistently and appropriately *within* the style they are expected to use in school or at work. To use COS style, simply follow it consistently for all the electronic sources in a project, choosing the COS form best suited to the documentation style you are using for printed sources. To make this adaptation simple, COS offers forms for both major types of documentation, the author–page number form favored in humanities systems (MLA, CMS) and the author-date style preferred in the sciences (APA, CBE). In this chapter we provide separate COS Models for humanities-style citations (Section 52b) and science-style citations (Section 52d).

Like the MLA and APA systems, Columbia Online Style documentation itself involves just two basic steps: inserting a note at each point where a paper or project needs documentation (Section 52a-1) and then recording all sources used in these notes in a Works Cited or References list (Section 52a-2).

■ 1 (Step 1) In the body of your paper, place a note in the appropriate form for every item you must document.

For a humanities paper in MLA style, the in-text note will usually be an author's last name and a page number in parentheses.

    (Weinberg 38)

But most electronic sources do not have page numbers—which are, after all, a convention of printed texts. So, for electronic sources without page numbers or other consistent divisions, simply place the author's last name in parentheses after a passage that requires documentation.

    Jim Lehrer may be America's most trusted newsperson,

    its new Walter Cronkite (Shafer).

If a Web site or Web page has no conventional author (a common occurrence), identify the source by placing a shortened version of its title within parentheses.

    USA Today was among those to editorialize against the

    tobacco industry's continuing influence on Congress

    ("Tobacco").

When you cite a source without page numbers multiple times, repeat the author's name (or short title, if there is no author) for each citation. But try to keep intrusions to a minimum—for example, by using a single note at the end of a paragraph when one source is cited throughout it. You can eliminate a parenthetical note by naming the author or title of a source in the body of the paper.

    Shafer claims in a Slate column that PBS's Jim Lehrer

    is the new Walter Cronkite, America's most trusted

    newsperson.

    In "Tobacco Wields Its Clout," USA Today

    editorializes against the tobacco industry's

    continuing influence on Congress.

When citing a message from email, listservs, or other electronic forums, you may have to cite an author's alias or nickname.

```
In a recent posting to the newsgroup

alt.sport.paintball, jireem argued . . .
```

For scientific papers, the in-text note will include an author's last name followed by a date of "publication" in parentheses. Give only the year even if the source furnishes day and date.

```
Jim Lehrer may be America's most trusted newsperson,

its new Walter Cronkite (Shafer, 1996).
```

You can also simply name the author in the body of your text, following the name with year of publication in parentheses.

```
Shafer (1996) claims in a Slate column that PBS's Jim

Lehrer is the new Walter Cronkite, America's most

trusted newsperson.
```

Some electronic sources such as pages on the World Wide Web will not have dates of publication or any dates at all. In such cases for science-style references, record the date you accessed the source, giving date, month, and year.

```
Slipstream (21 May 1997) argues that the research

design is flawed, but ksmith (22 May 1997) rejects

that claim.
```

As a general rule, make all parenthetical notes as brief and inconspicuous as possible. Remember that the point of a note is to identify a source of information, not to distract readers.

For a humanities paper using Chicago Manual of Style (CMS) footnotes or endnotes, the note consists of a raised number in the text of the paper keyed to a full note either at the bottom of the page or on a separate "Notes" page at the end of the paper.

```
     20. Paul Skowronek, "Left and Right for
Rights," Trincoll Journal, 13 March 1997;
http://www.trincoll.edu/~tj/tj03.13.97/articles/
comm2.html (23 July 1997).
```

Note that electronic addresses are not enclosed in parentheses or angle brackets in COS style.

52a
COS

The COS form for CMS notes can be adapted from the COS Humanities Models in Section 52b. You will need to study both MLA forms in that section and the CMS footnote forms in Sections 50a and 50c.

■ 2 (Step 2) On a separate page at the end of your paper, list every source you cited in a parenthetical note. This alphabetical list of sources is usually titled "Works Cited" in humanities papers and "References" in scientific papers. You must have a Works Cited/References page for MLA and APA papers; in Chicago style, such a page is optional because the notes themselves include all essential bibliographical information. (We do not include specific CMS models among the COS Models in Section 52b.)

Like citations in other systems, COS items are assembled from a few basic components.

- **Author.** Many electronic sources do not have authors in the conventional sense. A Web site, for example, may be a collaborative effort or represent an entire institution or a corporation. List an "author" when you can clearly identify someone as responsible for a source, text, or message. List an alias if you don't know the actual name of the person sending an online message. For example, the author of an email message from cerulean@mail.utexas.edu would be cerulean.

  ```
  cerulean. "Re: Bono Rocks." Personal email

      (25 Jul. 1997).
  ```

  Note that COS style does not hyphenate the word e-mail. When no author can be identified, list the source on a Works Cited/References page by its title.
- **Title.** Depending on whether you are adapting COS to MLA or APA documentation, titles of electronic works might be italicized, placed between quotation marks, or left without any special marking. But titles in COS citations are never underlined because in many computer environments, underlining is used for hypertext links.
- **Publication information.** Many online works are based on printed sources with conventional publication histories, and this information can be included in a citation just before the electronic address. But for other online sources, the electronic address or pathway is the essential publication information. Specifying a "publication medium" (CD-ROM, Internet, online, WWW) for an electronic source is usually unnecessary since the information is evident in the electronic address.
- **Date of publication and/or access.** While print publications are routinely dated and archived, these conventions don't always suit

52a
COS

electronic sources, which are less stable and are revised more frequently (see Section 45a-4 on the timeliness of research materials). When an online or electronic source is based on a printed source or appears in a dated format (such as the online version of a newspaper or magazine), give the original publication date of the material. For Web sites, check the home page for information about original dates of posting and updates.

For most electronic sources, provide a date of access—the day, month, and year you actually examined the material. This date is important for establishing the version of the material you looked at in an environment that might be changing rapidly. When the date of publication of a source is the same as the date of your access to it (as it might be when you're reading an online news source), you need to give only the date of access.

- **Electronic address.** In citations of online items, the information most important to a researcher may be the pathway or electronic address, the means by which a given source can be located. For many sources in undergraduate research projects, that electronic address is likely to be a World Wide Web uniform resource locator (URL), that is, the familiar Web address beginning http://www. URLs must be copied accurately so researchers can locate the material you are documenting. To ensure accuracy, you can usually cut and paste an address directly from a Web browser into your project document.

Unfortunately, some URLs are quite long and will produce odd line breaks. Don't, however, introduce a space into a URL just to fill an awkward gap in your citation. That empty space will ruin the citation for researchers who might copy and paste it directly from your document to their Web browsers. Let the word wrap capability of your word processor break the URL (but turn off the auto hyphenation feature).

Holmes, Steven. "Black English Debate." *The New York*
Times 30 Dec. 1996. http://search.nytimes.com/
search/daily/bin/fastweb?getdoc+site+site+8836+
4+wAAA+%28suspension%29%26OR%26%28bridges%29%26
OR%26%28%29 (28 July 1997).

52a
COS

In the sample COS entries in the Models sections (52b and 52d), we follow this convention.

COS style does not surround electronic addresses with angle brackets (< >). This additional and potentially confusing punctuation is not necessary to separate an electronic pathway from other elements in an entry. Moreover, these characters could cause problems if you were to copy and paste them into a hypertext composition.

There are many variations to these general entries, so you will want to check any particular item with the COS models in Sections 52b (Humanities) and 52d (Sciences).

52b COS models—HUMANITIES (MLA)

Below you will find the COS humanities-style forms for a variety of electronic sources. Use these forms when you are writing a paper in which you use an author–page number citation system (such as MLA) for nonelectronic sources. Note that the items in this section adhere to MLA style for the names of authors and the titles of works but follow COS guidelines for the electronic portion of the citation.

To find the form you need, look in the Models Index for the type of source you want to document and then locate that item by number in the list of COS Models. To handle more complex electronic sources and to learn more about developing standards for online style, consult *The Columbia Guide to Online Style* by Janice R. Walker and Todd Taylor (New York: Columbia University Press, 1998) or its online updates at <http://www.columbia.edu/cu/cup/cgos/idx_update.html>.

COS Models Index— HUMANITIES (MLA)

World Wide Web Citations

112. Web site—COS/MLA
113. Web site, revised or modified—COS/MLA
114. Web site with a group or institutional author—COS/MLA
115. Web site, no author or institution—COS/MLA
116. Web site maintained by an individual—COS/MLA
117. Web site, government—COS/MLA
118. Web site, corporate—COS/MLA
119. Web site—book, printed, available online—COS/MLA
120. Web site—book, published electronically—COS/MLA
121. Web site—online article—COS/MLA
122. Web site—article from a news service—COS/MLA

52b
COS

123. Web site—article from an archive—COS/MLA
124. Web site—with frames—COS/MLA
125. Web site—graphic or audio file—COS/MLA

Email, Listservs, Newsgroups
126. Personal email—COS/MLA
127. Listserv—COS/MLA
128. Newsgroup—COS/MLA
129. Message from an archive—COS/MLA

Gopher, FTP, and Telnet Sites
130. Material from a Gopher or FTP site—COS/MLA

131. Material from a telnet site—COS/MLA
132. Synchronous communications (MOOs, MUDs)—COS/MLA

References and Databases
133. Online encyclopedia article—COS/MLA
134. Online dictionary entry—COS/MLA
135. Material from a CD-ROM—COS/MLA
136. Material from an online database—COS/MLA

Software
137. Software—COS/MLA

112. **Web Site—COS/Humanities (MLA)** The title of a particular Web page appears in quotation marks, and the title of the entire site is italicized. Provide author (if any), title of the page, publication information and date, electronic address, and date of access in parentheses.

Works Cited

Prosek, James. "Fishing." *Troutsite.* 1999.

http://www.troutsite.com/fishing/index.html (18

Mar. 2000).

113. **Web Site, Revised or Modified—COS/Humanities (MLA)** You may specify a date that a page or site was revised or updated if such a date is given. Your date of access follows the electronic address.

Works Cited

Stasi, Mafalda. "Another Deadline, Another Miracle!"

La Pagina Casa Di Mafalda. Rev. Mar. 1997.

http://www.cwrl.utexas.edu/~mafi/present/ (5

May 1997).

52b
COS

114. **Web Site with a Group or Institutional Author—COS/Humanities (MLA)**

Works Cited

Texas Department of Economic Development. "Rio

　　　Grande Float Trips." *TravelTexas*. 1998.

　　　http://www.traveltex.com/region_viewer.asp?

　　　region_id=271 (19 May 2000).

115. **Web Site, No Author or Institution—COS/Humanities (MLA)**
When no author or institution can be assigned to a site, begin the
entry with the title of the page or the site. In the example, the title
is italicized because it identifies an entire Web site.

Works Cited

The British Monarchy: The Official Web Site. Rev. 14

　　　Mar. 2000. http://www.royal.gov.uk/

　　　(15 Mar. 2000).

116. **Web Site Maintained by an Individual—COS/Humanities
(MLA)** A maintained site is one that usually contains links,
routinely updated, to materials not created by the author(s) of
the site. The site can be listed either by the person(s) maintaining it or by its name, depending on which emphasis suits your
project.

Works Cited

Clark, Stephen, et al., maint. "Philosophy at

　　　Large." University of Liverpool Department of

　　　Philosophy. http://www.liv.ac.uk/Philosophy/

　　　philos.html (28 Feb. 2000).

"Philosophy at Large." Maint. Stephen Clark, et al.

　　　University of Liverpool Department of

　　　Philosophy. http://www.liv.ac.uk/Philosophy/

　　　philos.html (15 Mar. 2000).

52b
COS

117. **Web Site, Government—COS/Humanities (MLA)** In this example, no date is given for this frequently updated Web site because it is the same as the date of access.

Works Cited

United States Congress. "Floor Activity in Congress

This Week." *Thomas: Legislative Information on*

the Internet. http://thomas.loc.gov/home/hot-

week.html (28 July 1997).

118. **Web Site, Corporate—COS/Humanities (MLA)** The corporation or institution should be listed as the author.

Works Cited

Cedar Point, Inc. "Whoa! Cedar Point Tops Off the

World's Tallest and Fastest Roller Coaster." 3

Jan. 2000. http://www.cedarpoint.com/thrill/

millennium/topping.htm (29 Feb. 2000).

119. **Web Site—Book, Printed, Available Online—COS/Humanities (MLA)** Give the name of the author, the title of the work, and the publication information for the printed version if known. Then provide the title of the electronic version, if different from the original title, and the electronic publication information.

Works Cited

Austen, Jane. *Pride and Prejudice.* 1813. *Pride and*

Prejudice Hypertext. Ed. H. Churchyard. 1994.

http://www.pemberley.com/janeinfo/pridprej.html

(3 Mar. 2000).

120. **Web Site—Book, Electronic—COS/Humanities (MLA)** Provide an author, title, and date of publication. In this example, the publication of the book is sponsored by an organization listed after the title.

52b
COS

Works Cited

```
Baker, Catherine. Your Genes, Your Choices. American

    Association for the Advancement of Science.

    1997. http://ehrweb.aaas.org/ehr/books/

    (15 Mar. 2000).
```

121. **Web Site—Online Article—COS/Humanities (MLA)** The title of the article in quotation marks is followed by the italicized title of the journal in which it appears. The volume number of the periodical is given, followed by a colon and an issue number (if available) and date of publication.

Works Cited

```
Williamson, Iain. "Internalized Homophobia and

    Health Issues Affecting Lesbians and Gay Men."

    Health Education Research 15:1 (Feb. 2000).

    http://her.oupjournals.org/cgi/content/full/15/

    1/97 (1 Mar. 2000).
```

122. **Web Site—Article from a News Service or Online Newspaper—COS/Humanities (MLA)** Provide author, title of the article, the name of the news service or online newspaper, the date of the article (if different from the date accessed), the electronic address, and the date accessed.

Works Cited

```
Matthews, Karen. "Demand Outstrips Server Capacity

    in King Story's Online Debut." FoxNews.com.

    http://www.foxnews.com/entertainment/031500/kin

    g.sml (15 Mar. 2000).
```

If no author's name is given, list the name of the news source (such as Reuters or Associated Press).

Works Cited

```
Associated Press. "Pathfinder's Battery Power

    Dwindles." CNN Interactive. http://www.cnn.com/
```

52b
COS

TECH/9707/29/pathfinder.ap/index.html (29 July
1997).

123. **Web Site—Article from an Archive—COS/Humanities (MLA)**
Provide author, title, journal, and date as you would for a printed
article, followed by the name of the archive site, the electronic address, and the date of access. In the example below, "The Compost Pile" is the name *Slate* gives to its archive of previously published articles.

Works Cited

Achenbach, Joel. "The Unexamined Game Is Not Worth

Watching." *Slate* 9 May 1997. "The Compost

Pile." http://www.slate.com/goodsport/97-05-

09/goodsport.asp (1 June 1999).

124. **Web Site—with Frames—COS/Humanities (MLA)** A Web site
that uses frames may present material from other sites as well as
material from within its own site. When you cannot determine
the original URL of such material, list the documents by author
and title and other publication information, and then give the
name of the site where the source appears in a frame. Provide the
electronic address of the site with frames, followed by a comma,
and the path or links necessary to access the specific article or site.
Conclude the entry with the date of access.

Works Cited

Burney, Fanny. *Fanny Burney and Dr. Johnson.* London,

1842. *Women of the Romantic Period.*

http://www.cwrl.utexas.edu/~worp/worp.html,

Frances Burney/Dr. Johnson and Fanny Burney

(13 July 1997).

125. **Web Site—Graphic or Audio File—COS/Humanities (MLA)**
You may want to cite a graphic file in one of two ways: either
by its own URL (which you can usually find in the *Netscape
Navigator* browser by selecting "view document info") or by the
Web page on which the image appears. For the graphic alone,

identify the author, photographer, or artist (if known); and give its title (italicized as a work of art) or its file name without italics. Then furnish an electronic address and the date of access.

Works Cited

Sandberg, Bob. *Jackie Robinson in Dodgers Uniform.*

  http://rs6.loc.gov/pnp/ppmsc/00000/00047r.jpg

  (12 Mar. 2000).

To cite the graphic as it appears on a particular page, once again identify the artist and the title of the graphic. Then name the site on which the graphic appears and give the electronic address for the page.

Works Cited

Sandberg, Bob. *Jackie Robinson in Dodgers Uniform.*

  "Baseball, the Color Line, and Jackie Robinson--

  About the Collection." *American Memory.*

  http://memory.loc.gov/ammem/jrhtml/jrabout.html

  (12 Mar. 2000).

126. Personal Email—COS/Humanities (MLA) Identify the author of the email and give the title of the message in quotation marks. Then identify the communication as "Personal email" and date it. In most cases, the date of access will be the same day you receive it. Do not give the writer's email address.

Works Cited

Sherman, Lee. "Coffee Shops." Personal email (5 Mar.

  1997).

127. Listserv—COS/Humanities (MLA) Identify the author of the message to a listserv. If no author's name is given, use the author's alias or email name. Then give the subject line of the message as the title, followed by a date (if different from the date of access), the address of the listserv, and the date of access.

52b
COS

Works Cited

```
Cook, Janice. "Re: What New Day Is Dawning?" 19 June

    1997. acw-l@ttacs6.ttu.edu (21 June 1997).
```

128. **Newsgroup—COS/Humanities (MLA)** Give the author's name (or alias), the subject line of the message as the title (enclosed in quotation marks), the date of the message (if different from the date of access), the address of the newsgroup, and the date of access.

Works Cited

```
Heady, Christy. "Buy or Lease? Depends on How Long

    You'll Keep the Car." 7 July 1997. news:clari

    .biz.industry.automotive (14 July 1997).
```

129. **Message from an Archive—COS/Humanities (MLA)** Identify the author, the title of the message, the date of posting, and the address of the list (if known). Then give the name of the archive if available, the electronic address, any other access information, and the date you read the message.

Works Cited

```
Butler, Wayne. "Re: Techno Literacy." 6 June 1996.

    acw-l@ttacs6.ttu.edu. ACW-L Archives.

    http://english.ttu.edu/acw/acw-l/archive.htm,

    Volume II (1996)/Issue 6 (29 July 1997).
```

130. **Material from a Gopher or FTP Site—COS/Humanities (MLA)** Give the name of the author; the title of the work; publication information if the work appears elsewhere; the date of the document; the protocol (Gopher, FTP); the electronic address, including any directory or path information; and the date of access. If the information is accessed via the World Wide Web, you may include the electronic address from the browser.

Works Cited

```
Harnad, Stevan. "Minds, Machines and Searle."

    Journal of Experimental and Theoretical

    Artificial Intelligence 1 (1989). gopher://
```

```
gopher.liv.ac.uk:70/00/phil/philos-l-

files/searle.harnad (30 July 1997).
```

Or the electronic address can be written to indicate the links that lead to a particular document.

```
gopher://gopher.liv.ac.uk, phil/philos-l-files/

searle.harnad (30 July 1997).
```

131. **Material from a Telnet Site—COS/Humanities (MLA)** Give the author of the material you are citing (if available); the title of the material; the date (if available); the protocol (*telnet*); the telnet address, including any steps or commands necessary to access the site; and the date of access.

Works Cited

```
"Manners." Connections. telnet://connections

.sensemedia.net:3333, help manners

(1 Mar. 1997).
```

132. **Synchronous Communications (MOOs, MUDs)—COS/Humanities (MLA)** Identify the speaker, the type of communication and/or the title of the session, and the title of the site (if available). Then give the electronic address and date of access. In giving an address, furnish any pathways, directories, or commands necessary.

Works Cited

```
Inept_Guest. Personal interview. The Sprawl.

telnet://sensemedia.net:7777/ (21 May 1997).
```

133. **Online Encyclopedia Article—COS/Humanities (MLA)** Give the author of the article (if available), the title of the article, and the name of the encyclopedia. If the encyclopedia is based on a printed work, give place of publication, publisher, and date. Give any publication information about the electronic version; the service offering it (for example, *America Online*); the electronic address, including any directories and pathways; and the date accessed.

52b
COS

Works Cited

Brown, James R. "Thought Experiments." *Stanford*

Encyclopedia of Philosophy. Stanford

University, 1999. http://plato.stanford.edu/

entries/thought-experiment/

thought-experiment.html (17 Mar. 2000).

134. Online Dictionary/Thesaurus Entry—COS/Humanities (MLA) List the entry by the word looked up, followed by the name of the dictionary. If the dictionary is based on a printed work, give place of publication, publisher, and date. Give any publication information about the electronic version, the service offering it (for example, *America Online*), the electronic address if available, and the date accessed.

Works Cited

"Drudge." *WWWebster Dictionary.* Merriam-Webster,

2000. http://www.m-w.com/dictionary.htm

(17 Mar. 2000).

135. Material from a CD-ROM—COS/Humanities (MLA) Provide an author (if available), the title of the entry or article, and the name of the CD-ROM program or publication. Furnish any edition or version numbers, a series title, and available publication information.

Works Cited

Bruckheim, Allan H. "Basic First Aid." *The Family*

Doctor. Vers. 3. Portland: Creative Multimedia,

1993.

136. Material from an Online Database—COS/Humanities (MLA) Identify the author and the title of the entry or article, and give publication information for items that have appeared in print. Identify the database or information service, and furnish retrieval data and a date of access.

Works Cited

Vlasic, Bill. "In Alabama: The Soul of a New

Mercedes?" *Business Week* 31 Mar. 1997:70.

InfoTrac SearchBank File #A19254659. (27 July

1997).

137. **Software—COS/Humanities (MLA)** List software by its individual or corporate author. If no author is given or if the corporate author is the same as the publisher, list the software by its title. Then identify the version of the software unless the version number is part of its name (Windows 95, Word 6.0). Give place of publication (if known), publisher, and date of release.

Works Cited

Virtual PC. Vers. 3.0. San Mateo: Connectix, 1999.

52c Sample Columbia Online Style (COS) Works Cited page—HUMANITIES (MLA)

On the following pages we have reprinted in its entirety the Works Cited page from the sample MLA paper on pages 770–72, reworking its electronic citations to conform to COS style. If you compare the two pages, you will notice that the nonelectronic items continue to follow MLA guidelines and that the COS entries themselves resemble MLA entries in arrangement, capitalization, and punctuation. You will also notice that all the underlined items in the sample MLA paper are now italicized, even in the nonelectronic entries. Since COS does not permit underlining, a paper conforming to COS/MLA style would, for consistency, italicize all appropriate items in the body of the paper as well as on the Works Cited page.

Works Cited

Arni, Sherry. "I Can Live With It." *English Journal*

79 (Nov. 1990): 76.

Corbett, H. Dickson, and Bruce L. Wilson. *Testing,*
    Reform, and Rebellion. Norwood: Ablex, 1991.

Dinan, John. "Standardized Tests: Multiple Choices
    of the Wrong Kind." *English Journal* 67 (Oct.
    1990): 54-56.

Garner, Donna. "RE: A Special Note on the TAAS
    Series." EducationNews.org Bulletin Board. 29
    Jan. 2000. http://www.educationnews.org/cgi/
    webbbs/article/article_list.pl (13 Feb 2000).

Irmscher, William F. *Teaching Expository Writing.*
    New York: Holt, 1979.

Kaufhold, Jack. "What's Wrong With Teaching for the
    Test?" *The School Administrator* 55 (Dec. 1998):
    14-16.

Linda/tx. "RE: Teaching to the TAAS Criticism
    Getting to Me." Texas Teachers Chatboard. 4
    Feb. 2000. http://texas.teachers.net/chatboard/
    (13 Feb. 2000).

Mary. "RE: Teaching to the TAAS Criticism Getting to
    Me." Texas Teachers Chatboard. 4 Feb. 2000.
    http://texas.teachers.net/chatboard/
    (13 Feb. 2000).

Melissa. "RE: Does Your School Give a Released TAAS
    Test?" Texas Teachers Chatboard. 14 Jan. 2000.
    http://texas.teachers.net/chatboard/
    (13 Feb. 2000).

Neill, Shirley Boes. *The Competency Movement:*
    Problems and Solutions. Sacramento: Educational
    News Service, 1978.

Rief, Linda. *Seeking Diversity*. Portsmouth:

   Heinemann, 1992.

Rison, A. D. *A. D. Rison's Teachers' and Parents'*

   Guide to Pass the TAAS Test: Language Arts,

   Reading and Writing. Austin: Sunbelt, 1990.

Shaughnessy, Anne. "Teaching to the Test: Sometimes

   a Good Practice." *English Journal* 83

   (Apr. 1994): 54-56.

Texas Education Agency. *Texas Education Agency*

   Administrative Rules. Chapters 110 and 128,

   subchapter c. Texas Education Agency. 1 Sept.

   1998. http://www.tea.state.tx.us/rules/

   tac/ch110_128c.html (6 Mar. 2000).

52d COS models—SCIENCES (APA)

Following you will find the COS science-style forms for a variety of electronic sources. Use these forms when you are writing a paper in which you use an author-date citation system (such as APA) for non-electronic sources. Note that the items in this section adhere to APA style for the names of authors and the titles of works but follow COS guidelines for the electronic portion of the citation.

To find the form you need, simply look in the Format Index for the type of source you must document and then locate that item by number in the COS Models Directory that follows. To handle more complex electronic sources and to learn more about developing standards for on-line style, consult *The Columbia Guide to Online Style* by Janice R. Walker and Todd Taylor (New York: Columbia University Press, 1998).

COS Models Index— SCIENCES (APA)

World Wide Web Citations

138. Web site—COS/APA

139. Web site, revised or modi-fied—COS/APA

140. Web site with a group or in-stitutional author—COS/APA

52d
COS

141. Web site, no author or institution—COS/APA
142. Web site maintained by an
individual—COS/APA
143. Web site, government—
COS/APA
144. Web site, corporate—COS/
APA
145. Web site—book, printed,
available online—COS/APA
146. Web site—book, published
electronically—COS/APA
147. Web site—online article—
COS/APA
148. Web site—article from a
news service—COS/APA
149. Web site—article from an
archive—COS/APA
150. Web site—with frames—
COS/APA
151. Web site—graphic or audio
file—COS/APA

Email, Listservs, Newsgroups

152. Personal email—COS/APA
153. Listserv—COS/APA

154. Newsgroup—COS/APA
155. Message from an archive—
COS/APA

Gopher, FTP, and Telnet Sites

156. Material from a Gopher or
FTP site—COS/APA
157. Material from a telnet
site—COS/APA
158. Synchronous communications (MOOs, MUDs)—
COS/APA

References and Databases

159. Online encyclopedia article—COS/APA
160. Online dictionary entry—
COS/APA
161. Material from a CD-
ROM—COS/APA
162. Material from an online
database—COS/APA

Software

163. Software—COS/APA

138. Web Site—COS/Sciences (APA) Capitalize the first word and
any proper names in the title. The title of the site is italicized.

References

Prosek, J. (1999). Fishing. *Troutsite.*

> http://www.troutsite.com/fishing/index.html

> (19 March 2000).

139. **Web Site, Revised or Modified—COS/Sciences (APA)** You
may specify a date that a page or site was revised or updated if
such a date is given. Your date of access follows the electronic
address.

52d
COS

References

Stasi, M. (1997, March). Another deadline, another

   miracle! *La pagina casa di Mafalda* (Rev. ed.).

   http://www.cwrl.utexas.edu/~mafi/present/

   (5 May 1997).

140. **Web Site with a Group or Institutional Author—COS/Sciences (APA)**

References

Texas Department of Economic Development. (1998).

   Rio Grande float trips. *TravelTexas*

   http://www.traveltex.com/

   region_viewer.asp?region_id=271 (19 May 2000).

141. **Web Site, No Author or Institution—COS/Sciences (APA)**
When no author or institution can be assigned to a site, begin the entry with the title of the page or the site. In the example, the title is italicized because it identifies an entire Web site.

References

The British monarchy: The official Web site. (2000,

   March 14). (Rev. ed.). http://www.royal.gov.uk/

   (15 March 2000).

142. **Web Site Maintained by an Individual—COS/Sciences (APA)** A maintained site is one that contains links, routinely updated, to materials not created by the author(s) of the site. The site can be listed either by the person(s) maintaining it or by its name, depending on which emphasis suits your project. Because this site is undated, no date follows the name of the author. In a parenthetical citation, however, give the date of access: (*Clark, 15 February 2000*).

References

Clark, S., et al. Philosophy at large. University of

   Liverpool Department of Philosophy.

52d
COS

```
http://www.liv.ac.uk/Philosophy/philos.html (15

February 2000).
```

143. **Web Site, Government—COS/Sciences (APA)** In this example, no date is given for this frequently updated Web site because it is the same as the date of access.

References

```
U.S. Congress. Floor activity in Congress this week.

    Thomas: Legislative information on the

    Internet. http://thomas.loc.gov/home/hot-

    week.html (28 July 1997).
```

144. **Web Site, Corporate—COS/Sciences (APA)** The corporation or institution should be listed as the author.

References

```
Cedar Point, Inc. (2000, January 3). Whoa! Cedar

    Point tops off the world's tallest and fastest

    roller coaster. http://www.cedarpoint.com/

    thrill/millennium/topping.htm (29 February

    2000).
```

145. **Web Site—Book, Printed, Available Online—COS/Sciences (APA)** Give the name of the author, the title of the work, and the publication information for the printed version if known. Then provide the title of the electronic version, if different from the original title, and the electronic publication information.

References

```
Austen, J. (1813). Pride and prejudice. Pride and

    prejudice hypertext. H. Churchyard (Ed.). 1994.

    http://www.pemberley.com/janeinfo/pridprej.html

    (3 March 2000).
```

52d
COS

146. Web Site—Book, Electronic—COS/Sciences (APA) Provide an author, title, and date of publication. In this example, the publication of the book is sponsored by an organization listed after the title.

References

Baker, C. (1997). *Your genes, your choices.* American

   Association for the Advancement of Science.

   http://ehrweb.aaas.org/ehr/books/

   (15 March 2000).

147. Web Site—Online Article—COS/Sciences (APA) Notice that in APA style, the volume number of the periodical is italicized. Provide an issue number (if available) in parentheses after the volume number. The issue number is not italicized.

References

Williamson, I. (2000, February). Internalized homo-

   phobia and health issues affecting lesbians and

   gay men. *Health Education Research, 15* (1).

   http://her.oupjournals.org/cgi/content/full/15/

   1/97 (1 March 2000).

148. Web Site—Article from a News Service or Online Newspaper— COS/Sciences (APA) If no author's name is given, list the name of the news source (such as Reuters or Associated Press), followed by the date of the article if different from the date accessed, the title of the article, the name of the news service or online newspaper, the electronic address, and the date accessed. If the date accessed differs from the date of publication, list the date of publication in parentheses after the name of the author or news service.

References

Matthews, K. Demand outstrips server capacity in

   King story's online debut. *FoxNews.com.*

52d
COS

```
http://www.cnn.com/TECH/9707/29/pathfinder.ap/

index.html (15 March 2000).
```

149. **Web Site—Article from an Archive—COS/Sciences (APA)** Provide author, title, journal, and date as you would for a printed article, followed by the name of the archive site, the electronic address, and the date of access. In the example below, "The Compost Pile" is the name *Slate* gives to its archive of previously published articles.

References

```
Achenbach, J. (1997, May 9). The unexamined game is

    not worth watching. Slate. The Compost Pile.

    http://www.slate.com/goodsport/97-05-09/

    goodsport.asp (1 June 1997).
```

150. **Web Site—with Frames—COS/Sciences (APA)** A Web site that uses frames may present material from other sites as well as material from within its own site. When you cannot determine the original URL of such material, list the documents by author and title and other publication information, and then give the name of the site where the source appears in a frame. Provide the electronic address of the site with frames, followed by a comma, and the path or links necessary to access the specific article or site. Conclude the entry with the date of access.

References

```
Burney, F. (1842). Fanny Burney and Dr. Johnson.

    London. Women of the Romantic Period.

    http://www.cwrl.utexas.edu/~worp/worp.html,

    Frances Burney/Dr. Johnson and Fanny Burney

    (13 July 1997).
```

151. **Web Site—Graphic or Audio File—COS/Sciences (APA)** You may want to cite a graphic file in one of two ways: either by its own URL (which you can usually find in the *Netscape Navigator* browser by selecting "View Document Info") or by the Web page on which the image appears. The first citation is for the photo-

graph itself. The second citation is to the page on which the graphic appears. APA style permits a description of the source in brackets, useful in this case.

References

Savoia, S. (1997). William F. Weld [Photograph].

   http://www.washtimes.com/news/images/news2.gif

   (29 July 1997).

Savoia, S. (1997). William F. Weld [Photograph]. *The*

   Washington Times. http://www.washtimes.com/

   index.html (29 July 1997).

Audio or video files can be treated the same way as graphics, either as separate documents or as files set in the context of particular Web pages.

152. **Personal Email—COS/Sciences (APA)** In APA style, you do not include personal email messages in the References list.

153. **Listserv—COS/Sciences (APA)** Identify the author of the message to a listserv. If no author's name is given, use the author's alias or email name. Then give the date followed by the subject line of the message as the title, the address of the listserv, and the date of access.

References

Cook, J. (1997, June 19). Re: What new day is dawn-

   ing? acw-l@ttacs6.ttu.edu (21 June 1997).

154. **Newsgroup—COS/Sciences (APA)** Give the author's name (or alias), the date of the posting, the subject line of the message as the title, the address of the newsgroup, and the date of access.

References

Heady, C. (1997, July 7). Buy or lease? Depends on

   how long you'll keep the car. news:clari.biz

   .industry.automotive (14 July 1997).

52d
COS

155. **Message from an Archive—COS/Sciences (APA)** Give the name of the author, the date of the message, the title of the message, and the address of the newsgroup or listserv (if known). Next, list the title of the archive site (if available), the electronic address, and the date of access.

References

```
Butler, W. (1996, June 6). Re: Techno literacy.

    acw-l@ttacs6.ttu.edu. ACW-LArchives. http://

    english.ttu.edu/acw/acw-l/archive.htm,Volume II

    (1996)/Issue 6 (29 July 1997).
```

156. **Material from a Gopher or FTP Site—COS/Sciences (APA)** Give the name of the author; the date; the title of the work; publication information if the work appears elsewhere; the protocol (*gopher, FTP*); the electronic address, including any directory or path information, and the date of access. If the information is accessed via the World Wide Web, you may include the electronic address from the browser.

References

```
Harnad, S. (1989). Minds, machines and Searle.

    Journal of Experimental and Theoretical

    Artificial Intelligence 1. gopher://

    gopher.liv.ac.uk:70/00/phil/philos-1-files/

    searle.harnad (30 July 1997).
```

Or the electronic address can be written to indicate the links that lead to a particular document.

```
gopher://gopher.liv.ac.uk, phil/philos-1-files/

searle.harnad (30 July 1997).
```

157. **Material from a Telnet Site—COS/Sciences (APA)** Give the author of the material you are citing (if available); the date (if available); the title of the material; the protocol (*telnet*); the telnet address, including any steps or commands necessary to access the site; and the date of access.

52d
COS

References

```
Manners. Connections. telnet://

    connections.sensemedia.net:3333, help manners

    (1 March 1997).
```

158. **Synchronous Communications (MOOs, MUDs)—COS/Sciences (APA)** Identify the speaker, the type of communication and/or the title of the session, and the title of the site (if available). Then give the electronic address and date of access. In giving an address, furnish any pathways, directories, or commands necessary.

References

```
Inept_Guest. Personal interview. The sprawl.

    telnet://sensemedia.net:7777/ (21 May 1997).
```

159. **Online Encyclopedia Article—COS/Sciences (APA)** Give the author of the article (if available), the date of the edition, the title of the article, and the name of the encyclopedia. If the encyclopedia is based on a printed work, identify the place of publication and the publisher. Give any publication information about the electronic version; the service offering it (for example, *America Online*); the electronic address, including any directories and pathways; and the date accessed.

References

```
Brown, J. R. (1999). Thought experiments. Stanford

    encyclopedia of philosophy. Stanford

    University. http://plato.stanford.edu/entries/

    thought-experiment/thought-experiment.html

    (17 March 2000).
```

160. **Online Dictionary/Thesaurus Entry—COS/Sciences (APA)** List the entry by the word looked up, followed by the date of publication and the name of the dictionary. If the dictionary is based on a printed work, give the place of publication and the publisher. Give any publication information about the electronic version,

52d
COS

the service offering it (for example, *America Online*), the electronic address if available, and the date accessed.

References

Drudge. (2000). *WWWebster dictionary*. Merriam-

    Webster. http://www.m-w.com/dictionary.htm

    (17 March 2000).

161. Material from a CD-ROM—COS/Sciences (APA) Provide an author (if available), the date of publication, the title of the entry or article, and the name of the CD-ROM program or publication. Furnish any edition or version numbers, a series title, and available publication information.

References

Bruckheim, A. H. (1993). Basic first aid. *The family*

    doctor (Version 3). Portland, OR: Creative

    Multimedia.

162. Material from an Online Database—COS/Sciences (APA) Identify the author, the date of publication, and the title of the entry or article, and give publication information for items that have appeared in print. Identify the database or information service, and furnish retrieval data and a date of access.

References

Vlasic, B. (1997, March 31). In Alabama: The soul of

    a new Mercedes? *Business Week, 70. InfoTrac*

    SearchBank. File #A19254659. (27 July 1997).

163. Software—COS/Sciences (APA) List software by its individual or corporate author. If no author is given or if the corporate author is the same as the publisher, list the software by its title. APA style does not italicize the title of software in a References list. Note also the placement of the version number in parentheses and the description of the source in brackets, both following the title.

52d
COS

References

The Norton utilities (Version 3.0) [Computer soft-

ware]. (1995). Cupertino, CA: Symantec.

52e Sample Columbia Online Style (COS) References page—SCIENCES (APA)

On the following pages we have reprinted in its entirety the References page from the sample APA paper on pages 800, 802, reworking its electronic citations to conform to COS style. If you compare the two pages, you will notice that the nonelectronic items continue to follow APA guidelines and that the COS entries themselves resemble APA entries in arrangement, capitalization, and punctuation. However, COS electronic entries are more compact than comparable APA entries.

References

Baker, C. (1997). *Your genes, your choices.* American

Association for the Advancement of Science.

http://www.nextwave.org/ehr/books/index.html

(16 July 2000).

Caskey, T. C. (1994). Human genes: The map takes

shape. *Patient Care, 28,* 28-32.

Davis, J. (1990). *Mapping the code: The human genome*

project and the choices of modern science. New

York: Wiley.

Ethical, legal, and social issues. (2000, July)

Human Genome Project information.

http://www.ornl.gov/hgmis/elsi/elsi.html

(29 July 2000).

52e
COS

Gardner, W. (1995). Can human genetic enhancement be

   prohibited? [Abstract]. *Journal of Medicine and*

   Philosophy, 20, 65-84. http:// www.med.upenn.edu/

   ~bioethic/genetics/articles/2.gardner.can.human

   .html (29 July, 2000).

Human genome project frequently asked questions.

   (2000, July). *Human Genome Project information.*

   http://www.ornl.gov/hgmis/faq/faqs1.html (5

   July 2000).

Magnus, D. (1996). Gene therapy and the concept of

   genetic disease. *Ethics and genetics: A global*

   conversation. Center for Bioethics electronic

   discussion site. http://www.med.upenn.edu/

   ~bioethic/genetics/articles/12.gen.disease.html

   (28 June 2000).

Matsubara, K. (1993). Background of human genome

   analysis. *The human genome: Toward*

   understanding ourselves. http://www

   .genome.ad.jp/brochure/english/

   Background.html#part4 (29 July, 2000).

New goals for the U.S. Human Genome Project: 1998-

   2003. (1998). *Science, 282*, 682-689.

Suzuki, D., & Knudtson, P. (1989). *Genethics: The*

   clash between the new genetics and human

   values. Cambridge, MA: Harvard University Press.

Swinbanks, D. (1992). When silence isn't golden.

   Nature, 368, 368-370.

The White House. (2000). Text of remarks on the

   completion of the first survey of the entire

Human Genome Project. *The White House Office of the Press Secretary.* http://www.whitehouse.gov/ WH/New/html/genome-20000626.html (29 July 2000).

Zylke, J. (1992). Examining life's code means re-examining society's long-held codes. *Journal of the American Medical Association, 267,* 1715-1716.

For more on doing research, be sure to see the Web site for this handbook at <http://www.ablongman.com/sfhandbooks>.

52e
COS

Glossary of Terms and Usage

This glossary covers grammatical terms, rhetorical terms, and items of usage. Whether you require the definition of a key term (*verbals, proper noun*), an explanation of a rhetorical concept (*cliché, idiom*), or some advice about correct usage (What's the difference between *eminent* and *imminent?*), you'll find the information in this single, comprehensive list. For convenient review, key grammatical terms are marked by the symbol *.

a, an.   Indefinite articles. **A** and **an** are **indefinite articles** because they point to objects in a general way (**a** book, **a** church), while the **definite article the** refers to specific things (**the** book, **the** church). **A** is used when the word following it begins with a consonant sound: **a** *house,* **a** *year,* **a** *boat,* **a** *unique* experience. **An** is used when the word following it begins with a vowel sound: **an** *hour,* **an** *interest,* **an** *annoyance,* **an** *illusory* image.

Notice that you choose the article by the *sound* of the word following it. Not all words that begin with vowels actually begin with vowel sounds, and not all words that begin with consonants have initial consonant sounds.

* **absolute.**   A phrase that modifies an entire sentence. Absolutes are often infinitive or participial phrases. Unlike other modifying phrases, absolutes do not necessarily modify a word or phrase standing near them.

> **To put it politely,** Connie is irritating.
>
> She will publish the entire story, **space permitting.**
>
> **Scripts discarded, props disassembled, costumes locked away in trunks,** the annual Shakespeare festival concluded.

See **misplaced modifier** and **dangling modifier;** see Section 30a.

* **absolute adjective.**   A word such as *unique, dead,* or *equal* that ought not to be qualified to suggest some degree. Logically speaking, something cannot be *more* unique, *less* equal, or *very* dead.

* **abstract noun.**   A noun that names ideas, concepts, and qualities without physical properties: *softness, Mother Nature, democracy, humanism.* Abstract nouns exist in the mind as ideas. They are defined in contrast to **concrete nouns.**

accept/except.   Very commonly confused. **Accept** means "to take, receive, or approve of something." **Except** means "to exclude, or not including."

> I **accepted** all the apologies **except** George's.

accidently/accidentally.   **Accidently** is a misspelling. The correct spelling is **accidentally.**

acronym.   A single term created by joining the first letters of the words that make up the full name or description. Acronyms are pronounced as single words and are ordinarily capitalized.

> **NATO**—North Atlantic Treaty Organization
> **NASA**—National Aeronautics and Space Administration

Some common acronyms are written as ordinary words without capitalization: *laser, radar.* See also **initialism.**

* active verb/voice.   See **voice.**

ad/advertisement.   In academic and formal writing, you should use the full word: **advertisement.**

* adjectival.   A word, phrase, or clause that modifies a noun or pronoun.

>   noun   adjectival
> the *engagement* of Ike and Bernice
>   adjectival   noun   adjectival
> the **never-ending** *battle* **between the sexes**
>   noun   adjectival
> the *ceremony* **they would have preferred**

* adjective.   A word that modifies a noun or pronoun. Some adjectives describe the words they modify, explaining how many, which color, which one, and so on.

> an **unsuccessful** coach   a **green** motel
> the **lucky** one   a **sacred** icon

Such adjectives frequently have comparative and superlative forms.

> the **blacker** cat   the **happiest** people

Other adjectives limit or specify the words they modify.

> **this** adventure   **every** penny
> **each** participant   **neither** video

Proper nouns can also serve as adjectives.

> **Texan** wildlife   **Eisenhower** era

See also **coordinate adjective, demonstrative adjective, noncoordinate adjective,** and **predicate adjective.**

* adjective clause.   A dependent (or subordinate) clause that functions as an adjective, modifying a noun or pronoun. See **clause** for definition of a dependent clause; see Section 17d-2.

> Margery Hutton, the woman **who writes mystery stories,** lives in the mansion **that Dr. Horace Elcott built.**
>
> Her gardens were tended by Bud Smith, **who learned to garden from his father.**

* **adverb.** A word that modifies a verb, an adjective, or another adverb. Adverbs explain where, when, and how.

adverb   verb

Bud **immediately** *suspected* foul play at the Hutton mansion.

adverb adjective

It seemed **extremely** *odd* to him that Mrs. Hutton should load a large burlap sack into the trunk of her Mercedes.

adverb   adverb

Mrs. Hutton replied **rather** *evasively* when Bud questioned her about what she was up to.

Some adverbs modify complete sentences.

adverb

Obviously, Mr. Hutton had been murdered!

* **adverb clause.** A subordinate clause that functions as an adverb. See Section 17b-2; see also **clause.**

> **After Mrs. Hutton left,** Bud slipped into the Hutton mansion.
> Bud was startled **when Mr. Hutton greeted him in the living room.**

* **adverbial.** An expression that functions like an adverb but is not actually an adverb. Adverbials can be nouns, clauses, and phrases.

> **NOUN AS ADVERBIAL**
> They are going **home.**   Explains *where.*

> **CLAUSE AS ADVERBIAL**
> They go jogging **whenever they can.**   Explains *when.*

> **PHRASE AS ADVERBIAL**
> They go jogging **in the morning.**   Explains *when.*

adverse/averse. Often confused. Adverse describes something hostile, unfavorable, or difficult. Averse indicates the opposition someone has to something; it is ordinarily followed by *to.*

> Travis was **averse** to playing soccer under **adverse** field conditions.

advice/advise. These words aren't interchangeable. **Advice** is a noun meaning "an opinion" or "counsel." **Advise** is a verb meaning "to give counsel or advice."

> I'd **advise** you not to give Maggie **advice** about running her business.

affect/effect. A troublesome pair! Each word can be either a noun or a verb, although **affect** is ordinarily a verb and **effect** a noun. In its usual sense, **affect** is a verb meaning "to influence" or "to give the appearance of."

> How will the stormy weather **affect** the plans for the outdoor concert?
> The meteorologist **affected** ignorance when we asked her for a forecast.

Only rarely is **affect** a noun—as a term in psychology meaning "feeling" or "emotion." On the other hand, **effect** is usually a noun, meaning "consequence" or "result."

> The **effect** of the weather may be serious.

Effect may, however, also be a verb, meaning "to cause" or "to bring about."

> The funnel cloud **effected** a change in our plans.
> Compare with: The funnel cloud **affected** our plans.

African American.   A term now preferred by many Americans of African ancestry, although it has not displaced *black*. *Negro* is used very rarely and then for specific historical reasons. **African American** is usually not hyphenated as a noun; usage is divided when it is an adjective. You will see both **African American literature** and **African-American literature**. Whichever form you prefer, use it consistently throughout a project.

aggravate/irritate.   Many people use both of these verbs to mean "to annoy" or "to make angry." But formal English preserves a fine—and useful—distinction between them. **Irritate** means "to annoy" while **aggravate** means "to make something worse."

> It **irritated** Greta when her husband **aggravated** his allergies by smoking.

* **agreement, pronoun and antecedent.**   A grammatical principle which requires that singular pronouns stand in for singular nouns (*his* surfboard = *Richard's* surfboard) and plural pronouns stand in for plural nouns (*their* surfboard =*George and Martha's* surfboard; *everyone's* place = *his or her* place). When they do, the pronoun and its antecedent agree in **number;** when they don't, you have an agreement problem. See Chapter 27.

Pronouns and their antecedents also must agree in **gender.** That is, a masculine pronoun (*he, him, his*) must refer to a masculine antecedent, and a feminine pronoun (*she, her, hers*) must refer to a feminine antecedent.

Finally, pronouns and antecedents must agree in **case,** whether objective, subjective, or possessive. For example, an antecedent in the possessive case (*Lawrence's* gym) can be replaced only by a pronoun also in the possessive case (*his* gym). See Chapter 28.

* **agreement, subject and verb.**   Verbs and nouns are said to agree in number. This means that with a singular subject in the third person (for example, *he, she, it*), a verb in the present tense ordinarily adds an -s ending to its base form. With subjects not in the third person singular, the base form of the verb is used.

Third person, singular, present tense:	Barney sits.
	He sits.
	She sits.
First person, singular, present tense:	I sit.
Second person, singular, present tense:	You sit.

First person, plural, present tense:	We sit.
Second person, plural, present tense:	You sit.
Third person, plural, present tense:	They sit.

Most **verbs**—with the notable exception of *to be*—change their form to show agreement only in third person singular forms (*he, she, it*). See Chapter 22.

ain't. The word isn't appropriate in academic or professional writing.

all ready/already. Tricky, but not difficult. **All ready**, an adjective phrase, means "prepared and set to go."

> Rita signaled that the camera was **all ready** for shooting.

Already, an adverb, means "before" or "previously."

> Rita had **already** loaded the film.

all right. **All right** is the only acceptable spelling. **Alright** is not acceptable in standard English.

allude/elude. Commonly confused. **Allude** means "to refer to." **Elude** means "to escape."

> Kyle's joke **alluded** to the fact that it was easy to **elude** the portly security guard.

allude/refer. To **allude** is to mention something indirectly; to **refer** is to mention something directly.

> Carter **alluded** to rituals the new students didn't understand.

> Carter did, however, **refer** to ancient undergraduate traditions and the honor of the college.

allusion/illusion. These terms are often misused. An **allusion** is an indirect reference to something. An **illusion** is a false impression or a misleading appearance.

> The entire class missed Professor Sweno's **allusion** to the ghost in *Hamlet*.

> Professor Sweno entertained the **illusion** that everyone read Shakespeare as often as he did.

a lot. Often misspelled as one word. It is two. Many readers consider **a lot** inappropriate in academic writing, preferring **many, much,** or some comparable expression.

already. See **all ready/already.**

alright. See **all right.**

American. Though often used to describe citizens of the United States of America, the term can also refer to any citizen of the Americas, North or South. Be careful how you use this term when writing to audiences that may include Americans not from the United States.

among/between.   Use **between** with two objects, **among** with three or more.

> Francie had to choose **between** Richard and Kyle.
>
> Francie had to choose from **among** a dozen actors.

amount/number.   Use **amount** for quantities that can be measured but not counted. Use **number** for things that can be counted, not measured: the **amount** of water in the ocean; the **number** of fish in the sea. The distinction between these words is being lost, but it is worth preserving. Remember that **amount of** is followed by a singular noun, while **number of** is followed by a plural noun.

amount of money	**number of** dimes
amount of paint	**number of** colors
amount of support	**number of** voters

an.   See **a, an.**

analogy.   An extended comparison between something familiar and something less well known. The analogy helps a reader visualize what might be difficult to understand. For example:

> analogy
> A transitional word in a paper serves **as a road sign, giving readers directions to the next major idea.**

and etc.   A redundant expression. Use **etc.** alone or **and so on.** See **etc.**

and/or.   A useful form in some situations, especially in business and technical writing, but some readers regard it as clumsy. Work around it if you can, especially in academic writing. **And/or** is typed with no space before or after the slash.

Anglo.   A common term in some areas of North America for designating white or nonminority people. The term is inaccurate in that many people considered white are not, in fact, *Anglo-Saxon* in origin.

angry/mad.   The distinction between these words is rarely observed, but strictly speaking, one should use **angry** to describe displeasure, **mad** to describe insanity.

* **antecedent.**   The person, place, or thing a pronoun replaces in a sentence. The antecedent is the word you would have to repeat if you couldn't use a pronoun. In the following sentence, *Marissa* is the antecedent of *she* and *radio* is the antecedent of *it.*

> **Marissa** turned off the **radio** because *she* was tired of listening to *it.*

See Chapter 26 for more details.

antonyms.   Words with opposite meanings: *bright/dull; apex/nadir; concave/ convex.*

anyone/any one. These expressions have different meanings. Notice the difference highlighted in these sentences.

> **Any one** of those problems could develop into a crisis.
>
> I doubt that **anyone** will be able to find a solution to **any one** of the equations.

anyways. A nonstandard form. Use **anyway.**

> WRONG   It didn't matter **anyways.**
>
> RIGHT   It didn't matter **anyway.**

* **appositive.** A word or phrase that stands next to a noun and modifies it by restating or expanding its meaning. Note that appositives ordinarily are surrounded by commas.

> Connie Lim, **editor of the paper and a liberal,** was furious when ex-President Clinton gave his only campus interview to Sue Wesley, **chair of the Young Republicans.**

See Section 17c-4.

* **articles.** The words **the, a,** and **an** used before a noun. **The** is called a **definite article** because it points to something specific: **the** book, **the** church, **the** criminal. **A** and **an** are **indefinite articles** because they refer more generally: **a** book, **a** church, **a** criminal. See Sections 25d and 33b.

as being. A wordy expression. You can usually cut **being.**

> In most cases, telephone solicitors are regarded **as (being)** a nuisance.

Asian American. The term now preferred by many Americans of Asian ancestry, replacing *Oriental.*

* **auxiliary verbs.** Verbs, usually some form of *be, do,* or *have,* that combine with other verbs to show various relations of tense, voice, mood, and so on. All the words in boldface are auxiliary verbs: **has** seen, **will be** talking, **would have been** going, **are** investigating, **did** mention, **should** prefer. Auxiliary verbs are also known as *helping verbs.* See Chapter 23.

averse/adverse. See **adverse/averse.**

awful. **Awful** is inappropriate as a synonym for **very.**

> INAPPROPRIATE   The findings of the two research teams were **awful** close.
>
> BETTER   The findings of the two research teams were **very** close.

awhile/a while. The expressions are not interchangeable. **Awhile** is an adverb; **a while** is a noun phrase. After prepositions, always use **a while.**

> Bud stood **awhile** looking at the grass.
>
> Bud decided that the lawn would not have to be cut for **a while.**

bad/badly. These words are troublesome. Remember that **bad** is an adjective describing what something is like; **badly** is an adverb explaining how something is done.

> Stanley's taste in music wasn't **bad**.
> Unfortunately, he treated his musicians **badly**.

Problems usually crop up with verbs that explain how something feels, tastes, smells, or looks. In such cases, use **bad**.

> The physicists felt **bad** about the disappearance of their satellite.
> The situation looked **bad**.

balanced sentence. A sentence containing two or more independent clauses that have parallel structure and are joined by a conjunction or a semicolon.

> Chapman arrived in a cloud of glory; he departed in a mist of shame.

because of/due to. Careful writers usually prefer **because of** to **due to** in many situations.

CONSIDERED AWKWARD	The investigation into Bud's sudden disappearance stalled **due to** Officer Bricker's concern for correct procedure.
REVISED	The investigation into Bud's sudden disappearance stalled **because of** Officer Bricker's concern for correct procedure.

However, **due to** is often the better choice when it serves as a **subject complement** after a **linking verb**. The examples illustrate the point.

> subj.   l. v.   subj. comp.
> Bricker's discretion seemed **due to** cowardice.
> subj.   l. v.   subj. comp.
> His discretion was **due to** the political and social prominence of the Huttons.

being as/being that. Both of these expressions sound wordy and awkward when used in place of **because** or **since**. Use **because** and **since** in formal and academic writing.

INAPPROPRIATE	**Being that** her major was astronomy, Jenny was looking forward to the eclipse.
BETTER	**Since** her major was astronomy, Jenny was looking forward to the eclipse.

beside/besides. **Beside** is a preposition meaning "next to" or "alongside"; **besides** is a preposition meaning "in addition to" or "other than."

> **Besides** a sworn confession, the detectives also had the suspect's fingerprints on a gun found **beside** the body.

Besides can also be an adverb meaning "in addition" or "moreover."

> Professor Bellona didn't mind assisting the athletic department, and **besides,** she actually liked coaching volleyball.

between.   See **among/between.**

black.   A term that has fallen somewhat out of favor as a term to describe people of African descent. Many American blacks now prefer the term **African American.** The terms *black* and *white* are ordinarily not capitalized, though some writers do prefer to capitalize *Black.*

British.   The term refers to the people of Scotland and Wales in addition to those of England. *English* refers chiefly to those people of the British Isles who come from within the borders of England itself.

can/may.   Understand the difference between the auxiliary verbs **can** and **may.** (See also **modal auxiliary.**) Use **can** to express an ability to do something.

> Charnelle **can** work differential equations.
>
> According to the *Handbook of College Policies,* Dean Rack **can** lift the suspension.

Use **may** to express either permission or possibility.

> You **may** want to compare my solution to the problem to Charnelle's.
>
> Dean Rack **may** lift the suspension, but I wouldn't count on that happening.

cannot.   **Cannot** is ordinarily written as one word, not two.

can't.   Writers sometimes forget the apostrophe in this contraction and others like it: **don't, won't.**

can't hardly.   A colloquial expression that is, technically, a double negative. Use **can hardly** instead when you write.

> DOUBLE NEGATIVE   I **can't hardly** see the road.
> REVISED   I **can hardly** see the road.

* **cardinal numbers.**   Numbers that express an amount: *one, two, three.* In contrast, **ordinal numbers** show a sequence: *first, second, third.*

* **case.**   The form a noun or pronoun takes to indicate its function in a sentence. Nouns have only two cases: the **possessive** form, to show ownership (*girl's, Greta's, swimmers'*), and the **common** form, to serve all other uses (*girl, Greta, swimmers*). See Section 25b.

Pronouns have three forms: **subjective, objective,** and **possessive.** (See Chapter 28.) The **subjective** (or **nominative**) **case** is the form a pronoun takes when it is the subject of a sentence or a clause. Pronouns in this case are the doers of actions: *I, you, she, he, it, we, they, who.*

A pronoun is in the **objective case** when something is done to it. This is also the form a pronoun has after a preposition: (*to*) *me, her, him, us, them, whom.* For the pronouns *you* and *it,* the subjective and objective forms are identical.

A pronoun is in the **possessive case** when it shows ownership: *my, mine, your, yours, her, his, its, our, ours, their, theirs, whose.*

censor/censure. These words have different meanings. As verbs, **censor** means "to cut," "to repress," or "to remove"; **censure** means "to disapprove" and "to condemn."

> The student editorial board voted to **censor** the four-letter words from Connie Lim's editorial and to **censure** her for attempting to publish the controversial piece.

* **clause.** A group of related words that has a subject and verb. Clauses can be independent or dependent.

> Whenever it could, **the Astronomy Club scheduled meetings at an isolated hilltop observatory.**

An **independent clause** can stand alone as a complete sentence.

> The Astronomy Club scheduled meetings at an isolated hilltop observatory.

A **dependent** (or **subordinate**) **clause** is a group of words that cannot stand alone as a sentence even though it contains a subject and a verb.

> **Whenever it could,** the Astronomy Club scheduled meetings at an isolated hilltop observatory.

See Section 17d.

cliché. A tired expression or conventional way of expressing something: *guilty as sin, hungry enough to eat a horse, sleep like a log, dumb as a rock.*

coherence. Unity in a paragraph or longer piece of writing. See Section 13a.

* **collective noun.** A noun that names a group: *team, orchestra, jury, committee.* Collective nouns can be either singular or plural, depending on how they are used in a sentence.

* **comma splice.** The mistaken use of a comma to join two groups of words, each of which could be a sentence by itself. Also called a comma fault. See Sections 35c and 36c-2.

> COMMA SPLICE   David liked Corvettes, they were fast cars.
>
> CORRECTED   David liked Corvettes because they were fast cars.

common knowledge. Facts, dates, events, information, and concepts that belong generally to an educated public.

* **common noun.** A noun that names some general object, not a specific person, place, or thing: *singer, continent, car.* Common nouns are not capitalized.

* **comparative and superlative.** Adjectives and adverbs can express three different levels or degrees of intensity—the positive, the comparative, and the superlative. The positive level describes a single condition; the comparative ranks two conditions; the superlative ranks three or more.

POSITIVE	COMPARATIVE	SUPERLATIVE
cold	colder	coldest
bad	worse	worst
angry	more angry	most angry
angrily	more angrily	most angrily

* **complement.** A word or phrase that completes the meaning of a verb, a subject, or an object. A **verb complement** is a **direct** or **indirect object.** A **subject complement** is a noun, pronoun, or adjective (or a comparable phrase) that follows a linking verb (a verb such as *to be, to seem, to appear, to feel,* and *to become*) and modifies or explains the subject, as in these examples.

> Eleanor is Bruce's **cat.**
> Eleanor is grossly **overweight.**
> Eleanor is the **one** on the sagging couch.

Object complements are nouns or adjectives (or comparable phrases) that follow direct objects and modify them.

> A pet food company named Eleanor **"Fat Cat of the Year."**
> Mackerel makes Eleanor **happy.**

complement/complementary, compliment/complimentary. The words are not synonyms. **Complement** and **complementary** describe things completed or compatible. **Compliment** and **complimentary** refer to things praised or given away free.

> Travis's sweater **complemented** his green eyes.
>
> The two parts of Greta's essay were **complementary,** examining the same subject from differing perspectives.
>
> Travis **complimented** Greta on her successful paper.
>
> Greta found his **compliment** sincere.
>
> She rewarded him with a **complimentary** sack of rice cakes from her health food store.

* **complex sentence.** A sentence that combines an independent clause and one or more dependent (subordinate) clauses. See also **clause.**

> dependent clause + *independent clause*
> ***When Rita Ruiz first saw the announcements for the job fair,*** she began to get nervous.

* **compound sentence.**   A sentence that combines two or more independent clauses, usually joined by a coordinating conjunction (*and, or, nor, for, but, yet, so*) or a semicolon.

  independent clause + independent clause
  Recruiters from industry have set up booths on campus, *and* several corporations are sending recruiters to interview students.

* **compound-complex sentence.**   A sentence that combines two or more independent clauses and at least one dependent (subordinate) clause. See also **clause.**

  dependent clause + independent clause + independent clause
  Although business is slow, recruiters from industry have set up booths on campus, *and* several corporations are sending recruiters to interview students.

* **concrete noun.**   A noun that names objects or events with physical properties or existences: *butter, trees, asteroid, people.* Concrete nouns are defined in contrast to **abstract nouns.**

* **conjugation.**   The forms of a given verb as it appears in all numbers, tenses, voices, and moods. See Anatomy of a Verb, pages 432–34.

* **conjunctions, coordinating.**   The words *and, or, nor, for, but, yet,* and *so* used to link words, phrases, and clauses that serve equivalent functions in a sentence. A coordinating conjunction is used to join two independent clauses or two dependent clauses; it would not link a subordinate clause to an independent clause. See also **conjunctions, subordinating.**

  Oscar **and** Marie directed the play.
  Oscar liked the story, **but** Marie did not.

* **conjunctions, subordinating.**   Words or expressions such as *although, because, if, since, before, after, when, even though, in order that,* and *while* that relate dependent (that is, subordinate) clauses to independent ones. Subordinating conjunctions introduce subordinate clauses.

  subordinate clause
  Although Oscar and Marie both directed parts of the show, Marie got most of the blame for its failure.
  subordinate clause
  Oscar liked the story **even though** no one else did.
  subordinate clause
  When the show opened, audiences stayed away.

  See Section 17d-2.

* **conjunctive adverbs.**   Words such as *however, therefore, nevertheless,* and *moreover,* used to link one independent clause to another. Conjunctive adverbs are weaker links than **coordinating conjunctions** (such as *and, but, or,* and *yet*) and must be preceded by a semicolon when used to join independent clauses.

  Darwin apologized; **nevertheless,** Rita considered suing him.

  See Sections 17f-4 and 37a-3.

connotation.   Connotation is what a word suggests beyond its basic dictionary meaning—that is, the word with all its particular emotional, political, or ethical associations. While any number of words may describe a *fight*, for example, and so share the same **denotation** (generic meaning), such words as *scrap, brawl, battle, fisticuffs, altercation*, and *set-to* differ significantly in what they imply—in their **connotations**. When using a list or collection of synonyms—such as you would find in a thesaurus—be sure you understand the connotation of any words you decide to use. See Section 16b.

conscience/conscious.   Don't confuse these words. **Conscience** is a noun referring to an inner ethical sense; **conscious** is an adjective describing a state of awareness or wakefulness.

> The linebacker felt a twinge of **conscience** after knocking the quarterback **unconscious.**

consensus.   This expression is redundant when followed by **of opinion**; **consensus** by itself implies an opinion. Use **consensus** alone.

> REDUNDANT   The student senate reached a **consensus of opinion** on the issue of censorship.
>
> REVISED   The student senate reached a **consensus** on the issue of censorship.

* **contraction.**   A word shortened by the omission of a letter or letters. In most cases, an apostrophe is used to indicate the deleted letters or sounds: *it is* = **it's**; *you are* = **you're**; *who is* = **who's.**

* **coordinate adjective.**   Coordinate adjectives are adjectives that modify the nouns they precede, not each other.

> Mali is a **bright, creative,** and **productive** artist.

See **noncoordinate adjective** and Sections 17b-1 and 36c-4.

* **coordinating conjunction.**   See **conjunctions, coordinating.**

* **correlatives.**   Words that work together as conjunctions: *either . . . or, neither . . . nor, whether . . . or, both . . . and, not only . . . but also.*

> **Whether** Darwin **or** Travis plays makes little difference.
>
> Brian attributed the failure of the play **not only** to a bad script **but also** to incompetent direction.

could of/would of/should of.   Nonstandard forms when used instead of **could have, would have,** or **should have.**

> WRONG   Coach Rhoades imagined that his team **could of** been a contender.
>
> RIGHT   Coach Rhoades imagined that his team **could have** been a contender.

* **count noun.**   A noun that names any object that exists as an individual item: *car, child, rose, cat.*

couple of.   Casual. Avoid it in formal or academic writing.

> INFORMAL   The article accused the admissions office of a **couple of** major blunders.
>
> REVISED   The article accused the admissions office of **several** major blunders.

credible/credulous.   **Credible** means "believable"; **credulous** means "willing to believe on slim evidence." See also **incredible/incredulous.**

> Officer Bricker found Mr. Hutton's excuse for his speeding **credible.** However, Bricker was known to be a **credulous** police officer, liable to believe any story.

Criteria, criterion.   **Criteria,** the plural form, is more familiar, but the word does have a singular form—**criterion.**

> John Maynard, age sixty-four, complained that he was often judged according to a single **criterion,** his age.
>
> Other **criteria** ought to matter in hiring.

cumulative sentence.   A sentence in which an independent clause is followed by a series of modifiers.

> Dr. Coles praised the volunteers as an outstanding group of young people, energetic, knowledgeable, and dependable.

See Section 17j.

curriculum, curricula.   **Curriculum** is the singular form; **curricula** is the plural.

> Dean Perez believed that the **curriculum** in history had to be strength-ened.
>
> Indeed, she believed that the **curricula** in all the liberal arts depart-ments needed rethinking.

* **dangling modifier.**   A modifying phrase that doesn't seem connected to any word or phrase in a sentence. Dangling modifiers are usually cor-rected by rewriting a sentence to provide a better link between the modifier and what it modifies. See Section 30a. See also **absolute.**

> DANGLING   **After finding the courage to ask Richard out,** the evening was a disaster.
>
> IMPROVED   After finding the courage to ask Richard out, Francie had a disastrous evening.

data/datum. **Data** is the plural form of *datum*. But in informal writing and speech, you will typically see *data* treated as if it were singular.

The *data* **is** not convincing.

In academic writing use **datum** when a singular form is expected. If **datum** seems awkward, rewrite the sentence to avoid the singular.

SINGULAR The most intriguing **datum** in the study was the rate of population decline.

PLURAL In all the **data,** no figure was more intriguing than the rate of population decline.

* **demonstrative adjective.** An adjective that points to a specific object: *this* house, not *that* one; *those* rowdies who disrupted *these* proceedings last month.

* **demonstrative pronoun.** A pronoun that points something out: *this, that, these, those.*

denotation. The specific meaning of a term. Sometimes called the dictionary meaning, the denotation of a word attempts to explain what the word is or does, stripped of particular emotional, political, cultural, or ethical associations. See **connotation.**

* **dependent clause.** See **clause.**

* **determiner.** A word indicating that a noun must follow. Determiners in English include articles (*a, an, the*) and certain possessive pronouns (*my, your*).

dialect. A spoken variation of a language. See Section 16e.

diction. See **word choice.**

different from/different than. In formal writing, **different from** is usually preferred to **different than.**

INFORMAL Ike's account of his marriage proposal was **different than** Bernice's.

FORMAL Ike's account of his marriage proposal was **different from** Bernice's.

* **direct discourse.** The actual words of a speaker or writer. Direct discourse is enclosed within quotation marks. See **indirect discourse.**

DIRECT As she approached the altar, Bernice yelled, "I won't marry you!"

INDIRECT As she approached the altar, Bernice declared that she would not marry Ike.

discreet/discrete. Discreet means "tactful" or "sensitive to appearances" (*discreet* behavior); **discrete** means "individual" or "separate" (*discrete* objects).

> Joel was **discreet** about the money spent on his project.
> He had several **discrete** funds at his disposal.

disinterested/uninterested. These words don't mean the same thing. **Disinterested** means "neutral" or "uninvolved"; **uninterested** means "not interested" or "bored."

> Alyce and Richard sought a **disinterested** party to arbitrate their dispute.
> Stanley was **uninterested** in the club's management.

don't. Writers sometimes forget the apostrophe in this contraction and others like it: **can't, won't.**

* **double negative.** Two negatives in a sentence that emphasize a negative idea. Such expressions are considered nonstandard in English.

> INCORRECT   Don't **never** use a double negative.
>   Ike **won't** say **nothing** about his wedding plans.

To correct a double negative, eliminate one of the negatives in the sentence.

> CORRECT   **Never** use a double negative.
>   **Don't** use a double negative.
>
> CORRECT   Ike will say **nothing** about his wedding plans.
>   Ike **won't** say anything about his wedding plans.

* **double possessive.** A form such as *a friend of Ruth's,* which includes two indications of possession—an *of* and an *'s.*

due to/because of. See **because of/due to.**

due to the fact that. Wordy. Replace it with **because** whenever you can.

> WORDY   Coach Meyer was fired **due to the fact that** he won no games.
>
> REVISED   Coach Meyer was fired **because** he won no games.

effect/affect. See **affect/effect.**

elicit/illicit. These words have vastly different meanings. **Elicit** means to "draw out" or "bring forth"; **illicit** describes something illegal or prohibited.

> The detective tried to **elicit** an admission of **illicit** behavior from Bud.

* **elliptical construction.** A phrase or sentence from which words have been deleted without obscuring the meaning. Elliptical constructions are common.

When [she is] asked about Rodney, Sue Ellen groans.
She likes reading books better than [she likes] writing them.
Curtis is a tough guy at heart, but [he is] a softie on the surface.
He senses [that] he was wrong.

elude/allude. See **allude/elude.**

eminent/imminent. These words are sometimes confused. **Eminent** means "distinguished" and "prominent"; **imminent** describes something about to happen.

The arrival of the **eminent** scholar is **imminent.**

enthused. A colloquial expression that should not appear in academic or professional writing. Use **enthusiastic** instead.

INFORMAL	Francie was **enthused** about Wilco's latest album.
BETTER	Francie was **enthusiastic** about Wilco's latest album.

Never use **enthused** as a verb.

equally as. Redundant. Use either **equally** or **as** to express a comparison—whichever works in a particular sentence.

REDUNDANT	Sue Ellen is **equally as** concerned as Hector about bilingual education.
REVISED	Sue Ellen is **as** concerned as Hector about bilingual education.
REVISED	Sue Ellen and Hector are **equally** concerned about bilingual education.

Eskimo. Falling out of favor as a term to describe the native peoples of Northern Canada and Alaska. Many now prefer *Inuit.*

* **essential modifier.** See **restrictive element.**

etc. This common abbreviation for *et cetera* should be avoided in most academic and formal writing. Instead, use **and so on** or **and so forth.** Never use **and etc.**

even though. **Even though** is two words, not one.

everyone/every one. These similar expressions mean different things. **Everyone** describes a group collectively. **Every one** focuses on the individual elements within a group or collective term. Notice the difference highlighted in these sentences.

Every one of those problems could develop into an international crisis **everyone** would regret.

I doubt that **everyone** will be able to attend **every one** of the sessions.

except/accept. See **accept/except.**

* **expletive construction.** The words **there** and **it** used as sentence lead-ins.

> **It is** going to be a day to remember.
> **There were** hundreds of spectators watching the demonstrators.

Expletive constructions often contribute to wordiness. Cut them whenever you can.

> REVISED Hundreds of spectators were watching the demonstrators.

fact that, the. Wordy. You can usually replace the entire expression with **that.**

WORDY	Bud was aware of **the fact that** he was in a strange room.
REVISED	Bud was aware **that** he was in a strange room.

faith/fate. A surprising number of writers confuse these words and their variations: **faithful, fateful, faithless. Faith** is confidence, trust, or a religious belief; **fate** means "destiny" or "outcome."

farther/further. Although the distinction between these words is not always observed, it is useful. Use **farther** to refer to distances that can be measured.

> It is **farther** from El Paso to Houston than from New York to Detroit.

Use **further,** meaning "more" or "additional," when physical distance or separation is not involved.

> The detective decided that the crime warranted **further** investigation.

fate/faith. See **faith/fate.**

* **faulty predication.** A term used to describe verbs that don't fit their subjects. In faulty predication, a subject could not logically perform the action specified by the verb.

POSSIBLE PROBLEM	The purpose of radar detectors **is banned** in a few states. What is forbidden—radar detectors or their purpose?
POSSIBLE REVISION	Radar detectors **are banned** in a few states.

At other times a linking verb is used incorrectly to connect words that aren't really equivalent. In the following example, the noun *problem* cannot be linked to the adverb *when.*

PROBLEM	A common problem with some foreign bikes **is** *when* you have them serviced.
REVISED	A common problem with foreign bikes **is** getting them serviced.

fewer than/less than.   Use **fewer than** with things you can count; use **less than** with quantities that must be measured or can be considered as a whole.

> The express lane was reserved for customers buying **fewer than** ten items.

> Matthew had **less than** half a gallon of gasoline.

> He also had **less than** ten dollars.

figurative language.   Language that includes analogies, metaphors, and similes that create images for the readers or listeners. See Section 18e.

* **finite verb.**   A verb that changes form to indicate person, number, and tense. A complete sentence requires a finite verb. Finite verbs stand in contrast to **nonfinite verb** forms such as **infinitives, participles,** and **gerunds,** which do not change form and which cannot stand as the only verb in a sentence. (See Section 24b.) Compare the following finite and nonfinite forms.

FINITE VERBS	He **ensures** freshness.
	The baker **kneads** the dough.
NONFINITE VERBS	**To ensure** freshness, Jean-Pierre buys eggs from local farms.
	The baker **kneading** the dough sneezed.

flaunt/flout.   These words are confused surprisingly often. **Flaunt** means "to show off"; **flout** means "to disregard" or "to show contempt for."

> To **flaunt** his wealth, Mr. Lin bought a Van Gogh landscape.

> **Flouting** a gag order, the newspaper published its exposé of corruption in the city council.

* **fragment.**   A group of words that does not fully express an idea even though it is punctuated as a sentence. A fragment may also be called a broken sentence. See Section 35a.

FRAGMENT	Despite the fact that Professor Chase had an impressive portfolio of investments.
COMPLETE SENTENCE	Despite the fact that Professor Chase had an impressive portfolio of investments, she was still careful with her money.
FRAGMENTS	Bonds. A safe investment most of the time.
COMPLETE SENTENCE	Bonds are a safe investment most of the time.

fun, funner, funnest.   Used as an adjective, **fun** is not appropriate in academic writing; replace it with a more formal expression.

| INFORMAL | Skiing is a **fun** sport. |
| FORMAL | Skiing is an **enjoyable** sport. |

The comparative and superlative forms, **funner** and **funnest**, while increasingly common in spoken English, are inappropriate in writing. In writing, use **more fun** or **most fun.**

INFORMAL Albert found tennis **funner** than squash.
FORMAL   Albert found tennis **more fun** than squash.

SPOKEN   He thought racquetball the **funnest** of the three sports.
WRITTEN   He thought racquetball the **most fun** of the three sports.

* **fused sentence.**   See **run-on sentence.**

gay.   A term now widely used to mean "homosexual." Less formal than *homosexual,* **gay** is still appropriate in most writing when used as an adjective. (As a noun— *a gay* or *the gays*—the term is inappropriate and should be avoided.) While **gay** is often used without regard to gender, some prefer it as a term that refers mainly to homosexual men, with **lesbian** the appropriate term for homosexual women.

* **gender.**   A classification of nouns and pronouns as masculine (*actor, muscleman, he*), feminine (*actress, midwife, she*), or neuter (*tree, it*).

* **gerund.**   A verb form used as a noun: *smiling, biking, walking.* (See Section 24a-3.) Most gerunds end in **-ing** and, consequently, look identical to the present participle.

GERUND   **Smiling** is good for the health.
PARTICIPLE A **smiling** critic is dangerous.

The difference is that gerunds function as nouns while participles act as modifiers. Gerunds usually appear in the present tense, but they can take other forms.

Having been criticized made Brian angry.
gerund in past tense, passive voice, acting as subject of the sentence

Being asked to play an encore was a compliment Otto enjoyed.
gerund in present tense, passive voice, as subject of sentence

get/got/gotten.   The principal parts of this verb are:

PRESENT	PAST	PAST PARTICIPLE
get	got	got, gotten

Gotten usually sounds more polished than **got** as the past participle in American English, but both forms are acceptable.

Aretha **has gotten** an *A* average in microbiology.
Aretha **has got** an *A* average in microbiology.

Many expressions, formal and informal, rely on **get.** Use the less formal ones only with appropriate audiences.

get it together
get straight
get real

good and.   Informal. Avoid it in academic writing.

> INFORMAL   The lake was **good and** cold when the sailors threw Sean in.
> BETTER   The lake was **icy** cold when the sailors threw Sean in.

good/well.   These words cause many problems. (See Section 30c-2.) As a modifier, **good** is an adjective only; **well** can be either an adjective or an adverb. Consider the difference between these sentences, where each word functions as an adjective.

> Katy is **good.**
> Katy is **well.**

Good is often mistakenly used as an adverb.

> WRONG   Juin conducts the orchestra **good.**
> RIGHT   Juin conducts the orchestra **well.**
>
> WRONG   The bureaucracy at NASA runs **good.**
> RIGHT   The bureaucracy at NASA runs **well.**

Complications occur when writers and speakers—eager to avoid using **good** incorrectly—substitute **well** as an adjective where **good** used as an adjective may be more accurate.

> WRONG   After a shower, Coach Rhoades smells **well.**
> RIGHT   After a shower, Coach Rhoades smells **good.**
>
> RIGHT   I feel **good.**
> ALSO RIGHT I feel **well.**

handicapped.   Falling out of favor as a term to describe people with physical disabilities. However, euphemistic alternatives such as *differently abled* and *physically challenged* have been roundly criticized. (See Section 16d-3.)

hanged, hung.   **Hanged** has been the past participle conventionally reserved for executions; **hung** is used on other occasions. The distinction is a nice one, probably worth observing.

> Connie was miffed when her disgruntled editorial staff decided she should be **hanged** in effigy.
> Portraits of the faculty were **hung** in the student union.

* **helping verbs.**   See **auxiliary verbs.**

he/she.   Using **he/she** (or *his/her* or *s/he*) is a way to avoid a sexist pronoun reference. Many readers find expressions with slashes clumsy and prefer *he or she* and *his or her.*

Hispanic.   A term falling somewhat out of favor among some groups, in part because of its imprecision. Groups that have fallen under the Hispanic label now often prefer to be identified more precisely: *Chicano/Chicana, Cuban American, Latin American, Mexican American, Puerto Rican.*

hisself. A nonstandard form. Don't use it.

homonyms. Words of different meanings and spellings pronounced alike: *straight/strait, peace/piece, their/there.*

hopefully. Some readers object to using the adverb *hopefully* as a sentence modifier. They would consider the following sentences ambiguous and incorrect.

> **Hopefully,** the stock market will grow.
> The government, **hopefully,** will not impose price controls.

Hopefully, they argue, should be used to mean only "with hope."

> Traders watched **hopefully** as stock prices approached yet another record.

However, English includes many adverbs like *hopefully* that function as sentence modifiers, including words such as *understandably, mercifully, predictably,* and *honestly,* By precedent and general usage, *hopefully* seems entrenched as a sentence modifier.

idiom. A widely accepted expression that does not seem to make literal sense. Idioms often mean more than the sum of their parts.

> The jet fighter **bit the big one** over Montana.
> Let's **get cracking.** We're late.
> Alyce hoped Richard would **cough up** the money.

Idiom can also describe a vocabulary and language style shared within certain groups or professions: the *idiom* of medical personnel, the *idiom* of computer specialists, the *idiom* of literary critics.

illicit/elicit. See **elicit/illicit.**

illusion/allusion. See **allusion/illusion.**

imminent/eminent. See **eminent/imminent.**

* **imperative mood.** The form of a verb that expresses a command (see **mood**).

> **Go! Find** that missing canister of film. **Bring** it back to the lab.

imply/infer. Think of these words as opposite sides of the same coin. **Imply** means "to suggest" or "to convey an idea without stating it." **Infer** is what you might do to figure out what someone else has implied: you examine evidence and draw conclusions from it.

> By joking calmly, the pilot sought to **imply** that the aircraft was out of danger. But from the crack that had opened in the wing, the passengers **inferred** that the landing would be harrowing.

incredible/incredulous. **Incredible** means "unbelievable"; **incredulous** means "unwilling to believe" and "doubting." See also **credible/credulous.**

The press found the governor's explanation for his wealth **incredible.** You could hardly blame them for being **incredulous** when he attributed his vast holdings to coupon savings.

* **indefinite pronoun.** A pronoun that does not refer to a particular person, thing, or group: *all, any, each, everybody, everyone, one, none, somebody, someone,* and so on. See Section 27b.

* **independent clause.** See **clause.**

* **indicative mood.** The form of a verb that states facts or asks questions (see **mood**).

Did he **find** the canister of film? It **was** in the lab yesterday.

indirect discourse. The substance of what a speaker or writer has said, but not the exact words. Indirect discourse is not surrounded by quotation marks. See **direct discourse.**

DIRECT	At the altar Ike told Bernice, "If you don't marry me, I'll sue."
INDIRECT	At the altar Ike told Bernice he would sue her if she didn't marry him.

infer/imply. See **imply/infer.**

* **infinitive.** A verbal that can usually be identified by the word **to** preceding the base form of a verb: *to strive, to seek, to find, to endure.* Infinitives do take other forms to show various tenses and voices: *to be seeking, to have found, to have been found.* Infinitives can act as nouns, adjectives, adverbs, and absolutes (see Section 24a).

INFINITIVE AS NOUN	**To capture** a market is not easy. subject of the sentence
INFINITIVE AS ADJECTIVE	Greta had many posters **to redesign.** modifies the noun *posters*
INFINITIVE AS ADVERB	Mr. Stavros laughed **to forget** his troubles. modifies the verb *laughed*
INFINITIVE AS ABSOLUTE	**To be blunt,** the paper is plagiarized.

* **inflection.** A change a word undergoes to specify its meaning or to reflect a relationship to other words or phrases in a sentence. For instance, verbs change to reflect shifts in tense, person, and number (*walk, walks, walked*). Nouns change to indicate number and possession (*antenna, antennae; Pearl, Pearl's*). Adverbs and adjectives show degrees of comparison (*cold, colder, coldest; happily, more happily, most happily*).

initialism. A single term created by joining the first letters of the words that make up the full name or description. Unlike acronyms, however, initialisms are pronounced letter by letter.

> IRS—Internal Revenue Service
> CIA—Central Intelligence Agency
> HBO—Home Box Office

See **acronym** and Section 42a-2.

* **intensifier.** A modifier that adds emphasis: *so, very, extremely, intensely, really, certainly.*

> **so** cold   **very** bold   **extremely** complex

* **intensive pronoun.** A pronoun form, created when **-self** or **-selves** is added to personal pronouns (*myself, yourself, herself, itself, oneself, ourselves, yourselves, themselves*), that modifies a noun to add emphasis. See Section 29a

> Otto **himself** admitted he was the winner.
> The managers did all the printing **themselves.**

* **intentional fragment.** A group of words that does not have all the usual parts of a sentence but can act as a sentence because it expresses an idea fully. See Section 35b.

> INTENTIONAL FRAGMENTS   So what?   Big deal!

* **interjection.** A word that expresses emotion or feeling, but that is not grammatically a part of a sentence. Interjections can be punctuated as exclamations (!) or attached to a sentence with a comma. Interjections include *oh, hey, wow,* and *well.*

* **interrogative pronoun.** A pronoun used to pose a question: *who, which, what, whose.*

* **intransitive verb.** A verb that does not take a direct object. This means that the action of an intransitive verb does not pass on to someone or something; the sentence is complete without an object.

> INTRANSITIVE   I **slept** well.
>   Lawrence **wept.**

Linking verbs are intransitive.

> INTRANSITIVE   I **am** happy.
>   You **have been** absent.

Compare intransitive verbs to **transitive** verbs, which require an object to complete the action of a sentence.

> TRANSITIVE   Travis accidentally **pushed** *Kyle.*
>   Sister Anne **bit** her *lip.*

* **inversion.** A reversal in the normal subject-verb-object order of a sentence.

> Off came the wheel.
>
> Our lives we hold less dear than our honor.

irregardless. A nonstandard form. Use **regardless** instead.

* **irregular verb.** A verb that does not form its past and past participle forms by adding *-d* or *-ed* to the infinitive (see **principal parts of a verb**). Irregular verbs are both numerous and important (see the full chart in Section 23d). They change their forms in various ways; a few even use the same form for all three principal parts.

INFINITIVE	PAST	PAST PARTICIPLE
burst	burst	burst
drink	drank	drunk
arise	arose	arisen
go	went	gone

irritate/aggravate. See **aggravate/irritate**.

its/it's. Don't confuse these terms. **It's** is a contraction for *it is*. **Its** is a possessive pronoun meaning "belonging to it." See Section 28g for a discussion of this problem.

jargon. The term has two meanings: (1) the specialized language of a profession or craft, and (2) wordy, impersonal writing full of abstract terms and long sentences. See Section 16c-3.

judgment/judgement. The British spell this word with two *e*'s. Americans spell it with just one: **judgment**.

kind of. This expression is colloquial when used to mean "rather." Avoid *kind of* in formal writing.

> COLLOQUIAL   The college trustees were **kind of** upset by the bad publicity.
>
> MORE FORMAL The college trustees were **rather** upset by the bad publicity.

less than. See **fewer than/less than**.

lie/lay. These two verbs cause much trouble and confusion. Here are their parts.

PRESENT	PAST	PRESENT PARTICIPLE	PAST PARTICIPLE
lie (to recline)	lay	lying	lain
lay (to place)	laid	laying	laid

Notice that the past tense of **lie** is the same as the present tense of **lay**. It may help you to remember that **to lie** (meaning "to recline") is *intransitive*—that is, it doesn't take an object. You can't lie *something*.

> Travis **lies** under the cottonwood tree.
> He **lay** there all afternoon.
> He was **lying** in the hammock yesterday.
> He had **lain** there for weeks.

To lay (meaning "to place" or "to put") is *transitive*—it takes an object.

> Jenny **lays** a *book* on Travis's desk.
> Yesterday, she **laid** a *memo* on his desk.
> Jenny was **laying** the *memo* on Travis's desk when he returned.
> Travis had **laid** almost three *yards* of concrete that afternoon.

like/as.   Many readers object to **like** used to introduce clauses of comparison. **As, as if,** or **as though** are preferred in situations where a comparison involves a subject and verb.

> NOT   Mr. Butcher is self-disciplined, **like** you would expect a champion weightlifter to be.
>
> BUT   Mr. Butcher is self-disciplined, **as** you would expect a champion weightlifter to be.

> NOT   It looks **like** he will win the local competition again this year.
>
> BUT   It looks **as if** he will win the local competition again this year.

Like is acceptable when it introduces a prepositional phrase, not a clause.

> Yvonne looks **like** her mother.
> The sculpture on the mall looks **like** a rusted Edsel.

* **linking verb.**   A verb, often a form of *to be,* that connects a subject to a word or phrase that extends or completes its meaning. Other common linking verbs are *to seem, to appear, to feel,* and *to become.*

> Bob King **is** Dean of Humanities.
> She **seems** tired.

See Section 17a-3.

literally.   When you write that something is **literally** true, you mean that it is exactly as you have stated. The following sentence means that Bernice emitted heated water vapor, an unlikely event no matter how angry she was.

> Bernice **literally** steamed when Ike ordered her to marry him.

If you want to keep the image (*steamed*), omit **literally.**

> Bernice steamed when Ike ordered her to marry him.

lose/loose.   Be careful not to confuse these words. **Lose** is a verb, meaning "to misplace," "to be deprived of," or "to be defeated." **Loose** can be either an adjective or a verb. As an adjective, **loose** means "not tight"; as a verb, **loose** means "to let go" or "to untighten."

Without Martin as quarterback, the team might **lose** its first game of the season.

The strap on Martin's helmet had worked **loose**.

It **loosened** so much that Martin **lost** his helmet.

mad, angry.   See **angry/mad**.

majority/plurality.   There is a useful difference in meaning between these two words. A **majority** is more than half a group; a **plurality** is the largest part of a group when there is *less than* a *majority*. In an election, for example, a candidate who wins 50.1 percent of the vote can claim a **majority**. One who wins a race with 40 percent of the vote may claim a **plurality**, but not a majority.

man, mankind.   These terms are considered sexist by many readers since they implicitly exclude women from the human family.

> **Man** has begun to conquer space.

Look for alternatives, such as *humanity, men and women, the human race,* or *humankind.*

> **Men and women** have begun to conquer space.

many times.   Wordy. Use **often** instead.

may/can.   See **can/may**.

media/medium.   **Medium** is the singular of **media**.

> Connie believed that the press could be as powerful a **medium** as television.
> The visual **media** are discussed in the textbook.

The term **media** is commonly used to refer to newspapers and magazines, as well as television and radio.

> President Xiony declined to speak to the **media** about the fiscal problems facing the college.

metaphor.   A comparison that does not use the word *like* or *as.*

> All the world's a stage.
> I'm a little teacup, short and stout.

See also **mixed metaphor**.

Mexican American.   A preferred term for describing Americans of Mexican ancestry.

might of.   A nonstandard form. Use **might have** instead.

> NOT   Ms. Rajala **might of** never admitted the truth.
> BUT   Ms. Rajala **might have** never admitted the truth.

* **misplaced modifier.** A modifying word or phrase that is ambiguous because it could modify more than one thing. See Section 30a. See also **absolute.**

> MISPLACED MODIFIER   Some of the actors won roles **without talent.**
> IMPROVED   Some of the actors **without talent** won roles.

mixed metaphor. A metaphor in which the terms of the comparison are inconsistent, incongruent, or unintentionally comic.

> Unless we tighten our belts, we'll sink like a stone.
>
> The fullback was a bulldozer, running up and down the field on winged feet.

See Section 18e-2.

* **modal auxiliary.** An auxiliary verb that indicates possibility, necessity, permission, desire, capability, and so on. Modal auxiliaries include *can, could, may, might, will, shall, should, ought,* and *must.* See Section 32d.

> Hector **can** write.
> Hector **might** write.
> Hector **must** write.

* **modifier.** A word, phrase, or clause that gives information about another word, phrase, or clause. Writers use modifiers, mainly adjectives, adverbs, and modifying phrases, to make important qualifications in their writing, to make it more accurate, and sometimes to give it color and depth. See Chapter 30.

* **mood.** A term used to describe how a writer regards a statement: either as a fact (the **indicative** mood), as a command (the **imperative** mood), or as a wish, desire, supposition, or improbability (the **subjunctive** mood). Verbs change their form to show mood. See Section 23f.

> INDICATIVE   The engineer **was** careful.
> IMPERATIVE   **Be** careful!
> SUBJUNCTIVE   If the engineer **were** careful . . .

moral, morale. Don't confuse these words. As a noun, **moral** is a lesson. **Morale** is a state of mind.

> The **moral** of the fable was to avoid temptation.
> The **morale** of the team was destroyed by the accident.

must of. Nonstandard. Use **must have** instead.

> NOT   Someone **must of** read the book.
> BUT   Someone **must have** read the book.

Native American. The term now preferred by many people formerly described as American Indian.

nice. This adjective has little impact when used to mean "pleasant": **It was a nice day; Sally is a nice person.** In many cases, **nice** is damning with faint praise. Find a more specific word or expression. **Nice** can be used effectively to mean "precise" or "fine."

There was a **nice** distinction between the two positions.

* **nominal.** A word, phrase, or entire clause that acts like a noun in a sentence. **Pronouns** and **gerunds** often function as nominals.

The wild applause only encouraged **them.**   Pronoun *them* acts as an object.
Keeping a straight face wasn't easy.   Gerund phrase acts as a subject.

* **nominalizations.** Nouns created by adding endings to verbs and adjectives: *acceptability, demystification, prioritization,* and so on. Clumsy nominalizations of several syllables can usually be replaced by clearer terms. See Section 18c-2.

* **noncoordinate adjective.** Noncoordinate adjectives are adjectives or adjectivals that work together to modify a noun or pronoun. As a result, they cannot be sensibly rearranged.

her six completed chapters
a shiny blue Mustang convertible
our natural good humor

See **coordinate adjective** and Section 36c-5.

* **noncount noun.** A noun that names something that does not exist as a separable or individual unit: *blood, money, work, time.*

* **nonessential modifier.** See **nonrestrictive element.**

* **nonrestrictive (or nonessential) element.** A modifier, often a phrase, not essential to the meaning of a sentence. If the nonrestrictive element is removed, the basic meaning of the sentence is not altered.

The senator, **who often voted with the other party,** had few loyal friends and a weak constituency.

The agent, **a tall fellow from the FBI,** looked a bit self-conscious when he introduced himself.

Nonrestrictive phrases are ordinarily set off by commas. See **restrictive element** and Sections 36b-1 and 36b-2.

* **noun.** A word that names a person, place, thing, idea, or quality. In sentences, nouns can serve as subjects, objects, complements, appositives, and even modifiers. There are many classes of nouns: **common, proper, concrete, abstract, collective, noncount,** and **count.** See individual entries for details of each type.

nowheres. Nonstandard version of **nowhere** or **anywhere.**

COLLOQUIAL The chemist couldn't locate the test tube **nowheres**. It was **nowheres** to be found.

REVISED The chemist couldn't locate the test tube **anywhere**. It was **nowhere** to be found.

* **number.** The form a word takes to indicate whether it is singular or plural. See Section 25a.

SINGULAR boy his this
PLURAL boys their these

number/amount. See **amount/number**.

* **object, direct/indirect.** A word or phrase that receives the action of a verb. An object is **direct** when it states to whom or what an action was done.

direct obj.
Kim gave us **the signal**.

An object is **indirect** when it explains for whom or what an action is done or directed. It usually precedes the direct object.

indirect obj.
Kim gave **us** the signal.

* **objective case.** The form a noun or pronoun takes when it serves as a direct or an indirect object in a sentence or as the object of a preposition. See **case**.

off of. A wordy expression. **Off** is enough.

Arthur drove his Jeep **off** the road.

O.K., OK, okay. Not the best choice for formal writing. But give the expression respect. It's an internationally recognized expression of approval. OK?

* **ordinal numbers.** Numbers that express a sequence: *first, second, third*. In contrast, **cardinal numbers** express an amount: *one, two, three*.

Oriental. A term falling out of favor as a description of the people or cultures of East Asia. Terms preferred are *Asian* or *East Asian*.

paragraph. A cluster of sentences working together for some purpose: to develop a single idea, to show relationships between separate ideas, to move readers from one point to another, to introduce a subject, to conclude a discussion, and so on. Paragraphs are marked by separations (indentions or open spaces). Paragraphs vary greatly in length but may be as short as a single sentence. See Chapters 13 and 14.

The symbol ¶, meaning "paragraph," is sometimes inserted by editors and instructors where a new paragraph is needed in a paper. *No* ¶ indicates that an existing paragraph should be combined with another.

* **parallelism/parallel structure.** Ideas or items expressed in matching grammatical forms or structural patterns. Words, phrases, sentences, and even paragraphs can demonstrate parallelism. See Sections 10a-3 and 15b-5, and especially Section 17h.

PARALLEL VERBS	The child was **waving, smiling, jumping,** and **laughing**—all at the same time.
PARALLEL PHRASES	**On the sea, in the air, on the ground,** the forces of the Axis powers were steadily driven back.
PARALLEL CLAUSES	He was **the best of clowns;** he was **the worst of clowns.**
PARALLEL SENTENCES	The child was **waving, smiling, and laughing**—all at the same time. Her mother was **screaming, berating, and threatening**— **all to no avail.**

* **parenthetical element.** A word or phrase that contributes to a sentence but is not an essential part of it. Parenthetical items are usually separated from sentences by commas, dashes, or parentheses. When the element occurs in the middle of a sentence, it is set off by punctuation.

Orlando, **a wiry fellow,** climbed the sycamore tree easily.

Francie decided to climb an elm and—**still clutching her purse and camera**—soon waved from its topmost branches.

All the while, Richard **(the most vocal advocate of tree climbing)** remained on *terra firma.*

* **participle.** A verb form that is used as a modifier (see Section 24a-2). The present participle ends with **-ing.** For regular verbs, the past participle ends with **-ed;** for irregular verbs, the form of the past participle will vary. Participles have the following forms.

TO PERFORM (A REGULAR VERB)
Present, active:	performing
Present, passive:	being performed
Past, active:	performed
Past, passive:	having been performed

Participles can serve as simple modifiers.

Smiling, Officer Bricker wrote the traffic ticket. Modifies *Officer Bricker.*

But they often take objects, complements, and modifiers of their own to form verbal phrases, which play an important role in shaping sentences.

<u>Writing the ticket for speeding,</u> Bricker laughed at his own cleverness in catching Arthur.

<u>Having been ridiculed</u> often in the past by Arthur, Bricker now had his chance for revenge.

Arthur, <u>**knowing** what his friends were doing to Officer Bricker's patrol car,</u> smiled as he took the ticket.

Like an infinitive, a participle can also serve as an **absolute**—that is, a phrase that modifies an entire sentence.

All things **considered**, the prank was worth the ticket.

* **parts of speech.** The eight common categories by which words in a sentence are identified according to what they do, how they are formed, where they are placed, and what they mean. Those basic categories are **nouns, pronouns, adjectives, verbs, adverbs, prepositions, conjunctions,** and **interjections.**

passed/past. Be careful not to confuse these words. **Passed** is a verb form; **past** can function as a noun, adjective, adverb, or preposition. The words are not interchangeable. Study the differences in the following sentences.

PASSED AS VERB, PAST TENSE
Tina **passed** her economics examination.

PASSED AS VERB, PAST PARTICIPLE
Earlier in the day she had **passed** an English quiz.

PAST AS NOUN
In the **past,** she did well.

PAST AS ADJECTIVE
In the **past** semester, she got straight *A*'s.

PAST AS ADVERB
Smiling, Tina walked **past** the teacher.

PAST AS PREPOSITION
Past midnight, Tina was still celebrating.

* **passive verb/voice.** See **voice.**

persecute/prosecute. **Persecute** means "to oppress" or "to torment"; **prosecute** is a legal term meaning "to bring charges or legal proceedings" against someone or something.

Connie felt **persecuted** by criticisms of her political activism.

She threatened to **prosecute** anyone who interfered with her First Amendment rights.

* **person.** A way of classifying personal pronouns in sentences.

1st person: the speaker—*I, we*
2nd person: spoken to—*you*
3rd person: spoken about—*he, she, it, they* + all nouns

Verbs also change to indicate a shift in person.

1st person: I see.
3rd person: She sees.

personal/personnel. Notice the difference between these words. **Personal** refers to what is private, belonging to an individual. **Personnel** are the people staffing an office or institution.

Drug testing all airline **personnel** might infringe on **personal** freedom.

* **personal pronoun.** A pronoun that refers to particular individuals, things, or groups: *I, you, he, she, it, we, you, they.*

phenomena/phenomenon. You can win friends and influence people by spelling these words correctly and using **phenomenon** as the singular form.

The astral **phenomenon** of meteor showers is common in August.
Many other astral **phenomena** are linked to particular seasons.

* **phrase.** A group of related words that does not include both a subject and a finite verb. Among the types of phrases are **noun phrases, verb phrases, verbal phrases** (infinitive, gerund, and participial), **absolute phrases,** and **prepositional phrases.** See Section 17c.

NOUN PHRASE	**The members of the Astronomy Club** will be going to the observatory in a van.
VERB PHRASE	The members of the Astronomy Club **will be going** to the observatory in a van.
VERBAL PHRASE— INFINITIVE	Their intention is **to observe the planet Mars.**
VERBAL PHRASE— GERUND	**Driving to the observatory** will be half the fun.
VERBAL PHRASE— PARTICIPIAL	The instructor **sponsoring the trip** will drive the van.
ABSOLUTE PHRASE	**All things considered,** the trip was time well spent.
PREPOSITIONAL PHRASE	Whenever it could, the Astronomy Club scheduled its meetings **at the hilltop observatory.**

plurality/majority. See **majority/plurality.**

plus. Don't use **plus** as a conjunction or conjunctive adverb meaning "and," "moreover," "besides," or "in addition to."

NOT	Mr. Burton admitted to cheating on his income taxes this year. **Plus** he acknowledged that he had filed false returns for the last three years.
BUT	Mr. Burton admitted to cheating on his income taxes this year. **Moreover,** he acknowledged that he had filed false returns for the last three years.

possess.   Don't forget the final *s* in *possess*.

* possessive case.   The form a noun or pronoun takes to show ownership: *Barney's, Jean-Pierre's, mine, yours, hers, theirs.* See Sections 25b (nouns) and 28f (pronouns).

* possessive pronoun.   The form a pronoun takes when it shows ownership: *my, mine, your, yours, her, his, its, our, ours, their, whose, anyone's, somebody's.* See Section 28f.

* predicate.   A verb and all its auxiliaries, modifiers, and complements.

> The pregnant cat, enormous and fierce, **kittened in the back seat of Officer Bricker's car, where she planned to set up housekeeping.**

* predicate adjective.   An adjective that follows a linking verb and describes the subject.

> Coach Rhoades is **inept.**
> It was **cold.**

* predicate nominative.   A noun or pronoun that follows a linking verb and tells what the subject is.

> Rhoades is the **coach.**
> It was **she.**

prejudice/prejudiced.   Many writers and speakers use **prejudice** where they need **prejudiced**. **Prejudice** is a noun; **prejudiced** is a verb form.

> WRONG   Joe Kamakura is **prejudice** against liberals.
>
> RIGHT   Joe Kamakura is **prejudiced** against liberals.
>
> WRONG   **Prejudice** people are found in every walk of life.
>
> RIGHT   **Prejudiced** people are found in every walk of life.
>
> COMPARE   **Prejudice** is found in every walk of life.

* preposition.   A word that links a noun or pronoun to the rest of a sentence. Prepositions point out many kinds of basic relationships: *on, above, to, for, in, out, through, by,* and so on.

* prepositional phrase.   The combination of a preposition and a noun or pronoun. The following are prepositional phrases: *on our house, above it, to him, in love, through them, by the garden gate.* See Section 17c-1.

* principal parts of a verb.   The three basic forms of a verb from which all tenses are built. See Section 23d.

> **Infinitive (present).** This is the base form of a verb, the shape it takes when preceded by **to: to walk, to go, to choose.**
>
> **Past.** This is the simplest form a verb has to show action that has already occurred: **walked, went, chose.**
>
> **Past participle.** This is the form a verb takes when it is accompanied by an **auxiliary verb** to show a more complicated past tense: **had walked, might have gone, would have been chosen.**

principal/principle. Two terms commonly confused because of their multiple meanings. **Principal** means "chief" or "most important." It also names the head of an elementary or secondary school (remember "The **principal** is your pal"?). Finally, it can be a sum of money lent or borrowed.

> Ike intended to be the **principal** breadwinner of the household.

> Bernice accused Ike of acting like a power-mad high school **principal.**

> She argued that they would need two incomes just to meet their mortgage payments—both interest and **principal.**

A **principle,** on the other hand, is a guiding rule or fundamental truth.

> Ike declared it was against his **principles** to have his wife work.

> Bernice said he would just have to be a little less **principled** on that issue.

prioritize. Some readers object to this word, regarding it as less appropriate than its equivalents: **rank** or **list in order of priority.**

proceed to. A wordy and redundant construction when it merely delays the real action of a sentence.

> WORDY   We **proceeded to** open the strongbox.
>
> TIGHTER   We **opened** the strongbox.

* **progressive verb.** A verb form that shows continuing action. Progressive tenses are formed by the auxiliary verb *to be* + the present participle. See Sections 23a and 32a.

> *to be* + present participle
> Nelda **is conducting** her string orchestra.
> *to be* + present participle
> Nelda **had been conducting** the orchestra for many years.
> *to be* + present participle
> Nelda **will be conducting** the orchestra for many years to come.

* **pronoun.** A word that acts like a noun but doesn't name a specific person, place, or thing—*I, you, he, she, it, they, whom, who, what, myself, oneself, this, these, that, all, both, anybody,* and so on. There are many varieties of pronouns: **personal, relative, interrogative, intensive, reflexive, demonstrative, indefinite,** and **reciprocal.** See Chapters 26–29 and individual entries for details about each type.

* **proper adjective.** An adjective based on the name of a person, place, or thing. Proper adjectives are capitalized.

> **British** cuisine
> **Machiavellian** politics
> **Cubist** art

* **proper noun.** A noun that names some particular person, place, or thing: *Bryan Adams, Australia, Ford.* The first letter in proper nouns is capitalized.

* **qualifier.**   A modifier. Sometimes the word refers to particular classes of modifiers: **intensifiers** (*so, too, surely, certainly*), **restrictive expressions** (*many, most, both, some, almost*), or **conjunctive adverbs** (*however, nevertheless*).

* **quantifier.**   A word that precedes nouns and tells *how much* or *how many:* **some, several, a little.**

quote.   Some people do not accept **quote** used as a noun. To be safe, use **quotation** in formal writing.

real.   Often used as a colloquial version of **very:** "I was **real** scared." This usage is inappropriate in academic writing.

really.   An adverb too vague to make much of an impression in many sentences: **It was <u>really</u> hot; I am <u>really</u> sorry.** Replace **really** with a more precise expression or delete it.

reason is . . . because.   The expression is redundant. Use one half of the expression or the other—not both.

REDUNDANT	The **reason** the cat is ferocious is **because** she is protecting her kittens.
REVISED	The **reason** the cat is ferocious is **that** she is protecting her kittens.
REVISED	The cat is ferocious **because** she is protecting her kittens.

* **reciprocal pronoun.**   A compound pronoun that shows a mutual action: *one another, each other.*

The members of the jury whispered to **one another.**

redundancy.   Unnecessary repetition in writing.

refer/allude.   See **allude/refer.**

* **reference.**   The connection between a pronoun and the noun it stands in for (its **antecedent**). This connection should be clear and unambiguous. When a reader can't figure out who *he* is in a sentence you have written, or what exactly *this* or *it* may mean, you have a problem with unclear reference.

UNCLEAR REFERENCES
The sun broke through the mists as Jim and Jack, fully recovered from their accident, arrived with news about the award and the ceremony. **This** pleased us because **he** hadn't mentioned anything about **it.**

REFERENCES CLARIFIED
The sun broke through the mists as Jim and Jack, fully recovered from their accident, arrived with news about the award and the ceremony. **The news** pleased us because **Jim** hadn't mentioned anything about **a ceremony.**

See Chapter 26.

* **reflexive pronoun.** A pronoun form created when **-self** or **-selves** is added to personal pronouns (*myself, yourself, herself, himself, itself, oneself, ourselves, yourselves, themselves*). Use the reflexive form when both the subject and the object of an action are the same (see Section 29a).

> subj.   obj.
> **Chunyang** had only *himself* to rely on.
> subj.   obj.
> **They** took *themselves* too seriously.

* **regular verb.** A verb that forms its past and past participle forms (see **principal parts of a verb**) simply by adding **-d** or **-ed** to the infinitive. See Section 23a.

INFINITIVE	PAST	PAST PARTICIPLE
talk	talked	talked
coincide	coincided	coincided
advertise	advertised	advertised

* **relative clause.** See **adjective clauses** and **relative pronoun.**

* **relative pronoun.** A pronoun such as *that, which, whichever, who, whoever, whom, whomever, whose,* and *of which* that introduces subordinate clauses. In the following example, the relative pronoun *whichever* introduces a noun clause that forms the subject of the sentence.

> subordinate clause
> **Whichever** car you buy will cost a small fortune.

In this second example, the relative pronoun *which* introduces an adjective clause modifying *club.*

> subordinate clause
> Mr. Rao sold the club, **which** he had owned for twenty years.

A clause introduced by a relative pronoun is called a **relative clause.**

* **restrictive (or essential) element.** A modifier, usually a phrase, essential to the meaning of the subject or noun it modifies. If the restrictive element is removed, the sentence no longer makes sense.

> Only the senator **who voted "nay"** remained in the chamber.
> The agent **from the CIA** was the one who called.

Restrictive phrases are *not* set off by commas. See **nonrestrictive element** and Sections 36b-1 and 36b-2.

* **run-on sentence.** A faulty sentence in which two independent clauses (groups of words that could stand alone as sentences) are joined without appropriate punctuation marks or conjunctions. It may also be called a **fused sentence.** See Section 35d.

> RUN-ON   Reading *Ulysses* is one thing understanding it is another.
> CORRECTED   Reading *Ulysses* is one thing; understanding it is another.

* **sentence.**   A group of words that expresses an idea and is punctuated as an independent unit.

> Whenever it could, the Astronomy Club scheduled meetings in an isolated hilltop observatory.
>
> Is that true?
>
> Explain the situation to me.

* **sentence fragment.**   See **fragment.**

* **sentence structure.**   The way a sentence is put together—its organization or arrangement of phrases and clauses. Sentences can be described in many ways—for example, as *simple, complex, compound,* or *compound-complex; periodic* or *cumulative;* or *direct, complicated, tangled,* and so on. See Chapters 17 and 18.

* **sequence of tenses.**   The way the tense of one verb in a sentence limits or determines the tense of other verbs.

set/sit.   These two verbs can cause problems. Here are their parts.

PRESENT	PAST	PRESENT PARTICIPLE	PAST PARTICIPLE
set (put down)	set	setting	set
sit (take a seat)	sat	sitting	sat

It may help you to remember that **to sit** (meaning "to take a seat") is *intransitive*—that is, it doesn't take an object. You can't sit *something.*

> Haskell **sits** under the cottonwood tree.
> He **sat** there all afternoon.
> He was **sitting** in the hammock yesterday.
> He had **sat** there for several weeks.

To set (meaning "to place" or "to put") is *transitive*—it takes an object.

> Jenny **set** a *plate* on the table.
> At Christmas, we **set** a *star* atop the tree.
> Alex was **setting** the *music* on the stand when it collapsed.
> Connie discovered that Travis **had set** a *subpoena* on her desk.

sexist language.   Language that reflects prejudiced attitudes and stereotypical thinking about the sex roles and traits of both sexes. See Sections 16d and 29d.

s/he.   Most readers object to this construction which, like *he/she* and *she/he,* is an alternative to the nonsexist but clumsy *he or she.* Avoid **s/he.**

should of.   Mistaken form of **should have.** Also incorrect are **could of** and **would of.**

simile.   An explicit comparison between two things. In a simile, a word such as *like* or *as* underscores the comparison.

> Driving a Porsche 911 is **like** riding the surf at Waikiki.
> Graziella is **as** flaky **as** Wheaties.

simple sentence.   A sentence that has only one clause.

independent clause
Mardi Gras is celebrated just before Ash Wednesday.

sit/set.   See **set/sit.**

slang.   Casual, aggressively informal language.

The punk wanted to bum a cigarette off us, but we told him to get lost.

Slang expressions are out of place in most academic and business writing. See Sections 16a-3 and 16a-4.

so.   Vague when used as an intensifier, especially when no explanation follows **so:** *Sue Ellen was so sad.* **So** used this way can sound trite (how sad is **so** sad?) or juvenile: *Professor Sweno's play was so bad.* If you use **so,** complete your statement.

Sue Ellen was **so** sad she cried for an hour.

Professor Sweno's play was **so** bad that the audience cheered for the villains.

* **split infinitive.**   An infinitive interrupted by an adverb: *to boldly go; to really try.* Though correct, split infinitives offend some readers. To alter a split infinitive, simply place the adverb somewhere else in your sentence: *to go boldly.* See Section 24c.

stationary/stationery.   **Stationary,** an adjective, means "immovable, fixed in place." **Stationery** is a noun meaning "writing material." The words are not interchangeable.

* **subject.**   A word or phrase that names what a sentence is about. The **simple subject** of a sentence is a single word; the **complete subject** is the simple subject and all its modifiers.

SIMPLE SUBJECT
        subj.   verb
The **captain** of the new team quit.

COMPLETE SUBJECT
        subj.   verb
The captain of the new team *quit.*

* **subject complement.**   A word or phrase that follows a **linking verb,** completing its meaning. Subject complements can be nouns, pronouns, or adjectives.

        subj.   l.v.   subj. comp.
Sanjay Sacomdri is **student representative.**
        subj.   l.v. subj. comp.
The director is she.
        subj.   l.v.   subj. comp.
Kelly McKay seems **mysterious.**

* **subjunctive mood.** The form of a verb that expresses a wish, desire, supposition, or improbability (see **mood** and Section 23f).

    If he **were to find** the canister of film, we would be delighted.
    It is necessary that the film **be** locked in the vault.

* **subordinate clause.** See **clause.**

* **subordinating conjunctions.** See **conjunctions, subordinating.**

  such. Vague when used as an intensifier, especially when no explanation follows **such:** *Shakespeare achieves such dramatic heights in his tragedies.* If you use **such,** complete your statement.

    Shakespeare achieves **such** dramatic heights in his tragedies that he is regarded as the finest playwright in English.

* **superlative.** The highest degree in a comparison of at least three things.

    The **worst** play in thirty-seven years . . .
    The **most vicious** of three published reviews . . .

  supposed to. Many writers forget the *d* at the end of **suppose** when the word is used with auxiliary verbs.

    INCORRECT Calina was **suppose to** check her inventory.
    CORRECT Calina was **supposed to** check her inventory.

* **synonyms.** Words of approximately the same meaning: *street/road, home/domicile.* While synonyms may share their **denotation,** or basic meaning, they often differ in **connotation**—that is, what the words imply. Both *skinny* and *svelte* denote thinness, but the terms differ significantly in how they would be used. In most situations, *skinny* sounds disparaging, while *svelte* is a positive, even glamorous description.

* **syntax.** The arrangement and relationship of clauses, phrases, and words in a sentence.

* **tense.** That quality of a verb which expresses time and existence. Tense is expressed through changes in verb forms and endings (*see, seeing, saw; work, worked*) and the use of auxiliaries (*had seen, will have seen; had worked, had been working*). Tense enables verbs to state complicated relationships between time and action—or relatively simple ones. See Sections 23a and 32a.

  than/then. These words are occasionally confused. **Than** is a conjunction expressing difference or comparison; **then** is an adverb expressing time.

    If the film is playing tomorrow, Shannon would rather go **then than** today.

  theirselves. A nonstandard form. Use **themselves** instead.

    INCORRECT All the strikers placed **theirselves** in jeopardy.
    CORRECT All the strikers placed **themselves** in jeopardy.

then/than.   See **than/then.**

this.   As a pronoun, **this** is sometimes vague and in need of clarification (see Section 26c-1).

VAGUE	We could fix the car if you had more time or I owned the proper tools. Of course, **this** is always a problem.
CLEARER	We could fix the car if you had more time or I owned the proper tools. Of course, **my lack of proper tools** is always a problem.

This (and **these**) may be inappropriate when used informally as demonstrative adjectives that refer to objects not previously mentioned.

INAPPROPRIATE *THIS*	Jim owns **this** huge Harley motorcycle.
INAPPROPRIATE *THESE*	After she moved out, we found **these** really ugly roaches in her apartment.

Such forms are common in speech but should not appear in writing.

BETTER	Jim owns **a** huge Harley motorcycle.
BETTER	After she moved out, we found ugly roaches in her apartment.

throne/thrown.   A surprising number of writers use **thrown** when they mean **throne.**

Charles I was **thrown** from his **throne** by an angry army of Puritans.

thusly.   A fussy, nonstandard form. Don't use it. **Thus** is stuffy enough without the *-ly.*

till/until.   **Until** is used more often in school and business writing, though the words are usually interchangeable. No apostrophe is used with **till.** You may occasionally see the poetic form 'til, but don't use it in academic or business writing.

to/too.   Most people know the difference between these words. But a writer in a hurry can easily put down the preposition **to** when the adverb **too** is intended. If you make this error often, check for it when you edit.

INCORRECT	Coach Rhoades was **to** surprised to speak after his team won its first game in four years.
REVISED	Coach Rhoades was **too** surprised to speak after his team won its first game in four years.

topic sentence.   A sentence that states the main idea of a paragraph. See Section 13a-2.

toward/towards.   **Toward** is preferred, though either form is fine.

transitions. Connecting words, phrases, and other devices (repetitions, headings) that help readers move from one unit to the next in your writing. Transitions help to hold a piece of writing together, bridging gaps and linking sentences and paragraphs. **Transitional words** are individual terms used to link ideas: *therefore, moreover, nevertheless, nonetheless, consequently,* and so on. See Chapter 15.

* **transitive verb.** A verb that takes an object. The action of a transitive verb passes on to someone or something; the sentence would be incomplete without an object.

TRANSITIVE	Travis accidentally **pushed** *Kyle.* You can **push** someone.
	Sister Anne **wrecked** the *van.* You can **wreck** something.

Transitive verbs (unlike intransitives) can usually be changed from the active to passive voice.

ACTIVE	Travis accidentally **pushed** *Kyle.*
PASSIVE	*Kyle* **was** accidentally **pushed** by Travis.

Compare transitive verbs to **intransitive** ones, which do not require an object to complete the action of a sentence.

INTRANSITIVE	I **slept** well. You cannot **sleep** something.
	Lawrence **sat** down. You cannot **sit** something.

try and. An informal expression. In writing, use **try to** instead.

INCORRECT	After its defeat, the soccer team decided to **try and** drown its sorrows.
REVISED	After its defeat, the soccer team decided to **try to** drown its sorrows.

TV. This abbreviation for *television* is common, but in most writing it is still preferable to write out the entire word. The abbreviation is usually capitalized.

type. You can usually delete this word.

WORDY	Hector was a polite **type** of guy.
REVISED	Hector was polite.

uninterested/disinterested. See **disinterested/uninterested.**

unique. Something **unique** is one of a kind. It can't be compared with anything else, so expressions such as *most unique, more unique,* or *very unique* don't make sense. The word **unique,** when used properly, should stand alone.

INCORRECT	Joe Rhoades's coaching methods were **very unique.**
REVISED	Joe Rhoades's coaching methods were **unique.**

Quite often **unique** appears where another, more specific adjective is appropriate.

INCORRECT	The **most unique** merchant on the block was Tong-chai.
IMPROVED	The **most inventive** merchant on the block was Tong-chai.

until/till. See **till/until.**

used to. Many writers forget the **d** at the end of **use.**

INCORRECT	Leroy was use to studying after soccer practice.
CORRECT	Leroy was **used to** studying after soccer practice.

utilize. Many readers prefer the simpler term **use.**

INFLATED	Mr. Ringling **utilized** his gavel to regain the crowd's attention.
BETTER	Mr. Ringling **used** his gavel to regain the crowd's attention.

* **verb.** The word or phrase that establishes the action of a sentence or expresses a state of being (see Chapters 22–23).

               verb
The music **played** on.

                       verb
Turning the volume down **proved** to be difficult.

A verb and all its auxiliaries, modifiers, and complements is called the **predicate** of a sentence.

  complete subj.   predicate
David's band **would have played throughout the night.**

              complete subj.   predicate
Turning the volume down on the band **proved to be much more difficult than the neighbors had anticipated it might be.**

* **verbals.** Verb forms that act like nouns, adjectives, or adverbs (see Chapter 24). The three kinds of verbals are **infinitives, participles,** and **gerunds.** Like verbs, verbals can take objects to form phrases. But verbals are described as nonfinite (that is, "unfinished") verbs because they cannot alone make complete sentences. A complete sentence requires a **finite** verb—that is, a verb that changes form to indicate person, number, and tense.

NONFINITE VERB—INFINITIVE	**To have found** security . . .
FINITE VERB	I **have found** security.
NONFINITE VERB—PARTICIPLE	The actor **performing** the scene . . .
FINITE VERB	The actor **performs** the scene.

very. Many teachers and editors will cut **very** almost every time it appears. Overuse has deadened the impact of the word. Whenever possible, use a more specific term or expression.

> WEAK   I was **very angry.**
> STRONGER I was **furious.**

* **voice.** Transitive verbs can be either in the **active voice** or in the **passive voice.** They are in the **active voice** when the subject in the sentence actually performs the action described by the verb.

> subj.   action
> *Professor Chase* **donated** the video camera.

They are in the **passive voice** when the action described by the verb is done to the subject.

> subj.   action
> *The video camera* **was donated** by Professor Chase.

See Section 23e.

well/good. See **good/well.**

who/whom. Use **who** when the pronoun is a subject; use **whom** when it is an object.

> **Who** wrote the ticket?
> **To whom** was the ticket given?

See Section 28e.

-wise. Don't add **-wise** to the end of a word to mean "with respect to." Many people object to word coinages such as *sportswise, weatherwise,* and *healthwise.* However, a number of common and acceptable English expressions do end in **-wise:** *clockwise, lengthwise, otherwise.* When in doubt about an expression, check the dictionary.

with regards to. Drop the **s** in regards. The correct expression is **with regard to.**

won't. Writers sometimes forget the apostrophe in this contraction and in others like it: **can't, don't.**

word choice. A marginal annotation used by many instructors to suggest that the writer could find a more appropriate or effective word or phrase.

would of. Mistaken form of **would have.** Also incorrect are **could of** and **should of.**

you all. Southern expression for *you,* usually plural. Not used in academic writing.

your/you're.   Homonyms that often get switched. **You're** is the contraction for *you are;* **your** is a possessive form.

> **You're** certain Maxine has been to Iran?
> **Your** certainty on this matter may be important.

Credits

TEXT CREDITS

Abbey, Edward. *Desert Solitaire.* New York: McGraw-Hill, 1968.

Ackerman, Diane. *A Natural History of the Senses.* New York: Random House, 1990.

AltaVista. "AltaVista-help-Search" at <http://doc.altavista.com/help/search_help.html>. Copyright © 2001 AltaVista® Company. Reproduced with permission of AltaVista®. AltaVista® is a registered trademark and the AltaVista® logo is a trademark of AltaVista Company.

American Psychological Association. *Publication Manual of the American Psychological Association,* Fourth Ed., 1994.

Angelou, Maya. *I Know Why the Caged Bird Sings.* New York: Random House, 1969.

Angier, Natalie. "Mating for Life?" in *The Beauty and the Beastly.* New York: Houghton Mifflin Company, 1995.

Anzaldúa, Gloria. From "How to Tame a Wild Heart" in *Borderlands/La Frontera: The New Mestiza.* Copyright © 1987, 1999 by Gloria Anzaldúa. Reprinted by permission of Aunt Lute Books.

Austen, Jane. "Pride and Prejudice," 1813.

Baker, Catherine. Illustration from *Your Genes, Your Choices,* a publication of Science & Literacy for Health, a project of the AAAS Directorate for Education and Human Resources. Copyright © 1997 by the American Association for the Advancement of Science. Reprinted by permission.

Barnett, Lincoln. *The Universe and Dr. Einstein.* New York: William Morrow and Co., 1968.

Barry, Dave. From "Neither Man Nor Rat Can Properly Fold the Laundry" as appeared in *The Miami Herald,* July 2, 2000. Reprinted by permission of the author.

Bernstein, Richard. *Dictatorship of Virtue.* New York: Alfred A. Knopf, 1994, p. 11.

Berry, Wendell. *Sex, Economy, Freedom & Community.* New York: Pantheon Books, 1993.

Blake, William. "The Divine Image," 1789.

Bloodworth, Dennis. *The Chinese Looking Glass.* New York: Farrar, Straus & Giroux, 1980, p. 155.

Bork, Robert H. "Give Me a Bowl of Texas," *Forbes,* September 1985, p. 184.

Boyer, Ernest L. "Creating the New American College," *The Chronicle of Higher Education,* 1994.

Briggs, Chad, and Fred Ribich. From "The Relationship Between Test Anxiety, Sleep Habits, and Self-perceived Academic Competency." *Psych-E,* Vol. 1, 12/1/98. Reprinted by permission of Chad Briggs.

Brunvard, Jan. *The Vanishing Hitchhiker: American Urban Legends and Their Meaning.* New York: W. W. Norton, 1982.

Burke, James Lee. *Black Cherry Blues.* Boston: Little, Brown and Company, 1989.

Carville, James. *We're Right, They're Wrong: A Handbook for Spirited Progressives.* New York: Random House, 1996.

Chesler, Ellen. *Women of Valor.* New York: Simon & Schuster, 1992.

Churchill, Winston. From a speech to the House of Commons, January, 1952.

Codell, Esmé Raji. From *Educating Esmé: Diary of a Teacher's First Year.* Copyright © 1999. Reprinted by permission of Algonquin Books of Chapel Hill and by permission of the author.

Cofer, Judith Ortiz. *Silent Dancing: A Partial Remembrance of a Puerto Rican Childhood.* Houston: Arte Publico Press–University of Houston, 1990.

Costas, Bob. "Eulogy for Mickey Mantle," August 15, 1995.

Council of Biology Editors. *Scientific Style and Format: The CBE Manual for Authors, Editors, and Publishers,* Sixth Edition. Copyright © 1994 by the Council of Biology Editors. Reprinted by permission.

Crouch, Stanley. "Blues for Jackie," *All American Skin Game, or the Decoy of Race: The Long and the Short of It, 1990–1994.* New York: Pantheon Books, 1995.

Dabelko, Geoffrey. From "The Environmental Factor," *The Wilson Quarterly,* Autumn 1999. Reprinted by permission.

DI: Communicator. From newsletter *DI: Communicator,* Issue No. 1, May 2000. Reprinted by permission of Design International, Dallas, TX.

Didion, Joan. "Georgia O'Keeffe," *The White Album.* New York: Simon & Schuster, 1979.

Ebert, Roger. *The Great Movies: Casablanca.*

Edelman, Marian Wright. "It's Time for America to Protect and Put Children First," *CDF Reports* June/July 1999. © Children's Defense Fund. Reprinted with permission.

Edge, John T. From "I'm Not Leaving Until I Eat This Thing," *Oxford American Magazine,* September/October 1999. Reprinted by permission of the author.

Epstein, Daniel Mark. "The Case of Harry Houdini" in *Star of Wonder.* Woodstock, NY: Overlook Press, 1986.

Goodman, Robert. *The Luck Business.* New York: Free Press, 1995.

Gould, Stephen Jay. "The Power of Narrative" in *The Urchin in the Storm.* New York: W. W. Norton, 1987, p. 77.

Grady, Sandy. "Tobacco Deal Reduced to Ashes," *Austin-American Statesman,* September 22, 1997.

Hart, Joseph. From "Chimps Are People Too," *Utne Reader,* August 16, 2000. Reprinted with permission of the author and Utne Reader.

Himmelfarb, Gertrude. "Second Thoughts on a Civil Society," *The Weekly Standard,* September 6, 1996. Reprinted by permission of the author.

Hoberman, Barry. "Translating the Bible," as originally published in the February 1985 issue of *The Atlantic Monthly,* Vol. 255, No. 2. Copyright © 1985. Reprinted by permission.

Hofstadter, Douglas. *Gödel, Escher, Bach: An Eternal Golden Braid.* New York: Vintage Books/Random House, 1979, p. 603.

Johnson, Paul. *Intellectuals.* New York: Harper & Row, Inc., 1988, p. 73.

Kadaba, Lini. "No Beef," *Philadelphia Inquirer,* February 8, 1998.

Kennedy, John F. *Inaugural Address,* January 20, 1961.

Kerouac, Jack. *On the Road.* New York: Penguin Books, 1968, p. 8.

Kingsolver, Barbara. *High Tide in Tucson.* New York: HarperCollins Publishers, 1995.

Kleine, Ted. "Living the Lansing Dream," *NEXT: Young American Writers on the New Generation,* Eric Liu, ed. New York, W. W. Norton, 1994, p. 95.

Kristoff, Nicholas. "Where Children Rule," *The New York Times Magazine,* August 17, 1997.

Lapham, Lewis. "Notebook," *Harper's,* October 1997.

Lewon, Dennis. From "Malaria's Not So Magic Bullet," *Escape,* July 1999. Reprinted by permission of the author.

McMurtry, Larry, and Diana Ossana. *Zeke and Ned.* New York: Simon & Schuster, 1997.

Mellix, Barbara. "From Outside, In" originally appeared in *The Georgia Review*, Volume XLI, No. 2 (Summer 1987), © 1987 by The University of Georgia / © 1987 by Barbara Mellix. Reprinted by permission of Barbara Mellix and *The Georgia Review.*

The Modern Language Association Style Manual. "Rules." Reprinted by permission. Thanks to the *MLA Style Manual and Guide to Scholarly Publishing*, Second Edition. Copyright © 1998 Modern Language Association of America.

Moffatt, Michael. *Coming of Age in New Jersey.* New Brunswick, NJ: Rutgers University Press, 1989.

Morrison, Toni. *The Bluest Eye.* New York: Simon & Schuster, 1970, p. 97.

Mowat, Farley. *Never Cry Wolf.* Boston: Little, Brown and Company, 1963.

Negroponte, Nicholas. From "Get a Life?" © 1995 by Nicholas Negroponte. This article originally appeared in *Wired.* Reprinted by permission of the author.

Netscape. Netscape Communications browser window and Netscape Composer © 1999 Netscape Communications Corporation. Used with permission. Netscape Communications has not authorized, sponsored, endorsed, or approved this publication and is not responsible for its content.

New Student Services. Screen shot from <www.utexas.edu/depts/dos/nss> reprinted with permission of The University of Texas at Austin, Office of the Dean of Students.

New York Times on the Web. "Search" page from <www.nytimes.com>. Copyright © 1998 by the New York Times Company. Reprinted by permission.

News Service. "News Service Usenet Access," <http://www.news-service.to/>.

Nuland, Sherwin B. "Medical Fads: Bran, Midwives, and Leeches," *The New York Times*, June 25, 1995, p. E16

Olds, Sharon. "The One Girl at the Boy's Party" from *The Dead and the Living* by Sharon Olds. Copyright © 1987 by Sharon Olds. Used by permission of Alfred A. Knopf, a division of Random House, Inc.

The Onion. "The Queen Mum's 100th."

Patoski, Joe Nick. "Three Cheers for High School Football." Reprinted with permission from the October 1999 issue of *Texas Monthly.*

Professional Communications Center Brochure. Reprinted by permission of the Professional Communications Center at the University of South Carolina College of Engineering & Information Technology.

Quindlen, Anna. "Between the Sexes, a Great Divide" from "Life in the 30's" column, *The New York Times Magazine*, March 24, 1988. Copyright © 1988 by The New York Times Company. Reprinted by permission.

Ramage, John, and John Bean. *Writing Arguments.* New York: Allyn & Bacon, 1995, Third Ed.

Reid, T. R. From "Sumo," *National Geographic*, Vol. 192, Issue 1, July 1997. Reprinted by permission of the National Geographic Society and the author.

Roland, Alex. "Leave the People Home," *USA Today Online*, July 3, 1997. Reprinted by permission of the author.

Rose, Mike. *Lives on the Boundary.* New York: The Free Press, 1989.

Sagan, Carl. *The Demon-Haunted World.* New York: Random House, 1995.

Schriver, Karen. *Dynamics in Document Design.* New York: John Wiley & Sons, 1977.

Samaras, Thomas T. "Let's Get Small," *Harper's*, January 1995, p. 32. Reprinted from *The Truth About Your Height: Exploring Myths and Realities of Human Size and Its Effects on Performance, Health, Pollution, and Survival.* San Diego: Telecote Publications.

Santiago, Chiori. "The Fine and Friendly Art of Luis Jiménez," *Smithsonian*, 1993.

PHOTO CREDITS

Index

A

a

and count nouns, 535–536
ESL writer, 535–536
in titles, capitalization of, 608
use before words, 449–450, 856, 862
a couple of, as quantifier, 538
a good deal of, as quantifier, 538
a great deal of, as quantifier, 538
a lack of, as quantifier, 538
a little, little, as quantifiers, 538
a lot, correct usage, 860
a lot of, as quantifier, 538
Abbreviations, 615–620
    academic degrees, 612, 617
    acronyms, 615, 616. *See also*
        Acronyms
    agency names, 617
    capitalization of, 616
    dates, 618
    divisions of books, 620
    editor's mark for, 615
    at end of sentence, 542
    geographic place names, 618–619
    initialisms, 616
    Latin expressions, 605, 619–620
    months of year, 615
    for *mount,* 619
    for *number,* 618
    period in, 542–543, 615–620
    plural of, 444
    for *saint,* 619
    states in United States, 619
    symbols as, 620
    technical terms, 617
    of terms for *street,* 619
    titles of persons, 616–617
    weights/measures, 618
About.com, 654
Absolute, 273, 435, 436, 856
Absolute adjectives, 494–495
    correct use of, 494–495, 856
    list of, 494, 856
Absolute phrases, 273, 490, 888
    comma with, 561
    compared to dangling modifiers, 490
    functions of, 273

from infinitives, 273, 435, 878
from participles, 273, 436, 887
use in sentences, 273, 856
Abstract
    content, APA style, 789, 793
    example of, 792
    parenthetical note (APA), 787
    purpose of, 789
    References (APA, online abstract), 787
Abstract nouns
    defined, 856
    examples of, 534, 856
Abstract terms
    capitalizing, 612–613
    use of, 67
Abstract writing, avoiding, 241–242
Academic degrees
    abbreviations, 612, 617
    capitalization, 612
    comma with, 574
Academic ranks, capitalization rules, 611
Academic responsibility, 696–701
Academic writing, 83–115. *See also* Literary analysis; Research project; Subject areas
    appearance of papers, 106–107
    assessment of project requirements, 100–101
    denotative language in, 237
    documenting sources, 104
    letter grades for, 83–89
    possessives before gerunds in, 448–449
    research sources, 102
    service-learning projects, 125–129
    smaller topic, benefits of, 101
    supporting reasons and evidence in, 101–102
accept/except, correct usage, 856
accidentally, common misspelling of, 857
Acronyms
    abbreviations, 615, 616
    capitalizing, 614, 616
    defined, 857
    form for, 543, 857
    as ordinary words, 857
    plural of, 444
    pronunciation of, 857

ACS Style Guide: A Manual for Authors and Editors (2nd edition), 820
Action verbs, ESL writer, 519–520
Active voice
  defined, 258, 419, 899
  examples of, 420, 433
  revising passive voice to, 430
  and verb tense, 419–420, 429
A.D.
  as abbreviation, 618
  capitalization of, 615
  small caps for, 616
ad/advertisement, correct usage, 857
Ad hominem arguments, 170
Addresses
  commas in, 574
  email, 385
  state names, abbreviating, 619
  World Wide Web. *See* Electronic address
Adjectivals, 857. *See also* Noncoordinate adjectives
Adjective(s), 264–265, 488–495
  -ed and *-ing* ending, 507–508
  absolute adjectives, 494–495, 856
  adverbs as modifiers, 266
  comparative and superlative forms, 500–501, 857
  compound modifiers, 265
  coordinate adjectives, 264, 567–568, 868
  in cumulative sentences, 300
  demonstrative adjectives, 870
  ESL writer, 507–508
  functions of, 264–265, 488, 857
  infinitive phrases as, 272
  infinitives as, 272, 878
  as modifiers, 264–265, 488–495
  pairs of, 508
  parallelism in, 293
  participle phrases as, 271
  participles as, 271
  placement in sentences, 491–492
  predicate adjectives, 492–494, 889
  proper nouns as, 857, 890
  and subject and object complements, 265
  subordinate clauses as, 277
  verbals as, 271–272
Adjective (relative) clauses, 277, 897
  commas in, 277
  in cumulative sentences, 301
  relative pronouns in, 277

as sentence fragment, 548–549
use in sentences, 277, 857
Adverb(s), 266, 495–498
  and adjective clauses, 277
  almost and *even,* 497
  comparative and superlative forms, 500–501
  compound modifiers, 265
  in concise writing, 318
  conjunctive. *See* Conjunctive adverbs
  in cumulative sentences, 300
  ESL writer, 509
  formal versus informal usage, 495–496
  functions of, 266, 858
  infinitive phrases as, 272
  infinitives as, 272, 878
  as intensifiers, 318
  as modifiers, 266, 492–493, 495–498, 858
  only, 498
  parallelism in, 293
  placement in sentences, 266, 496–498, 509
  predicate adjectives instead of, 492–494
  short and long form, use of, 495–496
  subordinate clauses as, 277
  verbals as, 272
Adverb clauses
  functions of, 278
  use in sentences, 278
Adverbials
  examples of, 858
  functions of, 858
adverse/averse, correct usage, 858
Advertisements
  MLA style, 755
  visual appeal of, 150–151
advice/advise, correct usage, 858
affect/effect, correct usage, 858–859
African Americans
  Black English and, 254–255
  terms used for, 249, 859, 864
after
  in adverb clauses, 278
  as subordinating conjunction, 288, 560–561
Afterword
  parenthetical note (MLA), 734–735
  Works Cited (MLA), 734–735
Age, eliminating biased language toward, 250
Agency names, abbreviating, 617
Agent/action sentences, 303–309

nature of, 303
people as subjects in, 303–305
verbs in, 305–309
writing guidelines, 303–309
aggravate/irritate, correct usage, 859
Agreement
in number, 457–459, 534–538
pronoun agreement, 457–464
subject-verb agreement, 406–418
ain't, avoiding use of, 860
AIP Style Manual (4th edition), 820
Aircraft
capitalizing name of, 613
italics, 605
Album titles, italics, 605
Alignment, in document design, 343, 353–354
all
in nonsexist language, 486
possessive form, 475
and pronoun agreement, 460
and subject-verb agreement, 411
all ready/already, correct usage, 860
all right, correct usage, 860
AlltheWeb, 654
allude/elude, correct usage, 860
allude/refer, correct usage, 860
allusion/illusion, 860
Almanacs, 649, 650
almost, placement in sentences, 497
along with, and subject-verb agreement, 409
already/all ready, correct use, 860
AltaVista, 653, 654, 663
although
in adverb clauses, 278
in compound and complex sentences, 281
as subordinating conjunction, 276, 288, 289, 290, 560–561
A.M.
as abbreviation, 618
capitalization of, 615
numerals with, 623
small caps for, 616
American Indian, use of term, 249
American Medical Association Manual of Style (9th edition), 820
American Psychological Association (APA), 693. *See also* APA style
Web site for, 773
American, use of term, 860
among/between, correct usage, 861

amount/number, correct usage, 861
Ampersand (&), 620, 779
an
and count nouns, 535–536
ESL writer, 535–536
in titles, capitalization of, 608
use before words, 449–450, 856, 862
Analogy
defined, 861
false analogy, 173–174
in paragraphs, 203
Analyze, essay question, 112
and
ampersand (&) as abbreviation of, 620, 779
avoiding overuse of, 282–283
comma before, 566, 567
compound subjects and subject-verb agreement, 408
in compound subjects/verbs/objects, 262–263
linking independent clauses, 282–283
and etc., 861
and/or, use in writing, 861
and so on
correct usage, 861, 872
Latin expression for, 619, 872
Anecdote, in opening paragraph, 211–212
Anglo, use of term, 861
angry/mad, correct usage, 861
Annotated bibliographies
developing, 103–104
purpose of, 644
Annotations
example of, 133
in literary analysis, 183–184
in online reading, 135
during reading, 132–134
of research materials, 682–683, 685
Annual bibliographies, purpose of, 644
Antecedents
examples of, 451–452
nature of, 451, 861
pronoun agreement, 457–464, 859
and pronoun reference problems, 451–452, 891
Anthologies
Bibliography/Works Cited (CMS) for selection, 809
Notes (CMS) for selection, 809
parenthetical note (APA) for book, 781
parenthetical note (MLA) for book, 736–737

Anthologies *(Continued)*
  parenthetical note (MLA) for selection,
    741–742
  References (APA) for book, 781
  References (APA) for selection, 781
  Works Cited (MLA) for book, 736–737
  Works Cited (MLA) for selection,
    741–742
Antonyms, defined, 861
any
  possessive form, 475
  and pronoun agreement, 460
  and subject-verb agreement, 411
any one/anyone, correct usage, 862
anybody
  in nonsexist language, 486
  possessive form, 475
  and pronoun agreement, 460
  and subject-verb agreement, 411
anyone
  possessive form, 475
  and pronoun agreement, 460
  and subject-verb agreement, 411
anything
  and pronoun agreement, 460
  and subject-verb agreement, 411
anyway/anyways, correct usage, 862
anywhere/nowhere, correct usage, 884–885
AOL Anywhere, 654
APA style, 773–802. *See also* Parenthetical
    notes (APA style); References (APA
    style)
  abstract, 789, 792, 793
  APA form directory, 777–788
  body of paper, 795
  direct quotations, 693–694, 708
  and electronic sources. *See* COS/APA
    (sciences) style
  for figures and tables, 714–715
  final copy, 776
  headings, 716–717
  indenting long quotations, 708
  numbers, figures for, 622
  pagination, 789
  prose quotations, 707
  quotations, 693–694, 708
  sample paper, 788–802
  subjects for APA style, 773
  title of project, 716, 717
  title page, 790, 791
Apostrophe
  contraction versus possessive form,
    475–476, 900
  indefinite pronouns, 474–475

plurals, 444, 623
possessives, 445–447
Appendix
  in document design, 350–351
  of social science report, 789
Apply, essay question, 112
Appositives, 274–275
  comma with, 563–564
  in cumulative sentences, 301
  essential, 563–564
  functions of, 274, 467–468, 862
  gerunds as, 437
  introductory words to, 274
  nonessential, 563–564
  and pronoun case, 467–468
  as sentence fragments, 548–549
  use in sentences, 274–275
Architectural structures, capitalizing name
    of, 613
Archive article (online)
  COS/APA (sciences) style, 848
  COS/MLA (humanities) style, 836
Archive message (online)
  COS/APA (sciences) style, 850
  COS/MLA (humanities) style, 838
are, ineffectiveness in sentences, 307
Arguments, 153–175
  and audience, 160–163, 169
  characteristics of, 153–154
  in closing paragraph, 217
  concessions, 169
  connotative language in, 238–239
  and credibility of writer, 162–163
  critique of argument, 163
  development, steps in, 158–160
  essay question, 112
  evidence in, 154–155, 156, 158–159,
    163
  examples of, 119–120, 164–169
  faulty reasoning in. *See* Fallacies
  for inquiries about grades, 97
  introduction/body/conclusion pattern
    for, 36–37
  opposing arguments, dealing with, 37,
    162–163
  oversimplifying in, 162
  qualifiers in, 157
  refuting opposing argument, 163
  and shared values of writer/reader, 161
  structure of, 154–155
  and tone, 68
  warrants as basis of, 155–156,
    159–160, 163
  writing guidelines, 158–169, 169

Argus Clearinghouse, 656, 671
Art. *See* Visual information
ArticleFirst, 646
Articles (grammatical). *See also u; an; the*
  correct usage of, 856, 862
  as determiners, 870
  number agreement, 534–538
Articles in periodicals. *See* Magazine articles; Periodicals; Scholarly articles
Artistic terms, capitalization of, 613–614
Artwork
  italics for titles of, 605
  parenthetical note (MLA), 756
  Works Cited (MLA), 756
as
  in adverb clauses, 278
  and appositives, 274
  in comparisons, 469–470
  and parallelism, 294
  in similes, 327
  as subordinating conjunction, 288,
    560–561
as being/being, 862
as follows, at beginning of list, 582
as if, as subordinating conjunction, 288
as/like, correct usage, 881
as though, as subordinating conjunction,
  288
as well as, and subject-verb agreement,
  409
Asian/American, use of term, 862
Asians, use of term, 248
Ask an Expert, 665
Ask Jeeves, 655
Assignments, 4–6. *See also* Literary analysis; Research project; Writing projects
Assumptions, recognizing in written piece,
  138–139
at any rate, semicolon before, 578–579
Attachments, email, 385
Attributions, 703
Audience
  and argument, 160–163, 169
  audience adaptations, 9
  audience analysis questions, 10
  common ground with, 244
  and document design, 330, 334, 344
  expectations of, 118, 119
  and language level, 230–231, 233,
    242–244, 256
  and paragraph writing, 194, 209
  and presentation of viewpoint, 11–13
  revising for, 63–64

  for service-learning projects, 126–127
  and title selection, 48–49
  and topic selection, 9–10
Audio file
  COS/APA (sciences) style, 848–849
  COS/MLA (humanities) style, 836–837
  MLA style, 754
Auxiliary verbs
  ESL writer, 506
  function of, 862
  list of, 421
  modal auxiliaries, 421–422, 523–527,
    883
  past participle, 426
  verb phrases from, 427
  and verb tense, 421–422, 426
averse/adverse, 858
awful/very, correct use, 862
awhile/a while, correct use, 862

B
bad/badly, correct use, 863
Balanced sentence, 298–299, 863
Bandwagon appeal, 174
Bar graphs, interpretation of, 144–145
barely, and double negatives, 499
Base form, of verbs, 406, 532
B.C.
  as abbreviation, 618
  capitalization of, 615
  small caps for, 616
be able to, as modal auxiliary, 524
because
  in compound and complex sentences,
    281
  as subordinating conjunction, 276,
    288, 289, 560–561
because of/due to, correct usage, 863
because . . . reason is, correct usage, 891
before
  in adverb clauses, 278
  as subordinating conjunction, 288,
    560–561
Begging the question fallacy, 170–171
Beginning writing. *See* Draft
being as/being that, correct use, 863
beside/besides, correct use, 863–864
between/among, correct usage, 861
Bias, of research sources, 675
Biased language, 13, 245–253
  acceptable use of, 245, 252–253
  age-related, 250
  and arguments, 162–163
  about class distinctions, 251–252

Biased language *(Continued)*
  detecting in written piece, 139–140
  about disabled persons, 251
  emotional language, 68, 162–163
  hostile language, 13, 68, 162–163
  occupational labels, 251–252
  racial and ethnic bias, 248–249
  sexist language, 246–248
  stereotypes, 162–163, 247–248,
    248–249
  toward sexual orientation, 251
Bible passages
  colon in, 583
  Notes (CMS), 810
  parenthetical note (MLA), 751–752
  period in, 543
  Works Cited (MLA), 751–752
Bibliography, 641, 644–645
  annotated bibliography, 103–104
  software for preparing, 639, 695–696
  subjects/bibliographies, listing of, 645
  types of, 644
  Web sites listing, 645
  working bibliography, 633–634
Bibliography/Works Cited (CMS style),
    806
  book (online), 811
  book in series, 808
  book with editor, focus on editor,
    807–808
  book with editor, focus on original au-
    thor, 808
  book with four or more authors or edi-
    tors, 807
  book with no author, 808
  book with one author, 807
  book with two/three authors or editors,
    807
  book written by group, 808
  chapter in book, 809
  electronic sources, 810–811
  email, 811
  italics versus underline, 812
  magazine article (online), 811
  magazine article (printed article), 809
  multivolume works, 808
  newspaper, 810
  scholarly article (printed article), 809
Biographical information
  in literary analysis, 178
  print resources for, 648
  subjects/reference works, listing of, 649
  on World Wide Web, 648–649
Black English, 254–255

Black, versus *African American,* 249, 864
Block format letters, 387
Block style paragraphs, 354
-body, as word ending, possessive form,
    475
Body of paper
  APA style, 795
  function of, 36
  MLA style, 763
Body of Web page, 364, 374
Boldface, type style, 355, 356
Book(s)
  abbreviation of divisions of, 620
  Bibliography/Works Cited (CMS, on-
    line books), 811
  Bibliography/Works Cited (CMS,
    print books), 807–808
  capitalization of titles, 607–608
  COS/APA (sciences) style, 846–847
  COS/MLA (humanities) style, 834–835
  Notes (CMS), 807–808
  online catalog information, 642–643
  parenthetical notes (APA), 778–781
  parenthetical notes (MLA), 732–738
  References (APA), 778–781
  References (CBE), 822–823
  sections of book, abbreviations for, 620
  Works Cited (MLA, online books),
    746–747
  Works Cited (MLA, print books),
    732–738
Book reviews
  guides to, 652
  parenthetical note (APA), 782
  parenthetical note (MLA), 738–739
  References (APA), 782
  Works Cited (MLA), 738–739
Book titles
  capitalization in, 607–608
  italics for, 605
Bookmarking, Web sites, 135, 636, 682
Books on the Internet, 656
Boolean searching, 661–662
Borders, in document design, 359
both . . . and, and parallelism, 294
Brackets, 595–596
  angle brackets, Web address, Works
    cited (MLA), 745
  editor's mark for, 595
  with ellipses to show omitted material,
    589, 590, 591, 596, 705–707
  at end of sentence, 705
  for inserted comments in direct quota-
    tions, 595

around material added to quotations, 707
within parenthetical expression, 595
with *sic* to indicate errors in quoted material, 596
Brainstorming
ideas used for outline, 44–45
for topic, 15–16
Brand-name products, capitalizing name of, 613
British conventions
dates, 574
judgment/judgement, 880
quotation marks, 589
British, use of term, 864
Brochures, 400–401
components of, 401
denotative language for, 237–238
examples of, 401
white space, 354
writing/design guidelines, 400
Browsers, 654
Buildings, capitalizing name of, 613
Bulletins
parenthetical notes (MLA), 744
Works Cited (MLA style), 744
Businesses
abbreviating names of, 617
capitalizing names of, 611
Web site documentation, 834, 846
but
in balanced sentences, 299
comma before, 566
in compound and complex sentences, 282
linking independent clauses, 282

C
Calendar, for research project, 638
Call numbers, 623
Campus groups, writing related to, 117
can, as modal auxiliary, 421, 422, 524, 525
can/may, correct usage, 864
cannot, correct usage, 864
can't, correct usage, 864
can't hardly, correct usage, 864
Capitalization, 606–614
abbreviations, 616
abstract terms, 612–613
academic degrees, 612
acronyms/initialisms, 614, 616
brand-name products, 613
buildings/structures/monuments, 613

businesses/organizations/unions/ clubs/schools, 611
document titles, 613
editor's mark for, 607
first word in lines of poetry, 608
first word of direct quotation, 607
first word of sentence, 607
following colon, 607
geographic place names, 612
initials of people, 609
-ism expressions, 613–614
misuse of, 607, 611
musical groups, 613
names of people, 609–610
national/political/ethnic groups, 610
north/south/east/west, 612
religious figures/religious groups/sacred groups, 611
school subjects/classes, 614
ships/planes/automobiles, 613
small caps, 355, 356, 616
special events, 613
time periods, 613
titles, 607–608
titles of people, 609–610
trademarks, 611
Card catalog, 640–641, 642. *See also* On-line catalogs
Cardinal numbers, words used for, 864, 885
CARL Uncover, 646
Cartoons, Works Cited (MLA), 743
Case. *See also* Pronoun case
defined, 864–865
of nouns, 864
Casual language, 233–234
characteristics of, 234
situations for use, 233–234
Cause-and-effect pattern
organization of paper, 41–42
paragraphs, 202–203
CBE style, 820–825. *See also* References (CBE style)
citations in text, 820
citations relationship to References, 821
general guidelines for, 825
name-year system versus citation-sequence system, 820
References (citation-sequence-style), 821–825
several citations in same note, 821
subject area style manuals and, 820
subsequent citations, 821

CD-ROM
    COS/APA (sciences) style, 852
    COS/MLA (humanities) style, 840
    parenthetical note (MLA), 750–751
    Works Cited (MLA), 750–751
censor/censure, correct usage, 865
certainly, as intensifier, 891
Chapter of book
    Bibliography/Works Cited (CMS), 809
    Notes (CMS), 809
    parenthetical note (APA), 781
    parenthetical note (MLA), 737
    quotation marks around title, 586, 605
    References (APA), 781
    Works Cited (MLA), 737
Charts, 143–144, 313
    computer-generated, 357–358
    evaluating accuracy of, 148
    pie chart, 143–144
Chemistry reports, style manual for, 820
Chicago Manual of Style, 693, 803. *See also*
        CMS style
Chunking, sentences, for clarity, 311–312
circa, 695
Circular reasoning, 170–171
Citation of sources. *See specific documenta-*
        tion systems
Citation-sequence system. *See* CBE style
Civil language, 13–14, 242–244
Claims
    in arguments, 154–155, 156, 158–159,
        163
    of definition, 710
    evaluating in written piece, 138
    of fact, 710
    of policy, 711
    supporting reasons and evidence,
        101–102
    of value, 710–711
Clarinet, 652
Clarity in writing, 310–313
    charts and graphs for, 313
    chunking sentences, 311–312
    and commas, 562
    and details, 310
    downshifting, 310
    and positive statements, 311
Classification, paragraphs of, 201
Classification pattern, organization of pa-
        per, 41
Clauses, 275–278. *See also specific types of*
        clauses
    adjective (relative) clauses, 277

adverb clauses, 278
    as adverbial, 858
    commas with, 560–561, 566
    condensing to phrases, 321–322
    and cumulative sentences, 301
    ESL writer, 506
    essential clauses, 480–481
    functions of, 275–276, 865
    independent clauses, 276, 865
    nonessential clauses, 480–481, 504
    noun clauses, 279
    parallelism of, 279, 292–297, 885–886
    semicolon with, 576–579
    as sentence fragments, 547–549
    as subject of sentence, 410
    and subject-verb agreement, 410
    subordinate (dependent) clauses,
        276–277, 865
Cliché, defined, 865
Closing paragraphs, 215–218
    argument in larger contrast, 217
    conclusions, 218
    examples of, 216–217
    linking to opening paragraph, 216–217
    recommendation in, 216
    as summary, 216
Closing tag, 372, 381
Clubs, capitalizing name of, 611
Cluttered writing. *See* Concise versus clut-
        tered writing
CMS style. *See also* Bibliography/Works
        Cited (CMS style); Notes (CMS
        style)
    CMS form directory, 806–811
    and electronic sources. *See* COS/CMS
        style
    information in entries, 803–806
    for literary analysis, 187
    sample paper, 812–819
    title page, 813
Coherence, and paragraphs, 194, 865
Collaboration
    benefits of, 51
    and disagreements, 59
    division of assignment, 58–59
    and drafting, 57–59
    and goals of group, 58
    peer editing, 73–81
    rules established for, 701
    in service-learning projects, 128
Collective nouns
    function of, 413, 462–463, 865
    and pronoun agreement, 462–463

singular and plural nouns, 413
and subject-verb agreement, 413, 414
Colons, 581–584
in Bible passages, 583
in bibliographic entries, 584
capitalization following, 607
editor's mark for, 581
introduction to list, 571–572, 581–582
joining sentences with, 583
linking independent clauses, 284–285
misuse of, 582, 583
with quotation marks, 587
before quotations or dialog, 583
in salutation of letter, 584
in time, 583
between title and subtitle, 583
Color
in document design, 335, 342, 359–361
and Web page design, 374–375, 379, 380–381
Columbia Guide to Online Style (COS), 693, 826. *See also* COS style
Web site for, 831
Comma(s), 559–574
and absolute phrases, 561
with academic degrees, 574
in addresses, 574
and adjective clauses, 277
and appositives, 274–275
avoidance of, with essential modifiers, 502–504
and clusters of adjectives, 265
and comma splices, 552–555
in compound subjects/verbs/objects, 263
with conjunctive adverbs, 285–286, 578
and contrasts, 560–561, 562
with conversational expressions, 562
with coordinate adjectives in series, 567–568
before coordinating conjunctions, 282–283, 566
correcting run-on with, 557
in dates, 574
and distinct ideas, 562
editor's mark for, 559
functions of, 559
before incidental/additional/contrasting thought, 560–561
with interrupting words/phrases/clauses, 564–565

after introductory phrases, 559–560
after introductory subordinate clauses, 560
with items in a series, 567–568
linking independent clauses, 566–567
with nonessential appositives, 563–564
with nonessential modifiers, 502–504, 563–564
in numbers, 573, 621
after parentheses, 594
with quotation marks, 587
in quotations, 573
after salutation in letter, 574
and transitions, 562
unnecessary commas, 569–572
Comma splices, 71, 552–555, 566–567
characteristics of, 552, 865
correction of, 553–555, 865
editor's mark for, 553
in modern fiction, 555
Commands
exclamation mark at end of, 545
imperative mood, 431, 433, 877, 883
period at end of, 542
Commitment and response pattern, organization of paper, 36–37
Common knowledge, defined, 694, 865
Common nouns, function of, 866
Community
community issues as topic, 16–17
writing related to, 117
Companies. *See* Businesses; Corporations; Organizations
Comparative and superlative forms, 500–501, 866, 895
-er and *-est* endings, 500–501
more and *most*, 500–501
Compare, essay question, 112
Comparison and contrast pattern
feature by feature, 39–40
organization of paper, 38–40
paragraphs, 202
parallelism in, 293–294
subject by subject, 38–39, 40
Comparisons
pronoun case in, 469–470
than and *as in*, 469–470
Compass directions, capitalization rule, 612
complement, complementary, correct usage, 866
Complements. *See also* Object complement; Subject complement
function of, 866

Complex sentence, 225, 280, 866
  subordination in, 282, 287–291
compliment/complimentary, correct usage, 866
Compound-complex sentence, 280, 867
  subordination in, 282, 287–291
Compound modifiers, 265
  hyphenated, 265, 600–601
  identification of, 601
Compound nouns, hyphenated, 599
Compound objects, 263
Compound phrases, hyphenated, 600–601
Compound sentence, 280, 282, 867
  and correlatives, 284
  question mark at end of, 544
Compound sentences, balancing, 299
Compound subjects, 262
  subject-verb agreement, 408–409, 410
Compound verbs, 262–263
  hyphenated, 600
Compound words
  plurals, 443–444
  possessives, 446
Computer software. *See* Software
Computers. *See also* Electronic media; Electronic sources
  annotation with, 682
  document design with, 347–349, 361–382
  drafting with, 52
  in evaluation process, 95
  outlining with, 47
  quotation marks with, 588
  for revision, 65
  spelling checker, 71
  style checker, 69
Concession, in arguments, 169
Concise versus cluttered writing, 313–322
  condensing sentences, 313–314, 321–322
  doublings, 317
  expletives, 318–319
  intensifiers, 318
  nominalizations, 315
  paragraphs, 206–207
  prepositional phrases, 319–320
  redundancies, 317
  relative pronouns, 321
  verb phrases, 316
Conclusion
  in closing paragraph, 218
  and drafting, 54
  editing, 69

essay examination response, 114
  function of, 36
  of social science report, 789
  testing against introduction, 712
Concrete language, 67, 241–242
Concrete nouns
  defined, 867
  examples of, 867
Conjugation, defined, 867
Conjunctions
  and compound objects, 263
  and compound subjects, 262
  and compound verbs, 262
  coordinate adjectives and, 264
  coordinating. *See* Coordinating conjunctions
  correcting comma splice with, 553
  correlatives, 263, 284
  linking independent clauses, 284–285
  subordinating conjunctions, 276–277, 867
Conjunctive adverbs
  comma with, 285–286, 578
  linking independent clauses, 285–286
  list of, 285, 578, 867, 891
  semicolon with, 285–286, 578, 867
Connotation, 237–239
  cautions in use of, 239
  defined, 236, 868
  situations for use, 237–238
conscience/conscious, correct usage, 868
consensus, correct usage, 868
consequently
  commas with, 561, 564
  in independent clauses, 285
  semicolon before, 578
Content notes, 132
Content of paper. *See also* Topic selection
  library for information, 17, 25–26
  marginal comments of editor, 74
  marginal comments of instructor, 87–89
  revising for, 64–65
Content pages, 365
Context notes, 132
Contractions
  apostrophe in, 475–476, 868
  defined, 868
  versus possessive form, 475–476, 900
Contradictions, in written piece, 139
Contrast
  and commas, 560–561, 562
  in document design, 341
  essay question, 112

Coordinate adjectives
  commas in series of, 567–568
  functions of, 567–568, 868
  identification of, 567–568
  use in sentences, 264
Coordinating conjunctions
  in balanced sentences, 298–299
  comma before, 282–283, 566
  correcting comma splice with, 554
  correcting run-on with, 557
  functions of, 282, 867
  linking independent clauses, 282–283
  list of, 282, 867
  use in sentences, 282–283
Coordination in sentences, 282–286
  compound and complex sentences, 281
  conjunctive adverbs, 282, 285–286
  coordinating conjunctions, 282–283
  correlatives, 284
  methods for, 282–283
  punctuation for, 282, 284–285
Copyright
  electronic media, 344–345, 636
  obtaining, 344–345
  software, 345
Corporate Web site
  COS/APA (sciences) style, 846
  COS/MLA (humanities) style, 834
Corporations
  abbreviated names of, 543
  capitalizing names of, 611
Correlatives
  in compound subjects/verbs/objects, 263
  functions of, 284, 868
  linking independent clauses, 284
  list of, 284, 868
  and parallelism, 294
COS/APA (sciences) style, 843–855
  archive article, 848
  archive message, 850
  audio file, 848–849
  books, 846–847
  CD-ROM, 852
  corporate Web site, 846
  database, 852
  dictionary/thesaurus entry, 851–852
  email, 849
  encyclopedia article, 851
  form directory, 843–853
  gopher/FTP site, 850
  government Web site, 846
  graphic file, 848–849
  information in entry, 829–831

institutional/group Web site, 845
listserv, 849
magazine articles, 847
newspaper/news service, 847–848
sample References page, 853–855
software, 852–853
synchronous communications, 851
Telnet site, 850–851
Usenet newsgroup, 849
Web site, generic, 844
Web site, revised, 844–845
Web site of individual, 845–846
Web site with frames, 848
Web site with no author, 845
COS/CMS (humanities) style
  footnotes/endnotes, 828
  information in entry, 829–831
COS/MLA (humanities) style, 831–843
  archive article, 836
  audio file, 836–837
  books, 834–835
  CD-ROM, 840
  corporate Web site, 834
  database, 840–841
  dictionary/thesaurus entry, 840
  email, 837
  encyclopedia article, 839–840
  form directory, 831–841
  gopher/FTP site, 838–839
  government Web site, 834
  graphic file, 836–837
  information in entry, 829–831
  institutional/group Web site, 833
  listserv, 837–838
  magazine article, 835–836
  newspaper/news service, 835–836
  sample Works Cited page, 841–843
  software, 841
  synchronous communication, 839
  Telnet site, 839
  Usenet Newsgroup, 838
  Web site, generic, 832
  Web site, revised, 832
  Web site of individual, 833
  Web site with frames, 836
  Web site with no author, 833
COS style, 76, 826–855. *See also* entries
    for specific systems [e.g., COS/APA
    (sciences) style]
  alias/nickname of author, 828, 829
  compared to MLA style, 826–827
  date of access, situations for use, 828,
    829–830

COS style *(Continued)*
  electronic addresses, format for, 828,
    830–831
  parenthetical notes, 827–828
  publication date, 828, 829–830
  publication information in citation,
    829
  source with no author, 827
  source with no page numbers, 827, 828
  source with no publication date, 828,
    829–830
  titles of electronic works, 829
  use with other documentation systems,
    828
  Works Cited/References, 829–831
could, as modal auxiliary, 421, 524, 525
could have, as modal auxiliary, 526–527
could have/could of, correct usage, 868,
  899
Council of Biology Editors (CBE), 693,
  820. *See also* CBE style
Count nouns
  and *a, an, the,* 535–536
  characteristics of, 534–535, 869
  ESL writer, 534–535
Country names
  abbreviating, 618
  capitalizing, 612
couple of/several, use in writing, 869
Cover letter, 388–389
  components of, 389
  examples of, 389
  writing guidelines, 388
CQ Researcher, 651
Credibility of writer
  and argument, 160–163
  aspects of, 11–12
credible/credulous, correct usage, 869
Credit lines, dash before name, 598
criteria/criterion, correct usage, 869
Critical reading, 136–141
  belief and doubt during, 136–137
  bias detection, 139–140
  checking claims of writer, 138
  evaluation of assumptions, 138–139
  evaluation of supporting evidence,
    137–138
  evaluation of writer's problem solving,
    140–141
  qualifications of writer, 137
  recognizing contradictions, 139
Critical thinker, characteristics of, 130

Critique, essay question, 112
Cultural movements, capitalization of,
  613–614
Cumulative sentences, 299–301
  examples of, 299–301
  structure of, 299–300, 869
curriculum/curricula, correct usage, 869

D
-d. See -ed, -d
Dances, italics, 605
Dangling modifiers, 488–490
  characteristics of, 488–489, 869
  compared to absolute phrases, 490
  correction of, 489
  editor's mark for, 489
  examples of, 489, 490
Dashes, 597–598
  before additional idea sentence, 597
  capitalization of word following dash,
    607
  editor's mark for, 597
  for inserted information in sentences,
    597–598
  interruptions in dialogue, 597
  linking independent clauses, 284–285
  misuse of, 598
  before name in credit line, 598
  with quotation marks, 588
  to set off items, 598
  to set off phrases, 598
  and verbal phrase, 438
data/datum
  correct usage, 870
  subject-verb agreement, 414
Databases
  APA style, 785–786
  COS/APA (sciences) style, 852
  COS/MLA (humanities) style, 840–841
  listing of, 646–647
  organizing research material with,
    633–634
  parenthetical note (MLA), 750–751
  scheduling software, 639
  search of, 646–648
  Works Cited (MLA) style, 750–751
Dates
  abbreviation of, 618
  A.D./B.C. with, 615, 618
  at beginning of sentence, 622–623
  in body of paper, 695
  British form, 574

commas in, 574
numbers in, 623
unestablished, question mark for, 544
Days of week
abbreviation of, 618
capitalization of, 613
Deadlines, research project, 637–639
Decimals, periods in, 543
Decorative fonts, 355
Define, essay question, 112
Definite articles. *See the*
Definition, paragraphs of, 201
Definition-based claims, 710
Definition-based question, 24, 25
dejanews.com, 18
Demonstrative adjectives
function of, 870
list of, 870
Demonstrative pronouns
function of, 225, 870
list of, 225, 870
as transitions, 225
Denotation, 236–237
defined, 236, 868, 870
situations for use, 236–237
Dependent clauses. *See* Subordinate (dependent) clauses
Description, in opening paragraph, 212
Details
and clarity in writing, 310
parenthetical, 593
research project, 717–719
for sentence variety, 323–324
Determiner
articles as, 870
defined, 870
possessive pronouns as, 870
Dialect, 253–256
correct use of, 255–256
defined, 253, 870
importance of, 254
limitations of, 254–255
uses in writing, 253–256
Dialogue. *See also* Direct quotations
dashes for interruptions in, 597
quotation marks around, 585–586
Dictionary
online, COS/APA (sciences) style, 851–852
online, COS/MLA (humanities) style, 840

plural form of noun, 442
and reading assignments, 131
different from/different than, correct usage, 870
Dingbats, fonts for, 355, 356
Direct discourse, 870
defined, 870
example of, 870
Direct object
compound object, 263
and compound verbs, 263
function of, 258, 885
noun clause as, 279
and passive construction, 258
and sentence patterns. *See* Sentence structure
and transitive verbs, 257–258, 518–520
verbals as, 271, 437
Direct questions, question mark at end of, 543
Direct quotations, 701–708
adding information to, 707
APA style, 693–694, 708
attributions with, 703
bracketed comments in, 595
capitalization of first word, 607
colon as introduction, 583
comma as introduction, 573
commas in, 573
dialogue, 585–586
ellipses in, 589–590, 704–707
end punctuation, 543, 587–588
fitting into text, 704
frame for, 702–703
indenting longer quotations, 708
lines of poetry as, 608
MLA style, 693–694, 697, 727
omitted material from, 589–591, 596, 704–707
in opening paragraphs, 213
prose quotations, 707, 708
quotation marks, 585–589
reasons for use, 702
sic to indicate errors in quoted material, 596, 707
on World Wide Web, 648–649
Directions, in parentheses, 593
Disabled persons, eliminating biased language toward, 251
Discourse
direct, 870
indirect, 878

discreet/discrete, correct usage, 871
Discuss, essay question, 110–111, 112
disinterested/uninterested, correct usage, 871
Dissertations
  parenthetical note (MLA), 738
  Works Cited (MLA), 738
Division pattern, organization of paper, 40–41
Document(s)
  capitalizing name of, 613
  titles, capitalization, 613
Document design, 329–404. *See also* Document format; Document style
  and audience, 330, 334, 344
  brochure example, 401
  charts and graphs, 357–358
  color, use in, 335, 342, 359–361
  with computer, 347–349, 361–382
  draft, 338–341, 344
  model documents in. *See* Model documents
  newsletter example, 399
  organizing long documents, 349–351
  photographs and illustrations, 358–359, 367
  proofreading in, 72
  storyboarding, 366–367
  typography, 342
  white space, 340, 343, 354
Document format, 331–334
  basic principles, 331–332
  combined print and electronic, 334
  correctness of, 712–717
  defined, 331
  electronic, 332–333
  identifying suitable, 336–337
  page layout in, 351–354
  print, 332–333
Document style, 334–336
  basic principles, 334–336
  consistency of, 343
  defined, 334
  experimenting with, 339–340
  exploring possible, 337–338
Documentation of sources, 104, 693–708. *See also specific documentation systems*
  dates of important events, 695
  direct quotations, 693–694, 697
  information outside of common knowledge, 694
  parenthetical notes, 693–694, 697
  plagiarism and, 104, 687, 690
  systems for, 695–696
  and writing for nonspecialists, 694–695

Dogpile, 655
Dollar sign ($), use in writing, 620
don't, correct form for, 871
Double negatives, 498–499
  avoiding, 498–499, 871
  defined, 498–499, 871
Double possessive, defined, 871
Doublings
  avoiding for conciseness, 317
  defined, 317
Downloading, of electronic sources, 635–636, 713
Downshifting, for clarity, 310
Draft, 5, 50–59
  beginning writing, 50–52
  collaborative drafting, 57–59
  on computer, 52
  conclusion in, 54
  continuity in writing, 52–54
  document design, 338–341, 344
  editing, 60–61, 67–70
  editing for standard English, 255
  example of, 53
  example of process for developing, 55–56
  HTML documents in Web design, 369–381
  length and proportion of, 53–54
  literary analysis, 186–187
  main ideas in, 52–53
  pace for writing, 51
  in peer editing, 73–81
  proofreading, 61, 71–81
  revising, 60, 61–67
  solid draft, features of, 56–57
  taking breaks, 54–55
  and thesis development, 25, 52–54
  time management, 55
  typing/printing guidelines, 57
  zero draft, 25
due to/because of, correct usage, 863
due to the fact that, revision of, 871

E

each
  in nonsexist language, 486
  possessive form, 475
  and pronoun agreement, 460
  and subject-verb agreement, 408, 411, 412
each other, as reciprocal pronoun, 891
Economical writing. *See* Concise versus cluttered writing
-ed, -d
  adjective ending, 507–508

ESL writer, 507–508
   past/past participle of verbs, 426,
      435–436, 507–508, 886–887
Edited works
   Bibliography/Works Cited (CMS),
      807–808
   Notes (CMS), 807–808
   parenthetical notes (APA), 780
   parenthetical notes (MLA), 732,
      733–734
   References (APA), 780
   Works Cited (MLA), 732, 733–734
Editing, 5, 67–70
   computer for, 69
   for concise writing, 313–322
   conclusion, 69
   for concrete/specific language, 67
   defined, 60–61, 67
   document design, 341–344
   example of, 70
   introduction, 69
   marginal comments, 74
   peer editing, 73–81
   premature, 51
   for style, 67–68
   for tone, 68
   transitions, 68
   in Web design, 381–382
   for wordiness, 68
Editions of book
   parenthetical notes (MLA), 737
   Works Cited (MLA), 737
Editorials
   connotative language for, 238–239
   parenthetical note (MLA, printed edi-
      torials), 743
   Works Cited (MLA, online editorials),
      748
   Works Cited (MLA, printed editorials),
      743
Editorials on File, 651
effect/affect, correct usage, 858–859
e.g., 619
either
   and pronoun agreement, 411, 460
   and subject-verb agreement, 411
Either/or arguments, 172
either . . . or
   in compound subjects, 262
   in compound verbs, 262
   linking independent clauses, 284
   and parallelism, 294
   and pronoun agreement, 464
   and subject-verb agreement, 409–410

Electronic address
   angle brackets in, 745
   COS style, 828, 830–831
   email, 385
   parenthetical note (APA), 775,
      785–787
   References (APA), 785–787
   References (CBE), 824–825
   slashes in, 603
   Works Cited (MLA), 745–751, 748
Electronic indexes, 646–648
Electronic mail. *See* Email
Electronic media. *See also* COS style; Elec-
      tronic sources; Internet; Web de-
      sign; World Wide Web
   copyright issues, 344–345
   email, 384–385
   listservs, 18, 26, 657–659
   online discussions, 657–659
   and quality of writing, 3
   Usenet newsgroups, 17–18, 26,
      657–659
   Web page creation. *See* Web design
Electronic scanning, photographs and il-
      lustrations, 367
Electronic sources, 344–345, 653–659.
      See also COS style
   Bibliography/Works Cited (CMS),
      810–811
   electronic information issues, 693
   hyperlinks in electronic sources, 695
   image collections, 653
   Notes (CMS), 810–811
   parenthetical notes (MLA), 750–751
   References (APA), 785–787
   References (CBE), 824–825
   Works Cited (MLA), 745–751, 748
elicit/illicit, correct usage, 871
Ellipses, 589–591
   bracketed ellipses, 589, 590, 591, 596,
      705–707
   full line for deletions, 591
   MLA style for, 589–591
   for omitted material, 589–591, 596,
      704–707
   for pauses or incomplete action, 590
   punctuation with, 590
   in quoted material, 589–590,
      704–707
   spacing before/after, 590
Elliptical construction, 871–872
   defined, 871
   examples of, 871
elude/allude, correct usage, 860

Email
    address, 385
    Bibliography/Works Cited (CMS), 811
    for classmate correspondence, 26
    components of, 385
    COS/APA (sciences) style, 849
    COS/MLA (humanities) style, 837
    examples of, 385
    letter of application, 389
    memorandums, 395
    Notes (CMS), 811
    parenthetical note (APA), 787
    quotation marks in, 585
    References (APA), 787
    résumé, 391
    Works Cited (MLA), 750
    writing guidelines for, 384
eminent/imminent, correct usage, 872
Emotional language, 235–239
    in arguments, 162–163
    use of, 68
Emphasis
    capitalization for, 607, 612–613
    dashes in sentences, 597
    italicized words/phrases, 604, 605
    parallelism for, 295, 296
    quotation marks in sentences, 586
    subordination to shift, 289
Encyclopedia
    Bibliography/Works Cited (CMS), 810
    COS/APA (sciences) style (online article), 851
    COS/MLA (humanities) style (online article), 839–840
    Notes (CMS), 810
    parenthetical note (MLA) for article, 743–744
    parenthetical note (MLA) for volume, 735
    and research topic selection, 630
    specialized, listing of, 630
    Works Cited (MLA, online article), 743–744
    Works Cited (MLA, printed article), 743–744
    Works Cited (MLA) for volume, 735
Endnotes
    CBE-style, 821–825
    CMS style, 803–805, 817
    COS/CMS style, 828
    MLA style, 757–759
    software for preparing, 695–696
English (nationality), use of term, 864

English as a second language. *See* ESL writer
enthusiastic/enthused, correct use of, 872
Enumerate, essay question, 113
equally as, misuse of, 872
-er, comparative form, 500–501
-es, plurals, 441–443
Eserver, 656
Eskimo, use of term, 249, 872
ESL writer, 505–540
    a, an, the, 535–536
    adjective pairs, 264–265, 508
    adverbs, 509
    auxiliary verbs, 506
    clauses, 506
    common problem areas, 506–509
    count and noncount nouns, 534–535
    -ed ending, past participle, 507–508
    general problems, list of, 510
    gerunds, 529–533
    idioms, 520–522
    indirect object, 520
    infinitives, 529–532
    intransitive verbs, 519–520
    modals, 523–527
    nonaction verbs, 515
    proofreading guidelines, 506–509
    quantifiers, 537–538
    reference books for, 511
    repetition in sentence elements, 508–509
    -s with third person singular/present tense verbs, 506–507
    separable and inseparable verbs, 520–522
    transitive verbs, 518–519
    two and three word verbs, 520–522
    verb tense, 512–517
especially, at beginning of list, 550
Essay examinations, 108–115
    analysis of questions, 110–111
    compared to papers, 108
    components of good response, 113–114
    example question/response, 114–115
    grammatical errors and scoring, 114
    key terms used in questions, 110–113
    knowing parameters of exam, 109, 114
    knowledge of material, 108–109
    outline of response, 113–114
    planning and, 113–114
    and stress, 110
    study time, 109–110
    time management during, 111–112
    writing guidelines, 110–111, 113–114

Essays, quotation marks around title, 586
Essential appositives, 563–564
Essential clauses
    that in, 480
    which in, 481
Essential modifiers, 502–504, 892
    commas with, 572
    functions of, 503
    that in, 504
-*est,* superlative form, 500–501
et al., 605, 619, 733
etc., 605, 619, 861
    avoiding in writing, 872
Ethnic groups
    capitalizing names of, 610, 612
    eliminating biased language toward, 248–249
    stereotypes, 248–249
Ethnic News Watch, 646
Evaluate, essay question, 112
Evaluating sources, 670–677
Evaluating World Wide Web sites, 672–674
Evaluation process, 83–98
    letter grades in, 83–89, 96–97
    portfolios in, 89–95
    for service-learning projects, 127–128
    student rights and responsibilities in, 95–98
even if, as subordinating conjunction, 288
even, placement in sentences, 497
even though
    correct usage, 872
    as subordinating conjunction, 288, 289
every, and subject-verb agreement, 408
every, in nonsexist language, 486
everybody
    and pronoun agreement, 460
    and subject-verb agreement, 411
everyone
    and pronoun agreement, 460, 461
    and subject-verb agreement, 411
everyone/every one, correct usage, 872
everything
    and pronoun agreement, 460
    and subject-verb agreement, 411
Evidence
    in academic papers, 101–102
    in arguments, 154–155, 156, 158–159, 163
    criteria for solid evidence, 159
    for essay examination response, 114
    evaluation in written piece, 137–138

Examples
    dashes before, 597
    in parentheses, 593
except/accept, correct usage, 856
Excite, 655, 663
Exclamation marks, 545–546
    with abbreviations at end of statement, 542
    editor's mark for, 545
    end of command, 542, 545
    at end of strong reaction, 545
    with other punctuation marks, 546
    overdoing use of, 545
    with quotation marks, 546
Expanded Academic ASAP, 646
Expanding sentences, subordination in, 289–290
Explain, essay question, 110–111, 112
Expletives
    avoiding for conciseness, 318–319, 873
    defined, 221, 318, 873
    in transitions, 221–222
Export, HTML options, 363, 380–381

F

Fact-based claims, 710
Fact-based question, 24, 25
fact that, the, 873
Facts on File, 651
Fahrenheit, abbreviation of, 618
faith/fate, correct usage, 873
Fallacies, 170–175
    ad hominem arguments, 170
    bandwagon appeal, 174
    circular reasoning, 170–171
    either/or arguments, 172
    fallacy of insufficient options, 172
    fallacy of special pleading, 163
    false analogies, 173–174
    false cause arguments, 171–172
    hasty generalization, 171
    non sequitur, 174
    red herrings, 172–173
    slippery slopes fallacy, 173
    straw man fallacy, 162
False analogies, 173–174
False cause arguments, 171–172
False dilemma fallacy, 172
Farmer's Almanac, The, 650
farther/further, correct usage, 873
fate, faith, correct usage, 873
Faulty parallelism, correction of, 295–297, 423–424

Faulty predication
  defined, 306–307, 873
  revision of, 873
Feature by feature pattern, in compare
  and contrast paper, 39–40
few
  possessive form, 475
  and pronoun agreement, 460
  and subject-verb agreement, 411, 412
few, a few, as quantifiers, 538
fewer than/less than, correct usage, 874
Field research, 664–669
  interviews, 664–665
  observations, 669
  questionnaires, 665–668
Figurative language, 326–327, 874
  metaphors, 327
  similes, 327
Figures (graphic)
  APA style, 714–715
  documenting borrowed images, 345,
    653
  image collections, 653
  MLA style, 713–714
  in research paper, 713–714
Figures (numeric). *See also* Number(s)
  plural of, 444
Filming, in online reading, 135
Films
  parenthetical note, 787
  References (APA), 787
  reviews (MLA style), 738–739
  reviews, guides to, 652
  titles, italics, 605
  Works Cited (MLA), 752
Filtering, in online reading, 134
Final portfolios, 90
Finite verbs, 438, 874, 898
First person, 433, 887
flaunt/flout, correct usage, 874
flout, flaunt, correct usage, 874
Folders, of Web sites, 367–368, 636, 682
Fonts, 355–357
Footers, in document design, 339
Footnotes
  CMS style, 803–805, 818, 819
  COS/CMS style, 828
  MLA style, 757–759
  software for preparing, 695–696
for
  comma before, 566
  linking independent clauses, 282
  present perfect with, 516

for example
  as appositive, 274
  at beginning of list, 550
  Latin expression for, 619
  semicolon before, 578–579
for instance, at beginning of list, 550
Foreign language book
  parenthetical note (MLA), 736
  Works Cited (MLA), 736
Foreign terms
  italics for, 605
  Latin expressions, 605, 619–620
Formal language, 229–231
  characteristics of, 231
  possessive form of noun in, 448–449
  situations for use of, 230–231
Formal outline, 46–47
Format of document. *See* Document de-
  sign
Formatting, proofreading for, 72
Forward
  parenthetical note (MLA), 734–735
  Works Cited (MLA), 734–735
Fractions
  hyphenated words for, 599
  slashes in, 603
Fragment. *See* Sentence fragments
Frames (document design), 353
Frames (Web sites)
  COS/APA (sciences) style, 848
  COS/MLA (humanities) style, 836
Free modifiers, 301
Freewriting
  defined, 23
  ideas used for outline, 44–45
  topic development, 23–24
FTP (File Transfer Protocol) site
  COS/APA (sciences) style, 850
  COS/MLA (humanities) style, 838–839
fun/funner/funnest
  comparative/superlative forms,
    874–875
  use in writing, 874–875
further/farther, correct usage, 873
Fused sentences. *See* Run-on sentences
Future perfect progressive tense
  and active voice, 420
  ESL writer, 514
Future perfect tense, 433
  and active voice, 420
  ESL writer, 513
  and passive voice, 421
Future progressive tense, 433

and active voice, 420
ESL writer, 514
Future tense, 433
and active voice, 420
ESL writer, 513
and passive voice, 421

G
gay, use of term, 251, 875
Gender
biased language. *See* Sexist language
defined, 875
and pronoun agreement, 859
Generalizations, use of, 67
Geographic place names
abbreviations, 618–619
capitalization, 612
Geology reports, style manual for, 820
Gerund(s), 270–271, 436–437
-*ing* as identifier, 436–437
as complement, 271, 437
as direct object, 271, 437
ESL writer, 529–533
following prepositions, 533
functions of, 437, 875
as nominals, 884
possessive form, 448–449
in sentence fragments, 549
as subject, 271, 437
tense, 434, 437
verbs followed by gerunds, 530–532
Gerund phrases
as appositives, 274
as direct object, 271
as subject, 271
get/got/gotten, correct usage, 875
Glossaries, in document design, 350–351
Go, 655
Goals
drafting and, 58
and purpose for writing, 7–8
in topic selection, 22
good and, avoiding in writing, 876
good/well, correct use of, 493–494, 876
Google, 18, 655, 659
Gopher sites
COS/APA (sciences) style, 850
COS/MLA (humanities) style,
838–839
got/gotten, correct usage, 875
Government agencies
abbreviated name of, 543
Web sites on, 652–653

Government documents
parenthetical notes (MLA), 744–745
Works Cited (MLA), 744–745
Government Web site
COS/APA (sciences) style, 846
COS/MLA (humanities) style, 834
Grading criteria, 83–89
Graphics. *See* Visual information
Graphs, 144–145, 313
bar graphs, 144–145
computer generated, 357–358
evaluating accuracy of, 148
interpreting, 142–148
line graphs, 145
Group writing. *See* Collaboration
Guillemets, 589

H
had better, as modal auxiliary, 524
had, ESL writer, 532
handicapped, use of term, 876
hanged/hung, correct usage, 876
Hard points, research project, 637
hardly, and double negatives, 499
Hasty generalization, 171
have to, as modal auxiliary, 524, 526
he
ESL writer, 506–507
in nonsexist language, 485–487, 876,
893
in sexist language, 246
he/him, pronoun case, 469–470, 471
Headers
in document design, 339
Web page, 364
Headings, 715–717
APA style, 716–717
in document design, 339
maximum levels of, 715
MLA style, 715–716
as transitions, 226–227
Helping verbs. *See* Auxiliary verbs
her, in nonsexist language, 485–487, 876
her/she, pronoun case, 469–470, 471
here, and subject-verb agreement, 416
Hierarchical pattern, in Web design, 365,
366
him
in nonsexist language, 485–487
in sexist language, 246
him/he, pronoun case, 469–470, 471
his, in nonsexist language, 485–487
Hispanics, use of term, 248–249, 876

index

hisself, avoiding, 479, 877
Historical epochs, capitalization of, 613
Holidays, capitalization of, 613
Home page, 365
Homonyms
  examples of, 877
  nature of, 877
homosexual, use of term, 251
Honesty, in presentation of material, 12–13
hopefully, correct usage, 877
HotBot, 655
how many, as quantifier, 891
how much, as quantifier, 891
however
  comma with, 561, 564, 565
  as connection in paragraph, 223
  in independent clauses, 285
  as qualifier, 891
  semicolon before, 578
HTML (Hypertext Markup Language),
  361–364
  HTML text editors, 363, 364, 369–376
  visual HTML text editors, 363, 364,
  376–380
HTML text editors, 363, 364, 369–376
Hub structure, in Web design, 365, 366
Humanities reports. *See also* Subject
  areas
  characteristics of, 105
  documentation of. *See* CMS style;
  COS/MLA (humanities) style; MLA
  style
Humor, in writing, 252–253
hung/hanged, correct usage, 876
Hypertext links, of Web pages, 365, 375,
  378–379, 381, 695
Hyphens, 599–602
  to clarify word meaning, 599
  compound modifiers, 265, 600–601
  compound nouns, 600
  compound phrases, 600–601
  compound verbs, 600
  misuse of, 598, 601–602
  in numbers, 599, 621
  in possessives, 446
  after prefixes of proper nouns, 600
  in suspended modifiers, 601
Hypothesis
  defined, 21
  development for research project, 631
  nature of, 21–22
  of social science report, 789
  in topic selection, 21–22

I, correct use of, 482
I/me, pronoun case, 468–469, 470, 471
I/you, pronoun case, 467
ibid., CMS style for subsequent citations,
  805
-ics endings, subject-verb agreement, 414
ICYouSee, 671
ID numbers, 623
Idea map, topic selection/refinement,
  20–21
Idioms
  clusters of adjectives, 264–265
  defined, 877
  ESL writer, 520–522
  examples of, 877
  nature of, 264–265
i.e., 605, 619
if
  in adverb clauses, 278
  as subordinating conjunction, 276,
  288, 560–561
if only, as subordinating conjunction, 288
if . . . then, linking independent clauses, 284
illicit/elicit, correct usage, 871
illusion/allusion, 860
Illustration, paragraphs of, 199–200
Illustrations. *See* Visual information
Image collections, 653
imminent/eminent, correct usage, 872
Imperative mood
  defined, 877, 883
  use of, 431
Imperative mood, use of, 433
imply/infer, correct usage, 877
Imposing, in online reading, 134
Imprint of publisher
  abbreviations of publisher name,
  725–726
  parenthetical note (MLA), 738
  Works Cited (MLA), 738
in fact, semicolon before, 578–579
in order that, as subordinating conjunction, 288
in other words, as appositive, 274
including these, at beginning of list, 582
incredible/incredulous, correct usage, 878
Incubation period, 5, 54–55
indeed, semicolon before, 578–579
Indefinite articles. *See a; an*
Indefinite pronouns
  functions of, 411–412, 878
  list of, 411, 460

modification of, 412
possessive forms, 447, 475
pronoun agreement, 460–462
pronoun case, 474–475
singular/plural/variable, 411–412,
    460–462
subject-verb agreement, 411–412
Indentions
lines of poetry in passage, 707–708
longer quotations, 708
paragraphs, 354, 885
Independent clauses
in balanced sentences, 298–299
colon as link, 284–285
comma as link, 566–567
in comma splices, 552–555
in complex sentences, 280, 281
in compound-complex sentences, 280
in compound sentences, 280, 281
conjunctions as link, 282–283, 284–285
conjunctive adverbs in, 285–286
coordination of, 282–286
and correlatives, 284
dashes as link, 284–285
function of, 276, 566, 865
parts of, 276
semicolon as link, 284–285, 577–579
in simple sentences, 280–281
subordination of, 281, 287–291
Indexes, in document design, 350–351
Indexes to periodicals, 646–648
electronic indexes, 646–648
information in, 646–648
newspapers, 650
printed volumes, 646
searching index, 646
subjects/indexes, listing of, 646–647
Indicative mood, use of, 433, 878, 883
Indirect discourse
defined, 878
example of, 878
Indirect object
ESL writer, 520
function of, 260–261, 885
noun clause as, 279
and transitive verbs, 260–261, 520
use in sentence, 260–261
Indirect questions
defined, 544
period at end of, 542, 544
infer/imply, correct usage, 877
Infinitive phrases
as adjectives, 272

as adverbs, 272
as direct object, 271
as subject, 270
Infinitives, 270–272, 432, 433, 435
absolute phrases from, 273, 435, 878
as adjectives, 272
as adverbs, 272
defined, 426, 435
as direct object, 271, 529
ESL writer, 529–532
following transitive verbs, 532
functions of, 270–272, 529, 878
to as identifier, 435, 878
as nouns, 878
in sentence fragments, 549
split infinitives, 438–439, 894
as subject, 529
as subject complement, 271, 530
tense, 433, 435
verbs followed by infinitives,
    530–532
Inflammatory language, 13, 68
Inflection, defined, 878
Infomine, 656
Informal language, 231–233
characteristics of, 233
possessive form of noun in, 448–449
situations for use of, 231–233
Informal outline, 45–46
Informative brochure, denotative language
    for, 237–238
InfoSurf, 656
-ing
adjective ending, 507–508
ESL writer, 508
gerunds, 436–437, 549, 875
participles, 435–436, 886–887
Initialisms, 614, 879
abbreviations, 616
capitalizing, 614, 616
periods in, rule for, 616
pronunciation of, 879
Initials of people, capitalization,
    609–610
Inseparable verbs, 520–522
and ESL writer, 520–522
example of, 521
listing of, 521–522
Institutional Web site
COS/APA (sciences) style, 845
COS/MLA (humanities) style, 833
Intellectual property, 344–345, 693,
    698–701

Intensifiers
avoiding for conciseness, 318
list of, 891
nature of, 318, 879, 891
Intensive pronouns, 478–479, 879
Intentional fragment, sentence as,
551–552, 879
Interchange, 658
Interjection, defined, 879
Internet. *See also* Electronic media; Electronic sources; World Wide Web
for input about project, 26
for research, 158–159, 631
research project posted on, 627–628,
631
for topic selection, 17–18
Internet Public Library, 650
Interrogative pronouns, list of, 879
Interruptions
comma with, 564–565
dashes with, 597
Interviews
guidelines for, 665
online, 665
as research tool, 664–665
types of questions for, 665
Works Cited (MLA), 753
Intransitive verbs, 519–520, 879
action verbs as, 519–520, 520
ESL writer, 519–520
examples of, 897
linking verbs as, 519, 520, 879
use in sentence, 257–258
Introduction/body/conclusion pattern, organization of paper, 36–37
Introduction of book
parenthetical note (MLA), 734–735
Works Cited (MLA), 734–735
Introduction of paper
editing, 69
function of, 36
testing conclusion against, 712
thesis statement in, 32–33, 34–35
Introductory phrases, comma after,
559–560
Inuit, use of term, 249, 872
Inversion of sentence, defined, 880
Inverted sentence order, and subject-verb
agreement, 417
irregardless/regardless, correct usage, 880
Irregular verbs, 421, 426–429
list of, 427–429, 880
participle of, 436

and subject-verb agreement, 407
and verb tense, 421, 426–429
Irregular words, and plurals, 441
irritate/aggravate, correct usage, 859
is, ineffectiveness in sentences, 307
-ism expressions, capitalization rule, 613–614
it
in beginning of sentence, 873
ESL writer, 506–507
and pronoun reference, 454–455
it is, as expletive, 221, 319, 873
it was, as expletive, 318–319
Italics, 604–606
album titles, 605
book titles, 605
dances, 605
editor's mark for, 604
film titles, 605
foreign words/phrases, 604, 605
journal titles, 605
letters of alphabet, 606
magazine titles, 605
musical pieces (long works), 605
newspaper titles, 605
paintings, 605
phrases, 606
play titles, 605
poetry (long poems), 605
radio shows, 605
sculptures, 605
ship names, 605
software programs, 605
spacecraft, 605
television shows, 605
train names, 605
type style, 355, 356, 604
underlining for, 604
words as words, 606
Items in a series. *See* Series
it's, contraction, 447, 475
its/it's
possessive form versus contraction,
475–476, 880
pronoun case, 475–476

J

Jargon
avoiding, 242
defined, 880
Journal articles. *See also* Magazine articles;
Scholarly articles
capitalization in, 607–608
quotation marks around title, 605

Journal titles, italics, 605
Journalist's questions, and topic development, 24
judgment/judgement, American/British spellings, 880
just as . . . so, linking independent clauses, 284

K

Keyword search, 642, 654–657, 659–664
Boolean searching, 661–662
by exact phrase, 663–664
simple search, 660–661
and specific search engines, 657
time frame for, 663–664
Web domain for search, 664
kind of/rather, correct usage, 880

L

Labor unions, abbreviations, 617
Landscape page orientation, 351
Language
and audience, 230–231, 233, 240–241, 256
bias in. *See* Biased language
casual language, 233–234
civil language, 13–14, 242–244
and college writing, 233
concrete language, 67
connotative language, 236, 237–239
denotative language, 236–237
dialect, 253–256
editing of, 67–68
figurative language, 326–327
formal language, 229–231
idioms, 264–265, 520–522, 877
inclusive language, 256
informal language, 231–233, 448–449
jargon, 242, 880
levels of, 229–230
neutral language, 237
and respect for reader, 240–241
slang, 894
specific language, 67
Latin expressions, abbreviation of, 605, 619–620
lay/lie, correct usage, 880–881
Layout of page, and reader response to text, 149
Learning Record, 95
Lectures, MLA style, 755
Length
of paper, 53–54

of paragraphs, 207–210
of sentences, 311–312, 324–325
lesbian, use of term, 251, 875
less than/fewer than, correct usage, 874
let, ESL writer, 532
Letter grades, 83–89, 96–97
Letters (correspondence)
business letters, 386–389
components of, 387
cover letter, 388–389
electronic. *See* Email
examples of, 387
letter of application, 388–389
letter to the editor, parenthetical note (MLA), 743
letter to the editor, Works Cited (MLA), 743
parenthetical note (MLA), 756
published and unpublished, Works Cited (MLA), 756
salutation, 574, 584
writing guidelines for, 386
Letters (of alphabet)
italics, 606
parentheses with listed, 593–594
plural of, 444
LEXIS-NEXIS, 646, 648, 664
Librarians' Index to the Internet, 656, 671
Library, 640–652
almanacs, 649, 650
bibliographies, 641, 644–645
biographical resources, 648–649
book reviews, 652
card catalog, 640–641, 642
encyclopedia, 630
film reviews, 652
indexes, 646–648
literary analysis works, 181–182
news sources, 650–652
online catalogs, 640
periodical literature, 646–648
reference books, guides to, 646–647
statistical information, sources for, 649–650
for thesis development, 25–26
for topic selection, 17
Library of Congress Subject Guide to Internet Resources, 656
lie/lay, correct usage, 880–881
like/as, correct usage, 881
like, in similes, 327
Line graphs, 145
interpretation of, 145

Linking verbs
  ESL writer, 519, 520
  function of, 259–260, 471, 881
  as intransitive verbs, 519, 520, 879
  list of, 881
  and predicate adjectives, 493–494
  and pronoun case, 466, 471–472
  and subject complement, 259–260,
    471–472, 894
  subject-verb agreement, 416–417
Links in Web pages, 365, 375, 378–379,
    381, 695
List, essay question, 113
Lists
  colon before, 571–572, 581–582, 583
  developing outlines from, 44–45
  in document design, 339, 352
  introductory words to, 550, 582
  numbers in, 593–594
  parallelism in, 293
  in sentence fragments, 550
  for technical information, 312
Listservs, 18, 26, 657–659
  characteristics of, 658
  COS/APA (sciences) style, 849
  COS/MLA (humanities) style, 837–838
  parenthetical note (APA), 785
  pros/cons of information, 658
  References (APA), 785
  searching, 658
  threads, 397
  Works Cited (MLA), 749
literally, correct usage, 881
Literary analysis, 176–192
  character/setting analysis, 177
  close readings for, 177, 182–184
  conventions used in, 187–188
  denotative language for, 237
  examples of, 179–180, 188–192
  first draft, 186–187
  gender-focused analysis, 178
  historical/cultural analysis, 178
  life of writer and works, 178
  literary archetypes analysis, 177
  literary genre analysis, 177–178
  literary Web site, 178
  outline for, 186–187
  plot analysis, 177
  primary source for, 180–181
  reference works for, 181–182
  secondary sources for, 181
  theme analysis, 177
  thesis development, 184–186

Literary periods, capitalization of, 613–614
Literature review, in social science report,
    789
little, a little, as quantifiers, 538, 891
Logical fallacies. *See* Fallacies
Looksmart, 655
loose/lose, correct usage, 881–882
-ly
  adverbs ending in, 266, 495–496, 500,
    601
  colloquial and formal usage, 495–496
  in double negative, 499
  in long forms of adverbs, 495
  use in writing situations, 495
Lycos, 18, 655

M
mad/angry, correct usage, 861
made, ESL writer, 532
Magazine articles
  capitalization in, 607–608
  COS/APA (sciences) style, 847
  COS/MLA (humanities) style, 835–836
  index search for, 646–648
  Notes (CMS), 809
  parenthetical note (APA), 783
  parenthetical note (MLA), 740–741
  quotation marks around title, 586, 605
  References (APA), 783
  References (CBE), 824
  Works Cited (MLA, online magazines),
    747
  Works Cited (MLA, printed maga-
    zines), 740–741
Magazine titles, italics, 605
Magellan, 655
Main clauses. *See* Independent clauses
majority/plurality, meaning and usage of,
    882
man, in sexist language, 246–247, 882
mankind
  alternatives to, 882
  in sexist language, 882
*Manual for Authors of Mathematical Pa-
    pers, A,* 820
*Manual for Writers of Term Papers, Theses,
    and Dissertations* (6th edition), 803
*Manual of Style, Government Printing Of-
    fice,* 600
many
  and pronoun agreement, 460
  as quantifier, 538
  and subject-verb agreement, 411, 412

many times/often, correct usage, 882
Marginal comments, 74, 87–89
Margins
    MLA style, 763
    white space, 340, 343, 354
Married women, titles for, 247, 616–617
Mass nouns, examples of, 534
Mathematics reports, style manual for,
    820
may, as modal auxiliary, 421, 524, 525
may/can, correct usage, 864
me/I, pronoun case, 468–469, 470, 471
Measurement units. *See* Weights and mea-
    sures
media/medium, correct usage, 882
Medical reports, style manual for, 820
Memorandums, 394–395
    components of, 395
    examples of, 395
    writing guidelines for, 394
Messages to online forums, 396–397
    archived, 631, 658, 838, 850
    components of, 397
    examples of, 397
    writing guidelines for, 396
Metaphors
    defined, 327, 882
    examples of, 327, 882
    mixed metaphors, 327
Methods section, of social science report,
    789
Mexican Americans, use of term, 882
Microfilm/microfiche, 650–651
    parenthetical note (MLA), 751
    Works Cited (MLA), 751
Microsoft Internet Explorer, 654
might, as modal auxiliary, 421, 422, 525
might of/might have, correct usage, 882
Misplaced modifying phrases, 488–489,
    883
    compared to absolute phrases, 490
    correction of, 488–489
    example of, 489
Mixed metaphors
    avoiding, 327
    defined, 883
*MLA Handbook for Writers of Research Pa-
    pers* (Gibaldi), 722
MLA style, 76, 722–772. *See also* Paren-
    thetical notes (MLA style); Works
    Cited (MLA style)
    compared to COS style, 826–827
    direct quotations, 693–694, 697

and electronic sources. *See* COS/MLA
    (humanities) style
    footnotes and endnotes, 757–759
    headings, 715–716
    indenting long quotations, 708, 727
    for literary analysis, 187
    MLA form directory, 728–759
    numbers, spelling of, 622
    omitted material, brackets and ellipses
        for, 591, 596, 705–707
    pagination, 763
    prose quotations, 707, 708
    punctuation, 718
    quoted lines of poetry, 707–708
    sample paper, 759–772
    subsequent citations, 728
    for tables and figures, 713–714
    title of project, 715
    title page, 761
MLA Style Manual, The. See also MLA
    style
Modals, 421–422, 523–527
    ESL writer, 523–527
    functions of, 421–422, 523, 883
    future form, 524–525
    list of, 421–422, 883
    past form, 524–525, 526–527
    perfect form, 526–527
    present form, 524–525, 526
    tips for use of, 526
Model documents, 383–404
    APA-style paper, 788–802
    brochures, 400–401
    business letters, 386–389
    CMS-style paper, 812–819
    email, 384–385
    letters of application, 388–389
    messages to online forums, 396–397
    MLA-style paper, 759–772
    newsletters, 398–399
    professional memos, 394–395
    résumés, 390–393
    Web pages, 402–404
Modern Language Association (MLA),
    693, 722. *See also* MLA style
    Web site for, 722
Modified block format letters, 387
Modifiers, 263–268
    absolute phrases, 490
    adjectives as, 264–265, 488–495. *See
        also* Adjective(s)
    adverbs as, 266, 492–493, 495–498,
        858. *See also* Adverb(s)

Modifiers *(Continued)*
  appositives as, 274–275
  compound, 265, 600–601
  in cumulative sentences, 300
  dangling modifiers, 488–490, 869
  double negatives, 498–499
  essential, 502–504, 572, 892
  free modifiers, 301
  functions of, 263–264, 883
  guidelines for use, 509
  misplaced modifying phrases, 488–489, 883
  nonrestrictive. *See* Nonessential modifiers
  nouns as, 267
  participles as, 268, 435–436, 886
  suspended modifiers, 601
  verbals as, 268
Money
  decimal points in, 543
  dollar sign ($), 620
  numerals for sums of, 622
Months of year
  abbreviation of, 615, 618
  capitalization of, 613
Monuments, capitalizing name of, 613
Mood
  defined, 431, 883
  imperative mood, 433, 877, 883
  indicative mood, 433, 878, 883
  subjunctive mood, 431–432, 433, 883, 895
MOOs (Multi-User Domain, Object Oriented), 658
  COS/APA (sciences) style, 851
  COS/MLA (humanities) style, 839
  Works Cited (MLA), 750
moral/morale, correct usage, 883
more
  comparative form, 500–501
  and pronoun agreement, 460
  and subject-verb agreement, 411
moreover
  comma with, 564
  to link independent clauses, 285
  semicolon before, 578
moreover/plus, correct usage, 888
most
  possessive form, 475
  and pronoun agreement, 460
  and subject-verb agreement, 411
  superlative form, 500–501
most, most of, as quantifiers, 538

most of the, as quantifier, 538
mount, abbreviation for, 619
Movies. *See* Films
m.p.g.(miles per gallon), 616, 618
m.p.h.(miles per hour), 616, 618
Mr., 616–617
Mrs., 616–617
Ms., 247, 616–617
Mt., 619
MUD (Multi-User Domain)
  COS/APA (sciences) style, 851
  COS/MLA (humanities) style, 839
  Works Cited (MLA), 750
Multivolume works. *See also* Encyclopedia
  Bibliography/Works Cited (CMS), 808
  Notes (CMS), 808
  Works Cited (MLA), 735
Musical compositions
  italics for title of longer works, 605
  parenthetical note (APA), 788
  References (APA), 788
  Works Cited (MLA), 753–754
Musical groups, capitalizing name of, 613
must, as modal auxiliary, 421, 524, 525
must have, as modal auxiliary, 526–527
must have/must of, correct usage of, 883
Myths about writing, 3–4

N
Name-calling, 13, 68
namely, at beginning of list, 550
Names of people. *See also* Title of person
  capitalization of, 609–610
  unestablished, question mark for, 544
Narrative
  dialect in, 254–255
  in opening paragraph, 211–212
Narrative pattern
  organization of paper, 37–38
  paragraphs, 200–201
National groups, capitalizing name of, 610, 612
Native American, use of term, 249, 883
Negative statements
  avoiding in writing, 311, 499
  double negatives, 498–499, 871
neither
  and pronoun agreement, 460
  and subject-verb agreement, 411
neither . . . nor
  in compound subjects, 262
  in compound verbs, 262
  and parallelism, 294

index

and pronoun agreement, 464
and subject-verb agreement, 409–410
Netscape Navigator, 654
Networks, abbreviated name of, 543
Neutral language, 237
never, and double negatives, 499
nevertheless
  comma with, 561, 564
  as connection in paragraph, 223
  to link independent clauses, 285
  as qualifier, 891
  semicolon before, 578
New York Times, The, 650, 675
  index to, 650
  on Web, 651, 652
News, print sources for, 650–651
News service (online)
  COS/APA (sciences) style, 847–848
  COS/MLA (humanities) style, 835–836
NewsBank, 650–651
Newsgroups. *See* Usenet newsgroups
Newsletters, 398–399
  components of, 399
  denotative language for, 237–238
  examples of, 399
  parenthetical note (APA), 783–784
  References (APA), 783–784
  writing/design guidelines, 398
Newspaper articles, 650–652. *See also* Editorials
  characteristics of, 650
  COS/APA (sciences) style, 847–848
  COS/MLA (humanities) style, 835–836
  index search for, 646–648, 650–652
  Notes (CMS), 810
  online resources to, 650–652
  parenthetical note (APA, online article), 786–787
  parenthetical note (APA, print article), 784
  parenthetical note (MLA), 742
  quotation marks around title, 586, 605
  References (APA, online article), 786–787
  References (APA, printed article), 784
  Works Cited (MLA), 742
Newspaper sections, quotation marks around title, 605
Newspaper titles, italics, 605
nice, correct usage, 884
No., 618
no, and double negatives, 498–499

no one
  and pronoun agreement, 460
  and subject-verb agreement, 411
nobody
  and double negatives, 499
  in nonsexist language, 486
  and pronoun agreement, 460
  and subject-verb agreement, 411
Nominalizations
  avoiding for conciseness, 315
  examples of, 315, 884
  nature of, 315, 884
Nominals
  functions of, 884
  gerunds as, 884
  pronouns as, 884
Nominative case. *See* Subjective case
Non sequitur, 174
Nonaction verbs, 515
  ESL writer, 515
  list of, 515
Noncoordinate adjectives, 568
  function of, 568, 884
  identification of, 568
  order of, 568, 884
Noncount nouns
  article problems with, 537
  characteristics of, 534–535, 537, 884
  ESL writer, 534–535, 537
none
  possessive form, 475
  and pronoun agreement, 460
  and subject-verb agreement, 411
Nonessential appositives, 563–564
Nonessential clauses, *which* in, 480–481
Nonessential modifiers, 502–504, 563–564
  commas with, 563–564
  function of, 502–503, 884
  which in, 504
nonetheless, semicolon before, 578
Nonfinite verbs, 438, 874
Nonrestrictive modifiers. *See* Nonessential modifiers
nor
  comma before, 566
  linking independent clauses, 282
  and pronoun agreement, 464
NorthernLight.com, 655
not, and double negatives, 499
not have to, as modal auxiliary, 524
not much, as quantifier, 538
not need to, as modal auxiliary, 524

not only . . . but also
   linking independent clauses, 284
   and parallelism, 294
Note cards
   research information on, 634–635
   working bibliography on, 633–634
Note-taking
   content notes, 132
   context notes, 132
   electronic, 639, 691
   interviews, 665
   observations, 669
   response notes, 132
Notes (CMS style)
   biblical citations, 810
   book (online), 811
   book in a series, 808
   book with editor, focus on editor,
      807–808
   book with editor, focus on original au-
      thor, 808
   book with four or more authors or edi-
      tors, 807
   book with no author, 808
   book with one author, 807
   book with two/three authors or editors,
      807
   book written by group, 808
   chapter in book, 809
   electronic sources, 810–811
   email, 811
   examples of, 804–805
   footnotes versus endnotes, 804
   Ibid., for subsequent citations, 805
   magazine article, 809
   magazine article (online), 811
   multivolume works, 808
   newspaper article, 810
   page reference for subsequent citations,
      805
   relationship to footnotes/endnotes, 804
   same work cited several times, 805
   scholarly article (printed article), 809
   several sources in single sentence, 804
   software, 810
   superscript for number keyed to,
      803–804
nothing
   and double negatives, 499
   and pronoun agreement, 460
   and subject-verb agreement, 411
Noun(s). *See also* Proper nouns
   abstract nouns, 534, 856

adjective modifiers of, 264–265,
   488–492
as adverbial, 858
as appositives, 275
case of, 864
collective nouns, 413, 414, 462–463,
   865
common form, 866
compound modifiers, 265
compound nouns, 600
concrete nouns, 867
count and noncount nouns, 534–535,
   869, 884
gerunds functioning as, 437
infinitives as, 878
mass nouns, 534
as modifiers, 267
parallelism in, 293
plurals, 441–444
possessive form, 445–447
subordinate clauses as, 277
Noun clauses, 279
   functions of, 279
   use in sentences, 279
Noun phrases, example of, 888
now that, as subordinating conjunction,
   288
nowhere/anywhere, correct usage, 884–885
number
   abbreviation for, 618
   subject-verb agreement, 414
Number(s), 621–623
   APA style for, 622
   at beginning of sentence, 622–623
   cardinal numbers, 864, 885
   combining words and figures in, 622
   commas in, 573
   comparing numbers, 622
   dates, 623
   decimals, 543
   fractions, 603
   hyphenated, 599–600, 621
   large numbers, 621
   MLA style for, 622
   numerals for, 621–622
   ordinal numbers, 621, 864, 885
   parentheses with listed, 593–594
   percentages/statistics/scores, 623
   plural of, 444, 623
   street numbers/page numbers/sums of
      money/ID and call numbers, 623
   subject-verb agreement, 414
   in technical writing, 621

time of day, 623
two-word numbers, 622
weights and measures, 623
words for, 621–622, 621–623, 864
number/amount, correct usage, 861
Number of word
  article agreement, 534–538
  pronoun agreement, 457–459, 859

O

Object complement
  adjectives as, 265
  function of, 261, 866
  use in sentence, 261
  verbals as, 271, 437
Object of sentence. *See* Direct object
Objective case
  defined, 466, 865, 885
  list of objective forms, 467
  situations for use, 466, 467, 470,
    472–473
Observations
  guidelines for, 669
  recording information, 669
  as research tool, 669
o'clock, words with, 623
of course, comma with, 565
off/off of, correct usage, 885
often/many times, correct usage, 882
O.K., OK, okay, 885
on the one hand . . . on the other hand, and
  parallelism, 294
on the other hand, semicolon before,
    578–579
once, as subordinating conjunction, 288
one another, as reciprocal pronoun, 891
one, as indefinite pronoun, 483–484
one of those who, subject-verb agreement,
    418
-one, as word ending, possessive form, 475
Online catalogs, 642–643
  information in, 640
  keyword search, 642
  Web site for list of, 642
  on World Wide Web, 642–643
Online writing and publishing. *See* Elec-
    tronic media
only, placement in sentences, 498
Opening paragraphs, 211–215
  anecdote in, 211–212
  closing paragraphs linked to, 216–217
  description in, 212
  examples of, 214–215

importance of, 211
narrative in, 211–212
question in, 200, 212–213
quotations in, 213
statement of thesis in, 213–214
Opening question, beginning paragraphs
  with, 200
Opening tag, 372
Opinion pieces, connotative language for,
    238–239
or
  and appositives, 274
  comma before, 566, 567
  in compound subjects/verbs/objects,
    262–263
  linking independent clauses, 282
  and pronoun agreement, 464
  and subject-verb agreement, 409–410
or/and, use in writing, 861
Ordinal numbers, words for, 621, 864, 885
Organization of paper, 29–49
  cause-and-effect pattern, 41–42
  classification pattern, 41
  commitment and response pattern,
    36–37
  comparison and contrast pattern, 38–40
  division pattern, 40–41
  feature by feature pattern, 39–40
  introduction/body/conclusion pattern,
    36–37
  narrative pattern, 37–38
  problem and-solution pattern, 42–43
  process pattern, 37–38
  revising for, 64
  subject by subject pattern, 38–39, 40
  thesis construction in, 29–35
Organizations
  abbreviating name of, 617
  capitalizing name of, 611
  COS style for Web sites, 833, 845
Oriental, terms preferred to, 885
Orphans, 343
ought to, as modal auxiliary, 421, 524, 525
Outline, 43–47
  with computer, 47
  literary analysis, 186–187
  for response in essay examination,
    113–114
  scratch outline, 45–46, 113–114, 186–187
  sentence outline, 46–47
  working list, 44–45
  writer preferences for, 47
Ownership. *See* Possessive(s); Possessive case

P

Page footer, in Web design, 375
Page numbers, numerals for, 623
Pagination
   APA style, 789
   MLA style, 763
Paintings, italics for name of, 605
Pamphlets
   parenthetical note (MLA), 744
   Works Cited (MLA), 744
Paragraphs, 194–210. *See also* Closing
      Paragraphs; Opening paragraphs
   analogy in, 203
   appearance of, 207–210, 226–227
   and audience, 194, 209
   cause-and-effect pattern, 202–203
   of classification, 201
   comparison and contrast pattern, 202
   of definition, 201
   in document design, 354
   editor's mark for, 885
   focus in writing, 194–195
   gaps between, 222
   of illustration, 199–200
   indentions, 354, 385
   internal transitions, 197–198
   length of, 207–210
   linking paragraphs, 225–226
   narrative, 200–201
   one-sentence paragraphs, 208–209
   parallelism in, 198, 225–226
   pointer words in, 223
   question and answer, 200
   question at beginning of, 200
   repetition of words in, 198
   revising, 204–207
   sentence variety in, 322–325
   signals for beginning paragraphs, 211
   topic sentence, 195–197, 896
   transition words, 198, 223–225
   unified paragraphs, writing guidelines,
      194–198
   verb tense, consistency of, 425
Parallelism
   in clauses, 279, 292–297, 885–886
   and correlatives, 294
   defined, 292, 885–886
   for emphasis, 295, 296
   examples of, 292–297
   faulty, correction of, 295–297, 423–424
   and paragraphs, 198, 225–226
   in phrases, 292–293, 885–886
   in sentences, 292–297, 885–886

   as transition, 225–226
   and verb tense, 423–424
   of words, 292–293, 885–886
Paraphrase
   avoiding, in literary analysis, 187
   defined, 684
   plagiarized, 687
   of research materials, 684, 687–691,
      698
Parentheses, 593–594
   bracketed information with, 596
   commas after, 594
   editor's mark for, 593
   end punctuation with, 594
   inserted directions/examples, 593
   separated details from main informa-
      tion, 593
   for short sentence within longer sen-
      tence, 594
   in test for essential modifiers, 504
Parenthetical element
   examples of, 886
   nature of, 886
Parenthetical notes (APA style), 693–694,
      774–776
   abstract (online), 787
   anthology, 781
   anthology selection, 781
   basic form, 773
   book review, 782
   book with no author, 780
   book with one author, 778
   book with three or more authors, 779
   book with two authors, 779
   chapter in book, 781
   for direct quotations, 774
   electronic sources, 785–787
   email, 787
   listserv, 785
   magazine article, author not named,
      784
   magazine article from monthly maga-
      zine, 783
   magazine article from weekly/biweekly
      magazine, 783
   movie/videotape, 787
   musical recording, 788
   newsletter article, 783–784
   newspaper article (online), 786–787
   newspaper article (printed), 784
   page numbers in, 774
   revised book, 780
   scholarly article (online), 786

scholarly article (printed), 782–783
several sources in one sentence, 775
several works in one note, 775
single source for series of references, 775–776
software, 784–785
Usenet newsgroups, 785
Web page (generic), 786
Web site, 775
Parenthetical notes (COS style), 827–828
Parenthetical notes (MLA style), 693–694, 697, 723–724
anthology, 736–737
anthology selection, 741–742
biblical citation, 751–752
book in foreign language, 736
book in series, 736
book published before 1900, 737
book reviews, 738–739
book revised by second author, 733
book with focus on forward/introduction/preface/afterword, 734–735
book with four or more authors or editors, 732–733
book with no author, 734
book with one author, 732
book with one editor, focus on author, 733
book with one editor, focus on editor, 733–734
book with several editors, 734
book with two/three authors or editors, 732
book written by group, 734
bulletins, 744
cartoons, 743
CD-ROM, 750–751
chapter in book, 737
dissertation, 738
encyclopedia, volume, 735
encyclopedia article, 743–744
at end of sentence, 587, 723
and end punctuation, 723
government document, 744–745
later editions, 737
letter to the editor, 743
letters, 756
magazine article from monthly magazine, 741
magazine article from popular magazine, 740
magazine article from weekly/biweekly magazine, 740

microfilm/microfiche, 751
newspaper article, 742
newspaper editorial, 743
pamphlets, 744
plays, 756–757
purpose of, 723
relationship to Works Cited, 722, 724
republished book, 736
same author of different works, 727–728
scholarly article, 739–740
several sources in single sentence, 726
several within one sentence, 726
several works in one note, 726
software, 745
translated book, 735–736
volume in multivolume set, 735
work with no author, 724, 726
Participle phrases
as adjectives, 271
as modifier, 271
Participles, 435–436, 886–887. *See also* Past participle
absolute phrases from, 273, 437, 887
as adjectives, 271
forms of, 433–434, 436
and irregular verbs, 436
as modifier, 268, 435–436, 886
tense, 433–434, 436
as verbal phrases, 886
Parts of speech. *See also specific categories*
categories of, 887
defined, 887
passed/past, correct usage, 887
Passive voice
avoiding use of, 308–309, 430
and *to be* verbs, 430
defined, 258, 420, 899
examples of, 421, 433
identifying passive verb, 430
revising to active voice, 430
situations for use, 430
and verb tense, 420–421, 429
Past participle, 432, 886, 889
defined, 426
ESL writer, 507–508
irregular verbs, 426–429
verb phrases from, 427
past/passed, correct usage, 887
Past perfect progressive tense, ESL writer, 514
Past perfect tense, 422, 433
and active voice, 420, 429–430

Past perfect tense *(Continued)*
  ESL writer, 513
  and passive voice, 421, 429–430
Past progressive tense, 433
  and active voice, 420
  ESL writer, 514
  and passive voice, 421
Past subjunctive, 431–432
Past tense, 422, 433
  and active voice, 420
  defined, 426
  ESL writer, 513, 516
  irregular verbs, 426–429
  and passive voice, 421
Pecking, in online reading, 134
Peer editing
  example of, 76–81
  guidelines for, 73–75
People. *See* Persons
Percentages, numerals in, 621, 623
Perfect tense
  ESL writer, 513–514
  forms of, 422
  future perfect tense, 420, 421, 433
  guidelines for use, 422
  past perfect tense, 422, 433
  present perfect tense, 433
Periodical Abstracts, 646
Periodicals. *See also* Journal articles; Magazine articles; Newspaper articles; Scholarly articles
  indexes to, 646–648
  titles, italics for, 605
  types of, 646
Periods, 542–543
  in abbreviations, 542–543, 615–620
  after commands, mild, 542
  correcting comma splice with, 554
  correcting run-on with, 556
  in decimals, 543
  editor's mark for, 542
  with ellipses, 590
  at end of commands, 542
  at end of indirect questions, 542, 544
  at end of statements, 542
  numbers in bible passages, 543
  after parentheses, 594
  with quotation marks, 587
persecute/prosecute, correct usage, 887
Person (grammatical), 432–434, 887
  ESL writer, 506–507
  first person, 432, 433
  second person, 432, 433, 887

singular and plurals, 433
and subject-verb agreement, 859–860
and subjunctive form, 432
third person, 431–432, 433, 887
Personal opinion, essay examination response, 114
personal/personnel, correct usage, 888
Personal pronouns
  -self/-selves added to, 478–479
  case of, 474
  nature of, 888
  nonsexist use of, 485–487
  person, 432–434
  possessives, 447, 474, 475–476
Personal writing projects, 117
Persons
  in agent/action sentences, 303–305
  capitalizing names of, 609–610
phenomena/phenomenon, correct usage, 888
Photographs
  in electronic documents, 358–359, 367
  parenthetical note (MLA), 756
  Works Cited (MLA style), 756
Phrases, 268–275, 888
  absolute phrases, 273, 888. *See also* Absolute phrases
  adverbial phrases, 858
  appositive phrases, 274–275
  dashes with, 598
  functions of, 268–269
  gerund, 271, 274
  hyphenated compound phrases, 600–601
  infinitive, 270–272
  italics for emphasis, 606
  noun phrases, 888
  parallelism of, 292–293, 885–886
  participle, 271
  prepositional phrases, 268–269, 888, 889. *See also* Prepositional phrases
  semicolon with, 576, 578–579
  as sentence fragments, 550
  as subject of sentence, 410
  and subject-verb agreement, 410
  verbals and verbal phrases, 270–272, 888
Physics reports, style manual for, 820
Pictures, effects on readers, 150
Pie chart, interpretation of, 143–144
Place names. *See* Geographic place names
Plagiarism
  avoiding when writing, 687

defined, 104, 696
in paraphrase, 687, 690
in summary, 687
Planning stage, 5, 7–8, 15–28, 338, 361–363
Plays
  parenthetical note (MLA), 756–757
  providing act and scene divisions of,
    188
  titles, italics for, 605
  Works Cited (MLA), 756–757
plenty of, as quantifier, 538
plurality/majority, meaning and correct usage, 882
Plurals, 441–444
  of abbreviations, 444
  of acronyms, 444
  apostrophe, 444
  compound words, 443–444
  and derivation of words, 443
  editing errors, 442
  -es ending, 441–443
  -f or *-fe* at end of word, 443
  of figures, 444
  -full at end of word, 444
  and irregular words, 441
  of letters, 444
  of numbers, 444, 623
  o at end of word, 442
  and person, 433
  possessive form, 446
  pronouns. *See* Pronoun agreement
  proper nouns, 442–443
  -s ending, 441–444
  subjects of sentences. *See* Subject-verb
    agreement
  y at end of word, 442–443
plus, incorrect use of, 888
P.M.
  as abbreviation, 618
  capitalization of, 616
  numerals with, 623
  small caps for, 616
Poetry
  capitalizing first word of lines, 608
  as direct quotation, 608
  ellipses for deletions from, 591
  identifying passages by line number,
    188
  slashes between quoted lines within
    sentences, 603
Poetry titles
  capitalization in, 607–608
  italics for longer poems, 605

quotation marks for short poems, 586,
  605
Point size of type, and purpose of docu-
  ment, 355
Pointer words, as transitions, 223
Points, 355
Policy-based claims, 711
Policy-based question, 24, 25
Political groups, capitalizing name of, 610
Portfolio page orientation, 351
Portfolios, 89–95
Positioning, in document design, 343
Positioning sources, 677–681
Positive statements, and clarity in writing,
  311
Possessive(s), 445–447, 889
  apostrophe, 445–447
  compound words, 446
  defined, 445
  as determiners, 870
  double possessives, 447, 871
  before gerunds, 448–449
  hyphenated words, 446
  living things, 446–447
  nonliving things, 446–447
  nouns, 445–447
  nouns ending in *-s* or *-z,* 445
  personal pronouns, 447, 474,
    475–476, 889
  plural nouns ending in *-s,* 446
  pronouns, 448, 889
  proper names, 446
  titled works, 446–447
  two nouns sharing ownership, 446
Possessive case
  defined, 466, 865, 889
  list of possessive forms, 467
  situations for use, 466, 467, 474–476
Possessive pronouns, 447, 474, 475–476,
  889
Post hoc, ergo propter hoc fallacy, 171–172
Predicate
  in agent/action sentences, 305–309
  function of, 257, 889, 898
  in independent clause, 276
  logical connection to subject, 306–307
Predicate adjectives, 492–494
  correct use of, 492–494, 889
  good and *well,* 493–494
  instead of adverbs, 492–493
Predicate nominative
  function of, 889
  pronouns, 466

index

Preface
    parenthetical note (MLA), 734–735
    Works Cited (MLA), 734–735
Prefixes, hyphenation for proper nouns, 600
prejudice/prejudiced, correct usage, 889
Preparation stage, 5, 7–8, 15–28
Preposition(s)
    in adjective pairs, 508
    functions of, 468, 889
    gerunds used with, 533
    list of, 468
    in titles, capitalization of, 608
Prepositional phrases, 268–269, 888, 889
    avoiding for conciseness, 319–320
    in cumulative sentences, 300–301
    like as introductory word, 881
    parts of, 268–269, 468
    and pronoun case, 468–469
    use in sentences, 269
Present perfect progressive tense, ESL
    writer, 514, 516–517
Present perfect tense, 433
    and active voice, 420
    ESL writer, 513, 516–517
    and passive voice, 421
Present progressive tense, 433
    and active voice, 420
    ESL writer, 513, 514, 515
    and passive voice, 421
Present subjunctive, 431
Present tense, 433
    and active voice, 420
    defined, 426
    ESL writer, 512, 515
    irregular verbs, 426–429
    and passive voice, 421
    quoting events from literature, 188,
    708
    subject-verb agreement, 859–860
Press release, denotative language for,
    237–238
Previewing text, 131
Primary sources. *See* Research sources
Principal clause. *See* Independent clauses
Principal parts of verb, 426, 432–433, 889
principal/principle, 890
prioritize, alternatives to, 890
Problem-and-solution pattern, organiza-
    tion of paper, 42–43
proceed to, avoiding, 890
Process pattern
    organization of paper, 37–38
    paragraphs, 200–201

Profession
    eliminating biased language toward,
    251–252
    eliminating sexist language toward,
    247
Professional organizations. *See also* Orga-
    nizations
    getting addresses for, 652
    as research source, 652–653
Profusion, 655
Progression of ideas, and parallelism,
    294–295
Progressive tense
    construction of, 890
    ESL writer, 513–514
    future perfect progressive tense, 420, 514
    future progressive tense, 420, 433, 514
    past perfect progressive tense, 514
    past progressive tense, 420, 421, 433,
    514
    present perfect progressive tense, 514,
    516–517
    present progressive tense, 420, 433,
    513–515
Project folder, in Web design, 367–368
Pronoun(s), 890. *See also specific types of*
    pronouns
    adjective modifiers of, 264–265, 488
    antecedents of, 451–452, 861
    demonstrative pronouns, 225, 870
    indefinite pronouns, 411–412
    intensive pronouns, 478–479, 879
    interrogative pronouns, 879
    as nominals, 884
    nonsexist use of, 485–487
    possessive form, 447, 448
    as predicate nominative, 466
    in prepositional phrases, 468–469
    reciprocal pronouns, 891
    reflexive pronouns, 478–479, 892
    relative pronouns, 225
Pronoun agreement, 457–464, 859
    and case, 859
    and collective nouns, 462–463
    and gender, 859
    and indefinite pronouns, 460–462
    and number, 457–459, 859
    and *or, nor, either . . . or, neither . . .
    nor*, 464
    with singular or plural antecedents,
    458–459
Pronoun case, 466–477, 864–865
    and appositive after pronoun, 467–468

in comparisons, 469–470
indefinite pronouns, 474–475
its/it's, 475–476
after linking verbs, 466, 471–472
listing of pronoun forms, 467
objective case, 467, 470, 472–473, 865, 885
possessive case, 466, 467, 474–476, 865
and pronoun agreement, 859
and pronoun in prepositional phrases, 468–469
of subject complements, 471–472
subjective case, 467, 468, 469–473, 864
and *who* and *whom*, 472–473
whose/who's, 476
Pronoun reference, 451–455, 891
and ambiguous antecedents, 453
defined, 451, 891
and lack of antecedents, 451–452
and *they* or *it*, 455
and *this, that, which* and *it*, 454–455
Proofreading, 5, 71–81
areas to check, 71–72
defined, 61
document design, 341–344
ESL writer, 506–509
example of, 75
peer editing, 73–81
proofreading symbols, 74–75
in Web design, 381–382
Proper names
with academic degree, 574
dash in credit line, 598
possessive form, 446
Proper nouns
as adjectives, 857, 890
as appositives, 275
capitalizing names, 609–610
defined, 890
hyphen after prefix of, 600
as modifiers, 267
plurals, 442–443
Proportion of paper
drafting, 53–54
revising, 61, 63
Proposal
paper proposal example, 27–28
research project, 631–632
prosecute/persecute, correct usage, 887
Prove, essay question, 112
provided, as subordinating conjunction, 288
public, subject-verb agreement, 414

Public writing, 116–125
and audience expectations, 118, 119
dialect in, 254–255
example of, 121–124
models for, 119–120. *See also* Model documents
nonacademic, types of, 116–117
professionalism in, 121
public versus academic writing, 116, 120–121
service-learning projects, 125–129
spotting opportunities for, 118
Publication date
in COS style, 828, 829–830
in literary analysis, 188
Publication Manual of the American Psychological Association, 714, 773, 776. *See also* APA style
Punctuation. *See also specific marks*
brackets, 595–596
colons, 581–584
commas, 559–574
dashes, 597–598
ellipses, 589–591
exclamation marks, 545–546
hyphens, 599–602
MLA style, 718
parentheses, 593–594
periods, 542–543
proofreading, 71
question marks, 543–545
quotation marks, 585–589
semicolons, 576–580
slashes, 602–603
Purpose for writing
and goal of piece, 7–8
questions in establishment of, 8
and revising, 61, 62

Q
Qualifiers
in arguments, 157
categories of, 891
list of, 494
Quantifiers
ESL writer, 537–538
list of, 538, 891
and noncount nouns, 534
Question(s)
abbreviations at end of, 542
indirect, period at end of, 542, 544
in topic selection, 21–22
Question and answer paragraphs, 200

Question marks, 543–545
  compound sentences, 544
  in direct versus indirect questions, 544
  editor's mark for, 543
  at end of questions, 543
  to mark unestablished fact/date/name, 544
  in middle of sentence, 544
  with other punctuation marks, 545
  with quotation marks, 544, 545
Questionnaires
  composing questions, 665–668
  guidelines for, 668
  as research tool, 665–668
Questions and writing
  journalist's questions, 24
  in opening paragraph, 200, 212–213
  questions of definition, 24, 25
  questions of fact, 24, 25
  questions of policy, 24, 25
  questions of value, 24, 25
  rhetorical questions, 24–25
Quotation marks, 585–589
  British convention, 589
  chapters of books, 586, 605
  colons with, 587
  commas with, 587
  dashes with, 588
  in dialogue, 585–586
  editor's mark for, 585
  to emphasize words, 586
  essays, 586
  with exclamation points, 546
  guillemets, 589
  journal article, 605
  magazine article, 586, 605
  newspaper article, 586, 605
  newspaper sections, 605
  periods with, 587
  poetry titles, shorter works, 605
  question marks with, 544, 545
  radio episodes, 605
  running into sentence, 587
  semicolons with, 579, 580, 587
  short story titles, 605
  to signal ironic/sarcastic/derisive words, 586
  song titles, 586, 605
  speeches, 586
  television episodes, 586, 605
  titles of short works, 586, 605
  around words from sources, 585, 694
quote/quotation, correct usage, 891
Quoted material. *See* Direct quotations

R
Race, eliminating biased language toward, 248–249
Radio
  episodes, quotation marks around, 605
  programs, Works Cited (MLA), 753
  titles of shows, italics, 605
rather/kind of, correct usage, 880
rather than, as subordinating conjunction, 288
Readers. *See* Audience
Readers' Guide Abstracts, 646
Readers' Guide to Periodical Literature, 646
Reading assignments, 130–136. *See also* Critical reading
  dictionary, use of, 131
  features of text, 131
  and goals of reader, 130
  note-taking during, 132–134
  online, 134–135
  pace for reading, 132
  previewing text, 131
real/very, correct usage, 891
really, avoiding, 891
reason is . . . because, 891
Reasoning errors. *See* Fallacies
Reciprocal pronoun, function of, 891
Recommendation, in closing paragraphs, 216
Recordings, Works Cited (MLA), 754
Red herrings, 172–173
Redundancies
  avoiding for conciseness, 317
  defined, 317, 891
refer/allude, correct usage, 860
Reference (pronouns). *See* Pronoun reference
Reference works. *See also* Library; Research sources; Subject areas
  guides to, 646–647
  literary analysis, 181–182
  specialized encyclopedias, 630
  Web-based reference sites, 656
References (APA style), 776–777
  abstract (online), 787
  anthology, 781
  anthology selection, 781
  basic guidelines, 801
  book review, 782
  book with no author, 780
  book with one author, 778–779
  book with three or more authors, 779
  book with two authors or editors, 779
  chapter in book, 781

electronic sources, 785–787. *See also*
    COS/APA (sciences) style
email, 787
final copy style, 776
hanging indents for, 776
information in entries, 773
italics versus underline, 776
listserv, 785
magazine article, author not named,
    784
magazine article from monthly maga-
    zine, 783
magazine article from weekly/biweekly
    magazine, 783
movie/videotape, 787
musical recording, 788
newsletter article, 783–784
newspaper article, author named,
    784
newspaper article, author not named,
    784
newspaper article, online, 786–787
purpose of, 776–777
revised book, 780
scholarly article (online), 786
scholarly article (printed), 782–783
software, 784–785
spacing of items, 776
Usenet newsgroup, 785
Web page (generic), 786
References (CBE style), 821–825
    books, 822–823
    electronic sources, 824–825
    magazine article, 824
    scholarly article, 823
Reflexive pronouns, 478–479
    function of, 478–479, 892
    list of, 478, 892
    problems with, 478–479
regardless/irregardless, correct usage, 880
Regular verbs, 892
    participle of, 435–436
    principal parts of, 426
Relationship words, as transitions, 223
Relative clauses. *See* Adjective (relative)
    clauses
Relative pronouns
    in adjective clauses, 277
    avoiding for conciseness, 321
    case of, 472–473
    list of, 225, 287, 892
    and subordination in sentences,
        287–291
    as transitions, 225

Religious affiliation
    capitalizing name of, 611
    terms for, 249
Religious figures, capitalizing name of,
    611
Repetition in writing
    doublings, avoiding, 317
    redundancies, avoiding, 317
    repeated words as transitions, 224
    sentence elements, ESL writer, 508–509
    as transitions within paragraphs, 198,
        224
Republished book
    parenthetical note (MLA), 736
    Works Cited (MLA), 736
Research project, 5, 11–12
    academic responsibilities related to,
        696–701
    checking final product, 717–719
    claims in, 709–711
    collaborative projects, 636
    details of, 717–719
    direct quotations in, 701–708
    documentation, general guidelines,
        693–708
    framework for, 626–639
    headings, 715–717
    hypothesis for, 631
    influence of electronic media on form,
        627–628, 631
    narrowing topic, 631, 709–711
    neutral language in, 237
    planning, 631–636
    scheduling, 637–639
    structure of, 709–712
    submission of, 718
    tables and figures in, 713–714
    time management, 637–639
    topic selection, 628–631
    typing of, 712–713
    understanding assignment, 628–629
Research sources
    for academic writing, 102
    annotation of, 682–683, 684
    biases of, 675
    classifying, 632–633
    commercial intrusions into, 676
    documentation, general guidelines,
        693–708
    downloading electronic sources,
        635–636, 713
    electronic media-based resources,
        657–659
    evaluation of, 670–677

index

Research sources *(Continued)*
  field research, 664–669
  keyword search, 654–657
  library, 640–652
  note cards, information on, 634–635
  paraphrase, 684, 687–691, 698
  photocopying sections, 634–635
  positioning of, 677–681
  professional organizations, 652–653
  purpose of sources, 670–671
  relating and connecting, 691–692
  summarizing, 684–687, 698
  timeliness of, 674–675
  working bibliography, 633–634
  World Wide Web, 654–657
Response notes, 132
Restrictive modifiers. *See* Essential modifiers
Results section, of social science report, 789
Résumés
  components of, 391, 393
  cover letter, 388–389
  examples of, 391, 393
  online, 393
  writing guidelines for, 392
Review, essay question, 113
Reviews
  book reviews, 652, 738–739
  connotative language for, 238–239
  film reviews, 652, 738–730
Revised book
  parenthetical notes (APA), 780
  References (APA), 780
Revised Web site
  COS/APA (sciences) style, 844–845
  COS/MLA (humanities) style, 832
Revising, 5, 61–67
  audience adaptation, 63–64
  for content, 64–65
  defined, 60
  document design, 340–341
  example of, 65–67
  for focus, 61, 62
  hard copy versus computer screen, 65
  for length and proportion, 61, 63
  new draft versus revising, 61–62
  for organization, 64
  paragraph, 204–207
  peer revision, 73–81
  for purpose, 61, 62
  of thesis, 33
  title, 48
Rhetoric, defined, 7

Rhetorical questions, 24–25
r.p.m.(revolutions per minute), 616
Rules, in document design, 359
Run-on sentences, 556–557, 892
  characteristics of, 556, 892
  correction of, 556–557
  editor's mark for, 556
Running heads, 353, 399

S
's
  contractions, 475–476
  indefinite pronouns, 474–475
  plurals, 623
  possessives, 445–447
-s
  ESL writer, 506–507
  plurals, 441–444
  present tense verbs/third person singular, 407
s/he, 893
Sacred books. *See also* Bible passages
  capitalizing name of, 611
saint, abbreviation for, 619
Salutation in letter, 387
  colon in, 584
  comma in, 574
Salutation of email, 385
Sans serif fonts, 355
"Save as" HTML options, 363
Scanning graphics and text, 367
scarcely, and double negatives, 499
Scholarly articles
  Bibliography/Works Cited (CMS), 809
  Notes (CMS), 809
  parenthetical note (APA), 782–783, 786
  parenthetical note (MLA), 739–740
  References (APA style, online journal), 786
  References (APA style, printed journal), 782–783
  References (CBE), 823
  Works Cited (MLA, online journal), 747
  Works Cited (MLA, printed journal), 739–740
School courses, capitalizing title of, 614
School name, capitalizing, 611
School subjects, capitalization rule, 614
Scientific reports. *See also* Subject areas
  characteristics of, 106
  documentation of. *See* CBE style; COS/APA (sciences) style
  style manuals for, 820

Scientific Style and Format: The CBE Manual for Authors, Editors, and Publishers (6th edition), 820. *See also* CBE style
Scores, numerals in, 623
Scratch outline, 45–46
  in literary analysis, 186–187
  for response in essay examination, 113–114
Screen literacy, 134–135
Sculptures, italics for name of, 605
Search engines, 18, 654–657
  category search, 654–655
  keyword search, 642, 654–657, 659–664
  listing of, 654–655
  for Usenet newsgroups, 631
Searches of indexes/databases. *See* Keyword search
Seasons of year, capitalization rule, 613
Second person, 432, 433, 887
Secondary sources. *See* Research sources
Selective bibliography, purpose of, 644
Self-assessment, in portfolios, 91–94
Self-presentation, and writing, 11–12
-self, -selves, adding to personal pronouns, 478–479
Semicolons, 576–580
  with conjunctive adverbs, 285–286, 578, 867
  correcting comma splice with, 553, 554
  correcting run-on with, 556–557
  editor's mark for, 576
  with items in series, 579
  linking independent clauses, 284–285, 285–286, 577–579
  misuse of, 579
  with quotation marks, 579, 580, 587
  as transitional device, 226
Sentence(s)
  action in. *See* Agent/action sentences
  balanced sentence, 298–299, 863
  capitalization of first word, 607
  clauses, 275–278
  condensing to clauses, 321–322
  coordination in. *See* Coordination in sentences
  cumulative sentences, 299–301, 869
  dates at beginning of, 622–623
  defined, 257, 893
  intentional fragment, 551–552, 879
  joining with colons, 583
  length, 311–312, 324–325
  modifiers, 263–268

  numerals at beginning of, 622–623
  parallelism in, 292–297, 885–886
  phrases, 268–275
  predicate, 257
  structure of. *See* Sentence structure
  subject, 257
  subordination in. *See* Subordination in sentences
  verb tense, consistency of, 425
Sentence fragments, 547–552
  adjective clause as, 548–549
  appositive as, 548–549
  characteristics of, 547, 874
  correction of, 547–550
  disconnected phrases as, 550
  editor's mark for, 547
  intentional fragments, situations for use, 551–552, 879
  lists in, 550
  subordinate clauses as, 547
  verbals in, 438, 549
Sentence outline, 46–47
Sentence patterns, varying in writing, 323–324
Sentence problems
  comma splices, 552–555, 865
  faulty predication, 306–307, 874
  run-on sentences, 556–557, 892
  sentence fragments, 438, 547–552, 874
Sentence structure, 257–263, 893
  complex sentence, 225, 280, 281, 287–291, 866
  compound-complex sentence, 280, 282, 287–291, 867
  compound objects, 263
  compound sentence, 280, 281, 284, 299, 867
  compound subjects, 262
  compound verbs, 262–263
  inversion, 880
  and parallel construction, 292–297
  simple sentence, 280–281, 894
  subject-verb-direct object-object complement pattern, 261
  subject-verb-direct object pattern, 258
  subject-verb-indirect object-direct object pattern, 260–261
  subject-verb pattern, 257
  subject-verb-subject complement pattern, 259–260
Sentence variety, 322–325
  importance of, 322
  and length of sentences, 324–325
  and sentence patterns, 323–324

index

Separable verbs, 520–521
  and ESL writer, 520–522
  example of, 521
  listing of, 521–522
Sequence of tenses, 893
Sequential pattern, in Web design, 365, 366
Series
  comma separating coordinate adjectives, 567–568
  comma separating items, 567–568
  dash in, 598
  noncoordinate adjectives in, 567–568
  semicolon in, 579
Series of books
  Bibliography/Works Cited (CMS), 808
  Notes (CMS), 808
  parenthetical note (MLA), 736
  Works Cited (MLA), 736
Serif fonts, 355
Service-learning projects, 125–129
  audiences for, 126–127
  collaboration in, 128
  dual purpose of, 126
  evaluation of, 127–128
  nature of, 125
set/sit, correct usage, 893
several
  and pronoun agreement, 460
  as quantifier, 538, 891
  and subject-verb agreement, 411
several/couple of, use in writing, 869
Sexist language, 246–248, 893
  nonsexist pronouns, guidelines for use, 485–487
  revising, guidelines for, 246–248
Sexual orientation, eliminating biased language toward, 251
Shadow, type style, 356
she
  ESL writer, 506–507
  in nonsexist language, 485–487, 876, 893
she/her, pronoun case, 469–470, 471
Ship names
  capitalization, 613
  italics, 605
Short story titles, quotation marks around, 605
should, as modal auxiliary, 421, 422, 524, 525
should have, as modal auxiliary, 526–527
should have/should of, correct usage, 868, 893

sic, to indicate errors in quoted material, 596, 707
similarly, to link independent clauses, 285
Similes
  defined, 327, 893
  examples of, 327
Simple sentence, 280–281, 894
since
  in adverb clauses, 278
  present perfect with, 516
  as subordinating conjunction, 288, 560–561
Singular terms, and subject-verb agreement, 417–418
sit/set, correct usage, 893
Site map, 365
Skimming, in online reading, 134
Slang, nature of, 894
Slashes, 602–603
  in expressions indicating a choice, 602
  in fractions, 603
  between lines of poetry quoted within sentences, 603
  in World Wide Web addresses, 603
Slippery slopes fallacy, 173
Small caps
  for *A.D./B.C.,* 616
  for *A.M./P.M.,* 616
  type style, 355, 356
so
  comma before, 566
  as intensifier, 891, 894
  linking independent clauses, 282
so that, as subordinating conjunction, 288
Social class, eliminating biased language toward, 251–252
Social science reports. *See also* Subject areas
  characteristics of, 105
  components of, 789
  documentation of. *See* APA style
Software
  for bibliography preparation, 639, 695–696
  copyright, 345
  COS/APA (sciences) style, 852–853
  COS/MLA (humanities) style, 841
  italics for name, 605
  Notes (CMS), 810
  parenthetical note (APA), 784–785
  References (APA), 784–785
  Web design, 349, 363–364, 369–381
  Works Cited (MLA), 745

Solutions, evaluating in written piece, 140–141
some
  possessive form, 475
  and pronoun agreement, 460
  as quantifier, 538, 891
  in restrictive expressions, 891
  and subject-verb agreement, 411, 412
somebody
  possessive form, 475
  and pronoun agreement, 460
  and subject-verb agreement, 411
someone
  possessive form, 475
  and pronoun agreement, 460
  and subject-verb agreement, 411
something
  and pronoun agreement, 460
  and subject-verb agreement, 411
Song titles, quotation marks around, 586, 605
Sources. *See* Documentation of sources; Electronic sources; Library; Research sources; *specific documentation styles*
Spacecraft, italics, 605
Special events, capitalization, 613
Specialized encyclopedias, 630
Specific language, 67
Speeches
  quotation marks around title, 586
  Works Cited (MLA), 754–755
Spelling
  proofreading for, 71
  spelling checker, 71
Split infinitives, 438–439, 894
  nature of, 438–439
  revision of, 439, 894
Standard English, versus dialect, 253–256
State names
  abbreviations for, 619
  capitalization of, 612
Statement, in opening paragraph, 213–214
stationary/stationery, correct usage, 894
Statistical information
  numerals in, 623
  print sources for, 649–650
  reference works, listing of, 649–650
  on World Wide Web, 650
Stereotypes
  about age, 250
  in arguments, 162–163
  about disability, 251

male/female, 247–248
  racial/ethnic, 248–249
  about sexual orientation, 251
Stories, quotations for titles of, 605
Storyboarding, document design, 365–367
Straw man fallacy, 162
Street
  -related terms, abbreviation for, 619
  numbers, 623
Stress, and essay examinations, 110
Strikethrough, type style, 356
Study, and essay examinations, 108–109, 109–110
Style
  agent/action sentences, 303–309
  clarity in writing, 310–313
  concise writing, 313–322
  editing for, 67–68
  figurative language, 326–327
  sentence variety, 322–325
Style checker, 69
Style sheets, 343
Subject areas
  academic writing conventions of, 104–106
  bibliographies, 645
  biographical information, 649
  capitalizing names of, 614
  indexes and databases, 646–647
  literary analysis references, 181–182
  professional organizations, 652–653
  science style manuals, 820
  specialized encyclopedias, 630
  statistical information sources, 649–650
  Web-based subject guides, 645
Subject-by-subject pattern, in compare and contrast paper, 38–39, 40
Subject complement
  adjectives as, 265
  function of, 866, 894
  pronoun case of, 471–472
  use in sentence, 259–260
  verbals as, 271, 437, 530
Subject of sentence
  in agent/action sentences, 303–309
  agreement with verb. *See* Subject-verb agreement
  clauses as, 410
  comma separating verb from, 570
  complete subject, 894
  compound subject, 262
  function of, 257, 894
  in independent clause, 276

Subject of sentence *(Continued)*
  logical connection to predicate,
    306–307
  noun clause as, 279
  phrases as, 410
  and sentence patterns. *See* Sentence
    structure
  simple subject, 894
  verbals as, 270–271, 437
Subject-verb agreement, 406–418,
    859–860
  along with, as well as, together with in
    sentences, 409
  collective noun as subject, 413, 414
  compound subjects, 408–409, 410
  editing faulty verb, 408
  every and *each* subject modifiers, 408
  here and *there* in sentences, 416
  indefinite pronoun as subject, 411–412
  and inverted sentence order, 417
  linking verbs, 416–417
  one of those who in sentences, 418
  or, neither . . . nor, either . . . or joining
    subjects, 409–410
  and person, 859–860
  and singular or plural subject, 406–407
  singular terms, 417–418
  and subject-verb separation, 415
Subjective case
  defined, 466, 864
  list of subjective forms, 467
  situations for use, 466, 467, 468,
    469–473
Subjunctive mood, 431–432, 433, 883
  functions of, 431, 895
  past subjunctive, 431–432
  present subjunctive, 431
  in *that* clauses, 432
Subordinate (dependent) clauses
  comma after, 560
  in complex sentences, 280, 281, 288
  in compound-complex sentences, 280,
    287–291
  in cumulative sentences, 301
  function of, 276, 865
  introductory words of, 276, 287, 547,
    867
  parts of, 277
  relationship to independent clause, 276
  as sentence fragments, 547
  signal words for, 560
  as transitions, 223, 224
  who/whom in, 473

Subordinating conjunctions, 287–291
  in adverb clauses, 278
  correcting comma splice with,
    554–555
  correcting run-on with, 557
  functions of, 287, 867
  list of, 276, 288, 548, 867
  in subordinate clauses, 276–277, 287,
    548
Subordination in sentences, 287–291
  compound and compound-complex
    sentences, 281, 287–291
  methods for, 287–291
  and relative pronouns, 287–291
  and subordinating conjunctions,
    287–291
Subsections, in document design, 352
Subtitles, colon before, 583
such as, as appositive, 274
such as, at beginning of list, 550, 582
such, as transitional word, 225, 895
*Suggestions to Authors of Reports of the
    United States Geological Survey* (7th
    edition), 820
Summarize, essay question, 113
Summary
  closing paragraph as, 216
  defined, 684
  plagiarized, 698
  of research materials, 684–687, 698
Superlative form. *See* Comparative and su-
    perlative forms
Superscript
  CBE-style citations, 820–821
  CMS-style footnotes and endnotes,
    803–804
  MLA-style footnotes, 758
Support for ideas. *See* Evidence
suppose to/supposed to, correct usage, 895
surely, as intensifier, 891
Surveys. *See* Questionnaires
Suspended modifiers, hyphen in, 601
Symbols
  abbreviations for, 620
  fonts for, 355, 356
Synchronous communication
  COS/APA (sciences) style, 851
  COS/MLA (humanities) style, 839
  Works Cited (MLA), 750
Synonyms
  denotation/connotation of, 895
  nature of, 895
Syntax, defined, 895

T

Table of contents, in document design, 350

Tables, 145–147, 713–714
APA style, 714–715
in document design, 339, 352
evaluating accuracy of, 148
interpretation of, 145–147
MLA style, 713–714

Technical information
abbreviating technical terms, 617
hyphens in, 600
lists for, 312
numbers in, 621
symbols in, 620

television, abbreviation for, 897

Television programs
episodes, quotation marks around title, 586, 605
italics for name of, 605
Works Cited (MLA), 752–753

Telnet site
COS/APA (sciences) style, 850–851
COS/MLA (humanities) style, 839

Temperature
abbreviation in, 618
numerals in, 623

Tense. *See* Verb tense

than
in comparisons, 469–470
and parallelism, 294
as subordinating conjunction, 288

than/then, correct usage, 895

that
in adjective clauses, 277, 548–549
in essential clauses, 480, 504
and pronoun reference, 454–455
as relative pronoun, 225, 277, 287, 321
and subjunctive mood, 432
as subordinating conjunction, 287, 288
as transitional word, 225

that is, Latin expression for, 605, 619

the
coordinate adjectives ahead of, 264
and count nouns, 535–536
ESL writer, 535–536
in titles, capitalization of, 608
use before words, 856, 862

their, in nonsexist language, 486

themselves/theirselves, correct usage, 479, 895

then/than, correct usage, 895

there, and subject-verb agreement, 416

there are, as expletive, 221, 318–319

there is, as expletive, 221, 319

there was, as expletive, 873

therefore
comma with, 561, 564, 565
as connection in paragraph, 223
to link independent clauses, 285
semicolon before, 578

Thesaurus
and editing for word choice, 68
online, COS/MLA (humanities) style, 840, 851–852

these
incorrect use of, 896
as transitional word, 225

Thesis (dissertation). *See* Dissertations

Thesis construction
for essay examination response, 113
focus in, 31–32
in literary analysis, 184–186
placement of thesis, 32–33, 34–35
revision in, 33
strength of thesis, 29–30

Thesis statement
defined, 29
in opening paragraph, 213–214

they
in nonsexist language, 486
and pronoun reference, 455

Third person, 431–432, 433, 887

this
and pronoun reference, 454–455, 896
as transitional word, 225

this is, as expletive, 318–319

those, as transitional word, 225

though
in adverb clauses, 278
as subordinating conjunction, 288

Threads, listserv, 397

throne/thrown, correct usage, 896

thus/thusly, correct usage, 896

till, as subordinating conjunction, 288

till/until, correct usage, 896

Time management
draft writing, 55
for essay examination, 111–112
for research project, 637–639
for study, 109–110

Time of day
A.M./P.M., 616
colon in, 583
numerals in, 623
o'clock, 623

Time periods
  abbreviation of, 618
  A.D./B.C., 616, 618
  capitalization of, 613, 616
Time words
  list of, 223, 224
  and transitions, 223, 224
Title of paper, 48–49
  and audience, 48–49
  capitalization in, 607–608
  revision, 48
  two-part title, 49
  working title, 48
Title of person
  abbreviation of, 616–617
  capitalization, 609–610
  comma with, 574
  minor versus prestigious titles, 609–610
Title of works. *See also specific types of works*
  article and prepositions in, 607–608
  capitalization in, 607–608
  colon before subtitle, 583
  italicized titles, 605
  possessive form, 446–447
  short works, quotation marks around titles, 586, 605
Title page
  APA style, 790, 791
  CMS style, 813
  MLA style, 761
to
  in base form of verb, 406
  in infinitives, 435, 438–439, 878
  and parallelism, 296–297
  in split infinitives, 438–439
to be
  ineffectiveness of, 307
  as irregular verb, 421
  as linking verb, 881
  passive voice, 430
  in progressive tense, 890
  subjunctive form, 431–432
  and verb tense, 421
to have
  as irregular verb, 421
  and verb tense, 421
to lay, correct usage, 881
to/too, 896
together with, and subject-verb agreement, 409
Tone
  civil, importance of using, 13, 242–244

  editing for, 68
  in opening paragraph, 212
too, as intensifier, 896
Topic development, 29–35
  classical rhetorical questions for, 24–25
  and draft writing, 25, 52–54
  freewriting, 23–24
  journalist's questions, 24
  learning about topic, 25–26
  literary analysis, 184–186
  thesis construction in, 29–35
Topic refinement, 29–35
Topic selection, 15–28
  and audience, 9–10
  brainstorming for, 15–16
  community issues for, 16–17
  encyclopedias, use of, 630
  example topics, 15
  goal statement in, 22
  hypothesis in, 21–22
  idea map, 20–21
  and interest of writer, 16
  Internet for, 17–18, 631
  library search, 17
  narrowing topic, 631, 709–711
  paper proposal example, 27–28
  personal experience and, 16
  questions in, 16, 21–22
  refining topic, 18–23
  for research project, 628–631
  timeliness of topic, 17
  tree diagram for, 19–20
Topic sentence, paragraphs, 195–197, 896
Toulmin, Stephen, 154–155, 157
toward/towards, correct usage, 896
Trace, essay question, 113
Trademarks, capitalization, 611
Train names, italics, 605
Transitions, 220–228
  comma as mark of, 562
  common transitional words/phrases, 224
  demonstrative pronouns as, 225
  editing, 68
  functions of, 68, 220, 897
  internal, 197–198
  and linked paragraphs, 225–226
  in paragraphs, 197–198
  parallelism as, 225–226
  pointer words as, 223
  relationship words as, 223
  relative pronouns as, 225
  repetition as, 198, 224

and semicolon, 226
and subordinate clauses, 223, 224
time and sequence markers as, 223,
    224
weak transitions, signs of, 220–222
Transitive verbs
and active voice, 258, 897
ESL writer, 518–519
followed by infinitive, 532
functions of, 518–519, 897
and passive constructions, 258, 897
separable and inseparable verbs,
    520–522
two-word verbs, 520–522
type of, 520
use in sentence, 258, 260–261, 879
and voice, 429
Translated book
parenthetical note (MLA), 735–736
Works Cited (MLA), 735–736
Tree diagram, topic selection/refinement,
    19–20
try to/try and, correct usage, 897
TV, use in writing, 897
Type size, 355, 356–357
Type styles, 342, 355–357, 356–357
guidelines for use, 356
most commonly used, 356
purpose of, 356
type, use in writing, 897
Typing research papers, 712–713
Typography, 342
errors in, 72
fonts, 342, 355–357
importance of, 342
size of type, 355, 356–357
type styles, 342, 355–357, 356–357

U
Underlining
for italics, 604
type style, 356
Uniform resource locator (URL), 746,
    748. *See also* Electronic address
uninterested/disinterested, correct usage,
    871
Unions, capitalizing name of, 611
unique, correct usage, 897–898
United States, abbreviations for state
    names, list of, 619
Units, breaking material into, 351–353
unless, as subordinating conjunction, 288,
    560–561

until
in adverb clauses, 278
as subordinating conjunction, 276, 288
until/till, correct usage, 896
Uploading, of page to Web server, 382
URL (uniform resource location), 746,
    748
us/we, pronoun case, 468
use/utilize, correct usage, 898
used to/use to, correct usage, 898
Usenet newsgroups, 17–18, 26, 657–659
archived material, access to, 631, 658
COS/APA (sciences) style, 849
COS/MLA (humanities) style, 838
messages to, 396–397
parenthetical note (APA), 785
pros/cons of information, 658
References (APA), 785
searching, 631, 658
Works Cited (MLA), 749
utilize/use, correct usage, 898

V
Value-based claims, 710–711
Value-based question, 24, 25
Verb(s)
action verbs, 519–520, 520
active voice, 258
adverbs as modifiers, 266
in agent/action sentences, 305–309
of attribution, 703
auxiliary verbs. *See* Auxiliary verbs
base form of, 406, 532
comma separating subject from,
    570–571
compound verbs, 262–263, 600
ESL writer, 506, 512–527
finite and nonfinite, 438, 874, 898
function of, 257, 898
intransitive verbs, 257–258, 519–520,
    879
irregular verbs, 421, 426–429, 436, 880
linking verbs, 259–260. *See also* Link-
    ing verbs
nonaction verbs, 515
parallelism of, 885–886
passive constructions, 258, 308–309
principal parts of, 426, 889
progressive verbs, 890
regular verbs, 426, 892
and sentence patterns. *See* Sentence
    structure
separation from subject, 415

Verb(s) *(Continued)*
  transitive verbs. *See* Transitive verbs
  two- and three-word verbs, 520–522
Verb complements. *See* Direct object; In-
    direct object
Verb phrases, 270–271, 888
  in concise writing, 316
  participles in, 886
Verb tense, 419–429
  and active voice, 419–420, 429–430
  and auxiliary verbs, 421–422, 426
  consistency in paragraphs, 425
  consistency in sentences, 425
  defined, 419, 895
  ESL writer, 512–517
  gerunds, 434, 437
  infinitives, 433, 435
  irregular verbs, 421, 426–429
  listing of tenses, 433
  and modals, 421–422, 523–527
  participles, 433, 436
  and passive voice, 420–421, 429–430
  and principal parts of verb, 426
  sequence of, 893
Verbal phrases, 438, 888
Verbals, 270–272, 433–434, 435–439
  as adjectives, 271–272
  as adverbs, 272
  as direct object, 271
  functions of, 270, 435, 898
  gerunds, 270–271, 435, 436–437
  infinitives, 270–272, 435
  as modifiers, 268
  as nonfinite verbs, 438
  participles, 268, 435–436
  in sentence fragments, 438, 549
  as subject, 270–271
  as subject and object complements,
    271, 437
  verbal phrases from, 270–271, 438
very/awful, correct use, 862
very/real, correct usage, 891
very, use in writing, 899
Videotape
  parenthetical note (APA), 787
  References (APA), 787
  Works Cited (MLA), 752
Visual HTML editors, 363, 364, 376–380
Visual information, 142–152
  in advertisements, 150–151
  charts, 143–144
  COS/APA (sciences) style, 848–849
  COS/MLA (humanities) style, 836–837

and document design, 342–343,
    357–359
documenting borrowed images, 345,
    653
in electronic documents, 357–358
evaluating accuracy of, 148
graphs, 144–145
layout of page, 149, 351–354
pictures, 150
tables, 145–147, 713–714
in transitions, 226–227
value of, 142, 313
visual literacy, 150–151
viz., 605
Voice of verbs, 899. *See also* Active voice;
    Passive voice

W

Wall Street Journal, The, 675
Warrants
  in argument, 155–156, 159–160, 163
  examples of, 155–156
we, correct use of, 483
we/us, pronoun case, 468
Web browser, in Web design, 369, 370,
    377–378, 381
Web design, 361–382
  document presentation. *See* Document
    design
  draft HTML documents in, 369–381
  editing in, 381–382
  HTML in, 361–364
  hyperlinks in, 365, 375, 378–379, 381,
    695
  importance of, 676
  planning in, 361–363
  proofreading in, 381–382
  single-page or multi-page format,
    364–365
  uploading page to Web server, 382
Web forums
  archived, 631, 658
  messages to, 396–397
Web pages, 402–404
  components of, 403
  examples of, 403
  writing guidelines for, 402
Web site documentation
  APA style, 786–787
  CMS style, 811
  COS/APA (sciences) style, 844–849
  COS/MLA (humanities) style, 832–837
  MLA style, 745–749

WebCrawler, 655
Weights and measures
  abbreviations for, 618
  numerals in, 623
  subject-verb agreement, 414
well/good, correct use of, 493–494, 876
what
  as relative pronoun, 287
  and subordination, 287
whatever
  as relative pronoun, 287
  and subordination, 287
when
  in adjective clauses, 277
  in adverb clauses, 278
  as subordinating conjunction, 276,
    288, 560–561
whenever, as subordinating conjunction,
  276, 288
where
  in adjective clauses, 277, 548–549
  as relative pronoun, 225
  as subordinating conjunction, 277, 288
  as transitional word, 225
whereas, as subordinating conjunction, 288
wherever, as subordinating conjunction,
  288
whether, as subordinating conjunction, 288
which
  in adjective clauses, 277, 548–549
  in essential clauses, 481
  in nonessential clauses, 480–481, 504
  and pronoun reference, 454–455
  as relative pronoun, 225, 277, 287, 321
  as subordinating conjunction, 287, 288
  as transitional word, 225
while
  in adverb clauses, 278
  as subordinating conjunction, 276,
    288, 289, 290, 560–561
White space, document design, 340, 343,
  354
who
  in adjective clauses, 277, 548–549
  modifier of human subject, 481
  possessive form, 476
  pronoun case, 472–473
  as relative pronoun, 225, 277, 287, 321
  in subordination, 287
  as transitional word, 225
who/whom, correct usage, 321, 472–473,
  899
whoever/whomever, pronoun case, 473

whom
  in adjective clauses, 277
  pronoun case, 472–473
  as relative pronoun, 277, 287, 321
  and subordination, 287
whom/who, correct usage, 321, 472–473,
  899
whomever
  in adjective clauses, 277
  as relative pronoun, 277, 287
  and subordination, 287
whomever/whoever, pronoun case, 472–473
who's, contraction, 447, 475, 476
who's/whose
  possessive form versus contraction,
    475–476, 476
  pronoun case, 476
whose
  in adjective clauses, 277
  as possessive of who, 476
  as relative pronoun, 277, 287
  and subordination, 287
whose/who's
  possessive form versus contraction,
    475–476, 476
  pronoun case, 476
Widows, 343
will, as modal auxiliary, 525
-wise, as word ending, 899
with regard to/with regards to, 899
Women, titles for, 247, 616–617
won't, as contraction, 899
Word choice, 899
Word processing. *See* Computers
Wordiness, editing for, 68
Words. *See also* Language
  acronyms as, 857
  connotative, 239, 868
  denotative, 236–237, 868
  inflection, 878
  initialisms as, 614, 879
  interjections, 879
  nominalizations, 315, 884
  parallelism of, 292–293
  quotation marks for emphasis, 586
  repetition in writing, 224
  words as words, italics, 606
Work, writing related to, 117
Working bibliography, 633–634
  database for, 633–634
  note cards for, 633–634
  printouts from Web, 634
  purpose of, 634

index

Working list, outline from, 44–45
Working portfolios, 90
Working title, 48
Works Cited (CMS style). *See* Bibliography/Works Cited (CMS style)
Works Cited (MLA style), 724–728
  advertisements, 755
  anthology, 736–737
  anthology selection, 741–742
  artwork, 756
  basic guidelines, 771
  biblical citation, 751–752
  book (online), 746–747
  book in foreign language, 736
  book in series, 736
  book published before 1900, 737
  book reviews, 738–739
  book revised by second author, 733
  book with focus on forward/introduction/preface/afterword, 734–735
  book with four or more authors or editors, 732–733
  book with no author, 734
  book with one author, 732
  book with one editor, focus on author, 733
  book with one editor, focus on editor, 733–734
  book with several editors, 734
  book with two/three authors or editors, 732
  book written by group, 734
  bulletins, 744
  cartoons, 743
  CD-ROM, 750–751
  chapter in book, 737
  database, 750–751
  dissertation, 738
  electronic sources, 745–751, 748. *See also* COS/MLA (humanities) style
  email, 750
  encyclopedia, volume, 735
  encyclopedia article (online), 743–744
  encyclopedia article (printed), 743–744
  films, 752
  format of page, 725
  government documents, 744–745
  information in entries, 724–725
  interviews, 753
  later editions, 737
  lectures, 755
  letter to the editor, 743
  letters, 756

listserv, 749
magazine article from monthly magazine, 741
magazine article from popular magazine (online), 747
magazine article from popular magazine (printed), 740
magazine article from weekly/biweekly magazine, 740
microfilm/microfiche, 751
musical compositions, 753–754
newspaper article, 742
newspaper editorial (online), 748
newspaper editorial (printed), 743
pamphlets, 744
plays, 756–757
publishers' name, shortening of, 725–726
radio programs, 753
recordings, 754
republished book, 736
same author of several works, 727–728
scholarly article (online journal), 747
scholarly article (printed journal), 739–740
software, 745
special imprints, 738
speeches, 754–755
synchronous communication (MOOs, MUDs), 750
television programs, 752–753
translated book, 735–736
Usenet newsgroup, 749
videotape, 752
volume in multivolume set, 735
Web page (generic), 745–746
Web page (home page), 748–749
work with no author, 724, 726
World Wide Web, 654–657. *See also* COS style; Electronic media; Electronic sources; Internet; Web design; Web pages; Web site documentation
  annotation of sites, 682
  APA Web site, 773
  biographical information on, 648–649
  bookmarking, 135, 636, 682
  browsers, 654
  commercial intrusions on, 676
  copying files to disc, 632, 635–636
  copyright of site, 636
  COS Web site, 831
  credentials/expertise of writers, evaluation of, 671–674